1991

P9-ASN-777

Introduction
to
Learning Disabilities

Thomas C. Lovitt
University of Washington, Seattle

ALLYN AND BACON
Boston ■ London ■ Sydney ■ Toronto

Editorial-production service: Technical Texts, Inc.
Text designer: Sylvia Dovner
Cover administrator: Linda Dickinson
Cover designer: Dick Hannus
Production administrator: Lorraine Perrotta

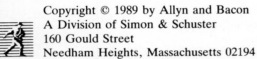

Copyright © 1989 by Allyn and Bacon
A Division of Simon & Schuster
160 Gould Street
Needham Heights, Massachusetts 02194

Library of Congress Cataloging-in-Publication Data

Lovitt, Thomas C.
  Introduction to learning disabilities / Thomas C. Lovitt.
    p.   cm.
  Includes index.
  ISBN 0–205–11949–2
  1. Learning disabilities.   2. Learning disabled children—
Education.   3. Learning disabled teenagers—Education.   I. Title.
LC4704.L52   1989
371.92′6—dc19   88–38949
                                                                        CIP

Printed in the United States of America.
10 9 8 7 6 5 4 3 2 1   93 92 91 90 89

CONTENTS

PREFACE

Introduction to Learning Disabilities is intended for upper division or beginning graduate students in education. The ongoing research I have been conducting in learning disabilities for over twenty-five years established the foundation for the book. My goal in writing it was not only to provide a comprehensive framework for study in this field, but to share the excitement and satisfaction that comes from working in it.

I have been personally involved in studies on most of the topics in the book: reading, writing, mathematics, spelling, social adjustment, self-management, adapting materials, and study skills. The scope of the book does go beyond these areas, however, to include such areas as language development and the education of handicapped preschoolers.

Although the book does not give equal weight to each and every idea that has come along in the field, it is not a "single-strand" approach. That is, I have not presented learning disabilities from one viewpoint—not neurological, not cognitive, and not as a bedrock behaviorist. I have referenced a wide variety of ideas and themes throughout the book, including some about which I had some disagreement.

Throughout the text, I have attempted to remain unbiased and to present multiple views of the topics at hand. My personal opinions are clearly identified in a comments section that appears at the end of each chapter, and where I felt the need to present another perspective within the body of a chapter, my commentary is clearly identified.

Outline of the Book

The book consists of four major parts and an epilog, which contains recommendations and perspectives for the future.

Part I, Chapters 1 and 2, provides an overview of learning disabilities. Chapter 1 is a review of the historical trends and developments in the field. I have tried to capture the enthusiasm of the early experts by quoting from their works, rather than dryly paraphrasing their beliefs and theories. Chapter 2 is a fairly sophisticated chapter on neurological and pharmacological aspects of learning disabilities. It also covers genetics, heredity, toxic agents, and dietary aspects as well.

Part II, Chapters 3 through 5, is on assessment and services for learning disabled students. Chapter 3 looks at the reasons for assessing these youngsters and reviews various assessment techniques. Chapter 4 provides a unique review of the various locations in which LD students may be educated—regular classrooms, self-contained classes, or resource rooms—and discusses the positive and negative aspects of each location. Chapter 5 has to do with consultation and communication. It covers the interactions of those involved in the management and instruction of LD youngsters, including professionals, community groups, parents, and students themselves.

Part III, Chapters 6 through 11, provides details on areas of specific learning disabilities. Chapters 6 through 9, which cover language and communications, reading, writing and spelling, and mathematics, each contain information on normal development and the comparative performances of LD learners. These chapters also review current programs and the latest research in each area.

Chapter 10 describes instructional approaches for LD students. It includes strategies and tactics that cut across academic areas and age levels. This chapter can be considered a "stand alone" chapter in that it can be used as the basis for in-service training programs for all teachers—not just those who work with mildly handicapped students.

The final chapter in Part III, Chapter 11, covers the social and emotional characteristics of LD students. It includes techniques for assessing various behaviors and reviews intervention strategies.

Part IV, Chapters 12 and 13, expands the discussion of LD youngsters to include early childhood (Chapter 12) and secondary school students (Chapter 13). Each of these chapters contains a discussion of characteristics, assessment techniques, and intervention programs. Chapter 13 also includes considerable material on delivery systems and curricular options for LD adolescents.

Features of the Book

Each chapter begins with an outline of the chapter headings, a list of the main ideas within the chapter, and a brief introduction to the chapter contents. These materials provide a guide to the most significant aspects of the chapter topic.

Many of the chapters contain a section on the ever-expanding role of microcomputers in the field of learning disabilities. The computer has become a valuable aid to teachers and other professionals for keeping records, planning, and developing strategies. The computer is also increasingly being used as an interactive learning device, with software programs available for various subjects (for example, reading or spelling) at various age and skill levels. Specific software packages are reviewed in the appropriate chapters, and a few of the research studies on this approach to teaching LD youngsters are summarized.

The comments section at the end of each chapter provides discussion points for students. Many of the comments can serve as the focus of lively classroom discussion, a stimulus for further reading, or the basis for more formal research reports.

An instructor's manual is available that provides multiple-choice and essay questions.

Illustrations are used throughout the text to help clarify certain concepts. In the appropriate chapters, actual samples of tests, recommended procedures, and teaching techniques are provided to familiarize readers with the instructional materials being discussed.

Throughout the book, photographs of researchers, past and present, who have contributed significantly to the field of learning disabilities appear along with a few comments about the individuals.

Each chapter opens with a painting by a famous artist. The selection is intended to convey not only the beauty of children but the feelings and moods of childhood as seen by the artist. I have included these pictures—all from galleries in the United States—in the hope they will help readers gain an appreciation for the special children we refer to as learning disabled.

Acknowledgments

As with every undertaking of this type there are a number of individuals who must be acknowledged, many of whom actually helped to develop the project. First of all, I want to thank Ray Short, the editor I worked with at Allyn and Bacon, who saw to it that we came up with a book. I also thank Sylvia Dovner at Technical Texts, where this book was produced. Sylvia has a keen eye and a quick mind, both of which she brought to bear on this volume.

For much of the library work, I thank Kathleen Opie. She looked up countless books, journals, dissertations, and unpublished papers. She certainly knows the library system at the University of Washington and the interlibrary affiliations throughout the country. I also thank Susan Isoshima and her colleagues in the word processing room at the Experimental Education Unit at the University of Washington. They typed and retyped dozens of drafts of the chapters for this book. And among others at the University, I thank Joan Ronk and Lisa DeWitt who rushed the many packages I sent to Boston and environs, and I am grateful to Pat Vadasy for writing the study questions.

I also extend my appreciation to some of the people who reviewed various drafts of the manuscript: Carol Weller, University of Utah; William Wolking, University of Florida; Bill Watson, University of New Mexico; and Edward Polloway, Lynchburg College. They spent many hours pouring over these chapters, and their comments were always helpful and encouraging.

Thanks also go to all of my colleagues in learning disabilities throughout the country who sent me materials, references, and pictures. I never called anyone, but what it wasn't a matter of great urgency ("I need it right now!"), and bless them, they all came through.

I wish to thank my wife for pushing me to include the pictures in this book. She has a good idea now and then. Lastly, I acknowledge the University of Washington for allowing me to fuss with this book for almost three years—never scolding me for taking extra time off to write or for being grumpy when I did show up for work.

PART I

OVERVIEW OF
LEARNING DISABILITIES

Chapter 1

Mother and Child by Gary Melchers (*c.* 1906). Courtesy of The Art Institute of Chicago, gift of James Deering.

BACKGROUND

MAIN IDEAS

- Fundamental concepts about learning disabilities: who is learning disabled, who is interested in learning disabilities, what causes learning disabilities, where and how LD pupils are educated

- Three definitions of learning disabilities and points of similarity: neurological dysfunction, difficulty in academic tasks, discrepancy between achievement and potential, exclusion of other causes

- Statistical data on the number of LD youngsters and the reasons for the increasing incidence of learning disabilities in recent years

- Classification of LD students: diversity, subtypes, and reasons for classification

- Key points and participants in the six major approaches to managing learning disabilities: neurological and perceptual functions, neurological and multisensory functions, neurological impairment and language development, linguistics and modality matching, behavioral and direct instruction, cognitive and meta-cognitive approaches

OVERVIEW

Learning disabilities is a most exciting, confusing, and important field. This book is intended to provide an understanding of learning disabilities, as well as information about the latest developments in the area and some changes that could come about in the future.

This chapter is intended as a first step toward those ends. The first section contains a set of responses to common questions about learning disabilities. Next is a brief summary of the important definitions of learning disabilities and some data on prevalence. A discussion of attempts to classify LD students follows. The fifth section summarizes the history of this relatively new field. The final section contains comments on the topics covered in the chapter.

GENERAL ISSUES

As an introduction to the field of learning disabilities, this section begins with some basic questions and responses. They are not at all comprehensive. The intent is simply to provide a framework from which to begin a study of learning disabilities.

Who is learning disabled?   As a whole, individuals with learning disabilities are a diverse group of people with a wide variety of characteristics. This section briefly identifies some common types of LD pupils. The following comments are from *Because of My Persistence I've Learned From Children* (Lovitt, 1982).

Generally slow.   One subset of LD youngsters includes those who are a bit slow in many ways. They have problems in a number of areas: reading, writing, spelling, computing, playing games, and socializing.

Specifically slow.   Other LD children have a specific disability. Some are able to compute, write, and socialize, but have great difficulty reading. Others are specifically disabled in spelling or handwriting, and a few are off the mark only in mathematics.

Socially clever.   Some LD pupils have highly developed social skills, but are behind their peers academically. Many of these socially clever youngsters have traveled widely and interacted a great deal with adults. They have been given toys and games of several types and have been taken regularly to concerts, museums, and parks. They may even have been tutored privately or attended exclusive schools. For many of these youngsters, even their problems in reading, math, and spelling are more sophisticated than those of other youngsters.

Frequently disruptive.   Still other children in the LD category are so classified because they behave inappropriately. In most LD classes there are two or three youngsters who barely qualified for special services; they would not have been eligible had they behaved more suitably. These children can read, write, and perform other academic skills as well as many of their classmates who were not referred for special services, but they were dubbed learning disabled because they talked without permission too often in the classroom, fought too much on the playground, or in other ways disrupted their classrooms too frequently. Most of these children are boys.

Environmentally impoverished.   Some LD children come from poor environments. A considerable number grew up with only one parent; others were shifted from one home to another. Still others were physically or emotionally abused. Many were raised in homes where there were only a few books and reading and other academic pursuits were not encouraged. Some LD youngsters have not been cared for physically. They haven't been fed properly; they haven't been encouraged to bathe; they've had to wear ragged and dirty clothes; and they haven't gotten enough sleep. Some of these children, quite understandably, cannot read, spell, or compute too well.

Variably talented.   Some LD children give the impression that they simply were not in school when certain skills were taught. They have a number of specific gaps in many areas. For example, they may be able to perform certain skills in reading and math, but lack other specific skills normally associated with these subjects: They read well orally but not silently; they can add but not subtract. Many of these children have missed several days of school. They were absent because they or someone else in their family was ill. They didn't attend when they were shifted from one foster home to another. Many of them missed a number of days when they were taken from clinic to clinic in an effort to find the alleged cause of their disability.

Who is interested in learning disabilities?   Learning disabilities are perhaps the most popular of all the areas of exceptionality. One reason for this interest is that a number of famous people have been referred to as learning disabled: Albert Einstein, Woodrow Wilson, Nelson Rockefeller, Thomas Edison, to name a few. Recently, some new names have been added to that group: Tom Cruise and Bruce Jenner (Schulman, 1986). Whether any of these prestigious people were actually learning disabled is not terribly important. What does matter is that their names lend touches of class to the field. Many parents, particularly those of middle- to upper-class status, are willing to have their children labeled "learning disabled" when some academic or social problem has been detected in their children if they feel the rich and famous have also been affected.

The academically and socially conscious parents are extremely interested in learning disabilities and are eager to keep up with advances and trends in the field. Accordingly, the media devote considerable attention to learning disabilities. Rarely does a month pass without a feature article on learning disabilities or dyslexia in one or more of the popular magazines. Likewise, most of the large city daily newspapers regularly run lengthy stories on learning disabilities or dyslexia. Television and radio stations often interview parents of LD youth, as well as teachers and other professionals who work with them.

Interest in learning disabilities also extends to people in a number of professional disciplines: pediatrics, family medicine, neurology, psychiatry, psychology, nutrition, pharmacology, optometry, kinesthesiology, toxology, and of course, education.

What causes learning disabilities?   There is quite an ongoing debate about the causes of learning disabilities. Many experts believe that some neurological difference or impairment is the cause. Other authorities link learning disabilities to environmental factors such as poor diet, certain toxins, and fetal exposure to alcohol, nicotine, or other toxic agents. Still other experts maintain that some disorders are related to inadequate instruction. Not a few authorities argue that learning disabilities run in a family. To date, these reasons and others are little more than alleged causes. (See Chapter 2 for details on these presumed etiologies.)

Where and how are LD students educated and by whom?   Most LD pupils are educated in either resource rooms or regular classrooms. Some are managed in self-contained classrooms or in clinics. (See Chapters 4 and 5 for more detail.) A wide variety of techniques is used, some more specialized than others. (See Chapters 6 through 10 for discussions of these methods.) When it comes to instructors, most LD youngsters are taught by specially trained teachers. In many instances, those specialists work directly with LD pupils; at other times they assist other teachers who directly serve the students.

—————— DEFINING LEARNING DISABILITIES ——————

This section is by no means a definitive listing and discussion of the many definitions of learning disabilities that have been written over the past twenty years. Only three definitions are cited here: Those that have had, or will probably have, significant influence on the field.

The first definition comes from the United States Office of Education. It includes the regulations for defining and identifying LD students under Public Law (PL) 94–142:

> Specific learning disability means a disorder in one or more of the basic psychological processes involved in understanding or in using language, spoken or written, which may manifest itself in an imperfect ability to listen, think, speak, read, write, spell, or to do mathematical calculations. The term includes such conditions as perceptual handicaps, brain injury, minimal brain dysfunction, dyslexia, and developmental aphasia. The term does not include children who have learning problems which are primarily the result of visual, hearing, or motor handicaps, or mental retardation, or emotional disturbance, or of environmental, cultural, or economic disadvantage. [USOE, 1977, p. 65983]

According to Mercer, Hughes, and Mercer (1985), 44% of the states are using the USOE definition without modification, whereas another 28% have adopted it with slight variation.

Not every organization has been pleased with the USOE definition, however. The National Joint Committee for Learning Disabilities (NJCLD), comprised of professionals from six groups, argued with five features of the federal definition:

1. The term "children" was unnecessarily restrictive, since a major trend in the field has been the development of secondary-level and adult programs.
2. The inclusion of the phrase "basic psychological processes" generated extensive and needless debate in the field.
3. It was troublesome to include spelling as a separate category, because it is typically subsumed under written expression.
4. The definition of LD is not enhanced by the list of conditions, which include perceptual handicaps, brain injury, minimal brain dysfunction, dyslexia, and developmental aphasia.

5. The wording of the exclusion clause has contributed to the widespread misconception that learning disabilities can occur neither in conjunction with other handicapping conditions nor in the presence of "environmental, cultural, or economic disadvantage."

Consequently, the coalition issued the following definition in 1981:

> Learning disabilities is a generic term that refers to a heterogeneous group of disorders manifested by significant difficulties in the acquisition and use of listening, speaking, reading, writing, reasoning, or mathematical abilities. These disorders are intrinsic to the individual and presumed to be due to central nervous system dysfunction. Even though a learning disability may occur concomitantly with other handicapping conditions (e.g., cultural differences, insufficient/inappropriate instruction, psychogenic factors), it is not the direct result of those conditions or influences. [Hammill, Leigh, McNutt, & Larsen, 1981, p. 336]

After some deliberation, five of the six groups approved the definition. The Board of the Association for Children and Adults with Learning Disabilities (ACALD), however, disapproved it and wrote their own:

- □ Specific Learning Disabilities is a chronic condition of presumed neurological origin which selectively interferes with the development, integration, and/or demonstration of verbal and/or non-verbal abilities.
- □ Specific Learning Disabilities exists as a distinct handicapping condition in the presence of average to superior intelligence, adequate sensory motor systems, and adequate learning opportunities. The condition varies in its manifestations and in degree of severity.
- □ Throughout life the condition can affect self-esteem, education, vocation, socialization, and/or daily living activities. [*Special Education Today,* 1985, p. 1]

The ACALD definition differs in important ways from the 1977 federal definition and the NJCLD statement. It is different from both in its contention that a learning disability can go beyond the academic domain, as expressed in the final sentence of the ACALD definition. Also, the ACALD definition, like that from the NJCLD, differs from the federal statement in that it presumes learning disabilities to be of neurological origin.

Points of Similarity

There are, however, four points of agreement in the three definitions. These points tend to agree with most other definitions of learning disabilities that have been advanced. This section discusses each of the four points.

Neurological Dysfunction.   The NJCLD and ACALD definitions directly state that learning disabilities are presumably caused by some neurological disorder, and this condition is implied in the federal definition. All agree, to some extent, that other factors such as experiences at school or home can exacerbate this condition.

It has been difficult to state unequivocally that many learning disabilities are the result of brain injury, for the traditional means for making such deter- minations—medically administered electroencephalograms and psychological tests, such as the Bender-Gestalt—have proven to be rather imprecise.

In recent years considerable advances have been made in the diagnostic tests of neurologists and others; hence, statements can be made about brain injury with more precision than formerly was possible. (Chapter 2 discusses advances that are used in documenting brain injuries or neurological differences.)

Difficulty in Academic Tasks.   The ACALD, NJCLD, and USOE definitions all indicate that learning disabilities could be revealed as a deficit in one or more academic areas, either in specific subjects such as reading, writing, mathematics, or spelling, or in more general skills such as listening, speaking, or thinking. The ACALD definition goes beyond even those conditions by stating that a learning disability could appear in the form of social or vocational adjustment, daily living skills, or self-esteem. (Chapters 6 through 11 present considerable information on the academic, social, and emotional characteristics of LD youth.)

Discrepancy Between Achievement and Potential.   All three definitions also agree that LD youth experience problems in one or more areas in spite of the fact that these young people are of normal intelligence. To determine this discrepancy has posed problems for school personnel who are trying to put the various definitions into practice, for in order to calculate a discrepancy they must grapple with three questions.

How is a pupil's potential identified?   Ordinarily, a school psychologist admin- isters an IQ test—frequently the *Wechsler Intelligence Scale for Children–Revised* (WISC–R)—to determine potential intelligence. Therein lies a problem, for the scores from these tests are not as constant and accurate as their proponents would like us to believe. Several factors could affect a youngster's score on a test; for example, lack of sleep, depression, hunger. A far more serious criticism of such tests is that they measure intelligence only insofar as it is defined by the assorted questions and games that make up the test.

How is achievement measured?   School psychologists, speech therapists, teachers, or others administer a battery of tests to determine achievement. A common package given to LD youth in Washington state, for example, includes the *Woodcock Reading Mastery Tests,* the *KeyMath Diagnostic Test,* and the *Peabody Individual Achievement Test.* Hundreds of other tests exist in every area. (See Chapter 3, Chapters 6 through 9, and Chapters 11, 12, and 13 for more detail on tests.) Scores from those tests pose another set of problems; a pupil's score on one reading test will not necessarily be the same as his score on another. Such inconsistency has been noted a number of times (for example, in Lovitt, 1986).

How is a discrepancy specified? Discrepancies are generally determined by relating the scores from the tests measuring intelligence and achievement. It has been pointed out that neither the data required to determine potential nor those needed to indicate achievement are too stable. Serious problems can therefore arise when it comes to making sensible statements about a youngster's discrepancy. Even if we could count on solid data from intelligence and achievement tests, we would still have to select a discrepancy score that certified someone to be "truly learning disabled." Should that difference be two years behind, or three, or four, or more? Furthermore, should the discrepancy score be greater the older the LD youth happens to be? (This issue and others related to assessment are discussed in Chapter 3.)

Exclusion of Other Causes. The three definitions of learning disabilities presented above, along with most others, are insistent that a child's learning disability cannot be attributed to such handicapping conditions as mental retardation, emotional disturbance, hearing or visual impairment, or cultural or social disadvantage. Furthermore, those definitions state or infer that a learning disability must either be caused by a neurological impairment or be linked to an assumed neurological difference. It is difficult to meet either demand. In many instances it is impossible to state with assurance that the disability was not brought on by one of the conditions listed earlier. Furthermore, as has been indicated, the means for indicating neurological impairment have been somewhat unreliable.

───────── PREVALENCE OF LEARNING DISABILITIES ─────────

The number of LD youngsters is largely dependent on the definition used and correspondingly, the methods selected for implementing the definition. (More information on methods is given in Chapter 3.) The statistics on LD youth are greatly influenced by which tests are administered, how they are interpreted, and which formulas are relied on to determine discrepancy. Because of the built-in variations, the incidence of learning disabilities over the years has ranged from 2% to over 30%.

Recently, there has been a national concern over the rising incidence of learning disabilities. In 1984 Gerber reported some revealing statistics about three states over a seven-year period, as shown in Table 1.1.

Another informative group of statistics is the percentage of LD pupils within the total handicapped population served in schools, which is shown in Table 1.2 from Gerber's article.

The percentages of LD pupils from California, Texas, and New York are fairly representative of what has occurred throughout the country. In every state, the number of LD pupils served has increased since 1976. In 1985–86 an estimated 1.8 million LD youngsters were being served in the public schools.

In a report on special education programs (USOE, 1983) state directors of special education identified five reasons that may account for the increased percentages of students classified as learning disabled:

■ TABLE 1.1 ■   Percentage of All Students Classified as Learning Disabled in Three Large States

School Year	California	Texas	New York
1976–77	1.7	1.8	1.0
1977–78	2.0	4.1	.9
1978–79	2.2	4.5	.6
1979–80	2.9	4.3	1.0
1980–81	3.9	4.5	1.6
1981–82	4.7	4.8	2.5
1982–83	5.0	5.4	4.5

Source: Reprinted by permission from M.M. Gerber, "The Department of Education's Sixth Annual Report to Congress on PL 94–142: Is Congress Getting the Full Story?" *Exceptional Children, 51*, 1984, p. 214.

— Improvements in identification and assessment procedures
— Liberal eligibility standards applied by local districts
— Diminishing instructional options other than special education for students with learning problems
— Greater social acceptance and preference to be classified as learning disabled, as opposed to mentally retarded
— Judicial interference with identification procedures for students thought to be mentally retarded

As noted by Frankenberger and Harper (1987), the U.S. Department of Education identified a rapid increase in the prevalence of LD children during the eight years from 1976 to 1984. In 1978, the LD population constituted approximately 29% of the handicapped children, and in 1982, 40%. Frankenberger and Harper pointed out that the increased number of students with learning disabilities was the cause for considerable concern in the Department of Education and at the state and district levels.

■ TABLE 1.2 ■   Percentage of All Handicapped Students Classified as Learning Disabled in Three Large States

School Year	California	Texas	New York
1976–77	22.4	21.8	14.4
1977–78	26.4	41.2	11.9
1978–79	27.8	47.5	9.3
1979–80	33.2	46.2	14.2
1980–81	44.1	47.4	19.4
1981–82	53.0	50.4	27.8
1982–83	54.5	52.1	44.1

Source: Reprinted by permission from M.M. Gerber, "The Department of Education's Sixth Annual Report to Congress on PL 94–142: Is Congress Getting the Full Story?" *Exceptional Children, 51*, 1984, p. 215.

Frankenberger and Harper were of the opinion that states could reduce these numbers by resorting to one or more of the following plans. First, alter their definition of learning disabilities. Second, specify higher IQ cutoffs. Third, specify stringent discrepancy formulas between achievement and intelligence. Data from their surveys of the states in 1982 and 1986, with regard to those practices, revealed that few states had resorted to the first and second approaches for reducing numbers, but many were relying on the third method. In 1986, 57% of the states specified achievement discrepancy criteria, and several had published sophisticated expectancy formulas and regression analysis techniques.

CLASSIFYING LD STUDENTS

Agreement on Diversity

Those who write definitions of learning disabilities and most others associated with the field agree on one matter: LD youngsters are a heterogeneous lot. The great majority of researchers, teachers, and parents do not believe that there is only one type of learning disability. They generally concur that some pupils have difficulty in certain areas, while others have difficulty in different areas. They might argue about the causes of learning disabilities, how many there are, where they should be served, by whom, and with what, but they would all admit that LD youngsters are extremely diverse.

Identification of Subtypes

A number of researchers have set out to identify subgroups of learning disabilities within the total set. McKinney (1984) identified four subtypes, which are described in the following paragraphs.

Subtype I, representing 33% of the sample, were determined by their average verbal skills with deficits in sequential and spatial tasks. They were lacking in independence and task orientation. Teachers rated them as more considerate and less hostile than other subtypes. Academically, they were mildly impaired in reading and math.

Subtype II (10% of the sample) showed the greatest scatter on the WISC–R. They were rated the lowest by their teachers on all behavioral scales. Furthermore, they were judged to be less considerate, more hostile, less competent academically, and less oriented toward tasks than children in the other subgroups.

Subtype III represented the largest collection at 47%. Although they had above-average conceptual skills, their scores on the WISC–R were not outstanding. Children in this subgroup were rated low on task orientation. While they were as extroverted as non-disabled pupils, they were rated as less considerate and more hostile than youngsters in other LD categories.

Subtype IV students (10%) were much like those in Subtype I, but did not display behavioral disorders. This group was also more impaired in achievement than were either Subtypes I or III.

Spreen and Haaf (1986) sought to replicate findings of previous research on subtypes of learning disability and to determine the consistency of those subtypes from childhood to adulthood. They found their data generally agreed with those of others, when test scores of a number of learning disabled children with a mean age of ten years were submitted to cluster analysis. To achieve their second goal, the authors followed up and tested some of those individuals at a mean age of twenty-four. According to them, data regarding the tracing of individual characteristics from childhood to adulthood suggested that those who had displayed visual-spatial deficits as children maintained those impairments into their adult years and that problems with reading and arithmetic also persisted into adulthood. Furthermore, those who exhibited severely impaired or nonimpaired performances as children continued to display those characteristics as adults. Those who fell into a subtype with linguistic impairment as children, however, appeared in clusters of overall low-performance as adults. Spreen and Haaf contended that this pattern generally supported the prediction that language deficits would worsen during teen and early adult years. It may be that children with primary linguistic impairments at ages eight to twelve never catch up and thus emerge into a generally impaired subtype in their early adult years.

Reasons for Classifying

The primary reason for classifying youngsters in education is to put them in a certain place, with a particular kind of teacher, who will teach them in a specific way. If there were children of types X, Y, and Z, and if there were ways to sort them out—to put the all X's together and so forth—and then place them in situations corresponding to their letters, supplying them with teachers trained especially to deal with them, and who presented the children with materials, techniques, and procedures specifically suited for them, and particularly, if all this would lead to the greatest improvement in learning, then there would be a point to classifying students.

The diagnostic/classification schema for some disciplines actually make sense. Dermatologists at several universities, for example, are seeking to identify various forms of skin cancer and accordingly come up with cures. To date, they have learned that some types of treatment are more effective with certain types of cancer. Apparently there is a specific technique for the *carcinoma* type that is not as appropriate for the *lymphoma* and *melinoma* forms. For this reason, it is important to locate the precise type of cancer. Another reason for determining the exact form would be to isolate the conditions that caused the cancer and then avoid those conditions. In other words, whether we are interested in classifying types of cancer or types of youngsters, there should be reasons for those classifications.

Specialists in learning disabilities have not been as effective as the dermatologists in locating specific treatments. The recommended treatment—books, techniques, procedures, strategies—have not proven to be exclusively beneficial for LD children. For certain, there are some good reading, mathematics, and social skills practices (see Chapters 6 through 13), but they have not been exclusive practices for the learning disabled. An approach effective for instructing the learning disabled ordinarily turns out to be a creditable technique with Chapter I children (those qualifying for federally funded programs for the disadvantaged), slow learners, and often regular students as well. When it comes to selecting specific practices for the subtypes of LD youngsters identified by McKinney, there is even less support to indicate that distinct programs are appropriate for specific sets of youngsters. Furthermore, there is little evidence to suggest that any of the subtypes was caused by anything different: environmentally, genetically, or otherwise. Conversely, and fortunately, if a beneficial technique is discovered for nonhandicapped children, or for those not designated as learning disabled, chances are that it will work with many LD children.

Historically, when an exemplary technique is developed for youngsters of one type, it often turns out to be suitable for students of other classifications. For example, the Montessori Method, originally designed for children from lower socio-economic areas, is now, paradoxically, one of the favorite approaches for preschoolers from higher income families. Another example of the generalization of practices is the Distar program, also developed originally for children of low-income parents. Although apparently well suited for those target children, that method is now arranged with children of all types: wealthy, not so wealthy, special, and regular. In the same vein, a number of techniques designed to adapt content materials to handicapped learners have been useful with nonhandicapped children (a few of those are discussed in Chapter 10). Conversely, there are any number of good reading approaches—advance organizers, mapping, framed outlines, study guides—that have found their way into situations with LD students although they were originally designed for nonhandicapped or gifted children.

A BRIEF HISTORY OF LEARNING DISABILITIES

The search for techniques appropriate to LD individuals is nearly two centuries old. Interest in learning disabilities as a field of study began about 1800. This section contains a survey of six major theories and their efforts to deal with this disability. A more detailed account, written by Wiederholt (1974), divides the saga into three periods:

- —*Foundation phase* (1800 to 1930): marked by basic scientific investigations of brain function
- —*Transition phase* (1930 to 1960): application of research findings about brain dysfunction to the clinical study of children with learning problems and professional development of assessment and treatment methods for those children
- —*Integration phase* (1960 to 1980): characterized by rapid growth of school programs for the learning disabled; the emergence of a variety of theories, assessment techniques, and teaching strategies; and the enactment of legislation designed to protect the rights of handicapped children and youth

In the historical sketch included here, we will consider the major themes that have in the past or are currently influencing the practice of learning disabilities. We will also note individuals associated with those themes and tie together those ideas and individuals whenever possible. Finally, we will look at the contributions of those individuals with respect to the literature and practices of learning disabilities. In order to accomplish these objectives, the following stylistic features are incorporated in the following sections.

First, while the story of learning disabilities has been simplified, no attempt has been made to smooth out the rough edges. Although there have been a number of individuals and circumstances that contributed to the development of the field, the evolution has been anything but orderly.

Second, characterizations of ideas and individuals in the field are included only to the extent they contributed at one time or another. In a number of LD textbooks, dozens of names and a few themes have been kept alive simply because early historians noted them and others saw fit to continue the litanies even though the characters had never significantly influenced the field. Such a practice is bothersome and confusing to the student of learning disabilities. Third, a number of quotations are used to present the ideas of the field's founding mothers and fathers in their own words. On rereading the old accounts, it becomes obvious that the Lehtinens, Ortons, Cruickshanks, and others best presented their cases themselves. That should not be surprising, for after all, they were caught in the enthusiasm of their discoveries, theories, and recommendations. Much of that spirit is lost when their ideas are paraphrased by others.

Six major themes are featured in the following historical sketch: Neurological and Perceptual Functions, Neurological and Multisensory Functions, Neurological Impairment and Language Development, Linguistics and Modality Matching, Behavioral and Direct Instruction, and Cognitive and Metacognitive Approaches.

Neurological and Perceptual Functions

The line of theory that deals with neurological and perceptual functions has been the most long lasting and possibly the most influential in the field of learning disabilities. It generally begins with the work of Kurt Goldstein (1939), a physician who treated brain-injured soldiers during World War I. Goldstein concluded that those men behaved abnormally with respect to visual perception (noted by foreground–background difficulties), attending to unimportant objects (being distracted by numerous external stimuli), and perseveration (being locked into repeated action).

As the story of perceptual deviation due to brain injury unfolds, Goldstein influenced Heinz Werner, a developmental psychologist, and Alfred Strauss, a neuropsychiatrist who worked with brain-injured individuals at the Wayne County Training School in Northville, Michigan. Their studies with brain-injured mentally retarded children (Strauss & Werner, 1942; Werner & Strauss, 1941) revealed to them the following behavioral and biological characteristics:

Alfred A. Strauss came to the United States as a research psychiatrist at the Wayne County School in Michigan in 1937. He later founded the Cove School in Wisconsin. Strauss made major contributions to both diagnosis and education of brain-injured children. His best known studies dealt with children who were retarded but who showed behavioral characteristics of brain injury.

— Perceptual disorders—that is, seeing certain parts of a picture rather than the whole
— Figure-ground distortions—that is, confusing background and foreground
— Perseveration—that is, having difficulty stopping activities or switching to others
— Conceptual disorders—that is, inability to organize materials and thoughts
— Behavioral disorders—that is, being hyperactive, explosive, or otherwise unruly
— Soft neurological signs—that is, displaying subtle evidences of neurological dysfunctioning such as awkwardness
— Neurological impairment—that is, having some evidence of actual brain injury or having no history of mental retardation in the family

Strauss, in collaboration with Laura Lehtinen, a teacher, developed a set of instructional practices for brain-injured youngsters. Their rationale for concentrating on instructional and environmental matters stated: "Since the organic lesion is medically untreatable, our efforts may extend in two directions: in manipulating and controlling the external, overstimulating environment and in educating the child to the exercise of voluntary control" [Strauss & Lehtinen, 1947, p. 131].

As for the control of the external environment, they offered this description of the proper classroom:

> The class group is small—twelve children is the maximum number. . . . The classroom for these children is large enough to permit each child to be seated at a considerable distance from any other. There is only a minimum of pictures, murals, bulletin boards. . . . We would even recommend entire absence of these materials for the first half-year of a child's attendance in the special class. Since the never absent sights and sounds outside the classroom form another great source of distraction, the most suitable classroom is one on the second floor or one in which the windows face an infrequently used court.
>
> [The teacher] . . . will soon discover the distracting influence of ornamentation such as bracelets, earrings, dangling necklaces. . . . For the brain-injured child she will be no less attractive and more effective as a teacher if these distractions are avoided. . . . In order to curtail further the number of distracting influences, the child may be removed to the periphery of the group by placing his work table in contact with the wall, so that his back is toward the other children. [Strauss & Lehtinen, 1947, p. 131]

In addition to this rather somber atmosphere, Strauss and Lehtinen also recommended that materials be stripped of unnecessary detail and made to focus only on important items:

> The learning handicap of the child who is not hyperactive or disinhibited but who is distracted by the multiplicity of detail he finds in his books can be similarly alleviated by applying our knowledge of the general control of distractibility. If the child's materials are divested of everything but the merest essentials—by actually cutting away borders or pictures or by enclosure within a cover which exposes only a small area at a time—the child is able to accomplish his task with relatively little distraction. [1947, p. 131]

These collaborators were concerned, however, about weaning children from this austere type of program:

> The direction of the child's behavior, however, should eventually be effected from within himself rather than from externally regulated conditions. As the organic disturbances are lessened, the protections are gradually removed; a child's desk is placed within the class group, pictures and bulletin boards make their appearance, and experiences in which a group participates become more numerous. After another period of adjustment with further reduction of the general disturbances as well as possession of the requisite skills and knowledges, the child can return to a regular class group which is suited to his needs. [1947, p. 135]

Strauss and Lehtinen summarized their beliefs on the implications of brain injury in these words:

The brain-injured organism must be seen from a different aspect [than a nonbrain-injured individual]. The organic damage produces disturbances of figure-ground perception, disintegration in the perception of visual form and space, disturbances of auditory perception, and disturbances of general integration which render the pathological organism unable to perceive stimuli in the same relationship as do most normal children or to respond to patterns of the expected complexity. [1947, p. 136]

About half of the Strauss and Lehtinen book is devoted to examples and descriptions of activities for instruction in arithmetic, reading, and writing. Underlying all their practices are recommendations that children must develop visual, auditory, and kinesthetic perceptions before they can progress to the basic skills. In keeping with that belief, they provide numerous suggestions on how to present these "readiness" activities.

Another person involved with the perceptual saga was Newell Kephart, who was greatly influenced by Werner and Strauss while he was a student at the Wayne County School. In 1955 he collaborated with Strauss (Strauss & Kephart, 1955) to revise the original Strauss and Lehtinen volume. His most significant contribution to the field, however, was *The Slow Learner in the Classroom,* published in 1960 and revised in 1971. In that text Kephart presented his philosophy on child development and spelled out numerous remedial and educational techniques for children with perceptual-motor difficulties. In his preface he described the behaviors of the children featured in his book:

Newell C. Kephart was for many years at the University of Northern Colorado. Prior to that, he was a trainee at the Wayne County School and collaborated with Strauss to revise the original Strauss and Lehtinen volume. His most significant contribution to learning disabilities was "The Slow Learner in the Classroom," which presented his philosophy of educating children with perceptual–motor difficulties.

Too often these aberrant performances are attributed to willful misbehavior, stupidity or lack of interest. Actually, in many cases, the child's problems are not his fault. His central nervous system processes information in a little different way than that of other children. The organization among the items of information is disturbed, so that he does not see what we think we show him; he sees something different. He does not hear what we think we are saying to him. He does not make the connections as we do between bits of information which we think we are presenting in such a beautifully organized fashion. His central nervous system is treating these items in a different way. [Kephart, 1971, Preface]*

Kephart's principal hypothesis on educating these children was that a perceptual-motor match must be made. His rationale for that belief states:

Perception supplies the information upon which behavior is based. Motor responses supply the movements which are the overt aspects of the behavior. Unless these two functions can be related to each other, behavior has little or no relation to information. Perceptual information does not influence behavior but merely proliferates its own processes independent of the responses of the child.

The motor learning described above has resulted in a body of motor information. This body of information is concerned with what movements are possible, how you make them, and what are their results. Tactual and kinesthetic data are used to monitor the course of the movement and to provide knowledge of its results. Tactual and kinesthetic data are closely allied to (possibly inseparable from) movement, since they occur only in the presence of movement and since movement always produces one or the other or both. The body of motor information, therefore, is largely tactual and kinesthetic in nature. It is a body of action information, by and about movement.

Visual and auditory information, on the other hand, have initially no movement implication. They provide static information which needs no response for its fulfillment. Sometimes they trigger action, as in the signal qualities suggested by Werner. . . . Even such triggered responses, however, are only related to the perceptual data at the instant of inception. A continuing relationship to the perceptual data or modifications in the course of the response on the basis of such data do[es] not occur.

Unless some relationship is established between the motor functions and the perceptual functions, the child builds up a body of perceptual information, resulting from the manipulation among themselves of the perceptual elements which he has differentiated, but this body of perceptual information will not be related to his motor information and hence will not influence it. [pp. 19–20]*

Kephart then hypothesized on the developmental sequences of activities: "The perceptual-motor match paves the way for perceptual control of motor responses. When accuracy and consistency of perceptual information has been assured, it can be used to determine and guide the overt responses of the child"

---

*Reprinted by permission from Newell C. Kephart (Ed.), *The Slow Learner in the Classroom,* 2nd edition (Columbus, OH: Merrill, 1971).

(p. 24). When a figure-ground relationship has been established, a basis for movement control is available, which in turn facilitates systematic exploration, perception, and intersensory integration, ultimately leading to the formation of concepts. According to Kephart,

> [t]he slow learning child is one in whom progress through these stages of development has either broken down or is noticeably delayed. If progress appears to be normal but slow in its course, the condition is usually associated with borderline mental retardation or with cultural deprivation. If the progress is disrupted in its course, the condition is usually associated with diagnosed or assumed disturbances of neurological functioning. In either event, if the delay is sufficient or if the disturbance is severe enough, mental retardation will accompany the condition. [p. 42]*

As for instruction, he claimed that

> [w]hen a gap in development is identified, it is not enough merely to go back and teach as one would teach a younger child. These earlier occurring learnings must be recast in terms of the highest developmental stage the child has achieved, even though this higher stage is very disturbed. [p. 46]*

Kephart recommended a perceptual, not merely a remedial program. Although he understood the rationale for multisensory programs, he was cautious about their use:

> Every individual has a sense avenue which is particularly efficient for him. Some people learn more readily through vision; some through audition; some through tactual-kinesthetic avenues. In like manner, every multi-sensory presentation has a core sensory avenue around which the other avenues are related. If the core avenue of the presentation is different from the most efficient avenue of the child, the presentation may well confuse more than it helps. Therefore, no standard multisensory presentation can be developed, and each presentation must be tailored to the individual child. [p. 73]*

Kephart emphasized the importance, in the process of learning, of developing laterality (knowing about the left and right sides of our bodies), of establishing directionality (knowing which way to move), and of control and accurate images of our bodies in space. Consistent with his philosophies, he recommended instructional approaches and techniques based on acquiring perceptions that were particularly related to physical development.

William Cruickshank, who also began his career at the Wayne County Training School, continued this theoretical line and maintained that learning disabilities were the result of neurological impairment and perceptual deficits.

---

*Reprinted by permission from Newell C. Kephart (Ed.), *The Slow Learner in the Classroom,* 2nd edition (Columbus, OH: Merrill, 1971).

William M. Cruickshank trained at the Wayne County facility and was a student of Strauss'. He was for many years at the University of Syracuse and more recently at the University of Michigan. His most influential book, "A Teaching Method for Brain-Injured and Hyperactive Children," describes his research in Maryland with such youngsters. For that research, he adapted the teaching methods of Strauss and Lehtinen.

Cruickshank applied Strauss and Lehtinen's instructional suggestions to his work with nonretarded brain-injured youth.

One of his early studies at Syracuse University with a doctoral student (Dolphin, 1950) sought ". . . to corroborate much of what Werner and Strauss had done with exogenuous mentally retarded boys." Dolphin's data indicated that there were ". . . marked similarities between the responses of her intellectually normal cerebral-palsied subjects and those of the retarded subjects of Werner and Strauss and their associates." Dolphin's findings thus illustrated that the perceptual and perceptual-motor problems of neurologically handicapped children were not a function of mental retardation alone, but of some type of neurophysiological dysfunction. A series of doctoral dissertations at Syracuse University, based on research with children who were organically deaf, aphasic, and or suffering from various types of epilepsy, provided similar evidence that perceptual deviations were associated with neurological impairment.

Later, Cruickshank and a number of colleagues (1961) arranged Strauss and Lehtinen techniques in a public school setting with youngsters who were of normal or near-normal intelligence. Although most of these pupils displayed behaviors characteristic of brain injury—distractibility, motor disinhibition, dissociation, disturbance of figure-background relationship, and perseveration—and were accordingly labeled as having perceptual problems, many of them did not have a defined brain injury.

Cruickshank and his fellow investigators set up a two-year study in which experimental and control classrooms were arranged. Ten youngsters were assigned to each of four classes: two experimental and two control. Some of the children were believed to be brain injured and others were not; all of them exhibited the same perceptual deficits and other characteristics of brain injury.

Based on Strauss and Lehtinen's recommendations for instruction, Cruickshank and colleagues (1961) hypothesized that four elements comprised the essentials of a good teaching environment for brain-injured children: ". . . reduced environmental stimuli, reduced space, a structured school program and life plan, and an increase in the stimulus value of the teaching materials which are constructed to cope with the specific characteristics of the psycho-pathology under consideration" (p. 14). They incorporated their ideas in their experimental classrooms:

> . . . the two experimental rooms were painted a uniform color closely matching the honey-colored woodwork. Individual work cubicles with built-in desk tops were constructed to meet the height and weight requirements of the individual children in each group. Open coat closets and supply cabinets were provided with sliding doors. Windows were made opaque with a plastic medium. Individual two-shelf lockers equipped with snap-lock doors were built for each child. . . . Every assignment during the day was checked by the teacher and only when the task was correctly completed was the child allowed to file his work on the bottom shelf. This practice introduced into the classroom learning situation a rigid order of sequential procedures for both the child and teacher. . . . [Cruikshank et al., 1961, p. 119].

Many of the teaching materials Cruikshank and his colleagues used were similar to the ones designed for preschools, including peg boards, puzzles, form boards, stencils, and blocks. The researchers maintained that it was vital to instruct children in readiness and perceptual tasks before teaching them reading and other basic skills. Teachers of children in control group classes could use any of the teaching methods that were available in experimental classes.

At the end of one year, children in experimental situations were returned to more ordinary settings, where most of the experimental conditions were no longer in effect. According to Cruikshank and his co-authors, the study revealed two major results:

1. At the end of the project year, the experimental classes had made *temporary* gains in comparison to the control group on several of the scoring categories of the perceptual tests. . . . By the end of the second year . . . after the classes had been regrouped and the teaching approach had been varied, the children who had originally been in the experimental classes had lost these gains.

2. The total group of 39 children, disregarding their placement in experimental or control classes, made significant academic improvement and showed considerably fewer errors on the perceptual and visuo-motor tests. [1961, pp. 374–375]

Cruickshank's views on brain injury and perception may be summarized by the following logic: If there is perceptual dysfunction, there must be neurological dysfunction, whether or not it is possible to identify such a neurological base with the crude instrumentation presently available to both neurology and psychology.

■ COMMENTARY ■   Too bad Cruickshank didn't provide more description about the control class-rooms, for those youngsters improved as much as did those in the experimental situations. Furthermore, it would be interesting to analyze Cruickshank's data using more sophisticated measures (they used only *t*-tests). To continue, it's too bad they didn't break out their data as to children who were brain injured and those who were not. It's possible that the larger gains were from one subset or the other.

Summary.   Goldstein, who began the research into neurological and perceptual functions, noted a number of unusual characteristics in brain-injured adults. Some of these characteristics, collectively referred to as perceptual difficulties, were hyperactivity, perseveration, impulsivity, and figure-ground disturbances. Goldstein influenced Strauss, Werner, and Lehtinen who worked with brain-injured and nonbrain-injured children, many of whom displayed the same perceptual disturbances. These researchers designed instructional programs, characterized by their austerity, that were reportedly effective with these children. Later, Cruickshank and his colleagues arranged the same techniques with brain-injured youngsters of several types and with others who displayed perceptual problems. They reported modest success with those structured techniques. Kephart advocated the use of perceptual training with slow learners generally, whether or not they were actually brain injured.

Influence.   The publication of Cruickshank's work in 1961 and Kephart's in 1960 had a considerable impact on public school instruction of youngsters with learning disabilities. Up until a few years ago, when there were more self-contained classrooms for LD children, it was common to see classrooms designed on the premise that possible distractions should be shielded, that children should work in small groups, and that perceptual materials should be the order of the day. Similarly, during that period, there were numerous situations that relied heavily on the perceptual-motor materials developed by Kephart and later arranged by Marianne Frostig. Thus the perceptual camp has not only influenced classroom and clinical practice, but has greatly altered the course of diagnosis and assessment.

Neurological and Multisensory Functions

The next oldest theme is perhaps neurological and multisensory functions, and it has had the next most influence on teaching practices for LD youth. This theory had its beginning with Samuel Orton, a specialist in neurology and neuropathology.

According to Geschwind (1982), a noted neurologist, some of Orton's beliefs with respect to dyslexia and brain injury have been proven true:

Samuel T. Orton, a specialist in neurology and neuropathology, theorized that dyslexia was attributed to some form of brain injury and that special techniques were required to instruct those individuals. One of his more influential books is "Reading, Writing, and Speech Problems in Children." In that volume, he describes a systematic phonics program reinforced with kinesthetic aids. He coined the term "word blindness."

- The visual perception of dyslexic or brain-injured children is generally normal.
- Childhood dyslexia is the result of an impairment in the same area of the brain that causes adult alexia.
- Childhood dyslexics can occasionally read as easily when the text is upside down or seen in a mirror.
- Ambidexterity is a characteristic of many dyslexic children.
- Stuttering is sometimes related to dyslexia.
- Many dyslexics are left-handed.
- Dyslexia is often apparent in the children's families.
- Dyslexic children are often slow in developing speech.
- Dyslexic children are frequently clumsy.
- Some dyslexic children read fairly well but have great difficulty spelling.
- Emotional disturbance is not necessarily the result of dyslexia, but it can be the result of changes in the brain.
- Disorders in other areas are not necessarily causes of dyslexia, since, in many instances, there may be other indications of the process that led to dyslexia.

Orton emphasized the importance of developing lateral dominance because of its effect on reading and writing:

From the fact that loss of the capacity to read follows a unilateral lesion only when this occurs in the dominant hemisphere may we assume that irradiation is necessary into only one of the two third level cortices to produce a linkage between visually presented symbols and their meaning. That one or the other hemisphere or one locus in one hemisphere must have an initiatory function for all volitional motor responses seems obvious. Were it not for this placing of the lead or control in one side, the two hemispheres might originate opposed or conflicting responses to a given situation. In man's brain the entire initiatory control of certain major functions, such as speech, writing and reading, seems to be in one hemisphere, as is illustrated by the occurrence of . . . aphasia, agraphia, alexia, etc., following unilateral lesions. Dominance of this degree has not, I believe, been demonstrated in the lower animals, but some form of initiatory control would seem necessary to prevent confusion of responses such as would result if either hemisphere were competent to lead without reference to the activities of the other. [Orton, 1925, p. 606]

In his later book, *Reading, Writing, and Speech Problems in Children,* Orton (1937) described a number of remediation programs that utilized a systematic phonics program reinforced with kinesthetic aids that followed the instructional recommendations given in his 1925 publication:

The tentative envisagement of the disability herein outlined would suggest that . . . training for these children would be that of extremely thorough repetitive drill on the fundamentals of phonic association with letter forms . . . until the correct associations were built up and the permanent elision of the reversed images and reversals in direction was assured. The flash method would seem from this point of view not only to be inadequate to correct early mistakes in orientation, but also to put these children under an unnecessary and unjust handicap. . . . The child has no opportunity to puzzle out whether a symbol means "p" or "q" by the flash method, and many such initial errors might well be perpetuated. When a child looks at "not" and reads it "ton," the teacher's first reaction is that the child is inattentive or is not trying, and she is apt to apply either discipline or ridicule, which in turn engender an emotional blocking or a feeling of inferiority without, however, correcting the difficulty. . . . According to our hypotheses, the training should aim at teaching the child to focus the attention on the correct set of images, and for this purpose the repetitive "a-b = ab" sort of kindergarten drill would seem to offer the most promise. [1925, p. 614]

Among the investigators who developed techniques based on Orton's recommendations and put them into practice were Marion Monroe, Anna Gillingham, Bessie Stillman, Grace Fernald, and the Spaldings. Monroe, a research assistant of Orton's, tested his educational theories. In her 1932 publication, *Children Who Cannot Read,* she laid out a teaching plan referred to as the "synthetic phonetic approach." This method begins with pictures mounted on cards from which children identify initial consonants and then vowels. After a few elements are learned, youngsters are instructed to blend consonants, and gradually, they begin to read short stories. Throughout these drills, kinesthetic activities are arranged: Children move their hands and arms to form letters and other symbols.

Gillingham and Stillman (1965) used remedial reading procedures that focused on developing language-pattern associations between the visual, auditory, and kinesthetic mechanisms in children's dominant hemisphere. It was their belief that unless these sensory mergers were accomplished, a language disability would result. They recommended a multisensory approach as a means of achieving those affiliations.

Fernald was another contributor to this line of activity. She established a clinic at UCLA where she developed a remedial approach to teach reading and spelling. This method was not particularly concerned about process, dominance, or brain injury; instead, Fernald's techniques involved the visual-auditory-kinesthetic-tactile approaches to instruction.

Fernald identified four stages in her remedial plan (Fernald, 1943). In the first stage, children selected the words they wanted to learn. These words were written with crayon in plain, blackboard-sized print. Children said each part of the word while tracing the word with a finger. In the next stage, children looked at words in print, said them while looking at them, and wrote them without copying. In the third stage, children looked at words and wrote them without vocalizing or copying them. They began reading from books and were assisted on words they were unable to pronounce. Finally, children were encouraged to generalize and form new words from their resemblance to known words. (There is more detail on both the Gillingham and Stillman and the Fernald approaches in Chapter 7.)

The Spaldings' contribution was an approach to written language disability entitled "Unified Phonics Methods." According to their description,

> [t]he core of the method is a technique by which the child learns how to write down the sounds used in spoken English as they are combined into words. Thus, conversely, he can pronounce any printed word. Meaning is thoroughly taught hand-in-hand with the writing and by using new words in original sentences. It begins with correct pronunciation of words and the writing of their component sounds in accordance with the rules of English spelling. By this means the saying, writing, reading, and meaning of words are well learned and understood. [Spalding & Spalding, 1962, p. 8]

Summary.   There are three important points to remember with regard to the studies focusing on neurological and multisensory functions. First, from their roots—that is, from the work of Orton—the adherents of this school were convinced that language/reading disability was due to a neurological impairment. Second, the clients with whom they were concerned were generally of normal intelligence and were often referred to as dyslexics. Third, they recommended a multisensory—visual, auditory, and kinesthetic—approach to instruction.

Influence.   Beth Slingerland extended the Orton–Gillingham recommendations for multisensory education into classrooms. Previously, most of the ideas of the pioneers in the field were offered to youngsters only at clinics. Slingerland, based in suburban Seattle, established several classrooms that relied on multisensory instruction in the public schools.

The districts adopting the Slingerland method served children of normal intelligence, many of whom display characteristics cited by Orton and others. Slingerland referred to these youngsters as dyslexic and categorized them as "Specific Language Disabled." Writing about the symptoms of these children, she said that

> [y]ounger children may reverse letters, numbers, their names and words in reading. Their recall may be short or erratic, sometimes recognizing a word while, at another time, being completely baffled by its appearance. They may or may not speak fluently, mispronounce words or forget the names of objects. Sentences may be disordered, if used at all. Penmanship may be unreadable and untidy, with letters distorted. Others express ideas and general knowledge so well that failure to learn to read comes as a shock to all concerned, including the child.
>
> As the boys and girls grow older reading achievement falls further behind grade levels, spelling becomes increasingly difficult or unreadable, penmanship is illegible or, if satisfactory, done too slowly for functional use. The reversing may disappear but words are misread, not recalled, and little words are omitted. Comprehension is lost in the struggle to recognize the words. They are without feeling for rhythm or phrasing. Written work cannot keep pace with advancing requirements. Difficulties with directional orientation in time and space may continue into adulthood. Some are clumsy and many are hyperactive to the point of exhausting themselves as well as those working or living with them. Usually there will be a lack of well established lateral dominance, possibly insecure handedness and a family pattern of language problems. Not to be overlooked are those giving the appearance of not hearing although acuity is entirely normal and the ones unable to say what they want to say, often exclaiming, "Oh, skip it," when unable to express ordered thoughts. [pp. 66–67]*

The following story about how Slingerland adapted Orton's work is from her 1962 address to the Orton Society:

> I read Dr. Orton's *Reading, Writing and Speech Problems in Children* over and over. Miss Gillingham's *Remedial Training* was always at hand. I knew my goal . . . [adapting their techniques so that they might be used with groups of youngsters in classrooms]. I wanted to be sure my application would be psychologically sound. . . . Dr. Orton [pointed out] from his studies of the syndromes of delay or disorder in acquisition of language—alexia, special disability in writing, developmental word deafness, motor speech delay, stuttering, and . . . developmental apraxia . . . [that] "only one factor is common to the entire group and that is a difficulty in repicturing or rebuilding in the order of presentation, sequences of letters, of sound, or of units of movement." This would have to be kept in mind while planning an adaptation

---

*Reprinted by permission from Beth H. Slingerland, "Meeting the Needs of Dyslexic Children," *Academic Therapy Quarterly*, *1*(2), 1965, pp. 66–72.

of the Orton–Gillingham method that would be workable in classroom situations. Also more than twenty-five years of experience had shown me that recognition of both graphic and sound units is not enough, thus bearing out what is to be found . . . [in Orton's] book.

Unless disability children are shown *how* to use phonics as a stepping stone, its use is without purpose. Teachers need to know phonics but just a "phonics system" alone is not enough. Thus, training by way of the three channels of learning—visual, auditory and kinesthetic—must never be eliminated for the sake of short cuts or lack of knowledge. . . . Furthermore, children need a "thought pattern" as I choose to call it, the use of which enables them to help themselves. [p. 5]*

Largely because of Slingerland, the teachings of Orton and his followers have had a significant impact on the education of learning disabled or dyslexic children. In Washington state alone, it was estimated in 1986 (Andrews, 1986) that there were at least 54 Slingerland classes serving 1000 children in 13 school districts. There are concentrations of Slingerland activity throughout the United States. Some of the other states in which there are large numbers of classes are Alaska, Arizona, California, Colorado, Hawaii, Idaho, Missouri, New Hampshire, Oregon, Texas, and Utah.

In addition to Slingerland's influence through her scripted lessons, training courses, tests, and other publications, other disciples of multisensory instruction have left their traces. Certainly, evidences of the techniques recommended by Fernald and Spalding and other interpreters of Orton and Gillingham can be seen in clinics and classrooms throughout the land.

Neurological Impairment and Language Development

Helmer R. Myklebust, who theorized and conducted research at Northwestern University, has been the unquestioned prime influence on studies focusing on neurological impairment and language development. Originally recognized for his writings about deafness and aphasia, Myklebust later drew on his hypotheses and findings in those fields to formulate a comprehensive theory of learning disorders.

Like many other theorists in learning disabilities, Myklebust attributed learning problems to some sort of neurological impairment, coining the term "psychoneurological learning disorder" to describe such disabilities. He maintained that, unless the central nervous system is intact, there may be a learning disorder of one or more of the following types:

1. Perceptual disturbance: Inability to identify, discriminate, and interpret sensation. Indicated by poor recognition of everyday sensory experiences.

---

*Reprinted by permission from Beth H. Slingerland, "A Public School System Recognizes Specific Language Disability," address given at the Orton Society annual meeting, November 2, 1962, New York.

Helmer R. Myklebust was for a number of years at Northwestern University. He introduced the term "psychoneurological learning disorders" to refer to youngsters with reading and other language impairments. Myklebust, with his long-time associate, Doris Johnson, co-authored a number of books and articles, one of the more significant being "Learning Disabilities: Educational Principles and Practices."

2. Disturbance of imagery: Inability to recollect common experiences although they have been perceived. Indicated by deficiencies in hearing and vision.

3. Disorders of symbolic processes: Inability to acquire facility to express experiences symbolically. Seen as aphasia, dyslexia, dysgraphia, dyscalculia, and as language disorders.

4. Conceptualizing disturbances: Inability to generalize and categorize experiences. Seen as a deficiency in grouping ideas that have a logical relationship. [Myklebust, 1964, p. 359]

In collaboration with Doris Johnson at Northwestern University, Myklebust identified five specific areas in which learning disorders might be noticed in classrooms (Johnson & Myklebust, 1967).

1. *Disorders of auditory language.* This disability is more handicapping than speech problems because normal symbolic language development is impaired. The types of language disorders noted were generalized auditory learning, auditory receptive language, and auditory expressive language.

2. *Disorders of reading or dyslexia.* Such problems may disrupt a child's total language development. Commonly, a reading problem is detected in combination with one or more of the following impairments: memory, memory for sequence, left-right orientation, time orientation, body image, spelling and writing, dyscalculia,

motor disturbances, and perceptual disorders.[1] According to Johnson and Myklebust, dyslexia could be visual or auditory. They recommended, therefore, that instruction should be arranged via the strong modality.

3. *Disorders of written language.* Myklebust and Johnson maintained that written language is the culminating verbal achievement because it requires the integration of many prerequisite skills. They recognized three types of problems in the area of writing: inability to copy symbols, inability to write spontaneously or from dictation, and difficulty in putting ideas onto paper.

4. *Disorders of arithmetic.* Johnson and Myklebust referred to two types of arithmetic inadequacies—those related to other language disorders and those associated with disturbances in quantitative thinking. According to them, pupils with the former disorder may have difficulty hearing and understanding their teachers' directions and explanations. Those with the latter difficulty may have inadequate body images and poor visual-motor integration and may be unable to discriminate between left and right.[2]

5. *Nonverbal disorders of learning.* Youngsters with these disorders may have difficulty with gesturing, motor learning, body image, spatial orientation, right-left orientation, social perception, distractibility, perseveration, and disinhibition.[3] [Excerpted from Myers & Hammill, 1982.]

Myklebust contended that because the brain is comprised of systems that at times function semi-independently, in conjunction with, and in supplement to other systems, precise and differential diagnosis should be arranged for children who may suffer from psychoneurological learning disorders. He believed educational programs for LD children should begin with a thorough survey of the brain's capacity to receive, categorize, and integrate information as well as of the sensitivity of the auditory, visual, motor, and tactile modes. The evaluation might include clinical teaching to obtain the additional information that makes possible the modification of training programs and the verification of test data.[4]

Summary. The general instructional considerations of those concerned with neurological impairment and language put emphasis on the following points:

— Teaching that is as individualized as possible
— Teaching according to readiness in a balanced program
— Teaching that is as close to the level of involvement as possible
— Input preceding output as a basis for grouping or classification
— Teaching that reaches to the tolerance level, but not the point of overloading

---

1. Note the similarities to other LD experts with respect to identifying symptoms of learning disabilities.
2. Note the similarities to the views of Kephart and Orton.
3. Note the similarities to the characteristics cited by Strauss, Werner, and Cruickshank.
4. Throughout, there are familiar rings from the writings of Orton and Kirk.

— The administration of multisensory instruction
— The raising of deficits without undue demand on the disability itself
— Blending of the senses
— Perceptual training as needed
— Control of important variables such as attention, rate, proximity, and size
— Development of both the verbal and nonverbal areas of experience
— Instruction guided by behavioral and psychoneurological considerations

Influence.   The suggestions of Myklebust, Johnson, and others of this type on learning disabilities have been directed more to speech, language, and communication therapists than to classroom teachers. A number of suggestions for teachers of LD children, however, are noted in Johnson and Myklebust's book, *Learning Disabilities: Educational Principles and Practices* (1967).

Linguistics and Modality Matching

The founder and most influential representative of the theoretical line dealing with linguistics and modality matching is Samuel Kirk. Incidentally, most attribute the very name "learning disabilities" to Kirk, noting its use in a speech he delivered to the Conference on Exploration into Problems of the Perceptually Handicapped Child in 1963. Following are excerpts from that historical message.

> The term "brain injury" [when used with children] has little meaning to us from a management or training point of view. It does not tell me if the child is smart or dull. . . . It does not give me any clues to management or training. . . . Recently I have used the term "learning disabilities" to describe a group of children who have disorders in development, in language, speech, reading, and associated communication skills needed for social interaction. In this group I do not include children who have sensory handicaps such as blindness or deafness, because we have methods of managing and training the deaf and the blind. I also exclude from this group children who have generalized mental retardation. [Kirk, 1976, pp. 255–256]

One of Kirk's early experiences relating to learning disabilities was at a school for delinquent boys in Oak Forest, Illinois. There, he studied and was influenced by the instructional techniques of Marion Monroe and Grace Fernald. He used the phonic method advocated by Monroe to instruct "regular" words, and Fernald's kinesthetic method to teach "irregular" words.

Like Cruickshank, Kephart, Lehtinen, and others, Kirk received training at the Wayne County facility. While there, he taught and conducted research with children who had reading, language, perceptual, and behavioral disabilities. His studies reflected the influence of Monroe's instructional ideas and her *Reading Aptitude Tests,* which analyze reading errors in a variety of situations. Kirk relied on that type of assessment for profiling abilities when he developed the *Illinois Test of Psycholinguistic Abilities* (ITPA).

The ITPA is a unique test that seeks to tap selected psychological and linguistic abilities that are assumed to contribute to academic achievement. According to Kirk, McCarthy, and Kirk the twelve ITPA subtests are intended to

. . . isolate defects in three processes of communication, two levels of language organization, and/or, two channels of language input and output. Performance on specific subtests of this battery should pinpoint specific psycholinguistic abilities and disabilities. The identification of specific deficiencies in psycholinguistic functions leads to the crucial task of remediation directed to the specific areas of defective functioning. This is the *sine qua non* of diagnosis. [1968, p. 13]

Summary.   Kirk and his followers sought to identify, through testing or observation, the pupil's preferred and nonpreferred means for receiving and processing information—that is, visually or aurally. Once those determinations were made, teachers were expected to find suitable means for instructing, ideally relying on a student's strengths to promote that student's weaknesses. Some clinicians and teachers (not necessarily Kirk and his associates) interpreted Kirk's ideas as meaning that if a pupil was a visual learner, his instruction should be keyed primarily through that sense, and if another student had demonstrated an aural preference, she should be dealt with accordingly.

Influence.   In their book *Psycholinguistic Learning Disabilities: Diagnosis and Remediation* (1971) Kirk and Kirk offered suggestions for instruction based on data from the ITPA. They presented examples of activities designed to teach abilities measured by the ITPA and offered nine principles for teachers to consider as they remediate psycholinguistic disabilities:

□ Differentiate testing from teaching, and consider routine teacher evaluations as testing. Assessment should be frequent and educational decisions should be based on those data.
□ Train the deficit areas. Overcome deviations, do not merely compensate for them.
□ Utilize areas of strength. Design tasks that blend strong and weak areas.
□ Arrange multisensory presentations judiciously.[5]
□ Remediate prerequisite deficits first when there is a logical order of events.
□ Utilize two forms of feedback: Provide information to children on the quality of their performances, and promote self-delivered feedback when possible. When multisensory instruction is arranged, pupils should see, say, and trace the words.
□ Teach initially those skills that pupils can most immediately put into practice.

---

5. They take a page from Kephart's warning in this regard.

☐ Begin remedial programs early; don't wait for children to fail before beginning psycholinguistic instruction.

☐ Individualize instruction for LD children, who are educationally unique.

■ **COMMENTARY** ■   *Several of the points made by Kirk and Kirk are in agreement with other approaches. Note, for example, the similarities with the next group, the school of behavioral, direct instruction.*

Minskoff, Wiseman, and Minskoff were also interested in linguistics and disabilities. They developed *The MWM Program for Developing Language Abilities* (1972), the intent of which was to provide remediation in twelve psycholinguistic areas: auditory reception, visual reception, auditory association, visual association, verbal expression, manual expression, auditory sequential memory, visual sequential memory, grammatic closure, visual closure, auditory closure, and sound blending.

A number of other materials and projects have been designed to alter various psycholinguistic components. Hammill and Larsen (1974), in fact, reviewed 39 studies in which researchers attempted to teach certain of these elements. They concluded that, generally, the belief was not demonstrated that psycholinguistic constructs, as measured by the ITPA, could be trained by existing techniques (Myers & Hammill, 1982).

Arter and Jenkins conducted a survey (1977) to indicate the extent that modality matching was practiced. When 700 teachers of exceptional children were asked whether they were familiar with the modality model, 87% said they were. When asked whether a child's modality strengths and weaknesses should be a major consideration when devising educational prescriptions, 99% agreed. When asked whether research studies did or did not validate the notion of modality matching, 95% believed that it did. Asked whether one of the most important outcomes of diagnosis was to determine a child's learning modality, 93% said that it was. Asked whether they should attempt to remediate modality weaknesses directly, 82% agreed. And when asked which test was most frequently administered to detect modality strengths and weaknesses, 58% listed the ITPA.

Behavioral and Direct Instruction

Norris G. Haring could easily be tagged the major figure who advocated the use of behavioral techniques with LD youngsters. A doctoral student of Cruickshank's at Syracuse University, Haring was understandably influenced by him. He was particularly impressed by his mentor's research in Montgomery County, Maryland, where a structured program was arranged for youngsters who displayed symptoms of brain injury (Cruickshank, 1961). Haring found several features in that program of particular significance: The investigators individualized instruction as far as possible and gave frequent and direct feedback to students with regard to performance. They also arranged certain consequences; for example, if a child did not complete an assignment satisfactorily, that child was not allowed to go out for recess.

Norris G. Haring was a student of Cruick-shank's at Syracuse University. Later, he collaborated with Phillips in a landmark study in Virginia that investigated the effects of the Cruickshank/Lehtinen plan for educating mildly handicapped youngsters. Haring was for some years the director of the Children's Rehabilitation Unit in Kansas and the Experimental Education Unit in Washington.

The year following Cruickshank's study, Haring and E. Lakin Phillips (1962) designed an investigation in Arlington, Virginia. For that research, they formed three types of instructional situations for emotionally disturbed children with learning problems. One was a self-contained class; another was regular classrooms into which handicapped youngsters were mainstreamed. In both those situations, the instructional plan was described as traditional: There was a minimum of individualized attention, few consequences were arranged, and so forth. For the third type of instruction, children were assigned to a self-contained classroom in which Cruickshank's teaching practices were followed. It was a structured classroom where firm consequences were scheduled; there was a great deal of individualized programming, and the youngsters were given frequent and direct feedback regarding their performances.

The results of that study at the end of one year indicated that the children in the third group outperformed those in the other two settings in academic achievement and were also rated higher socially. Haring (1963) commented, "The results of this study were strikingly in favor of the structured educational experience with firm expectations from the children and small special classes" (p. 316).

Shortly after that research study Haring was named director of the Children's Rehabilitation Unit (CRU) at the University of Kansas Medical Center in Kansas City, Kansas. There were half a dozen classrooms for handicapped youngsters in that experimental setting. One was taught by Richard Whelan, another by Eugene Ensminger, and another by the author. The youngsters in those situations all had learning disorders of one form or another, and their instructional plans were based on many of the ideas advanced first by Lehtinen, then Cruickshank, and later by Haring.

Although Haring was leaning more and more to the behavioral side with respect to the instruction of handicapped youngsters, he was not unfamiliar with the literature regarding neurological influences on behavior.[6] He maintained that although the brain had significant influences on behavior, there was little that could be done about it presently. Haring argued that we could, however, deal with observable behaviors, and by arranging certain events contingent on specified behaviors, we could effect worthwhile changes.

In the quest to refine further the involvement of behavioral approaches with the education of handicapped children, Haring and others at the University of Kansas arranged for Ogden R. Lindsley to join their faculty. Lindsley, a doctoral student of B. F. Skinner's, had been carrying out research with psychotic adults. His studies pertained to social communications, the effects of anesthetics, and other matters.

Lindsley was a technician highly skilled with the tools of operant conditioning, and for some years he had wanted to ply his craft to education. He was confident that if the principles of operant conditioning were arranged in schools, children would learn more and at faster rates than they would otherwise. He believed also that if the basic tenets of operant conditioning were arranged in the common schools, there would have to be adaptations. Lindsley was aware that it was one thing to work with psychotic patients in hospitals and quite another to instruct various types of youngsters in schools.

Lindsley's translation of operant conditioning techniques in laboratories to a working approach in classrooms was referred to as "precision teaching" (PT). Four features comprise that method (Lindsley, 1971):

1. Pinpoint the behavior of concern. If the target behavior is oral reading, then monitor the number of words read.

2. Count the frequency of the identified behaviors. If oral reading was the target behavior, the teacher would count the number of words read in a period of time. Furthermore, two rates would be tallied, the number of correctly read words and the number of words read incorrectly.

3. Chart the daily rates of the children on six-cycle logarithmic graphs.[7]

4. Try again. If the teacher attempted an intervention in reading or something else, and it wasn't effective, then some other technique should be attempted.

---

6. See Haring's (1963) review of studies on emotional disturbance in Kirk and Weiner's *Behavioral Research on Exceptional Children.*

7. Lindsley and others argued that plotting data on these charts greatly facilitated the making of decisions in respect to educational treatments.

In addition to these four points, Lindsley recommended heavy doses of contingency management. Like Skinner, he was a firm believer that if a reinforcer could be located and then properly arranged with the desired behavior, the frequency of that behavior would be altered.

Lindsley was particularly creative in this latter vein. Heretofore, most teachers had thought of reinforcers in terms of candies or other items that are often unnatural to school settings. Lindsley and his followers, however, showed how rather common and available objects and events—for example, having a favorite seat or being first in line—could, when properly arranged, affect behavior.

Meanwhile, Haring had moved from Kansas to Seattle, Washington in 1965. There, he was the director of the Experimental Education Unit (EEU), a part of the University of Washington's Child Development and Mental Retardation Center. One of his first administrative moves was to appoint Harold Kunzelmann, a former student of Lindsley's, as the school principal.

The majority of the children at the EEU at that time were learning disabled. Originally, there were about five classes. Later, when the EEU moved to its larger and permanent facility in 1969, there were a dozen classrooms. With the exception of two or three preschool classes, Kunzelmann insisted that teachers in the other rooms base their instructional approaches on Lindsley's PT practices. Teachers carefully pinpointed the important instructional behaviors, monitored the pupils' efforts in respect to those behaviors, and plotted their rates on six-cycle charts.

In 1966 Lovitt joined Haring and Kunzelmann at the EEU and proceeded to conduct research with LD youngsters. Prior to moving to Seattle, he had studied with Lindsley at Kansas. His investigations have dealt with self-management, reading, arithmetic, and other curricular matters (Lovitt, 1981). (More detail is given on these studies in chapters 6, 7, 8, 9, and 10.)

When Haring's professional interests shifted away from the emotionally disturbed and learning disabled in 1979, he left the EEU to take on other responsibilities. Joseph Jenkins, from the University of Illinois, became the new director. Prior to and throughout his tenure in Washington, Jenkins has made a considerable contribution to the research literature in learning disabilities (for example, Jenkins & Pany, 1981; Jenkins & Mayhall, 1976).

Although Jenkins's research with LD youngsters had not featured the characteristics of precision teaching, he did follow another behavioral approach, direct instruction (DI). Direct instruction has been used throughout the country and has significantly influenced the education of learning disabled children. The DI procedures were developed by Sigfried Engelmann, who collaborated with Carl Berieter at the University of Illinois. Later, when Engelmann shifted his operation to the University of Oregon, his principal colleagues were Wesley Becker and Douglas Carnine. Bateman, a student of Kirk's at the University of Illinois, has also worked with Engelmann.

The major contributions of DI researchers have been instructional materials such as DISTAR. (More coverage of direct instruction programs can be found in Chapter 7.) Following are the general structure and rationale for DI materials and instruction:

1. Specify objectives. Decide on the long-term objectives, and determine what students should do when they have completed the program.

2. Devise problem-solving strategies. Instructional programs should teach students problem-solving or generalization strategies rather than merely to memorize information.

3. Determine necessary preskills. Instruction should be sequenced so that component skills are taught one step at a time.

4. Sequence skills. The order in which information and skills are introduced should be carefully considered.

5. Select a teaching procedure. The most suitable procedure for instructing tasks in various academic areas must be chosen.

6. Design formats. Once appropriate teaching procedures have been selected, presentation formats should be written.

7. Select examples. Examples should be selected that are in accord with the chosen formats.

8. Provide practice and review. Teach skills to a point of mastery so they are retained over time. [Excerpted from Silbert, Carnine, & Stein, 1981]

Summary.   Several instructional features are involved in both PT and DI:

☐ Place emphasis on direct instruction; focus teaching on the exact behavior of concern.

☐ Stress the notion of active and frequent responding.

☐ Emphasize the importance of setting precise educational goals.

☐ Base curriculum planning on the sequencing and systematic instruction of behaviors.

☐ Place great importance on performing the desired behavior a number of times until it is thoroughly mastered.

Influence.   The influences of the DI approach in classrooms where LD youngsters are educated are considerable. For example, DI materials are widely used in resource rooms and in other situations where small groups can be formed. Many programs have been developed by DI researchers, and more important, most users have been pleased with their results.

Similarly, pockets of teachers throughout the country have included PT procedures into their classrooms. Many regular teachers have been working with mainstreamed LD pupils. A number of resource teachers have also put PT techniques into operation. Raymond Beck (1986) and his colleagues have done more than any others to popularize PT practices. From a base of operations in classrooms in Great Falls, Montana, with the aid of numerous research grants and the National Diffusion Network, they have started up and maintained hundreds of PT classrooms in practically every state. (There is more information on this operation in Chapter 4.)

Cognitive and Metacognitive Approaches

Cognitive behavior modification (CBM) and metacognition are two lines of research with the common concern of instructing students, both learning disabled and others, to learn about learning—that is, to be able to act as their own instructors.

The major contributor to the CBM approach, as it relates to mildly handicapped youngsters, has been Donald Meichenbaum at the University of Waterloo in Ontario, Canada. According to him (Meichenbaum, 1980), the primary impetus for the development of cognitive behavior modification was the increasing evidence that available treatments for mildly handicapped students, especially behavior modification procedures, had not fostered changes that were generalizable or durable. Second, many researchers and practitioners were rethinking the reasons for the deficits and deviations of the mildly handicapped. One group, according to Meichenbaum, became concerned about verbal development and its pervasive influence on other attributes. Another set of theorists speculated that many of the shortcomings of mildly handicapped individuals could be attributed to their inability to solve social problems. A third set of researchers maintained that the primary reason for many academic failures of mildly handicapped youth was that they lacked the ability to rely on strategies for solving problems. According to Meichenbaum, these three lines of inquiry had in common the belief that underlying traits were primarily responsible for many social and academic behaviors, and mildly handicapped youth had often not developed those attributes.

The goal of CBM practitioners is to train children to spontaneously generate and employ cognitive strategies and self-instructions—that is, to use verbal statements and images that prompt, direct, or maintain behaviors. Meichenbaum (1985) outlined the following steps for such training of youngsters:

1. An adult model performs a task while talking to himself or herself (cognitive modeling).
2. The child performs the same task under the direction of the model's instructions (overt, external guidance).
3. The child performs the task while instructing himself or herself aloud (overt, self-guidance).
4. The child whispers the instructions to himself or herself while going through the task (faded, overt, self-guidance).
5. The child performs the task while guiding performance via nonverbal self-direction (covert, self-instruction).

Meichenbaum (1985) maintains there is a natural relationship between cognitive training and affect, and that association should be recognized. In this respect, he said, ". . . helpless children tend to attribute failures to the lack of ability and view them as insurmountable. Mastery-oriented children, in contrast, tend to emphasize motivational factors and to view failure as surmountable"

(p. 419). It is reasonable to imagine, Meichenbaum continued, ". . . how poor performance could lead to affective disturbance and negative self-statements and, in turn, to further poor performance as the cycle continues" (p. 420). Meichenbaum believes that training programs that are designed to teach thinking must take into account the children's feelings and the accompanying images, self-statements, attributions, appraisals, and expectations.

A parallel movement to the CBM approach is metacognition, which refers to what a person knows about what he or she knows. A major contributor to this theoretical position was Ann Brown from the University of Illinois. She summarized (1978) metacognitive processes as including the identification and analysis of the problem at hand, the reflection on what one does and does not know about the situation that may be necessary for solving the problem, the designing of a plan for dealing with the problem, and the monitoring of one's progress toward solving the problem. In short, metacognitive activities are those deliberate reflections on one's cognitive abilities and activities that are concerned with self-regulatory mechanisms during an attempt to learn or solve problems (Meichenbaum, 1980).

Techniques for teaching thinking from either a CBM or metacognitive perspective are set forth in the following guidelines (condensed from Meichenbaum, 1985):

1. Teachers should adopt metacognitive outlooks. They should have the attitude that thinking skills should and can be taught.
2. Teachers should be aware of their attributions when instructing metacognitive skills. If they fail to assist students to develop those strategies, they should attribute that failure to their instructional program.
3. Teachers should conduct a task analysis of the skills to be taught, analyzing the desired target behavior into its component strategy and capacity requirements.
4. Teachers must be aware that generalization of the learned skills will not simply occur; techniques must be employed to see that it happens.

As Meichenbaum had indicated, one of the criticisms of simple behavior modification and other treatment programs that led to the development of alternate strategies was that they did not address generalization of skills. Following are some suggestions[8] for developing that important feature of behavior:

☐ The training on specific skills must often be prolonged and in depth. For many behaviors, it is necessary to train students to a high degree of com-

---

8. These suggestions have been compiled from a number of sources related to either CBM or metacognitive approaches. It's more than a little interesting to note that many of the suggestions offered here were recommended by Stokes and Baer (1977), two stalwarts of the behavior modification camp.

petency. Furthermore, it is generally necessary, during training, to provide them with feedback as to which strategy to employ and the extent to which they are using it.

☐ The students should be involved in their own instruction wherever possible. They should certainly be informed as to why they are being instructed in certain behaviors.

☐ The cognitive strategies that are initially taught should be usable in a wide variety of activities. They might include self-interrogation, self-checking, analyzing tasks, breaking problems into manageable steps and then proceeding sequentially, and scanning one's strategic repertoire to match task demands.

☐ Students should be helped to identify and alter existing maladaptive and idiosyncratic self-statements and to develop more effective ones. The teacher should discuss with pupils the conditions and factors that may interfere with their use of cognitive strategies.

☐ The timing of when to teach cognitive strategies is important. Some researchers have suggested that cognitive training may be most appropriate for children who have developed basic performance skills, but who fail to self-regulate their use of those skills. Researchers believe pupils need to spend some time engaged in training activities before they can develop correspondence between verbalizations and the behaviors that are to be controlled by them. In other words, students should practice a skill as they are being informed about how to do it.

☐ The training tasks should ensure a sequential gradation of difficulty. Pupils must recognize the fact that they can call into play the strategy they just learned on a new, related, and perhaps more difficult task. Meichenbaum noted that tasks should be chosen that have a high "pull for the strategy that is the focus of training."

☐ The training tasks should actively involve the students and should require mental transformation of the instructed strategies. Although pupils should not be encouraged to recite by rote the steps involved in the strategies, they should be able to identify the steps and explain the reasons for them in their own words.

☐ Teachers should consciously fade from involvement in strategy instruction as the pupils begin to take on more responsibility.

☐ The instruction of cognitive strategies should take place in multiple settings. Furthermore, several instructors should be involved, and many other circumstances should be altered from one setting to the next.

☐ The naturally occurring environmental contingencies should be arranged, whenever possible, to reinforce the use of cognitive strategies.

Summary. Meichenbaum, Brown, and many others in the CBM and metacognitive camps maintain that youngsters need to develop strategies for learning;

they need to know how to identify and solve academic and social problems. These researchers also claim that many mildly handicapped pupils lack these skills and should be instructed in their use. When pupils are provided these learning strategies, those theorists believe, they will be better able to generalize learning from one situation to another.

Influence.   The general CBM and metacognitive approach has had a tremendous influence on education. The group that has been most responsible for translating the research of metacognition, and to some extent that of CBM, has been that involved in special education at the University of Kansas, where Donald Deshler and colleagues (Deshler and Schumaker, 1986) have developed a learning strategies curriculum based on ideas from Brown, Meichenbaum, and others. The basis for this set of strategies is that youth are given plans for reading, taking notes, writing passages, taking tests, and for performing other school tasks. Like the founders of cognitive behavior modification and metacognition, the researchers believe that students, especially those that are learning disabled, must learn how to learn by being given approaches that will be generalized across multiple situations and settings. (A great deal of Deshler's work and that of his colleagues is covered in Chapter 10.)

——————— COMMENTS AND DISCUSSION POINTS ———————

- Many of the theorists in learning disabilities have maintained that the problems of the learning disabled can be attributed to some neurological damage or difference. And accordingly, a few of them have recommended treatments that ostensibly take those deviations into account. On occasion, some data were compiled with respect to diagnosis and treatment of "brain injured individuals." What with the new advances in neurological assessment, research design, and strategies for instructing LD students (see Chapters 6 through 10), we can only hope that researchers will continue to acquire data that might lead to treatments geared to particular neurological functions.

- Other theorists in the field have advanced a perceptual hypothesis: the idea that there are traits underlying the basic skills that should be developed before the academic behaviors are instructed. While their argument for some fundamental structure sounds reasonable, the data to support those beliefs are shaky. In behalf of the perceptual proponents an argument can be made that if the measures of perception were improved and perhaps made more sensitive, their hypothesis could, in fact, be verified.

- A number of early LD theorists advanced the multisensory cause. They believed that the best way to teach youngsters who were disabled academically was to present information to them through several senses—visual, auditory, kinesthetic, and tactile. This theory seems logical, but, once again, the data to support it are weak. Like the perceptual theorists, however, the multisensory advocates might contend that if the treatments and measures were more sensitive and perhaps more direct, their ideas might be upheld.

- There are also the modality-matching theorists. This group maintains that if a person is a visual learner, information should be presented to that person visually, with the same correspondence holding true for auditory and other types of learners. Recently, learning-style advocates have renewed interest in this theory by saying, more generally, if we determine an individual's preferences or styles for learning and accommodate them, that person will learn more, or better, or easier. But this group, too, needs more sensitive measures to provide substantiating data.

- Those who champion direct instruction aren't distracted by the indirect approaches of the perceptual, multisensory, or modality-matching camps; they go right to the heart of the matter. If one wants to teach X, say advocates of direct instruction, then one should set up instruction to teach X. While there are ample data to support this idea, the direct instruction people are roundly criticized for their "micro-instructional attitude"—that is, their tendency to focus only on tiny bits of behaviors, and thus failing to deal with larger processes.

- Finally, the metacognitive supporters believe that LD youth must learn about learning; these youngsters should have strategies and processes available for performing tasks. Few would argue with that message, we all need to have a few plans. The metacognitive theorists are criticized, however, by those who believe that it is not a good idea to divert instructional time from learning about actual skills. Those critics maintain that LD and other youth would not be in such a need of learning strategies if they had more content, if they were more proficient in the skills that others want to "strategize." These critics may have a point.

REFERENCES

Andrews, H. (1986). A look at the Slingerland approach: Yesterday, today, and tomorrow. Unpublished manuscript, University of Washington, Seattle.

Arter, J.A., & Jenkins, J.R. (1977). Examining the benefits and prevalence of modality considerations in special education. *Journal of Special Education, 11,* 281–298.

Beck, R. (1986). *Precision teaching project.* Skyline Center, Great Falls, MT.

Brown, A. (1978). Knowing when, where, and how to remember: A problem of metacognition. In R. Glaser (Ed.), *Advances in instructional psychology.* Hillsdale, NJ: Lawrence Erlbaum Associates.

Cruickshank, W.M.; Bentzen, F.A.; Ratzeburg, R.H.; & Tannhauser, M.T. (1961). *A teaching method for brain-injured and hyperactive children.* Syracuse, NY: Syracuse University Press.

Deshler, D.D., & Schumaker, J.B. (1986). Learning strategies: An instructional alternative for low-achieving adolescents. *Exceptional Children, 52,* 583–590.

Dolphin, J.E. (1950). A study of certain aspects of the psychopathology of children with cerebral palsy. Unpublished doctoral dissertation, Syracuse University, Syracuse, NY.

Fernald, G.M. (1943). *Remedial techniques in basic school subjects.* New York: McGraw-Hill.

Frankenberger, W., & Harper, J. (1987). States' criteria and procedures for identifying learning disabled children: A comparison of 1981–82 and 1985–86 guidelines. *Journal of Learning Disabilities, 20,* 118–121.

Gerber, M.M. (1984). The Department of Education's sixth annual report to Congress on PL 94–142: Is Congress getting the full story? *Exceptional Children, 51,* 209–224.

Geschwind, N. (1982). Why Orton was right. *Reprint No. 98, Annals of Dyslexia,* Vol. 32. The Reprint Series, The Orton Dyslexia Society, Baltimore, MD.

Gillingham, A., & Stillman, B. (1965). *Remedial training for children with specific disability in reading, spelling and penmanship,* 7th ed. Cambridge, MA: Educators Publishing Service. (Originally published in 1936 by Hackett & Wilhelms in New York.)

Goldstein, K. (1939). *The organism.* New York: American Book Company.

Hammill, D.D., & Larsen, S. (1974). The efficacy of psycholinguistic training. *Exceptional Children, 41,* 5–14.

Hammill, D.D.; Leigh, J.E.; McNutt, H.; & Larsen, S.C. (1981). A new definition of learning disabilities. *Learning Disability Quarterly, 4*(4), 336–342.

Haring, N.G. (1963). The emotionally disturbed. In S.A. Kirk & B.B. Weiner (Eds.), *Behavioral research on exceptional children.* Washington, DC: The Council for Exceptional Children, NEA.

Haring, N.G., & Phillips, E.L. (1962). *Educating emotionally disturbed children.* New York: McGraw-Hill.

Jenkins, J.R., & Mayhall, W.F. (1976). Development and evaluation of a resource teacher program. *Exceptional Children, 43*(1), 21–29.

Jenkins, J.R., & Pany, D. (1981). Instructional variables in reading comprehension. In J. Guthrie (Ed.), *Reading comprehension and teaching: Research views.* Newark, DE: International Reading Association.

Johnson, D., & Myklebust, H.R. (1967). *Learning disabilities: Educational principles and practices.* New York: Grune & Stratton.

Kephart, N.C. (1971). *The slow learner in the classroom,* 2nd ed. Columbus, OH: Merrill.

Kirk, S.A. (1976). Samuel A. Kirk. In J.M. Kauffman & D.P. Hallahan (Eds.), *Teaching children with learning disabilities: Personal perspectives.* Columbus, OH: Merrill.

Kirk, S.A., & Kirk, W.D. (1971). *Psycholinguistic learning disabilities: Diagnosis and remediation.* Urbana: University of Illinois Press.

Kirk, S.A.; McCarthy, J.J.; & Kirk, W.D. (1968). *The Illinois test of psycholinguistic abilities,* rev. ed. Urbana: University of Illinois Press.

Lindsley, O.R. (1971). From Skinner to Precision Teaching: The child knows best. In J.B. Jordan & L.S. Robbins (Eds.), *Let's try doing something else kind of thing.* Arlington, VA: Council for Exceptional Children.

Lovitt, T.C. (1981). Charting academic performances of mildly handicapped youngsters. In J.M. Kauffman & D.P. Hallahan (Eds.), *Handbook of special education.* Englewood Cliffs, NJ: Prentice-Hall.

———. (1982). *Because of my persistence, I've learned from children.* Columbus, OH: Merrill.

———. (1986). Oh! that this too too solid flesh would melt . . . the erosion of achievement tests. *The Pointer, 30*(2), 55–57.

McKinney, J.D. (1984). The search for subtypes of specific learning disability. *Journal of Learning Disabilities, 17*(1), 43–50.

Meichenbaum, D. (1980). Cognitive behavior modification with exceptional children: A promise yet unfulfilled. *Exceptional Education Quarterly, 1*(1), 83–88.

————. (1985). Teaching thinking: A cognitive-behavioral perspective. In S.F. Chipman & J.W. Segal (Eds.), *Thinking and learning skills: Research and open questions,* Vol. 2. Hillsdale, NJ: Lawrence Erlbaum Associates.

Mercer, C.D.; Hughes, C.; & Mercer, A.R. (1985). Learning disabilities definitions used by state education departments. *Exceptional Children, 8,* 45–55.

Minskoff, E.; Wiseman, D.E.; & Minskoff, J.G. (1972). *The MWM program for developing language abilities.* Ridgefield, NJ: Educational Performance Associates.

Monroe, M. (1932). *Children who cannot read.* Chicago: University of Chicago Press.

Myers, P.I., & Hammill, D.D. (1982). *Learning disabilities: Basic concepts, assessment practices, and instructional strategies.* Austin, TX: PRO-ED.

Myklebust, H.R. (1964). Learning disorders: Psychoneurological disturbances in childhood. *Rehabilitation Literature, 25,* 354–359.

Orton, S.T. (1925). "Word-blindness" in school children. *Archives of Neurology and Psychiatry, 14*(5), 581–615.

————. (1937). *Reading, writing and speech problems in children.* New York: Norton.

Schulman, S. (1986). Facing the invisible handicap. *Psychology Today* (February), 58–65.

Silbert, J.; Carnine, D.; & Stein, M. (1981). *Direct instruction mathematics.* Columbus, OH: Merrill.

Slingerland, B.H. (1962). A public school system recognizes specific language disability. Address given at the Orton Society Annual Meeting, New York.

————. (1965–1966). Meeting the needs of dyslexic children. *Academic Therapy Quarterly, 1*(2), 66–72.

Spalding, R.B., & Spalding, W.T. (1962). *The writing road to reading: A modern method of phonics for teaching children to read.* New York: Morrow.

Special Education Programs, U.S. Department of Education. (1983). To assure the free appropriate public education of all handicapped children. *Fifth annual report to Congress on implementation of PL 94–142.* Washington, DC.

Special Education Today. (1985). ACALD definition of learning disabilities. 2(1), 1–20.

Spreen, O., & Haaf, R.G. (1986). Empirically derived learning disability subtypes: A replication attempt and longitudinal patterns over 15 years. *Journal of Learning Disabilities, 19,* 170–180.

Stokes, T., & Baer, D. (1977). An implicit technology of generalization. *Journal of Applied Behavior Analysis, 10,* 349–367.

Strauss, A.A., & Kephart, N.C. (1955). *Psychopathology and education of the brain-injured child,* Vol. II. New York: Grune & Stratton.

Strauss, A.A., & Lehtinen, L. (1947). *Psychopathology and education of the brain-injured child,* Vol. I. New York: Grune & Stratton.

Strauss, A.A., & Werner, H. (1942). Disorders of conceptual thinking in the brain-injured child. *Journal of Nervous and Mental Diseases, 96,* 153–172.

U.S. Office of Education. (1977). Assistance to states for education of handicapped children: Procedures for evaluating specific learning disabilities. *Federal Register, 42,* 65082–65085.

Werner, H., & Strauss, A.A. (1941). Pathology of figure-background relation in the child. *Journal of Abnormal and Social Psychology, 36,* 236–248.

Wiederholt, J.L. (1974). Historical perspectives on the education of the learning disabled. In L. Mann & D. Sabatino (Eds.), *The second review of special education.* Philadelphia: Journal of Special Education Press.

Chapter 2

Louis Guillaume by Paul Cezanne: (*c*. 1882). Courtesy of the National Gallery of Art, Washington, Chester Dale Collection.

MEDICAL ASPECTS

MAIN IDEAS

- Neurological theories: neurological sites of learning disabilities and embryological theory

- Heredity studies and research on sex-linked abnormalities

- Teratogenic influences that might cause learning disabilities: alcohol, smoking, lead, other causes

- Influences of nutrition on behavior: sugar and other foods, food additives, vitamins, caffeine

- Problems associated with prescribing drugs: nutritional status, hyperactivity, academic performance, left hemisphere disorders, attention deficit disorders

OVERVIEW

When it comes to most health problems, "conditions," or "ailments," we want to know the cause. And relatedly, we want to know whether there is a pill, diet, or exercise that can be prescribed to take care of the problem. We often call on the medical profession to provide answers. Similarly, in the case of learning disabilities, we ask: "Why did this happen?" and "What can be done about it?"

This chapter provides a discussion of the role the medical profession plays in the diagnosis and treatment of learning disabilities. It contains five sections. The first is a discussion of neurological bases of learning disabilities. The second section has to do with genetic and hereditary influences, while the third is a discussion of some teratogenic influences. The fourth section deals with nutritional influences, and the fifth, with pharmacological treatments and diagnoses. In the last section, there are a number of comments regarding the medical aspects of learning disabilities.

NEUROLOGICAL BASES

As indicated in Chapter 1, a number of researchers and educators have argued for the neurological bases of learning disabilities. Many of them are of the opinion that brain dysfunction is the cause of learning disabilities or dyslexia, even if common techniques for diagnosing brain functioning do not indicate obvious abnormalities. To these researchers, a child who behaves as an LD youngster *is* learning disabled and therefore must be at least minimally brain damaged.

Early and traditional techniques for assessing brain functioning—electro-encephalograms and tests such as the *Halstead-Reitan Neuropsychological Test Batteries* (1987)—are relatively global attempts to explain neurological functions. But within the past ten years, several sophisticated approaches, including *diagnostic imaging,* have been developed to assess brain functioning. These include computerized tomography (CT), sonography (SONO), digital substraction augiography (DSA), positron emission tomography (PET), single photon emission computed tomography (SPECT), magnetic resonance imaging (MRI), and the latest, magneto-encephalography (MEG) (Ward, 1987). (Some of those techniques are described briefly in Chapter 3.)

Theories on Neurological Sites of Learning Disabilities

Over the past ten to fifteen years, researchers relying on traditional and advanced approaches for assessing neurological functioning have learned considerable amounts about which sections of the brain serve which functions, and how some individual's brain structures may differ from those of most others without being damaged.[1] From Broca's speculation to modern confirmation, it is now generally accepted that for the majority of individuals, the left hemisphere of the brain is dominant for language. For approximately 99% of right-handers and 60–70% of left-handers the left hemisphere is dominant for language. Of the remaining left-handers, the right hemisphere is dominant for language for 20–30%, whereas 10–15% have bilateral representation of language (Ojemann, 1985). It has also been recognized that while language skills are usually lateralized to the left hemisphere, spatial skills are lateralized to the right (Witelson, 1977). This is not to claim that spatial skills are as strongly lateralized as those of language, nor to discount the importance of communication between the hemispheres.

As knowledge of the anatomical basis of language increased, many researchers became interested in the relationship between neurological involvement and disordered language. They believed that it would be profitable to examine the brains of LD individuals to determine whether they differed from those of non-

---

1. Some of the research summarized here was reported by Bergerud (1986), a doctoral student of Lovitt's at the University of Washington.

handicapped persons. Such examinations became more feasible as the technology for observing human brains advanced (for example, Galaburda & Kemper, 1979).

With the development of computerized axial tomographic (CAT) scans—the first of many modern techniques—researchers were provided a noninvasive method for examining the development and activity of living brains. Hier, LeMay, Rosenberger, and Perlo (1978) relied on this method to observe the brains of twenty-four individuals who had been labeled developmentally dyslexic. Accepting Geschwind and Levitsky's assumption (1968) that the asymmetry of the cerebral hemispheres represented a functional asymmetry for language, they analyzed those patterns in a group of dyslexic patients. On examining the computerized tomograms for differences in the width of the parieto-occipital regions of the brain, they reported that for ten patients these regions were wider on the right, eight were wider on the left, and six were about the same. For those whose right hemispheres were wider, four had been delayed in acquiring language, while only one patient with a wider left hemisphere had similar difficulties. Furthermore, those with wider right hemispheres had lower mean verbal IQs than those with wider left sides.

Hier and his colleagues maintained that the number of dyslexic patients with wider right hemispheres—that is, reversed asymmetry—was significantly higher than would be found in the normal population. They concluded that reversed asymmetry might be related to the patients' reading problems.

The research suggestion that the difficulties of poor readers may be related to a reversal in the brain's normal asymmetry for language has been substantiated by studies comparing the electrical activity of normal brains and those of learning disabled youngsters. This research has consistently shown different electrical activities in the language-related areas of the brains of students with and without reading disorders. John's research group (John et al., 1977), relied on a series of electroencephalograms and evoked potential measures, for example, and found highly significant differences between the electrical activity of nonhandicapped and LD groups. (Other references to this form of assessment are discussed in Chapter 3.) Likewise, Johnstone and associates (Johnstone et al., 1984) observed differences in the amplitude and latency of certain event-related potential (ERP) features, and reported that these variations were noted in the central and parietal areas of the brain.

Hynd and Hynd (1984) argue for the existence of the *functional system of reading*—that is, one based on neurological activities in various parts of the brain. According to them, this system is supported not only by data from numerous case studies, but from the electroencephalographic literature as well. As for the latter, the work of Duffy and colleagues (for example, Duffy et al., 1980) is important because they developed a computerized program to investigate electrical activity of regional brain differences between dyslexics and nondyslexics during reading and tasks associated with reading. Those researchers claimed that the brains of the nonhandicapped and dyslexics at rest did not differ in terms of the distribution of electrical activity. During reading and listening tasks, however, the brains of dyslexics in regions hypothesized to be involved in reading showed less appropriate electrical activity than was present in the nondyslexics' brains. The areas of greatest difference in electrical activity were observed in Broca's area, the left temporal region, and in an area roughly equivalent to Wernicke's area and that of the angular gyrus. (See Figure 2.1.) Hynd and Hynd claim that the important point to underscore from these studies is that the abnormalities are not due to brain damage. A second, related point from their research is that the pattern of the neurodevelopmental deficits appears primarily in the region involved in the act of reading.

Studies of the electrical activity of the brain have generally supported the theory that the neurological site of learning disorders is in the language areas of the temporal and parietal lobes. (See Figure 2.2, which shows the areas of the cerebral cortex that represent language-related systems.) Revealing studies of the actual neurological substrate for learning disabilities have been conducted by Galaburda and associates at Harvard University and Beth Israel Hospital in Boston. The findings of their postmortem studies of LD individuals' brains revealed striking abnormalities in the language-related areas of the cortex and thalamus (Galaburda & Kemper, 1979). They claim that the most pronounced areas of abnormality were restricted to the left hemisphere; more specifically, to the structures involved with language.

Galaburda and associates argued that the specific structural abnormalities in the cortex and thalamus of an LD brain might explain the origin of the learning difficulties. Moreover, they were of the opinion that the abnormalities were

■ FIGURE 2.1 ■   Areas of the Brain in which Differences in Electrical Activity Between Dyslexics and Nondyslexics Have Been Observed

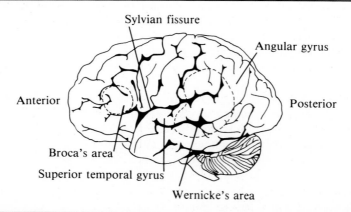

Source: Reprinted by permission from Donna B. Bergerud, "The Neurological Basis of Learning Disabilities," unpublished manuscript, University of Washington, College of Education, Seattle, 1986.

■ FIGURE 2.2 ■   Neurological Sites of Language and Learning Disorders

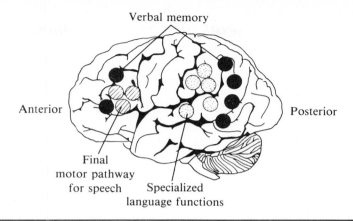

Source: Reprinted by permission from Donna B. Bergerud, "The Neurological Basis of Learning Disabilities," unpublished manuscript, University of Washington, College of Education, Seattle, 1986.

Albert M. Galaburda is a neurologist on the staff of the Beth Israel Hospital in Boston. He and Behan have advanced the embryological theory that forms associations between lefthandedness, immune system diseases, and learning disabilities. Other collaborators in Boston have been Geschwind, Kemper, and Eidelberg.

developmental in nature and were not the result of lesion or trauma:

> [t]he patient with developmental dyslexia had not only abnormalities in the left-sided language-relevant cortex, but also bilateral, language-relevant thalamic abnormalities, thus helping to explain the severe, unremitting language disorder he exhibited during life. [Galaburda & Eidelberg, 1982, p. 336]

Embryological Theory

Geschwind and Behan (1982) advanced the *embryological theory,* an elaborate theory that forms associations between left-handedness, immune system diseases, and learning disabilities. Their theory stemmed from the fact that neurons of the cerebral cortex were not actually formed in that area. Before the twenty-first gestational week, neurons developed in a central area of the brain, then migrated to their final positions in the cortex. A contributing point to their theory is that the right hemisphere develops one to two weeks earlier than the left in the normal brain (for example, LeMay & Culebras, 1972), and this developmental asymmetry causes the right temporal region to develop earlier and the left to become larger.

Geschwind's theoretical explanation continued with the speculation that before the thirty-first gestational week, the fetal brain of individuals with learning disabilities might be subjected to an unusual surge of the hormone *testosterone.* This surge would occur more frequently in boys, because that hormone is secreted by fetal testes. As a result of this excess testosterone, the growth of the left hemisphere could be delayed while the right hemisphere remained unaffected. It followed, then, that the migration of immature neurons in the left hemisphere would be arrested, thus causing the abnormalities observed in the LD brain.

The embryological theory accounted for several puzzling phenomena associated with learning disabilities:

1. It would be logical that more boys should be learning disabled than girls if the abnormalities were caused by fetal testosterone.
2. It would be reasonable that once the left hemisphere stopped developing normally, peripheral functions such as handedness would become controlled by the stronger hemisphere—that is, the right—thus accounting for the unusually high proportion of left-handers among LD students (Galaburda & Kemper, 1979).
3. The testosterone surge would have the effect of suppressing the development of a normal immune system, since it affects the development of the thymus, which is a structure of early life and necessary for normal immunological function. This could explain the high proportion of immune disorders among learning disabled children and adults.
4. The association that some have advanced between learning disorders and heredity (for example, Baker, 1984) may be explained by the embryological theory. Geschwind and Behan speculated that abnormal testosterone activity was likely to be controlled by gene complexes that could explain the "genetic factors in the familial clustering of handedness, immune disorders, and learning disabilities" (Geschwind & Behan, 1982, p. 5100).

HEREDITARY AND GENETIC INFLUENCES

For generations there has been controversy over the degree to which environmental and genetic factors operate to influence intellectual functioning. Although some researchers credit one feature more than others, most agree that there is some interaction between the two in the majority of cases. That majority group would argue that because genetic endowment imposes a range of intellectual potential, it plays an important role in the genesis of some learning disabilities.

Heredity Studies

Some years ago, a group of Swedish researchers provided evidence to support the theory of inheritability of some learning disabilities. In a study of 276 dyslexic cases, Hallgren (1950) revealed a high prevalence of reading and language problems among relatives and concluded that genetic factors were involved. Hermann (1959) compared a dozen pairs of nonreading identical twins to thirty-three pairs of fraternal twins in which at least one member had difficulty reading. His results showed that if reading problems were noted, they were more likely to occur for identical twins than for fraternal twins. Based on those data, Hermann concluded that reading, spelling, and writing disabilities had a genetic relationship. Matheny, Dolan, and Wilson (1976) also found a higher concordance of learning disability for identical than for fraternal twins.

Two modes of transmission have been hypothesized to explain the influence of genetic factors. One mode is the group of single-gene disorders of which there are three basic patterns: autosomal dominant, autosomal recessive, and sex-linked. The second mode of transmission—multifactorial (polygenetic) traits—reflects the combined effects of genetic factors acting in concert with prenatal environmental factors. It is believed that the majority of congenital disorders result from the interaction of genes and the intra-uterine environment (Sparks, 1984). Morrison and Stewart (1974) found support for this inheritance pattern by analyzing family histories in a group of hyperactive children and their families.

Other studies have also linked the causes of learning disabilities to genetic factors. Safer (1973), for example, found a higher susceptibility for minimal brain injury among full siblings than among half-siblings. More recent work by Decker and Defries (1980 and 1981) has provided strong evidence for the familial nature of dyslexia. In one study, the researchers matched 125 reading-disabled children and their immediate families with 125 control children and their families and administered a battery of reading and cognitive tests to all the youngsters. The results showed dramatic evidence to support the inheritability of reading disability with respect to three factors: reading, spatial/reasoning, and coding.

Studies on Sex-Linked Abnormalities

The basic building blocks of living systems are their cells. The nucleus of a cell is a spherical body that functions as the control center. Genes are located in the nucleus on pairs of microscopic bodies called chromosomes. The twenty-three pairs of human chromosomes differ in size and shape as well as in the genes they contain. In a standardized system for the classification of human chromosomes, twenty-two of the twenty-three pairs are termed autosomes. The largest autosomal pair is labeled 1, the next largest 2, and so on to the smallest pair, labeled 22. The remaining pair of chromosomes is the sex chromosomes. That pair is not numbered, but its members are labeled X and Y. Females have 2X chromosomes (XX), and males have 1 X and 1 Y chromosome (XY).

There are a number of sex chromosome abnormalities—that is, cases where individuals have more X or Y chromosomes than the usual. Many of those conditions are associated with various impairments, the extent of which are dependent on the type of abnormality and a number of contributing factors, genetic and otherwise. Although many youngsters with sex-linked abnormalities are mentally retarded, some are learning disabled (Sparks, 1984).

With respect to the relationship of sex-linked chromosome abnormalities and mild to moderate impairment, Nielsen et al., (1979) reported that children with sex chromosome abnormalities XXX, XXY, or XYY in all cells deviated from other children in several aspects. As for academic achievement, they reported that these youngsters had disabilities in reading and mathematics, visual perceptual problems, and poor abstract reasoning, auditory discrimination problems, and auditory memory deficits.

With respect to language development, especially expressive language, delays are often found in XXX girls and XXY boys, and there are indications of some delays in boys with XYY. The delay in language development, in children with an extra X and to a certain extent in children with an extra Y chromosome, would imply that these children would have difficulties verbalizing experiences. The tendency for girls with XXX and boys with XXY to withdraw from group activities might be associated with their language disabilities. As for emotional development, Nielsen and his colleagues claimed that a number of youngsters with extra X or Y chromosomes were delayed; many of them had minor psychiatric problems. Nielsen and his coauthors also reported that children with an extra X or Y chromosome had poorer gross and fine motor coordination than did children without sex chromosome abnormalities. These authors maintain that it is important to provide hormone treatment to boys and girls with sex-linked abnormalities and to give them information about their hormone and chromosome disorder at a proper age, which is usually around puberty.

TERATOGENIC INFLUENCES

According to Thompson and Thompson (1980), teratogens are agents that produce or raise the incidence of congenital malformations. Until recently, it was believed that the placenta served as a protective shield for the developing fetus. It is now known that nearly all substances taken by the mother during pregnancy are transferred across the placenta to the fetus.

Needleman has warned that

> [t]he belief that the infant was protected by nature, the placenta, and his or her
> mother from the vicissitudes of life dies hard. We now know that the period of rapid
> cell growth and specialization is a time of increased vulnerability to nutritional
> shortage or toxic excess. . . . It seems equally clear that a prudent society will not
> await the achievement of impeachable proof before removing these agents from the
> proximity of our children. [1986, p. 25]

Not all fetuses exposed to potential teratogens will exhibit developmental
abnormalities, and the pattern of any abnormality as a consequence of a teratogen
may vary. This variation may result from exposure at different critical periods
during gestation. Another factor that contributes to the variation of the teratogens'
effects is threshold, the minimum amount of teratogen required for a birth defect
to occur. This threshold differs from one individual to another, depending on the
health, nutrition, and genetics of the mother and the uterine environment and
genetics of the fetus (Sparks, 1984).

Alcohol

Alcohol has been a suspected teratogen for centuries, but only recently has the
relationship between maternal alcohol intake and learning disabilities been recognized. The major impact of alcohol is growth deficiency resulting from a
diminished number of cells. This growth deficiency is more evident in brain and
eye development than in linear growth and more pronounced in midfacial growth
than in general skeletal growth. Because alcohol freely crosses the placenta,
concentrations of alcohol in the fetus are at least as high as in the mother and
probably have a toxic effect upon fetal organ development (Sparks, 1984).

Gold and Sherry (1984) examined the professional literature in regard to
the history of and research on alcohol consumption of pregnant women. They
concluded that those studies gave evidence that learning problems, delayed psychomotor development, impulsiveness, behavioral problems, and emotional disorders can all be traced to maternal use of alcohol during pregnancy.

Shaywitz, Cohen, and Shaywitz (1980) provided further evidence to indicate
that alcohol was related to the development of hyperactivity or learning disabilities
in children. In their study, they found that in a group of 87 children with learning
problems, there were 15 who were born to heavy drinking mothers. All children
exhibited "hyperactivity" in spite of their normal intelligence. By first grade, 13
of the 15 had been recommended for special education, and by third grade, all
of them had been.

According to Hanson, Streissguth, and Smith (1978), fetal alcohol syndrome
(FAS) represents only one end of a continuum of alcohol-related birth defects.
Several studies suggest that there are probably twice as many children who could
be called partial FAS or FAE (Fetal Alcohol Effects), but in the absence of the
full syndrome, an identification becomes difficult. Erb and Andresen (1981) agree,

suggesting that besides the adverse effects resulting from high alcohol ingestion, even infrequent social drinking may contribute to learning disabilities or hyperactivity. Mild alcohol consumption may lower fetal glucose to near fatal levels, even though a hypoglycemic episode would not be displayed by the mother. A serious lowering of fetal serum glucose and subsequent loss of valuable energy stores for rapidly dividing cells may produce varying degrees of cellular damage. Fetal cellular damage and deficiencies would then manifest themselves as disproportionate skeletal features as well as lowered metabolic and mental capacities, all common diagnostic patterns of FAS children.

In a follow-up study of four-year-old children born to mothers interviewed during pregnancy, children of moderate drinkers had significantly shorter attention spans, more periods of inattention, and more instances of noncompliance with parents' commands compared to children of infrequent drinkers or nondrinkers (Landesman-Dwyer, Ragozin, & Little, 1981).

Smoking

Several studies have addressed the question of the long-term association between maternal smoking during pregnancy and various aspects of child behavior and development that may relate to learning disabilities. According to Sparks (1984), two components of smoke, nicotine and carbon monoxide, are the agents most likely to affect fetal growth. Nicotine is associated with decreased uterine blood flow and decreased fetal breathing, and carbon monoxide reduces fetal oxygen when it crosses the placenta. Butler, Goldstein, and Ross (1972) reported maternal cigarette smoking associated with an average reduction of 170 gm in birthweight. Their finding that mothers who stopped smoking by the fourth month of pregnancy had infants indistinguishable from nonsmokers suggested a direct effect of smoking.

Maternal smoking after the fourth month was significantly related to decreased reading ability at age seven, even after statistically adjusting for mother's age, social class, and sex of the child. Nichols and Chen (1981) examined scores of a large sample of seven-year-old children on a battery of intellectual, achievement, and behavioral tests. Factor analyses of the test scores revealed that three factors—learning difficulties, hyperactivity–impulsivity, and neurological soft signs—were related to maternal smoking during pregnancy.

Dunn, McBurney, Ingram, and Hunter (1977) studied a number of low-birthweight infants and an equal number of normal birthweight controls at age six and one-half. Their data indicated that children of nonsmokers had significantly higher IQ scores than did the smokers' children. Teachers' behavior rating scores also differentiated smokers' children from nonsmokers', but only for boys. According to them, minimal brain dysfunctioning occurred nearly twice as often among smokers' children, but the results were not statistically significant. Electroencephalograms showed that abnormalities also occurred more frequently, particularly among low-birthweight smokers' children, but were not statistically significant.

Denson, Nanson, and McWatters (1975) studied the effects of maternal smoking during pregnancy on a small group of children five to fifteen years old. When compared to control children, youngsters of smokers were more prone toward hyperkinesis. Streissguth and her colleagues (1984) found that maternal smoking was related to childhood attention deficits, as assessed with a computer-operated vigilance apparatus. This finding was true even after adjustments were made for maternal alcohol and caffeine use during pregnancy, as well as for maternal nutrition and education, and for birth order.

Lead

The toxic effects of lead at high doses have been recognized for some time. In the past, public health agencies, through lead-poisoning prevention programs, have focused primarily on severe lead exposure. More recently researchers have shown that important biochemical changes are brought on by lead levels well below those generally associated with clinical symptoms of lead poisoning. There is also evidence that low-level lead exposure can result in altered neuropsychological behaviors, which may exhibit themselves as attention disorders, emotional disorders, or learning disabilities that impair classroom progress (Needleman, 1980). (Some lead toxicity studies are reported in Chapter 3.)

Laws enacted to limit the amount of lead in indoor paint have cut down on the problem of children ingesting large amounts of lead. Now more concern is directed toward children who live in high-lead environments and may be ingesting excess lead from sources other than paint and plaster. Byers and Lord, in an early study (1943), followed twenty children who had been hospitalized with a diagnosis of lead poisoning. Their data, which spanned several years, indicated that those children had deficits in intelligence, perception, and memory. Moreover, their results showed that nineteen of the twenty children were failing in school or were behaviorally disordered.

David, Clark, and Voeller (1972) suggested a relationship between increased exposure to lead and behavioral problems in children. Results from their research showed that even low-level chronic exposure to lead during early life may be responsible for hyperactivity.

Lansdown and his research group (1974) examined the total population of children under the age of seventeen who lived in an area exposed to undue amounts of lead, looking for relationships between blood-lead levels, general intelligence, reading ability, and rate of behavior disorders. Their data indicated that the distance from a factory producing the lead pollution was related to blood-lead level, but there was no relationship between blood-lead level and any measure of mental functioning. Lower levels of intelligence and higher rates of disturbance were found to be more related to social factors.

Needleman (1980) classified the exposure of children to lead by measuring the amount of lead in deciduous teeth (teeth they had shed). High- and low-lead children were then evaluated in a blind study using a large battery of neuropsychological instruments. Needleman also measured a number of lead covariates known to influence development and evaluated their effects. The results showed that children with high-lead levels demonstrated a statistically significant impairment in verbal performance, auditory discrimination, language processing, and attention. These performance deficits also appeared to be reflected in the classroom behavior of the children.

Other Teratogens

Faustman-Watts, at the University of Washington, has studied the actions of a series of N-nitroso compounds that produce toxic effects in embryos (*University Week,* 1986). Her findings indicate N-nitroso compounds are pervasive in our environment; they are found in cosmetics, urban air, car exhaust, cigarette smoke, and several industrial settings, including the rubber and plastics industries. Faustman-Watts is now seeking to identify common chemical properties of the N-nitroso compounds that relate to the patterns, frequency, and severity of their effects. She will also investigate critical biochemical alterations within embryonic cells. Her interest in developing new systems that could provide valid information on the birth-defect potential of chemicals has led to another recent project: a computer mathematical modeling system that uses data already available on chemicals to evaluate the potential for developmental effects.

According to Sparks (1984), the major physical agent that can cause birth defects is radiation. Radiation changes the chemical properties of the atoms and molecules within living cells and results in birth defects. The critical period for a fertilized egg to be killed by radiation is before it is implanted in the uterus. Either the embryo is destroyed or it develops normally. Radiation doses in critical periods of development later can cause malformations, growth retardation, and some embryo deaths. It is generally believed that there is no threshold level below which radiation does no damage, although there are levels below which the effects cannot be measured.

NUTRITIONAL INFLUENCES

The idea that an improper diet can adversely affect central nervous system functioning has recurred throughout the history of medicine. In 1545, Thomas Phaer wrote the following in "The Boke of Children":

> Not only other ages but also lytle children are often times afflycted with this gryevouse syckenes, some time by nature received of the parents and than it is impossible or difficile to cure, sometime by evil and unholsome diet whereby there is engendred many cold and moist humors in the brayne whereupon this infirmity procedeth, which if it be in one that is young and tender it is very hard to be removed, but in them that are somewhat strong as of seven yeres and upward, it is more easy. [Levine and Liden, 1976, p. 145]

Sugar and Other Foods

Sugar, in particular cane sugar, has been implicated as a leading cause of hyperactivity. Crook (1974), a pediatrician who specializes in allergies, in one year of his practice identified fifty-five children whose hyperactivity was related to overuse of sugar. According to him, the following foods should be restricted in the diets of hyperactive children: milk, chocolate, cola, cane sugar, beet sugar, cereal grains, eggs, citrus products; foods containing additives and colorings should be avoided.

In a later study, Crook (1978) claimed that hyperactivity was decreased in more than 75% of his patients who were treated with elimination diets—that is, certain foods were eliminated from their diets. Sugar and milk were the major items that were withheld, but other foods were also restricted, such as eggs, corn, wheat, citrus products, beef, and pork.

Crook is closely allied with Feingold in his recommendation of an elimination diet to improve hyperactivity and other disorders affecting youngsters. He differs from Feingold, however, in a few important respects. For one, Crook's dietary concerns are more general; whereas Feingold is particularly emphatic about the elimination of food additives and foods containing salicylates, Crook claims that, depending on the individual, any number of foods may be related to behavior disorders. Another difference between the two physicians is that Crook is somewhat more rigorous in his methods for determining the behavioral influences of particular foods.

Crook has recommended an applied behavior analysis–type of design to parents and other caregivers who believe that some type of food is associated with a child's inappropriate behavior, namely, hyperactivity or inattention. He asks them to observe the child's behavior during a period when they are eating ordinary kinds of foods. During the next phase, the caregivers are asked to eliminate all the foods suspected of causing the problem and to continue keeping data. During a third phase, they are asked to reintroduce some, if not all, of the foods that were eliminated and to continue their behavioral observations.

Over the years Crook has suggested this type of regime to nearly two hundred families and has gathered considerable questionnaire data regarding their children's actions.

— Boys made up 75% of the sample.
— 70% of the parents reported that their child's hyperactivity was definitely related to specific foods in the diet.
— 9.3% of the parents said that hyperactivity was probably related to the diet.
— 56% of the cases were allegedly caused by sugar; 35%, by additives; 30%, by milk; 22%, by corn; and 20%, by chocolate.[1]

---

1. The percentages add up to more than 100% because some respondents believed more than one type of food contributed to the behavior problem.

— Other foods reported as contributing to hyperactivity were eggs, wheat, potatoes, soy, citrus, and pork.

When asked why many physicians such as Harley, Matthews, and Eichman (1978) do not support his views or those of Feingold, Crook (1980) offered three possible reasons:

1. Many of those who doubt the findings have been concerned with only food colors and other additives, not with the wide range of foods that could possibly contribute to hyperactivity or other inappropriate behaviors.
2. Many critics have not conducted experiments for long enough periods of time for either the offending or the experimental diet to take effect.
3. Some of the critics have not administered the possibly offending food in normal amounts; instead, they often study amounts that are below the average daily intake.

Although Crook recommends that diets must be individually determined, he offers some general guidelines for those concerned that diet may be influencing a child's behavior:

> A good starting place for such a diet is one that permits the child to eat any meat except hot dogs, bacon, sausage, ham, and the luncheon meats, any vegetable except corn, and any fruit except orange. He may also eat cereals, breads, cakes, and crackers that contain only rice or oats. He should avoid most or all commercially processed and prepared foods since so many of them contain sugar, dextrose, or food dyes, colors, and other additives. He should also avoid milk, wheat, sugar, egg, corn, chocolate, and orange. [1980, p. 286]

With respect to the effects of sugar on hyperactivity, Kolata (1982) reported that at a 1982 conference on food and behavior, held at the Massachusetts Institute of Technology, scientists claimed that although folk wisdom says that refined sugars and carbohydrates cause children to be hyperactive, rigorous studies show that the more likely effect is to make people sleepy due to the role of the sugars and carbohydrates in the formation of serotonin, a neurotransmitter that induces sleep.

Food Additives

Benjamin Feingold, a widely known and controversial figure in the world of nutrition and learning disabilities, linked certain diets with learning and behavioral problems in an address he delivered in 1973 at an American Medical Association conference. The medical and educational communities have been debating his pronouncements ever since. Feingold argued that one of the most widespread and critically important group of pollutants in the environment is food additives, and of those, synthetic colors and flavors are the most common. He contended further that synthetic colors and flavors are the most pronounced causes of adverse reactions, in that they affect practically every system of the body (Feingold, 1976).

Feingold has gone so far as to suggest that artificial colors and flavors ingested by mothers during pregnancy may be teratogenic, and possibly induce covert neurological alterations that, if not detected at birth, may appear later as behavioral disturbances and learning disabilities.

On the positive side, Feingold claimed that a complete reversal of behavioral and learning deficits is likely, following the elimination of artificial food colors and flavors. To support such a position, he has been quoted as saying that striking behavioral improvements were observed in from 30% to 50% of a group of youngsters who were treated with his additive-free diet (Bierman & Furukawa, 1978).

Burlton-Bennet and Robinson (1987) conducted an evaluation of the Feingold Kaiser Permanente (K–P) diet in the treatment of a six-year-old hyperkinetic boy. There were five phases in this applied behavior analysis–type study that ran for about seven weeks. During the baseline phase, the special diet was not in effect; it was instituted throughout a second period. In the third phase, the diet was discontinued, but put in effect throughout the fourth phase. The final period was a follow up some weeks after the fourth phase, during which time the diet was in effect.

The researchers took three daily measures in school throughout all phases of the study: attention-to-task, out-of seat, and movement. In addition to those measures, data were obtained from teacher rating scales. Overall, the data indicated that the K–P diet was effective in controlling the boy's hyperkinesis. The authors concluded, however, that although the diet was nutritionally adequate, it was rather difficult to implement.

Kavale and Forness (1983) conducted a meta-analysis of the research on the Feingold diet, and concluded that the diet was not an effective intervention for hyperactivity, as evidenced by the fact that treatment effects were only slightly greater than those expected by chance. They argued that since research had not validated the Feingold hypothesis, diet modification should be questioned as a treatment for hyperactivity.

Weiss, affiliated with the School of Medicine and Dentistry at the University of Rochester, took a dim view of the Kavale and Forness analysis:

> To take a pastiche of studies, and expect that a massive statistical analysis will compensate for their intrinsic absurdities and neglect of crucial variables, is akin to combining the predictions of 20 gypsy fortune-tellers to extract a strategy for stock market investment. . . .
>
> The ultimate importance of Feingold's hypothesis is not that he contributed an additional approach (of unknown dimensions) to the treatment of a poorly defined cluster of behavioral disturbances, but that he uncovered one more clue to their diverse mechanistic origins, and, at the same time, demonstrated how primitive our standards of food additive safety remain. [1983, p. 575]

Vitamins

Many physicians suggest that vitamin deficiency may be a cause of learning and behavioral disabilities, and megavitamins have been recommended by some as a mode of treatment (for example, Hoffer, 1974). Increased doses of Vitamins C, B3, B6, B12, and E have been given in megavitamin treatments for various disorders.

Brenner (1982) investigated the effects of megadoses of selected B-complex vitamins on children with hyperkinesis. In that study, one hundred children with hyperkinesis and cerebral dysfunction were given individual trials of large doses of thiamine, calcium pantothenate, pyridoxine, and placebo. Data indicated that some children dramatically responded to doses of thiamine, whereas others responded to pyridoxine. Meanwhile, other children responded to niacin or combinations of B-complex vitamins with minerals. Furthermore, half the children found to be "dependent" on pharmacological doses of thiamine worsened with the administration of vitamin B6. Conversely, half of the pyridoxine responders worsened when given large doses of thiamine; blood zinc levels dropped substantially with administration of that element. The experience suggested that hyperactivity may be the result of several factors, one of which may be an improper diet, and that children's reactions to various treatments vary widely.

Crook (1983) reported that the work of Horrobin, Rubin, and others had indicated that deficiencies of essential fatty acids such as those obtained from cold-pressed vegetable oils (for example, linseed, sunflower, safflower, and primrose), plus associated deficiencies of vitamins and minerals, may also lead to hyperactivity and disordered behavior. In addition, according to Crook, the clinical observations of Truss suggest that widespread systemic and nervous system illness, including hyperactivity and disturbed behavior, can occur through still another mechanism: colonization with *candida albicans* in the gastrointestinal tract. Crook recommended the dietary program devised by Truss, which consists mainly of putting patients on a yeast-free, sugar-free diet with some restrictions of other carbohydrates, since these dietary ingredients promote candida growth. To further discourage candida growth, the diet requires that patients be orally given nystatin, an anti-fungal agent.

■ COMMENTARY ■   *The existing data suggests that professionals in learning disabilities should exercise considerable caution in recommending megavitamin therapy, but we should be on the alert for future research findings on this topic.*

Caffeine

The use of caffeine as a stimulant has, on occasion, been prescribed for the treatment of hyperactivity (Harvey & Marsh, 1978). The addition of whole coffee to diets has been recommended because of its relief of symptoms and lack of side effects. Harvey and Marsh compared the effects of whole coffee with decaffeinated coffee with twelve hyperactive children. Their data indicated that the performances of eight children improved on tests of concentration, digit recall, and visual–motor coordination during periods when they ingested whole coffee. Furthermore, the scores of those children on parents' and teachers' rating scales were higher during phases when they drank whole coffee. From those results, the authors suggested that hyperactive children be given three or four cups of coffee a day.

Goulart (1979) argued against such advice, warning that coffee drinking may lead to serious thiamine deficiency. He maintained that when coffee is ingested, large amounts of the water-soluble vitamins are removed including the entire B complex and ascorbic acid.

EFFECTS OF PHARMACOLOGICAL TREATMENTS

Perhaps the most controversial therapy for hyperactive LD youngsters has been the prescription of psychopharmacological agents, or drugs. This section discusses some of the arguments and data on this controversy.

Nutritional Status

It is interesting to note that the medications most often prescribed for the treatment of hyperactivity may affect the nutritional status of LD children. According to Harvey and Marsh (1978), dextroamphetamines and methylphenidate are the most widely recommended medications. It has been suggested that dextroamphetamines suppress the appetite (*Nutrition Reviews,* 1973), and the long-term use of methylphenidate may lead to anorexia and weight loss.

One study (*Nutrition Reviews,* 1973), which compared the effects of various dosages of dextroamphetamines and methylphenidate, reported that the weight gain of children on these medications was about 60% of normal. The rate of weight gain of children who did not receive medication over the summer vacation increased to 130% of normal. The research report concluded that the effect of medication on growth was least marked for children who received the lowest dosages of methylphenidate.

Hyperactivity

In an attempt to unravel some of the facts and myths surrounding the issue of prescribing stimulant drugs to hyperactive children, Kavale (1982) conducted a meta-analysis on 135 drug studies. The studies represented approximately 5,300 youngsters, who averaged eight years and nine months of age, with an average IQ of 102, and who had been on medication for an average of eighteen weeks. Kavale's examination of the literature yielded three major classes of outcomes: behavioral, cognitive, and physiological. With respect to the first two categories, the data revealed that drug-treated youngsters would be better off than about

70% of the control students, those who had not received drugs. The results were not as positive for the third category; the differences were not appreciably different for drug-treated or control pupils.

Further analyses revealed that all major drugs were equally effective, with the exception of caffeine. Those findings indicated little to choose from among the most popular stimulant drugs: methylphenidate, dextroamphetamine, magnesium pemoline, levoamphetamine, and benzedrine. His analysis indicated that, although the studies performed by medical investigators showed more significant results than those performed by nonmedical personnel, there did not appear to be serious methodological problems, which some had suggested might affect the outcomes of the drug literature.

Academic Performance

Gadow (1983) wrote a comprehensive review of the effects of stimulant drugs on academic performance on LD children. According to him, the most controversial treatment variable was dosage, since the optimal dosage to allow some hyperactive children to perform cognitive tasks is less than one-half the optimal amount for the suppression of conduct problems. The dosage issue is further complicated by the fact that the ideal cognitive dose is not the same for all children, which somewhat limits the desirability of fixed-dosage studies. The essence of the dosage issue is that it is impractical to reduce dosage gradually with a measure that is not sensitive to short-term effects.

■ COMMENTARY ■   *Another problem is that most investigators have relied on standardized achievement tests to determine the effects of a drug on academic performance. The fact that such tests are given infrequently and are often indirectly related to what youngsters are being taught makes them insensitive to all but the most profound of changes.*

Some studies have been done on the effects of drugs on specific academic skills. Aman (1978) analyzed the results of ten investigations that assessed the effects of drugs on reading achievement and concluded that there was no justification for the use of stimulants to treat reading disorders. Other investigators (for example, Rapport, Murphy, & Bailey, 1982) reported that the arithmetic performances of hyperactive youngsters improved when they were administered stimulant drugs. As for handwriting, a handful of researchers (among them, Yellin, Hopwood, & Greenberg, 1982) have concluded that stimulant drugs have also helped LD students improve their handwriting.

With respect to the relationship of drugs and academic performances, Gadow urged caution:

> Whether enhanced academic productivity, when demonstrated, is attributable to increased motivation, sustained attention, information processing ability, or some combination of these or other variables is unknown. [1983, p. 294]

He further claimed that, according to the literature, there are at least four potential iatrogenic effects of stimulant therapy on academic achievement: One is that drugs may actually induce academic retardation. A second possible iatrogenic effect pertains to the relationship between school failure and hyperactivity. Some critics have suggested that the latter is often a consequence of the former. A third possible effect is that pharmacotherapy may suppress conduct problems so effectively that school personnel find it easier to ignore children's academic deficits. The fourth possible effect is that the drug treatment process may communicate to children the idea that they play only a minor role in the remediation of their own academic and behavioral difficulties. (See comments on attribution retraining in Chapter 10.)

Left Hemisphere Disorders

According to Wilsher (1986), the term "nootropic" (noo = mind, tropic = towards) was coined by Giurgea in reference to a new type of psychoactive compound. Drugs of this type were believed to act primarily on the so-called "nooetic" functions of the brain—that is, they were supposed to be selective in activating the higher functions of the brain while leaving lower functions largely untouched. Wilsher claims that hundreds of studies have been conducted on various patient populations with Piracetam, one of the nootropic drugs, and researchers have consistently found only a low incidence of adverse effects.

Wilsher quotes some researchers as referring to Piracetam as a "left hemisphere drug" because activities commonly controlled by that hemisphere seem to be more sensitive to the drug. He felt there was considerable evidence to suggest that the drug affects such left hemisphere activities as vigilance, coding, short-term verbal memory, naming, and verbal learning. Wilsher added, however, that a definitive study has yet to be performed to show a particular hemispheric effect of Piracetam.

Attention Deficit Disorders

Recently, a number of physicians have referred to a condition they call attention deficit disorders (ADD). They claim that children with this affliction are not mentally handicapped; in fact, many of them are naturally bright, but their mode of learning is quite different from that of nondisabled youngsters.

Dr. Constance Macdonald, a pediatrician in the Seattle area, believes that ADD is a biochemical imbalance that causes a range of behavioral problems, hyperactivity, and learning disabilities. She estimates that about 800,000 children in the United States suffer from this disorder (Parshall, 1988).

As a treatment for ADD, Macdonald and other physicians often prescribe Ritalin, maintaining that this drug helps youngsters focus their attention, behave better, and generally improve their academic performance. Macdonald claims that Ritalin is a perfectly safe drug for youngsters with ADD because it will not affect children unless they have a neurotransmitter imbalance, which is the commonly accepted cause of ADD. She claims the drug serves as a stimulant to non-ADD individuals. Critics of prescribing Ritalin argue that the drug is a "chemical straitjacket" for misbehaving children, and they quickly point to the potential side effects of Ritalin, which may include temporary appetite loss, insomnia, or Tourette's syndrome.

———— COMMENTS AND DISCUSSION POINTS ————

- Teachers, in fact all professionals who work with LD youngsters, should keep up with medical advances with respect to the diagnosis of the brain—that is, the attempts to determine whether the brain of the learning disabled is damaged in some way or is remarkably different from others. The most practical implication of this work would have to do with differential treatments that would coincide with differential diagnosis. While such efforts have been futile to this point, that won't always be the case. It could be that as diagnoses become more sophisticated, so will the treatments. These diagnostic efforts could also be significant with respect to prevention and treatments that are medical, surgical, or otherwise.

- The same advice goes for studies on the influences of genetics and heredity. Teachers and caregivers of LD youngsters should be aware of all the latest discoveries and their possible effects on learning disabilities. Meanwhile, they have to keep nurturing and instructing their students as best they can, and even though they are busy teaching and providing care day after day, they shouldn't be ignorant of current research.

- Teachers should also be on the alert when it comes to teratogenic influences. Whereas they probably can't do much about the neurology or genetics of their charges, they *can* do something about their environments. Teachers now can give mothers ample data regarding the use of alcohol and nicotine and can provide some data to suggest that other toxic agents should be avoided since they can adversely affect behaviors related to learning.

- Teachers also need to keep up with current data on nutrition. They must be cautious when it comes to passing on advice about what to eat and drink. There have been hundreds of diet and food fadists who have burned lots of people. In this area, the buyer should definitely beware.

- Teachers must be keen observers when it comes to offering advice on the influences of drugs and learning disabilities. They should not be skeptical of all drugs for hyperactive or LD youngsters, for some drugs, used with care, are probably helpful to certain of their students. On the other hand, teachers should not believe that all their woes will vanish (Piracetem notwithstanding) if the proper drug can be prescribed for certain behavioral problems. They should arrange applied behavior analysis–type designs, as recommended by Crook and others, in order to assay a variety of behaviors under conditions where drugs were and were not administered.

- Teachers and others must be aware that there are great individual differences with respect to tolerances for teratogens, drugs, and various diets.

- Teachers should be attuned to the fact that there are bound to be considerable interactions among many of the factors affecting the growth and development of individuals. It is unlikely that the alteration of one variable will have an observable affect on just one behavior.

- Of necessity, teachers of LD children will interact with a number of medical professionals—pediatricians, neurologists, optholmologists, pharmacologists, psychiatrists—and should do so with respect but without being intimidated. Medical people are often just as uneasy with teachers as teachers are with them. (See comments in Chapter 5.)

- Teachers of LD youngsters should have considerable knowledge about the various agencies, hospitals, clinics, and schools in their area, for they will be called on often to make referrals. Teachers need to know which of these "helping agencies" are truly helpful.

REFERENCES

Aman, M.G. (1978). Drugs, learning, and the psychotherapies. In J.S. Werry (Ed.), *Pediatric psychopharmacology: The use of behavior modifying drugs in children.* New York: Brunner/Mazel.

Baker, D. (1984). The neurological basis of the talents of dyslexics. *Perspectives on Dyslexia* (August), 1–4.

Bergerud, D.B. (1986). The neurological basis of learning disabilities. Unpublished manuscript, College of Education, University of Washington, Seattle.

Bierman, C.W., & Furukawa, C.T. (1978). Food additives and hyperkinesis: Are there nuts among the berries? *Pediatrics, 61,* 932–934.

Brenner, A. (1982). The effects of megadoses of selected B-complex vitamins on children with hyperkinesis: Controlled studies with long-term follow-up. *Journal of Learning Disabilities, 15,* 258–264.

Burlton-Bennet, J.A., & Robinson, V.M.J. (1987). A single subject evaluation of the K-P diet for hyperkinesis. *Journal of Learning Disabilities, 20,* 331–335, 346.

Butler, N.R.; Goldstein, H.; & Ross, E.M. (1972). Cigarette smoking in pregnancy: Its influence on birth weight and perinatal mortality. *British Medical Journal, 2,* 127–130.

Byers, R.K., & Lord, E.E. (1943). Late effects of lead poisoning on mental development. *American Journal of Diseases of Children, 66,* 471–494.

Crook, W.G. (1974). An alternate method of managing the hyperactive child (letter). *Pediatrics, 54,* 656.

———. (1978). Adverse reactions to food can cause hyperkinesis (letter). *American Journal of Diseases in Children, 132,* 819–820.

———. (1980). Can what a child eats make him dull, stupid, or hyperactive? *Journal of Learning Disabilities, 13,* 281–286.

———. (1983). Behavior disorders and diet, allergy, etc. (letter). *Journal of Learning Disabilities, 16,* 383.

David, O.; Clark, J.; & Voeller, K. (1972). Lead and hyperactivity. *The Lancet, 12,* 900–903.

Decker, S.N., & DeFries, J.C. (1980). Cognitive abilities in families of reading disabled children. *Journal of Learning Disabilities, 13,* 517–522.

Decker, S.N., & DeFries, J.C. (1981). Cognitive ability profiles in families of reading disabled children. *Developmental Medicine and Child Neurology, 23*(2), 217–227.

Denson, R.; Nanson, J.L.; & McWatters, M.A. (1975). Hyperkinesis and maternal smoking. *Canadian Psychiatric Association Journal, 20,* 183–187.

Duffy, F.H.; Denckla, M.B.; Bartels, P.H.; Sandini, G.; & Kiessling, L.S. (1980). Dyslexia: Automated diagnosis by computerization classification of brain electrical activity. *Annals of Neurology, 7,* 421–428.

Dunn, H.G.; McBurney, A.K.; Ingram, S.; & Hunter, C.M. (1977). Maternal cigarette smoking during pregnancy and the child's subsequent development: II. Neurological and intellectual maturation to the age of 6½ years. *Canadian Journal of Public Health, 68,* 43–50.

Erb, L.E., & Andresen, B.D. (1981). Hyperactivity: A possible consequence of maternal alcohol consumption. *Pediatric Nursing, 94,* 30–34.

Feingold, B.F. (1976). Hyperkinesis and learning disabilities linked to the ingestion of artificial colors and flavors. *Journal of Learning Disabilities, 9*(9), 551–559.

Gadow, K.D. (1983). Effects of stimulant drugs on academic performance in hyperactive and learning disabled children. *Journal of Learning Disabilities, 16,* 290–299.

Galaburda, A.M., & Eidelberg, D. (1982). Symmetry and asymmetry in the human posterior thalamus. *Archives of Neurology, 39,* 333–336.

Galaburda, A.M., & Kemper, T.L. (1979). Cytoarchitectonic abnormalities in developmental dyslexia: A case study. *Annals of Neurology, 6,* 94–100.

Geschwind, N., & Behan, P. (1982). Left-handedness: Association with immune disease, migraine, and developmental learning disorder. *Proceedings of the National Academy of Science, 79,* 5097–5100.

Geschwind, N., & Levitsky, W. (1968). Human brain: Left-right asymmetries in temporal speech region. *Science, 161,* 186–187.

Gold, S., & Sherry, L. (1984). Hyperactivity, learning disabilities, and alcohol. *Journal of Learning Disabilities, 17*(1), 3–6.

Goulart, F.S. (1979). Frightening facts about coffee. *Bike World* (March), 46–47.

Hallgren, B. (1950). Specific dyslexia ("congenital word-blindness"): A clinical and genetic study. *Acta Psychiatrica et Neurologica Scandinavia* [Supplementum], *65,* 1–287.

Hanson, J.W.; Streissguth, A.P.; & Smith, D.W. (1978). The effects of moderate alcohol consumption during pregnancy on fetal growth and morphogenesis. *The Journal of Pediatrics, 92*(3), 457–460.

Harley, J.P.; Matthews, C.G.; & Eichman, P. (1978). Synthetic food colors and hyperactivity in children: A double-blind challenge experiment. *Pediatrics, 62,* 975–983.

Harvey, D.H., & Marsh, R.W. (1978). The effects of de-caffeinated coffee versus whole coffee on hyperactive children. *Developmental Medicine and Child Neurology, 20,* 81–86.

Hermann, K. (1959). *Reading dyslexia: A medical study of word-blindness and related handicaps.* Springfield, IL: Charles C. Thomas.

Hier, D.B.; LeMay, M.; Rosenberger, P.B.; & Perlo, V.P. (1978). Developmental dyslexia: Evidence for a subgroup with a reversal of cerebral asymmetry. *Archives of Neurology, 35,* 90–92.

Hoffer, A. (1974). Hyperactivity, allergy, and megavitamins (letter). *Canadian Medical Association Journal, 111,* 905–907.

Hynd, G.W., & Hynd, C.R. (1984). Dyslexia: Neuroanatomical/neurolinguistic perspectives. *Reading Research Quarterly, 19,* 482–498.

John, E.R.; Karmel, B.Z.; Corning, W.C.; Easton, P.; Brown, D.; Ahn, H.; John, M.; Harmony, T.; Prichep, L.; Toro, A.; Gerson, I.; Bartlett, F.; Thatcher, R.; Kaye, H.; Valdes, P.; & Schwartz, E. (1977). Neurometrics. *Science, 196,* 1393–1410.

Johnstone, J.; Galin, D.; Fein, G.; Yingling, C.; Herron, J.; & Marcus, M. (1984). Regional brain activity in dyslexic and control children during reading tasks: Visual probe event-related potentials. *Brain and Language, 21,* 233–254.

Kavale, K. (1982). The efficacy of stimulant drug treatment for hyperactivity: A meta-analysis. *Journal of Learning Disabilities, 15,* 280–289.

Kavale, K.A., & Forness, S.R. (1983). Hyperactivity and diet treatment: A meta-analysis of the Feingold hypothesis. *Journal of Learning Disabilities, 16,* 324–333.

Kolata, G. (1982). Food affects human behavior. *Science, 218,* 1209–1210.

Landesman-Dwyer, S.; Ragozin, A.S.; & Little, R.E. (1981). Behavioral correlates of prenatal alcohol exposure: A four-year follow-up study. *Neurobehavioral Toxicology and Teratology, 3*(2), 187–193.

Lansdown, R.G.; Clayton, B.E.; Graham, P.J.; Shepherd, J.; Delves, H.T.; & Turner, W.C. (1974). Blood-lead levels, behaviour, and intelligence: A population study. *The Lancet, 1,* 538–541.

LeMay, M., & Culebras, A. (1972). Human brain—morphologic differences in the hemispheres demonstrable by carotid arteriography. *The New England Journal of Medicine, 287,* 168–170.

Levine, M.D., & Liden, C.B. (1976). Food for inefficient thought. *Pediatrics, 58,* 145–148.

Matheny, A.P.; Dolan, A.B.; & Wilson, R.S. (1976). Twins with academic and learning problems: Antecedent characteristics. *American Journal of Orthopsychiatry, 46*(3), 464–469.

Morrison, J., & Stewart, M. (1974). Bilateral inheritance as evidence for polygeneticity in the hyperactive child syndrome. *Journal of Nervous and Mental Disease, 158,* 226–228.

Needleman, H.L. (1980). Human lead exposure: Difficulties and strategies in the assessment of neuropsychological impact. In R.L. Singhal & J.A. Thomas (Eds.), *Lead Toxicity.* Baltimore: Urban & Schwarzenberg.

Needleman, H.L. (1986). Prenatal exposure to pollutants and neural development. In M. Lewis (Ed.), *Learning Disabilities and Prenatal Risk.* Chicago: University of Illinois Press.

Nichols, P.L., & Chen, T.C. (1981). *Minimal brain dysfunction: A prospective study.* Hillsdale, NJ: Lawrence Erlbaum Associates.

Nielsen, J.; Sillesen, I.; Sørensen, A.M.; & Sørensen, K. (1979). Follow-up until ages 4 to 8 of 25 unselected children with sex chromosome abnormalities, compared with sibs and controls. *Birth Defects: Original Article Series, 15,* 15–73.

Nutrition Reviews. (1973). The growth of children given stimulant drugs. *31,* 91–92.

Ojemann, G.A. (1985). Language and the brain. Paper presented at the Mason Clinic, Seattle, WA.

Parshall, S. (1988). Disorderly conduct: Attention disorder may be cause of behavior problem. *Journal American* (Bellevue, WA). Tuesday, April 5, p. D1.

Rapport, M.D.; Murphy, H.A.; & Bailey, J.S. (1982). Ritalin vs. response cost in the control of hyperactive children: A within-subject comparison. *Journal of Applied Behavior Analysis, 15,* 205–216.

Reitan, R.M., & Wolfson, D. (1985). *The Halstead-Reitan neuropsychological test battery.* Reitan Neuropsychological Laboratory, Tucson, AZ.

Safer, D. (1973). A familial factor in minimal brain dysfunction. *Behavior Genetics, 3,* 175–186.

Shaywitz, S.E.; Cohen, D.J.; & Shaywitz, B.A. (1980). Behavior and learning difficulties in children of normal intelligence born to alcoholic mothers. *The Journal of Pediatrics, 96*(6), 978–982.

Sparks, S. (1984). *Birth defects and speech-language disorders.* San Diego: College-Hill Press.

Streissguth, A.P.; Martin, D.C.; Barr, H.M.; Sandman, B.M.; Kirchner, G.L.; & Darby, B.L. (1984). Intrauterine alcohol and nicotine exposure: Attention and reaction time in four-year-old children. *Developmental Psychology, 20,* 533–541.

Thompson, J.S., & Thompson, M.W. (1980). *Genetics in Medicine,* 3rd ed. Philadelphia: Saunders.

University Week. (1986). Health forum speaker seeks birth defect information. Seattle, WA., September 11, p. 6.

Ward, B. (1987). Medicine's new supersleuths. *SKY* (Delta Air Lines Inflight Magazine), *16*(8), 42–53.

Weiss, B. (1983). Feingold diet research seen as inadequate (letter). *Journal of Learning Disabilities, 16,* 574–575.

Wilsher, C.R. (1986). The nootropic concept and dyslexia. *Annals of Dyslexia, 36,* 118–137.

Witelson, S.F. (1977). Developmental dyslexia: Two right hemispheres and none left. *Science, 195,* 309–311.

Yellin, A.M.; Hopwood, J.H.; & Greenberg, L.M. (1982). Adults and adolescents with attention deficit disorder: Clinical and behavioral responses to psychostimulants. *Journal of Clinical Psychopharmacology, 2,* 133–136.

PART II

ASSESSMENT AND SERVICES

Chapter 3

Child in a Straw Hat by Mary Cassatt: (*c.* 1886). Courtesy of the National Gallery of Art, Washington, collection of Mr. and Mrs. Paul Melon, 1983.

ASSESSMENT

MAIN IDEAS

- General reasons for frequent testing and specific purposes of assessment: screening, placement, program planning, program evaluation, student progress review

- Controversial issues: the use of discrepancy measures, the need for distinguishing slow learners from LD pupils, the effects of examiner familiarity

- Five types of assessment: formal assessment, including a listing of the most popular tests; informal assessment, including criterion referenced tests, rating scales, checklists, case studies, and ecological studies; curriculum-based assessment; neurological assessment, including neurometrics and various computerized tomographic techniques; microcomputer approaches to assessment

- PL 94–142 requirements for Individual Education Programs and assessment responsibilities

OVERVIEW

Assessment is the process of evaluation and diagnosis that is undertaken to form a judgment on students that may be learning disabled. Gathering precise information about such students is extremely important because of the crucial decisions that must be made about their placement and instruction.

This chapter discusses the reasons for assessment, reviews various types of assessment, and relates assessment to current laws. The chapter ends with comments and recommendations about issues and practices of assessment.

--------------------- REASONS FOR ASSESSMENT ---------------------

LD assessment practices are particularly important since LD youngsters are probably tested, probed, monitored, and evaluated more than children of any other type, handicapped or otherwise. The first reason is that the federal and state requirements to qualify students as learning disabled call for an assessment process that is likely to involve a fair number of tests. In order to qualify as learning disabled, individuals must be of average intelligence and yet off the mark in some academic task as noted in Chapter 1. Some states and locales demand other characteristics, all of which require a test or two. A second reason for the frequent testing of these youth is that a number of disciplines are concerned with learning disabilities, and most of them have developed their own tests to assess learning abilities. The third reason for the quantity of tests given learning disabled students is the eagerness of a variety of organizations and professionals to test them. Public and private schools administer tests, and so do clinics, hospitals, and any number of pediatricians, family medicine specialists, psychologists, optometrists, and therapists of numerous types.

Salvia and Ysseldyke (1981) have specified five purposes of assessment that are pertinent for learning disabilities:

James E. Ysseldyke is on the faculty of the University of Minnesota, where he was the director of its federally funded LD institute. Ysseldyke has written a number of articles and books on special education topics, including testing practices, policy matters, and role of school psychologist. One of his more important books, in collaboration with John Salvia, is "Assessment in Special and Remedial Education." He is the editor of *Exceptional Children*.

— *Screening:* to identify which students qualify for learning disabilities services (Ordinarily, pupils would be tested more carefully following this screening, before initial placement or instructional decisions are made.)

— *Placement:* to determine the most appropriate location in which to provide services for LD youth (Those options—self-contained classrooms, resource rooms, regular classrooms, and others—are discussed in Chapters 4 and 5.)

— *Program planning:* to find the best, or at least an acceptable program, that is appropriate for the youngster (It is important to identify not only an appropriate program—for example, Slingerland in reading— but the level in that program at which to begin instruction.)

— *Program evaluation:* to obtain data about the effectiveness of programs (It is often a good idea to keep data on two or more programs to determine which one is the most suitable for a particular youngster.)

— *Review of student progress:* to determine the extent to which youngsters are reaching their goals (Performance should be monitored frequently in order to make adjustments in pupils' programs.)

CONTROVERSIAL ISSUES

A number of controversial issues pertain to assessment. In fact, there is more controversy than we can explore in an introductory book on learning disabilities. Three assessment matters, however, are particularly related to learning disabilities and will be discussed here.

The Use of Discrepancy Measures

In most definitions of learning disabilities, a key statement indicates that in order for an individual to be classified as learning disabled, there must be a significant difference between the person's potential (as measured by an intelligence test) and achievement in some area (as measured by an achievement test). In an effort to come up with a number, ratio, or other statistic to indicate that there is such a difference, several states have devised discrepancy formulas.

Fuller and Alsdorf (1986) observed that fewer tests were required after Washington state adopted a severe discrepancy criterion, but the tests had to be administered on an approved list calibrated on the state's discrepancy table. Their survey of psychologists in eight Seattle area school districts noted the following tests were most frequently administered to individuals who were possibly learning disabled:

— General intelligence: *Wechsler Intelligence Scale for Children—Revised* (WISC-R)

—General achievement: *Woodcock–Johnson Psycho-Educational Battery, Wide Range Achievement Test* (WRAT), and *Peabody Individual Achievement Test* (PIAT)

—Reading: *Woodcock Reading Mastery Test, Durrell Analysis of Reading Difficulty,* and *Spache Diagnostic Reading Scales*

—Written expression: *Test of Written Language* (TOWL)

—Specialized areas: *KeyMath Diagnostic Arithmetic Test, Bender Visual–Motor Gestalt Test, Illinois Test of Psycholinguistic Abilities* (ITPA), and *Berry Developmental Test of Visual-Motor Integration*

Since the procedure for determining a discrepancy involves a complex set of computations, the criterion values defining a severe discrepancy must be calculated, put in tables, and made available for test evaluators (Schrag, Kirsch, & Dailey, 1984). Four steps are followed to determine whether or not there is a severe discrepancy:

1. Determine the intellectual ability score.
2. Determine the age-based achievement score.
3. Determine the criterion discrepancy score by looking it up on the appropriate table.
4. Determine whether a severe discrepancy exists—that is, the standard score obtained in Step 2 is equal to or smaller than the criterion value obtained in Step 3.

The Council for Learning Disabilities has taken a strong position against the use of discrepancy formulas such as that used in Washington and other states. The eight reasons listed by the board to support their dissent include the following:

1. Discrepancy formulas tend to focus on a single aspect of learning disabilities (e.g., reading, mathematics) to the exclusion of other types of learning disabilities.
2. The use of discrepancy formulas often creates a false sense of objectivity and precision among diagnosticians who feel that their decisions are statistically based when formulas are employed.
3. Although promoted as a procedure for increasing accuracy in decision-making, discrepancy formulas often represent a relatively simplistic attempt to reduce incidence rates of learning disabilities. [Council for Learning Disabilities, 1986, p. 245]

The trustees of the Council for Learning Disabilities made six recommendations, three of which follow:

1. Reductions in incidence rates of learning disabilities, when warranted, should be accomplished through comprehensive diagnostic evaluations conducted by

multidisciplinary teams in accordance with the concept of learning disability stated in the definition of learning disabilities adopted by the National Joint Committee on Learning Disabilities.

2. Alternative service delivery programs for students who are misdiagnosed as learning disabled must be developed if all persons are to be served appropriately in the least restrictive environment.

3. Where the use of discrepancy formulas is mandated by state agencies, the results derived from formulas should be reported in accordance with current professional standards. Even then, discrepancy formulas should be used with extreme caution, and viewed as only one course of information concerning the degree of discrepancy between ability and achievement. The results of using such formulas cannot dictate whether or not individuals have a learning disability. [1986, p. 245]

The Need for Distinguishing Slow Learners from LD Pupils

According to the state of Washington, it is important to discriminate between youngsters who are learning disabled and those who are simply slow learners, for the latter students ". . . should be taught differently, even though they may have the same academic achievement level. The learning disabled student requires instructional techniques available in special education. The slow learning student who does not have a specific handicap is the responsibility of regular education and should not be placed in programs designed to help those with specific learning disabilities. Other services should be provided, such as remediation assistance, Chapter I, or local district support services." [Schrag et al., 1984, p. 10]

The state of Washington guidelines continue: ". . . in obtaining documentation that the student has an academic achievement problem in the regular education program, it is important to take into consideration any previous attempts to remediate the student's learning problems in the regular education program, as well as results obtained. Interventions may include classroom strategies such as cross-age peer tutoring, small group or individualized instruction, alteration of curriculum, modification of instructional techniques, and itinerant consultation services, participation in transition classrooms, the Chapter I program, remedial academic programs, or other district compensatory educational services" (Schrag et al., 1984, p. 17).

Fuller and Alsdorf (1986) obtained data relevant to this point when they noted that the percentage of those pupils referred, then tested, was high; the percentage of those tested who qualified as LD was also high; and more psychologists were giving suggestions to teachers for dealing with youngsters in their classes prior to involving them in the assessment process.

■ COMMENTARY ■   *This probably accounts for the fact that the percentage of those pupils who were tested and were eventually qualified as learning disabled was so high.*

Their survey revealed that time for administering tests and writing up the results ranged from 2.5 to 24 hours, an average of 10 hours.

The board of trustees of the Council for Learning Disabilities agrees with the opinion that nonhandicapped low achievers and underachievers should not be included with LD youngsters for instructional purposes. The Board's position statement gives the following reasons:

1. The major reason for excessive incidence rates in learning disability programs is the inclusion of students whose low achievement or underachievement reflects factors other than a learning disability (e.g., depressed intellectual functioning, lack of motivation, inadequate or inappropriate instruction, environmental disadvantage, cultural differences);

2. Students with appropriately diagnosed learning disabilities may be denied needed services in programs with incidence rates that have been previously inflated due to the inclusion of nonhandicapped low achievers and underachievers;

3. Placement of nonhandicapped "slow learners" and other low achievers and underachievers in learning disability programs seriously compromises the quality of services provided to students who have appropriately diagnosed learning disabilities;

4. Placement of such nonhandicapped students in special education programs funded through PL 94–142 is a violation of the eligibility provisions of the law;

5. Placement of nonhandicapped low achievers and underachievers in learning disability programs propagates the misperception that a learning disability is a relatively mild problem that can be addressed simply through remedial or enrichment programs. [Council for Learning Disabilities, 1986, p. 246]

The board of trustees of the Council for Learning Disabilities makes the following recommendations:

1. School personnel should not view learning disability as synonymous with "slow learner," "mild learning problem," or low achievement or underachievement. Multidisciplinary evaluation teams must ensure that all eligibility criteria, not only provisions pertaining to underachievement, are satisfied prior to providing a student with learning disability services;

2. Nonhandicapped low achievers and underachievers who have already been misdiagnosed and misplaced should be removed immediately from learning disability services;

3. Nonhandicapped low achievers and underachievers should generally be served within the domain of regular education. Building-level teacher assistance teams should be available to help classroom teachers serve the needs of underachievers who do not qualify for special education services;

4. "Slow learners" and other low-achieving or underachieving students should not be denied special education services when the multidisciplinary evaluation team determines that a specific learning disability exists. [1986, p. 246]

Although a number of professionals believe strongly in the importance of discriminating between LD and slow learners, that has not been an easy matter. Ysseldyke and his colleagues at the University of Minnesota have conducted a number of studies which demonstrate that when school psychologists are asked to make these discriminations based on standardized test information, they are not at all accurate.

In one such study (Epps, Ysseldyke, & McGue, 1984), researchers sought to determine the degree to which groups of individuals, when given patterns of scores from psychometric measures, could decide which youngsters were LD and which ones were simply slow learners. There were three groups of evaluators in their study: school psychologists, special education teachers, and a number of "naive" individuals who were enrolled in programs unrelated to either education or psychology. Results of their study confirmed the difficulty of differentially diagnosing students with learning disabilities: All three groups of judges were in agreement with the school classifications only half of the time; and no significant differences were found between the teachers, the school psychologists, and the naive group in their overall agreement with the schools. Based on the difficulty of the professionals to make discriminations between LD and non-LD pupils from standardized psychometric information, the authors recommended that other ways be found to evaluate students' abilities.

The Effects of Examiner Familiarity

There have been a few studies on the effects of examiner familiarity and related factors that could affect test scores of certain youngsters. Fuchs, Fuchs, and Power (1987), for example, studied the effects of examiner familiarity on LD and MR students' language performance. In their research, students were assessed on *The Clinical Evaluation of Language Functions* (CELF) by familiar and unfamiliar testers. Results showed that LD students performed significantly better with familiar, rather than unfamiliar, examiners. Across ten CELF subtests, the mean score for LD students was 30.4 points greater in the familiar condition. Meanwhile, mentally retarded students generally scored the same in both conditions.

In a related study, Brown and Rosenbaum (*New York Times*, 1983), of Georgetown University, learned that certain types of stress can influence children's scores on standardized tests. They reported that, in general, youngsters' test scores decreased by 13% when they were experiencing stress. According to them, one stress factor was being held back in school; another was being assigned to a special education class. This effect should be of some concern, since many of our LD youngsters experience both factors (Lovitt, 1986).

TYPES OF ASSESSMENT

As we have seen, learning disabled youngsters are assessed frequently. This section discusses five types of assessment: formal, informal, curriculum based, neurological, and microcomputer.

Formal Assessment

Formal assessment makes use of tests that have been standardized and given to large numbers of children of different ages from various parts of the country. The resulting scores are the norms from which youngsters being assessed are compared. The test scores are often reported in terms of grade level equivalents, for example, fourth grade or sixth grade.

There are hundreds of standardized tests on the market, and dozens of them have been administered to LD youngsters. Several tests are described elsewhere in this book (see Chapters 6 through 8 and 11 through 13). Only a few general tests and those not discussed elsewhere are covered in this chapter.

A few years ago a graduate student (Kuta, 1981) surveyed the formal tests given in a number of districts in the Seattle area. Following is a summary of her report. In addition to formal tests, subtests from a number of tests were routinely administered for reading: *Spache Diagnostic Reading Scales, Durrell Analysis of Reading Difficulty, Woodcock Reading Mastery Tests—Revised* (WRMT-R), *Wide Range Achievement Test* (WRAT), *Woodcock–Johnson Psycho-Educational Battery, Peabody Individual Achievement Test* (PIAT), and *Gates-McKillop Reading Diagnostic Tests.* Subtests from the WRAT and *Tests of Written Language* (TOWL) were the favorite testing devices for written expression. Educators relied on subtests from WRAT, *KeyMath Diagnostic Arithmetic Tests,* or *Woodcock–Johnson. Wechsler Intelligence Scale for Children—Revised* (WISC-R) was administered

Richard W. Woodcock has developed several tests that are widely used with learning disabled youth, primarily *Woodcock Reading Mastery Tests* and *Woodcock-Johnson Psycho-Educational Battery.* He also developed the Rebus reading program referred to in this text. He has been on the faculty of the University of Arizona and has just taken a position at the University of Southern California.

most often when measuring general intelligence. Other measures used included *Stanford–Binet Intelligence Scale, McCarthy Scales of Children's Abilities, Leiter International Performance Scale, Bayley Scale for Infant Development, Slosson Intelligence Test,* and *Peabody Picture Vocabulary Test* (PPVT).

Five years later, Fuller and Alsdorf (1986) reported that many of the same tests were still being used. Moreover, reports from other parts of the country indicate that these tests are among the most popular.

Wechsler Intelligence Scale for Children—Revised (WISC-R).   This individually administered intelligence test is designed for children from the ages of six to sixteen. From this test a single IQ score is derived along with verbal and performance scores. Five subtests comprise the verbal scale:

1. *Information* (tests general knowledge): "How many legs does a dog have?"
2. *Similarities* (tests knowledge of analogies and similarities): "In what way are a candle and lamp alike?"
3. *Arithmetic* (tests arithmetic reasoning): "If you buy two dozen pencils at 45 cents a dozen, how much change should you get back from a dollar?"
4. *Vocabulary* (measures ability to describe spoken words): "clock," "alphabet," "obliterate"
5. *Comprehension* (tests ability to make judgments about social situations): "What is the thing to do when you cut your finger?"

There are also five subtests in the performance scale:

— *Picture completion,* which tests ability to detect missing elements in pictures—for example, missing ear, missing telephone cord
— *Picture arrangement,* which tests ability to rearrange a set of pictures to relate a sequenced and sensible story
— *Block design,* which requires students to arrange colored blocks to copy geometric designs
— *Object assembly,* which asks students to assemble parts of a puzzle that represent objects
— *Coding,* which tests the ability to remember association between numbers and geometric symbols and quickly record these associations

Wide Range Achievement Test (WRAT).   The WRAT is designed for students from age 5 to 74 years, 11 months. There are two levels of the test, one for youngsters from 5 to 11 years, 11 months and one for older individuals. Three subtests make up this individually administered test: reading, which tests the ability to name letters and words; spelling, which assesses the ability to write words that are dictated; and arithmetic, which tests the ability to count and solve problems.

Woodcock–Johnson Psycho-Educational Battery.   This test is designed for individuals from the ages of three to eighty. It is a comprehensive test and is made up of three parts and numerous subtests. Part 1 (Cognitive Ability) is made up of the following subtests: picture vocabulary, spatial relationships, memory for sentences, visual matching, antonyms-synonyms, analysis-syntheses, numbers reversed, concept formation, and analogies. The subtests in Part 2 (Achievement) are letter-word identification, word attack, passage comprehension, calculation, applied problems, dictation, proofing, science, social studies, and humanities. Part 3 is a collection of the following subtests: reading interest, mathematics interest, language interest, physical interest, and social interest.

Slosson Intelligence Test (SIT).   The SIT is designed to estimate the intellectual potential of children and adults. It is administered individually and verbally and does not require special preparation of the examiner. According to its publisher, Pro-Ed, the SIT has been shown to yield results that are statistically equivalent to those derived from other tests of intelligence.

Informal Assessment

Informal assessment makes use of tests that are not standardized and can be administered in the classroom. The tests are generally more related to a school's curricula and are often developed by teachers. This section summarizes nonstandardized tests and other types of informal assessment.

Criterion Referenced Tests.   These tests have established criteria; a student's skills are compared to them and not necessarily to other students' performances. A widely used test of this type is the *Brigance Diagnostic Inventories* (1982).

There are five steps for developing criterion referenced tests:

1. Select content to be taught.
2. Sequence the content in the order that it exists in the materials.
3. Put the easier items first and gradually increase the difficulty of the items.
4. Construct an item to assess each skill on the list.
5. Use the device and determine if modifications should be made.

Rating Scales.   Scales of this type record teachers' judgments of students in a measurable fashion. The teacher may judge students' ability on some task by rating them on a five-point scale. Generally, a score of one represents the lowest rating of a function; whereas a score of five indicates the highest level was achieved. Skills that could be rated on such a scale include auditory comprehension (ability to follow oral directions, comprehend class discussion, retain auditory information, and comprehend word meaning), and spoken language (ability to use complete and accurate expression, vocabulary ability, and ability to recall words, relate experience, and formulate ideas).

Checklists.   For this type of assessment, statements that infer questions about students' performances or learning characteristics are assembled. Checklists are flexible because they can be developed and administered in about any area of interest. General checklists might refer to academic traits such as paying attention, turning in work, or participating in discussions; specific checklists might refer to types of comprehension skills such as sequencing, stating the main idea, or discriminating fact from fiction. When the teacher observes that a skill is mastered, that skill statement is checked off.

Case Studies.   These are written reports that should include information on a number of developmental milestones—for example, the age when the pupil first sat up, walked, was toilet trained; data on the student's language development; and information about the child's health, eyesight, hearing, absences from school, family moves, and school changes. Teachers' comments, grades, and summaries of school performances would also be included in the case history. Furthermore, a case study should include social and educational information about other family members.

Ecological Assessment.   Ecological assessments take both the student and the environment into consideration and focus on their interactions (Bulgren & Knackendoffel, 1986). Assessments of this type provide ways to analyze patterns of behavior and interrelationships between individuals and their surroundings. Because this type of evaluation is an ongoing process, students in special placement can benefit from the continual assessment to verify placement decisions, to diagnose areas of weakness, and to plan and evaluate educational plans.

According to Bulgren and Knackendoffel, six steps are involved in the ecological assessment process:

1. Set goals—that is, consider the purpose of the assessment, what information will be necessary to attain the goals, and how the information will be attained.
2. Develop conceptual framework—that is, determine how the learning environment will be assessed.
3. Implement assessment plan—that is, identify primary learner goals.
4. Evaluate results.
5. Form hypotheses.
6. Develop a learning plan.

Among the classroom elements that could be involved in an ecological assessment are physical milieu (spatial arrangement, classroom seating, size and density of the classroom), classroom patterns (movement, parallel activities, transition), personal interactions, learning styles, academic deficits, and expectancy factors (student, teacher, peer, parental). Ecological data also can be obtained from a variety of resources outside the classroom—student records, interviews, observations, checklists, teacher-administered tests.

Curriculum Based Assessment (CBA)

CBA is a type of informal assessment that has become quite popular as an alternative to relying on information from standardized tests for making important decisions—who is handicapped; where that person should be educated, by whom, and with which type of program—regarding youngsters' welfare.

In defining CBA, Tucker (1985) informs us that it ". . . is a new term for a teaching practice that is as old as education itself [that is,] using material to be learned as the basis for assessing the degree to which it has been learned" (p. 199). To illustrate, if a teacher wanted a child to read from an American Book Company basal reader at the fourth grade level, to compute multiplication problems of the type $67 \times 33 =$ ____, spell words from a Botell program, and write sentences at a certain level, the teacher would assess the students' ability to perform those exact tasks and measure the student's performance directly.

Blankenship has stated:

> CBAs are usually given at the beginning of the school year, with the results being used to place students into curriculum materials and to identify specific skills each student needs to learn. All or part of a CBA may be re-administered immediately following instruction on a topic to assess skill mastery and to determine whether additional instruction or continued practice is warranted. Following mastery, CBAs may be used periodically throughout the year to measure long-term retention. [1985, p. 234]

Stimulated by the concern that standardized tests were not sensitive to subtle differences between LD and slow learners and by the suggestion that alternative measures be considered, Shinn and Marston (1985) arranged an investigation with curriculum-based assessments in reading, spelling, written expression, and math. In their study, pupils read from a Ginn reader for reading assessment; in spelling, they wrote words from a grade four book; in math, they computed problems in multiplication and division; and in written expression, they wrote simple stories. The study assessed three groups of students—mildly handicapped, low-achieving, and regular—from three grade levels: fourth, fifth, and sixth. The results indicated that

> . . . low-achieving students performed higher than the mildly handicapped group yet significantly lower than regular education students receiving no remedial services. These differences were reliable across the content areas of reading, spelling, multiplication and division basic skills, eight of nine contrasts in grade level computational tasks, and eight of nine contrasts in written expression. [Shinn & Marston, 1985, p. 36]

Lovitt and Fantasia (1980) arranged a study to compare reading evaluation by standardized tests and by CBA. For their research, they obtained pretest and posttest measures of both types from several LD youngsters. The standardized test was the *Spache Diagnostic Reading Scales;* for the direct assessment, youngsters read passages from Holt and Lippincott basal readers. The data indicated that, with respect to statistical significance, the approaches were much alike. Nevertheless, the authors recommended that teachers follow the CBA approach because it allows the evaluator to know more exactly what youngsters can read and how well they read; it places the evaluator in a better position to determine when to consider new interventions; and it clearly communicates progress to pupils and their caregivers.

Although Tucker (1985) mentioned that CBA was a new term for a teaching and assessment practice that has been around for a long time, he neglected to identify its origins. Considerable debate could be stirred by this issue, but several educators would argue that when it comes to assessing pupils' performance directly, Lindsley was a significant contributor.

Lindsley's approach, referred to as precision teaching (PT), has four characteristics. First is its directness. Like CBA, PT measures pupil performance on materials and programs that are actually being taught. If a teacher is instructing a student to read orally from a particular basal text, data would be gathered as the pupil read orally from that text. The second feature of precision teaching is frequency. Data on important educational and social behaviors are obtained quite often, if not daily. A third PT component is that data are gathered and charted as rate of responding—that is, correct and incorrect responses per minute. A fourth important feature is that if the first attempt to change a behavior is unsuccessful, another can be tried fairly quickly. (There was a brief review of precision teaching in Chapter 1; for a definitive explanation, see White and Haring, 1980.)

■ COMMENTARY ■   *When the features of the "new" CBA are compared with those of the "old" PT approach, the latter is more sophisticated and detailed than the former. Whereas both approaches recommend direct and repeated measures, precision teaching advocates that pupil data be graphed on a specific type of paper, that aims be specified, and that instructional decisions be based on those data. In this case, it appears that progress was made when an old sophisticated idea was reduced to a less complex, perhaps more usable state.*

Neurological Assessment

Neuropsychological Test Battery.   According to Rourke (1981), a broad range of neurological tests can help determine to what extent brain dysfunction is responsible for a youngster's performance deficiencies. Making a systematic assessment with these tests, says Rourke, enhances the chance of arriving at a preferred mode of treatment and prognosis.

Rourke indicated that the principal criterion for selecting tests and procedures for neuropsychological test batteries is that the adaptive abilities tapped should constitute a broad spectrum of those subserved by the human brain and should include those thought to be impaired when various systems within the brain are dysfunctional. To this end, researchers have chosen a variety of measures of sensory–perceptual, motor, psychomotor, linguistic, and cognitive skills, believed to be sensitive to the functional integrity of the cerebral hemispheres in children. Tests and procedures of this type have been developed and standardized by Reitan (Reitan & Davison, 1974; Reitan & Wolfson, 1986).

Neurological test batteries that are particularly important in the neuropsychological assessment of children with learning disabilities include the following features:

— Tests that require auditory and visual discrimination under conditions of passive attending, since they yield information regarding this important dimension of classroom situations
— Measures that allow for an assessment of the child's ability to benefit from feedback regarding the accuracy of his or her performance
— Measures that involve novel problem solving, because they are particularly sensitive to the functional integrity of the cerebral hemispheres in humans
— Tests that require a particular psychological "set" be maintained throughout performance or tests that necessitate the shifting of psychological sets, since Cognitive flexibility is a crucial variable to assess.
— Tests that include "power" as well as "speed" measures—that is, both untimed and timed tasks.

On the basis of research on neuropsychological assessment, Rourke (1981) offered the following general observations:

1. There appears to be a significant, positive correlation between severity of reading, spelling, and arithmetic retardation and severity of impairment on a large number of tests known to be sensitive to the functional integrity of the cerebral hemispheres.
2. The brain-related abilities that are impaired in learning disabled children are not the same for all such children.
3. Between the ages of five and fifteen, the neuropsychological abilities most likely to be deficient in the retarded reader vary considerably, with visual–spatial disorders declining, the psycho-linguistic problems increasing with age.
4. It is clear that the same levels of deficient performance in reading, spelling, and arithmetic can be the result of different patterns of brain-related abilities and deficits.

It has also been demonstrated that differing types of reading, spelling, and arithmetic disabilities can be defined in terms of patterns of neuropsychological abilities and deficits. Therefore, according to Rourke, it is no longer justifiable to speak of general characteristics of learning disabled children or even of those with reading, spelling, or arithmetic deficiencies.

Other Types of Medical Assessment.   This section includes a description of four ways, other than the usual paper-and-pencil or standardized tests, to assess learning disabled youngsters.

Neurometrics.   Neurometrics includes computerized electroencephalogram (EEG) and evoked potential (EP) means of evaluation. Following is a sketch of the procedure used when these assessment techniques are combined (Johnstone et al., 1985). The subject sits at a table on which there is a checkerboard panel that can be illuminated from below. Visual probes in the form of light flashes are presented from this surface, and a loudspeaker presents tones that alternate with the flashes. During a session, the probes are administered and EEG readings are taken while the subject is engaged in a variety of tasks and while not busy with tasks. Activities performed during a session include assembling blocks from patterns, silent reading and oral reading (at difficult and easy levels), listening to tapes of stories, and telling about favorite TV shows.

A primary goal of neurometrics, according to Thatcher and Lester (1985), is the application of an accurate and relatively unbiased or culturally fair technique for detecting learning disabilities and evaluating remediation strategies. The application of neurometrics is intended to complement psychometric assessments with a psychological measure that is sensitive to underlying neurological processes that may be responsible for learning disorders.

Thatcher and Lester have used neurometrics and hair analysis techniques to help identify environmental and nutritional factors that may have either deleterious or beneficial effects on child development. They noted that higher concentrations of lead or cadmium in the hair were associated with a slow wave activity and a decrease in the amplitude of the EEG, and they found that these measures were related to intelligence and achievement, as measured by standardized tests.

Evoked potential studies of several researchers have shown consistently different electrical activity in the language-related areas of the brains of students with reading disorders. Conners (1971), for example, demonstrated that poor readers showed attenuation of the visual evoked response in the left parieto-occipital area. Fuller (1977) reported deficits in the parieto-occipital area in a group of LD boys. Preston, Guthrie, and Childs (1974) reported that a group of LD readers showed significantly different visual evoked responses in the left angular gyrus. John and colleagues (1977) found highly significant differences between normal and LD groups on the basis of neurometric profiles. Johnstone and associates (1984) observed differences in the amplitude and latency of certain evoked potential features and found these differences to be related to the central and parietal areas of the brain.

Computerized Axial Tomography (CAT).   Computerized axial tomography is a technique whereby an X-ray beam, rotated in full circles around the body, produces images of thin cross-sectional segments of the brain. (See Figure 3.1.) A computer then assembles the segments into an overall picture (Case, 1986). Thompson, Ross, and Horwitz (1980) conducted tomographic assessments on

■ FIGURE 3.1 ■   A Computerized Axial Tomography (CAT) Scanner

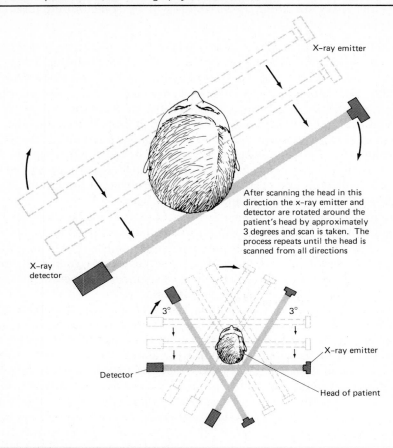

X–ray emitter

After scanning the head in this direction the x-ray emitter and detector are rotated around the patient's head by approximately 3 degrees and scan is taken. The process repeats until the head is scanned from all directions

X–ray detector

3°   3°

Detector

X–ray emitter

Head of patient

Source: Carlson, N.R., *Physiology of Behavior,* Third Edition. © 1986 by Allyn and Bacon. Reprinted by permission.

forty-four children with minimal brain dysfunction. The scans were then evaluated individually by two radiologists, neither of whom had access to clinical information about the children at the time of the interpretations. The researchers came to several conclusions. First, most children evaluated with CAT will have normal scans. Second, little additional information will be provided from CAT scans beyond neurologic and psychomotor testing. Third, computed tomography of the brain is indicated in a child with minimal brain damage (MBD) and specific learning disabilities *only* if there is a focal neurologic deficit.

Hier, LeMay, Rosenberger, and Perlo (1978) reported on scans of twenty-five LD youngsters. In addition to qualifying legally as learning disabled, the children between seven and fifteen years of age met the biomedical criterion for

"MBD-LD." For their investigations, two radiologists independently interpreted the scores. One radiologist designated fifteen scans as normal, nine as slightly abnormal, and one as borderline atrophic. The other radiologist designated thirteen scans as normal and twelve as slightly abnormal. Five scans out of the total were read as slightly abnormal by both radiologists. Most of the learning disabled children had normal scans. (More information on this type of assessment appears in Chapter 2, Medical Aspects.)

Hair analyses.   For this type of assessment, hair samples are taken from the nape of the neck and analyzed to determine the amounts of lead, cadmium, or other metals present. Thatcher and colleagues (1983) reported that the significant relationship between lead hair concentrations and intelligence indicated that higher levels of cognitive functioning were the most susceptible to lead poisoning. They indicated furthermore, that this relationship was not a threshold phenomenon, but rather represented a continuum of subtle deleterious effects.

Thatcher and Lester (1985) reported that a dietary deficiency of zinc, copper, iron, calcium, and vitamin C enhanced the toxicity of lead or cadmium. They noted also that the refining of foods significantly reduced the content of many protective micro-nutrients. Moreover, they found that the nutrients of refined and unrefined carbohydrates, together with vitamins C and D, were related to IQ, that lead was not significantly correlated with diet, but that cadmium showed a strong positive correlation with the proportion of refined carbohydrates in the diet. They claimed, furthermore, that most intellectual measures showed significant negative correlations with the proportion of refined low-nutrient foods in the diet. Finally, their results suggested that zinc may protect or reduce the deleterious effects of cadmium, a heavy metal pollutant.

Rimland and Larson (1983) reviewed 51 studies and concluded the following:

1. LD youngsters seemed to be characterized by a general pattern of high cadmium, lead, copper, and manganese.
2. Mentally retarded youngsters tended to show high levels of lead and low levels of sodium.
3. Juvenile delinquents exhibited high cadmium and magnesium, copper, calcium, aluminum, and lead, along with deficiencies in potassium, manganese, and sodium.
4. Brain damaged youngsters tended to exhibit high lead, chromium, and molybdenum, along with low cobalt and vanadium.
5. Bright youngsters tended to exhibit low levels of lead and cadmium and high levels of zinc.

Rimland and Larson offered a number of cautions, however, to drawing conclusions from hair analysis data. First, hair mineral levels do not necessarily reflect levels in other tissues. Second, high or low mineral levels may have little meaning, since the ratios of the various minerals may be more important. Third, averaging the data may mask different configurations of hair mineral levels that could be meaningful for individuals.

Eye movements.   For this type of assessment, the number of forward and regressive eye movements are recorded. Pavlidis (1985) pointed out that the primary eye movements during visual scanning and reading are saccadic eye movements. He stated that although vision depended on the efficiency of eye movements, it would be erroneous to equate eye movements with vision, as the function of eye movement goes beyond vision and reflects higher intellectual processes. Although the relatively high cost of eye movement devices, combined with the need for specialized technical skills for their operation, has restricted their use, this approach, according to Pavlidis, is a highly sensitive, non-invasive method. Findings from these assessments suggest that whereas advanced, normal, and retarded readers belonged to the same continuum, dyslexics were a distinct group. Pavlidis indicated that dyslexic youngsters made significantly more regressive eye movements and fixations while they read text appropriate to their reading age than did any of the other three groups.

Microcomputer Approaches

Hofmeister and colleagues at Utah State University have done considerable work with microcomputers and assessment. One of their projects has been to design "expert systems" that engage the user in a dialogue (Hofmeister & Lubke, 1986). In many ways this interaction with a microcomputer program parallels the type of conversation a person might have with an expert consultant, since the computer is programmed to present the user with questions, accept the user's responses, and match those responses with information in the program. Based on the programmed logic, conclusions are then displayed to the user.

The researchers at Utah State University also developed an artificial intelligence (AI) unit and explored its applications to special education. This system, the Mandate Consultant (Parry & Hofmeister, 1986), was designed to provide a second opinion about the accuracy of placement decisions for learning disabled students and to help special educators review the procedures followed in developing Individualized Education Programs (IEPs). The expert system consists of two components: a *knowledge base* and an *inference engine.* The former is made up of rules derived from research findings as well as state and federal regulations, whereas the inference engine guides the knowledge base to bear on a specific case being reviewed.

Colbourn and McLeod (1983) also developed an expert system intended to serve as a consultant in the process of diagnosis and prescription. Their program guided the user through the various stages and levels of diagnosis, from the initial suspicion that a reading problem might exist to the point at which sufficient information had been gathered to plan an appropriate remedial program. The results of their program were encouraging in that the expert system's diagnoses were accurate. Furthermore, because of the system's speed at analyzing error patterns, its diagnostic reports included more information than those of human diagnosticians.

One of the most perplexing problems facing special education program administrators in the United States is the frequent misclassification of students as learning disabled. In response to that issue, Hofmeister (1984) developed an expert system, referred to as CLASS.LD. That program enables individuals who diagnose children as learning disabled to check their reasoning and conclusions against decision rules programmed into the computer.

There are now available a number of microcomputer services for various tests. For example, there is a *WISC-R* computer program that provides the tester with a printed psychological report of students' performances. It is intended to facilitate report writing and to make better interpretations and recommendations (Nicholson, 1986). Paparella and Piazza (1986) reported on a program designed to inform testers or teachers as to what they should do once they have the scores from the WISC-R. Also available are computer scoring disks for the *Slosson Intelligence Test* and the *Stanford Binet Intelligence Scale* and error analysis disks for the *PIAT* and *Woodcock Reading Mastery Tests.*

In addition, there are microcomputer programs designed to help write comprehensive reports. Psychological/Social History Report (PSHR), for example, conducts a structural psychological intake interview and generates a narrative report. With that program, basic information that is gathered covers a number of areas: presenting problems, family/developmental history, education, financial history/status, employment history, alcohol/drug history, medical history, diet/ exercise, and other information.

The Screening and Tracking Corporation of America has developed a sophisticated system for monitoring IEPs called MICRO-SPED (Kunzelmann, 1988). According to Kunzelmann, it contains the entire special education process: pre-referral information (intervention attempts and decisions to evaluate or intervene), evaluation reports for all disciplines, staffing report (including current performance levels, evaluation summaries, and recommended objectives), and an IEP. Kunzelmann maintains that the most important contribution of their system is the inclusion of over 6,000 behavior statements that generate both current performance levels and specific objectives. Those statements force evaluators to connect their findings to the objectives in the IEP as stated by the teacher. Another contribution of MICRO-SPED is that the behavior statements will print either current or performance levels or objectives only if the evaluator has included information on the conditions and criteria for reaching the objectives.

THE ROLE OF ASSESSMENT IN PL 94–142

Since Public Law 94–142, The Education for All Handicapped Children Act, was signed in 1975, all handicapped youngsters—and that includes those who are learning disabled—must have an Individualized Education Program (IEP). The law requires that an IEP include the following features:

— A statement of the child's present levels of educational performance
— A statement of annual goals, including short-term instructional objectives

— A statement of specific special education and related services to be provided to the child, including the extent to which the child will be able to participate in regular educational programs

— The projected dates for initiating services and the anticipated duration of the services

— Appropriate objective criteria, evaluation procedures, and schedules for determining, on at least an annual basis, whether the short-term instructional objectives are being achieved

To summarize, an IEP should describe how the child is doing right now, what and how the child should be taught, where the teaching will take place and by whom, how long it should take, and, finally, how to tell whether the program is working.

Following are the steps required for developing and implementing an IEP (Lovitt, 1980):

□ *Initial referral made:* A teacher, parent, or someone else who knows the child's abilities makes the initial referral.

□ *Parents notified:* The principal or other building representative asks the parents for permission to continue with an evaluation of their youngster.

□ *Case reviewed:* If the parents give permission to proceed, the group of evaluators reviews existing data and decides whether or not to gather additional information.

□ *Parental consent requested:* If further information is desired, the parents are asked to give their permission.

□ *Evaluation continued:* If the parents agree, the evaluation team proceeds to acquire the additional data, including data from some of the assessment techniques described in this and in other chapters.

□ *Summary written:* The evaluation team writes a summary of all the data available.

□ *Parents contacted:* After the data are summarized, parents are asked to come to the school for a meeting regarding their child's placement and instructional program.

□ *Planning conference held:* If the parents agree, a meeting is arranged with the school personnel, both those who are familiar with the child's data as well as those who will work with the child in the future.

□ *Plan reviewed:* If the parents agree with the summary report of the evaluation team, the group discusses tentative goals for the child.

□ *IEP developed:* Parents and school personnel develop an IEP for the child that indicates not only how the pupil will be taught, but where, by whom, and for how long.

□ *IEP approved:* All parties who wrote the IEP—that may include the youngster—sign the document.

☐ *Plan implemented:* The IEP is put into operation.

☐ *Parents notified of review:* After a period of time the parents are asked to participate in a review of the IEP.

☐ *Program reviewed:* Ideally, all the personnel who work with the child and the child's parents go over all available data and decide whether to continue various aspects of the IEP or to make revisions.

At any time in the process of writing and putting the IEP into operation a parent may request more information or disagree on certain features of the plan. At that point, additional meetings are scheduled between the school, parents, and perhaps representatives of the parents in an attempt to supply more information or to reconcile the disagreements. If the parents and school officials continue to be at odds, an impartial hearing officer may be called in to arbitrate the case. If that fails, the parents or the school can take the case to court.

A unique feature of PL 94–142 when it comes to qualifying youngsters as learning disabled is that their assessments must be carried out by a multidisciplinary team. The team must include at least one special education teacher and at least one person qualified to conduct individual diagnostic assessments in the area of suspected disability. The other member of the team is ordinarily the student's regular classroom teacher. Each member must be licensed, registered, credentialed, or certificated according to his or her professional standards in accordance with state statutes and rules.

Following are the major responsibilities of the multidisciplinary assessment team for most states:

1. Collect—or aid in the collection of—data relevant to the determination of eligibility.

2. Appoint a team member (other than the student's teacher) to observe the student in the regular classroom.

3. Summarize (in writing), date, and sign the assessment data collected as required in the rules and regulations.

4. Review all available data with consideration given to ways in which the suspected learning disability may be manifested in test performance and in other student behaviors.

5. Make a collaborative team decision about whether or not the student meets the learning disability eligibility criteria.

6. Prepare a written report that addresses all eligibility criteria according to the summary analysis requirements.

7. Sign and date the summary analysis, with individual members certifying concurrence with the eligibility decision, or provide a minority report.

As discussed in Chapter 1, in many states there are three general conditions which must be demonstrated before a student with academic achievement problems may be identified as learning disabled; they relate to exclusion, discrepancy, and the need for special education. A number of tests should be given in order to respond to those points.

Also, according to the law, the students should be assessed across all areas of suspected disability, for a severe discrepancy between intellectual ability and academic achievement may result from a number of other handicapping and sociological conditions, such as visual, hearing, motor handicap, mental retardation, serious behavioral disability, environmental, cultural, or economic factors.

————— COMMENTS AND DISCUSSION POINTS —————

- Assess directly. In many instances, it is more sensible for teachers to measure something they are teaching than to gather inappropriate data from standardized tests. As noted, many of the items on standardized tests are not the ones being taught.

- Assess frequently. If teachers want to know how a student is doing on a certain skill or behavior, it is important to gather pertinent data frequently, rather than rely on standardized tests, which are generally given only once or twice a year.

- Assess the most important and most critical behaviors most often. Teachers should decide on which behaviors are the most in need of change and then gather as much data as possible on them.

- Inform pupils about the assessment process. Teachers can help pupils by explaining not only the reasons for various measurements, but in many cases the meaning of the results. Too often, pupils are not told their intelligence or achievement test scores, which are generally filed and spoken of only in multidisciplinary team conferences.

- Conduct assessments in the students' classrooms or homes under normal circumstances. When pupils are taken to testing chambers outside their familiar surroundings, they are generally not at ease, even if efforts have been made to establish rapport.

- Assess skills and behaviors that are part of the pupils' IEPs. It makes sense for teachers to rely on the IEPs for guidance on instruction and measurement. Too often, items included in IEPs are not instructed.

- Rely on published standardized tests only to the extent that it is absolutely necessary. Some of them may be required in order to qualify youngsters as learning disabled, and it may be important to qualify pupils as learning disabled in order to provide them with appropriate services; but standardized tests shouldn't be administered any more than necessary.

- Learn as much as possible from standardized tests when they have to be given. Teachers administering tests are in a good position to listen to pupils, watch them carefully as they respond to the test queries, and note their reactions. Some of the pupils' behaviors and comments may help in subsequent instruction.

- Don't be overly impressed by the reports that come from standardized tests. Some school psychologists try to dazzle teachers with their talk of stanines and grade-level equivalents. (For more details on the standardized test versus direct measurement argument, see Lovitt, 1986.)

■ Become familiar with the techniques for conducting ecological assessments. If detailed reports about certain pupils are desired, the ideas from that approach, coupled with ongoing data, blend together quite nicely.

■ Keep up with the findings from neurological and other medical assessments. Although the jury is still out when it comes to these measures, information from such approaches can provide a great deal of information about diet, nutrition, allergies, and possibly, about differential treatments for children of various neurological types.

■ Keep up with the uses of microcomputers when it comes to assessment. This is true with respect to gathering, displaying, analyzing, and reporting data.

■ Communicate with parents and other interested caregivers frequently and directly about the progress of their children. Be open to suggestions from them about behaviors that should be assessed that are not being monitored.

REFERENCES

Blankenship, C.S. (1985). Using curriculum-based assessment data to make instructional decisions. *Exceptional Children, 52,* 233–238.

Brigance, A.H. (1982). *Brigance Diagnostic Comprehensive Inventory of Basic Skills.* North Billerica, MA: Curriculum Associates.

Bulgren, J.A., & Knackendoffel, A. (1986). Ecological assessment: An overview. *The Pointer, 30*(2), 23–30.

Case, F. (1986). Scan power. *Seattle Times.* January 26, Section D (Scene), pp. 4 and 5.

Colbourn, M., & McLeod, J. (1983). Computer guided educational diagnosis: A prototype expert system. *Journal of Special Education Technology, 6*(1), 30–39.

Conners, C.K. (1971). Cortical visual evoked response in children with learning disorders. *Psychophysiology, 7,* 418–428.

Council for Learning Disabilities. (1986). Inclusion of nonhandicapped low achievers and underachievers in learning disability programs: A position statement by the board of trustees of the Council for Learning Disabilities. *Learning Disability Quarterly, 9,* 245–246.

Epps, S.; Ysseldyke, J.E.; & McGue, M. (1984). "I know one when I see one"—differentiating LD and non-LD students. *Learning Disability Quarterly, 7,* 89–101.

Fuchs, L.S., & Fuchs, D. (1986). Effects of systematic formative evaluation: A meta-analysis. *Exceptional Children, 53,* 199–208.

Fuchs, D.; Fuchs, L.S.; & Power, M.H. (1987). Effects of examiner familiarity on LD and MR students' language performance. *Remedial and Special Education, 8*(4), 47–52.

Fuller, F., & Alsdorf, B. (1986). Learning disabilities: Assessments and programs in eight school districts. Paper submitted to a learning disabilities class, University of Washington, Seattle.

Fuller, P.W. (1977). Computer-estimated alpha attenuation during problem solving in children with learning disabilities. *Electroencephalography and Clinical Neurophysiology, 42,* 149–156.

Hier, D.B.; LeMay, M.; Rosenberger, P.B.; & Perlo, V.P. (1978). Developmental dyslexia: Evidence for a subgroup with a reversal of cerebral asymmetry. *Archives of Neurology, 35,* 90–92.

Hofmeister, A.M. (1984). CLASS.LD: An expert system for classifying learning disabilities (Computer program). Logan: Utah State University.

Hofmeister, A.M., & Lubke, M.M. (1986). Expert systems: Implications for the diagnosis and treatment of learning disabilities. *Learning Disability Quarterly, 9,* 133–137.

John, E.R.; Karmel, B.Z.; Corning, W.C.; Easton, P.; Brown, D.; Ahn, H.; John, M.; Harmony, T.; Prichep, L.; Toro, A.; Gerson, I.; Bartlett, F.; Thatcher, R.; Kaye, H.; Valdes, P.; & Schwartz, E. (1977). Neurometrics. *Science, 196,* 1393–1410.

Johnstone, J.; Galin, D.; Fein, G.; Yingling, C.; Herron J.; & Marcus, M. (1984). Regional brain activity in dyslexic and control children during reading tasks; visual probe event-related potentials. *Brain and Language, 21,* 233–254.

Kunzelmann, H. (1988). MICRO-SPED. Customized software for schools. Brookline, MA: Screening and Tracking Corporation of America.

Kuta, N. (1981). Assessments for special education eligibility. Paper submitted to a learning disabilities class, University of Washington, Seattle.

Lovitt, T.C. (1980). *Writing and implementing an IEP: A step-by-step plan.* Belmont, CA: Pitman Learning, Inc.

———. (1986). Oh! That this too too solid flesh would melt . . . the erosion of standardized tests. *The Pointer, 30*(2), 55–57.

Lovitt, T.C., & Fantasia, K. (1980). Two approaches to reading program evaluation: A standardized test and direct assessment. *Learning Disability Quarterly, 3,* 77–87.

New York Times. (1983). Study ties I.Q. scores to stress. Tuesday, May 31, p. 15.

Nicholson, C.L. (1986). *WISC-R computer report (WISC-RCR).* East Aurora, NY: Slosson Education Publications, Inc.

Paparella, C., & Piazza, C. (1985). *WISC-R compilation (WISC-RC): What to do now that you know the score.* East Aurora, NY: Slosson Educational Publications, Inc.

Parry, J.D., & Hofmeister, A. (1986). Development and validation of an expert system for special educators. *Learning Disability Quarterly, 9,* 124–132.

Pavlidis, G.T. (1985). Eye movements in dyslexia: Their diagnostic significance. *Journal of Learning Disabilities, 18*(1), 42–50.

Preston, M.A.; Guthrie, J.T.; & Childs, B. (1974). Visual evoked responses (VERs) in normal and disabled readers. *The Society for Psychophysiology Research, 11,* 452–457.

Reitan, R.M., & Davison, L.A. (Eds.), (1974). *Clinical neuropsychology: Current status and applications.* Washington, D.C.: V.H. Winston & Sons.

Reitan, R.M., & Wolfson, D. (1986). *Traumatic brain injury Vol. 1: Pathophysiology and neuropsychological evaluation.* Tucson, AZ: Neuropsychology Press.

Rimland, B., & Larson, G.E. (1983). Hair mineral analysis and behavior: An analysis of 51 studies. *Journal of Learning Disabilities, 16,* 279–285.

Rourke, B.P. (1981). Neuropsychological assessment of children with learning disabilities. In Fiskov, S.B., & Boll, T.J. (Eds.), *Handbook of Clinical Neuropsychology.* New York: Wiley.

Salvia, J., & Ysseldyke, J. (1981). *Assessment in special and remedial education.* Boston: Houghton Mifflin.

Schrag, J.; Kirsch, G.; & Dailey, J. (1984). The identification of students with learning disabilities. Olympia, WA: Division of Special Services and Professional Programs, State of Washington, Office of the Superintendent of Public Instruction.

Shinn, M., & Marston, D. (1985). Differentiating mildly handicapped, low-achieving, and regular education students: A curriculum-based approach. *Remedial and Special Education, 6*(2), 31–38.

Thatcher, R.W., & Lester, M.L. (1985). Nutrition, environmental toxins and computerized EEG: A mini-max approach to learning disabilities. *Journal of Learning Disabilities, 18,* 287–295.

Thatcher, R.W.; Lester, M.L.; McAlaster, R.; Horst, R.; & Ignasias, S.W. (1983). Intelligence and lead toxins in rural children. *Journal of Learning Disabilities, 16,* 355–359.

Thompson, J.S.; Ross, R.J.; & Horwitz, S.J. (1980). The role of computed axial tomography in the study of the child with minimal brain dysfunction. *Journal of Learning Disabilities, 13*(6), 48–51.

Tucker, J.A. (1985). Curriculum-based assessment: An introduction. *Exceptional Children, 52,* 199–204.

White, O.R., & Haring, N.G. (1980). *Exceptional Teaching,* 2nd ed. Columbus, OH: Merrill.

Chapter 4

Detail from *Jungle Tales (Contes de la Jungle)* by James J. Shannon (1895). Courtesy of The Metropolitan Museum of Art, Arthur Hoppock Hearn Fund, 1913. (13.143.1).

DELIVERY SYSTEMS AND SERVICES

————————————— MAIN IDEAS —————————————

- Social, educational, and other reasons for educating LD children with nonhandicapped pupils and the primary mandate of the concept of least restrictive environment

- Description and history of self-contained classrooms, including advantages and disadvantages and an overview of research in this setting

- Description and history of resource rooms, including advantages and disadvantages and an overview of research in this setting

- Description and history of regular classrooms with respect to integrating LD pupils, including advantages and disadvantages and an overview of research in this setting

- Rationale and explanation of the Regular Education Initiative and how this movement relates to the placement of LD youngsters

————————————— OVERVIEW —————————————

This chapter describes delivery systems for educating LD youngsters and focuses on the locations in which they are generally educated: self-contained classrooms, resource rooms, and regular classrooms. The matter of location is central to the concept of providing the least restrictive environment (LRE) when placing LD pupils in instructional programs.

The first section of the chapter places some of the benefits of educating LD and non-LD youngsters together in the context of LRE. The next three sections cover the three locations in which LD youngsters are ordinarily placed. The discussions include the research on these situations and the possible advantages and disadvantages of each of the placements. The next section looks at the Regular Education Initiative and three approaches that help make it effective. The final section provides comments and discussion points on the topic of location of instructional programs.

RATIONALE FOR LRE

The benefits of educating LD youngsters with their nonhandicapped peers have been summarized by various researchers. In making a case for social skills training, Gresham (1982), for example, cited reasons others have offered for the merger of LD and non-LD pupils:

- When LD youngsters are integrated into regular classrooms, they will be able to imitate the more acceptable behaviors of their nonhandicapped mates.
- When youngsters of both types are educated together, they will begin to interact and socialize with one another.
- The mingling of LD and non-LD children encourages the latter to become more accepting of their less-endowed "chums."

Ivarie, Hogue, and Brulle (1984) have pointed out additional motives for integrating LD youngsters with other pupils.

— Federal legislation stemming from the Civil Rights laws of the 1960s
— Parental concerns for equal opportunities for their children
— Implications that LD pupils will not be negatively labeled by nonhandicapped children if they associate more

■ COMMENTARY ■   Comments on most of these reasons appear throughout this chapter. Moreover, some discussion relevant to a few of these points will be found in other parts of the book (for example, Chapter 11).

Despite the merits of integrating LD and non-LD students cited by many researchers, one important dimension of the concept of least restrictive environment (LRE) must not be overlooked: the adjustment of both the LD and non-LD children must be taken into account when placement choices are considered. It would be foolish to assign LD children to instructional situations with nonhandicapped pupils if the LD pupils were uncomfortable and hence nonproductive in that location. It would be equally foolish if their nonhandicapped classmates or teachers were disturbed to the point of being nonproductive. Therefore, in order to sensibly implement the concept of LRE, educators and parents must take into account the net effect of any placement. There should be specific reasons for placing LD youngsters in one situation or another—reasons that go beyond the usual vague and general justifications of aiding youngsters to improve educationally and socially.

In order to respond to the primary mandate of LRE, three placement situations are ordinarily arranged: self-contained classrooms, resource rooms, and regular classrooms. As one might imagine, each of these delivery systems has dozens of variations, most of which are reviewed in the next three sections. The fourth section that follows provides details on three approaches to providing services—blending resources, consultation teachers, and teacher assistance teams—within the context of the regular classroom. (Other services and systems are covered in Chapter 13.)

_____ SELF-CONTAINED CLASSROOMS _____

Description

Self-contained classrooms have been established in elementary and secondary schools for some time. In this delivery system, a group of from 10 to 20 LD pupils is assembled in the same classroom. The number of students depends on the particular state's guidelines, the severity of the youngsters' problems, and other factors.

In one type of approach, LD youngsters remain together and are taught by the same teacher all day long. They might interact with non-LD youngsters only in hallways, lunchrooms, or play yards. Self-contained classrooms of this type are the most restrictive option for serving LD students in the regular school, although there are more restrictive placements for children who are more severely handicapped.

Another approach to self-contained classrooms in regular elementary and secondary schools calls for assigning LD students to self-contained classes for the majority of the day and placing them in integrated classes for certain periods. The integrated classes vary from school to school, depending on the willingness and abilities of the regular teachers to manage LD pupils. At the secondary level, vocal music, industrial arts, home living, physical education, and art are among the more usual integrated classes.

Ideally, teachers of self-contained classes are specially trained to manage mildly handicapped children or, more specifically, LD youngsters. In practice, however, the type and thoroughness of the preparation varies widely from state to state. Several states require a specific credential in the category to which teachers are assigned; some demand more general credentials, whereas others do not require special education credentials at all, although they may at least expect teachers to take a few courses in special education. Under such nonuniform circumstances, the quality of preparedness—hence the instruction—varies considerably from one locale to another.

Although the type of instruction in self-contained classes differs depending on the ages and abilities of the youngsters, the needs of the local situation, the type of training the teachers received, and other factors, the great majority of self-contained classes offer a basic skills program of one form or another. Considerable time is generally allocated to instruction in reading, spelling, writing, and arithmetic, particularly at the elementary level. Along with this emphasis on the fundamentals, some teachers schedule time for instructing social skills (see Chapter 11) or selected aspects of language (see Chapter 6).

History

Self-contained classes for LD pupils have been around for approximately 25 years. They were extremely popular in the early 1960s, when learning disabilities was a new concept. It is estimated that in 1966, for instance, 67 percent of the total LD population throughout the country were enrolled in them. Due to the reasons for integrated classes given earlier in this chapter and other factors, however, self-contained classes have become less and less popular over the years. In 1985–1986, only 21 percent of the LD population were served in this way.

Advantages and Disadvantages

The primary advantage of self-contained classes pertains to the homogeneity of the pupils. The thinking is that if students are homogeneously grouped, they can be instructed more efficiently. Logically, it *would* seem to be easier to teach reading or mathematics or most any other skill to pupils if they were all at about the same ability level and equally motivated to learn that skill than if they were a more diverse group. Numerous professionals agree with this position, including the Council for Learning Disabilities, which has maintained that LD youngsters should not be educated alongside slow-learners or nonachievers (see the discussion in Chapter 3).

■ COMMENTARY ■   *The practical problem with such a scheme is that even when youngsters are grouped on the basis of ability in one area (for example, reading), it is highly unlikely that they will be equally talented and motivated in another (say, mathematics).*

Another advantage for placing LD youngsters in self-contained classes is that ordinarily there are fewer students in those situations than in regular classrooms. As mentioned, special classes for the LD generally range from 10 to 20 pupils, whereas regular classrooms have as many as 35 youngsters. Because of the smaller groups, we might assume that LD pupils in these special rooms would receive more individual attention from teachers than they would in regular classes. According to a study by Ivarie et al. (1984), LD youngsters in regular classes received only one minute of individualized help a day. This finding tends to confirm the suspicion that LD students aren't provided much one-on-one assistance in regular classrooms.

■ COMMENTARY ■   *We don't know, from this study how much time comparable LD children received in self-contained classrooms. They might not have been any better off there. Nor do we know from the study how much individualized help the non-LD pupils were given in regular classrooms.*

Another advantage of special classes centers around the degree of variability among the students within a class. Accordingly, LD pupils who are educated separately from regular students should be better served than those in integrated classes because the teacher will not have to deal with extreme variability. However, some researchers claim that there is as much variability among non-LD students as there is among LD pupils (Weener, 1981).

■ COMMENTARY ■   *It would be informative to arrange a study whereby researchers obtained data on an entire class of pupils that included a few LD pupils, then removed them and continued keeping data in order to determine the impact of the LD pupils. Or, turn that process around.*

This advantage is not a reason for isolating LD pupils that is expressed in many books or keynote addresses; nonetheless, it is and has been one of the primary reasons for removing LD and other handicapped youngsters from "mainstream" classes and preventing their readmittance.

A disadvantage for placing LD youngsters in self-contained classes is that they are often given negative labels because of the special placement. A number of educators maintain that because of such labels, LD pupils' self-confidence is impaired. Macmillan, Jones, and Aloia (1974), for example, identified five areas in which the stigma of a label might affect children: self-concept, peer rejection, future vocational adjustment, family attitudes, and teacher expectancies. Based on reviews of the literature in each of these areas, however, they concluded that there was little support for the fears. (Further comment on this and other matters relating to adjustment appear in Chapter 11.)

Another disadvantage to self-contained placement is one expressed by numerous educators—that is, when LD pupils are educated only with themselves, there are few proper models for them to imitate. Critics of self-contained classrooms maintain that it is important for LD students to observe non-LD students as they achieve, socialize, and generally maneuver about the room. According to Gresham (1982), however, research evidence does not support the notion that beneficial modeling effects will occur simply as a result of mainstreaming. (More details on Gresham's views regarding effects of mainstreaming on the social interaction and acceptance of mildly handicapped youth are included in Chapter 11.)

Research on Effects

For the past fifty years there has been considerable research on special class placement for educable mentally retarded (EMR) children (see, for example, Polloway, 1984). Those "efficacy studies" sought to determine whether it was better to place EMR children in self-contained classes or to leave them in regular situations. Although more than 600 studies had this purpose in mind, the data are inconclusive. A number of investigations reported that EMR children were better off academically in regular classes, but did better with respect to social development in special settings. Other researchers came up with different conclusions.

■ COMMENTARY ■   *When one stops to think about these efficacy studies, it is not difficult to understand the reasons for the absence of firm conclusions. To begin with, there is tremendous* variability, as noted earlier, in the expertness of LD teachers; some are highly skilled, whereas others are not so expert. The same can be said for regular classroom teachers; there are hundreds of marvelous instructors and nearly as many who are not. It is small wonder that the results differ from one study to the next.

Meanwhile, a few studies concerned specifically with LD youngsters have been undertaken. At the University of Washington, a series of investigations, involving LD seventh graders in physical science, responded to the matter of LD placement. In one study, LD youngsters were enrolled in regular science classes instructed by regular teachers (Lovitt et al., 1986). In another, students were engaged in physical science activities in a self-contained classroom taught by a doctoral student or a special education teacher (Benedetti, 1984). Dependent measures were the same in both experiments. Results from these two and similar studies, indicate that LD youngsters acquired considerable information about physical science in either situation, when effective teaching practices were in effect. (See Chapter 10 for more detail.)

■ COMMENTARY ■   Chances are, most students—LD or otherwise—would thrive in regular or special situations with teachers who individualized instruction, were highly motivating, and exercised other qualities of excellence. Similarly, the probability is high that most LD pupils would languish if placed in regular or special rooms with inept teachers.

Beck, Lindsey, and Frith (1981) conducted a study to determine the progress of two groups of students enrolled in self-contained LD classes for one- and two-year periods. Their major finding was that the students who were in special classes for two years attained higher mathematics scores than did their one-year class-mates. All other comparisons were insignificant, however. The data from a study involved with reading (Lovitt & Fantasia, 1980) were similar: Students enrolled in a special program for two years outperformed those who were in the program for only one.

RESOURCE ROOMS

Description

Resource rooms have been established in elementary and secondary schools for some time. They have been an extremely popular approach for delivering services to LD youngsters. Some programs are designed to accommodate a variety of handicapped youngsters—that is, learning disabled, emotionally disturbed, educable mentally retarded—as well as some visually or hearing impaired children. Other resource room programs, however, cater only to LD students.

Some resource rooms are in operation for only a part of the day, either in the morning or afternoon; most are run the entire day. Accordingly, the number of children served throughout the day varies. Full-time resource teachers generally see from 15 to 30 youngsters each day. A few states specify the number of children that can be assisted by resource teachers; others dictate the amount of time pupils can spend in resource rooms.

A typical resource room schedule in an elementary school is for small groups of youngsters to come into the room, one group at a time. The first set might consist of five youngsters who are just beginning to read. They may all be from the same class or from different classes and grades. Following that group, another small collection would arrive for instruction in reading or another subject. As with the first students, these youngsters might come from the same class or from different ones. This sort of arrangement could continue throughout the day, with each group of students being seen for 30 to 45 minutes. Some of the pupils would stay in the resource room for only one period, whereas others would be enrolled for two or more periods. Resource room schedules depend on factors such as the needs of the school, the availability of support staff such as remedial reading teacher, and other special programs.

Resource teachers in elementary schools ordinarily concentrate on reading and related subjects, such as writing and spelling, although many of them also assist children in other subjects. The expectations of classroom teachers, administrators, and others regarding the role of resource teachers vary considerably from one program to another. In some instances, resource teachers are expected to *supplant* the services of regular teachers. For example, if children are referred for reading problems, the resource teacher is expected to be totally responsible for helping them in reading. Under such an arrangement the classroom teacher takes care of all other activities.

In other programs, resource teachers are expected to *supplement* the services of regular teachers. In such cases, resource teachers must determine what assignments or subjects the LD children have trouble with in the regular classroom and assist the LD students to overcome those problems in the resource room, with the hope that they can keep up with other pupils in the regular class. In a number of schools, resource teachers are also expected to serve as educational consultants for the entire staff. Any teacher who has a problem with a child can request their help, whether or not the child is enrolled in the resource room. (The consulting aspect of the resource teacher's role is discussed further in Chapter 5.)

The scheduling of students into resource rooms differs somewhat in secondary schools from elementary situations, because the former operate on set schedules of five to seven daily periods. In many secondary schools, LD students spend one or more periods in the resource room and are enrolled in regular classes for the remainder of the day. The regular classes might be in the track leading toward graduation, with required courses in science, language arts, social studies, physical education, and electives in music, industrial arts, and home economics.

In several secondary programs, resource teachers concentrate on basic skills such as reading and mathematics; in others, they support classroom teachers by assisting students with assignments from their science, social studies, and other classes. In an increasing number of situations, resource teachers instruct LD pupils in *study skills* that are intended to help them in a variety of content-area classes. (More detail on the various approaches is included in Chapters 10 and 13.)

History

According to a survey by Friend and McNutt (1984), resource rooms have been in existence since the early 1960s; by the mid 1970s, there were programs of this type in practically every state. The survey also indicated that the resource room was the most frequently adopted alternative to the regular education classroom setting for special education students, and the one most often chosen to serve mildly-to-moderately handicapped students. The study further revealed that most states speculated that resource rooms would continue to be popular in the future. When queried as to the proportion of handicapped students served in resource rooms in their states, respondents reported from 17 to 98 percent. According to the Office of Special Education and Rehabilitation Services, 1,155,772 LD students, which is 62 percent of the total number of LD students, were educated in resource rooms in 1985–1986. It is estimated that there were 150,000 or only 25 percent served in those situations in 1966.

Advantages and Disadvantages

The primary advantage of resource room programs is that children in need of special help in a specific academic or social area will be given that help by specially trained teachers, and children might thus be able to maintain the expected academic and social pace of the regular program. A further advantage is that LD youngsters enrolled in resource programs will be in the regular class with their nonhandicapped classmates for a good part of the day, with time to interact socially and perhaps imitate certain behaviors.

A disadvantage to resource programs is that they are a "pull-out program."[1] In a number of elementary schools, classroom teachers rarely see all of their children at the same time. Four or five are pulled out for Chapter I classes, two or three for speech therapy, a half dozen for instrumental music, three for gifted classes, and others for a variety of different programs. Although children in such special programs may be receiving help in one area (such as reading), they may be missing out in another (for example, social studies).

Pull-out programs create scheduling and other types of problems. Lieberman, in an article entitled "The Nightmare of Scheduling" (1982), summarized the concerns associated with such an approach, noting that it

— Increases the time that children travel from one room to another
— Increases the movement of children in and out of classrooms
— Lessens the ability of teachers to keep track of individual children
— Raises the possibility of inconsistent instructional approaches
— Increases the number of specialists that work with youngsters, resulting in splintered services

---

1. See the comments of Will, later in this chapter, on pull-out programs.

— Augments the controversy of either holding or not holding children accountable for what they missed while receiving services elsewhere

— Increases the conflict between group and individual needs

Lieberman offered a few suggestions for overcoming certain of these problems, one of which was for LD children to keep daily records. According to him, they should be taught "to maintain logs in regard to tasks accomplished, objectives mastered, current work activities, materials to be used, and rate of progress. Such diaries would serve to lift the burden of memory for detail from the teachers" (p. 58). (See the discussion on self-management in Chapter 10.)

Research on Effects

Rust and Miller (1978) examined the effectiveness of a resource room program by testing 162 students in grades two through six who had learning problems. Half of them were randomly assigned to a resource room, while the others remained in a regular class. Results indicated that over a year, the children who received resource room services gained significantly in achievement, as did those who spent the entire day in the regular class. There was evidence on two of the four dependent variables (total reading and word knowledge) that resource room students gained more than those in the regular classroom, but the differences were relatively small.

Sindelar and Deno (1978) reviewed the results of seventeen investigations of resource programs and their effects on the academic achievement and personal–social development of exceptional children. They pointed out that many criticisms of the early "efficacy studies" regarding special class placement were applicable to research on resource room versus regular class placement. Nonetheless, it was noted that resource programs for LD and mildly disturbed children were generally effective when it came to academic gains. Positive effects of resource programs for personal and social development were not established, however.[2]

REGULAR CLASSROOMS

Among the reasons for attempting to educate LD youngsters in regular classrooms—that is, to mainstream them—are those listed earlier in this chapter given by Gresham (1982) and Ivarie et al. (1984). Stainback and Stainback (1984) have added to this list of reasons for mainstreaming LD and other handicapped youngsters into regular classrooms:

— To change the belief that there are two types of children, handicapped and nonhandicapped

---

2. Shades of the "efficacy studies" of thirty years ago.

— To provide individualized services to all children, nonhandicapped as
  well as handicapped
— To share instructional methods of the two groups with all children
— To temper or eliminate the use of labels
— To reduce or eliminate the competition among educators and cut down
  on the duplication of services

(Will's comments later in this chapter relate to many of these points.)

Description

Considerable variation of circumstances exists in regular classrooms. Enrollments,
for example, are not uniform. In some, there are as few as 20 children, whereas
in others, there may be as many as 35. Students' academic and social abilities
also vary considerably: In some classes, they are reasonably close, while in other
situations, youngsters' performances extend over a wide range. Indeed, a number
of regular classes in elementary schools combine two or more grades,[3] thus
increasing the degree of variability among students.

Just as there is tremendous variability in the makeup of regular classrooms
at the elementary and secondary level, there are great differences when it comes
to policies for mainstreaming LD or other handicapped children. Policies are
documented and supported by experience in a few programs, while in others,
there are no systematic procedures so that teachers and administrators must
improvise from one case to the next.

Policy issues that vary from school to school include the following:

— Informing regular teachers about how many exceptional students to
  expect in their classes
— Providing information about the characteristics of newly arriving children
— Providing in-service training on topics about exceptional children
— Identifying individuals who will provide assistance on academic and
  social matters

When it comes to the individuals who can offer help, here, too, there are great
differences across elementary and secondary schools. In some schools, there are
only resource room specialists, whereas others have remedial reading teachers,
speech therapists, counselors, and consulting or itinerant teachers.

Further variability applies to teacher preparation requirements. Some states
require all teachers to have had courses or experience in working with handicapped
students. In other states, individuals can complete teacher preparation programs
without course work or independent study focused on handicapped pupils. In

---

3. These "split classrooms" are becoming an increasingly popular option in districts with
   decreasing enrollments.

most states, in fact, the preparation for regular teachers to instruct handicapped pupils is minimal.

History

The proportion of LD youngsters who have been educated in regular classrooms has ebbed and flowed. In 1985–1986, 15 percent of LD youngsters were mainstreamed at least part of their day in regular classrooms. That compares to an estimated figure of 8 percent 20 years ago. As indicated earlier, the secondary level classes into which LD students are most often integrated are industrial arts, home economics, vocal music, and art.

Advantages and Disadvantages

In recent years, numerous advantages for mainstreaming LD youngsters have been put forth:

- LD youngsters are likely to use non-LD pupils as models for certain of their behaviors.
- Managing LD children in regular classrooms is less expensive than providing them with special services in other situations.
- Non-LD youngsters who share experiences with handicapped pupils are likely to become more understanding about individual differences.
- The materials and procedures of regular education are available to LD children.
- Regular teachers are likely to become more adept at individualizing instruction for *all* pupils.

On the other hand, there are some disadvantages to mainstreaming LD children:

- LD pupils do not receive as much individual assistance as they would in special classes.
- LD pupils are likely to be stigmatized because of their handicaps.
- LD students are likely to fail more often because of the difficulty of the material or assignments.
- LD pupils are deprived certain types of "special education" instruction, such as social skills or study skills training.
- LD pupils are likely to develop poor self-images, inaccurate or self-defeating attributions, and antagonisms toward non-LD pupils.
- The morale of classroom teachers may be negatively influenced, because many of them are ill-prepared to manage and instruct exceptional children.

Research on Effects

A number of studies have compared instruction of LD children in regular classes with instruction in resource rooms. Thurlow, Ysseldyke, and co-authors (1983) studied the instruction provided LD students in resource rooms and in regular classrooms by observing eight students in both settings on 53 events for two days of classroom instruction. They reported that, in general, opportunities for individualized instruction in subjects such as reading were more available to LD students in resource rooms. No significant differences were noted, however, as to the amount of time students were actively instructed in the two settings. Overall, LD students responded to academic tasks for short periods of time in either situation: 29 minutes per day in resource rooms and 19 minutes per day in regular classrooms. In addition, the authors observed considerably more concerns about task management, displays of inappropriate behavior, and instances of teacher-student discussion in the regular class.

Ivarie et al. (1984) conducted two experiments to ascertain the extent to which mainstreaming teachers spent time with LD and non-LD students. One study was conducted in a secondary setting and the other in an elementary school. The results of both studies indicated that teachers did not devote significantly more time to assisting LD students than they did to non-LD pupils.

Wang and Birch (1984) compared the instructional effects of a full-time mainstreaming program for handicapped students with a resource room approach for similar students (learning disabled, socially and emotionally disturbed, visually impaired, and gifted). Their full-time mainstreaming program—Adaptive Learning Environments Model (ALEM)—has four components:

— Early identification of learning problems
— Delabeling of special students and, instead, describing learning needs
  in instructional terms
— Individually designed educational plans
— Teaching self-management skills

This program, the study results suggested, exceeded the resource room approach in attaining desirable student attitudes and student achievement in basic skills.

Over the past decades, numerous educators have periodically argued for more integration of mildly handicapped pupils in regular classroom situations. Unquestionably, they have had some influence, but their efforts have been neither organized nor consistent. One movement, however, the Regular Education Initiative (REI)—which is backed by legislation and has the encouragement of high government officials and a group of respected and active special educators— merits further discussion, as is given in the following section.

■ COMMENTARY ■   In spite of the strong support of the movement, there are those who are wary
of the REI. Only time will tell whether it has had a significant impact on the education of LD
youngsters.

REGULAR EDUCATION INITIATIVE
Overview

As noted in Chapter 3, Madeleine C. Will, Assistant Secretary for the Office of Special Education and Rehabilitative Services in the Reagan administration, and others have advocated the Regular Education Initiative. This movement grew out of the fact that she and colleagues are critical of many special education policies. According to Will (1986), a number of negative consequences arise from current special education practices that educate handicapped youngsters apart from their nonhandicapped peers:

1. An undetermined number of students who do not fit into compartmentalized special programs may not receive needed extra services because they do not meet the eligibility requirements.

■ COMMENTARY ■   She is probably referring to students who are nearly learning disabled but not quite.

2. There is tendency to equate poor performance with a handicap.

■ COMMENTARY ■   Will may be implying that some youngsters behave as though they were handicapped because of cultural, motivational, social, or other reasons and should not be referred to as handicapped, and that there are more legitimate causes of learning disabilities.

3. There is a likelihood that students will be stigmatized because they have been placed in special programs that segregate them from their nonhandicapped classmates and activities in regular classrooms.

■ COMMENTARY ■   This reason for integration is often given, but the data to support the negative effects of labeling are slim.

4. There is an inclination to have lowered expectations for youngsters referred to as handicapped.

■ COMMENTARY ■   The literature on this topic, in spite of the Pygmalion premise, is not convincing.

5. The emphasis of special programs is on failure rather than prevention.

■ COMMENTARY ■   Will apparently means that more concern should be directed toward the child's early years. That idea certainly fits with requests for research proposals from the Office of Special Education and Rehabilitation Services (OSERS) in 1987, many of which pertained to primary age youngsters.

6. When youngsters are referred to special programs, their parents are affected. Many of them, according to Will, ". . . interpret the rigid rules and eligi-

bility requirements to which schools must adhere as an indication that school officials are not willing to help their child" (p. 412).

■ COMMENTARY ■   Some would see this statement as a bit peculiar, if not inaccurate; they might argue that since every effort is made to locate and then educate handicapped children, not only the youngsters but their parents are being served.

Will goes on to make recommendations with respect to the ways in which handicapped youngsters are educated:

1. Building principals should ". . . be empowered to assemble appropriate professionals and other resources for delivering effective, coordinated, comprehensive services for all students based on individual educational needs rather than eligibility for special programs" (p. 413).

■ COMMENTARY ■   This topic has been of concern for some time and has prompted some research. OSERS, for example, has funded a few projects on this matter.

2. Experiments should be set up whereby researchers explore a variety of ways in which services can be delivered to handicapped students.

■ COMMENTARY ■   OSERS has sponsored research on this topic also. One of these projects, Washington State University, is discussed later.

3. Increased attention should be directed toward the early identification of learning problems and to interventions that can ameliorate those problems.

■ COMMENTARY ■   Over the years, considerable attention has been devoted to preschool education, some of which is reviewed in Chapter 12.

4. More emphasis should be given to curriculum-based assessment. This approach emphasizes ". . . the assessment of each student's strengths and weaknesses for instructional planning purposes, rather than emphasizing categorization or labeling" (p. 415).

■ COMMENTARY ■   For a discussion on this approach, see Chapter 3 and Chapter 13.

5. Educational programs that have been proven to be effective should be put in practice by more teachers.

■ COMMENTARY ■   Not many would argue that point, but it is no small task to decide which programs are the best. To some extent the Joint Dissemination Review Panel has taken on this challenge. When that agency endorses a program, its developers can go throughout the country participating in "awareness sessions." There, they discuss their programs, which school systems can adopt. The U.S. Department of Education has a booklet on best practices entitled, *What Works: Research About Teaching and Learning* (1986).

6. Parents should be more involved in the education of their children: advisory boards should be set up to assist schools. School-parent programs should be established for developing an atmosphere of mutual responsibility between the home and school.

■ COMMENTARY ■   *Most would agree with this proposal, which is discussed in Chapter 5.*

7. Partnerships should be arranged between regular and special eduction. For one thing, procedures and techniques of the two sectors should be shared.

■ COMMENTARY ■   *There is a great deal of sharing of resources and practices in most schools today; few of them operate as distinct units. But Will's point is a good one; the ideas, techniques, programs, and procedures of one camp—particularly the good ones—should certainly be communicated to the other.*

The number of articles published on REI indicates the interest and concern the topic arouses. Indeed, an entire issue of the *Journal of Learning Disabilities* [*21* (1)] was devoted to REI in 1988.

Approaches

Following are descriptions of three general approaches that have been put into practice for accommodating remedial, LD, and other mildly handicapped youngsters in regular classrooms. The first is an administrative process whereby funds from three sources are blended and youngsters for whom those monies were allocated are served together. The second approach is the teacher consultation model, and the third, the teacher assistance team approach.

Blending Resources.   With a grant funded by OSERS (1984–1987) Washington State University conducted research on "Exemplary Instructional Program Options." A major purpose of the project was to blend finances and resources of three programs for the mildly handicapped and to serve all the individuals who fell in that category in regular classes (Jenkins, Pious, & Petterson, 1987). Two of the programs were federally funded—for the learning disabled and for Chapter I youngsters—and the third was a state-funded remedial assistance program for youngsters who were low achievers but were neither learning disabled nor qualified for Chapter I assistance.

An important goal of the project was to demonstrate that if instructional techniques found to be effective with one of the populations were arranged for the others, the techniques would be similarly effective. Among the general techniques included in the study were curriculum-based assessment, peer tutoring, materials adaptations, consulting teachers, and cooperative learning.

The project sponsored the plans of six school districts. The plans were all alike in that they reduced the number of pull-out programs as much as possible, attempted to adapt the regular program to meet the needs of divergent students,

Joseph R. Jenkins, University of Washington, has written on a number of topics in learning disabilities: reading, vocabulary development, and peer tutoring. In addition, he has conducted several research projects that dealt with resource rooms, mainstreaming, and the blending of facilities to educate mildly handicapped youngsters.

and gave building principals more fiscal and administrative responsibilities to support the programs. Each district's means for achieving these ends differed.

Data were gathered from the six districts throughout the three-year period of the grant in terms of student achievement, staff satisfaction, and student behavior. Additional data were acquired with respect to referral and placement. The data indicated, first, that effects from all six experimental models were about the same and, second, that the effects were not significantly greater than those of control groups in which youngsters were pulled out of their classes for instruction (Jenkins, 1988). The data did show, however, that when instructional procedures were effective, they were effective across the board—that is, they assisted not only the LD youngsters, but those who had been referred to as "Chapter I" or "remedial."

Bower and Meier (1981) also offered data to suggest that when educators look at performances of youngsters on actual school tasks, they cannot always discriminate among those who have been referred to as disabled, normal, or even gifted by standardized tests. In their study, a group of 21 fifth graders took a series of 10 one-minute tests that involved matching definitions to energy terms. Most of the youngsters were "regular," but some were "resource" or "gifted," according to scores on standardized tests. Data on their performances were plotted as number of correct answers per minute.

When the data were inspected across the 10 sessions, it was impossible to tell which students were which: The accelerations or trends of a few resource pupils were greater than those of some gifted pupils; the trends of some regular pupils were greater than those of some gifted pupils; the beginning points for some resource youngsters were higher than those for a few regular students; and the ending points for some resource pupils were higher than those for certain regular students. Generally, all the students made significant progress.

These two studies make clear that labeling or categorizing mildly handicapped youngsters is not a primary factor in whether or not they prosper as students. The quality of the instruction and the instructional procedures followed were more significant than how the children were grouped. In an approach that blends resources, youngsters can be grouped for instructional purposes according to their ability to perform school tasks—not other criteria that may be tied specifically to funding sources—and all funds can be pooled to support instructional personnel, equipment, and facilities to meet their needs.

Consulting Teacher. The consulting teacher approach, as indicated by Huefner (1988), is designed to keep as many youngsters, learning disabled or otherwise, in regular classes as possible. The model is a reaction to the many pull-out programs that have irritated so many individuals (for example, Will, 1986). Under this approach, the consultant gives advice to teachers on how to maintain youngsters in their classes, but that individual does not provide direct services to pupils. (See Chapter 5 for a detailed discussion of this approach.)

Beyond the benefits that are most often touted—decreased special education enrollment, more opportunity for handicapped students to compete satisfactorily in the mainstream, and reduced special education costs—Huefner noted seven potential benefits of the consulting teacher model.

Reduction of stigma. When all children are served in regular classes and none of them are sent to resource rooms or are seen directly by a specialist, there is a greater chance that they will not be labeled, hence be victims of possible negative consequences.

Better understanding across disciplines. As teachers from both sectors work with one another, there is a chance that they will become more knowledgeable and sympathetic for one another's situation and hence more helpful and tolerant toward one another.

On-the-job training for regular educators in special education skills. When consulting teachers are knowledgeable about effective procedures, they can assist teachers in learning about such processes. Their interactions with teachers under these circumstances could amount to individualized staff development sessions.

Reduction of mislabeling of nonhandicapped students. It is possible that some students are labeled as learning disabled simply to be provided certain types of assistance. If that same help can be offered in regular classes without the label, youngsters will gain from the preferred instruction without being subjected to possible ill effects from a label.

Spillover benefits to regular students.   It may be that as consultants assist teachers in dealing with handicapped youngsters, regular teachers can involve those practices with nonhandicapped pupils.

Suitability to needs of secondary school students.   Because students at the secondary level are assigned to several teachers, none of whom ordinarily assumes primary responsibility for the youngsters, including the mildly handicapped, the consultant can serve as an advocate and provide an element of continuity in the students' programs.

Prospect for master teacher staffing.   The consulting teacher model could fit with the recommendations of recent reports (for example, Carnegie and Holmes) that have suggested the involvement in education of master teachers. Huefner (1988) has also pointed out potential dangers of the consulting teacher model as well as some reasons why this approach can fail.

Ineffective caseload management.   In their efforts to save money with the consulting approach, districts could overload consultants. Or they could assign too few students or teachers to consultants and end up with fewer youngsters being served than were assisted by a former plan.

Conversion of the model to a tutoring or aide model.   Some districts may be tempted to involve their consultants as tutors for difficult-to-teach youngsters or as aides for regular teachers. Utilizing consultants in such capacities would probably not warrant the costs of the program.

Unrealistic expectations.   Some districts may view the consulting teacher model as the panacea for all their school problems. That attitude could result in significant disenchantment and perhaps the eventual cessation of the program.

Inadequate support from regular educators.   In order for consulting teacher programs to succeed, regular teachers must trust the consultants and make use of them. An underutilized program will cause dissension in the ranks and eventually lead to serious personnel and administrative problems.

Inadequate funding mechanisms.   Since many states and locales provide the most funds for youngsters who receive the most care in specialized settings, there is little reward for assisting them in environments that are less "restrictive." In instances such as these, schools would receive less and less money as they were able to manage more and more of their pupils in regular classrooms as opposed to self-contained settings or other expensive situations.

Faulty assumptions regarding cost savings.   Districts that decided to set up consulting teacher programs in order to save money on services to teachers and their youngsters should keep long-range planning in mind. Just as new businesses should be prepared for a couple of years or so of "negative cash flow," so should districts that begin consulting teacher programs.

Faulty assumptions regarding program effectiveness. Evaluations based on short-term goals are not effective in evaluating consulting teacher programs. Districts must collect data over time on the impact of the program on all persons involved—teachers, pupils, administrators, and parents. Further, schools should study the on-going data in order to make intelligent personnel and administrative decisions.

There has not been much major research on the process of consultation in special education. Some of the research that does exist is of the survey type: special education directors, regular teachers, or special education teachers asked to respond to lists of questions. Other investigations on consultation have been of the consumer satisfaction type: teachers, administrators, or others asked to comment on the services of consultants. Studies that have obtained data on participants in the process—consultants, consultees, and students—have been rare. Following are brief notes on eight investigations of that type.

Eglsaer (1979) studied effects and teachers' preferences for consultative styles. It was reported that an expert style was perceived as being more effective than a collaborative one in both crisis and noncrisis situations. In terms of preferences, however, an expert style was desired for crisis situations and a collaborative style for less critical situations.

In another study to assess regular classroom and special education resource teachers' preferences for consultation styles, West (1985) found that both groups significantly preferred a collaborative model over expert, medical, or mental health models. West warned that his data should be viewed with caution because the teachers he surveyed were involved in only a few actual consultations. The average number of consultation contacts for regular teachers was only six, and the resource teachers average was 46 consultations throughout the school year.

In a training project for consulting teachers in four Seattle area school districts, the consultants in training collected data on several aspects of the process (Lovitt & Haring, 1969). Throughout that project, data were kept on such aspects as number of consultations between consultants and teachers, number of times consultants communicated with building principals, and the number of times principals communicated with teachers. The trainee consultants also kept on-going data on the number of teachers who were taking data on pupils and the number of pupils for whom data were being acquired. By the end of a school year, 69 of about 100 teachers had acquired some data on 1,101 of the approximately 2,000 students. The majority of pupils on whom data were kept were those for whom the consultants in training had provided indirect consultation services.

■ COMMENTARY ■   *In teacher consultant programs, data such as collected in this training project should be the primary means for evaluating the effects, costs, and other aspects of the programs.*

Medway and Updyke (1985) conducted a meta-analysis of 54 school consultation studies. Most of the 192 effects they obtained were positive. The analysts concluded that despite the ultimate goal of improving student functioning, the most significant outcome effects were for the consultees. In another meta-analysis study, however, Sibley (1986) reported that effect sizes were higher for students than for the consultees. It may be important to note that Sibley included data from unpublished studies in his analysis, whereas Medway and Updyke did not.

According to West and Idol (1987), there have been only two experimental studies with regard to special education consultation. Miller and Sabatino (1978) compared teacher consultant and resource models on the basis of pupils' scores on word recognition and mathematics tests. Their data showed no significant group differences. Wixson (1980) compared direct and indirect services for learning disabled and behaviorally disturbed students and found that the average number of successful individual programs was higher for indirect than for direct services.

Idol-Maestas and Jackson (1983) surveyed 29 classroom teachers who were receiving consulting assistance. Their data indicated that all but one teacher believed that the consultations were beneficial. More specifically, the data revealed that 11 of the 29 consultations resulted in not referring students for special services, and nearly two-thirds of the teachers indicated that the consulting teachers offered innovative ways of managing student behaviors or selecting academic interventions.

Teacher Assistance Teams.   A reaction to the idea that more of the handicapped, particularly the mildly handicapped, should be educated in regular classrooms has been the advent of Teacher Assistance Teams (TAT). This plan, first advanced by Chalfant, Pysh, and Moultrie (1979), offers a means whereby the majority of mildly handicapped children, particularly those referred to as learning disabled, can be served in regular classes by regular teachers.

Following are the four aims of the plan:

1. Help teachers conceptualize and understand the nature of individual children's learning and behavior problems.
2. Provide immediate and helpful support to teachers who are trying to individualize instruction.
3. Improve follow up and evaluation of mainstreaming efforts.
4. Increase attention to referrals of the building level, reduce the number of inappropriate referrals, and utilize special education personnel more effectively.

The goal of the TATs is to deliver special help more efficiently and effectively to children by placing the initiative for assisting them in the hands of classroom teachers, the individuals who were initially and are ultimately responsible for their progress. With respect to implementing programs of this type, Chalfant and colleagues suggested that schools elect three regular classroom teachers to make up the team.

■ COMMENTARY ■ *According to one special education director in Salt Lake City, the idea of electing teachers to these teams, rather than having them appointed by building principals, is extremely important.*

Several criteria are used to select TAT members:

— Classroom experience
— Knowledge of curriculum and materials
— Ability to assess a wide range of learning and behavior problems and to individualize instruction
— Supportive personality
— Ability to communicate with pupils, parents, administrators, and staff
— Interest in and ability to help fellow teachers

Compensation for being a member of the TAT can come in many forms, for example, release from certain school duties, extra pay, advance on salary schedule, and trips to professional meetings.

The TAT approach has been implemented in a number of states. Utah, for example, has found it to be particularly suited to providing assistance to special children. Some procedural steps for putting the TAT into operation have been presented by Joan Sebastian (1984), former specialist at the Utah Learning Resource Center and currently an affiliate with the University of Utah:

☐ *Teacher referral:* The referring teacher fills out a written form describing the students' needs and what means have been used in attempts to overcome the problems.

☐ *Review of referral:* The TAT reviews the referral, identifies the problem, discusses tactics that might solve it, and recommends a few to the referring teacher.

☐ *Follow-up:* The TAT checks in with the referring teacher to determine how the recommended tactics are working. If there are still concerns, other techniques are recommended and the process continues.

TATs have also been set up in several elementary schools in Great Falls, Montana. The project, referred to as RIDE (Responding to Individual Differences in Education) is ". . . a staff development program [to] significantly enhance the knowledge and working skills of building staff [to] better accommodate atypical learners" (Beck, 1985, p. 3). Like other TAT programs the idea is to reduce pull-out programs and, alternatively, to provide education for handicapped learners in regular classes.

Each building has a TAT made up of three elementary teachers who provide support and advice to other teachers who refer problems to them. Unlike other TAT programs, however, the Great Falls program also maintains a set of pre-arranged tactics that are available to both teachers and consultants.

The first task in developing these tactics was to ask elementary teachers, special and regular, to identify the academic and social concerns with which they could use the most assistance. The teachers identified 25 topics in each of the two areas. The top 10 concerns in the social category were related to students' talking out, fighting, daydreaming, misbehaving out of classroom, stealing, not complying, bullying, blaming others, displaying inappropriate sexual behavior, and being out-of-seat. The top 10 academic concerns were related to students' failure to stay on task, complete school work on time, complete school work satisfactorily, follow oral directions, turn in completed school work, display adequate self-esteem, pay attention, attend to tasks, follow written directions, and develop better attitudes toward school.

Step two in the Great Falls plan was selecting a format for writing tactics in response to the identified problems. In the chosen format, which is similar to that in *Tactics for Teaching* (Lovitt, 1984), each tactic, approximately 350 words in length, consists of four sections: introduction, procedures, considerations, and approach for monitoring. Lovitt and Bornstein (formerly a member of the psychology department at the University of Montana) were engaged to write the 200 tactics, at least four for each topic. In writing up the tactics, the authors searched the extensive research literature for ideas. The great majority of their descriptions were paraphrased from published studies that had demonstrated that the approaches were effective.

Each of the participating schools in the RIDE program has a copy of these tactics in their library for use by consultants and teachers. In addition, the tactics have been entered on a program for Apple microcomputers, so that interested teachers and others can call up any tactic and read it on the screen or print it. As an additional aid to those searching for techniques to arrange with difficult-to-teach children, twenty of the written tactics have been filmed. Ten social and ten academic projects that lent themselves to visual description were scripted, filmed, and put on video cassettes.

Not only has the RIDE project been widely accepted in Great Falls and other Montana locations, but districts in other states have adopted this approach. As of December 10, 1987, there were adoptions in 154 elementary schools in Montana, New Mexico, Utah (116), Wyoming, Alaska, and Washington.

In Great Falls, data have been gathered on the number of referrals before and after their project. Before RIDE, 104 students were referred in the six elementary schools, and of those, 48 were placed in special education. Following RIDE, only 39 were referred for special education, and of those, 31 were placed. Thus the percentage of those referred and placed went from 46 percent to 79 percent, which clearly indicates that, to date, the goal of reducing inappropriate referrals has been met.

COMMENTS AND DISCUSSION POINTS

Arguments as to where to educate handicapped youngsters, and more specifically LD pupils, are to a great extent futile. These debates over the relative merits of self-contained classes, resource rooms, or regular classes have raged since the mid 1930s, and virtually nothing has come of them. With respect to sound instruction, it is probably irrelevant where an LD child is educated.

As is the case with so many instructional matters, we rarely ask for opinions from the students themselves. Jenkins and Heinen (1988) do have some data on this topic. They asked remedial youngsters, and others, if they would rather receive service from a specialist who came *into* their class or work with the specialist *outside* of the class. Most students opted for the latter approach, saying that they would be embarrassed if a specialist came in. It was interesting to note that the great majority of these youngsters, when asked if they would look down on or tease another youngster who was assisted by a specialist *in* the classroom, said that they would not.

Closely related are arguments that have focused on the type of teacher best suited for these LD pupils. Some maintain that the principal teacher should be the classroom teacher; others believe it should be either the resource or consulting teacher. Some suggest that cross-age or peer tutors are adequate instructors for LD pupils.

When it comes to educating youngsters, exceptional or otherwise, there are more important factors that should be addressed than *where* to teach and *who* should do it. Some of these factors follow.

- *It is a critical matter to select important behaviors for instruction. They should be negotiable ones, those that are either useful immediately or that will later foster the development of a related skill.*

- *It is important to identify proper placement levels. Regardless of where students are taught and by whom, their instruction should begin at a point that is suitable, neither too difficult nor too easy.*

- *Materials and instructional arrangements should be clear and concise. Regardless of where the instruction takes place and who offers it, the aspects of teaching should be well ordered and precise:*

  - *Pupils should be told what they are supposed to learn, the extent to which they are to learn it, why they are to learn it, and how they will be tested on whether or not they acquired it.*
  - *Pupils must be given appropriate amounts of feedback regarding their efforts to acquire the instructed skills, as well as ample doses of reinforcement when they do make progress.*
  - *Pupils must be given sufficient opportunities to practice the skills they are supposed to learn.*
  - *Pupils must be shifted to easier or different activities if they are not progressing and, conversely, passed on to other activities once they have mastered the initial skills.*
  - *Pupils must be helped to generalize skills they have acquired to other behaviors and locations.*
  - *Pupils must be assisted to remember the skills they have acquired once they were learned.*

REFERENCES

Beck, F. W.; Lindsey, J. D.; & Frith, G. H. (1981). Effects of self-contained special class placement on intellectual functioning on learning disabled students. *Journal of Learning Disabilities, 14,* 280–282.

Beck, R. (1985). Responding to individual differences in education: Project RIDE. Grant submitted to the Office of the Superintendent of Public Instruction, State of Montana, Helena.

Benedetti, D. M. (1984). The effectiveness of an instructional adaptation on the acquisition of science information by middle school learning disabled students. Unpublished dissertation, University of Washington, Seattle.

Bowen, R., & Meier, K. (1981) Will the real "slow learner" please stand up? *Journal of Precision Teaching, 2*(2), 25–27.

Chalfant, J. C.; Pysh, M. V.; & Moultrie, R. (1979). Teacher assistance teams: A model for within-building problem solving. *Learning Disability Quarterly, 2,* 85–96.

Eglsaer, R. F. (1979). The impact of crises on consultees' preferences for and evaluation of consultative style. Unpublished doctoral dissertation. University of Texas, Austin.

Friend, M., & McNutt, G. (1984). Resource room programs: Where are we now? *Exceptional Children, 51,* 150–155.

Gickling, E. E.; Murphy, L. C.; & Mallory, D. W. (1979). Teachers' preferences for resource services. *Exceptional Children, 45,* 442–449.

Gresham, F. M. (1982). Misguided mainstreaming: The case for social skills training with handicapped children. *Exceptional Children, 48,* 422–433.

Huefner, D. S. (1988). The consulting teacher model: Risks and opportunities. *Exceptional Children, 54,* 403–414.

Idol-Maestas, L., & Jackson, C. (1983). An evaluation of the consultation process. In L. Idol-Maestas (Ed.), *Special educator's consultation handbook*. Rockville, MD: Aspen.

Ivarie, J.; Hogue, D.; & Brulle, A. R. (1984). An investigation of mainstream teacher time spent with students labeled learning disabled. *Exceptional Children, 51,* 142–149.

Jenkins, J. R. Personal communication. March 24, 1988.

Jenkins, J. R., & Heinen, A. (1988). Students' preference for pull-out and in-class instruction. Unpublished manuscript, University of Washington, Seattle.

Jenkins, J. R.; Pious, C.; & Petterson, D. (1987). Explaining the validity of a unified learning program for remedial and handicapped students. Unpublished paper, University of Washington, Seattle.

Journal of Learning Disabilities. (1988). *21*(4), entire issue.

Lieberman, L. M. (1982). The nightmare of scheduling. *Journal of Learning Disabilities, 15*(1), 57–58.

Lovitt, T. C. (1984). *Tactics for teaching*. Columbus, OH: Merrill.

Lovitt, T. C., & Fantasia, K. (1980). Two approaches to reading program evaluation: A standardized test and direct assessment. *Learning Disability Quarterly, 3,* 77–87.

Lovitt, T. C., & Haring, N. G. (1969). Data from teacher consultant project. University of Washington, Seattle.

Lovitt, T.; Rudsit, J.; Jenkins, J.; Pious, C., & Benedetti, D. (1986). Adapting science materials for regular and learning disabled seventh graders. *Remedial and Special Education, 1,* 31–39.

MacMillan, D. I.; Jones, R. L.; & Aloia, G. F. (1974). The mentally retarded label: A theoretical analysis and review of research. *American Journal of Mental Deficiency, 79,* 241–261.

McLoughlin, J. A., & Kelly, D. (1982). Issues facing the resource teacher. *Learning Disability Quarterly, 5,* 58–64.

Medway, F. J., & Updyke, J. F. (1985). Meta-analysis of consultation outcome studies. *American Journal of Community Psychology, 13* (5), 489–505.

Miller, T. L., & Sabatino, D. (1978). An evaluation of the teacher consultation model as an approach to mainstreaming. *Exceptional Children, 45* (2), 86–91.

Polloway, E. A. (1984). The integration of mildly retarded students in the schools: A historical review. *Remedial and Special Education, 5,* 18–28.

Rust, J. O., & Miller, L. S. (1978). Using a control group to evaluate a resource room program. *Psychology in the Schools, 15,* 503–506.

Sebastian, J. (1984). The teacher assistance team. *The Special Educator, 4,* 2–4.

Sibley, S. (1986). A meta-analysis of school consultation research. Unpublished doctoral dissertation, Texas Women's University, Denton.

Sindelar, P. T., & Deno, S. L. (1978). The effectiveness of resource programming. *The Journal of Special Education, 12,* 17–28.

Stainback, W., & Stainback, S. (1984). A rationale for the merger of special and regular education. *Exceptional Children, 51,* 102–111.

Thurlow, M.; Ysseldyke, J. E.; Graden, J. L.; & Algozzine, B. (1983). What's "special" about the special education resource room for learning disabled students? *Learning Disability Quarterly, 6,* 283–288.

U.S. Department of Education. (1986). *What works: Research about teaching and learning.* Washington, D.C.

Wang, M. C., & Birch, J. W. (1984). Comparison of a full-time mainstreaming program and a resource room approach. *Exceptional Children, 51,* 33–40.

Weener, P. (1981). On comparing learning disabled and regular classroom children. *Journal of Learning Disabilities, 14,* 227–232.

West, J. F. (1985). Regular and special educators' preferences for school-based consultation models. Doctoral dissertation, University of Texas, Austin. *Dissertation Abstracts International, 47* (2). 504A.

West, J. F., & Idol, L. (1987). School consultation (Part I): An interdisciplinary perspective on theory, models, and research. *Journal of Learning Disabilities, 20* (7), 388–408.

Will, M. L. (1986). Educating children with learning problems: A shared responsibility. *Exceptional Children, 52,* 411–415.

Wixson, S. E. (1980). Two resource room models for serving learning and behavior disordered pupils. *Behavior Disorders, 5* (2), 116–125.

Chapter 5

Young Thomas and His Mother by Mary Cassatt (*c.* 1893). Courtesy of The Pennsylvania Academy of the Fine Arts, Philadelphia.

CONSULTATION AND COMMUNICATION

--- MAIN IDEAS ---

- Consultation and communication between special and regular education teachers: general considerations, ideas, and procedures for providing direct and indirect services

- Communications between special teachers and parents of LD youngsters, including suggestions for three levels of interactions: providing general information, encouraging advocacy, and offering assistance for training

- Communications between special education teachers and other professionals: physicians, psychologists and counselors, speech therapists, Chapter I and remedial teachers, and social workers

- Communications between special education teachers, schools, and industry in attempts to provide transition services for LD individuals

--- OVERVIEW ---

Many teachers of LD youngsters need to consult and communicate on a regular basis with other school personnel and professionals. Certainly all teachers of LD youngsters must communicate with parents. In order to communicate and interact effectively with others, LD teachers must be able to speak knowledgeably, candidly, and convincingly. They must be capable of reporting troublesome situations so that everyone understands them and be able to present plans that can be comprehended and agreed on by others involved in dealing with these situations. The first section in this chapter offers some considerations for communication between teachers of LD children and other teachers and school personnel. The second section presents techniques for facilitating communication between teachers and parents of LD youngsters. The third section is concerned with communications between LD specialists and community professionals, such as pediatricians and those in family practice, while the fourth section deals with communications between schools and industry. At the end of the chapter are comments relating to matters of communication and consultation.

COMMUNICATING WITH TEACHERS

This section begins with general considerations regarding consulting situations. Next is a discussion pertaining to resource teachers or others who provide *direct* services to youngsters and who do so, ordinarily, by pulling them out of regular classrooms and administering special services in other locations (for example, a resource room). Finally, communication suggestions are given for LD specialists who deal directly with teachers of referred children and hence *indirectly* with pupils.

General Considerations

Before commenting on some attributes of satisfactory consultation, a definition or two of the process is in order. Lippitt (1959) has defined the general process of consultation as follows:

> . . . [a] technique that at a minimum, always has the following six characteristics:
>
> 1. It is a helping, problem-solving process.
> 2. It occurs between a professional help-giver and the help-seeker who has responsibility for the welfare of another person.
> 3. It is a voluntary relationship.
> 4. The help-giver and the help-seeker share in solving the problem.
> 5. The goal is to help solve a current work problem of the help-seeker.
> 6. The help-seeker profits from the relationship in such a way that future problems may be handled more sensitively and skillfully. [p. 4]

When related more specifically to the school process and special education, Paolucci-Whitcomb and Nevin (1985) view the consultation process as interactions that occur among special education teachers, regular classroom teachers, principals, and others as a means of supporting mainstreamed students. Following is one definition of *collaborative* consultation:

> Collaborative consultation is an interactive process that enables teams of people with diverse expertise to generate creative solutions to mutually defined problems. The outcome is enhanced, altered, and produces solutions that are different from those that the individual team member would produce independently. The major outcome of collaborative consultation is to provide comprehensive and effective programs for students with special needs within the most appropriate context, thereby enabling

them to achieve maximum constructive interaction with their nonhandicapped peers [Idol, Paolucci-Whitcomb, & Nevin, 1986 p. 1]

In a survey of state departments of education, West and Brown (1987) sought to determine the prevalence of consultation programs in state policy as well as characteristics of those programs. Twenty-six of the respondents reported policies providing service delivery models that included consultation as an expected role of special educators. Twenty states reported the use of an indirect service model, with consultation provided to classroom teachers to assist handicapped students mainstreamed into regular classes. The delivery model of providing direct service to handicapped youngsters in regular classrooms was noted nearly as often. Ten states cited the resource room model as including consultation as an expected role of special education teachers. Nine respondents indicated that they had no service delivery models that included consultation as an expected role of special educators. Of those twenty-six states that did indicate consultation was included in their service delivery models, only thirteen listed specific consultation responsibilities for special educators.

West and Idol (1987b) reviewed the literature on delivery systems and identified six service options that involved the provision of consultative assistance to classroom teachers of mainstreamed students. The six programs they reviewed

Lorna Idol is currently associated with the University of Texas, Austin. She has conducted research and written widely in the area of teacher consultation. Two of her books are *Special Educator's Consultation Handbook* and *Collaborative Consultation*, the latter with P. Paolucci-Whitcomb and A. Nevin. She is editor of *Remedial and Special Education*.

were Teacher Assistance Team (Chalfant et al.), Pre-Referral Intervention System (Graden et al.), Consulting Teacher (for example, Egner & Lates), Resource/Consulting Teacher (for example, Idol-Maestas), Special Education Resource Teachers (Deno & Mirkin), and Resource Teacher (e.g., Jenkins & Mayhall). The programs were described with regard to five features: underlying theory, underlying knowledge base, goals, stages/steps, and responsibilities.

West and Idol (1987b) also discussed and provided some data on five important aspects of the consulting process, each of which could serve as either a barrier or a facilitator.

1. *Time to consult:* West and Idol maintained that the single most important feature in the initiation and maintenance of consultation programs was allowing consultants enough time to consult. In one study, they learned that consultants spent only 5 percent of their time in such activities; most of their day was taken up providing direct services to youngsters.

2. *Administrative support:* West and Idol cited a study in which 6 of 27 respondents named lack of administrative support as the primary reason their programs were not successful. Only 12 of those respondents believed that they had substantial administrative support from principals for their programs.[1]

3. *Teacher attitudes:* According to West and Idol, the fact that some teachers and administrators are generally uncooperative—more specifically, unwilling to share in the mutual care and education of handicapped youngsters—is a major factor in the failure of the consultation process as it relates to mainstreaming.

4. *Promoting consultation:* Consultation programs must be promoted and sold to faculty of elementary and secondary schools. One of the better ways to convince teachers to accept these programs is from the testimonies of other teachers who were assisted by the consultants and were pleased with the results.

5. *Consultation skills:* West and Idol maintain that a consultant who has only a scientific base may have much to share with teachers but have no means of effectively conveying that information. On the other hand, a consultant who possesses and uses effective communication/interactive skills may be able to establish rapport for sharing information but have nothing to share; the relationship between the consultant and the consultee will be pleasant but may result in ineffective outcomes.

Considerations for Providing Direct Services

When working with teachers and staff, resource teachers need to consider five practices. Most of them are policy matters that must be dealt with early on if effective and smoothly functioning resource programs are to be established.

---

1. There have been some federal- and state-sponsored programs designed to study the effects of principals as facilitators of special programs in general and particularly those that involve mainstreaming of one form or another. This is certainly an important area of research.

1. *Reach an agreement among the staff about the "ownership" of referred youngsters.* It might be decided, for example, that since resource teachers assist pupils for only part of the day, they are not *totally* responsible for them. In such cases the responsibility will be shared by the referring teacher and the resource teacher. Other schools might prefer different arrangements for designating responsibilities. But whatever the policy, it should be clearly communicated to all the staff.

2. *Come to an agreement among the staff as to the types of youngsters and behaviors resource teachers should attend to.* Some schools may decide that the resource teacher will help only with reading; others may want assistance on all the basic skills. In still other schools, the classroom teachers might be allowed to negotiate their own plans with the resource teacher. In such arrangements, one teacher might seek help with students in reading, another with pupils in math, a third with a variety of skills, and so forth.

3. *Arrive at an understanding on how resource teachers' instructions for various children are to blend with regular classroom programs.* Resource teachers could *replace* the efforts of classroom teachers; for example, take over the reading instruction for the pupils assigned to them. Alternatively, resource teachers could *supplement* the instruction of classroom teachers. In reading, the resource teacher might concentrate on oral or silent reading fluency, whereas the classroom teacher would focus on comprehension skills. In latter arrangements, classroom teachers would dictate, to a large extent, what the resource teacher works on.

4. *Deal with scheduling once the above agreements are firmed up.* Scheduling, which was partly discussed in Chapter 4, is the biggest problem of them all. The following five steps relate to it.

— Resource teachers should acquire detailed class schedules from teachers who intend to send youngsters to them.
— Classroom teachers should also submit lists of the children they want to be served, identify the subjects for which they are referred, note their performance levels in these skills, and provide other important facts. (The procedures for the "Focus of concern," the assessment, the approval letters, and other matters related to IEPs are discussed in Chapter 3.)
— Resource teachers should study referral lists and determine which children, regardless of class or grade, have been referred for the same subjects and have comparable levels of performance.
— Resource teachers must then be certain of the form of assistance the youngsters are to receive—that is, whether it is to replace or supplement the regular classroom work.
— Next, resource teachers must look at the requests for services to see whether there are schedule conflicts that require negotiation, such as asking teachers to change their schedules, to refer other youngsters who need help and will fit into available time slots, or to agree to keep

the referred youngsters in the classroom with consultation assistance from the resource teacher or some other plan to resolve the conflicts.

5. *Decide whether youngsters will be sent to the resource teacher or the resource teacher will go to the LD pupils.* Resource teachers can offer assistance to LD children in at least two ways: They can have youngsters sent to them (the most usual plan) or they can go to the youngsters' classrooms. There are advantages and disadvantages to either approach:

— Classroom teachers and children don't have to worry about schedules with the latter plan.
— Resource teachers can work with children other than those who are referred with the latter scheme.
— When resource teachers go into classrooms, they will learn about the instructional climate of the classroom, which can help them understand the total picture and perhaps some of the reasons for the referrals.
— Classroom teachers can tune in on the instructional techniques used by resource teachers when they come into the classrooms and may schedule those practices with other children who have not been referred for special help.
— Space may be a problem when resource teachers come into classrooms. Some rooms are crowded, and it is difficult to find tutorial space.
— If several instructional materials are required by resource teachers, they may have difficulty carrying the materials to the classroom.
— Some classroom teachers are uncomfortable when others come into their classrooms, even helpful resource teachers.
— Resource teachers who go into classrooms will not be able to group youngsters from several classrooms who need the same type of assistance.

The life of a resource teacher can be difficult, and the demands can be many. Following is a listing of resource teachers' perceptions of competencies required for effectiveness in that role from a survey by Davis (1983).*

— Knowledge of and skill in employing a variety of methods for teaching reading
— Ability to deal effectively with personal/professional frustrations related to the position
— Ability to communicate with parents
— Knowledge of and skill in employing a variety of pupil behavior management techniques
— Knowledge of and skill in employing a variety of methods for teaching math

---

*Reprinted by permission from W.E. Davis, "Competencies and Skills Required to Be an Effective Resource Teacher," *Journal of Learning Disabilities, 16*(10), 1983.

— Knowledge of instructional materials
— Consultation skills with regular class teachers
— Knowledge of various curriculum approaches
— Developing and monitoring IEP's
— Knowledge of informal pupil assessment techniques
— Ability to deal effectively with school administrators
— Ability to interpret formal pupil psychoeducational techniques
— Knowledge of pupil observation techniques
— Knowledge of the characteristics of the various categories of handicapped children
— Individual pupil counseling skills
— Competency in teaching spelling
— Overall program evaluation techniques
— Ability to administer formal pupil psychoeducational tests
— Knowledge of pertinent legislation relating to handicapped children

— Group counseling skills
— Knowledge of current research and professional literature regarding handicapped children
— Knowledge of public and private agencies serving handicapped children in the region, state, and so on
— Competency in teaching gross motor, sensory motor, and perceptual motor skills
— Knowledge of organization and physical layout of resource room
— Competency in teaching handwriting skills
— Ability in staff development/in-service training
— Ability to speak in public
— Supervisory and administrative skills
— Familiarity with use of audio-visual equipment
— Knowledge of budgetary and financial matters related to special education
— Skill in demonstration teaching
— Ability to write grants

To summarize this lengthy list, resource teachers are expected to know a great deal about instructional materials and procedures, about classroom management and assessment, and about legislation and communication.

Gickling, Murphy, and Mallory (1979) noted rather close agreement between resource and classroom teachers on their perceptions of some issues. For example, both groups believed that it was important for resource teachers to know about many techniques to promote individualized instruction, necessary for them to provide direct and indirect services to children, and vital for resource teachers to develop numerous ways to modify or adapt instructional materials used by classroom teachers.

Considerations For Providing Indirect Services

Included in this section are some ideas for teachers who offer direct services to teachers and thus provide indirect assistance to children. Whereas the preceding set of suggestions was intended to aid teachers to deal with youngsters in their classrooms or in resource rooms, the techniques detailed here are designed to help special teachers negotiate with classroom teachers and to provide *those* teachers with new or different information so that they might better deal with LD or other difficult-to-teach youngsters in their classrooms.

In that regard, Idol-Maestas (1983) has offered a list of six principles teacher consultants should adhere to in order to achieve successful consultation:

1. Ensure that the building principal provides strong support to the consultation model and positively communicates this to the teaching staff. Consultation should be communicated to teachers as a service that is available and one that administrators encourage them to use.
2. Do not become involved in any type of teacher evaluation.
3. Offer in-service workshops that address such topics as mainstreaming in the regular classroom, behavior management, and construction of curriculum-based assessments.
4. At faculty meetings early in the school year, offer a brief but comprehensive presentation of consultation services.
5. Emphasize the quality of contacts. The word will spread quickly if the consultant is doing a good job. It will spread even quicker if the service is of poor quality.
6. Share results of successful consultations with the teaching staff. Teachers will be particularly interested in strategies that produce results.

Friend (1984) proposed a more specific list of consulting skills. They are listed in their order of importance as perceived by groups of consulting teachers, classroom teachers, and principals:

☐ Evaluate interventions systematically to determine their effectiveness.
☐ Establish a climate of mutual trust.
☐ Explain the resource teacher's perception of a problem situation to the classroom teacher.
☐ Define the problems resource teachers and classroom teachers will address.
☐ Interview classroom teachers to obtain academic, social, and behavioral information about their students.
☐ Brainstorm to generate possible solutions to a child's classroom academic/social problems.
☐ Assist classroom teachers to identify potential positive/negative consequences of planned interventions.
☐ Schedule conferences regularly with classroom teachers to discuss shared students.
☐ Function as a link between classroom teachers and other individuals and agencies.
☐ Include classroom teachers as equal partners in planning and implementing programs for mainstreamed pupils.

- ☐ Resolve conflicts by using strategies that minimize hard feelings.
- ☐ Use a planned sequence for problem solving in working with classroom teachers on behalf of mainstreamed pupils.
- ☐ Probe to identify all the factors that contribute to a child's problem, including those involving the classroom teacher.
- ☐ Observe mainstreamed students in classrooms and other school settings.
- ☐ Use specific strategies to facilitate interpersonal communication with classroom teachers.
- ☐ Use a paraphrasing strategy to confirm the meaning of classroom teachers' communication.
- ☐ Conduct inservice training for classroom teachers.

Although Friend's survey noted fair agreement among those asked about the importance of these consultation skills, there was some disagreement as to the abilities of resource teachers to practice them. Classroom teachers rated the resource teachers as generally less skillful than they would like them to be, and scored them significantly low for four items: systematically evaluating interventions, seeing teachers as equal partners in planning, regularly scheduling conferences with teachers, and explaining their perceptions of problem situations to teachers. (For more information on the role of consulting teachers, see the comments in Chapter 4 with regard to teacher assistance teams.)

COMMUNICATING WITH PARENTS

Communicating with parents of LD youngsters can be difficult. Part of the reason for certain stressful communications of LD teachers is brought on by the fact that many parents of those youngsters are quite sophisticated. Indeed, a number of them are professional people. Several have taken their children to various clinics for assessments; read widely on learning disabilities and dyslexia; and are familiar with special treatments, approaches, and materials. They can, therefore, when speaking with LD teachers, be intimidating and threatening. These parents want action when it comes to solving their youngsters' problems, and sometimes seriously question the practices being used. Moreover, a number of parents actually recommend other treatments that they believe might better deal with their youngsters' excesses, deficits, or differences.

Following are a few additional reasons to account for parents' attitudes and hence, why communications with them can be difficult.

- ☐ Some parents feel guilty about their children. They ask, "What did I do wrong?"
- ☐ Some are generally disappointed with the services being provided to their youngsters.

- Some are bitter, believing this state of affairs should not have happened to them.
- Some parents are as handicapped as their youngsters; they too have problems with reading.
- Some have received only poor reports about their children when they visited schools.
- Some may have experienced considerable disappointment in the past because overzealous teachers, in their desire to help, made promises about the children's attaining academic or social goals that were impossible to attain.
- Some parents of LD youngsters are skilled organizers and lobbyists. Many are committed to AACLD-type organizations and spend several hours with directors of special education and politicians attempting to improve services for their youngsters. Not a few are quite astute in these areas.
- Some parents have given up on themselves, on schools in general, and on their children. They have been through so much, they simply quit.

Communication with parents can occur on at least three levels—informing, advocacy, and training. A description of each level follows.

Informing

Perhaps the most obvious type of communication with parents involves informing them about various aspects of their youngsters' education. For example, it is important to tell them about the features of IEPs and the procedures for developing them. Further, it is necessary to explain standardized tests to parents, to tell them why and how such tests are given, and to explain the meanings of such terms as grade level equivalent and percentile rank.

It is necessary to inform parents about related services for their LD youngsters. LD specialists must often apprise parents of the many theories, techniques, and therapies that are reputed to improve behaviors of LD children. Not infrequently, parents will ask resource or consulting teachers questions such as the following: Should we have our youngster retested to learn if he is *truly* learning disabled? Do you believe our son has dyslexia? Should we take our girl to an optometrist for eye training? Should we take our boy to a perceptual–motor specialist? Should we be using the so-and-so diet plan? What about medications? These are but a few of the tough questions that many parents will ask, and LD specialists must answer them concisely, accurately, and honestly.

There are a number of ways to provide parents with some of this information. Many schools have developed handbooks, some send out letters on special topics, while still other districts periodically mail out newsletters. In some schools, teachers telephone parents, mail them letters, and send messages home via the pupils. Furthermore, most schools schedule back-to-school nights when parents can visit with their children's teachers and see their classrooms. Some districts have begun to use computerized phoning services to check up on absent pupils, relay messages to homes, and perform similar duties.

In developing plans to communicate with parents, teachers and other school personnel should determine what it is that parents want to know. Sometimes educators tell parents things about which they are not interested and fail to interact with them on topics that concern them. In this respect, Dembinski and Mauser (1977) conducted a survey to determine what parents of LD children wanted from professionals. They learned that parents were most interested in how their children were getting along generally and if the children were trouble-makers. In addition, these parents wanted to be spoken to in plain English; they were "turned off" by professional jargon.

Promoting Advocacy

Another level of communication with parents of LD children involves encouraging and assisting them to assume advocacy roles for their children and others who are handicapped. This level of interaction is similar to the first, but differs in terms of the extent to which parents are involved in their children's programs. According to McLoughlin, McLoughlin, and Stewart (1979), LD specialists must consider ten steps for developing parent advocacy:

1. Know the rights of the parents of the handicapped thoroughly.
2. View parents of exceptional children as assets rather than liabilities. Parents can sense indulgence, impatience, and superiority on the part of teachers and will react accordingly.
3. Be willing to make accommodations for parents. There is no excuse for using professional jargon with them.
4. Share as much information as possible with parents. Categorizing information into "*for* and *not for* parents" is inappropriate.
5. Communicate with parents on a regular basis. It is unfortunate that they are contacted mainly in times of crises and for special meetings.
6. Involve parents actively in the schooling process. They can perform activities at school or at home that can benefit their children.
7. Organize parent-education programs. Parents need the opportunity to discuss issues and learn about their children's programs.
8. Encourage positive attitudes toward parents of the handicapped.
9. Reinforce principals, fellow teachers, and others who interact with parents.
10. See to it that referral and placement conferences are models of parent advocacy. Special educators must be assured that all due-process procedures are implemented.

Training

This level of communication with parents is an extension of the sixth point from the list by McLoughlin et al.: instructing parents to play an important part in their child's education. Growing numbers of parents and professionals contest the age-old belief that parents cannot educate their own children and, certainly, parents of handicapped youngsters cannot possibly help theirs.

Shapero and Forbes (1981) confirm that there has been a recent and distinct change in attitudes toward encouraging parents to tutor their own children. They cited a study by Edge, Fink, and Brause (1978), who surveyed a number of colleges and universities with teacher-training programs. The data showed that from 1973 to 1978, 65 percent of the programs had at least one course for training teachers to work with parents. They noted, furthermore, that all the institutions agreed that programs for parent education were essential to the total training programs.

A number of commercially available training manuals for parents are available. Bernal and North (1978), for example, reviewed 26 such packages. According to them, the programs varied greatly in the detail provided parents, the level of assumed sophistication required to administer them, and the target behaviors expected. Most of the manuals dealt with social or management behaviors, but a few focused on the development of academic skills.

Materials for parents published since 1978 include "Families of Handicapped Children" (Fewell & Vadasy, 1986) and "Teaching the Young Child with Motor Delays" (Hanson & Harris, 1986). A more recent resource for parents is "Becoming a Nation of Readers" (Anderson et al., 1985), which is a summary of research findings on reading instruction and recommendations. Although designed mainly for teachers, it includes a number of important points for parents to consider.

COMMUNICATING WITH OTHER PROFESSIONALS

Physicians

LD specialists often communicate with physicians about youngsters under their common care. Many LD youngsters are referred to doctors because of hyperactivity. Others are referred to physicians for allergy treatments, and not a few, for special diets. A great number of pupils are referred to pediatricians and family medicine specialists because of behavior or learning problems at school.

Communications between educators and physicians are frequently difficult for a number of reasons. For one thing, they speak different languages; educators and doctors each have their own jargon, guilds, and journals. For another, they are busy individuals. Both physicians and educators see dozens of people and deal with all sorts of problems every day.

Beck and a group of colleagues (1978), investigating interactions between physicians and educators, focused on two areas of concern:

— The types of school-related problems viewed by both teachers and physicians as areas of mutual concern
— The major problems in establishing mutually satisfying relationships between physicians and teachers

Questionnaires were sent to 120 regular and special education teachers and 250 pediatricians and general practitioners in Washington state. Responses were received from 57 percent of the teachers and 27 percent of the physicians.

The survey data indicated close agreement between teachers and physicians regarding the types of problems that were referred from schools to doctors (in order of frequency): hyperactivity, behavior problems, hearing and vision concerns, acute medical problems, emotional disturbance, musculo-skeletal problems, and seizures or epilepsy.

When asked if they would intervene in cases of behavioral problems, 82 percent of the physicians said that they would. The responses from teachers indicated that they turned to physicians for help in solving many school-related problems, and the physicians tended to accept these referrals as appropriate. When asked if they were pleased with these interactions, 60 percent of the teachers said they were, and 27 percent of the physicians responded similarly. When data regarding reasons for unsatisfactory interactions were examined, the complaints from both parties were similar. Each group accused the other of being arrogant, of not returning phone calls, of not supplying enough information about the referred client, and of delaying in providing data.

Obviously, there is room for improvement in communication between these professionals. Following are a few suggestions for professionals of both types, many of which also pertain to communications between other groups:

1. Learn more about the other persons' job, their hours, their language. Know which journals they read, which tests they give, and so forth.
2. Explore multiple ways to communicate. When someone you phone is not in, leave a message about the time that you can be reached. Try answering machines, modems and computers, or some other means.
3. Identify the person's hierarchy or chain of command; try not to jump over someone's head or disturb their "turf." Doctors should not call the teacher's principal until they have talked with the teacher; teachers should not call the director of the medical center until they have contacted the family's primary care physician.
4. Respect the other discipline when talking to a third party, particularly a parent. Either set of professionals could do damage to their cause and the entire communication process by downgrading the other discipline.

5. Invite professionals from the other discipline to visit you in your office, school, hospital, or wherever, and make it a point to visit them in their settings.

There are many other professionals with whom LD specialists must communicate, and some of these interactions can be just as tense as those with physicians for the same and other reasons. The following sections identify a few of the professionals with whom educators must communicate frequently, comment on some of the matters that might disrupt communications, and make suggestions for improving those situations.

Psychologists and Counselors

Special educators interact a great deal with psychologists and counselors. Once a child becomes a focus of concern, school psychologists are called on to administer tests required to qualify children for special services. They give most of the intelligence tests, many of the achievement tests, and others. Teachers must know why certain tests are given, how to interpret the scores from them, and other matters in order to communicate effectively with psychologists.

Quite a number of teachers become frustrated when working with psychologists who don't offer immediate and understandable suggestions for dealing with youngsters once they have been tested. Although this criticism can sometimes be valid, teachers should be aware that precise answers to a child's problem may not always exist. Teachers should also be sure that they clearly tell the psychologist exactly what kind of information they would like to have. They can also improve communications with psychologists by letting the psychologists know whenever a certain type of information has proven helpful.

Special education teachers must also communicate with counselors, whose primary responsibility, particularly at the secondary level, is assigning students to classes. It is of great importance for special education teachers to work with counselors so that the handicapped pupils are placed with teachers who are the most sensitive to their needs. In some districts, counselors in elementary and secondary schools assist regular and special teachers with problem children. In these settings, teachers should strive for effective communications with the counselors. They should not feel intimidated by counselors nor should they act to intimidate the counselors.

Speech Therapists

Several years ago speech therapists worked mainly with youngsters' speech problems—that is, articulation, stuttering, and voice disorders. There are still many therapists who attend to these matters, but more and more, speech therapists have begun to concentrate on language in general.[2] Instead of focusing only on

2. In some areas they are now known as communication disorders specialists.

discrete speech malfunctions, they now help youngsters to speak in practical situations.

This new role for speech therapists creates a greater need for communication between the therapists and teachers. Teachers must know the aspects of language on which the therapists will concentrate, and therapists must be aware of the language demands of the classroom. All too often these two sets of professionals work independently of one another: Teachers manage the programs in their classrooms, whereas speech therapists detail the offerings in their special chambers.

■ COMMENTARY ■   To be of more assistance to children, therapists should work *in* the classrooms with small groups of children on matters of functional communication. Of itself, that would do a lot to enhance communications between them and classroom teachers.

Chapter I and Other Remedial Teachers

In a number of schools, there are other specialists who work with remedial or mildly handicapped youngsters. Some schools engage remedial reading teachers and Chapter I teachers, for example, particularly in elementary schools. It is important for LD specialists to communicate with these instructors in order to best serve all the schools' remedial students. In locales where the remedial and special teachers deal only with certain youngsters in specific subjects (as is often the case), it is still important for all these teachers to communicate, for many ideas for assessment and instruction should be shared (particularly those that are effective). In those locales where the services of LD and Chapter I instruction and others are blended, it is even more important that instructors communicate with one another. Only thus can these instructors share techniques and regroup youngsters depending on their needs and on the teachers' skills to best serve the students.

Social Workers

Even though there aren't as many social workers in schools as there once were, this group of professionals can be immensely helpful to special education teachers. Social workers are concerned with entire families, not just problem children and their interactions at school. They are equally concerned with parents and siblings— along with everything else that affects the youngsters' behaviors. Social workers can play a critical role in facilitating communications with the families of handicapped youngsters. They can also provide insights into home situations that affect the children's education.

To ensure effective communications with social workers, teachers need to learn about the job demands of social workers, particularly their case loads and their procedures for dealing with the many systems and agencies that can assist handicapped youth and their families. Teachers must inform social workers of classroom observations that could provide clues about abuse that children may have suffered, their diets, their sleeping patterns, and their general hygiene.

COMMUNICATIONS BETWEEN SCHOOLS AND INDUSTRY

Weller, Crelly, and colleagues (see Crelly, 1987) have established a project linking the University of Utah, local agencies, and industry to determine the extent the skill levels of underserved secondary-age students (including many classified as learning disabled) can be raised. The major objective of their project is to increase the available labor force that can be employed by high-tech companies.

Their data with regard to the underserved are impressive. According to them, 3,000 students drop out of school in Utah prior to graduation, and of the 15,000 students who do graduate, approximately 60 percent of them are underserved in that they have not been prepared to work in high-tech industries. An underserved population of 12,000 students is alarming in a state that has a total population of only 1.5 million.

The Center for Base Technical Education and Transition was established to focus on this problem. Formed by units from the University of Utah and the Utah Advanced Technology Council, the Center set goals to collaborate with Utah industries to research, develop, validate, and commercially distribute base technical curriculum and assessment products that would have value for instructing underserved populations. Their goals were founded on six premises:

1. Education agencies, as "industries," produce a considerable number of underserved humans.
2. Educational settings must be provided and proven teaching technologies must be put into practice for developing individuals qualified to perform in high-tech industries.
3. Special educators have for some time relied on highly developed technologies to instruct a wide variety of skills.
4. Personnel from special education can collaborate with regular educators, educational administrators, and industrial representatives to develop assessment techniques and related curricula required to develop qualified workers.
5. These instruments and instructional programs will be effective with underserved populations, and as a result, several individuals and sectors will gain, not the least of which is the Utah economy.
6. Assessment and curricular products developed from the joint efforts of these groups can be distributed commercially throughout the United States.

Base technical skills include functional mathematics, science, verbal communication, written communication, and reading, augmented by skills of adaptation. The skills are intended to be generic, rather than job-specific skills. During a pilot program, for example, the investigators set out to enhance performances in six basic entry-level categories within high-tech industries: shipping and receiving, inventory, general assembly, electronic assembly, quality control, and product testing.

The researchers project that through direct interventions with students at the Center, the number of underserved individuals could be reduced by 17 percent. Further, if 1,000 teachers throughout Utah were trained to use their assessment and intervention techniques, the number of underserved could be reduced another 31 percent.

■ COMMENTARY ■   Whether or not those figures will be attained has yet to be determined, but the Utah plan is certainly an imaginative and innovative transition program when it comes to linking services from higher education, industry, and various service agencies.

COMMENTS AND DISCUSSION POINTS

- The demands on resource teachers in some situations are excessive. Some of them work with 25 to 40 youngsters each day. In those circumstances, it is impossible to deal effectively with the pupils, much less to consult with their referring teachers.

- The consulting teachers in some schools, particularly in secondary schools, could perform duties apart from their consulting, if they had the time. They could, for example, show teachers how to modify textbook passages and tests to make them suitable for slower pupils, select curriculum in areas such as study skills or vocational development, and suggest workshops or classes that teachers could take in special areas.

- Consulting teachers could also serve as "modeling teachers." They could actually go into various classes and show teachers how to carry out instructional or management programs. They could take over for a few days as the regular teacher watched. Then consultants could give feedback and support after the teacher took over the class again. Teachers serving in such consulting roles could go from one teacher to another in their schools or districts and see to it that regular teachers were involving certain programs. While initially more expensive because only one teacher could be assisted at a time and that help could take a number of days, in the long run, the modeling approach could be a most efficient process.

- Consider the possibility of the assistance of microcomputer programs in training consulting teachers. According to West and Idol (1987b), computer programs are available that give trainees problems to solve regarding least restrictive education of mildly handicapped students in regular classrooms and in resource programs.

- Researchers studying the effects of consulting programs should acquire data from all participants—the consultant, the consultee, and by all means, the pupil. Researchers should first obtain data on the number of contacts made by the consultants. Then, additional and more sophisticated information pertaining to satisfaction and achievement could be gathered.

- As West and Idol (1987b) suggested with respect to conducting research on consulting models, various stages and aspects of consulting should be considered. Researchers might seek, for example, what number of contacts are required to begin programs with teachers and what number is required to maintain their efforts.

- It is extremely important to involve building principals in any school program, especially when it comes to starting up teacher consulting programs. In a program described in Chapter 4 (Lovitt & Haring, 1969), one of the consultants being trained was working for a grim, nonreinforcing principal. To get this principal into a few classes to reinforce the teachers, the consultant set up exemplary situations in classes, told the principal about them, took him into those classrooms, and gained his support in reinforcing the teachers. Eventually, the principal began visiting a few classrooms without prompting from the consultant.

- Consulting teachers sometimes serve as staff development persons in their schools or districts. In such a role, they can provide instruction on a number of matters, ranging from classroom management to data collection to instructional techniques. Consultants could also provide information related to fundamental and recent medical advances, such as research on drugs and diets, that affect handicapped youngsters. Perhaps they might identify some physicians in the community who are particularly sensitive and knowledgeable about the medical needs of handicapped children.

- Consultants could provide noteworthy services if in-service and training programs were arranged to inform parents of handicapped youngsters and others about ways to assist their children at home. Many parents are willing to adopt management and instructional programs for their children if they are shown how to do so. A related benefit from these sessions would be that the parents can offer feedback and support to one another.

- A final point, implied throughout this chapter, is important enough to specifically state here: Special education teachers, consultants or otherwise, have a heavy responsibility. These teachers must keep on top of all the available data or testimony regarding old and new techniques. They must be able to give candid and concise advice, they must serve the children, neither delude nor discourage parents, and at the same time, protect themselves and their districts from litigation.

REFERENCES

Anderson, R. C.; Hiebert, E. H.; Scott, J. A.; & Wilkinson, I. A. G. (1985). Becoming a nation of readers: The report of the commission on reading. Washington, D.C.: The National Institute of Education, U.S. Department of Education.

Beck, G. R., Edgar, E., Kenowitz, L., Sulzbacher, S., Lovitt, T. C., & Zweibel, S. (1978). The physician-educator team: Let's make it work. *The Journal of School Health* (February), 79–83.

Bernal, M. E., & North, J. A. (1978). A survey of parent training manuals. *Journal of Applied Behavior Analysis, 11*(4), 533–544.

Bower, R., & Meier, K. (1981). Will the real "slow learner" please stand up? *Journal of Precision Teaching, 2*(2), 25–27.

Chalfant, J. C.; Pysh, M. V.; & Moultrie, R. (1979). Teacher assistance teams: A model for within-building problem solving. *Learning Disability Quarterly, 2,* 85–96.

Crelly, C. (1978). Entry of mildly handicapped and underserved secondary-age students into advanced technological industries: An educational/governmental/industrial endeavor. Paper presented at the International Division for Career Development Conference, Nashville, TN.

Deno, S. L., & Mirkin, P. K. (1977). *Data-based program modification: A manual.* Reston, VA: Council for Exceptional Children.

Davis, W. E. (1983). Competencies and skills required to be an effective resource teacher. *Journal of Learning Disabilities, 16,* 596–598.

Dembinski, R. J., & Mauser, A. J. (1977). What parents of the learning disabled really want from professionals. *Journal of Learning Disabilities, 10*(9), 578–584.

Edge, D.; Fink, A. H.; & Brause, M. (1978). Developing parent training programs for professionals. In D. Edge, B. J. Strenecky, & S. I. Mour (Eds.), *Parenting learning-problem children: The professional educator's perspective.* Columbus, OH: National Center, Educational Media and Materials for the Handicapped, Ohio State University.

Egner, A. N., & Lates, B. J. (1975). The Vermont consulting teacher program: A case presentation. In C. Parker (Ed.), *Psychological consultation: Helping teachers meet special needs.* Reston, VA: Council for Exceptional Children.

Fewell, R. R., & Vadasy, P. F. (1986). *Families of handicapped children.* Austin, TX: PRO-ED.

Friend, M. (1984). Consultation skills for resource teachers. *Learning Disability Quarterly, 7,* 246–250.

Gickling, E. E.; Murphy, L. C.; & Mallory, D. W. (1979). Teachers' preferences for resource services. *Exceptional Children, 45,* 442–449.

Graden, J. L.; Casey, A.; & Christenson, S. L. (1985). Implementing a prereferral intervention system: Part I. The model. *Exceptional Children, 51*(5), 377–384.

Hanson, M. J., & Harris, S. R. (1986). *Teaching the young child with motor delays: A guide for parents and professionals.* Austin, TX: PRO-ED.

Idol-Maestas, L. (1981). A teacher training model: The resource/consulting teacher. *Behavioral Disorders, 6,* 108–121.

Idol, L., Paolucci-Whitcomb, P., & Nevin, A. (1986). *Collaborative consultation.* Rockville, MD: Aspen.

Idol-Maestas, L. (1983). Special educator's consultation handbook. Rockville, MD: Aspen.

Idol-Maestas, L., & Jackson, C. (1983). An evaluation of the consultation process. In L. Idol-Maestas (Ed.), *Special educator's consultation handbook.* Rockville, MD: Aspen.

Jenkins, J. R., & Mayhall, W. F. (1976). Development and evaluation of a resource teacher program. *Exceptional Children, 41,* 21–30.

Lippitt, G. L. (1959). A study of the consultation process. *Journal of Social Issues, 15,* 43–50.

McLoughlin, J. A.; McLoughlin, R.; & Stewart, W. (1979). Advocacy for parents of the handicapped: A professional responsibility and challenge. *Learning Disability Quarterly, 2,* 51–57.

Paolucci-Whitcomb, P., & Nevin, A. (1985). Preparing consulting teachers through a collaborative approach between university faculty and field-based consulting teachers. *Teacher Education and Special Education, 8*(3), 132–143.

Shapero, S., & Forbes, R. (1981). A review of involvement programs for parents of learning disabled children. *Journal of Learning Disabilities, 4*(9), 499–504.

West, J. F., & Brown, P. (1987). State departments' of education policies on consultation in special education: The state of the states. *Remedial and Special Education, 8*(3), 45–51.

West, J. F., & Idol, L. (1987a). School consultation (Part I): An interdisciplinary perspective on theory, models, and research. *Journal of Learning Disabilities, 20*(7), 388–408.

West, J. F., & Idol, L. (1987b). Consultation in special education (Part II): Training and practice. *Journal of Learning Disabilities, 20*(8), 474–494.

PART III

SPECIFIC LEARNING
DISABILITIES

Chapter 6

Children Playing on the Beach by Mary Cassatt (1884). Courtesy of the National Gallery of Art, Washington, Ailsa Mellon Bruce Collection, 1970.

LANGUAGE AND COMMUNICATION

MAIN IDEAS

- Identification of the basic features of speech and language
- Normal language development: origins and development of vocabulary, semantic–syntactic structures, variations and complexities of language, language uses, interactions between understanding and speaking, language development throughout life, and cognitive deficits
- Language characteristics of LD individuals and comparisons of their development with nonhandicapped students with respect to cognition of auditory–symbolic units, cognition of semantic units, cognition of semantic classes, cognition of semantic relations, cognition of semantic systems, cognition of semantic transformations, cognition of semantic implications, memory, evaluation, language production, convergent production abilities, divergent production abilities, and pragmatics
- Overview of popular formal and informal assessments in various aspects of language development
- Language interventions: treatment and approaches, principles for setting up interventions, and evaluation of programs
- Microcomputer programs in the area of language: current applications, guidelines for involving microcomputer programs, emerging applications

OVERVIEW

No textbook on learning disabilities would be complete without seriously considering the many and varied language problems of LD youth. Indeed, to indicate the importance of this relationship, this chapter precedes all those that have to do with academic and social development. It sets the stage for those chapters.

In the first section of this chapter, some definitions of and distinctions between speech and language are offered. The second section outlines normal language development. The next three sections discuss characteristics of children with language problems, assessment techniques, and interventions. A review of microcomputer programs as aids to speech professionals and as tools for language assessment and development follows. At the end of the chapter are comments for teachers and clinicians about language assessment and development.

—————— COMPONENTS OF SPEECH AND LANGUAGE ——————

It is important to differentiate between the terms *speech* and *language*. Although some speech problems are due to physical limitations, they are not considered language disorders unless they affect the symbolic quality of the ideas, vocabulary, or grammar being expressed (Myers & Hammill, 1982).

Language can be defined as any ". . . socially shared code or conventional system for representing concepts through the use of arbitrary symbols and rule-governed combinations of those symbols" (Owens, 1984, p. 379). It is the entire process of human communication. According to Owens, American Sign Language, Morse code, Indian smoke signals, and Russian are all examples of language. Of those, however, only Russian can be classified as speech, for speech is a verbal means of transmitting language.

Speech

According to the American Speech–Language–Hearing Association (ASLHA, 1976), there are three types of speech disorders:

□ *Articulation* problems are indicated when children substitute, omit, or distort speech sounds. An example of substitution is saying "wascally wabbit" for "rascally rabbit."

□ *Voice disorders* are those that effect the pitch, loudness, or quality of speech. Pitch can be too high or low, loudness can be too weak or strong, and quality problems range from hoarseness to nasality.

□ *Fluency disorders* (stuttering) occur when the flow of speech is interrupted abnormally by repetitions or prolongations of a sound or syllable; these disorders are often marked by the avoidance of troublesome sounds.

Although speech problems are easier to recognize than language disorders, they are less common. Statistics from the ASLHA indicate that 54 percent of the caseloads of speech–language pathologists are those of individuals with language disorders. The remaining 46 percent consist of clients with speech or hearing problems (Shewan, 1986).

Language

The ASHLA recognizes two types of language disorders—aphasia and delayed language development. *Aphasia* is an impairment in comprehending or formulating messages, perhaps due to central nervous system damage. *Delayed language development* is manifested in vocabulary or grammatical deficits that prevent children from expressing themselves clearly. Phrased another way, the two major components of language are *receptive* (what we receive) and *expressive* (what we send).

Whereas speech pathologists, psychologists, educators, and others generally agree when it comes to the basic modes of language—receptive and expressive—they disagree on how to categorize expressive language. Recently, however, professionals representing several disciplines have reached some accord with the scheme advanced by linguists, who identified six elements of expression: phonemes, morphemes, syntax, semantics, prosody, and pragmatics.

☐ *Phonemes* are units of sound. They combine with other sounds to form words (the word "bat," for example, has three phonemes).

☐ *Morphemes* are the smallest units of language that convey meaning (the word "unnatural," for example, has two morphemes).

☐ *Syntax,* frequently referred to as grammar, is how words are joined to make sentences.

☐ *Semantics* refers to word meanings and requires an accurate and broad understanding of word categories (for example, verbs and adjectives) and their relationships. Semantics also refers to multiple word meanings and figurative language.

☐ *Prosody* involves an understanding and proper usage of the rhythm, intonation, and stress patterns of language. It has a function similar to the use of punctuation in writing.

☐ *Pragmatics* refers to the way in which language is used in social situations. Ordinarily, people alter the way they speak depending on the person to whom they are speaking, why they are speaking, and other factors.

NORMAL LANGUAGE DEVELOPMENT

The intent of this section is to provide a brief overview of normal language development to serve as a benchmark from which to judge language processes of LD youth.[1] The three components of language—content, form, and use—begin

---

1. The outline for this section is from the Bloom and Lahey text, *Language Development and Language Disorders* (1978).

as separate developmental threads in the child's first year, becoming more and more coordinated until the child induces relationships and integrates the three features of language into his or her environments.

The development of language *content,* or meaning, has to do with which objects and events are in the infants' environment and how children interact with them. Early on, infants learn that objects exist apart from their own movements and apart from the time and space in which they are perceived.

Precursors of language *form* are the infant's ability to perceive and produce sounds and, later, in the second year, to assemble and arrange these sounds into words. Infants, as young as one month old, are aware of speech in their environment and are sensitive to the social aspects of the context. Most parents are excited by signs of this awareness and feed into the process by imitating sounds and encouraging their babies to express even more sounds.

A few months later, infants *use* language as they exchange gazes and vocalizations with those about them. Language continues to develop when the precursors of content, form, and use become integrated and sensitive to the conventional language requirements in the environment. Although there is considerable range in the normal development of early language, many LD youngsters, for one reason or another, are quite slow in using and profiting from language.

Development of Language Content and Form

Vocabulary.   Children usually begin saying words and understanding them in their second year. Generally they start by saying one word at a time, and they often use that word in several contexts. They gradually add more words to their repertoires and begin using them in more discrete contexts. As their vocabularies expand, children learn different kinds of words that make reference to a variety of ideas about objects and relations between them. They begin to use words that name particular nouns (for example, "daddy") and classes of objects ("bread'). Later they learn more abstract words that have to do with existence ("there," for example, or "this"), disappearance ("gone," "away"), or reappearance ("again," "more"). In this period, children also learn social words such as "hi" and "bye-bye."

Children gradually learn words by trying them out in different situations; not surprisingly, they often use words inappropriately. From age two, the use of single-word utterances is continuous as children develop syntactically. Meanwhile, they begin learning about the semantic and syntactic structures of complex sentences.

This period too is exciting for most parents, as they continue to communicate verbally and gesturally with their children. They often engage their youngsters in "conversations" and request children to say their words for other relatives and friends, who, in turn, provide the youngsters with more reinforcement. Some LD children are not blessed with such doting parents or others who are thrilled by their abilities, language, or otherwise. Because of this lack, or for other reasons, some LD pupils get locked into this stage and have difficulty breaking into more sophisticated forms of speech.

Semantic–Syntactic Structure.   The semantic content of early sentences consists of information about relations among objects, in particular those that involve actions, locations, and persons. Children begin using such phrases as, "me go," "where my mummy," and "my daddy."

Based on those simple combinations, the syntactic structure of early sentences evolves in rather well-defined steps. Between using single- and multi-word utterances, many children pass through a transitional period when they say in succession several single words that do not always form a proper sentence. Some children, in an effort to carry out their end of a conversation, run out a string of their favorite words or sounds (Bloom & Lahey, 1978, p. 163).

When children begin to combine words consistently in sentences, they do so after acquiring a few prepositions, such as "in" or "on," and adverbs, such as "up" and "down." These words are then associated with nouns ("in car") and verbs (take up) and add richness and meaning to their communication.

Another early language structure is to use the same words in various settings and with various meanings. Take the word "cookie," for example. Children could say "cookie" to indicate that they see one, want one, have one, or (less likely), are ready to give up one.

Variation and Complexity.   Variation and complexity are two important features of children's language. As for *variation,* children neither add words to their vocabularies nor rules to their grammars in any uniform or simple way. Instead, there is a merging of each child's knowledge of various aspects of language content, form, and use.

Many LD youngsters are rather slow in developing new or different forms. Not a few of them appear to lack the confidence to try new words or phrases; moreover, some of them are not surrounded by parents and others who encourage these new linguistic variations.

Complexity occurs as children's sentences become more involved as they get longer. At first, children combine semantic-syntactic relations that had appeared in their earliest utterances. Later, they join simple sentences and bridge them with connectives (for example, "Give me juice so I can drink").

Between these two developments—beginning with two-word sentences and continuing until they are longer—children learn a great deal about grammar. In particular, they learn about past tense (often generalizing incorrectly to some verb forms), the relationships of morphemes to nouns (for example, "cups"), negation ("not," "none," "don't have any"), and asking words ("who," "why," "when") (Bloom & Lahey, 1978, p. 199).

Development of Language Use

Function.   A significant aspect of language has to do with function—that is, the kinds of things that people do with language. Another important aspect has to do with the rules that speakers acquire for deciding which forms and arrangements to select for achieving their goals.

From the age of three and thereafter, children become aware of the many functions of speech and practice on those several types. They first use speech to express their needs and feelings. Later, they use speech to initiate and sustain interaction. Still later, they learn to rely on language to acquire information. Later yet, they learn to identify the needs and backgrounds of their communicative partners. Thus, they are able to make the proper adjustments—that is, to ask questions of those who are likely to have desired information and to provide appropriate amounts and type of information to others.

As children carry out more conversations, they learn more about word usage, form, and style. In fact, the more varied the backgrounds, interests, and abilities of their partners, the more widely varied are the features of language to which they are exposed.

Unfortunately, many LD children do not profit a great deal from these interactions. For one thing, they are often reluctant to engage others in conversation, and when they do, those interactions are brief, terse, and at a rather low level. Accordingly, their partners tend to speak down to them, are not particularly reinforced by the interactions, and terminate them as soon as possible. The LD person is thus limited to the extent he or she can develop in substance or form to become a more engaging partner for the next interaction, and so on.

Interaction Between Understanding and Speaking.   It is readily apparent from the evidence in observational studies of children's language that the relationship between understanding and speaking is complex. Throughout the transition from single-word to multiword utterances, there is not a simple correspondence between understanding and speaking. For one thing, the words that children first understand and respond to are not necessarily the first words they say (Bloom & Lahey, 1978, p. 264).

Most parents and teachers would agree that there is a strong relationship between the words that children hear and those that they speak. As children listen to and comprehend the messages of others, they begin to understand the meanings and purposes of phrases, and as indicated earlier, they then begin to experiment in their own speech with those phrases and words. Then, as their communicative partners hear these words and phrases, they react either by correcting the youngsters or by adjusting their subsequent messages upward or downward in terms of complexity. Once again, LD individuals often come out on the short end, for they are not attentive listeners and are not as able to pull in new words or phrases from others that could increase their abilities as speakers.

As a Lifelong Process. It is possible to develop one's use of language throughout most of a lifetime. As individuals listen to more sophisticated and different speakers; attend more varied events; read more and varied papers, magazines, and books; attach more words and concepts to visual images; explain more complex behaviors or explain simple ones more succinctly; receive feedback from more and varied persons; and learn to listen more intently or for express purposes—they have opportunities to adjust, modify, and improve their language processes.

Many LD youngsters, however, are less adept at retrieving information from those situations and at setting them up and nurturing them in the first place. Thus they tend to fall further behind.

LANGUAGE DISORDERS

This section describes some components of language about which LD youngsters often experience difficulty. A few of those were noted generally in the preceding section, but considerably more detail is included here.[2]

Cognitive Deficiencies

Auditory–Symbolic Units (Speech Sounds). The ability to derive word structure from auditory stimuli constitutes the ability to comprehend or use those units, and LD children often have problems in auditory perception. The inability to abstract and categorize the distinctive features that make up significant speech sounds may combine with problems in integration and result in phoneme discrimination deficits. Reduced abstraction and classification abilities may also contribute to deficiencies in phoneme sequencing, segmentation, and discrimination of pitch, intensity, and duration, all of which may be observed in association with learning disabilities. These deficiencies take on considerable importance, for according to some (for example, Kavale, 1981), sound blending correlates with reading achievement and discriminates good from poor readers.

In an effort to compare the abilities of poor and good readers on speech production/phonological processing abilities, Catts (1986) set up a study in which readers of both types, between the ages of 12.5 and 15.5, participated in naming, word repetition, and phrase repetition tasks. The results of the group comparisons revealed that the poor readers made significantly more errors than good readers in the production of multisyllabic words and short phrases. Poor readers also made more errors on the naming task. The data also indicated a high correlation between performance on the speech production tasks and performance on the Word Attack subtest from the *Woodcock Reading Mastery Tests*.

---

2. The outline for this section is from Wiig and Semel's book, *Language Assessment and Intervention for the Learning Disabled Child* (1984).

Elizabeth H. Wiig, with her collaborator Eleanor M. Semel, has made a major contribution in the study of various language abilities of learning disabled youngsters. Most of their work was carried out at Boston University. Their most influential publication is Language Disabilities in Children and Adolescents.

Semantic Units (Words and Concepts).   The understanding of semantic units (words and concepts) indicates knowledge of the precise meaning of familiar words as well as broad knowledge of the meaning of less familiar words. Normal development with regard to concept formation depends upon the abilities to abstract, generalize, and categorize and to establish relationships between symbols and referents, among other factors.

Many LD individuals have problems with concept formation and in the development of semantic units. The fact that they may not have precise and comprehensive knowledge of familiar word meanings may contribute to those problems. For example, "diet" would only have one meaning—to cut down on eating in an attempt to lose weight.

Just as LD youngsters may not have precise knowledge of familiar words, they may have restricted knowledge of less familiar words (familiarity in terms of the general population). One example is the word "awesome." Although LD youngsters and their non-LD mates use this word a great deal, it's doubtful that many know its primary meaning ("inspiring"). As another example, many youngsters use the word "radical" as a synonym for awesome (meaning wonderful), and few of them know that it means "fundamental" or "extreme."

Because of such confusions, many LD youngsters have difficulty on standardized tests. If asked the meanings of "explosive" words such as "hit," "smack," or "bomb," it is quite likely that they would not come up with the preferred meanings. Likewise, these subtle and not so subtle confusions are partial reasons for the fact that so many LD youth have trouble following oral directions.

Wolf (1979) provided information about developmental relationships between reading problems and word-finding disorders. In that research, poor readers between the ages of 6 and 11 performed significantly lower than average readers on a variety of naming tasks. While average readers showed orderly developmental gains in naming ability, poor readers plateaued between 8 to 9 and 10 to 11 years of age.

Semantic Classes (Word Categories).   Individual words may be classified into larger groups, or semantic classes, according to several criteria. For example, "corn," "carrots," "peas," "lettuce," and "radishers" may be classified as vegetables, or they may be further categorized as to color. The ability to name the class name (superordinate) when given names of class members constitutes one feature of understanding classes, and the ability to name class members when given a class name is another feature. LD children are often troubled by either form of classification.

To extend this notion, non-LD children are better able than LD students, as groups, to use their classification abilities for interpreting meanings of ambiguous sentences. In the sentence, "Tom saw a raccoon on the way to school," non-LD students are more likely than LD students to classify "raccoon" as a member of the semantic class "animals" (which don't go to school).

In a study appropriate to this feature, Wiig and Semel (1975) compared the speed and accuracy with which the LD and non-LD adolescents named members of three classes—foods, animals, and toys—during one-minute periods. Results indicated that LD students gave significantly fewer names than their normal peers and also revealed that LD adolescents did not employ common grouping strategies as did their academically achieving peers. The latter grouped foods either by categories such as fruits or in relationship to meals such as breakfast.

Semantic Relations (Word Relationships).   Words may be placed adjacent to one another to form a logical semantic relation. For example, the concepts "plow," "harrow," "seed," "fertilize," and "harvest" form a relation with respect to a sequence that reflects time. Sentences that express comparison, or passive, spatial, temporal, familial relationships also convey a sequence in time or space. LD youngsters may not discern the underlying sequences when presented with such relations. Furthermore, LD youngsters may be confused by rather simple sentences that deal with time. In the sentence, "Randy went ahead of Kyle," they might not be able to get the order straight. Similarly, LD children, unlike achieving children, may not be able to complete rather basic analogies that have to do with time or space. The analogy "first is to third as one is to————" might bother them, as would the problem "floor is to ceiling as ground is to————."

In another example of subtle word confusions by some LD children, Seidenberg's (1984) data indicate that LD pupils in grades 2 through 6 were less accurate than their non-LD peers in providing verbal cues for similar word pairs such as "road"–"street," "car"–"auto," "magazine"–"journal," and "stove"–"oven."

Semantic Systems (Word Problems).   In order to solve verbal problems, it is necessary first to understand the inherent relations in the problem and the processes to be applied to arrive at a solution. Many LD children have difficulties in reading comprehension and in mathematical, spatial, and temporal reasoning. The cognitive problems underlying these deficits may also be evidenced in the processing of auditory language.

There are some particular features of "story problems" that are especially troublesome for many LD youngsters: extraneous information, numbers that are words (for example, four), aspects of time, converting units of measurement or time, and making change. Blankenship and Lovitt (1976) examined features of story problems that were particularly troublesome to LD youngsters, and Fantasia (1981) studied the effects of extraneous information on arithmetic performance of LD students. (Those studies are summarized in Chapter 9.)

Semantic Transformations (Changes in Meaning).   The information transmitted by any word may vary, depending upon the context, role, or significance of the utterance. The word "soft," for example, may describe texture or volume depending upon the attribute stressed. The recognition of and ability to make changes in the meanings of words reflects an understanding of semantic transformations (Wiig & Semel, 1984).

Numerous LD children have difficulty making semantic transformations. They may have limited knowledge of attributes or fail to generalize features from one situation to another. As a result, they may have difficulty processing multiple-meaning words, idioms, and metaphors.

Horton and Lovitt (1983) conducted a study in which they assessed pupils' abilities to explain the meaning of familiar idioms. There were LD, non-LD, and EMR youngsters in that research. The ten idioms in their study included: "raining cats and dogs," "barking up the wrong tree," and "hit the nail on the head." The results showed that the performances of the LD children were, as would be expected, slightly lower than those of non-LD students, but higher than those of the EMR pupil.

Semantic Implications (Implied Meaning).   One of the highest levels for comprehending language involves the ability to discern information that was implied, but not provided. That ability reflects an awareness of possible causes and is yet another area in which many learning disabled youngsters have problems. This particular deficit is reflected in the fact that a number of LD individuals have difficulty understanding fables, myths, parables, and proverbs. Paradoxically, when LD persons *do* remember a saying or two, they often use them too frequently and inappropriately.

Bruno, Johnson, and Simon (1987) investigated the perception of humor by regular class students and those with learning disabilities. Their results showed that LD students did not exhibit the increase in understanding humor at the intermediate or middle school age levels that the non-LD students showed. When it came to telling jokes, however, LD pupils told as many as the non-LD youngsters, but they were not as sophisticated linguistically. LD youngsters were particularly weak with respect to jokes that were "phonological," where humor was derived from slight sound changes resulting in multiple meanings (for example, "What did the judge say when the skunk entered the courtroom? Odor in the court.")

Deficiencies in Memory

Numerous researchers (for example, Chalfant & Scheffelin, 1969) have pointed out that children with learning disabilities frequently exhibit deficits in auditory memory. A variety of conclusions have been drawn from investigations regarding specific memory abilities. For example, nonverbal memory has been distinguished from verbal memory, as has visual from auditory memory. As for verbal memory, two separate components have been recognized—associative and span memory (French, 1951).

Learning disabled children may exhibit memory deficits that inhibit certain perceptual, linguistic, and cognitive abilities of language comprehension and production. Furthermore, they may show specific deficits in recalling phoneme sequences, retrieving words within selected categories, and understanding and remembering semantic relations such as verbal analogies, cause-and-effect relationships, and linguistic concepts (Wiig & Semel, 1984).

Memory strategies of school-age children with language disorders have been studied by several researchers. (See Chapter 10 for further discussion.) For example, Strand (1982) compared the performances of children with language impairments to those of children with normal language development. When memory strategies were compared under three conditions—recognition, cued, and free recall—a pattern of developmental delays was observed among the children with language impairments.

Wiig and Roach (1975) assessed short-term memory by asking LD and non-LD adolescents to repeat sentences. Their data indicated that the latter youngsters were better able to recall sentences accurately, indicating that they, unlike the LD pupils, used the structure of the sentences to facilitate recall. Rather than relying on the structures of sentences and clauses as memory aids, many LD students depended on consistencies in word and sentence meaning for their recall. When they encountered inconsistencies (for them), they simply changed the words to improve the meaning (for them).

Deficiencies in Evaluation Abilities

Evaluation is an integral part of language processing because it provides a link between language comprehension and production. Critical evaluation of verbal information calls for the comparison of new information with previously acquired information.

Some learning disabled children often have problems evaluating the consistency of a new word's meaning against information they have acquired in the past. As examples, they might accept the incorrect tense in the sentence "Yesterday he hitted the ball" or the incorrect preposition in the phrase "in the table" for "on the table."

Some learning disabled children and adolescents may continue using definite articles when nouns are first introduced in discourse past the ages expected (for example, "The Polly."). In contrast, nine-year-old children with normal language development use proper rules for articles in discourse (Warden, 1976).

At the sentence level, LD youngsters may exhibit deficits in the critical judgment of syntactic consistency by not recognizing the lack of subject–verb agreement in sentences such as "The men goes home," or they may fail to detect an incorrect auxiliary verb in sentences such as "I cannot be able to leave."

At the semantic implication level, they may not be able to evaluate cause-and-effect consistency, thus accepting statements such as "Strawberry ice cream is made with peaches." Moreover, they may not grasp inconsistencies between premise and conclusion, thus accepting a statement such as "She wore her mittens outside because it was so hot" (Wiig & Semel, 1984).

Liles, Shulman, and Bartlett (1977) compared the ability of language disabled and nondisabled youngsters to make judgments of proper and improper grammar and to correct ungrammatical sentences. Their data suggested that the language disordered students had difficulty in recognizing syntactic errors when they occurred and in knowing how to revise them once they were detected.

Language Production Deficiencies

According to Wiig and Semel (1984), language production may be facilitated by memory and retrieval as well as by affective behaviors (such as ideas, practices, standards, values) and psychomotor behaviors (sensory perception and mental, physical, and emotional set). Since these attributes are not generally highly developed by LD youth, their overall language production is adversely affected. The following studies serve to indicate a number of these deficiencies.

Idol-Maestas (1980) presented evidence of the syntactic deficits of reading disabled youngsters in spontaneous speech by noting that the language samples of those children contained significantly fewer words than those from normal youngsters. Disabled pupils have also received significantly lower "Developmental Sentence Scores" (Lee, 1974) than academically achieving peers. Among the grammatical morphemes, the relative absence of auxiliary verbs proved significant for children with reading disabilities. There was also a qualitative difference in the ease with which language samples were elicited; children with reading disabilities required substantially more prompts than did academic achievers.

Stahl and Erickson (1986) studied the language production of learning disabled and normally achieving children on a variety of tasks at the semantic, syntactic, and discourse levels of language. Their data indicated that, generally, the language performances of LD youngsters were similar to those of the younger, ability-matched controls but inferior to the age-matched LD youngsters. Further analysis revealed, however, that the stories told by the LD students were markedly different from those expressed by the ability-matched younger pupils. The stories of the LD students were often made up of fragments, did not include either a motivating conflict or a major character, and were disordered as to sequence.

When Donohue, Pearl, and Bryan (1982) compared the length and syntactic complexity of the sentences produced by LD and non-LD children, their data showed that there was no difference in the productivity measures for the two groups. Detailed analysis, however, suggested that although the LD students said as many words as their non-LD mates, the syntax of their utterances was not as complex.

Convergent Production Abilities. Language formulation and production often occur under imposed semantic, linguistic, or social restrictions; only one word will satisfy the restrictions imposed by a given context. An example of this would be to discriminate between the words "molecule," "element," "diatomic," and "cell." Although each word refers to something very small, each has a distinct meaning, particularly to a scientist. The ability to draw logical conclusions from verbal information and to produce unique semantic responses reflects a person's convergent semantic production ability (Wiig & Semel, 1984).

Not surprisingly, LD children may exhibit deficits in these areas. Their rate and accuracy scores for naming pictured objects or events and verbal opposites, completing verbal analogies, completing sentences, and redefining words and concepts are often lower than those scores of non-LD youngsters. To illustrate further, most LD youngsters would have problems generating a number of words to describe similar circumstances or objects and even more problems in defining the differences between such terms. Although "pole," "stake," "post," "spindle," "stick," and "rod" have several characteristics in common, for example, each has a unique meaning.

Divergent Production Abilities. The fluency, flexibility, originality, and elaboration with which language is produced reflect a person's divergent semantic abilities. Divergent production abilities can be indicated in the following tasks:

— Naming words and concepts
— Completing verbal associations and analogies
— Formulating ideas and verbal problems
— Reformulating concepts and ideas
— Formulating alternatives and solutions

According to Wiig and Semel (1984), divergent production abilities usually constitute an area of relative strength for LD youngsters. Specific deficits, however, may be observed in the rate and accuracy with which they name semantic units. Relevant to that observation, Wiig and Semel compared the speed and accuracy scores of LD and non-LD youngsters by administering two naming tests,

"Rapid Object Naming" and "Producing Names on Confrontation." Their data indicated that the performances of nondisabled students were significantly superior to those of their LD mates.

LD youngsters may also demonstrate limited flexibility in the formulation of sentences. They tend to express themselves in simple declarative sentences and verbal stereotypes. Lovitt and Smith (1972) conducted research on that matter as they studied the effects of simple instructions on an LD boy's ability to describe pictures. Throughout a baseline phase, when asked to describe pictures, the boy consistently began each phrase with "This is . . .," and most of his responses were four words in length ("This is a pencil"). In the second phase, he was told to use different ways to begin sentences. He immediately complied, but his response length was not markedly affected. In the third phase, when he was instructed to vary his sentence beginnings *and* to use more words, he again complied. Data from the study revealed that his average response length doubled, and his ratio of different sentence beginnings remained high.

Deficiencies in Pragmatic Areas (Functional Use of Language)

Although there have been only a few investigations with LD children in the functional area, the data suggest that they are just as inept in the pragmatics of language usage as they are in the other features of language development. For example, Bryan, Donohue, and Pearl (1981) concluded that LD children demonstrated more difficulty than their normally achieving peers in such skills as asking questions, responding to inadequate messages, sustaining a conversation, and disagreeing with and supporting an argument.

Knight-Arest (1984) studied the communicative effectiveness of LD and normally achieving boys of the same age. For their data, the experimenters asked pupils individually to teach them the game of checkers. Periodically, they asked the youngsters to clarify a point and to give them more information. Their data showed the following tendencies with respect to the LD boys:

1. They talked more but said less than the non-LD boys.

2. They appeared more comfortable "showing" than "describing."

3. They were less effective in adapting messages to the needs of the listener than their normally achieving peers.

4. They were even more inept than the non-LD boys when it came to interpreting and responding to subtle nonverbal feedback from their "students."

Boucher (1984) examined the verbal language complexity and styles of LD and non-LD boys of the same age in social interactions with an adult and a peer. The results, which were more positive than those of other studies, showed the following characteristics:

Tanis H. Bryan is at the University of Illinois in Chicago, where she has served as the director of one of the federally funded learning disabilities institutes. Bryan has made a significant contribution to the field with her studies of social interactions and social competencies of LD youth.

1. LD boys had less complex verbal language.
2. They were able to adjust verbal language and style to the listener.
3. Both groups showed complementary communication styles.
4. LD pupils made more statements that encouraged cooperation and showed a greater tendency to promote joint problem solving.

Donohue, Pearl, and Bryan (1980) studied the abilities of non-LD and LD children to request clarification of messages based on the informational adequacy of the message. The data revealed that LD children did not differ from non-LD pupils in their ability to use informative messages. LD pupils were, however, less likely to request clarification when provided with less-informative messages, even though they could recognize them as being inadequate communications. In another study of the communication process, Bryan, Donohue, and Pearl (1981) examined the persuasive skills of non-LD and LD children. In line with most other descriptive studies, their data showed that LD children were less conversationally persuasive than their non-LD peers. Furthermore, LD youngsters appeared to be more conversationally compliant than their peers and did not regulate the flow of dialogue.

ASSESSMENT OF LANGUAGE ABILITIES

A number of tests have been developed to tap various components and aspects of language. In this section, a few of the more popular standardized tests are reviewed. Information is also included on informal assessment.

Formal Assessment: Structured Language Tests

Clinical Evaluation of Language Functions Screening Tests (CELF) (Semel & Wiig, 1980).   These tests were designed to probe aspects of language comprehension and expression at two levels. The elementary level, covering grades K to 5, contains 48 items grouped in two sections on the basis of response mode. The first section of 31 items uses a "Simon says" format and requires action responses from students. The second section of 17 items requires verbal responses to a number of requests. The advanced level, designed for grades 5 to 11 or 12, contains 52 items in two sections. The first section, 34 items, uses a playing card identification format, and the second section of 18 items requires verbal responses to the examiner's requests.

Northwestern Syntax Screening Test (NSST) (Lee, 1971).   The NSST is designed to screen children for the ability to process and reproduce selected syntactic structures and transformations. It is made up of two sections, receptive and expressive, with items in each section. Each item consists of two semantically and syntactically contrasting sentences. The items are associated with four pictorial choices each for the receptive section and two pictorial choices each for the expressive section.

    The examiner reads the receptive items, and the child identifies the pictorial choices that best represent the two sentences that were read. The examiner reads the expressive items without indicating which of the two sentences in a pair is associated with each of the pictorial choices, and points to the pictorial representations of the sentences while asking "What is this one?" and "What's that one?"

Goldman-Fristoe-Woodcock Auditory Skills Test Battery (Goldman, Fristoe, & Woodcock, 1976).   This battery assesses a broad spectrum of skills, ranging from simple auditory attention and discrimination to the complex association of sounds with symbols in written language. It consists of 13 subtests for individuals from age 3 to adult and assesses such attributes as auditory attention, auditory discrimination, auditory memory, and sound–symbol relationships.

Peabody Picture Vocabulary Test—Revised (PPVT) (Dunn & Dunn, 1981).   The purpose of the PPVT, designed for individuals ranging in age from 2 ½ to 40, is to evaluate knowledge of single word meanings. The test contains 175 items in two forms. Each item consists of a single word associated with four pictorial choices. For administration, the examiner says a word, and the child points to the one picture among the four choices that represents the meaning of the word. The words are presented in increasing order of difficulty.

Boehm Test of Basic Concepts (BTBC) (Boehm, 1970). The BTBC is designed to evaluate knowledge and understanding of basic concepts of quantity and number, space (dimension, direction, orientation), time, and combinations of these aspects. There are two forms to the test, each containing fifty items arranged according to increasing difficulty. The items in both forms follow the same formats and feature identical terms for the basic concepts, which were selected from curriculum materials for kindergarten and first grade. For each item, an oral direction is given; it is associated either with a set of three horizontally displayed choices or with a composite picture. The child is given a pencil and a response booklet that contains the pictorial choices for three or four items on each page. The examiner reads each statement or oral direction, and the child either identifies the best representation of the featured concept or completes the action indicated in the oral direction.

Carrow Elicited Language Inventory (CELI) (Carrow, 1974). The CELI is a diagnostic instrument for evaluating verbal expression for individuals from 3 years to 7 years 11 months. When administered, the examiner says a sentence, and the student repeats it. One phrase and fifty-two sentences comprise the test; sentences range in length from two to ten words with an average of six words. Each sentence is scored on the basis of whether the student's imitation included various grammatical parts (such as pronouns, prepositions, and conjunctions).

Illinois Test of Psycholinguistic Abilities (ITPA) (Kirk, McCarthy, & Kirk, 1968). The ITPA, designed for children between the ages of 2 years 4 months and 10 years 3 months, contains 10 subtests and two supplementary tests. It attempts to measure psycholinguistic skills through three dimensions: channels of communication (auditory-vocal and visual-motor modalities), psycholinguistic processes (reception, organization, and expression), and levels of organization (representational and automatic).

Test of Language Development (TOLD) (Newcomer & Hammill, 1982). The purpose of the TOLD is to assess major aspects of spoken language, including phonology, syntax, and semantics. Five subtests and two supplementary tests are included for the primary level: subtests for picture vocabulary, oral vocabulary, grammatical understanding, sentence imitation, and grammatical completion, as well as supplementary tests for word discrimination and word pronunciation. The intermediate level has five subtests: *generals* and *characteristics* assess the understanding and meaningful use of spoken words, and *sentence combining, word ordering,* and *grammatic comprehension* assess differing aspects of grammar. The primary level is for youngsters from 4 through 9 years, and the intermediate level for children ages 8 years through 13 years.

Profile of Nonverbal Sensitivity (PONS) (Rosenthal, Hall, Archer, diMatteo, & Rogers, 1979). The PONS, which consists of 220 filmed scenes, assesses nonverbal perception abilities. When given, only intonational cues and facial/body movements of the film characters are provided. Students are asked to interpret the "wordless" communication that took place and choose one of two statements that best sums up the interactions.

Let's Talk Inventory for Adolescents (Wiig, 1982).   This inventory covers the age levels from 9 years to young adulthood. It was designed to probe the ability to speak in relation to the function of communication, its intent, and the type of audience. To assess these traits, situational-audience contexts were constructed. For each, a picture is shown of various peer interactions, and a short narrative describing the communication intent is read to the pupil. The student's task is to identify the appropriate remark for each occasion.

Informal Assessment: Spontaneous Speech Evaluation

Wiig and Semel (1984) suggested that clinicians address the following points when informally assessing youngsters' language behaviors:

— The best timing of a language evaluation
— The situational context of the evaluation
— The presence or absence of interpersonal interactions in the evaluation and the naturalness of the language observed
— The time required for the evaluation or the size of the language sample needed for a valid judgment of linguistic competence
— The critical linguistic structures that should be evaluated or the structural nature of the language sample needed for an evaluation
— The adequacy of the linguistic analysis used to evaluate the language observed

Among the procedures that are arranged to obtain spontaneous language samples, informal conversation is the preferred method, whereas eliciting speech by imperatives such as "Tell me all about . . ." is the second most popular. The third most popular method for obtaining speech samples is to ask wh- questions (who, what, why, when).

The more unstructured conversational method of eliciting speech can provide rich ideas and content as well as elaborate syntactic structures. In clinical interactions with LD students, Wiig and Semel consider it ideal to elicit an unstructured conversational sample as well as a structured sample in response to a question such as "Tell me about your favorite TV show." The former sample is frequently a terse, unelaborated response, whereas the sample about television is often more creative and structurally complex. This method also seems to elicit a greater quantity of utterances.

A method therapists and others might consider for obtaining informal language assessments is to give youngsters a tape recorder and ask them to talk. They could, of course, be offered a few more instructions, but the idea would be to leave them alone to talk freely—for as long as they wanted, about anything they wanted to address, and not be bothered by an examiner. The effectiveness of this method is indicated by an experience of the author, when his granddaughter made a tape for her great grandparents. When she made part of the tape she was alone, in her own room with her books, toys, and animals; she was the director, producer, and actress. For another part of the tape, her mother was around. There is a world of difference in the output: In the first taping session, she talked a mile a minute about lots of topics; in the second, her language was more stilted, and there was less of it.

Advantages and Disadvantages.   Analyzing children's spontaneous language has several advantages over more standardized testing methods. First, this method introduces fewer constraints on the child than do the structured language tests. Second, children may produce syntactic structures in spontaneous speech that may not be evident in elicited language samples. Third, sampling of type and the subsequent analysis provide evidence of children's productive language capacity in interactions occurring in natural settings. A spontaneous speech sample may be the most suitable method for determining which morphological and syntactic rules and structures children have learned.

The analysis of spontaneous speech samples has limitations, however. Among them is the size of the sample that is generally desired. Whereas spontaneous speech samples often consist of only from 50 to 100 utterances in clinical situations, speech samples in basic research studies of children's language acquisition often contain from 300 to 800 utterances. With these larger samples, situational cues such as the topic of conversation, the task at hand, the age, sex, and familiarity of the examiner, and the structure of the examiner's questions appear to have fewer negative effects. When relatively small language samples are analyzed, however, these factors may influence the quantity as well as the structural qualities of the child's speech.

A second limitation of the clinical analysis of spontaneous speech samples relates to the quality of the analysis. When research studies on syntactic development are designed, investigators often come up with a rather complete grammatical file for each child, based on the structural regularities in the language sample. In a clinical assessment, this task is not always practical. The size of the sample desired, the training required to learn the techniques, and the time needed to analyze the utterances may be prohibitive.

Methods of Analysis.   The methods of analyzing spontaneous speech in clinical settings have usually focused on selected aspects of language structure. Among these measures are the mean length of utterance and the developmental sentence analysis techniques. In natural settings, an observation and rating approach may be used.

Mean length of utterance (MLU) is obtained from a spontaneous speech sample of fifty consecutive utterances. The examiner counts the number of words or morphemes in each utterance in the sample, totals the count, and divides by fifty to calculate the MLU. For the *developmental sentence analysis* (DSA), the examiner gathers 50 complete sentences from spontaneous speech and analyzes the following grammatical categories: indefinite pronouns and noun modifiers, personal pronouns, main verbs, secondary verbs, negatives, conjunctions, interrogative reversals, and wh– questions (Wiig & Semel, 1984).

Observation and rating of interpersonal verbal interactions in natural settings such as the home or classroom can provide insight into which communication intents are expressed and what forms they take. A checklist may be developed to capture information in those situations (Wiig & Semel, 1984). Figure 6.1 contains selected items from a checklist for some interactive–interpersonal communication acts relevant to children ages 3 to 8 years. Figure 6.2 features types of communications in which preadolescents and adolescents are likely to engage. This checklist may be used to evaluate the relative skills of preadolescents, adolescents, or adults in formulating and carrying out selected communication functions and speech acts.

Each of the communication functions and speech acts featured in the communication checklists is evaluated by observing the speaker, among peers, in

■ FIGURE 6.1 ■   Communications Checklist for School-Age Children

	RITUALIZING	Pre date	During date	Post date	Comments
01	Greets peers and adults spontaneously (e.g., Hi/Hello.).				
	Responds verbally (e.g., Hi/Hello.) to verbal greetings.				
	Responds nonverbally (e.g., gesture/wave) to verbal greetings.				
02	Says farewell to peers and adults spontaneously (e.g., Good-bye.).				
	Responds verbally (e.g., Bye-bye/Good-bye.) to verbal farewells.				
	Responds nonverbally (e.g., gesture) to verbal farewells.				
03	Calls other spontaneously and verbally (e.g., Hi, Sue.) to get attention.				
	Gets the attention of others nonverbally (e.g., gesture/touch).				
04	Responds verbally (e.g., Yes/Hi.) to verbal calls for attention.				
	Responds nonverbally only (e.g., turns/gazes/waves) to verbal calls for attention.				
05	Initiates an introduction of himself/herself spontaneously to strangers (e.g., Hi, I'm Sue.).				
06	Initiates an introduction of two strangers known to him/her spontaneously (e.g., Sue, this is Ann. Ann, meet Sue.).				
07	Responds to verbal introductions initiated by others with name (e.g., I'm Sue.).				
	Introduces two strangers known to him/her when asked by others (e.g., Who is she? *That is Ann.*).				

Source: Elisabeth H. Wiig and Eleanor Semel, *Language Assessment and Intervention for the Learning Disabled* (Columbus, OH: Merrill, 1984), pp. 518 and 519. Reprinted by permission of the publisher.

natural settings. The categories on the school-age checklist relate to the dates the particular speech act was observed. The scoring categories for the adolescent checklist are based on the frequency of appropriate usage of a specific communication act.

The outcome of these assessments of communication skills may assist teachers to identify communication intents and functions and speech acts that are not always formulated appropriately. The assessments may also help teachers to identify the need for basic language and communication training within specific communication functions. Furthermore, this type of assessment may help teachers to identify relative areas of strength in communicative interactions and to assess and compare relative pre- and posttraining skill levels.

INTERVENTIONS

Intervention Approaches

According to Wiig and Semel (1984), there are five intervention and remediation approaches for LD youngsters: process, task-analysis, behavioral, interactive-interpersonal, and the total environmental system. Following is a brief explanation of each approach.

Process Approach. The objectives of this approach to language intervention are to strengthen and normalize processes considered basic to language acquisition and verbal communication. Processes that may be the target of intervention are auditory perception, memory, association, interpretation, and verbal expression. Remediation objectives may be directed toward strengthening language comprehension and use in and across various modalities—auditory, written, nonverbal language.

The psycholinguistic approach, which falls in this category, has the following assumptions:

— That the various psycholinguistic abilities can be identified and measured
— That development of these abilities is necessary for academic achievement in reading, writing, and other school tasks
— That academic performances will improve as a result of psycholinguistic training

(See the studies by Logan and Colarusso and by Sewell et al. later in this chapter that relate to this approach.)

Johnson and Myklebust (1967), influenced by work with adult aphasics, introduced neurosensory strategies and procedures to remediate language-learning disabilities of children. The researchers postulated that a learning disability may be apparent in auditory language, reading, written language, arithmetic, and nonverbal language and communication; they also outlined specific remediation

■ FIGURE 6.2 ■   Communications Checklist for Adolescents and Preadolescents

Communication Skills Checklist

Name _____ Birth Date _____ Sex _____

Address _____

Classroom _____ Teacher _____ Date _____

Other Information _____

_____

COMMUNICATION ACTS	Never	Seldom	Sometimes	Often	Always	QUALITY*
Ritualizing						
1. Greets others appropriately	1	2	3	4	5	
2. Introduces him/herself appropriately	1	2	3	4	5	
3. Introduces people to each other appropriately	1	2	3	4	5	
4. Greets others appropriately when telephoning	1	2	3	4	5	
5. Introduces him/herself appropriately when telephoning	1	2	3	4	5	
6. Asks for persons appropriately when telephoning	1	2	3	4	5	
7. Says farewell appropriately	1	2	3	4	5	
8. Asks others to repeat appropriately	1	2	3	4	5	
9. Gives name (first and last) on request	1	2	3	4	5	
10. Gives address (number, street, town, etc.) on request	1	2	3	4	5	
11. Gives telephone number on request	1	2	3	4	5	
Informing						
1. Asks others appropriately for name	1	2	3	4	5	
2. Asks others appropriately for address	1	2	3	4	5	
3. Asks others appropriately for telephone number	1	2	3	4	5	
4. Asks others appropriately for the location of belongings and necessities	1	2	3	4	5	
5. Asks others appropriately for the location of events	1	2	3	4	5	
6. Responds appropriately to requests for the location of events	1	2	3	4	5	
7. Asks others appropriately for the time of events	1	2	3	4	5	
8. Responds appropriately to requests for the time of events	1	2	3	4	5	
9. Asks others appropriately for preferences or wants	1	2	3	4	5	
10. Responds appropriately to requests for preferences or wants	1	2	3	4	5	
11. Tells others realistically about abilities	1	2	3	4	5	
12. Tells realistically about the levels of various abilities	1	2	3	4	5	
13. Asks appropriately for information by telephone	1	2	3	4	5	
14. Asks appropriately for permission to leave messages	1	2	3	4	5	
15. Tells appropriately who a message is for	1	2	3	4	5	
16. Leaves appropriately expressed messages	1	2	3	4	5	

Note: Quality of speech acts may be rated as informal, formal, direct, or indirect.

COMMUNICATION ACTS	Never	Seldom	Sometimes	Often	Always	QUALITY
Controlling						
1. Suggests places for meetings appropriately	1	2	3	4	5	
2. Suggests times for meetings appropriately	1	2	3	4	5	
3. Asks appropriately for permission	1	2	3	4	5	
4. Asks appropriately for reasons	1	2	3	4	5	
5. Tells reasons appropriately	1	2	3	4	5	
6. Asks appropriately for favors	1	2	3	4	5	
7. Responds appropriately to requests for favors:						
a. Accepts and carries out	1	2	3	4	5	
b. Evades or delays	1	2	3	4	5	
c. Rejects	1	2	3	4	5	
8. Offers assistance appropriately	1	2	3	4	5	
9. Makes complaints appropriately	1	2	3	4	5	
10. Responds to complaints appropriately:						
a. Accepts blame and suggests action	1	2	3	4	5	
b. Evades or refers	1	2	3	4	5	
c. Rejects blame	1	2	3	4	5	
11. Asks for intentions appropriately	1	2	3	4	5	
12. Responds appropriately to requests for intentions	1	2	3	4	5	
13. Asks to discontinue actions appropriately	1	2	3	4	5	
14. Asks appropriately for terms of contract:						
a. Pay	1	2	3	4	5	
b. Work hours	1	2	3	4	5	
c. Vacations, etc.	1	2	3	4	5	
d. Other	1	2	3	4	5	
15. Asks appropriately for changes in contractual terms:						
a. Pay	1	2	3	4	5	
b. Work hours	1	2	3	4	5	
c. Vacations, etc.	1	2	3	4	5	
d. Other	1	2	3	4	5	
Feelings						
1. Expresses appreciation appropriately	1	2	3	4	5	
2. Apologizes appropriately	1	2	3	4	5	
3. Expresses agreement appropriately	1	2	3	4	5	
4. Expresses disagreement appropriately	1	2	3	4	5	
5. Expresses support appropriately	1	2	3	4	5	
6. Compliments appropriately	1	2	3	4	5	
7. Expresses affection appropriately	1	2	3	4	5	
8. Expresses positive feelings and attitudes appropriately	1	2	3	4	5	
9. Expresses negative feelings and attitudes appropriately	1	2	3	4	5	

Source: Elisabeth H. Wiig and Eleanor Semel, *Language Assessment and Intervention for the Learning Disabled* (Columbus, OH: Merrill, 1984), pp. 518 and 519. Reprinted by permission of the publisher.

procedures that correspond to those disabilities. According to them, remediation progresses from receptive to expressive language training. (See Chapter 1 for more material on their work.)

Task-Analysis Approach.   The objectives of task analysis are to increase the complexity of meaning (semantics), structure (morphology and syntax), or function (pragmatics) of children's language. There are several programs of this type, one of which is the *Peabody Language Development Kit* (Dunn & Smith, 1965). Available for various levels, these programs are intended to develop word meanings and language concepts for labeling and to strengthen logical thinking with acquired concepts.

Another example, the *Developmental Syntax Program* (Coughran & Liles, 1974), provides programmed procedures for establishing word formation rules. Programming includes three phases: ear training, production and carry-over, and generalization to a different context. A third program of this type, the *Clinical Language Intervention Program* (Semel & Wiig, 1982), is designed to facilitate the use of semantic–syntactic structures, memory, and communication functions and to provide opportunities for maintenance and generalization of the acquired skills.

Behavioral Approach.   The objectives of the behavioral approach to language remediation are to modify and change overt language and communication behaviors. Those modifications are generally brought about by applying contingency management principles. A language program based on these principles that was popular some years ago is the "Monterey Program" (Gray & Ryan, 1973). The researchers arranged approaches to increase and structure the spontaneous speech of youngsters with word-finding problems, and to decrease the unacceptable and maladaptive verbal and nonverbal communication patterns that are often evident in the interpersonal interactions of language-learning disabled children.

Interactive–Interpersonal Approach.   The general objectives of the interactive–interpersonal approach are to strengthen pragmatic abilities and develop communicative competencies. A specific objective may be to enhance the interpretation of contextual cues that modify the meanings of verbal expressions in such requests as "Can you open the door?" Other objectives may be to improve children's role-taking and role-playing abilities, to develop nonverbal social perception, and to generally increase the range of verbal and nonverbal communication styles available for interpersonal interactions. An example of this type is *The ACCEPTS Program* (A Curriculum for Children's Effective Peer and Teacher Skills) (Walker et al., 1983), a curriculum for teaching peer-to-peer social skills to handicapped and nonhandicapped children in grades K through 6. (There is more detail on this program in Chapter 11.)

Total Environmental System Approach.   The objectives of this approach to language intervention are to set up environmental events and situations, and thus encourage varied and frequent language and communication experiences from which communication strategies can be acquired. The environmental system approach would seek to strengthen functional communication strategies, develop insights into compensatory and coping strategies, and develop awareness of the dynamics of interpersonal interactions. The ultimate objective of these holistic approaches would be to establish communicative competence for life in order to support the individual's potential for vocational or professional achievement and adjustment.

In the holistic approach, "no single dimension of language is considered to be more or less significant as a component of the total linguistic system" (Leigh, 1980, p. 63). Interventionists' use of this approach is reinforced by the reasoning that language is learned in the natural environment, rather than acquired through a variety of scheduled interventions that set out to artificially create this process. Advocates of the holistic approach arrange permissive linguistic environments where children are encouraged to communicate regardless of structure or style. "A whole language approach is especially appropriate for children who have effectively mastered the basic linguistic rules and structures of oral expression and comprehension, yet are unable to proficiently use written language" (Leigh, 1980, p. 65).

Intervention Principles

Semantics and Syntax.   Observations of normal developmental patterns in acquiring word meanings and of the characteristics of semantic deficits among LD youth suggest principles for intervention, a few of which are summarized here (Wiig & Semel, 1984).

Principle 1.   Unfamiliar or unestablished words, concepts, or relational terms should be introduced in sequences that follow normal developmental patterns and sequences.

Principle 2.   Unfamiliar words, concepts, and relationships should be introduced in their most familiar semantic and referential contexts (for example, "The balloon goes up"). The range of application of the words and concepts should then be extended to include less typical semantic and referential contexts.

Principle 3.   Semantically related words and concepts should be taught in sequences that introduce words with features that are more general or semantically less complex before words with features that are more specific or semantically more complex ("big"/"tall"/"wide" and "give"/"pay"/"trade").

Principle 4.   Antonyms should be introduced in sequences in which the unexpected member that denotes a change from the most common use is presented first (for example, "Turn the light off"). The expected opposite should be presented next ("Turn the light on").

Principle 5.   Sentences used to feature unfamiliar or unestablished words, concepts, and relationships should be rather short and simple.

Principle 6.   Materials and methods should feature real life or pictorial referents and relationships wherever possible.

Principle 7.   Unfamiliar or unestablished words, concepts, and relationships should be introduced in several familiar, typical, but different contexts. Pictorial representations of meaning should be featured along with the spoken labels. Features providing verbal definitions and elaboration of meaning should be given for the concepts in each of the different contexts.

Principle 8.   The range of application of new concepts should be extended to less familiar and typical and more specific semantically complex and abstract semantic contexts in a number of examples. A variety of task formats should be established to increase the opportunities to generalize.

Principle 9.   Descriptive communication tasks and role-playing activities should be scheduled to extend the range of application and control of newly established words, concepts, and relationships.

Principle 10.   Contexts with minimal redundancy and highly controlled vocabulary may be arranged to extend the range of application and control of specific concepts to subjects such as mathematics and the sciences.

Morphology and Syntax.   Wiig and Semel also set forth general clinical principles for selecting and designing materials for working on a child's knowledge and use of morphology and syntax (Wiig & Semel, 1984).

Principle 1.   Unfamiliar word and sentence formation rules should be introduced and sequenced according to normal developmental sequences.

Principle 2.   Familiar words should be featured in phrases, clauses, and sentences that are used for interventions.

Principle 3.   Sentence length—number of words—should be kept to a minimum; it should depend on the syntactic complexity of the units for which the rules apply.

Principle 4.   Pictorial or printed representations of words, phrases, or clauses should be given for all spoken sentences. Pictures of referents for content words with referential meaning may be shown in association with printed representations of nonreferential or function words.

Principle 5.   Rules for unfamiliar word or sentence formation should be introduced in several examples.

Principle 6.   Knowledge of rules for word or sentence formation should be established first in recognition and comprehension tasks.

Principle 7.   Knowledge and control of rules for word and sentence formation should be established first with highly familiar word choices, and should then be extended to contexts with less familiar vocabulary or with unfamiliar concepts.

Principle 8.   Knowledge and use of rules for word and sentence formation should be tested in a number of examples that feature vocabulary not previously used.

Verbal Communication.   The following principles extend the guidelines developed by Wiig and Semel to apply them to the area of enhancing verbal communication:

Principle 1.   Stress the importance of verbal communications.

Principle 2.   Study individuals who are skilled communicators and note their characteristics.

Principle 3.   Study not only the verbal traits of gifted communicators, but also their nonverbal communicating skills.

Principle 4.   Provide numerous opportunities for students to communicate with others.

Principle 5.   Arrange various types of situations in which students can communicate with a variety of people about several topics.

Principle 6.   Initially schedule interactions with individuals who will be helpful and generally reinforcing to students.

Principle 7.   Schedule debriefing sessions following planned interactions to inform students about the quality of their performances.

Principle 8.   Arrange for students to observe good conversationalists in action in a variety of situations.

Principle 9.   Demand several questions, statements, and replies from students in their daily routines.

Principle 10.   Provide large doses of individualized feedback and reinforcement to students with respect to their conversational abilities.

Program Evaluations

It is puzzling that so few intervention studies have been conducted with LD or other remedial youngsters for, as noted earlier, language may be the cornerstone to most academic and social endeavors. This state of affairs is echoed by Nye, Foster, and Seaman, who state:

> The vast majority of the research literature has focused on the acquisition and characteristics of certain language skills in children with language disorders, but there has been little systematic investigation of the effectiveness of the remediation of these characteristics. [1987, p. 348]

It should be added that the great majority of the studies available on the effects of interventions with LD children were undertaken with preschool youngsters or those in the primary grades.

■ **COMMENTARY** ■   Another perplexing matter is that so few intervention studies with LD youngsters
are published in journals, such as the *Journal of Learning Disabilities,* that relate specifically to
those individuals. Of the forty studies included in the Nye, Foster, and Seaman meta-analysis of
intervention studies with language/language disabled youngsters, only ten were published in
LD-type journals. And of those, only four were with youngsters of intermediate age or older.

Brief reviews of two of these intervention studies with LD youngsters follow: Logan and Colarusso (1978) studied the effectiveness of two programs developed from the ITPA model—the Minskoff, Wiseman, and Minskoff (1972) and GOAL programs—which were designed to develop general language abilities of kindergarten youngsters in lower socioeconomic areas. Youngsters were assigned to one or the other treatment group or to a control situation and were administered several tests to assess various language abilities. The Minskoff, Wiseman, and Minskoff (MWM) materials are intended to provide the basis for both developmental and remedial strategies for enhancing psycholinguistic skills. The GOAL materials are designed to promote language-processing skills. The results of the Logan and Colarusso study indicated that both the MWM and GOAL programs were effective in training certain psycholinguistic components, but they were no more influential than a regular kindergarten program in developing other language skills.

Sowell, Parker, Poplin, and Larsen (1979) also investigated the effects of psycholinguistic training on improving psycholinguistic skills. In their research, they used first graders who had low readiness for academic success according to tests and teacher perceptions. The youngsters were assigned to one of two treatments: the MWM program or a traditional first grade curriculum. To measure outcomes, the *MWM Inventory of Language Abilities,* the ITPA, and the *Otis-Lennon Mental Ability Test* (Otis & Lennon, 1967) were administered before and after the treatments. The data showed that the gains were small for students in either treatment, and there was not a significant difference in gains between the groups.

The Nye, Foster, and Seaman meta-analysis of intervention studies with children is summarized in the following paragraphs. Their data showed that the youngsters in experimental groups were moved from the 50th to the 85th percentile as a result of the treatments.

Seven types of treatments were labeled in the reviewed studies: imitation, elicitation, modeling, focused stimulation, general stimulation, comprehension, and psychosocial. There were more interventions of the imitation type than the others, and the most pronounced effects came from modeling interventions.

Nye et al. reported that the interventions focused on seven aspects of language: semantic, syntactic, pragmatic, auditory–visual perception, language achievement, academic achievement, and psychosocial. The great majority of the studies dealt with syntactic elements.

Outcome measures of five types were scheduled to determine the effects of the various interventions: rating scales, psychological tests, achievement tests, language tests, and language samples. Language tests were selected the most often, but the language samples appeared to be the most sensitive to performance changes.

THE ROLE OF MICROCOMPUTERS IN LANGUAGE DISORDERS

This section notes the current applications of the microcomputer in the area of communication disorders. It also provides some guidelines for using microcomputers in intervention approaches, as well as a review of potential uses in the area of language development.

Current Applications

Recordkeeping. The microcomputer, according to Goldman and Dahle (1985), is a valuable tool for generating reports and keeping records and is useful for scheduling appointments and monitoring clients' progress. Clinicians can use computers to catalog tests, therapy materials, and professional libraries; computers can also be used to track attendance, help develop IEP's, and monitor student progress.

Word Processing. Word processing provides an efficient way to write clinical reports. Some of them can be generated from stored prototypes—that is, typical objectives, interventions, standards, and other matters could be written into a program and coded for easy access by clinicians. Possible advantages of this scheme would be that clinicians would write more complete and detailed reports. A possible, and obvious, disadvantage would be that the descriptions and recommendations would be too standardized and not individualized.

Assessment. Computers can be used to score tests, provide information for test interpretation, and develop new language tests or to adapt some existing ones. Goldman and Dahle believe computers could be particularly useful when measuring receptive language abilities. A variety of stimuli—text, graphics, or synthesized speech—could be presented on the computer. Students could respond to these presentations by simply typing letters or numerals, moving a cursor with a key or mouse, or actually typing rather complex responses.

Training and Communication. The advent of inexpensive personal computers, modems, and communications programs (for example, BITNET) that are relatively simple to run could contribute significantly to training programs. The supervisor of speech therapists could, from an office or laboratory at the university, send out assignments to therapists in training throughout a city or state, and the trainees could reply via the communications linkage. Similarly, therapists, special and regular teachers, administrators, and others throughout a district or wider area could communicate with one another by computer on a variety of topics. They could confer on particular cases, send abstracts of recent investigations to one another, alert their colleagues about upcoming meetings or conferences, or respond to requests. In many situations, these computerized arrangements would save considerable time and be much more efficient than the frustrating games of telephone tag.

Research.   Microcomputers and accompanying software offer numerous possibilities for research on a wide variety of language and communication topics. When computers are linked with other types of instrumentation such as video or audio tape recorders, slide or filmstrip projectors, or other apparatus, a variety of interventions are possible. With this wide range of presentation modes, plus the variety of ways in which pupils can respond to these stimuli, any number of sophisticated studies of expressive or receptive language could be arranged. Initially, such studies could be in the form of comparisons—that is, pupils of different types could be exposed to the same situation—or different stimuli could be presented to the same students. Following such status studies, interventions could be arranged in order to influence certain of the behaviors.

Computer-Assisted Instruction.   Larson and Steiner (1985) discussed six activities for which microcomputers could enhance language instruction.

Drill and practice.   A number of new behaviors are learned best when a great deal of practice is scheduled. For example, the clinician might introduce the proper subcomponent of "Micro-LADS" to assist children to recognize present progressive, past, and future tenses of regular verbs.

Simulation.   Simulation activities are useful when real-life situations are either too expensive or dangerous to set up. An example simulation would be for youngsters to practice certain language behaviors related to the "lemonade industry" by working with the microcomputer-based program, "Sell Lemonade."

Tutorials.   Tutorials are valuable when it is desirable to teach a skill step-by-step, particularly when branching features are provided. An example of a tutorial program is "Prefixes," which progresses through several levels of difficulty to test understanding of those elements.

Instructional games.   Games are particularly useful when developing problem-solving skills. An example is the adventure game "Seastalker," which is intended to develop abilities in note-taking, mapmaking, following directions, recognizing cause-and-effect relationships, generating theories, developing hypothesis-testing abilities, and realizing the importance of behavioral sequences.

Problem-solving activities.   Programs using problem solving are often beneficial when instructing individuals to subdivide tasks into steps and to experiment with different patterns of information. An example program is "The Factory," in which users are presented with problems to solve in gamelike situations.

Exploration and discovery.   Programs of exploration and discovery create situations in which pupils can pose questions, make decisions, and solve problems. An example of such a program is LOGO, a procedure-oriented language that incorporates Piagetian theory and concepts from artificial intelligence.

Guidelines for Microcomputer Applications in Language Interventions

Larson and Steiner (1985) offer a number of guidelines for speech and language professionals to consider as they contemplate whether or not to rely on microcomputers in language intervention. Their suggestions, along with those of others, include the following:

1. Do not use microcomputers for language intervention unless it is advantageous to do so. Many activities can be accomplished "the old-fashioned way."

2. Do not involve microcomputer technology in language intervention programs to the exclusion of other, "low tech" procedures, some of which are quite recent.

3. Do not conceive of microcomputers as substitutes for human clinicians, for they cannot be programmed to make all the judgments and decisions that speech and language professionals must make.

4. Consider the principle of scaffolding when applying microcomputer technology to clients who have language disorders; the use of such devices may permit individuals to perform tasks that are otherwise impossible for them.

5. Incorporate microcomputer technology in language intervention within the context of functional communication. After skills have been taught by the computer, they must be substantiated later in the natural environment.

6. Affiliate with a group of other speech and language professionals who are using microcomputers in order to share ideas and resources on how to involve current software for assessment, interventions, and other purposes.

7. Assign an individual or small group the task of seeking out new advances in microcomputer and affiliated technologies. Encourage trainees to try out new hardware and software and peripherals to determine the appropriateness for speech and language development. If a new or different program or procedure is identified, arrange a series of organized in-service programs to instruct others on its use.

Emerging Applications

Most current applications in the area of communication disorders are self-contained within the microcomputer. However, a number of experts (such as Goldman & Dahle, 1985) have claimed that the usefulness of microcomputers in the area of communication disorders can be greatly enhanced through interfaces with other electronic instruments. They have indicated that digital/analog converters make it possible to interface many electronic devices with microcomputers.

Interactive Video.   The use of interactive video is particularly appealing when there is a need for program branching, rapid access, and visual motion sequences. Of major significance is the potential use of interactive video for creating simulated situations. If the instructor desired to teach pragmatic concepts, video could present simulations of the classroom, stores, home, playground, and other environments. The pupils' task, when viewing those situations, would be to select appropriate or possible responses from an array or to construct their own reactions to them.

Videotape Systems.   The integration of videotape players and microcomputers is useful in several areas. For example, test items could be presented audiovisually, thus incorporating the type of receptive assessment of the PPVT. The formats of other standardized tests could also be adapted to electronic collaborations. With such arrangements, test items could be presented audiovisually in mono or stereo in a standard order, while data could be obtained on the correctness of responses and the response latencies and could be stored and available for future analysis.

Videodisk Systems.   The videodisk can combine and randomly access video, audio, and computer data in both analog and digital form; the system is ideal for programs that require complicated branching. According to Goldman and Dahle (1985), the interactive videodisk system holds great promise for developing language intervention programs. "On a single side of one disk, thousands of still and motion picture sequences with accompanying speech can be stored and retrieved as needed. This capability opens the way for the development of innovative techniques for presenting and teaching language concepts" (Goldman & Dahle, 1985, p. 19). Among the examples of those uses that come to mind are teaching action verb concepts, expanding vocabulary, sequencing events, recognizing correctness of grammar, responding to questions, categorizing words and events, and constructing sentences.

_____ COMMENTS AND DISCUSSION POINTS _____

Based on the research and information regarding language assessment and development presented in this chapter, some comments for teachers and clinicians who work with LD youngsters are offered.

- Be aware of the tremendous impact that language has on the quality of life.
- Realize how inept many LD youth are when it comes to using language, and how these many and varied deficits influence their lives.

- Evaluate the language abilities of LD pupils frequently and in a number of settings. Study their abilities to use language in the classroom, playground, lunchroom, and by all means, in the home.

- Learn to observe and analyze the language behaviors of LD youth in these situations on a functional and informal basis. Don't rely solely on canned, standardized tests to evaluate language and its development. Be creative; design assessments to fit the pupils, their needs, and their circumstances.

- Instruct language in places where language is used. There are numerous real-life settings in which to develop language: in classrooms, in homes, and throughout the community. Attack the problems directly. Don't take LD youngsters to special chambers and assess or treat their language problems by pulling out cards, pictures, or engaging them in simpleminded games.

- Instruct language in every subject, not merely the language development hour. Help children acquire aspects of language during math periods, reading, spelling, writing, music, social studies, and physical education.

- Everyone who relates to LD youth should instruct language. This responsibility should not be the special province of speech therapists or specialists in communication disorders. Classroom teachers, parents, and all others should take on their share of the instructional burden.

- Be sensitive to the LD youngsters' abilities to receive language, as well as to their expressive performances. Occasionally, tap their abilities to listen, to follow directions, and to give other signals to indicate they are tuned in and understand.

- Be aware of the difficulties LD youngsters have in communicating nonverbally. Many of them are just as inept with these skills as they are with their verbal communications. Quite a number of LD youth have trouble "reading" others' gestures and cues, and not a few of them are unable to transmit proper nonverbal signals.

- Speech and language professionals should be particularly careful not to dazzle the unenlightened—that is, classroom teachers and parents—with their jargon. The language of the speech-, language-, and hearing- field is complex. Speech and language professionals should clearly inform individuals who are in frequent contact with LD children about the fundamental truths of language instruction.

- When communication is occurring naturally in classrooms, let it happen. Don't interrupt because it is 10:00 o'clock and time for reading. (Some time ago I was visiting a class for LD youngsters as the children were seated on the floor having a pleasant discussion with their teacher. In walked a speech therapist, led one of the pupils from the classroom to her chamber, and there, presumably, administered language therapy.)

- Use the microcomputer and any other available device to improve language features; but don't rely on medium- or high-tech aids simply to be fashionable. There are times when microcomputers are used to teach behaviors that could be better instructed by more common, less sophisticated means.

- Spend more time investigating the *effects* of various treatments on aspects of language. We don't need any more studies that compare the performance of LD youngsters with non-LD pupils on some language attribute. It's safe to say that, regardless of the feature being investigated, LD pupils as a group will come out on the short end. What we do need to know is how to change the behaviors of LD youngsters.

REFERENCES

American Speech–Language–Hearing Association. (1976). *Comprehensive assessment and service (CASE) information system.* Washington, D.C.

Blankenship, C., & Lovitt, T.C. (1976). Story problems: Merely confusing or downright befuddling. *Journal for Research in Mathematics Education, 7,* 290–298.

Bloom, L., & Lahey, M. (1978). *Language development and language disorders.* New York: John Wiley & Sons.

Boehm, A.E. (1970). *Boehm test of basic concepts.* New York: Psychological Corporation.

Boucher, C.R. (1984). Pragmatics: The verbal language of learning disabled and nondisabled boys. *Learning Disability Quarterly, 7,* 271–286.

Bruno, R.M.; Johnson, J.M.; & Simon, S. (1987). Perception of humor by regular class students and students with learning disabilities or mild mental retardation. *Journal of Learning Disabilities, 20,* 568–570.

Bryan, T.H.; Donahue, M.; & Pearl, R. (1981). Learning disabled children's peer interactions during a small-group problem-solving task. *Learning Disability Quarterly, 4*(1), 13–22.

Carrow, E. (1974). *Carrow elicited language inventory.* Austin, TX: Learning Concepts.

Catts, H.W. (1986). Speech production/phonological deficits in reading-disordered children. *Journal of Learning Disabilities, 18,* 504–508.

Chalfant, J.C., & Scheffelin, M.A. (1969). Central processing dysfunctions in children: A review of research. *NINDS Monograph No. 9.* Bethesda, MD: U.S. Department of Health, Education, and Welfare.

Coughran, L., & Liles, B.Z. (1974). *Developmental syntax program.* Austin, TX: Learning Concepts.

Donohue, M.; Pearl, R.; & Bryan, T. (1980). Learning disabled children's conversational competence: Responses to inadequate messages. *Applied Psycholinguistics, 1,* 387–404.

Donohue, M.; Pearl, R.; & Bryan, T. (1982). Learning disabled children's syntactic proficiency on a communicative task. *Journal of Speech and Hearing Disorders, 47,* 397–403.

Dunn, L.M., & Dunn, L. (1981). *Peabody picture vocabulary test—revised.* Circle Pines, MN: American Guidance Service.

Dunn, L.M., & Smith, J.O. (1965). *Peabody language development kit—level 1.* Circle Pines, MN: American Guidance Service.

Fantasia, K. (1981). An investigation of formal analysis as an intervention to improve word problem computation for learning disabled children. Unpublished doctoral dissertation, University of Washington, Seattle.

French, J.W. (1951). The description of aptitude and achievement tests in terms of rotational factors. *Psychometric Monographs, No. 5.* Chicago: The University of Chicago Press.

Goldman, R.; Fristoe, M.; & Woodcock, R.W. (1976). *Goldman-Fristoe-Woodcock auditory skills test battery*. Circle Pines, MN: American Guidance Service.

Goldman, R., & Dahle, A. (1985). Current and emerging applications of microcomputer technology in communication disorders. *Topics in Language Disorders, 6*(1), 11–26.

Gray, B., & Ryan, B. (1973). *A language program for the nonlanguage child*. Champaign, IL: Research Press.

Horton, S.V., & Lovitt, T.C. (1983). Leaving no stone unturned: An investigation of students' comprehension of idiomatic expressions, grades K–12 and special education. Unpublished manuscript, University of Washington, Seattle.

Idol-Maestas, L. (1980). Oral language responses of children with reading difficulties. *Journal of Speech Education, 14*, 386–404.

Johnson, D.J., & Myklebust, H.R. (1967). *Learning disabilities: Educational principles and practices*. New York: Grune & Stratton.

Kavale, K. (1981). The relationship between auditory perceptual skills and reading ability: A meta-analysis. *Journal of Learning Disabilities, 14*, 539–546.

Kirk, S.A.; McCarthy, J.; & Kirk, W.E. (1968). *Illinois test of psycholinguistic abilities*. Urbana, IL: University of Illinois Press.

Knight-Arest, I. (1984). Communicative effectiveness of learning disabled and normally achieving 10- to 13-year-old boys. *Learning Disability Quarterly, 7*, 237–245.

Larson, V.L., & Steiner, S. (1985). Language intervention using microcomputers. *Topics in Learning Disabilities, 6*(1), 41–55.

Lee, L.L. (1971). *Northwestern syntax screening text*. Evanston, IL: Northwestern University Press.

———. (1974). *Developmental sentence analysis*. Evanston, IL: Northwestern University Press.

Leigh, J.E. (1980). Whole language approaches: Premises and possibilities. *Learning Disability Quarterly, 3*, 62–69.

Liles, B.Z.; Shulman, M.D.; & Bartlett, S. (1977). Judgments of grammaticality by normal and language-disordered children. *Journal of Speech and Hearing Disorders, 42*, 199–209.

Logan, R., & Colarusso, R. (1978). The effectiveness of the MWM and GOAL programs in developing general language abilities. *Learning Disability Quarterly, 1*, 33–38.

Lovitt, T.C., & Smith, J.O. (1972). An analysis of the effects of instructions on an individual's verbal behavior. *Exceptional Children, 38*, 685–693.

Minskoff, E.; Wiseman, D.E.; & Minskoff, J.G. (1972). *The MWM program for developing language abilities*. Ridgefield, NJ: Educational Performance Associates.

Meyers, P.I., & Hammill, D.D. (1982). *Learning disabilities: Basic concepts, assessment practices, and instructional strategies*. Austin, TX: PRO-ED.

Newcomer, P.L., & Hammill, D.D. (1982). *Test of Language Development*. Austin, TX: PRO-ED.

Nye, C.; Foster, S.H.; & Seaman, D. (1987). Effectiveness of language intervention with the language/learning disabled. *Journal of Speech and Hearing Disorders, 52*, 348–357.

Otis, A.S., & Lennon, R.T. (1967). *Otis-Lennon mental ability test,* primary II. New York: Harcourt, Brace & World.

Owens, R.E. (1984). *Language development: An introduction*. Columbus, OH: Merrill.

Rosenthal, R.; Hall, J.; Archer, D.; diMatteo, M.; & Rogers, P. (1979). *Profile of nonverbal sensitivity*. New York: Irvington Publishing Inc.

Seidenberg, P.L. (1984). Referential communicative effectiveness of learning disabled children. Paper presented at the conference of the Northeastern Educational Research Association, Ellenville, NY.

Semel, E.M., & Wiig, E.H. (1980). *Clinical evaluation of language functions*, Columbus, OH: Merrill.

Semel, E.M., & Wiig, E.H. (1982). *Clinical language intervention program*. Columbus, OH: Merrill.

Shewan, C.M. (1986). Characteristics of clinical services provided by ASHA members. *ASHA*, January, 29.

Snyder, L.S. (1984). Developmental language disorders: Elementary school age. In A. Holland (Ed.), *Language Disorders in Children*. San Diego: College-Hill Press.

Sowell, V.; Parker, R.; Poplin, M.; & Larsen, S. (1979). The effects of psycholinguistic training on improving psycholinguistic skills. *Learning Disability Quarterly, 2*, 69–77.

Stahl, S.A., & Erickson, L.G. (1986). The performance of third grade learning disabled boys on tasks at different levels of language: A model-based exploration. *Journal of Learning Disabilities, 19*, 285–290.

Strand, K.E. (1982). The relation of metamemory to memory performance in normal and language-impaired children: A developmental study. Unpublished doctoral dissertation, Boston University.

Walker, H.M.; McConnell, S.; Holmes, D.; Todis, B.; Walker, J.; & Golden, N. (1983). *The ACCEPTS program*. Austin, TX: PRO-ED.

Warden, D.A. (1976). The influence of context on children's use of identifying expressions and references. *British Journal of Psychology, 67*, 101–112.

Wiig, E.H. (1982). *Let's talk inventory for adolescents*. Columbus, OH: Merrill.

Wiig, E.H., & Roach, M.A. (1975). Immediate recall of semantically varied "sentences" by learning disabled adolescents. *Perceptual and Motor Skills, 40*, 119–125.

Wiig, E.H., & Semel, E. (1975). Productive language abilities in learning disabled adolescents. *Journal of Learning Disabilities, 8*, 578–586.

Wiig, E.H., & Semel, E. (1976). *Language disabilities in children and adolescents*. Columbus, OH: Merrill.

Wiig, E.H., & Semel, E. (1984). *Language assessment and intervention for the learning disabled child,* 2nd Ed. Columbus, OH: Merrill.

Wolf, M. (1979). The relationship of disorders of word-finding and reading in children and aphasics. Doctoral dissertation, Harvard University Graduate School of Education, Cambridge, MA.

Chapter 7

A Young Girl Reading by Jean-Honore Fragonard (*c.* 1776). Courtesy of National Gallery of Art, Washington, gift of Mrs. Mellon Bruce in memory of her father, Andrew W. Mellon.

READING

MAIN IDEAS

- Foundations for instructing reading that include emphasis on prerequisites for reading, general approaches for reading instruction, strategies for developing such skills as decoding, vocabulary, and comprehension

- Characteristics of remedial readers in general and pertaining to several factors: physical, psychological, socioeconomic, educational, and various combinations

- Characteristics of LD readers in specific areas that include oral reading, short-term memory, and comprehension

- Assessment of reading abilities that includes formal and informal assessment

- Special remedial approaches: Fernald; Gillingham and Stillman; Hegge, Kirk, and Kirk; rebus; programmed reading; neurological impress; Distar; applied behavior analysis; and microcomputer programs

OVERVIEW

Reading, along with language, is significantly related to learning disabilities. Indeed, the inability to read and learning disabilities are synonymous to many educators. Whether or not that is true, it is important to know about the reading process in order to understand the nature of learning disabilities. This chapter contains a fair amount of preliminary material about reading generally before offering information on disabled readers.

The first section of the chapter presents a general overview of the instruction of reading. The second section, which pertains to remedial readers, includes comments on some reasons for failure to read. Section three discusses some characteristics of disabled readers, and section four, on assessment, presents an overview of some formal and informal tests. The fifth section contains brief discussions of nine reading techniques designed for LD or other remedial youngsters. At the end of the chapter are comments about strategies for teaching children to read.

——— DEVELOPMENTAL FRAMEWORK FOR READING ———

This section discusses reading readiness, outlines methods for teaching reading, and describes strategies for developing skills in decoding, vocabulary and comprehension. The section includes representative studies with LD students.

Prerequisites for Learning to Read

Reading readiness is an extremely important concept in American education. Most educators maintain that unless a child is ready to read, that child will not learn to read. Many argue that the best time for readiness is between the ages of five and six.

Over the years, however, experts have disagreed as to which elements constituted readiness for reading. Some maintained that readiness had to do with visual or auditory perception. Others argued that it was the ability to name letters of the alphabet, to know which sounds they generally make, to hear letter sounds, and to identify the letters that correspond to those sounds. Recently, some researchers have posited different ideas on what is meant by reading readiness.

Before offering those new opinions, however, a few studies are cited that dealt with perceptual or cognitive skills that allegedly indicated reading readiness. In a study with kindergartners, Stevenson, Parker, Wilkinson, Hegion, and Fish (1976) learned that visual tasks such as matching, remembering, and copying picture stimuli did not correlate highly with reading. They discovered, instead, that four verbal tasks were related to reading:

- *Naming letters:* The child names uppercase letters and matches letters.
- *Visual-auditory associations:* The child indicates which of several possible responses spoken by the examiner was the correct match to a visual stimulus.
- *Reversals:* The child selects a match for a two- or three-letter combination such as "nu" presented in correct and reversed orders: "un," "un," "nu," "un."
- *Categorization:* The child produces class names for groups of three words.

According to Richek (1977–1978), the ability to recognize letters was a general skill that predicted success among kindergartners.

Taylor and Taylor (1983) criticized current practices for developing readiness after they observed that it was not unusual for some children in the first grade to spend the entire year getting ready to read by performing exercises such as circling pictures of animals and drawing lines from one object to another. Arguing that this type of readiness training was less useful than reading instruction itself, they claimed that reading may actually foster readiness skills, rather than the other way around. In a similar vein, Singer and Balow (1981) pointed out that if teachers wanted pupils to learn particular reading skills, they should teach those skills directly rather than expect them to be transferred from other skills that were taught. Stevenson et al. (1976) maintained that the concept of reading readiness should apply mainly to the question of whether a child was old enough to withstand the rigor of formal instruction.

Searfoss and Readence (1985) argued that the following four rather nontraditional features were related to reading readiness.

1. *Print awareness:* Children see adults reading newspapers, magazines, cookbooks, road maps, and job-related material. They also see adults reading for information, pleasure, and relaxation. Many of them become aware that print means something, whether they understand it or not.

2. *Concepts about book print:* Most children learn that books are made up of such features as a title, pages, lines, letters, words, sentences, punctuation marks, and paragraphs. They also learn that books have a beginning, middle, and end; that pages go from top to bottom; and that lines move from left to right.

3. *Story sense:* Children with a well-developed sense of story, when taught to read, have an advantage over those who are not familiar with story structures. Knowing about common patterns often facilitates comprehension. Nurss, Hough, and Goodson (1981), for example, indicated that sequence of events was the story element most easy for children to develop, whereas knowing about main characters, settings, times, and having a sense of the story's feelings and plot were more difficult to achieve.

4. *Oral language:* Oral language has two roles as a foundation for reading instruction. Like reading, oral language is a form of communication. Second, oral language serves as a bridge between the language and experiences children bring to school and those they encounter at school.

■ COMMENTARY ■   When it comes to teaching LD youngsters to read, the implications of these current ideas of reading readiness are important. If accepted, teachers would immerse LD children with print and make certain that they understood the importance and functions of print. Furthermore, teachers would instruct LD youngsters to name the letters of the alphabet and to be conscious of letter sounds and grapheme–phoneme relationships. They would also devote considerable time teaching children to read and to understand what they read and perhaps less time getting youngsters ready to read.

Approaches for Teaching Reading

Some Basic Approaches.   According to Taylor and Taylor (1983), there are two primary approaches and three incidental ones for teaching reading. The former are the look–say and phonics approaches, whereas the latter are the ABC, linguistic, and the language–experience approach.

For the look–say approach, children learn to associate visual patterns of whole words with their meanings. They associate meaning directly to words without analysis of the words, phonetic or otherwise.

In the phonics method, children learn letter–sound relations and sound blends in order to figure out unfamiliar words. Individual sounds are associated with letters; sounds are combined into blends and syllables, which are then merged into words.

When the ABC approach is featured, a child spells a word by naming the letters, then pronounces the word. For example, "see-ai-tee" is *cat*. For the linguistic approach, teachers instruct children in the sounds of letters by using words of the same sounds and spelling patterns; for example, "can," "Dan," "fan," "man," "Nan," "pan," and "van." When using the language-experience approach, teachers have children tell them stories of their favorite activities. The words and passages the children relate form the basis for reading instruction.

Holistic or Skills Orientations.   Currently, educators advocate two plans—the skills view and the holistic plan—for instructing reading. Simply stated, advocates of skills believe that fluent reading is comprised of mastering different behaviors, just as a building is formed by putting bricks together. They reason that fluent reading occurs because of the smooth integration of these separate components.

By contrast, advocates of a holistic view maintain that reading is not learned in bits and pieces, and furthermore, children can become lost in the maze of skills lessons, and lose sight of the complete act of fluent reading. They argue that fragmented, paper-and-pencil skill lessons bear little resemblance to reading natural print.

John Manning, president of the International Reading Association (1985), argued that the emphasis on skills instruction should be seriously questioned. According to him, the amount of skill instruction taking place in the schools is entirely disproportionate to that necessary in learning to read. Many bright children do not need this instruction at all, and many lower ability children do not understand the language used to explain it.

Basal Reading Programs.   Artley (1965) characterized basal reading programs as comprehensive in the sense that they were concerned with all aspects of reading and had three major features—scope, sequence, and organization. *Scope* refers to the range of skills that must be acquired for a child to be a fluent reader, while *sequence* pertains to the order in which those skills are presented. *Organization* means the integration of components in a basal series: books, teachers' manuals, workbooks, audio visual materials, and other software.

Although there is wide variation in the format of the many basal programs, the following composite reflects the organization and content of most series.

Stage 1, the preparation for reading, includes these features: building background information for reading the selection, introducing new vocabulary, motivating children to read the selection, and setting purposes for reading.

Stage 2, guided reading, includes silent reading of the selection, comprehension questions on each unit, and some oral rereading for specific purposes.

Stage 3, postreading skill development and enrichment activities include: comprehension of entire selection, selected oral rereading for specific purposes, decoding skill teaching and practice, other skill development in comprehension, study skills and vocabulary, assessment of skills, reteaching and further practice of skills (if indicated), and enrichment language and other activities to extend story understanding.

Strategies for Developing Basic Skills

Decoding.   *Decoding* simply means the act of saying words; it doesn't necessarily mean that the words are understood, which is *encoding.* But it is safe to say that individuals must initially learn to "say" words, and toward that end, a number of instructional strategies have been advanced. Searfoss and Readence (1985) have provided the following steps for a general decoding strategy:

1. Ignore the mistake or unknown word while reading and continue, particularly if the missing word isn't critical to the overall comprehension.
2. If the lost word is necessary, it may be explained or clarified later in the text.
3. Predict the missing word, based on the context.
4. Reread the sentence in which the missing word is located; see if that clarifies the meaning.

Following are more detailed techniques for decoding words.

Context clues.   Early on, children must learn to rely on the language and meaning of other words to help unlock the pronunciation and meaning of unknown words.

Structural analysis.   Children are taught to break words into syllables and become informed about certain prefixes and suffixes. They are instructed also to combine words to make longer (compound) words. When teaching structural analysis, instruction should begin with children's personal or key words—that is, words already familiar to the child. Furthermore, only reliable generalizations about structure should be taught. Burmeister (1968) suggests the following guidelines for teaching structural analysis:

— Divide words between a prefix and a root or base word: *trans-continental, sub-heading.*
— Divide words between two root or base words: *cow-boy, some-time.*

— Divide words between a suffix and a root or base word: *bright-est, sail-ing.*
— When two vowels are separated by two consonants in longer words, divide between the two consonants: *mag-net, suc-cess.* (Note, however, that *ph, ch, th,* and *sh* are not separated.)
— Divide words that end in a consonant and *le: tri-ple, ma-ple.*

Phonics instruction. Most authors claim that decoding can be helpful if certain phonics generalizations are taught, although according to Frank Smith (1982), phonic strategies cannot be expected to eliminate all the uncertainty when the reader has no idea what the word might be. But if the reader can make use of nonvisual information related both to reading and to the subject matter of the text to reduce alternatives, then phonics analysis can be efficient.

Sorenson (1982) listed 38 phonic generalizations used in five basal reading programs and assessed the reliability of those generalizations. A sample is shown in Table 7–1. Most reading researchers agree that there is no sequence to phonics

■ TABLE 7.1 ■   Reliability of Phonic Generalizations in Teacher's Manuals of Five Basal Reader Series

Generalization	Number of Series	Reliability Percentage
In words in which the vowel is followed by a consonant and final *e*, the long sound of the vowel is usually heard: *mice, lone.*	5	77–87
If two or more consonants fall between two vowels in a word, divide the word between the consonants to make two syllables, with the first vowel being short: *mat-ter, sen-tence.*	5	78–88
If one consonant falls between two vowels in a word, try a long vowel first: *va-por* or *vap-or.* If that sound doesn't suggest a word that makes sense, try using a short sound of the first vowel: *no-vice* or *nov-ice.*	5	24–52
When a single vowel falls between two consonants in a word or syllable, the vowel usually has a short sound: *tap, tin-sel, stop.*	4	66–69
When the letter *r* follows a vowel, it changes the sound the vowel usually stands for: *fir, further, tire, car, for.* Note: In one series, separate generalizations are stated for each *r*-controlled vowel. The individual reliability percentages for that series are:	4	91–93
a. When *i* is followed by *r* (ir)	1	100
b. When *u* is followed by *r* (ur)	1	100
c. When *ire* occurs	1	100
d. When *a* is followed by *r* (ar)	1	74
e. When *o* is followed by *r* (or)	1	50
When *g* comes before *e, i,* or *y* in a word, the *g* stands for the sound of *j: gem, gin, gym.*	3	70–81

Source: N.L. Sorenson, "A Study of the Reliability of Phonic Generalizations in Five Primary-Level Basal Reading Programs," unpublished doctoral dissertation, Arizona State University, Tempe, 1982. Reprinted by permission.

instruction. Searfoss and Readence claimed, however, that some readiness would be useful. They argued that phonics instruction would be facilitated if children knew the letter names, and if they had already acquired certain auditory and visual discrimination abilities.

The process of decoding has been summarized by Taylor and Taylor (1983). According to them, skilled readers seem to use a visual route primarily to find a word's meaning and a phonetic route for unfamiliar or pseudowords. The researchers tried to trace a possible developmental sequence for the several paths to meaning. It was their belief that the foundation for the sequence is laid in the first auditory images children use to recognize spoken words. Later, children learn to read by reading aloud, gathering meaning through the well-practiced auditory channel. Still later, overt vocalization may be omitted, although covert control of the vocal musculature still occurs in the form of subvocalization. At the subvocalization stage, children's articulatory control patterns may complement the auditory images, and the two may gradually replace the sounds heard during the vocalization of the reading-aloud stage. Finally, "The visual path is a route to meaning, the phonetic path a route to remembering" (Taylor and Taylor, 1983, p. 232).

Decoding Studies. Jenkins and Larson (1979) investigated decoding with respect to LD youngsters. They examined the effects of error-correction techniques on oral reading abilities of LD junior high students. For their study, an alternating-treatments design was arranged to obtain data on five procedures: word supply, sentence repeat, end-of-page review, word meaning, and drill. Their results revealed that the drill technique was superior to the other correction procedures in measures of both word recognition and reading in context. Moreover, their analysis showed that the commonly used word-supply condition was the least effective of the five methods.

Rose, McEntire, and Dowdy (1982) also arranged an alternating-treatments design to study the relative effects of two error-correction approaches—word supply and phonic analysis—on oral reading. The students in their research were elementary level LD boys. Their results, contrary to those obtained by Jenkins and Larson, showed that word supply was the superior technique for most students.

Rosenberg (1986) designed a study similar to those of Jenkins and Larson and Rose et al. He too scheduled an alternating-treatments design and explored the relative merits of a number of error-correction procedures on aspects of oral reading. The students in his research were LD adolescents, and three procedures were evaluated: word supply (because of its superiority in the Rose et al. research), drill correction (because of its superiority in the Jenkins and Larson research), and phonic drill-rehearsal (because of demonstrated research and clinical success of the approach). Their data were similar to those of Jenkins and Larson in that drill was found to be more effective than word supply on a measure of isolated error-word identification. Drill was also the superior technique on a measure of oral reading.

Rosenberg concluded from the three studies that the contradictory results from previous studies might be attributed to a mismatch between the intervention goals and the measures used to assess effectiveness. More specifically, he maintained that the results of this set of investigations may

> . . . indicate that oral reading activities that stress speed and fluency may be best served by a rapid correction procedure that does not involve complex strategies (i.e., drill). In contrast, more deliberate and time-consuming procedures may be more appropriate when reading goals involve initial acquisition rather than fluency (i.e., word supply). [Rosenberg, 1986, p. 191]

Another approach researchers and practitioners have scheduled to enhance decoding has been *previewing*—that is, going over the material with pupils before they are expected to read it. A number of studies have investigated variations of this technique. Lovitt (1976), for example, reported that oral reading rates of LD youngsters were improved when material was read to them prior to their reading it orally or when pupils read the material silently before reading it orally. *AB* research designs were arranged in those studies to assess intervention effects: the *A* phase was a baseline during which no previewing was scheduled; during the *B* phase, some type of previewing was arranged.

Rose and Beattie (1986) studied the effects of two forms of previewing with a group of elementary age LD boys. They were concerned about the relative influence of teacher previewing—that is, the teacher reading a passage aloud or playing a tape recording of the teacher's reading of the passage before the pupils read it orally. An alternating-treatments design was employed for this study; following a baseline the two treatments were alternately and randomly scheduled. Results from this investigation showed that whereas both types of previewing improved youngsters' oral reading rates over the baseline phase, the more pronounced effects occurred when the pupils listened to the actual teacher, not a taped version. The improvements in oral reading rates were, however, rather insignificant.

Vocabulary.   Cunningham, Cunningham, and Arthur (1981) are of the opinion that vocabulary is acquired in one of the following ways: through the first-hand experience of interacting directly with the concept to be learned, through the vicarious experience of being indirectly exposed to concepts represented by words, and through the symbolic experience of interacting with a text. They maintain that vocabulary should be taught by relying on strategies that are either contextually or categorically based.

Contextual strategies.   Contextual strategies involve teaching vocabulary in the context of sentences. Brief descriptions of four contextual strategies follow:

❑ *Contextual redefinition:* First, the teacher introduces a new word. Next, he includes the word in a sentence and asks pupils to define it.

- *Preview in context:* The teacher presents new vocabulary in sentences drawn from the materials being used. By questioning and discussion, she assists children in discovering word meanings.

- *Cloze approach:* The teacher deletes every *n*th concept word in a passage and asks pupils to supply the missing words. The teacher then lengthens deletions to every seventh or tenth word and stresses the variety of words that may be used to maintain meaning, or he deletes every *n*th function word.

- *The possible sentence:* The teacher introduces new vocabulary words, which the pupils encounter in reading, along with familiar words. She then asks children to generate statements from the new words and to verify their accuracy as they read.

Categorical strategies.   Categorical strategies relate to words in categories and include the following:

1. *Word fluency:* The teacher and pupils name as many words as they can in a period of time.

2. *List–group–label:* Children identify words that relate to a target word (for example, *white),* categorize these words, and give them labels (such as "school things").

3. *Feature analysis:* Categories are first selected, then words are listed in each. Next, features are identified, and finally, the features that pertain to each word across categories are noted.

4. *Graphic organizer:* The key vocabulary is identified; then words are arranged into a diagram and presented graphically.

5. *Concept attainment strategy:* Students identify and list words in terms of supraordinate, coordinate, and subordinate aspects.

Vocabulary Studies.   Currently, a popular method for teaching vocabulary to youngsters, learning disabled and otherwise, is the "keyword strategy." When this method is scheduled, youngsters are given a word (the keyword) to associate with the word to be learned. Mastropieri and colleagues (Mastropieri, Scruggs, & Levin, 1985) have conducted a number of investigations with LD youth. The results show that when students are given phonetic links that serve as mnemonics for the words to be learned, their performances are enhanced. Furthermore, the data from these investigations have indicated the relative superiority of this technique over other established practices, such as direct instruction. (Chapter 10 provides further information on this approach.)

Condus, Marshall, and Miller (1986) conducted an investigation to replicate the findings of Mastropieri and cohorts and to determine the extent to which the keyword approach could be put in practice by special education teachers in their classrooms. (Heretofore, most of the research on this strategy had been carried out by professional experimenters, working with one child at a time in locations other than their classrooms.) Of the 64 12-year-old LD pupils in the study, half had high vocabulary scores on a pretest and half had low scores. Pupils from both sets were randomly assigned to one of four groups; a different strategy—keyword-image, picture context, sentence-experience context, and control—was used with each group. Tests given at various times following the treatments revealed that immediately following the instruction of vocabulary words, students in all groups were able to recall a high percentage of word meanings. Only the students in the keyword group, however, were able to remember a large number of word meanings for two and eight weeks following instruction. Results showed further that the students with initially low vocabulary scores who were assigned to the keyword method learned more definitions on average than students with high vocabularies assigned to all methods.

Pany, Jenkins, and Schreck have conducted a number of studies on the instruction of vocabulary to both nonhandicapped and LD youngsters of elementary age and offered this motivation for such studies:

> To date, relatively few training experiments have investigated either the absolute or the relative effects of various vocabulary teaching procedures. Further, no investigations have been published which demonstrate that teaching vocabulary to students affects their reading comprehension. [1982, p. 203]

These researchers conducted three related experiments to assess the effects of vocabulary instruction on word knowledge and reading comprehension. The three treatments varied in the amount of direct instruction—meanings from context, meanings given, and meanings practiced—and included a control group. All students participated in every condition. In the first study, students were average fourth graders, in the second and third experiments pupils were learning disabled and remedial readers of about the same age.

Results of the first two studies revealed that the treatments were differentially effective in teaching synonyms for unfamiliar words; more meanings were acquired as a result of increased direct instruction. Average students learned some word synonyms under all conditions except a noninstructional control condition. LD students, however, acquired fewer meanings across all conditions and required more direct instruction in order to acquire new vocabulary. In both experiments, procedures that were effective in teaching synonyms also produced fair amounts of transfer to sentence comprehension.

The third study examined the effect of vocabulary instruction on comprehension of connected discourse. Its results, like those of the previous studies, showed that vocabulary training transferred to comprehension of single sentences; however, no effects were observed on two of three measures of passage comprehension.

Comprehension

Questioning strategies.   Searfoss and Readence (1985) identified three types of questions for testing reading comprehension: explicit (can be answered from the exact wording or phrasing of the author), implicit (can be answered by making inferences from information in the text), and experiential (can be answered only by drawing on the pupil's experience).

They also offered three sets of questioning strategies for promoting active comprehension.

- ☐ *Teacher questioning:* An example of this strategy is the Directed Reading Activity (DRA), which is comprised of readiness, directed silent reading, comprehension questions and discussion, oral rereading, and follow-up activities.
- ☐ *Reciprocal questioning:* In this strategy, the teacher and students read a passage and take turns asking and answering questions.
- ☐ *Questioning by children:* An example of this strategy is the directed reading–thinking activity (DRTA), in which the children pose questions or make predictions about the text and then test these questions through reading to confirm, reject, or refine them. New questions are generated as reading progresses.

Guidance strategies.   Searfoss and Readence (1985) elaborated on four guidance strategies.

1. The anticipation guide is a prereading strategy that requires seven steps: identify the major concepts of a unit, determine how they support or challenge children's beliefs, create a few statements that support or challenge their beliefs, arrange them on an overhead transparency, present the guide to the children, discuss each statement briefly, and direct children to read the text.

2. Reading guides present a series of questions to be answered by the children as a result of their reading. The teacher develops a reading guide by following these steps: analyze content, construct statements, decide on assistance to be provided, give the assignment, and provide a follow-up discussion.

3. The planned inferential reading lesson (PIRL) is a two-part guidance strategy for which children are asked to recognize and react to statements rather than produce responses to questions. In the first part, they decide which statements about a text are explicit and which are implicit. In the second part, they are given a number of implicit statements and asked to determine which can be logically inferred from the text and which are unsupportable.

4. The guided reading procedure (GRP) has three features: collaborating to recall information from text, rereading to self-question and self-correct to fill in missing information, and organizing to facilitate retrieval of information from long-term memory. The GRP is implemented by prereading purpose setting, reading the selection, recalling the selection, rereading for corrections and additions, organizing the information, synthesizing the information, and revealing comprehension in a test.

Comprehension Studies.   Idol and Croll (1987) explored the effects of story-mapping training as a means to improve reading comprehension. The students in their research were intermediate-level pupils with mild learning handicaps and poor comprehension. For the intervention, youngsters were trained to develop an organizational framework for thinking about narrative stories. They were given a pictorial story map as the organizer for the stories and asked to fill in the map components—setting and characters, problem, goal, action, and outcome—as they read.

Researchers relied on the "model–lead–test" approach for instructing pupils to fill in and use the map. First, teachers modeled for the pupils, then led them through a few steps, then tested them on their ability to fill in the map independently and make use of the information. The primary dependent measure for the research was a set of responses to ten comprehension questions. Secondary dependent measures were length of story retell, comparison of story retell responses to comprehension-question responses, standardized reading tests, generalization probes, and listening comprehension. The authors reported that four out of five students improved on the primary dependent measure and that all students improved on most of the dependent measures.

Idol (1987) also conducted research on story-mapping with high school students who had difficulty with reading comprehension. Those pupils were reading from a U.S. history text and were instructed throughout an intervention phase to fill in the blanks in a story map. They provided information on important events/points/steps, main idea/lesson, other viewpoints/opinions, reader's conclusion, and the lesson's relevance to today. As in the study with elementary pupils, Idol acquired data on several variables.

Her results showed that all students improved substantially in daily comprehension. Most of them also improved on the other dependent measures: maintenance over time, generalization to another history text, generalization to a text in another content area, standardized test of vocabulary, and test of comprehension.

Darch and Kameenui (1987) investigated two approaches—direct instruction and discussion/workbook—for teaching critical thinking skills to LD students of elementary age. For the former procedure, pupils were trained to use specific rules and strategies to detect instances of faulty arguments. Students in the discussion/workbook group were engaged in interactions and exercises designed to instruct critical thinking. The study measured students' ability to detect false notions in different contexts. The results indicated that the students in the direct instruction group significantly outperformed their counterparts in the other group.

CHARACTERISTICS OF REMEDIAL READERS

There appear to be major sources of individual differences in reading ability in processes that influence both word decoding and higher level comprehension—that is, reading and understanding. The poor decoding ability of less skilled readers does not seem to be caused by a deficit in early visual processing skills. Many studies that vary widely—in the type of visual ability investigated, task methodology, ages of subjects, and range of reader skill—failed to find relation-ships between visual processing abilities and reading. Vellutino (1979) concluded that experiments that specifically isolated a visual processing operation tended to show no differences between good and poor readers.

Instead, much evidence suggests that poor readers suffer from a lack of phonological awareness (knowing about the sounds of letters), and that lack impairs their ability to segment, analyze, and synthesize the speech stream. The speed of naming nonsense words, a feature of this process, is one task that clearly differentiates good from poor readers (Hogaboam & Perfetti, 1978). A second feature of phonological awareness that separates good from poor readers is a lexical-decision skill (deciding whether a string of letters does or does not form a word). Barron (1978), for example, found that skilled readers were better at making these discriminations than less skilled readers.

A third aspect of phonological awareness that distinguishes the two groups of readers is phonological recoding—that is, the spelling-to-sound regularity of letters. In tasks that assess this ability, the difference in speed between saying regular and irregular words indicates the use of phonological coding in word recognition. Barron (1981) found that fifth- and sixth-graders who were skilled readers displayed larger spelling-to-sound regularity effects than less skilled read-ers. Barron maintained that this skill, crucially related to the ability to decode words by phonological recoding, accounted for the word-level processing deficits of poor readers.

Types of Reading Deficient Learners

Gentile (1985) has identified four types of remedial readers.

1. The *tense-inflexible learner* comes from a rigid home where rewards are provided for conforming to parental expectations and standards are inordinately high. In school, this youngster has difficulty carrying out assignments unless someone is there to provide clear guidance. His or her comprehension is marred by an inflexible application of an initial interpretation of a story.

2. The *fearful-accommodating learner* is the center of attention at home. This youngster, who has learned to please others but often at a personal loss, tries to be in control and becomes tense when unable to do so. Because this child sees reading as a means of getting attention, he or she is frequently too anxious, tries too hard, and operates under a good deal of stress. For this youngster, reading has no intrinsic worth, but is seen as a contest to be won.

3. The *scrambled-impulsive learner* comes from an inconsistent home setting in which the parents have failed to establish good lines of communication and may hold society responsible for child-rearing problems and thus expect schools to assume family responsibilities. This youngster, who feels rejected and distrusts authority, may be a behavioral problem and drop out of school when older. With an attitude towards reading instruction that is characterized by an "I won't" position, this child has little tolerance for tasks requiring sustained effort and is

talkative and balks during reading instruction. He or she often blames external circumstances for unsuccessful attempts to complete tasks or improve.

4. The *helpless-discouraged learner* comes from an overly protective home in which he or she is insulated and dependent. This child requires constant assurance and has an inadequate personality that allows others to manipulate him or her. Chronically depressed and unwilling to take risks, this youngster rejects responsibility in reading.

Causes of Reading Deficiencies

Physical Factors.   Following is a summary of reasons for reading failure based on Robinson's classic study (1946) and the work of Ekwall and Shanker (1983).

Visual difficulties.   Robinson's analysis indicated that 63.6 percent of the remedial pupils had some sort of visual difficulty. She concluded, however, that this difficulty was the cause of reading problems in only 50% of the cases.

Auditory difficulties.   Studies tend to show that there are more cases of impaired auditory acuity among groups of disabled readers than among average or good readers. Even though the differences may be statistically significant, the fact that a child has impaired auditory acuity does not necessarily predict that that child will become a disabled reader. Lyon (1977) reviewed the research in this area and concluded that the evidence did not support the view that auditory discrimination ability was necessary for later success in reading.

Laterality, mixed dominance, and directional confusion.   There is considerable research on the relationship of these factors with reading. There are no clear-cut answers, however, as to what we should test for or what we should do about the problems if they do exist. Therefore, a diagnosis for any of these factors seems of dubious value.

Neurological problems.   The field of cerebral mechanisms underlying reading disabilities is vast and complex. It is of interest to many disciplines—psychology, neurology, linguistics, education. Partly because of this wide and varied interest, the findings are not yet conclusive. As indicated in Chapter 2, however, there has been considerable progress in this area in recent years. Far more is now known about the relationship of neurological differences and impairments with reading than was the case a few years ago. We can expect even greater gains in the near future.

Psychological Factors

Emotional problems.   Robinson (1946) reported that 40.9 percent of her remedial readers had a significant degree of emotional maladjustment. She believed that it caused reading failure in 31.8 percent of her cases.

Intelligence.   According to George and Evelyn Spache (1977), research with first graders shows that intelligence test results are not highly predictive of early reading success. If pupils are arranged in the order of their reading test scores after a period of training, the ranking does not neatly parallel a ranking based on their intelligence quotient. The ranks of only very superior and mentally retarded pupils tend to agree in reading and intelligence.

Self-concept.   According to Cohn and Kornelly (1970), a significant positive relationship exists between reading achievement and self-concept. They maintained that a program of remediation for a low self-concept can product positive achievement in reading. According to Pryor (1975), perhaps the first step toward solving a child's academic problem is to change his self-concept.

Socioeconomic Factors.   Robinson reported that maladjusted homes contributed to 54.5 percent of her cases. The U.S. Commission on Civil Rights (1971) reported that from 50 to 70 percent of Mexican American and Black students in the fourth, eighth, and twelfth grades read below the grade level to which they were assigned. In contrast, only 25 to 34 percent of all Anglo youngsters in those grades read below grade level.

Educational Factors.   Brophy (1979) summarized research that evaluates the effects of teaching behaviors on pupil achievement and concluded the following:

1. Teachers' expectations for student learning are important.
2. Effective teachers are good classroom managers.
3. Effective teachers don't waste time; they provide a maximum amount of instruction on critical skills.
4. Students who receive great amounts of direct instruction on structured curriculum have the highest achievement.

Combined Factors.   Keogh (1974) reviewed the research on the effects of vision-training programs on academic readiness and remediation of reading difficulties and concluded that the value of such programs was questionable. Harber (1979) investigated the relationship of four skills—visual perception, visual-perceptual integration, sound blending, and visual closure—to two measures of reading achievement and found that perceptual deficits were not highly related to reading performances of LD students.

Seeking to determine the relationship between teacher expectations and self-concept, Carter (1970) studied the effects of teacher predictions on the self-esteem and academic performance of seventh grade students. He found that the expectations of teachers were in part determined by cumulative records, and those expectations subsequently affected students' levels of confidence and scholastic potentials.

Abrams (1970) claimed that there is no one single etiology for all learning disabilities; rather, learning problems can be caused by a number of factors, all of which may be highly interrelated.

Barbara K. Keogh is on the faculty of the University of California, Los Angeles. She has conducted research in several areas of learning disabilities, including the study of high-risk children, the identification of marker variables to describe learning disabilities, and the neurological bases of learning disabilities.

■ **COMMENTARY** ■   Unfortunately, the child who is experiencing learning disorders is often approached with a singular orientation so that important aspects of his or her unique learning problem are ignored. The tendency of each professional discipline to view the entire problem through its specialization often obscures vital factors that may contribute to the basic difficulty.

CHARACTERISTICS OF LD READERS

This section reviews some specific reading deficiencies of LD youngsters. It also reviews a number of studies that compare LD and non-LD readers.

Oral Reading Deficiencies

Loper (1984) conducted two experiments to investigate LD children's ability to predict and evaluate their own oral decoding performance. In the first, primary age LD and non-LD children predicted whether they could correctly pronounce words that varied in pronounceability. Some words were classified as high pronounceable, some low, and others were unpronounceable. The results indicated no significant differences between groups of youngsters on the low and unpronounceable word lists. LD children, however, evidenced substantially less confidence in their ability to pronounce words on the pronounceable word list.

In a second experiment, Loper's students were required to predict performance of nonsense words from a reading test whose items were of graduated difficulty. After their predictions, they were asked to read the words. Following that activity, a list of words was developed for each participant. The list included words that ranged from the easiest item on which a child made an error to the most difficult item to which he responded correctly.

Results from the two studies suggested ". . . that differences between LD and non-LD children's awareness of their own decoding performance may reflect differences in the groups' skill levels for the particular task. Unlike nondisabled children, the LD subjects were less able to distinguish between words that differed orthographically. However, when word lists were equalized and individualized according to relative difficulty, no differences were evident between groups in their prediction for either accurately or inaccurately decoded words" (Loper, 1984, p. 177).

■ COMMENTARY ■   *As Loper indicated, these results should prompt us to take another look at the presumed metacognitive deficits of LD children, for although many LD youth have deficits of that type, they have even greater deficits when it comes to substance.*

Shinn and Marston (1985) assessed the oral reading performances of mildly handicapped, low achieving, and regular education students from grades four, five, and six. Although some of the mildly handicapped youngsters were EMR, most of them were learning disabled. For the assessment, Shinn and Marston obtained word-per-minute data from one-minute timings as the pupils read passages orally from basal readers. The results indicate that the regular students' rates were higher than those of the low-achieving pupils, whose rates were better than those of the mildly handicapped for all grade levels.

Short-Term Memory Deficiencies

Deficient phonological recoding—that is, spelling to sound regularity—may also account for some of the inadequate performances of poorer readers in short-term memory tasks that are important to reading comprehension. Baddeley, (1966) provides some evidence that the most stable short-term memory code is a phonetic one. Thus, the ability to rapidly form a stable phonological code in short-term memory may be related to comprehension proficiency. The results are consistent with the hypothesis that skilled readers are more likely to store words in a phonological form in short-term memory.

It appears that the ability to form phonological codes rapidly conveys an advantage in addition to helping recall the sounds of letters. The second advantage is providing a more stable code that aids the reader to comprehend information in short-term memory. The inability to rapidly form and maintain relationships between letters and their sounds may hinder the comprehension and retention of information that is currently stored in short-term memory (for example, Perfetti & Lesgold, 1977).

It is likely that phonological recoding processes do not account for all the performance differences shown by poor readers on short-term memory tasks. Some of these readers may also be less inclined to employ mnenomics and more general memory strategies that facilitate performance (Torgesen 1978–1979).

Elliott and Gentile (1986) assessed the efficacy of a mnemonic technique for LD and non-LD adolescents. Their study included 60 students, half of whom were learning disabled and half were non-disabled. Half the students of each type were taught the peg-word rhyme—"one-bun, two-shoe, . . . ten-hen"—and practiced visualizing four target lists of words interacting with the rhyme words. The control students practiced on the word list in whatever way they chose. Retention tests were conducted immediately after the last list was learned, one week later, and five months later. The data revealed that the peg-word mnemonic device increased the memorability of paired associates for the students. Moreover, it increased the retention ability of LD students by almost the same amount as for the non-LD pupils, when compared to their respective control groups. The retention performances of the students favored the nondisabled.

Comprehension Deficiencies

In addition to any deficiency in syntactic abilities, there is mounting evidence that poor readers are less adept in their use of general comprehension strategies and that this deficit becomes particularly acute in the case of written text. These deficiencies may be related to the cognitive strategy differences that Torgesen (1978–1979) has uncovered in experiments on memory performance.

Poor readers appear to be less adept at comprehension monitoring, and they approach text in a more passive manner (Bransford, Stein, & Vye, 1982). Moreover, they display less efficient text scanning strategies (Garner & Reis, 1981) and are less sensitive to text structure (Pearson & Camperell, 1981). These strategic differences in the comprehension of text could result from a general lack of linguistic awareness on the part of the poorer reader (Downing, 1980).

Bos and Filip (1984) investigated the comprehension monitoring skills of LD and average seventh grade students. The students read expository passages with text inconsistencies under a standard condition and a cued condition—that is, where the students were cued to look for text inconsistencies. Their results indicated that average students spontaneously activated comprehension monitoring strategies, thereby noting the text inconsistencies regardless of the condition. LD students, however, drew on these strategies only when they were cued to do so. Their results were interpreted to support Torgesen's conceptualization of LD students as inactive learners.

Englert and Thomas (1987) designed research to study the extent to which LD and non-LD students could identify four text structures—description, enumeration, sequence, and comparison/contrast—in the contexts of reading and writing. Students at two age levels—from third or fourth grade and from 6th or 7th grade—participated in this study, which included LD youngsters, low achieving pupils, and normal achievers. Procedurally, the youngsters read a few statements, then identified sentences that either did or did not fit into one of the four text structures. For writing, they were given a beginning sentence and asked to complete paragraphs in the style of the four text structures.

Results in reading showed that older students, both regular and LD, were superior to younger ones in the recognition of both target and distractor statements. The results in writing were essentially the same. Englert and Thomas also reported that the scores of the LD pupils differed qualitatively and quantitatively from those of non-LD students. Further analysis revealed a moderate but significant relationship between students' reading and writing scores.

Chan, Cole, and Barfett (1987) also assessed the abilities of LD and non-LD students to detect and identify text inconsistencies. The LD students were about 11 years old, whereas their non-LD matches were, on the average, 8 years of age. Youngsters were assigned to either a general or a specific instruction condition. In both treatments, pupils were shown how to monitor text for internal inconsistency and were alerted to the presence of inconsistencies in some passages. In addition, pupils in the specific instruction condition were provided explicit instruction on how to use a cross-referencing technique to evaluate the internal consistency of a passage and were informed of the rationale for judging a passage as consistent or inconsistent. Results showed that the LD pupils in the specific instruction condition demonstrated significantly higher levels of detection, identification, and comprehension performance than their counterparts in the general instruction condition.

Although poor readers do seem to employ mechanisms for understanding text at the word level, they are less able to call on useful techniques at the text level. Due to deficient abilities to see the relationships of words in phrases and to a lack of more general metacognitive strategies, poor readers display comprehension deficits in both reading and listening performance. Thus, part of the comprehension deficit shown by less-skilled readers is not directly linked to decoding problems—that is, simply reading words. Some researchers, such as Smiley, Oakley, Worthen, Campione, and Brown, (1977), have reported large listening comprehension deficits for poor readers. Their results support the hypothesis that listening comprehension accounts for a large proportion of the reading variance at the higher levels of reading skill.

ASSESSING READING ABILITIES

Stoodt (1981) identified five purposes for assessing children within the scope of the reading curriculum:

— Determine the proper grouping of children for instruction
— Pinpoint the specific learning needs of children
— Evaluate the strengths and weaknesses of instructional programs
— Assess individual growth in reading
— Account to the community

Two types of assessment, formal and informal, are generally used to achieve these purposes.

Formal assessment is carried out with standardized tests—that is, tests having a uniform set of directions for administering them and that have been given to large groups of children at several grade levels. The purpose for standardizing tests is to establish norms against which the performance of individuals, assessed later, can be compared. The norms are computed by averaging the scores of children at each respective grade.

Informal assessment does not use norms as a means for interpreting the quality of a student's performance. A child's performance is judged solely on the basis of whether or not it meets a predetermined criterion. Informal tests are often developed by teachers and can be specifically tailored to the local school's reading curriculum.

Formal Assessment

Tests used for formal assessment can be described as survey, diagnostic, and achievement tests (comprehensive batteries).

Survey Tests.   Survey tests are given to groups; they measure general performance in a given area, rather than yield precise measures of each individual's performance. They are most useful when given at the beginning of the school year to identify children who are having problems in global areas such as word analysis, vocabulary, and comprehension. While survey tests can identify these children, they cannot indicate specifically what a particular child knows or has difficulty with (Gillet & Temple, 1982).

Gray Oral Reading Tests—Revised (GORT—R).   Originally developed by Gray and later edited by Robinson (Gray & Robinson, 1967), this test provides an objective measure of growth in oral reading. The GORT—R is comprised of two alternate, equivalent forms, each of which contains thirteen developmentally sequenced passages with five comprehension questions. The GORT—R provides examiners with a passage score that is derived by examining the reader's performance in rate (time taken to read each passage) and deviations from the text (errors). The passage score is reported in terms of standard scores and percentile ranks. A total score (oral reading quotient) is also provided. In addition to the quantitative scores, the manual provides a system for performing a miscue analysis of reader performance. This analysis provides the diagnostician with information in four areas: meaning similarity, function similarity, graphic phonemic similarity, and self-correction.

Diagnostic Tests.   Diagnostic tests yield more precise information. Ideally, they not only pinpoint an individual's specific areas of weakness, but inform teachers as to what should be done. Such tests assess a wide range of subskills, including letter identification, phonics, structural analysis, word knowledge, sound blending, and comprehension.

Woodcock Reading Mastery Tests. This series of tests (Woodcock, 1973), developed for grades K to 12, is designed to be individually administered. The five subtests are sequentially arranged from easy to difficult, and each has designated sections that are suggested starting points for each ability level from K through 12.

The *Letter Identification* subtest measures ability to name the letters of the English alphabet. The child is shown five to ten letters on a card and is asked, "Tell me the name of this letter." The print styles on the cards become more varied and more obscure as the test progresses. The author suggests that by the end of fourth grade, most pupils should receive perfect or nearly perfect scores.

The *Word Identification* subtest contains 150 words, listed 10 to a card. The range of difficulty begins with such words as *go, ball,* and *boy* and ends with such words as *gregarious, ptomaine* and *facetious.* The pupil's task throughout the levels is to name the words.

The *Word Attack* subtest measures ability to identify and pronounce nonsense words through the application of phonic and structural analysis. The 50 test items, 10 to a card, include most consonant and vowel sounds, common prefixes ("un," "re," "de"), common suffixes ("ed," "ing"), and frequently appearing irregular spellings of vowels and consonants ("kn" for *n*, "ph" for *f*, and "igh" for *i*.)

The *Word Comprehension* subtest measures knowledge of word meanings in an analogy format. Each analogy is a double pair: For the first pair, an example relationship is given; for the second, the student must fill in the missing word of the pair. The early part of the test offers analogies such as "*snow* is to *cold* as *sun* is to ————". For lower grades, the pairs are read to the students. At higher levels, the students read silently and complete the analogy aloud (for example, "*opulence* is to *wealth* as *deprivation* is to ————").

The *Passage Comprehension* subtest contains 85 passages meant to tap a wide variety of comprehension, word-attack, and word-meaning skills. There is a word missing in each of the passages, which range in difficulty from first grade to college level. Pupils read the items silently and tell the examiner which word belongs in the blank.

Achievement Tests. Achievement tests (comprehensive batteries) are often given at the end of the school year to measure whether children have mastered certain skills. Most achievement tests consist of subtests in such subjects as math, science, and reading. Some are very broad in scope, whereas others are quite specific. (A comprehensive achievement test is described in Chapter 3.)

Informal Assessment

Teachers and researchers rely heavily on four types of informal assessments described in this section. (Chapter 3 contains comments on curriculum-based assessment, which is another type of informal assessment.)

Informal Reading Inventories (IRI).   Although some IRIs have been standardized and published, many of them are made by teachers using regular classroom reading materials. An advantage of the latter is that they are tied in directly with curriculum. Ordinarily a few word lists, reading passages, and accompanying questions are prepared for each reading level. The tests are generally administered in the following steps:

1. Students are required to read a set of graded word lists.
2. Children begin oral reading of passages from the highest level at which 100 percent of the words are correctly identified on the corresponding word list.
3. Comprehension questions are asked after each passage is read.
4. Oral reading and corresponding comprehension questions are assigned in successively higher level passages as long as instructional criteria are met: 95 percent for word accuracy and 75 percent for comprehension questions. The process continues until independence criteria (99 percent for word accuracy and 90 percent for comprehension) or frustration criteria (less than 90 percent for accuracy and 50 percent for comprehension) are reached.
5. Silent and oral reading alternate from one passage to the next.
6. All three levels are established for both oral and silent reading.

Miscue Analysis.   This form of assessment has been advocated by Goodman (1976), who suggested that the quality of a student's reading errors can be determined by asking whether the errors limit the reader's comprehension of the text. According to him, some errors are more serious than others. Whereas some errors result in *meaning* changes, others in *language* changes, and still others in both, there are a few errors that result in neither. Goodman and Burke (1972) suggest that a minimum of 25 errors (miscues) should be obtained before an attempt is made to analyze the consequences of a student's miscues. Once the types of miscues are known, corresponding interventions should be arranged.

Cloze Procedure.   The well-known cloze procedure, which has fallen in and out of favor over the years, has been attributed to Taylor (1953). Following are the steps he and others have recommended for using this technique:

- ☐ Select a passage of from 250 to 500 words.
- ☐ Delete words (from every 5th word [narrative] to every 10th [expository]).
- ☐ Replace them with blank spaces.
- ☐ Don't delete words from first and last sentences in a passage.
- ☐ Require students to read the entire passage and guess at the missing words.
- ☐ Count the number of words that are exactly correct.
- ☐ Calculate the percentage of correctly inserted words.

Some practitioners and researchers claim a cloze test has several advantages:

— Measuring reading in process
— Requires higher levels of thinking than the ordinary factual type of questions
— Takes less time to construct than do some other measures
— Promotes objective scoring
— Takes little time to administer

Reading Interest Assessment.   It may be as important to determine children's reading interests and habits as it is to know about their reading levels and abilities. Farr and Roser (1979) identified four ways to obtain information about reading interests: observation, interest inventories, interviews with the children, and parent interviews. The researchers provided a list of behaviors and attributes to look for when observing children read and offered an interest inventory that is straightforward and simple to administer.

SPECIAL REMEDIAL APPROACHES

This section explores nine special reading techniques that were either designed specifically for LD or other remedial students or that have been widely used with them. The first two techniques (Fernald and Gillingham-Stillman) are multisensory approaches. Although they are not as popular as they once were, features of these approaches are still apparent in other reading programs. The Hegge, Kirk, and Kirk program, which relies on features of task analysis, had some impact years ago as a remedial method. The next approach, the rebus method, is now out of print, but since it represented a novel approach, it is included here. Although neither of the next two programs—programmed reading and neurological impress—is currently popular, they have influenced two other approaches. Traces of the neurological impress method are apparent in the repeated reading approach, and components of programmed reading approaches are obvious in current microcomputer programs. The final three approaches discussed in this section—direct instruction, applied behavior analysis, and microcomputer programs—are scheduled throughout the country as approaches for developmental or remedial reading.

Fernald Technique

There are four stages to the Fernald (1943) technique.

Stage One.   The first stage is a highly structured one in which students select the words they want to learn, regardless of their complexity. Each word is then written with crayon on a strip of paper in large cursive writing. Students trace the words with their fingers and pronounce each part as it is traced. Tracing is

Grace M. Fernald received her degree in psychology from the University of Chicago in 1907. She founded UCLA's Clinic School in 1921 and remained there until her death in 1950. Her lasting contribution to the field of learning disabilities was a method for instructing reading that utilized not only the conventional visual and auditory approaches, but kinesthetic and tactile cues as well.

repeated until the children can write the words on a separate piece of paper without looking at the copy. As new words are learned, they are placed in an alphabetized word file. After several words are taught, students are expected to realize that they can read and write. At that time, story writing activities are introduced. Subsequent learning of words occurs whenever the students cannot write a word for a story. Sometimes they may need to learn every word by the tracing technique before the story can be written. After the words are learned and the story is written, it is typed. The story is then read by the students, who proceed to file the words under the proper letter in their word file.

Stage Two.   Students are ready for stage two when there is no need for tracing. Words to be learned are derived from unfamiliar words in stories the students have written. The pupils learn the words simply by looking at them while saying them over and over. This process continues until the pupils can write the words by memory.

Stage Three.   At this stage, students learn words merely by looking at them and saying them. They are permitted to read anything they want. When an unknown word is encountered, pupils are told the word. During this period, students learn directly from the printed page; new words are no longer written on cards. Students look at words in print, pronounce them a number of times, and then write them from memory.

Stage Four.   During this final stage, students are expected to recognize new words from their resemblance to words or parts of words already learned. They should now be able to figure out many new words. Words might be learned from context or from generalization about words or word parts. Students are told that they should write out the words they cannot work out. In this phase, students are encouraged to scan paragraphs to clear up the meaning of unknown words prior to reading (ostensibly to prevent distractions and enable them to concentrate on the material). Fernald discouraged the sounding out of words during reading, either by the teacher or student, and suggested that any words that students did not know should be provided for them.

Gillingham and Stillman Method

Gillingham and Stillman (1966) argue that students with specific language disabilities learn to read successfully only when methods consistent with the evolution of language functions are employed. Their system is based on the work of Orton (1937), who maintained that specific language disabilities may be due to hemispherical dominance in specific areas of the brain. (For further discussion of this topic, see Chapter 1.)

The Gillingham and Stillman method is introduced by a story that traces the evolution of communications from spoken language to picture writing to alphabet writing. Accompanying the story, instructors explain to the students that the difficulty they are having with reading is not unique; many others have had similar problems. Following those preliminaries, a sequence of exercises is arranged, beginning with the introduction of letters and their sounds, then blending sounds to words, and ending with sentence and story reading.

Introduction of Letters.   Pupils are taught the sounds represented by letters and then to assemble the letters into words. Word families are taught by associations that involve visual, auditory, and kinesthetic processes. The teacher shows the students a letter and pronounces it, and the students repeat the letter. The same process is used for the sounds represented by letters.

To instruct letter forms, the teacher writes and explains the letter's form, students trace the lines, copy the letter, write the letter from memory, and finally write the letter without looking at what they write. Some guidelines for this approach are as follows:

1. Letters are introduced by a keyword; for example, *b* is presented in the context of *bat.*
2. Drill cards are used to introduce each letter.

3. Students learn to differentiate vowels and consonants by the manner of their production and their association with colored drill cards—that is, white for consonants, salmon for vowels.

4. The initial letters presented to students should represent clear sounds and nonreversible letter forms, such as *f* and *g*.

5. An echo speech procedure whereby the teacher drills the student in reproducing sounds is recommended for those who have pronunciation difficulties.

Blending Letters into Words.   When a pupil has learned 10 letters, they are blended into words. For this exercise, the students are shown several letter drill cards, and they blend the sounds of each letter to pronounce a word. The words are then printed on colored cards and placed in the student's "jewel case." When the pupils have a number of cards in the case, the procedure is reversed; students are required to separate the words into their component sounds. At this time, students might also write the words, and while doing so, name each letter.

Making Sentences and Stories.   When the students can read and write most three-letter phonetically regular words, sentence and story reading exercises are begun. The early stories that students read and write are simple and highly structured; they are to be read silently before reading them to the teacher. Here is an example:

> Pat sat on the mat.
>
> She had a hat.
>
> The hat was on Pat.
>
> A rat sat on the mat.
>
> Pat ran.
>
> The rat ran.

■ COMMENTARY ■   Although the Fernald and the Gillingham and Stillman reading approaches are similar, there are differences. One is that Gillingham and Stillman insist on a letter-by-letter, structured, synthetic phonics approach to reading. In contrast, Fernald recommends that students not proceed letter by letter, but select their own words to learn and initially learn through all modalities.

Hegge, Kirk, and Kirk

In the Hegge, Kirk, and Kirk (1972) method, students are initially provided auditory training in sound blending and practice in writing and vocalizing letter sounds. Later, students are shown cards on which 2- and 3-letter words are printed. They are expected to sound out each element separately before blending them into a word. Students are then required to write words as the sounds are pronounced and blended. There are three parts to the technique.

Samuel A. Kirk, who trained at the Wayne County facility, was for many years on the faculty at the University of Illinois. More recently he has been at the University of Arizona. He has contributed greatly to the field in assessment (the ITPA) and instructional matters (Hegge, Kirk, and Kirk reading drills). The term *learning disabilities* has been attributed to Kirk.

Preparation.   In this phase, students are expected to master most of the consonants and short vowel sounds and be able to blend these sounds into words. Following is a sample lesson:

> TEACHER: Writes *a* on the board. Tells students that it sounds like a baby's cry, "a-a-a-." Teacher erases letter.
>
> STUDENT: Writes letter from memory and says sound represented by the letter. (This activity may be repeated several times.)
>
> TEACHER: Other letters are introduced in similar fashion, and then a word composed of these letters is presented to the student. Teacher asks the student to name the sounds represented by the letters in the word.
>
> STUDENT: Names these sounds one at a time.
>
> TEACHER: Places other words on the board and asks students to blend the letter sounds to form a word. The teacher explains to students that knowing the sounds represented by letters allows them to form many words and that this can help improve their reading.

Implementing Sounds.   Practice in blending specific sounds is scheduled during this phase, with emphasis on accuracy. Students begin with the short *a* sound and proceed to blend orally long lists of words containing no other vowel sounds, such as *sat, fat,* and *rat.* Subsequent exercises deal with all common vowel sounds, consonant sounds, and combination sounds.

Forming Sentences and Reading Stories.   According to Hegge, Kirk, and Kirk, their drills are essential in developing correct responses to written symbols, attacking new words, and helping students to begin reading. They recommend that sentence and story reading be introduced to supplement the drill materials. They also suggest that students might be presented sentences composed of words on which they are being drilled. If the sentences include unknown or "phonetically irregular" words, they should be taught as whole words.

Hegge, Kirk, and Kirk advise teachers not to give students stories to read until they can read materials that are commensurate with their ages and interests and that the materials should be "phonetically regular." Teachers should assist pupils to generalize their learnings from the drills to story reading by aiding them either to name "phonetically irregular" words or to blend unknown "phonetically regular" words.

When story reading does begin in this approach, drills should continue to provide support with the introduction of new sounds and practice in blending larger units. As students move beyond sound blending, the drills and exercises are replaced by word study and reading.

Rebus Approach

The rebus approach to readiness and beginning reading instruction involves the use of picture words (rebuses) rather than spelled words. Since each picture has only one obvious meaning, reading is relatively easy; for example, "dog" is simply a picture of a dog and "in" is a dot inside a square.

The *Peabody Rebus Reading Program* (Woodcock, Clark, & Davies, 1979) includes three programmed workbooks and two readers. Each workbook contains 384 frames that present a simple question or reading task. To mark a response, the child uses a moistened pencil eraser. If the response is correct, the area changes color to green. If the response is incorrect, the area becomes red; the child does not move to the next frame until he has made a correct response. In this program, the student learns a rebus vocabulary and is taught to use context clues and structural analysis skills.

The program is designed so that, on completion, the student possesses the skills and reading vocabulary needed to move into the primer level of traditional programs. As the program progresses, the symbols are gradually replaced with printed words.

Programmed Reading Instruction

Programmed reading materials are presented either in a workbook format or via a teaching machine. Subject matter is presented in small steps that occur in a systematic, logical sequence. Pupils make responses to the questions in each frame, then check the responses by sliding down a marker. Students may respond by answering true-false or multiple-choice questions, completing sentences, writing a word, or completing a word by filling in letters.

Immediate feedback is a characteristic of all programmed materials. In workbooks, the answers are often printed in the margin. On teaching machines, a light or sound can give feedback, the answer can be uncovered, or the response can appear on the screen. In linear programs, students must correct an incorrect response before continuing. In branching programs, if an incorrect response is made, students are referred to another page, where the mistakes are explained before they continue.

Two programmed reading materials—*Programmed Reading* (Buchanan, 1966) and the *Sullivan Reading Program* (Sullivan, 1966)—though rarely used today, had a fair impact on the instruction of reading to remedial youngsters some years ago. A number of features of these early programmed methods have reappeared in the current microcomputer reading programs, for example:

— Providing several opportunities to respond
— Offering immediate feedback for correct and incorrect responses
— Allowing for opportunities to correct mistakes
— Showing data on the number of correct and incorrect responses

Neurological Impress

This reading approach of unison, rapid reading by the student and instructor was designed for severely disabled readers (Heckelman, 1969; Langford, Slade, & Barnett, 1974). For this program, the student sits in front of the instructor as they read, and the voice of the instructor is directed into the student's ear. While reading, the student or teacher points to the words as they are said. Occasionally, the instructor reads louder and faster than the student and, at other times, reads more softly than the student.

When the neurological impress approach is in effect, there are no preparations of the reading materials before the students see them. Furthermore, there is no attempt to teach phonics or word recognition skills or to monitor students' comprehension of materials they read. The basic concern of this approach is for the student to attain fluent reading automatically. To increase the probability of that occurring, instruction begins at a level slightly below where the students can read successfully. When that level is found, students are required to read several pages of text each day.

Like advocates of neurological impress who are concerned about reading fluency, Samuels (1987) believes that many LD youngsters are unable to decode textual material automatically and maintains that their reading rates are well below those of nondisabled youngsters. As a result of their slow rates for decoding material and the great amount of attention they must devote to that process, Samuels claims that they have little attention left to comprehend material they have read. Therefore, in an effort to assist LD youngsters to become more automatic as they read and hence understand more of that material, he has recommended the repeated readings technique (Samuels, 1979).

Repeated reading involves the selection of passages from 50 to 200 words in length at a difficulty level at which the student can recognize most of the words. When practical, the student reads the selection orally three or four times, often to a specified rate, before proceeding to a new passage. Word-per-minute rates are usually reported to the student after each reading, and daily practice is recommended.

Distar Reading Program

The *Distar Reading Program* (Engelmann & Bruner, 1984) consists of Books I and II of the SRA Reading Mastery basal reader series. It is a highly structured decoding program that emphasizes directed instruction, drill, and repetition. To administer the program the teacher is required to follow specific step-by-step procedures. Ordinarily, pupils are instructed in small groups for 30-minute periods, five times per week. Their performances are measured by criterion-referenced tests.

The reading mastery program is based on a synthetic phonics approach, whereby students are first taught to combine isolated sounds into words. The shapes of some alphabet letters are modified in order to provide clues to the letter sounds. For example, the letters of the digraph "th" are connected so that students realize that they are one sound, and the silent "e" at the end of a word is printed smaller than the other letters to emphasize that it is not pronounced. These and other special notations are gradually phased out as the student progresses.

The reading mastery program follows a behavioral management approach, in the sense that it progresses in small steps, and teachers are advised to praise students for acceptable performance. Because it contains both isolated drills and instructional reading, it is a complete reading program.

The *Corrective Reading Program* (Engelmann, Becker, Hanner, & Johnson, 1978) is based on the same premises as Distar, but is designed for older students, those from grades 4 through 12. The program is intended to develop primary and intermediate reading skills using material that is interesting to older students. As in the Distar program, instruction for corrective reading is detailed and carefully guided. Materials include a teacher's management and skill manual, presentation books, and assessment materials. Students use stories, student contracts, and progress charts. Another program in this series concentrates on comprehension.

Applied Behavior Analysis

The bases of applied behavior analysis (ABA) are from operant conditioning and behavior modification. The characteristics are briefly outlined, followed by four reading studies that relied on this approach.

Characteristics of ABA.

Direct measurement.   With this method, the behaviors of concern are measured directly. If, for example, the researcher is concerned with the pupil's ability to add facts of the class $2 + 2 =$ ————, those behaviors are measured.

Daily measurement.   The target behaviors are measured frequently in ABA. Throughout each phase of a project (for example, the baseline), the pupil has the opportunity to react several times to a set of responses.

Replicable teaching procedures.   An important feature of ABA is that the procedures scheduled to generate the research data are adequately described; generally enough detail is provided so that others might replicate the studies.

Individual analysis.   The very heart of the ABA technology is that the data from individuals are presented and analyzed.

Experimental control.   The ABA researcher uses experimental control to establish relationships between the independent and dependent variables. Ordinarily the "A" phase provides baseline data against which to compare effects of some imposed treatment throughout a "B" condition, although there are a few variations on this theme.

■ COMMENTARY ■   *For further information on the components of ABA and justifications for their selection, see Lovitt, 1976. Moreover, the reader may wish to compare the features noted for ABA with those listed and discussed for Precision Teaching in Chapters 1 and 3 and with Curriculum-Based Assessment in Chapter 3. There are a number of similarities.*

ABA-Based Studies.   The ABA approach has been arranged to assess interventions with LD youth in several academic and social areas. The pupils in four such studies were LD youngsters, mostly boys, of intermediate age.

Placing pupils in appropriate books (Lovitt & Hansen, 1976a).   Students read orally and answered comprehension questions from several levels of a basal reading series. They read from these levels for several days. Based on data from previous research, youngsters were placed, for subsequent instruction, in the highest level book in which their correct and incorrect rates and comprehension percentages were superior to established criteria.

Arranging contingent skipping and drilling (Lovitt & Hansen, 1976b).   Data were acquired as students read orally and answered comprehension questions. Following a baseline period, 25 percent improvement lines were drawn on the students' charts—one each for correct rate, incorrect rate, and comprehension percentage. During the next condition, youngsters could skip sections of their text if all three scores surpassed the criteria. If, however, one or more of their scores was not satisfactory, drill of some type was arranged. Significant improvement was noted for all students in the second condition.

Assessing effects of various reinforcement contingencies on oral reading (Lovitt, Eaton, Kirkwood, & Pelander, 1971). Pupils read orally from two textbooks. During a baseline phase, no particular reinforcement condition was arranged in either book. Following that period, some contingency was put in effect for one textbook; the other book served as a control. In two studies, the contingency was arranged for correct responses, and in one study, the contingency was arranged for errors. Data from the three projects indicated that pupils' correct and incorrect rates were superior during conditions when contingencies were in effect. Furthermore, the contingencies had the most pronounced effects on the rates to which they were applied.

Measuring comprehension of facts about a story (Hansen & Lovitt, 1977). During this project a girl read orally from a series of expository stories. Throughout, data were kept on her oral reading rates and her answers to prepared comprehension questions. Data were also acquired on the number of facts she said about the story; each bit of correct information was credited as a fact. Following a baseline, the teacher modeled for her how to say facts and instructed her to do likewise. Following that brief period, the girl was on her own. Data indicated that her rate of saying facts about the story accelerated significantly following instruction. Meanwhile, her scores on the prepared comprehension questions improved slightly.

Microcomputer Programs

Four microcomputer reading programs suitable for LD youth are described in this section. Also included are summaries of two studies with microcomputer programs.

Review of Programs. *Cloze Plus* (program published by Milliken Publishing Company and reviewed by Bogyo & Hardiman, 1985) has six levels of programs and four disks for each level. A reading level of fifth grade is recommended. For this cloze reading comprehension program, the presented paragraphs have been constructed to emphasize one idea and usually have one deletion. The eleven kinds of ideas with the associated deletions are synonyms, antonyms, associations, classifications, sequences, transitions, pronoun referents, similarities and differences, function words, summary words, and definitions. In most instances, the response mode is multiple choice; on occasion, the student must come up with a word and type it. Throughout the program, students are provided immediate feedback for correct and incorrect responses and opportunity to receive clues for correct answers.

The *Comprehension Power Program* (program published by Milliken Publishing Company and reviewed by Lindemann, 1985) consists of twelve levels. In levels HiA, HiB, and HiC, there are several activities. In one, complete sentences are presented. Following, vocabulary words to be learned are eliminated from the sentence. Next, all the words in the sentence are flashed on the screen, and students are asked to type in the missing word. The flash option can be taken away and students must type in the missing word from memory. With either option, students receive feedback on misspelled words. Two other program options may be arranged with these vocabulary words. With the first, the users can take as much time as they please to respond, but for the second, the presentation rate of the text is set by the teacher. The reviewer of this program finds it relevant to the instructional needs of many secondary LD students because of its varied activities and range of difficulty.

Critical Reading, Lesson Series A–H (program published by Borg-Warner Educational Systems and reviewed by Wilson, 1985) includes eight disks covering four units of instruction designed to provide individualized instruction in critical thinking and reasoning. The material is presented in a reading format written on the third- through sixth-grade reading level and designed for students at the secondary level. According to the reviewer, it is appropriate for students who read at the third-grade level. The lessons in the A–H series cover four instructional units: rule for *or* elimination, rule for *all* elimination, conditional statements, and inductive reasoning. Each lesson contains a pretest, lessons, progress checks, a posttest, and a management system. According to the reviewer, the programmed approach, the consistency of response modes, time requirements, opportunity for practice, and reading level combine to make this series well suited for LD students.

Edmark Reading Program, Level 1 Software (program published by Edmark Corporation, 1986) is designed to teach beginning reading and language development to handicapped students from age three to adult. It is available in two versions: The classroom version contains a sophisticated management system allowing the collection of data on student progress for up to thirty students; the resource version contains a management system for up to three students.

The publisher cites the following as notable features of the software for both versions:

☐ A human-quality voice, coded for the Edmark Reading Program and operated through the Echo+ or Cricket voice Synthesizer, that introduces words, gives cues, and reinforces students.

☐ A joystick that allows students to make responses to the materials without needing computer keyboard skills.

☐ High-quality color graphics that are appealing and provide student motivation.

Complete compatibility between the software and print version of the materials allows the teacher total flexibility in instruction. No prior computer knowledge is required of the teacher or student.

1. *Prereading lessons.* Throughout 63 prereading frames, students match illustrations, symbols, letters, and groups of letters. They are cued to "point" to the sample and to "find one like it."

2. *Word recognition lessons.* These lessons teach, on a sight-word basis, 150 words plus *-s*, *-ing*, and *-ed* endings. Throughout the word recognition lessons, students are cued to "point to the word————," then to "read the word————."

3. *Direction book lessons.* The purpose of these lessons is to teach students the meaning of the words. Students are presented words, phrases, and sentences that they are asked to "read" and told to then "find the pictures that go with the words." In addition to matching words with pictures, students learn left-to-right and top-to-bottom sequencing.

4. *Picture/phrase lessons.* In picture/phrase lessons, students are introduced to a more complex meaning of the words. A series of five phrases and one illustration are presented. Students are asked to "read the words and then point to the words that go with the picture."

5. *Storybook lessons.* These lessons present the words learned in illustrated, short stories.

6. *"Call Your Teacher."* This part of the program consists of a visual image of a student with his hand raised, and a voice stating "Call your teacher." The sequence is used to allow the teacher to intercede if the student is having difficulties and needs assistance.

Studies of Computer Methods.   Jones, Torgesen, and Sexton (1987) conducted a study with LD and non-LD students of elementary age to assess the effects of the *Hint and Hunt I Program* (Beck & Roth, 1984). Experimental students received instruction in the Hint and Hunt program, which provides practice on five short vowels and four vowel digraphs and diphthongs contained in single-syllable words. There are two instructional activities in the Hint and Hunt program. For the "hint" portion, vowel sounds are introduced and practiced in a quasi-instructional mode. Digitized speech is used to present the sounds associated with the vowels. The "hunt" feature is a game to provide practice in recognizing words and nonsense syllables that contain the vowel sounds introduced earlier. Students in the contrast group were assigned a different program, one that provided repetitive drill in spelling words from their current spelling lists. Both programs were presented on Apple IIe computers.

Following the week-long treatment, results revealed that children in the experimental group improved substantially in both speed and accuracy of word reading. This improvement occurred for generalization words as well as for target words. Performances of youngsters in the comparison group were not significantly altered by their treatment.

A second microcomputer study was conducted by researchers at Utah State University. That group has been exploring the applicability of interactive videodisc technology to learners with special needs and has designed several instructional discs. Before discussing one of those programs, however, some general information about the technology is in order:

A videodisc looks like a 33-rpm phonograph record. As with videotape, images and sounds can be recorded on the videodisc and reproduced on a television screen; however, the videodisc has several unique capabilities that make it a superior instructional medium compared to videotape. For example, a videodisc is capable of storing 54,000 individual picture frames resulting in 30 minutes of motion. It has two audio tracks per side; thus, the same visual information can be played with two different audio sequences. A videodisc produces high-quality still pictures when played in single-frame stop motion; it can also be played at regular speed or various slow-motion speeds. In addition, the "random access" capabilities of the videodisc player enable it to search from the first to the last frame in less than 3 seconds to locate and display particular frames requested by the user. [Thorkildsen & Friedman, 1986, p. 111]

One of the programs developed by the group at Utah State University is *Beginning Sight Reading* (BSR), which is designed to gather information on three dimensions of instructional technology. The first dimension focuses on the instructional potential of the technology—the extent to which the videodisc program results in students learning seven beginning sight-reading words. The second and third dimensions, which relate to the first, focus on the effects of two instructional variables—minimal versus extensive remediation and rate of instruction.

The researchers field tested two versions of BSR. Remedial students of elementary age were assigned to one of two groups: one received extensive remediation that corresponded to their performance, while the other received minimal remediation. The results indicated that both treatments were successful in that the students quickly learned to read the seven sight words in isolation and in context. Data further indicated that the pupils in the extensive remediation group required less time to reach their goal.

COMMENTS AND DISCUSSION POINTS

- As early as possible, children should learn to read in context. After all, that is what reading is: It isn't simply the babbling of unrelated sounds. Students should be taught sounds, letters, word parts, and isolated words only to the extent that the instruction will help them to read in context. There has been much too much task-analysis type of instruction given to LD students.

- Integrate the instruction of reading with the instruction of other academic skills, particularly those in the language arts group. The IEP process may have worked against such an integrated approach by calling for specific objectives and goals. Add to this the fact that most of us are none too imaginative when it comes to writing integrated programs. A great deal of spelling, writing, and handwriting instruction could take place along with reading instruction. Likewise, considerable functional language instruction could take place with the reading program.

- Early on, introduce expository reading. Give youngsters books to read that provide facts and information that is now or will soon be useful to them. They should read about their environments, their communities, about occupations, health, leisure time. They should be encouraged to read, as soon as possible, from science, social studies, and other content area books. When they read expository materials it makes comprehension instruction more meaningful, for there is something in the materials that should be remembered. Often, when children read narrative materials from basal texts, there is little of importance that should be comprehended, much less remembered.

- Teachers should emphasize a variety of comprehension skills and teach children to understand various aspects of the materials they read. Generally, not enough time is spent on comprehension, and what time is devoted to that skill is allocated to rather rudimentary forms. Children need to be taught first to identify or label the type of comprehension required for a certain passage—whether they should remember details, understand the sequence, make judgments, or what. Most of them don't have the faintest idea that there are various levels and types of comprehension.

- Related to the above, children should be taught to read for different purposes. They should learn, for example, to skim and scan.

- There should be great emphasis on functional reading. Children should be taught from and learn to read newspapers, maps, labels, directions, instructions, recipes, bulletins. These materials can be useful in instructing various types of comprehension.

- Youngsters should be taught to make use of directories such as the yellow pages, dictionaries, almanacs, and other general sources of information. They should, of course, be taught to locate them.

- A great deal of emphasis should be placed on reading a lot. Most adults who are poor readers simply do not read. Youngsters must be given opportunities to read several pages of various types of material every day. They need to practice in order to become fluent. They also need to read a great deal in order to develop a "schema," a body of knowledge and facts they can use to understand and comprehend new materials that they read. Most LD youngsters don't read enough to become fluent and don't acquire enough information on which to build new understandings.

- Children should spend less time completing workbook and skill sheets. There is little evidence that these activities are related to reading achievement.[*]

- Schools should introduce more comprehensive assessments of reading and writing. Standardized tests should be supplemented with assessments of reading fluency, ability to summarize and critically evaluate lengthy selections, amount of independent reading, and amount and quality of writing.[*]

REFERENCES

Abrams, J.C. (1970). Learning disabilities—a complex phenomenon. *Reading Teacher, 23,* 299–303.

---

[*] Comments taken from *Becoming a Nation of Readers* (Anderson et al., 1985).

Anderson, R.C.; Hiebert, E.H.; Scott, J.A.; & Wilkinson, I.A.G. (1985). *Becoming a nation of readers: The report of the commission on reading.* Washington, D.C.: The National Institute of Education, U.S. Department of Education.

Artley, A.S. (1965). Basal reading series. In H.K. Mackintosh (Ed.), *Current approaches to teaching reading.* Washington, D.C.: National Education Association.

Baddeley, A.D. (1966). Short-term memory for word sequences as a function of acoustic, semantic, and formal similarity. *Quarterly Journal of Experimental Psychology, 18,* 362–365.

Barron, R.W. (1978). Reading skill and phonological coding in lexical access. In M. Gruneberg, R. Sykes, & P. Morris (Eds.), *Practical Aspects of Memory.* London: Academic Press.

———. (1981). Reading skill and reading strategies. In A. Lesgold & C. Perfetti (Eds.), *Interactive Process in Reading.* Hillsdale, NJ: Erlbaum Associates.

Beck, I.L., & Roth, S.F. (1984). *Hint and Hunt I Program* Allen, TX: Developmental Learning Materials/Teaching Resources.

Bogyo, J., & Hardiman, P.M. (1985). Cloze plus: A context analysis program [Review]. *Journal of Learning Disabilities, 18,* 364–365.

Bos, C., & Filip, D. (1984). Comprehension monitoring in learning disabled and average students. *Journal of Learning Disabilities, 17,* 229–233.

Bransford, J.D.; Stein, B.S.; & Vye, N.J. (1982). Helping students learn how to learn from written texts. In M. Singer (Ed.), *Competent reader, disabled reader: Research and application.* Hillsdale, NJ: Erlbaum Associates.

Brophy, J. (1979). Teacher behavior and student learning. *Educational Leadership, 37,* 33–38.

Buchanan, C.D. (1966). *Programmed reading.* New York: McGraw-Hill, Sullivan Associates.

Burmeister, L.E. (1968). Usefulness of phonic generalizations. *The Reading Teacher, 21,* 349–356.

Carter, D.L. (1970). The effect of teacher expectations on the self-esteem and academic performance of seventh grade students. Doctoral dissertation, University of Tennessee, Knoxville.

Chan, L.K.S.; Cole, P.G.; & Barfett, S. (1987). Comprehension monitoring: Detection and identification of text inconsistencies by LD and normal students. *Learning Disability Quarterly, 10,* 114–124.

Cohn, M., & Kornelly, D. (1970). For better reading—a more positive self-image. *Elementary School Journal, 70,* 199–201.

Condus, M.M.; Marshall, K.J.; & Miller, S.R. (1986). Effects of the keyword mnemonic strategy on vocabulary acquisition and maintenance by learning disabled children. *Journal of Learning Disabilities, 19,* 609–613.

Cunningham, J.W.; Cunningham, P.M.; & Arthur, S.V. (1981). *Middle and secondary school reading.* New York: Longman.

Darch, C., & Kameenui, E.J. (1987). Teaching LD students critical reading skills: A systematic replication. *Learning Disability Quarterly, 10,* 82–91.

Downing, J. (1980). Learning to read with understanding. In McCullough, C.M. (Ed.), *Inchworm, Inchworm: Persistent Problems in Reading Education.* Newark, DE: International Reading Association, 163–178.

Edmark reading program, level 1 software. (1986). Edmark Corporation, Bellevue, WA.

Ekwall, E.E., & Shanker, J.L. (1983). *Diagnosis and remediation of the disabled reader,* 2nd ed. Boston: Allyn and Bacon.

Elliott, J.L., & Gentile, J.R. (1986). The efficacy of a mnemonic technique for learning disabled and nondisabled adolescents. *Journal of Learning Disabilities, 19(4), 237–241.*

Engelmann, S.; Becker, W.; Hanner, S.; & Johnson, G. (1978). *Corrective reading program.* Chicago: Science Research Associates.

Engelmann, S., & Bruner, E. (1984). *Distar reading program.* Chicago: Science Research Associates.

Englert, C.S., & Thomas, C.C. (1987). Sensitivity to text structure in reading and writing: A comparison between learning disabled and non-learning disabled students. *Learning Disability Quarterly, 10,* 93–105.

Farr, R., & Roser, N. (1979). *Teaching a child to read.* New York: Harcourt Brace Jovanovich.

Fernald, G.M. (1943). *Remedial techniques in basic school subjects.* New York: McGraw-Hill.

Garner, R., & Reis, R. (1981). Monitoring and resolving comprehension obstacles: An investigation of spontaneous text lookbacks among upper-grade good and poor comprehenders. *Reading Research Quarterly, 16,* 569–582.

Gentile, L.M. (1985). Remedial reading: A question of will as much as skill. In L.W. Searfoss & J.E. Readence (Eds.), *Helping children learn to read.* Englewood Cliffs, NJ: Prentice-Hall.

Gillet, J.W., & Temple, C. (1982). *Understanding reading problems: Assessment and instruction.* Boston: Little, Brown.

Gillingham, A., & Stillman, B. (1966). *Remedial training for children with specific difficulty in reading, spelling, and penmanship,* 7th ed. Cambridge, MA: Educators' Publishing Services.

Goodman, K.S. (1976). Reading: A psycholinguistic guessing game. In H. Singer & R.B. Ruddell (Eds.), *Theoretical models and processes of reading,* 2nd ed. Newark, DE: International Reading Association.

Goodman, Y.M., & Burke, C.L. (1972). *Reading miscue inventory: Manual for procedure for diagnosis and evaluation.* New York: Macmillan.

Gray, W.S., & Robinson, H.M. (1967). *Gray oral reading tests.* Austin, TX: PRO-ED.

Hansen, C.L., & Lovitt, T.C. (1977). An applied behavior analysis approach to reading comprehension. In J.T. Guthrie (Ed.), *Cognition, curriculum, and comprehension.* Newark, DE: International Reading Association, 160–186.

Harber, J.R. (1979). Are perceptual skills necessary for success in reading? Which ones? *Reading Horizons, 20,* 7–15.

Heckelmann, R.G. (1969). A neurological-impress method of remedial-reading instruction. *Academic Therapy, 4,* 277–282.

Hegge, T.G.; Kirk, S.A.; & Kirk, W.D. (1972). *Remedial reading drills,* 2nd ed. Ann Arbor, MI: George Wahr.

Hogaboam, T.W., & Perfetti, C.A. (1978). Reading skill and the role of verbal experience in decoding. *Journal of Educational Psychology, 70,* 717–729.

Idol, L., (1987). A critical thinking map to improve content area comprehension of poor readers. *Remedial and Special Education, 8(4),* 28–40.

Idol, L., & Croll, V.J. (1987). Story-mapping training as a means of improving reading comprehension. *Learning Disability Quarterly, 10,* 214–229.

Jenkins, J.R., & Larson, K. (1979). Evaluating error-correction procedures for oral reading. *Journal of Special Education, 13,* 145–156.

Jones, K.M.; Torgesen, J.K.; & Sexton, M.A. (1987). Using computer guided practice to increase decoding fluency in learning disabled children: A study using the Hint and Hunt I program. *Journal of Learning Disabilities, 20,* 122–128.

Keogh, B.K. (1974). Optometric vision training programs for children with learning disabilities: Review of issues and research. *Journal of Learning Disabilities, 7,* 219–231.

Langford, K.; Slade, K.; & Barnett, A. (1974). An explanation of impress techniques in remedial reading. *Academic Therapy, 9,* 309–319.

Lindemann, S.K. (1985). Comprehension power program [Review]. *Journal of Learning Disabilities, 18,* 495–496.

Loper, A.B. (1984). Accuracy of learning disabled students' self-prediction of decoding. *Learning Disability Quarterly, 7,* 172–178.

Lovitt, T.C. (1976), Applied behavior analysis techniques and curriculum research: Implications for instruction. In N.G. Haring & R.L. Schiefelbush (Eds.), *Teaching special children.* New York: McGraw-Hill.

Lovitt, T.C.; Eaton, M.; Kirkwood, M.E.; & Pelander, J., (1971). Effects of various reinforcement contingencies on oral reading rate. In E.A. Ramp & B.L. Hopkins (Eds.). *A new direction for education: Behavior analysis.* Lawrence, KS: Department of Human Development.

Lovitt, T.C., & Hansen, C.L. (1976a). Round one—placing the child in the right reader. *Journal of Learning Disabilities, 9,* 347–353.

Lovitt, T.C., & Hansen, C.L. (1976b). The use of contingent skipping and drilling to improve oral reading and comprehension. *Journal of Learning Disabilities, 9,* 481–487.

Lyon, R. (1977). Auditory-perceptual training: The state of the art. *Journal of Learning Disabilities, 10,* 564–572.

Manning, J.C. (1985). The reading teacher: Scholar and romanticist. *Reading Teacher, 2*(6), 3.

Mastropieri, M.A.; Scruggs, T.E.; & Levin, J.R. (1985). Mnemonic strategy instruction with learning disabled adolescents. *Journal of Learning Disabilities, 18,* 94–100.

Nurss, J.R.; Hough, R.A.; & Goodson, M.S. (1981). Prereading/language development in two day care centers. *Journal of Reading Behavior, 13,* 23–31.

Orton, S.T. (1937). *Reading, writing, and speech problems in children.* New York: Norton.

Pany, D.; Jenkins, J.R.; & Schreck, J. (1982). Vocabulary instruction: Effects on word knowledge and reading comprehension. *Learning Disability Quarterly, 5,* 202–215.

Pearson, P.D., & Camperell, K. (1981). Comprehension of text structures. In J.T. Guthrie (Ed.), *Comprehension and Teaching.* Newark, DE: International Reading Association.

Perfetti, C.A., & Lesgold, A.M. (1977). Discourse comprehension and sources of individual differences. In M. Just & P. Carpenter (Eds.), *Cognitive Processes in Comprehension.* Hillsdale, NJ: Erlbaum Associates.

Pryor, F. (1975). Poor reading—lack of self esteem? *Reading Teacher, 28,* 358–359.

Richek, M.A. (1977–1978). Readiness skills that predict initial word learning using 2 different methods of instruction. *Reading Research Quarterly, 13,* 200–222.

Robinson, H. (1946). *Why pupils fail in reading.* Chicago: University of Chicago Press.

Rose, T.L., & Beattie, J.R. (1986). Relative effects of teacher-directed and taped previewing on oral reading. *Learning Disability Quarterly, 9,* 193–199.

Rose, T.L.; McEntire, E.; & Dowdy, C. (1982). Effects of two error-correction procedures on oral reading. *Learning Disability Quarterly, 5,* 100–105.

Rosenberg, M.S. (1986). Error-correction during oral reading: A comparison of three techniques. *Learning Disability Quarterly, 9,* 182–192.

Samuels, S.J. (1987). Information processing abilities and reading. *Journal of Learning Disabilities, 20*(1), 18–22.

Samuels, S.J. (1979). The method of repeated readings. *Reading Teacher, 32,* 403–408.

Searfoss, L.W., & Readence, J.E. (1985). *Helping children learn to read.* Englewood Cliffs, NJ: Prentice-Hall.

Shinn, M., & Marston, D. (1985). Differentiating mildly handicapped, low-achieving, and regular education students: A curriculum-based approach. *Remedial and Special Education, 6*(2), 31–38.

Singer, H., & Balow, I.H. (1981). Overcoming educational disadvantagedness. In J.T. Guthrie (Ed.), *Comprehension and teaching: Research review.* Newark, DE: International Reading Association.

Smiley, S.S.; Oakley, D.D.; Worthen, D.; Campione, J.C.; & Brown, A.L. (1977). Recall of thematically relevant material by adolescent good and poor readers as a function of written versus oral presentation. *Journal of Educational Psychology, 69,* 381–387.

Smith, F. (1982). *Understanding reading: A psycholinguistic analysis of reading and learning to read,* 3rd ed. New York: Holt, Rinehart & Winston.

Sorenson, N.L. (1982). A study of the reliability of phonic generalizations in five primary-level basal reading programs. Unpublished doctoral dissertation, Arizona State University, Tempe.

Spache, G.D., & Spache, E.B. (1977). *Reading in the elementary school,* 4th ed., Boston: Allyn and Bacon.

Stevenson, H.W.; Parker, T.; Wilkinson, A.; Hegion, A.; & Fish, E. (1976). Longitudinal study of individual differences in cognitive development and scholastic achievement. *Journal of Educational Psychology, 68,* 377–400.

Stoodt, B.D. (1981). *Reading instruction.* Boston: Houghton Mifflin.

Sullivan, M.W. (1966). *Sullivan reading program.* Palo Alto, CA: Behavioral Research Laboratories.

Taylor, I., & Taylor, M.M. (1983). *The psychology of reading.* New York: Academic Press.

Taylor, W.L. (1953). "Cloze procedure": A new tool for measuring readability. *Journalism Quarterly, 30,* 415–433.

Thorkildsen, R.J., & Friedman, S.G. (1986). Interactive videodisc: Instructional design of a beginning reading program. *Learning Disability Quarterly, 9,* 111–117.

Torgesen, J.K. (1978–1979). Performance of reading disabled children on serial memory tasks: A selective review of recent research. *Reading Research Quarterly, 14,* 57–87.

U.S. Commission on Civil Rights. (1971). *The unfinished education.* Washington, D.C.: Government Printing Office.

Vellutino, F.R. (1979). *Dyslexia: Theory and research.* Cambridge, MA: MIT Press.

Wilson, J. (1985). Critical reading [Review]. *Learning Disability Quarterly, 8,* 64–66.

Woodcock, R.W. (1973). *Woodcock reading mastery tests.* Circle Pines, MN: American Guidance Service.

Woodcock, R.W.; Clark, C.R.; & Davies, C.O. (1979). *Peabody rebus reading program.* Circle Pines, MN: American Guidance Service.

Chapter 8

The Letter by Pierre Bonnard (*c* 1906). Courtesy of National Gallery of Art, Washington, Chester Dale Collection.

WRITING AND SPELLING

MAIN IDEAS

- Handwriting: traditional programs, assessment and standards, performances of LD students, and teaching approaches
- Spelling: traditional programs, assessment and standards, performances of LD pupils, and teaching approaches
- Expressive writing: traditional instructional plans, assessment and standards, performances of LD students, and teaching approaches

OVERVIEW

A number of researchers and practitioners have pointed out the relationship of reading, writing, and spelling. Indeed, Kamil, Langer, and Shanahan (1985) have written an excellent text on this subject and have called many of these relationships to our attention.

The first section of this chapter pertains to handwriting, the second to spelling, and the third to expressive writing. The coverage for each of the three subjects includes a review of how each subject is ordinarily taught in schools, formal and informal assessment measures, the comparative performances of LD and non-LD students on certain skills, and selected methods that have been arranged successfully with students, most of whom were LD. There is an additional discussion in the sections on spelling and expressive writing that has to do with typewriters or microcomputers. The chapter ends with comments on the subjects covered.

HANDWRITING

Although it generally is not necessary to make a case for instructing reading, mathematics, and other school subjects, it is sometimes necessary to do so for the instruction of handwriting.

According to Saltzman (1981), American business loses about $200 million a year because of illegible writing. Saltzman also claims that for the period he studied, the largest single cause of computer error was poor handwriting; thousands of tax returns were held up because figures, notes, and signatures could not be read; and indecipherable addresses accounted for millions of letters that ended up in dead-letter offices. Saltzman also points out that thousands of doctors' prescriptions can't be read or are misread each year.

Hagin has also made a strong case for the importance of handwriting:

> Even in these days of self-correcting typewriters and magic word processors, handwriting is a necessary competency. For pupils it represents the usual medium by which they convey to their teachers the progress they have made in learning what is being taught. Legible writing is a tool for learning; poor writing is a barrier. Unreadable numbers interfere with correct solutions in mathematics. Incomplete notes leave gaps in understanding in the content areas. Illegible examination papers bias test grades. It has been found that, regardless of the content, teachers assign higher grades to papers with clear handwriting.
>
> Nor can adults avoid the necessity for writing. There are official applications and forms to be completed, letters and notes to be written, as well as the record-keeping associated with one's personal affairs and the conduct of one's vocation, business, or profession. Finally, there is the importance of the written outline that guides the conceptualization of nearly any project or endeavor. Few people, indeed, can do their planning through mental operations only. [1983, p. 266]*

According to some, not much attention is paid in schools to the instruction of handwriting. Duvall (1981a) found only a small percentage of the average day in elementary school devoted to handwriting instruction. In her survey of the college preparation of 3,305 teachers, she reported that only thirteen had received any training to instruct handwriting. Hagin agreed with Duvall's grim statistics by saying that handwriting is one of the most poorly taught components in the school curriculum; only a few schools require their teachers to have some kind of handwriting training. Davis's data (1983) also supported the fact that knowing about handwriting was a low priority. When teachers were asked to rank order the skills they thought resource teachers should have, being knowledgeable about handwriting instruction was ranked 25 of 32 items.

Hagin indicated also that not much attention is given to handwriting in the educational literature, noting as an example that there was only a 32-word passage devoted to handwriting in the 1,400-page volume, *Second Handbook of Research on Teaching* (Travers, 1973).

---

* Reprinted by permission from R.A. Hagin, "Write Right—or Left: A Practical Approach to Handwriting," *Journal of Learning Disabilities, 16* (1983), pp. 266–271.

Traditional Instructional Plans

In most schools, handwriting instruction begins with the manuscript format—that is, printing. According to Hagin (1983), this form is advocated for beginners for at least five reasons:

1. It is regarded as being easier to learn because the letter forms are simpler.
2. It resembles the print in books; thus children do not have to accommodate two graphic styles.
3. Beginning writing in manuscript is more legible than cursive.
4. It is required throughout life for filling out applications and documents.
5. It promotes the independence of letters within words in teaching spelling. [p. 266]*

Traditionally, there is a shift to cursive writing at some time during the third grade. Thereafter, youngsters are expected to write in that form when they work on school assignments and are asked to use manuscript only when they write personal information items on forms or the like. A few educators have disagreed with this manuscript to cursive plan. Cruickshank (Cruickshank, Bentzen, Ratzeburg, & Tannhauser, 1961) and others have recommended that *only* the cursive form of writing be taught and that the manuscript stage should be skipped.

Hagin has summarized the reasons for recommending the cursive forms for beginning readers:

☐ The connected style permits learners to deal with words as units.

☐ Individual letters are more difficult to reverse than they are for manuscript writing.

☐ Cursive writing is faster than manuscript because it doesn't require separate pencil movements for each letter.

A few educators have recommended writing programs designed to make the transition from manuscript to cursive writing smoother. A few educators even argue that handwriting should be taught in only the italic form and that neither the classic manuscript nor cursive forms should be instructed. This group maintains that the italic method is easy to learn, is a rapid way to write, and is highly legible. Figure 8.1 shows examples of the four handwriting methods discussed in the following paragraphs.

Spelling and Writing Patterns (Botel, Holsclaw, Cammarota, & Brothers, 1971). This program has two levels: for grades 1 through 3 and for grades 4 to 6. The first level is designed to teach manuscript writing; the second is for cursive. In

---

* Reprinted by permission from R.A. Hagin, "Write Right—or Left: A Practical Approach to Handwriting," *Journal of Learning Disabilities, 16* (1983), pp. 266–271.

■ FIGURE 8.1 ■   Examples of Four Handwriting Programs

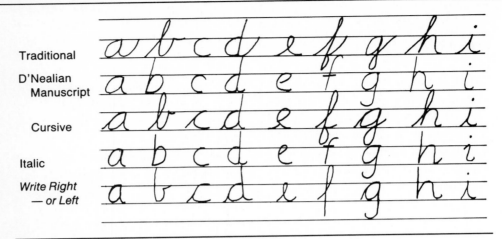

Traditional

D'Nealian Manuscript

Cursive

Italic

Write Right — or Left

both levels, letter forms are printed for youngsters to model. Arrows are drawn for each letter to show pupils the direction they are to follow when writing letters.

A four-step instructional procedure is featured throughout the program's books. In step one, pupils trace words and say each syllable while doing so. In step two, they copy the words, say the syllables, and then compare their efforts to the models. In step three, students cover the words, write them from memory, and compare them again with the model. In the fourth step, pupils draw lines through the words that do not match the models and start the process again. When a word is acceptable, they go on to the next one.

In workbook practice, pupils are initially required to write words such as *pen* and *sit*. Writing lines are divided by dotted red lines as cues for composing letters. Later in the program, more difficult and longer words, such as *thing* and *playing,* are requested. Midway through the book, children are expected to fill in missing words in stories and begin to practice cursive writing.

Handwriting with Write and See. (Skinner & Krakower, 1968).   Although this program is not used in many schools today, it is described here because it differs in many respects from other available approaches.

This manuscript–cursive program has six books, in which there are provisions for the transition from manuscript to cursive writing in either the second or third grade. Book 1 introduces manuscript writing—uppercase and lowercase letters, numerals, words and sentences. Book 2 emphasizes the manuscript form, requiring its use to write simple notes, stories, and poems. Book 3 reviews cursive letters and develops evaluation skills. In Book 4, pupils learn the handwriting vocabulary *(spacing, slant, form)* and rely on it to analyze handwriting samples and to evaluate their own work. Pupils learn to refine their handwriting in Book 5 by concentrating on important elements of legibility. Book 6 stresses legible handwriting for all written communication; pupils apply manuscript writing to designing posters and cursive writing to composing business and personal letters. The series also includes sections on learning to compress words into small spaces, to use abbreviations and proofreading marks, and to make graphs.

The Skinner and Krakower program includes a special pen that contains an ink that reacts with specially prepared paper to write either gray or yellow. The authors intend pupils to learn that gray marks are correct and yellow ones are incorrect, thus receiving immediate feedback on the quality of their writing. Such reactions would also provide teachers with records of students' performances.

Write Right—or Left (Hagin, 1983).   This program is derived from neuropsychological bases that suggest, according to its designer, some necessary conditions for a handwriting approach. Three of those conditions follow:

> 1. The style of writing should be appropriate to the child's level of motor control so that the initial chain of isolated motor impulses that produce the graphic form of the letter can gradually be mastered and transformed with a reasonable amount of training to the "kinetic melody" that is mature handwriting.
>
> 2. Handwriting should be taught not *just* as a visual task, nor *just* as a motor task, but as a process that involves body image, spatial orientation, awareness of kinesthetic feedback, and temporal sequencing; a handwriting program must take the full process into account.
>
> 3. The approach must give the child practice with visualizing and revisualizing the graphic form of the letters being taught. [Hagin, 1983, p. 268]*

Hagin points out that the *Write Right—or Left Program* combines the accuracy of manuscript writing with the speed of cursive. It is based on vertical downstrokes rather than the diagonal slant necessary for cursive writing. It builds on the motor patterns of manuscript letters taught in the early years, but adds connecting strokes to permit faster writing than is possible with the separated letters of print. Further, throughout the program provisions are made for the following aspects of handwriting: consideration of posture, position of the paper, the way the pencil is grasped, arm movements across the paper, visual matching of the letter patterns with graphic models, and timing of feedback.

In this program, letter forms are taught through simple motifs written on the chalkboard. These motifs include "ferryboats" (parallel lines), "waves" (connected "c's"), "pearls" (series of waves that are connected top and bottom), "wheels" (straight line with periodic downward loops), and "arrows" (straight line on which several arrows point to the left). Hagin suggests that a motif be practiced first on the chalkboard and then attempted at a desk. Five steps comprise those lessons at the desk—trace, try, match, mastery, and sample.

---

* Reprinted by permission from R.A. Hagin, "Write Right—or Left: A Practical Approach to Handwriting," *Journal of Learning Disabilities, 16* (1983), pp. 266–271.

D'Nealian Handwriting (Thurber & Jordan, 1978). This writing program is comprised of thirty sections with four lessons in each. In the D'Nealian plan, lowercase manuscript letters can be converted to cursive form by joining certain strokes, and writing is slanted from the beginning. According to its publisher, the program has a number of notable features:

☐ The form of most lowercase manuscript letters is the basic form of the corresponding cursive letters, thereby allowing for a continuous progression of skills.

☐ Individuality is accepted within the bounds of legibility.

☐ Complete letters are taught rather than component parts.

☐ Aspects of career-awareness are featured throughout the books.

☐ Emphasis on numbers, labeling, map use, and on health and reference sources helps reinforce the relationship between handwriting and school content areas.

☐ Letters are grouped by similarity of stroke and ample practice is provided, thereby helping to assure success for the learner.

Beginners start writing on one-half inch ruled paper with a dotted midline. The simple letter forms of the lowercase manuscript alphabet help children establish the essential rhythm for cursive writing from the beginning, according to the authors. The traditional steps in teaching handwriting—first the circle-and-straight-line manuscript letter forms, then the transition to the flowing, rhythmic, connected cursive letter forms—are difficult for students to cope with. "The transition from manuscript to cursive, with the latter's often rigidly perfectionist models, which few children—or adults, for that matter—can emulate, pose particularly severe and long-lasting problems for many learners" (Thurber & Jordan, 1978, p. 6).

Learning to Write—Italic Style (Duvall, 1981b). Geiszler, a Seattle area teacher, offers the following rationale for this writing program:

> Traditional print script lacks the four essential cursive characteristics—letter slope, compressed spacing, branching, and joining of letters. Moreover, the outdated switching from block printing to cursive in the third grade is traumatic for the typical student. The transition wastes a great deal of instructional time. The drawing of circles and lines is not really writing, and third graders must be taught writing all over again when they switch to cursive. Italic handwriting provides a superior system, because it offers continuity by using letter shapes designed for rapid handwriting, legibility, and beauty. [Schulz, 1984, p. G1]

This approach presents lowercase and uppercase letters, which are patterned after the lowercase letters, one at a time. Each is followed by a line on which to practice and the method for writing the letter is shown and described. A four-step plan for practicing the letters is given:

■ FIGURE 8.2 ■   Examples from Duvall's Italic Handwriting Program

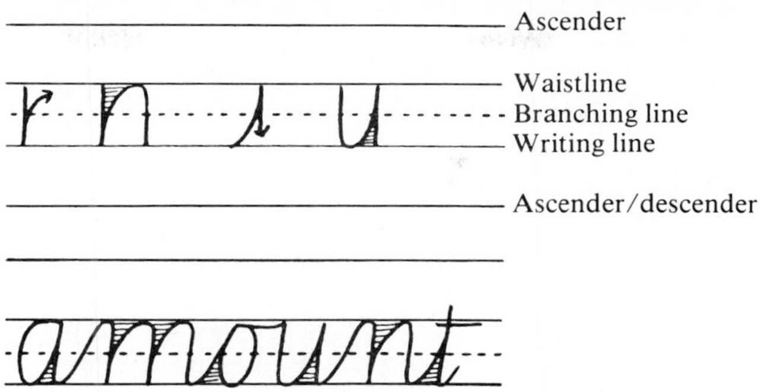

Source: Reprinted by permission from B. Duvall, *Learn to Write: Italic Style* (Great Falls, MT: Can Do Publications, 1981), p. 35.

1. Look carefully at each letter. Read the directions for making the letter, think about the directions, and mentally form the letter.
2. Practice the letter a few times when you have the formation in mind by thinking the letter and forming it "in the air."
3. Trace the letter several times at the beginning of the row.
4. Write a row of each letter on your own. As you complete each letter, compare it with the model. [Duvall, 1981b]

On linking letters to speed up writing, Duvall suggests that no more than three letters should be connected, but adds that the number is dependent on the size of the writing and on the student. She recommends that writers join as many letters as possible.

Pupils first practice on lowercase, then uppercase, then the two combined. Duvall suggests the use of four-line practice paper, to which a fifth line—a branching line—has been added. The branching line shows how far to retrace a stroke within a letter and also serves as a guide for the exit and entry strokes when joining letters to form words. The branching line allows pupils to check the triangular shapes that are formed, which should be the same in both cases. (See Figure 8.2.)

Assessment and Standards

Formal Assessment.   One of the more popular standardized assessments is the writing section of the *Basic School Skills Inventory—Diagnostic* (Hammill & Leigh, 1983). Norm-referenced for ages 4 to $7\frac{1}{2}$ years, the instrument is designed to assess children's handwriting ability in nine tasks:

— Writing from left to right
— Grasping a pencil
— Writing first name
— Maintaining proper writing position
— Writing letters on request
— Copying words
— Copying from chalkboard to paper
— Staying on the line
— Writing last name

The *Zaner-Bloser Evaluation Scales* (1979) are based on a national sampling of students' handwriting and are frequently given to assess manuscript and cursive handwriting. The evaluation includes scales for grades 1 and 2, written in manuscript style and scales for grades 2 through 8, written in cursive style. Each scale contains a sentence or paragraph that the teacher writes on the chalkboard. The students practice writing the model, then copy the sentences onto paper in their best handwriting. The teacher then compares each paper with five handwriting specimens—excellent, good, average, fair, and poor—for the child's grade level and judges five elements of writing—letter formation, vertical strokes in manuscript and slant in cursive, spacing, alignment, and proportion and line quality.

The *Test of Written Language* (Hammill & Larsen, 1983) a norm-referenced assessment, is sometimes administered to assess cursive handwriting. Students' handwriting abilities in grades 3 through 8 are estimated by rating samples of their spontaneous writing from 0 to 10 according to graded writing specimens included in the manual.

Informal Assessment. Hammill (1986) has suggested a method of assessment that evaluates the way pupils form letters according to the criteria listed in Figure 8.3. The extent to which students' letters match those in the "right column" indicates their degree of correctness. Hammill explains that the examples under the "wrong column" indicate the most common handwriting errors. These particular errors, referred to as "the fifteen handwriting demons," are said to cause or contribute to most of the illegibilities in children's cursive writing. It is interesting to note that when graduate students were asked to identify the letters they wrote that were the most illegible, they identified *d, h, m, r,* and *t*—letters that were all on the list of demons.

To obtain an informal assessment of handwriting legibility, Mann, Suiter, and McClung (1979) suggested that teachers obtain three samples: the students' usual, best, and fastest handwriting. The usual writing sample shows the students' work under normal conditions; for the best sample, students are told to take their time and write sentences as carefully as they can. To obtain samples of students' fastest writing, students are asked to write a given sentence as many times as they can during a 3-minute period. The reason for the three assessments is that some students write legibly only when specifically asked to do so, and others generally write well, but at extremely slow rates. By comparing the three writing

■ FIGURE 8.3 ■   *Criteria for Assessing Letter Formation*

	Wrong	Right
1. *a* like *o*	*o*	*a*
2. *a* like *u*	*u*	*a*
3. *a* like *ci*	*ci*	*a*
4. *b* like *li*	*li*	*b*
5. *d* like *cl*	*cl*	*d*
6. *e* closed	*e*	*e*
7. *h* like *li*	*li*	*h*
8. *i* like *e* with no dot	*e*	*i*
9. *m* like *w*	*w*	*m*
10. *n* like *u*	*u*	*n*
11. *o* like *a*	*a*	*o*
12. *r* like *i*	*i*	*r*
13. *r* like *n*	*n*	*r*
14. *t* like *l*	*l*	*t*
15. *t* with cross above	*t*	*t*

Source: D. D. Hammill, "Correcting Handwriting Deficiencies," *Teaching Students with Learning and Behavior Problems,* Fourth Edition, D. D. Hammill and N. R. Bartel, eds. © 1986 by Allyn and Bacon. Reprinted by permission.

samples, teachers can determine the student's ability with regard to speed *and* legibility.

Guerin and Maier (1983) developed a checklist (see Figure 8.4) for educators to use when assessing aspects of handwriting: letter size, proportion, figures, and fluency. Directions are provided for administering the checklist and for making specific judgments about the appropriateness of responses.

■ FIGURE 8.4 ■   Checklist for Assessing Handwriting

Directions: Analysis of handwriting should be made on a sample of the student's written work, not from a carefully produced sample. Evaluate each task and mark in the appropriate column. Score each task "satisfactory" (1) or "unsatisfactory" (2).

I. Letter formation
   A. Capitals (score each letter 1 or 2)

A _____	G _____	M _____	S _____	Y _____
B _____	H _____	N _____	T _____	Z _____
C _____	I _____	O _____	U _____	
D _____	J _____	P _____	V _____	
E _____	K _____	Q _____	W _____	
F _____	L _____	R _____	X _____	

                                                              Total _____

                                                              Score
                                                              (1 or 2)
   B. Lowercase (score by groups)
      1. Round letters
         a. Counterclockwise
            a, c, d, g, o, q   _____
         b. Clockwise
            k, p   _____
      2. Looped letters
         a. Above line
            b, d, e, f, h, k, l   _____
         b. Below line
            f, g, j, p, q, y   _____
      3. Retraced letters
         i, u, t, u, w, y   _____
      4. Humped letters
         h, m, n, v, x, z   _____
      5. Others
         r, s, b   _____

C. Numerals (score each number 1 or 2)

1 _____	4 _____	7 _____	10–20 _____
2 _____	5 _____	8 _____	21–99 _____
3 _____	6 _____	9 _____	100–1,000 _____
			Total _____

II. Spatial relationships

	Score (1 or 2)
A. Alignment (letters on line)	_____
B. Uniform slant	_____
C. Size of letters	
1. To each other	_____
2. To available space	_____
D. Space between letters	_____
E. Space between words	_____
F. Anticipation of end of line (hyphenates, moves to next line)	_____
	Total _____

III. Rate of writing (letters per minute)

	Score (1 or 2)
Grade 1: 20	
2: 30	
3: 35	
4: 45	
5: 55	
6: 65	
7 and above: 75	_____

Scoring

	Satisfactory	*Questionable*	*Poor*
I. *Letter formation*			
A. Capitals	26	39	40+
B. Lowercase	7	10	11+
C. Numerals	12	18	19+
II. *Spatial relationships*	7	10	11+
III. *Rate of writing*	1	2	6

Speed Standards.   An informal assessment for speed is shown in Table 8.1, which provides letters-per-minute data for intermediate grade pupils from surveys by Groff and Ayres (from Duvall, 1981a). Those data show that the majority of fourth graders wrote between 30 and 39 letters per minute; fifth graders, between 30 and 69 letters per minute; and sixth graders between 40 and 79 letters per minute. Note that the Ayres data are generally higher than those of Groff.

The *Precision Teaching Project* (Beck, 1986) suggests the following handwriting standards:

— See-to-write slashes = 200-400 per minute
— See-to-write circles = 100-150 per minute
— Think-to-write alphabet = 80-100 letters per minute
— See-to-write letters = 75 correct per minute
— See-to-write cursive letters connected = 125 correct per minute

Duvall (1981b) claimed that she could write 150 letters per minute in manuscript, 200 letters per minute in cursive, and 300 letters per minute in italic. Towle (1978) provided a practical scheme for evaluating handwriting based on these precision teaching techniques: count correct and incorrectly written letters per minute, chart those rates, and set rate standards derived from capable writers. In her assessment plan, procedures and standards were provided for writing letters, copying letters, copying letters in sequence that are near, and farpoint copying. Her suggested standards—50 legible letters per minute for copying letters—are much lower than those advanced by Duvall, another advocate of precision teaching.

■ TABLE 8.1 ■   *Pupils' Handwriting Speed, in Letters per Minute, from Studies by Ayres and Groff*

Letters per Minute	Percent of Pupils				
			Grade		
	4	5	5	6	6
	Groff	Ayres	Groff	Ayres	Groff
10–19	6.8	1	3.8	—	1.5
20–29	25.4	2	13.5	2	5.5
30–39	31.5	5	31.5	3	18.4
40–49	21.3	12	26.0	8	27.1
50–59	9.9	20	12.6	14	21.2
60–69	3.6	22	7.6	19	12.9
70–79	.8	19	3.2	21	7.9
80–89	.3	12	.8	16	3.6
90–99	.1	5	.4	10	.9
100–109	—	2	.4	5	.8
110–119	—	—	—	2	.4
	M = 35.06	M = 64	M = 40.65	M = 71	M = 49.65

Source: Data from Duvall (1981a, p. 15).

Performance of LD Youngsters

LD children have a variety of handwriting problems: slowness, incorrect direction of letters and numbers, too much or too little slant, poor spacing, inability to maintain a horizontal plane, illegible letters, too much or too little pencil pressure, and mirror writing. Newland (1932) examined the cursive handwriting of 2,381 individuals and discovered that half of the illegibilities involved the letters *a, e, r,* and *t,* (all members of the fifteen demons). Other common problems were the failure to close letters, closing top loops in letters such as *e,* not looping strokes that should be (writing *i* like e), using straight up strokes when they should not (for example, writing *n* for *u),* and exhibiting problems with end strokes. According to him, the numerals that were most often written illegibly were 3, 4, 5, 6, 7, and 9.

Figure 8.5 shows the writing of a seventh grade LD boy. He had read pages 139 to 144 in a social studies text and was asked to write notes on the passage. He was given 15 minutes for this task (he was not writing the entire time) and told to study what he had written in preparation for a test.

When his writing is analyzed, all the common handwriting errors pointed out by Newland, and many others, are apparent. Most of his letters are poorly formed, he often drifted away from the bottom line, his spacing of letters was erratic, and he often failed to cross *t's* and dot *i's.* Moreover, he misspelled a number of words, failed to include the proper punctuation at times, and neglected to capitalize words that should have been.

In contrast, Figure 8.6 shows some writing of a non-LD boy in that same class. These two samples are not intended to convey the idea that all LD writers write as poorly as Pete writes or that all non-LD writers write as well as Chris does. The samples, particularly that of the LD pupil, are intended to illustrate some of the problems such pupils have in writing.

Teaching Approaches

Eight techniques that have been arranged to improve the handwriting of pupils, many of whom were LD, are reviewed in the following paragraphs.

Lahey, Busemeyer, O'Hara, and Beggs (1977) used positive reinforcement and feedback to remediate severe perceptual–motor disorders in the handwriting of four LD boys. In their study, students copied words, geometric figures, and their names. Token reinforcement was contingent on correct responses, and corrective feedback was given following incorrect responses. Not only did the pupils improve on the instructed items, but showed generalizations to untrained symbols.

Hopkins, Schutte, and Garton (1971) studied the effects of access to a playroom on the rate and quality of printing and writing of first and second grade students. Their data demonstrated that when going to the playroom was contingent on the speed and quality of either manuscript or cursive writing, pupils' performances improved.

■ FIGURE 8.5 ■   Handwriting Sample from a Seventh Grade LD Boy

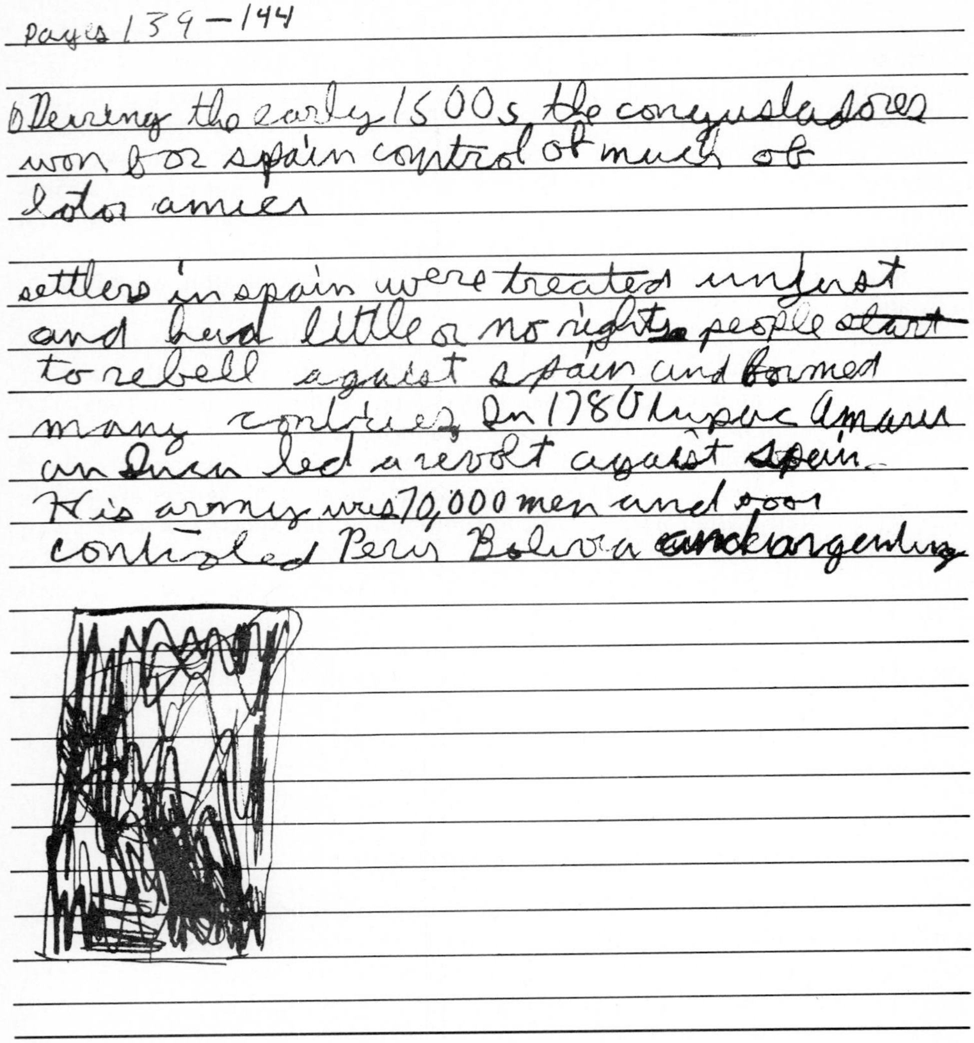

Pages 139 — 144

① Dureing the early 1500s the conquesladores won for spain control of much of latin amies

settlers in spain were treated unjust and had little or no rights. people start to rebell agaist spain and formed many contries In 1780 tupac Amaru an Inca led a revolt agaist spain. His army was 70,000 men and soon controled Peru Bolivia and argentina

Finholt and Hansen (1975) used contingent correction to improve the handwriting of LD pupils. In their project, students were required to practice the words in a passage they had copied illegibly, if more than five poorly written words were detected.

Harting (1974) demonstrated that feedback and a reinforcement contingency improved the handwriting of an LD boy in Mexico City. In her study, the pupil was provided corrective feedback following each session. He could avoid the next handwriting session if his correct rate exceeded 40 letters per minute and his incorrect rate was less than 2 per minute.

■ FIGURE 8.6 ■   Handwriting Sample from a Seventh Grade Non LD Boy

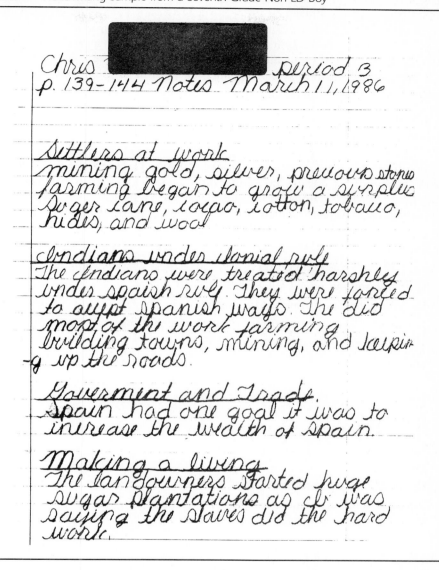

Trap, Milner-Davis, Joseph, and Cooper (1978) demonstrated the effects of feedback and consequences on transitional cursive letter formations of first graders. More specifically, they studied the effects of verbal and visual feedback, immediate rewriting of letters with incorrect letter strokes, and reinforcement on cursive letter strokes. Whereas students practiced on two sets of letters—trained and untrained—feedback and reinforcement were administered for only the former group. The results showed that the percentage of correctly formed letter strokes that were trained increased during all conditions. A consistent pattern of generalization to the untrained letter strokes was not demonstrated, however.

Kosiewicz, Hallahan, Lloyd, and Graves (1982) studied the effects of self-instruction and self-correction on the handwriting performance of a ten-year old LD boy. Self-instruction meant that the pupil said aloud the work to be written, then pronounced the first syllable, named each letter in the syllable three times, and repeated each letter as he wrote it. Self-correction meant that the student circled his errors from the previous day prior to copying the current day's assignment. The results showed that both techniques—self-instruction and self-correction—were highly effective, as was a combination of the two.

Blanford and Lloyd (1987) also investigated the effects of self-instruction on handwriting. They studied two LD boys, 10 and 11 years of age. Following a baseline condition, during an intervention phase the boys were given a card containing self-instructional questions designed to prompt the pupils to think about important aspects of handwriting. Following are the seven questions:

1. Am I sitting correctly?
2. Is my paper positioned correctly?
3. Am I holding my pencil correctly?
4. Are all my letters sitting on the line?
5. Are all my tall letters touching or nearly touching the top line?
6. Are my short letters filling only half of the space?
7. Am I leaving the right amount of space between words?

The study data showed the following results:

☐ The boys' handwriting improved markedly when the cards were introduced.
☐ The improvements persisted over time while the cards were still available to them.
☐ The effects were maintained after the cards were no longer available.
☐ The performance of one boy showed that his handwriting also improved in a regular classroom (those data were not gathered for the other boy).

The data also showed that the performances of the two boys were as good as those of average, nonhandicapped youngsters following the treatment.

Goldiamond (1965) described techniques arranged with a seventeen-year old boy to improve aspects of his handwriting. One problem was that he pressed too heavily with his pencil. To correct that, he was required to write on a stack of five sheets of onionskin paper, each separated by a piece of carbon paper, until his symbols were visible on only two sheets. Another writing problem was that his letters became smaller and smaller as he wrote. To remedy that, he was told to use the letter "T" as a guidepost. Every time he came to a "T" he was to write it as he had the one preceding and to use it to judge the letters that followed.

Another problem of the student's writing was that his "circle" letters were often ill-formed. For this, he was given small buttons to remind him of correct sizes.

SPELLING

Traditional Instructional Plans

According to Graham and Miller (1979), there are two major approaches for spelling instruction: the synthetic alphabet/whole word approach and the phonemic approach. The former implies that instruction is based on a special synthetic alphabet and whole words should form the core of the spelling curriculum. The phonemic approach views English orthography as a patterned but incomplete system. Supporters of the theory suggest that the systematic properties of orthography should be considered in spelling instruction. This view stresses the application of phonics and spelling rules as a means of developing spelling abilities.

Table 8.2 is a scope and sequence chart proposed by Graham and Miller. In this chart, they have suggested grades at which four general features of

■ TABLE 8.2 ■ Spelling Scope and Sequence

	Level 1	Level 2	Level 3	Level 4	Level 5	Levels 6–8
Spelling Vocabulary	25 words	275 words	400 words	460 words	460 words	460 words each
Phonic Skills	consonants ---------------					
		consonant clusters -----------------------------				
			digraphs ---------------------------------			
		vowels ---				
		base words ---				
		suffixes--				
			prefixes --			
Spelling Rules	capitalization					
			adding suffixes			
			punctuation-abbreviation			
			apostrophes			
				words do not end in v		
				letter q followed by u		
Proofreading Dictionary		spelling --				
	picture dictionary					
		alphabetical order				
			target word			
			alphabetical guide			
					independent dictionary work -----------------	

Source: Reprinted by permission of S. Graham and L. Miller, "Spelling Research and Practice: A Unified Approach," *Focus on Exceptional Children, 12* (October 1979), p. 6.

spelling—spelling vocabulary, phonic skills, spelling rules, and proofreading/dictionary—should be instructed.

One of the more popular spelling programs in the schools is *Basic Goals in Spelling* by Kottmeyer and Claus (1980), a series of books for eight levels. This program's goals include the following:

— Introduce most frequently used words in an orderly sequence
— Present words organized by the phonetic and structural characteristics which govern the anatomy of English vocabulary
— Make provisions for learning the irregularly spelled words
— Relate spelling to reading and writing
— Develop the habit of proofreading
— Incorporate dictionary skills

Information on Level 1 is provided to give an idea of the formats for the various levels. The level is organized into 36 weekly units because elementary school teachers are accustomed to teaching spelling in weekly units. Five pages of activities appear in each unit, one for each of the first four days of spelling instruction. The authors suggest that from 15 to 20 minutes each day be devoted to formal spelling instruction, generally one page per day. In this level, a standard set of stylized signs is introduced (it is repeated throughout the series). The consonant signs (for example, *ball, cat, dog)* are written to help pupils remember the sounds that the consonant letters spell. Thus pupils learn that *b* spells the sound that starts the word ball. The signs for the vowel sounds appear regularly *(apple, elephant, igloo, octopus-ostrich,* and *umbrella).* Pupils learn to identify letter names and to discriminate them visually in Unit 3. In Units 4 and 5, they are instructed to write lowercase letters; in Units 6 through 9, they learn the uppercase letter forms and key-picture words that will be used throughout the program. In Units 10 through 15 they are given practice in spelling consonant sounds.

Another popular spelling program is the one by Hanna, Hanna, Hodges, and Peterson (1971). The authors, who advocate the phonemic approach, claim that 49 percent of 17,000 words could be spelled correctly using phoneme-grapheme correspondences and another 37 percent could be spelled with only one error.

Assessment and Standards

Formal Assessment.   A widely used test for spelling is *Test of Written Spelling* (TWS) by Larsen and Hammill (1976). With that instrument, data are acquired on students' ability to spell words in three contexts: words that are readily predictable in sound-letter patterns, words whose spellings are less predictable, and both types of words considered together. The TWS is appropriate for students in grades 1 through 12, as well as for those in remedial programs. It can be administered in 20 minutes to either groups or individuals, and it yields a spelling quotient and percentile rank for each of the three subparts.

Another formal assessment is Kottmeyer's (1959) "Diagnostic Spelling Test," which measures a variety of spelling skills through a dictation format. Two tests are available—one for the second and third grades and one for fourth grade and above. The examiner says a word in isolation then gives a sentence in which that word is included. For both lists, each of the 32 items taps a specific spelling skill. For example, in list 1, words such as *not* and *get* are administered to assess pupils' abilities with short vowels; *boat* and *train,* to assess two vowels together; and *time* and *like,* for vowel-consonant-e. From list 2, *flower* is given to assess ability to deal with *ow-ou* spellings; *while,* for *wh* spelling and vowel-consonant-e; and *can't,* for contractions. Following administration of the test, the number of correct spellings is totaled and interpreted in a norm-referenced fashion. The results are then interpreted in a criterion-referenced manner. For example, if the student misspelled *shoot,* it is likely that she does not understand the use of long and short *oo* and *sh.* Analysis of the student's errors on the test should result in the development of a relatively data-based remedial program.

Informal Assessment. Edgington (1967) analyzed the writing of children and youth and compiled a list of the most frequent spelling errors in their writing, which included the following kinds of mistakes (examples shown in parentheses):

- Addition of unneeded letters *(sleevess)*
- Omissions of necessary letters *(now* for *know)*
- Reflection of dialectical speech patterns *(Imapala* for *Impala)*
- Reflection of mispronunciations *(wabbit* for *rabbit)*
- Reversal of letters in an entire word *(was* for *saw)*
- Reversal of consonant order *(cilp* for *clip)*
- Reversal of consonant or vowel placement *(peice* for *piece)*
- Reversal of syllables *(phonetele* for *telephone)*
- Phonetic spelling of nonphonetic words or parts thereof *(peple* for *people)*
- Neographisms, or letter placed in a word that bears no discernible relationship with the other letters in the word *(candlet* for *candle)*
- Varying degrees and combinations of these or other possible deficit spelling patterns

Speed Standards. Some years ago the author conducted a project with LD youngsters that relied on a rather unique way to assess spelling performance and to determine aims (Lovitt & Fantasia, 1983). Elementary age LD pupils were required to write spelling words from their proper placement level four times a year: October, December, March, and June. Thirty words were selected for each grade level. (Figure 8.7 shows samples of third grade words.)

The examiner said a word and the pupil wrote it, and as soon as the pupil was finished writing, the next word was pronounced. To obtain rate per minute

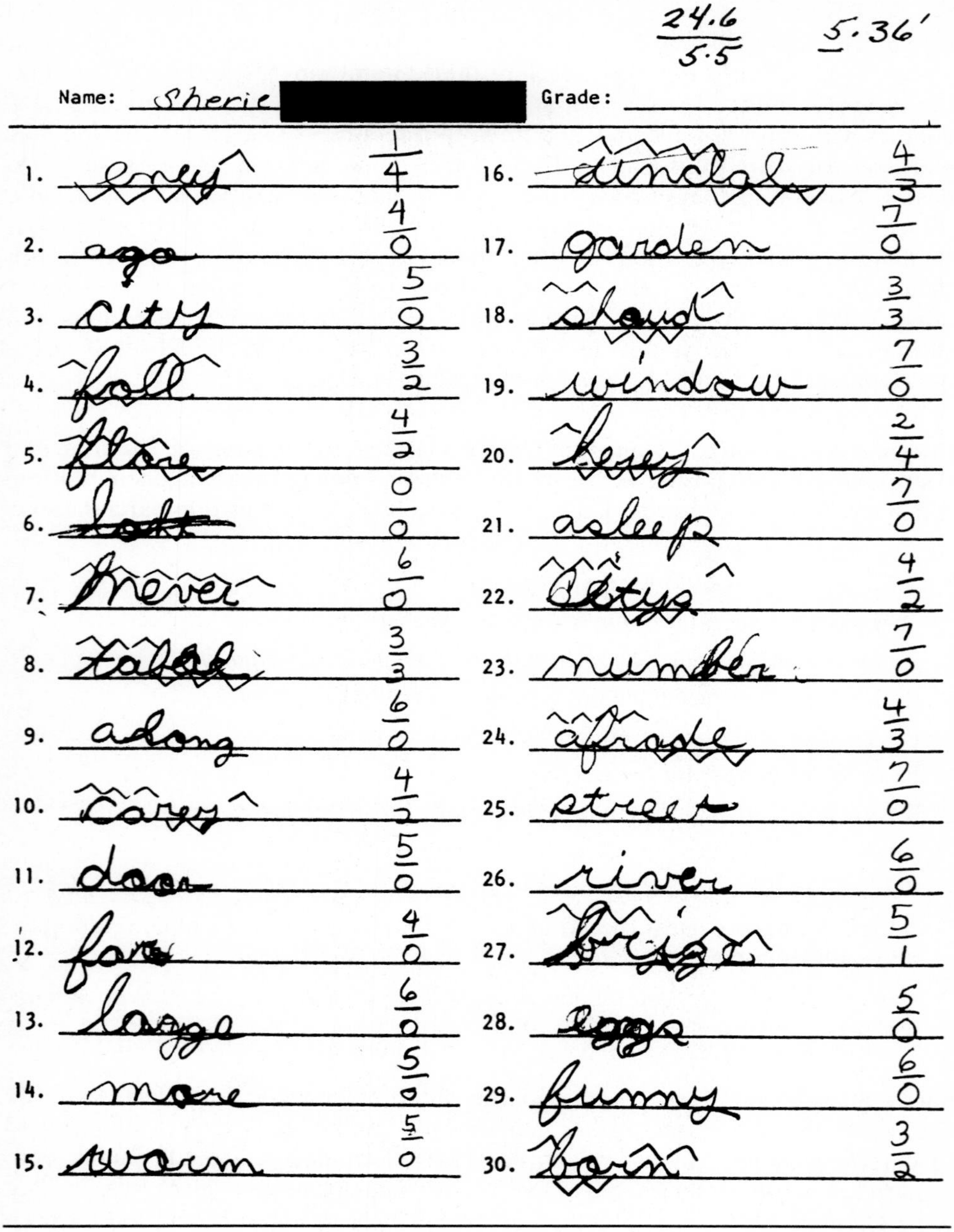

■ FIGURE 8.7 ■   Answer Sheet for Third Grade Spelling Performance Test

data the performances were timed and the number of correct and incorrect sequences was counted. The first word in the third grade list was *any*. As indicated by the carats on the word (see Figure 8.7), the pupil had one correct sequence (from "y" to space) and four incorrect sequences (from space to *e, e* to *v, v* to *e,* and *e* to *y).* The next word was correctly spelled, so she was credited with four correct sequences (one more than the number of letters in the word) and no incorrect sequences. As indicated at the top of the chart, it took her 5 minutes and 36 seconds to write all 30 words. Her correct and incorrect rates for writing sequences were 24.6 and 5.5 per minute. With respect to handwriting, some of her letter demons were *y, o, g,* and *t.* She also had some problems with the consistency of size. In some cases, her letters throughout a word became smaller; for example, *never.*

When the spelling performances of the LD pupils were studied throughout the year, the great majority of their correct rates doubled from first to last assessment, and their incorrect rates went down slightly. For example, if a pupil's rates were 30 and 5 for the first assessment, that pupil's rates in June would likely be around 60 and 3. This improvement was particularly true of the higher performing LD youngsters—that is, those who were placed at the fourth, fifth, and sixth grade levels.

To acquire aim rates on the words used, a group of graduate students was asked to spell the thirty words from the sixth grade list, with a new word pronounced every other second. The data indicated a range from 125 to 227 sequences per minute and an average rate of 196.5 sequences per minute.

Performance of LD Youngsters

Carpenter and Miller (1982) studied the spelling ability of LD students with reading deficiencies and able readers. The able readers were of two ages: averages of 8 and 11 years. The average age of the LD pupils, who were served in resource rooms, was 11. They were administered the following tests: *Peabody Picture Vocabulary Test, Peabody Individual Achievement Test,* and the *Test of Written Spelling.* The results of that study indicated that LD students performed significantly lower than nondisabled children in the same grades in the ability to spell phonic and nonphonetic words and in the ability to recognize misspelled words. The performance of reading disabled children was lower, though not significantly, than that of younger children who were more skilled at reading.

Carpenter (1983) studied the types of spelling errors of three groups of pupils: reading disabled (RD) from grades 3 through 6, reading able (RA) from the same grades, and a younger reading able (YRA) group matched with the RD pupils on a reading test. All pupils were administered the predictable words and unpredictable words subtests from the *Test of Written Spelling* (Larsen & Hammill, 1976). The results indicated that the RD and YRA pupils displayed similar spelling abilities, including the kinds of errors they made. The performances of the RD and RA pupils (those matched on grade level) were different; the RA youngsters used phonetic strategies more efficiently than did the RD students.

Donald D. Hammill was for some years on the faculty of the University of Texas. His major research interests have been in speech, language, perception, and reading. He has also been interested in policy matters in learning disabilities. Since 1977, Hammill has been president of PRO-ED, which publishes many of the tests summarized in this text. Most of the journals in the field of learning disabilities are also published by this company.

Gerber (1984) studied the spelling ability of LD and normally achieving students who were between the ages of 7 and 12. His results indicated that the spelling errors of LD students were no different from the errors of younger, normally achieving children. The errors of LD pupils were due to limited information and/or ability to formulate strategies for applying information to spelling words. In keeping with that conclusion, he recommended supplementary instruction in general problem-solving skills as they relate to the acquisition of basic academic skills.

DeMaster, Crossland, and Hasselbring (1986) analyzed the performances of LD students of intermediate age to determine the extent their errors were based on phonetic principles and predictable generalizations. Results showed that the students' spelling accuracy was consistent across the two dictated formats and was the same for good and poor spellers. Comparisons of the two forms of dictated presentations revealed that the specific types of spelling errors were about the same on both lists. The researchers concluded that this type of consistency indicated that LD pupils utilized systematic approaches to spelling dictated words. Their findings consequently supported the use of diagnostic error-analysis techniques with LD students, as well as teaching spelling by using a structured approach related to orthographic patterns.

James M. Kauffman is on the faculty of the University of Virginia. He has collaborated with Hallahan on a number of special education textbooks, one of the most recent being "Exceptional Children." Kauffman's primary interest has been with behavior disorders, but he has also published widely in a number of curricular areas including spelling and writing.

Traditional Teaching Approaches

The following paragraphs describe some techniques for teaching spelling to LD youngsters. Most of these methods are supported by data.

Kauffman, Hallahan, Haas, Brame, and Boren (1978) studied the effects of modeling and imitation on spelling performance. In the modeling phase, praise was given for each word correctly written on the chalkboard. When an error was made, the teacher said, "No, that's wrong," and erased the word. "Here's the way you spell it," and wrote the word correctly. The child was then required to copy the correct model. As for imitation, the teacher erased the word if an error was made and said, "No, that's wrong, here's what you wrote," (imitating the pupil's error) "and here's the way it should be spelled" (writing the word correctly and requiring the student to copy the correct model). Throughout, the teacher highlighted the particular letters that were incorrect. The data indicated that modeling aided spelling; when combined with imitation, the effects were even more pronounced.

Gerber (1986) replicated the research of Kauffman et al., but unlike that study, scheduled the imitation–modeling procedure with the youngsters until they had reached 100 percent accuracy on one list of words. To promote generalization,

a second list of words sharing the same orthographic features was then administered without specific instructions. A third list was next administered, and students
were instructed to use information about previous spellings in attempting words
on that list. Results showed the following: ten of eleven students reached mastery
in fewer than ten trials on List 1; students obtained more correct spellings on the
first trial of each new list; they required fewer trials on each successive list to
reach criterion; and students demonstrated systematic improvements in quality of
spelling attempts across both trials and lists.

McGuigan (see Hansen, 1978) devised a clever approach, referred to as the
"flow list method," for instructing spelling. This approach calls for a number of
words to be listed for pupils and for daily (or at least frequent) spelling tests on
those words to be given. When the pupil spells a word correctly three times in a
row, that word was eliminated from the daily testing and replaced by the next
word on the pupil's list. The list changed as rapidly as the pupil spelled words
correctly. Periodically, the "learned" words were presented to the pupil in a
retention test. If any of them is misspelled, it is again placed on the daily list to
be "relearned." When a pupil misspells a word, he or she practices it with the
"copy-cover-compare" technique: first copying the model word, then covering
the model word while writing it, and then comparing the word with the model.

Lovitt, Guppy, and Blattner (1969) investigated the use of reinforcement—
a free-time contingency—with fourth graders. They assessed spelling performances of the youngsters as a function of three conditions:

— When traditional procedures were in effect
— When contingent free time was individually arranged
— When a group contingency—listening to the radio—was added to the
    individually obtained free time

As a result of the reinforcement procedures, the majority of the pupils' spelling
performance improved, indicating that the use of contingent free time and radio
listening were effective reinforcers.

A number of other studies have also arranged reinforcement contingencies
to improve spelling performance. Zimmerman and Zimmerman (1962) demonstrated that when a teacher attended to only correctly spelled words, the spelling
accuracy of an eleven-year-old boy improved. Evans and Oswalt (1968) provided
evidence that a group consequence was effective in increasing the spelling accuracy
of two fourth grade students, and Karracker (1971) illustrated how a recess
contingency increased the spelling accuracy of a fifth grade boy.

Eisman (1962) compared pupil performance when words were supplied from
a commercial program and from an individualized program. Under the latter
program, students select the words to study and choose as many as they wanted
to learn each week. Pupils are tested each week; any words that are not passed
went on the following week's list. When given the *California Achievement Test,*
pupils on the individualized program scored about 1.5 grades higher in spelling
than children in the group program.

Hall (1964) recommended the "mark-out and corrected test method" as a way to improve spelling. For this technique, students evaluate their own spelling tests as the teacher spells each word aloud for them. The pupils mark out the letter or letters they missed in the words, write the correct letter or letters above the marked out letters, and rewrite the correct words beside the incorrectly written words.

Yudkovitz (1979) suggested a three-phase visual error-scanning approach for spelling disorders. During the first phase, the child reads sentences aloud and circles the errors he or she detects. In the next, the child is instructed to detect the errors he or she made. In the third phase, the student is taught to correct his or her errors.

Bryant, Drabin, and Gettinger (1981) studied the effects of varying unit size on spelling achievement of LD children with a mean age of 10 years and an average reading level of 2.2. The study used three groups who were taught three, four, or five phonetically irregular words a day. The study ran for three days and the instructional procedures were identical for all groups. The results indicated that

> Although total average achievement did not differ significantly among the three groups, they did differ on some aspects that are critical for LD children in terms of applicability of instruction in an ongoing classroom. There was greater variability in performance among children in the groups that were taught more words, with a higher overall percentage of failure. In addition, instructional time was greater (which may suggest the possibility of more fatigue and distractability), and fewer children were able to attain an acceptable (80%) mastery level. [Bryant et al., 1981, p. 203]

Gettinger, Bryant, and Fayne (1982) studied the effects of unit size, distributed practice, and training for transfer on the spelling abilities of LD youngsters. Experimental and comparison groups of nine-year-old LD pupils were formed for their study, and youngsters in both groups were instructed in a number of regular and irregular words. The experimental and comparison group experienced major instructional differences. The latter had a large total number of words introduced at one time and within one week of control instruction and lacked distributed and cumulative practice across the three weeks of instruction. Moreover, the teachers of the comparison group relied on instructional practices that included games and repetitive writing without providing corrective feedback, emphasizing mastery, or teaching for transfer. The researchers reported significant differences between the two groups. Pupils in the experimental setting were favored with respect to the accuracy of learning words in the first place and the ability to transfer to other words.

Stevens and Schuster (1987) studied the effects of a "constant time delay" procedure on the written spelling performance of an eleven-year-old LD pupil. According to the authors,

> The *constant time delay procedure* is a near errorless instructional method that transfers stimulus control from a controlling stimulus (a prompt that signals the

correct response) to a new stimulus (a target response). . . . For example, the new stimulus (the task request, "Spell *[target word]*") is given to the student. Simultaneously, a printed model of the target word (the controlling stimulus) is presented (zero-second delay) to allow the student to copy the model. After the model has been presented at the zero-second delay for a predetermined number of trials, the time between the task request and presentation of the model is systematically increased. This gives the student an opportunity to respond before the presentation of the model or to wait for the model if further prompting is required. [Stevens & Schuster, 1987, p. 10]

The results showed that the student acquired, maintained, and generalized 15 spelling words.

Graham and Freeman (1986) examined LD students' spelling performance in response to strategy training and variations in study conditions. Students were first trained in the use of a study strategy:

1. Say the word.
2. Write and say the word.
3. Check the word.
4. Trace and say the word.
5. Write the word from memory and check.
6. Repeat the first five steps.

Students were then divided into four study groups: directed-study, student-controlled, teacher-directed, and control. Students in the control group studied the words with any method they chose. Results revealed that students who were taught the study strategy recalled the correct spelling of more words than students in the control group; however, the spelling performances of students who received strategy training were about the same, regardless of the type of training.

Graham and Miller (1979) recommended the following five considerations for establishing an effective spelling program:

□ Instruction must be direct rather than incidental.
□ Instruction must be individualized.
□ Evaluation must be continuous.
□ Numerous instructional techniques must be available.
□ Attitudes of students and teacher must be positive.

Vallecorsa, Zigmond, and Henderson (1985) surveyed in the extent to which teachers were aware of spelling techniques and the extent they were involved in special education classrooms. The researchers found that teachers were reasonably well informed concerning spelling practices that were or were not supported by research. When it came to scheduling those techniques, a majority of the teachers selected eleven of the thirteen supported methods at least some of the time. Two of the supported methods, however—"daily testing" and use of a "test–study–test cycle"—were employed by fewer than 50 percent of the teachers. Many of the teachers also scheduled nonsupported practices, such as "presenting words initially in a sentence or paragraph format," "writing words several times to aid retention," "following a study-test cycle," "studying 'hard spots' in words," and "permitting students to devise their own word study methods."

Microcomputer Programs.   A number of microcomputer programs are available for instructing and monitoring spelling. The *Sensible Speller* (program published by Sensible Software, Inc., reviewed by Vanderwark, 1985), for example, is used to check the spelling in word processed files. With it, spellings can be compared with two electronic dictionaries, each containing 40,000 words. The program presents each misspelled word on the screen; it can display each misspelled word in three lines of surrounding text. The user may also select a wild card option and ask for the unknown letters in a word, whereupon a list of eight will be shown. This program enables the user to print out misspelled and corrected words.

Fitzgerald, Landis, and Milich (1986) compared the efficacy of computer-assisted instruction (CAI) with traditional instruction (TI) and a no-practice condition in the mastery of spelling words. The students in their study were nine elementary age students who had been identified as having attentional difficulties. The CAI software employed was the Spelling Machine. For that program, the student typed each word three times: copied from the model on the screen, typed after the model was removed, and entered from memory into a sentence. For the TI procedure, structured paper-and-pencil drill sheets guided the pupils through a "saying-writing-checking" sequence for each word. The results revealed that both CAI and TI were significantly more effective than the no-practice condition, but there was not a significant difference between the two treatments.

EXPRESSIVE WRITING

Traditional Instructional Plans

Hansen (1978) suggests the following purposes be taken into account when it comes to setting up programs to teach LD and non-LD students to write:

— Writing directions and announcements
— Writing reports about articles or stories
— Summarizing data from reading, oral, and written reports and from class discussions
— Communicating personal experiences
— Writing imaginative compositions
— Writing letters for social and business purposes

— Writing for school magazines or newspapers
— Writing to organize and develop one's ideas
— Writing reminders to oneself or others.

As teachers begin to instruct youngsters to write, they should consider the following suggestions:

Professional staff need to value writing as something more than opportunities for self-expression and communication, more than classroom contexts for practicing editing skills. They need to view composition and the composing process as a unique and powerful way for learning. Unless the cyclical relationship between writing and thinking is fully and systematically exploited, teachers will be deprived of a valuable teaching tool and growth in students' writing will never develop fully. In addition, all affected personnel need to accept a simple but incontrovertible fact—writing is a learned skill, best acquired in a school setting. [Alexander, 1983, p. 56]

Silverman, Zigmond, Zimmerman, and Vallecorsa (1981) surveyed a number of programs designed to teach writing to LD students. Their data showed that the LD students spent an average of 25 minutes a day in writing, and 19 minutes of that time was spent copying. They learned also that very young LD students were engaged in writing for less than 5 minutes a day, and most of that practice was devoted to filling in single words to blanks in worksheets. Their survey made it apparent that neither the purposes for writing noted by Hansen nor Alexander's guidelines for instructing writing were taken into account.

Roit and McKenzie (1985) projected three reasons for the failure of LD individuals to learn to write. First, they claimed that although the task-analysis approach may be appropriate for teaching mathematics and perhaps reading, it was not as suitable for developing writing. Second, they expressed agreement with the data of Silverman et al. and maintained that although LD children may have received ample drill on the elements of writing, they have never been allowed to write. Third, the reason LD pupils fail to write is that they lack the necessary metacognitive skills; they don't have the mental checklists that better writers have.

Roit and McKenzie offered three suggestions for designing writing programs for LD pupils:

1. Be sensitive to the misconceptions and consequent negative attitudes of LD students toward writing. Pay attention to the importance of motivating them to write. Help them realize that writing is an active, exploratory process that requires thinking about and organizing thoughts prior to writing.

2. Schedule writing in a variety of situations and contexts to foster the generalization of these skills to content classes.

3. Use orienting activities such as curiosity, arousal, prediction, and others to stimulate writing.

In *Writing Without Teachers* Peter Elbow (1973) advanced a rather nontraditional way to teach writing. He argued that pupils should engage in "freewriting exercises" in which they select a topic and write on it for about 10 minutes. During this period, all pupils should write something. If they could not think of anything to write, they should write, "I can't think of anything to write." Pupils should engage in several of these exercises, according to Elbow, so that words and phrases will "grow and cook" as they begin to write freely on a subject and are uninhibited by the thought of impending teacher criticism. He claimed that student's ideas and thoughts will begin to jell if they are allowed to express themselves freely.

Elbow believes that students often begin an editing process before they have written anything to edit. He is of the opinion that pupils should begin editing their work only when they have freely written on a topic for a number of times and when it has a focus. When pupils do edit, Elbow would encourage them to be brutal and throw out considerable material. In addition to keeping in mind all the usual editing approaches—rearranging, crossing out, correcting punctuation and spelling—students must learn to cut out all weak and unnecessary material.

Elbow hypothesized that if students were encouraged to write freely and without stopping, they would not be afraid later to cut out large sections of material they had written, for they would realize that words were relatively cheap. Elbow's belief that *only* when we write do we begin to think clearly agrees with Alexander's views.

■ COMMENTARY ■   Elbow's opinion that students would not hesitate to cut their writing is contrary to that of teachers who do not allow pupils to write until the students have made an outline and have "clearly" thought out what they will write. Words for those individuals are expensive. Although no data were found to support Elbow's contentions and his book was not written specifically for LD students, there are several reasons for considering his ideas: writing may improve thinking; reading one's own writing should be motivating; and writing freely without corrections may contribute to more writing.

Assessment and Standards

Following are a brief explanation of two tests for written expression, a discussion of some informal measures of writing, a description of a study comparing formal with informal measures of writing, and a report on some data that could be considered standards.

Formal Assessment.   A popular test for assessing writing is the *Test of Written Language* by Hammill and Larsen (1983). According to the authors:

The revised Test of Written Language (TOWL) identifies students who have problems in written expression and pinpoints specific areas of deficit. The TOWL yields information in six areas of writing competence: thematic maturity, spelling, vocabulary, word usage, style, and handwriting. Part of the information derived is from the analysis of a sample of continuous writing and part is from the analysis of subtest performance. Normative data in the form of percentiles and standard scores are provided for students between the ages of 7.0 through 18.11. Included in the manual is a section on informal methods for evaluating students' writing. Those techniques are intended to probe areas not covered by the TOWL and other formal writing tests. [Hammill & Larsen, 1983]

The *Written Expression Test* (Johnson, 1988) was designed for elementary school students. Youngsters are asked to write a story with a beginning, middle, and end. Tests are then scored for the following:

— Length of composition
— Spelling, punctuation and grammar
— Maturity and abstractness of theme
— Handwriting and letter formation
— Clause length and vocabulary development

Scoring rules are summarized and directions are provided for converting scores to percentiles and standard scores. Norms are available for grades 1 through 6. According to the publisher, the following are a few of the test's commendable features: It measures language skills as the child actually uses them; it may be administered to an entire class at the same time; and it provides a way to identify learning disabled students and diagnose certain of their language problems.

Informal Assessment.   Poteet (1980) developed an elaborate plan for assessing written expression but cautioned teachers, prior to conducting the assessment, to gather information on a broad spectrum of written expression skills, the requirements of specific writing tasks, and the characteristics of students being assessed as they relate to the developmental nature of their language system.

Poteet's checklist, illustrated in Figure 8.8, consists of sections on penmanship, spelling, grammar, and ideation. Poteet provided considerable detail in his write up on how to administer the checklist. He noted that teachers should mark in the appropriate codes for each youngster: TA = skill too advanced for instruction, A = skill adequately used, I = skill needs to be introduced, R = skill needs remediation.

To acquire writing data, Poteet suggested that pupils write several samples representing a variety of writing—letters, lists, reports, answers to questions— appropriate for their grade level, over a period of a few weeks. He suggested further, that students should read aloud what they have written, and the teacher should note any deviations from their writings.

Giordano (1984) discussed three informal techniques for analyzing generative writing samples. In the first technique pupils respond to five or so story starters, and the evaluator identifies the irregularities from these written samples. The evaluator then analyzes the writing with respect to grammatical accuracy and impact on comprehension and categorizes each sample into one of four quadrants.

Clusters of errors are interpreted as indications of certain types of writing disabilities. (See Table 8.3.)

Giordano's second technique for informally evaluating expressive writing is for pupils to respond to a few statements about writing, for example, "Writing makes me feel———." "When I have to write, I———." Results can differentiate pupils who are frustrated by writing activities from those who are not.

■ FIGURE 8.8 ■   Checklist for Assessing Written Expression*

Student's Name_____Grade Placement_____Teacher_____Grade_____

		TA	A	I	R	Notes
I.	PENMANSHIP					
	Rating: 1 2 3 4 5					
	A. Spacing on the page____					
	B. Spacing of the sentences___					
	C. Spacing of the words____					
	D. Spacing of letters____					
	E . Slant____					
	F . Letter formations____					
	G. Pressure on the paper____					
	H. Pencil grip ____					
II.	SPELLING					
	_____% misspelled					
	A. Miscalled rule____					
	B. Letter insertion ____					
	C. Letter omission ____					
	D. Letter substitution ____					
	E. Phonetic spelling____					
	F. Directional confusion____					
	G. Schwa or r-controlled vowels____					
	H. Letter orientation ____					
	I. Sequence____					
	J. Other ____					

Continues

Figure 8.8 Continued

III. GRAMMAR	TA	A	I	R	Notes
A. *Capitalization*					
1. proper noun					
2. proper adjective					
3. first word in a sentence					
4. first word in a line of verse					
5. first word in a quotation					
6. principal words in a title					
7. personal title					
8. use of "I" or "O"					
9. personification					
10. salutation in a letter					
11. complimentary close in a letter					
12. other					
B. *Punctuation*					
1. period					
2. comma					
3. apostrophe					
4. quotation marks					
5. question mark					
6. semicolon					
7. exclamation mark					
8. colon					
9. the dash					
10. parentheses					
11. brackets					
12. the slash					
C. *Syntax*					
1. parts of speech					
a. verbs					
b. nouns					
c. pronouns					
d. adjectives					
e. adverbs					
f. prepositions					
g. conjunctions					
h. interjections					
2. agreement					
3. case					
4. pronoun reference					
5. order/position of words					
6. parallelism					
7. abbreviations/numbers					
8. the paragraph					

Figure 8.8 Continued

IV. IDEATION
  A. *Type of writing*
    1. story_____ 2. poem_____ 3. letter_____ 4. report_____ 5. review_____
  B. *Substance*
    1. Naming_____ 2. Description_____ 3. Plot_____ 4. Issue_____.
  C. *Productivity*
    1. Number of words written_____ 2. Acceptable number_____ 3. Too few_____
  D. *Comprehensibility*
    Easy to understand_____ Difficult to understand_____ Cannot understand____
    _____perseveration of words   ____illogical
    _____perseveration of ideas   ____disorganized
  E. *Reality*
    _____Accurate perception of stimulus or task
    _____Inaccurate perception of stimulus or task

  F. *Style*
    1. Sentence Sense
      a. Completeness   Tallies:
        (1). complete sentences _____
        (2). run-on sentences _____
        (3). sentence fragments_____
      b. Structure
        (1). simple _____
        (2). compound _____
        (3). complex _____
        (4). compound/complex_____
      c. Types
        (1). declarative _____
        (2). interrogative _____
        (3). imperative _____
        (4). exclamatory _____
    2. Tone
      a. intimate_____ b. friendly_____ c. impersonal_____
    3. Word Choice (N=none, F=few, S=some, M=many)
      a. formality
        formal_____ informal_____ colloquial_____
      b. complexity
        simple_____ multisyllable_____ contractions_____
      c. descriptiveness
        vague_____ vivid_____ figures of speech_____
      d. appropriateness
        inexact words_____ superfluous/repetitions_____ omissions_____

Reprinted by permission from J.A. Poteet, "The Inventory of Written Expression and Spelling," *Learning Disability Quarterly, 3* (Fall 1980), pp. 90–92.

■ TABLE 8.3 ■   Interpreting Error Clusters

Quadrant	Examples	Characteristic	Interpretation
I	misspelled but recognizable word illegible but inferentially recognizable word	irregularities which are syntactically correct and comprehensible	author is not writing disabled; he is merely not responding to instruction
II	pronoun without a clear antecedent semantically inappropriate modifier	irregularities which are syntactically appropriate but incomprehensible	author may be writing disabled; or writer may be overattending to grammatical instruction to the point where he doesn't recognize that he isn't communicating
III	sentence fragment lacking a subject or a predicate adverb modifying a noun grammatically inappropriate and incomprehensible phrase pronoun not agreeing with a recognizable antecedent	irregularities which are syntactically inappropriate and incomprehensible	author is writing disabled
IV	double negative split infinitive inappropriate use of apostrophe run on sentence inappropriate punctuation alteration of an idiom	irregularities which are syntactically inappropriate but comprehensible	author is not writing disabled; he could be inattentive to instruction, or influenced by non-standard dialect

Source: Reprinted by permission from G. Giordano, "Analyzing and Remediating Writing Disabilities, *Journal of Learning Disabilities, 17* (1984), p. 82.

The third evaluation technique is a restoration exercise, in which children are asked to supply words deleted from passages they have written. Results from this technique, according to the author, indicate linguistic writing disabilities by confirming whether students can replicate the generation of grammatically and semantically appropriate words in their own writing.

Deno, Marston, and Mirkin (1982) related six approaches for scoring student performances in writing using subtests from three standardized writing tests—*Test of Written Language, Stanford Achievement Test,* and the *Developmental Sentence Scoring System.* The approaches for scoring writing included: mean T-unit length, "mature words," large words, words spelled correctly, letter sequences correct, and total number of words. The correlations shown in Table 8.4 indicated that four of the measures listed—total words written, words spelled correctly, correct letter sequences, and mature words—strongly and consistently related to the criteria, standardized tests. The authors recommended that, "Since counting words written is the simplest scoring procedure, recording that information is recommended for students who are writing words on cue. For beginning writers, however, counting correct letter sequences may be an appropriate alternative" (Deno et al., 1982, p. 370).

Speed Standards.   Throughout this chapter there have been a number of references to the speed of writing letters and words. In Table 8.1, for example, data were presented as letters per minute. They could be converted to words per minute by dividing the frequencies by five. From that table it is apparent, then, that .4 percent of the sixth graders in Groff's sample wrote about 20 words per minute, although we don't know how long they wrote. We also have Duvall's data on writing letters in manuscript, cursive, and italic. When her letters-per-minute data are converted to words, the rates for the three approaches are thirty, forty, and sixty for a period of only one minute each. Nodine, Barenbaum, and Newcomer (1985) reported that the top writers in their study wrote about seven words per minute over a period of 15 minutes.

■ COMMENTARY ■   Obviously, there are a number of factors to consider when setting word-per-minute aims for writing, among them age and intellectual level, time devoted to the task, preparation for the task, and mode of writing. For example, when a group of graduate students was asked to think for one minute about what they would later write for one minute with pen or pencil, their average rate was twenty-seven words per minute. When a doctoral student wrote her exam questions on a microcomputer for four hours a day for two days, her average rate was sixteen words per minute. While this information pertains to the speed with which a person can write with a pencil or a microcomputer for various durations, it doesn't inform us about the quality of the person's writing.

There are a number of ways to assess the quality of writing. Although most are highly subjective, a convenient approach is to use one of the many software programs for tabulating aspects of writing. One such program is *The Word* (published by Oasis Systems). This program gives the writer information on total number of words in the passage, the number of words used only once, and the number of unique words. In the preceding sentence, for example, there were twenty-seven total words, 13 words were used only once, and there were 17 unique words.

When those figures are divided by the total number of words, the ratios are .48 and .63. These figures are measures of variation, which is, to some extent, related to quality. There are many other ways, of course, to assess quality.

Another dimension of writing has to do with quantity. There are several ways to acquire such data. One could, for example, count the number of words, paragraphs, or pages written each day, week, month, or year. Over time, the sum of those counts would give an accurate account of the individual's output.

■ **TABLE 8.4** ■   Correlations Between Scores from a Writing Sample and Scores on Achievement Tests*

Achievement Measures	Measures of Written Expression					
	Mean T-Unit Length	Mature Words	Large Words	Words Spelled Correctly	Letter Sequences Correct	Total Words Written
Test of Written Language						
Vocabulary	.13[a]	.61	.43	.60	.63	.60
Thematic Maturity	.07[a]	.73	.57	.61	.65	.58
Spelling	.17[b]	.76	.67	.66	.70	.65
Word Usage	.15[a]	.77	.67	.71	.74	.69
Style	.20[b]	.62	.49	.57	.57	.59
Raw Total	.18[a]	.83	.75	.80	.75	.75
WLQ	.15[a]	.74	.60	.67	.71	.65
Stanford						
Word Usage	.29[c]	.72	.53	.67	.69	.62
Developmental Sentence Scoring	.29[c]	.74	.47	.76	.86	.84

*All correlations are significant at .001 unless otherwise noted.

[a]Not significant

[b]Significant at .05

[c]Significant at .01

Source: Reprinted by permission from "Valid Measurement Procedures for Continuous Evaluation of Written Expression" by Deno, S.L., Marston, D., & Mirkin, P., *Exceptional Children*, Vol. 48, No. 4, January 1982, p. 369. Copyright 1982 by The Council for Exceptional Children. Reprinted with permission.

Indeed, some famous authors have kept such records. Hemingway's daily output often ranged between 400 and 1,300 words a day. Trollope recorded his production in terms of pages per week and tried to maintain an average of 40. Skinner calculated the number of published words, and over a thirty-year period had written 175,000 of them (Lovitt, 1984).

Writing Performance of LD Youngsters

Following are summaries of a number of studies that compare certain writing performances of LD and non-LD students. In one such investigation, Poteet (1980) reported comparative data from Hermreck's (1979) master's thesis. In her research, nonhandicapped students, writing a story about a picture, wrote an average of 83 words in grade three, 94 words in grade four, 141 words in grade five, and 200 words in grade six. In comparison, she reported, LD students wrote an average of 40 words in grade three, 54 words in grade four, 70 words in grade five, and 170 in grade six. Depending on the grade, regular students wrote from 50 to 100 percent more than did the LD pupils.

There were also some comparative data in the report by Deno et al. (1982), referred to earlier. The authors presented a table showing the mean grade level performances for resource and regular students in grades four, five, and six for four direct measures of written expression. In every measure for every grade, the performances of the regular students exceeded those of the resource students. These differences were particularly significant at the third grade level where many of the differences were fivefold (see Table 8.5). However, we do not know how long the students wrote, nor do we know what the stimulus was (for example, story starter).

Morris and Crump (1982) studied the syntactic and vocabulary development in the written language of LD and non-LD students at four age levels. There were eighteen students of both types from four age levels: 9 to 10.5, 10.5 to 12, 12 to 13.5, and 13 to 15. These students wrote about two films that were shown. There were no significant differences between groups with respect to T-Units (a

■ TABLE 8.5 ■   Mean Grade Level Performance for Resource and Regular Students on Four Direct Measures of Written Expression

Measures of Written Expression	Resource Students			Regular Students		
	N	Mean	Standard Deviation	N	Mean	Standard Deviation
Total Words Written						
Grade 3	9	9.0	9.1	11	40.1	15.0
Grade 4	10	34.5	13.5	36	51.1	20.4
Grade 5	11	39.9	21.6	22	54.9	21.2
Grade 6	14	41.6	14.4	17	64.4	23.1
Mature Words						
Grade 3	9	1.7	2.7	11	9.6	4.1
Grade 4	10	5.1	3.6	36	11.9	6.7
Grade 5	11	8.5	5.9	22	12.5	6.0
Grade 6	14	9.4	4.0	17	14.6	7.0
Words Spelled Correctly						
Grade 3	9	5.8	7.2	11	36.8	15.1
Grade 4	10	28.9	15.2	36	45.1	20.6
Grade 5	11	32.0	21.0	22	52.0	22.2
Grade 6	14	34.0	17.5	17	61.5	23.5
Letter Sequences Correct						
Grade 3	6	18.3	29.7	9	153.5	74.0
Grade 4	5	113.4	72.9	27	213.9	89.2
Grade 5	8	208.0	101.3	17	258.1	101.1
Grade 6	10	164.8	55.2	15	270.0	80.9

Reprinted by permission from "Valid Measurement Procedures for Continuous Evaluation of Written Expression by Deno, S.L., Marston, D., & Mirkin, P., *Exceptional Children*, Vol. 48, No. 4, January 1982, p. 370. Copyright 1982 by The Council for Exceptional Children. Reprinted with permission.

quantitative measure of the average number of words in a main clause and any subordinate clauses attached to the main clause), but there was a significant main effect for age. The scores for syntactic density (a measure that takes into consideration T-unit length, clause length, number of subordinate clauses, embeddings, and verb expansions) were significantly different between groups and age levels. The corrected type/token ratio scores (derived by dividing the number of word types by the square root of twice the number of words in the sample) were significantly different between groups and among age levels. However, as in the report by Deno et al., we do not know how long students wrote.

Poplin, Gray, Larsen, Banikowski, and Mehring (1980) compared six components of written expression. There were three levels of LD and non-LD students in their study: grades 3 and 4, 5 and 6, and 7 and 8. The pupils were administered six subtests of the *Test of Written Language*. The results indicated that the performances of the non-LD youngsters were superior to those of the LD youngsters for all tests at all levels; the older the students, the more significant the difference. (See Table 8.6.)

Following is an interesting quote from that study:

> While some scores of the LD group (particularly at grades 7 and 8) were found to be significantly lower than those of normals in the more conceptual tasks of *Vocabulary* and *Thematic Maturity,* these mean scores did not at any grade level fall below one standard deviation from the norm. Since ideation and conveying of meaning is the most logical purpose of writing, the authors consider this a very promising finding. It might suggest that teachers of the LD should emphasize and reinforce these meaningful aspects of writing and de-emphasize the more mechanical aspects until a later date so that students can build confidence and positive attitudes toward writing activities before the more difficult and less meaningful activities are introduced. . . .
>
> Until otherwise proven, meaningful writing experiences with immediate, reasonable, and knowledgeable feedback still seem to offer the most effective method of improving mechanical, conventional knowledge of the writing process without interfering with and stifling the all-important ability to "get across" in writing what the student intends to communicate. [Poplin et al., 1980, p. 52]

Moran (1981) investigated the writing performances of LD and low-achieving (LA) secondary age students on several features of writing. These students were required to write four paragraphs and then edit them. On the average, the LD students took 9 minutes 13 seconds for the draft and 7 minutes 11 seconds for the copy. It took the LA pupils 7 minutes 23 seconds on the draft and 6 minutes 47 seconds on the copy. As for the four measures—syntactic maturity, mechanics, conventions, and spelling—there were significant differences between groups for only spelling. The author summarized the findings as follows:

> The finding that spelling performance as measured by analysis of elicited writing samples discriminated a group of secondary LD subjects from a group of LA subjects confirms earlier research reports that lowered spelling scores are characteristic of learning disabled students. [Moran, 1981, p. 279]

■ TABLE 8.6 ■   Summary of ANOVA and TOWL Subtest and Full-Scale Scores for Three Groups of
LD and NLD Students with Chronological Age Covaried

		Grade Levels								
		Elementary (3rd & 4th)				Middle (5th & 6th)				
		N	X	F	P	N	X	F	P	N
Vocabulary	LD	33	8.18	3.122	.08	33	8.73	5.314	.024	33
	NLD	33	10.42			33	10.73			33
Thematic	LD	33	8.85	3.092	.08	33	9.33	9.038	.004*	33
Maturity	NLD	33	10.39			33	11.48			33
Spelling	LD	33	6.94	37.293	.000*	33	6.03	86.538	.000*	33
	NLD	33	10.52			33	11.64			33
Word	LD	33	7.48	18.737	.000*	33	6.94	47.596	.000*	33
Usage	NLD	33	10.30			33	10.85			33
Style	LD	33	7.52	19.611	.000*	33	6.70	44.992	.000*	33
	NLD	33	10.67			33	10.85			33
Written	LD	33	88.42	23.888	.000*	33	87.82	54.144	.000*	33
Language										
Quotient	NLD	33	102.21			33	105.55			33

*df = 1, N = number, X = mean, F = a statistic, P = probability

Source: Reprinted by permission from M. S. Poplin, R. Gray, S. Larsen, A. Banikowski, and T. Mehring, "A
Comparison of Components of Written Expression Abilities in Learning Disabled and Non-Learning Disabled
Students at Three Grade Levels," *Learning Disability Quarterly*, 3 (Fall 1980), p. 50.

Nodine, Barenbaum, and Newcomer (1985) studied the story compositions
of LD, reading disabled, and nondisabled children; all of whom were 11 years
old and from families with a low socioeconomic standing. Students were shown
pictures and given 15 minutes to write. Results indicated that only 30 percent of
the LD students wrote passages that were classifiable as stories, as compared to
47 percent of the reading disabled, and 71 percent of the nonhandicapped youngsters. The nonhandicapped group wrote an average of 104 words per composition,
whereas the means for the other two groups were slightly over 50. (The top
writers wrote, on the average, 7 words per minute.) When it came to cohesiveness
of writing, the LD pupils were the least proficient.

Based on these data one may speculate that the learning disabled children, particularly those operating at the descriptive and expressive levels, lack the understanding
of story schema that, according to many theorists, is essential not only to writing
stories but to reading them with comprehension. [Nodine et al., 1985, p. 176]

Thomas, Englert, and Gregg (1987) analyzed the errors and strategies in
the expository writing of four groups of LD and non-LD students: 3rd and 4th

grade LD, 6th and 7th grade LD, 3rd and 6th grade non-LD matched to LD students on IQ and reading level (LD-M), and normal achieving 3rd and 6th graders (NA). Students in all four groups were required to write two stories for each of four types of text structures: description, sequence, comparison, and enumeration.

Results revealed that LD students had considerable difficulty in controlling the structures of expository prose. Of the five error categories that were analyzed, LD pupils surpassed NA students in the production of four types of error (redundancies, irrelevancies, early termination, and mechanical), and differed from LD-M in the production of two types (early termination and mechanical). When errors were summed across all categories, LD students differed substantially from both their LD-M and NA counterparts. The data further revealed that the comparison/contrast text structure was more difficult for students than the sequence format, and both were significantly more difficult than the description and enumeration structures.

Teaching Approaches

Traditional Methods.   The first two studies that follow were conducted with LD or remedial students. The remaining four investigations were scheduled with non-LD students.

Brigham, Graubard, and Stans (1972) analyzed how reinforcement contingencies affected aspects of composition with thirteen fifth graders, most of whom were more than two years behind academically. A token system was in effect in this classroom; points were alternatively given for the number of words written, new words, and different words. The average number of words written per session in the baseline was about 30, whereas it averaged about 90 in the phase when points were contingent on number of words. The number of new words per session went from an average of 15 in baseline to 22 when reinforcement was arranged for that feature. The baseline average for different words per session was 15, and it went to 30 when a contingency was associated with that type of writing.

Hansen and Lovitt (1973) studied the effects of feedback on several writing features. The LD students in their research were between the ages of 9 and 11. Following a baseline period, during which no feedback was provided, some youngsters received feedback on mechanical aspects of writing, whereas others were given feedback on content features. Later, all students were administered both types of feedback.

When data between baseline and treatment conditions were compared, results indicated the following:

1. Both groups improved in their use of punctuation and capital letters, but the group for whom feedback was given for mechanics improved more.
2. Average sentence length and the use of different words increased for most pupils irrespective of the intervention.

3. Both groups improved about the same on measures of quality.

4. The word-per-minute rates of the students remained about the same through-out the study. (The highest rates were about thirteen words per minute over 10 minutes.)

Gardstrom and Lovitt (1979) studied the effects of various interventions on the expressive writing of second graders. In their research, students wrote for 20 minutes each session on a theme of their choice. Throughout the study, the teacher gave minimal feedback on their efforts and counted the number of words and "thought units" (generally a sentence) written. During Phase I, students could read their compositions to their mates. In the next phase, pupils' charts were publicly posted, and they could also read their stories. In Phase 3, the charts were posted but the students did not read their stories. The last phase was like the first, the students could read their stories, but their data were not publicly available. Results indicated that, for most students, the biggest improvement in respect to both measures was during conditions when their charts were posted. Some of the writing rates during those phases were around five words per minute.

Glover (1979) studied the effectiveness of reinforcement and practice for enhancing the creative writing of elementary school children. In that research, team points and practice were applied to the written work of 16 fifth graders on five components of writing:

— *Fluency:* the number of different ideas listed in an idea list prepared prior to writing an essay
— *Idea list flexibility:* the number of different kinds of ideas that appeared in each day's list
— *Story flexibility:* the number of different approaches to the topic that the pupil used in the story itself
— *Idea list originality:* the statistical infrequency of ideas in the children's lists of ideas
— *Story originality:* the subjective ratings of stories conducted by independent raters

Data from that research indicated that all five measures were influenced by the contingencies. The procedures also raised students' scores on *Torrance Tests of Creative Thinking* (1974).

Maloney and Hopkins (1973) conducted a study with intermediate age students who wrote ten-sentence stories. In some phases, points were given contingent on various parts of speech. The data showed that when contingencies were arranged successively for adjectives and then action verbs, the frequencies for writing those parts of speech increased. Independent subjective ratings indicated that stories written during contingency conditions were generally rated as more creative than those written during baseline conditions.

In research by Maloney, Jacobson, and Hopkins (1975), third graders wrote five-sentence stories, and examiners counted the number of words, nouns, adjectives, adverbs, prepositions, and action verbs written. Data were also kept throughout the study on a subjective measure of quality. In various phases of their experiment, the examiners evaluated the effects on writing of teacher lectures, teacher requests, and points contingent for various parts of speech. Their data revealed that, generally, effects were noted for the parts of speech on which reinforcement was contingent, but little generalization to other features occurred. They also observed that lectures and requests had little effect on writing. The better compositions, according to subjective judgments, were those composed during the reinforcement phases.

Typewriters and Microcomputers.

Typewriters.   The typewriter has been considered by some as a way to teach writing to LD pupils. Two advantages to using typewriters—legibility and speed—have often been cited, particularly for LD students.

■ COMMENTARY ■   *Since most LD youngsters are not noted for their legible penmanship, it would certainly be an improvement were they to type. Not only would they and others be better able to read what had been written, but the typed message would probably have greater esthetic appeal.*

As indicated by data in this chapter, the average writing rate for graduate students is 27 words per minute when they wrote with pen or pencil for one minute. It would be very difficult to keep up that pace for even 10 minutes. Yet competent typists can produce around eighty words per minute over an extended period of time.
        Several years ago Blankenship and Hansen (1972) ran a project in which they instructed seven LD boys to type. The youngsters were between the ages of 10 and 12. They used a standard typing program and followed its directions and lesson format as closely as possible. The first skills to be taught were how to position the paper guide, how to operate the spacing regulator and margin stop, and how to insert paper. Over a period of about ten weeks most of the boys passed fifteen lessons. In that fifteenth lesson they were to learn the "Q" and "?" keys and to type 15 lines of letters such as the following: *aaa sss ddd fff jjj kkk lll ;;; ;/; :?: :/: :?:.* The rates of the youngsters during this brief instruction period were as high as fifteen "words"—that is, a group of three letters—per minute.

Microcomputers.   Currently there is great interest in instructing LD youngsters (and others) to use word processing programs and computers. Morocco and Neuman (1986), for example, are studying ways in which teachers use word processors to teach composition to fourth grade LD students. They claim that two possible advantages of using microcomputers stem from the public display of the message: teachers can readily assist youngsters with their writing, and groups of youngsters can write together in cooperative learning situations.

According to MacArthur and Shneiderman (1986), a number of features from word processors could aid writers, particularly those who are learning disabled. These features include the following:

1. The ability to produce neat, printed copy can affect students' perceptions of the quality of their writing and can increase their motivation to write.
2. The editing capabilities of word processing programs make revisions possible without tedious recopying. This capability makes it possible to teach writing as a process that involves repeated drafts.
3. With a word processor, students use typing rather than handwriting, which not only produces better looking copy, but may be easier for learning disabled students to produce.
4. A number of auxiliary features are available with word processing programs (for example, spell checkers and programs that help with outlining, generating, and refining ideas).

A word processing program recommended for LD youth is *QUILL* (reviewed by Vanderwark, 1985). It is a set of microcomputer writing activities designed for students in grades 2 through 12. *QUILL* includes two writing tools and two contexts for writing designed to promote communication by providing audiences for students' writing. The first writing tool is the "Planner," designed to help students plan and organize. The other tool is the "Writer's Assistant," a text editor designed to help students revise their text. One context for writing is "Mailbag," an electronic mail system for sending messages. The second context is "Library," a data-based management system which permits access to student writing via title, author, or keywords.

Another popular word processing program is the *Bank Street Writer* (program published by Broderbund Software). According to many, it is relatively simple to use; reminders are available on the top of the screen at all times to tell writers how to proceed. The program has three modes: write, edit, and transfer. In the write mode the writer composes the document, whereas in the edit mode he can make changes. The transfer mode is used to save, rename, delete, or print the document.

Kidwriter (reviewed by Mather, 1985) is a word processing program that allows students to create colorful graphic pictures and then write stories about them. The first step in creating a story is to make a picture. For this activity, a menu appears on the screen that enables students to select a background scene and ninety-nine different objects (such as people, animals, buildings). After the object is selected, students can alter the position, color, or size. When the picture is finished, students may then write a story in the lower part of the screen. The built-in word processor includes automatic line-wrap and allows students to edit, correct, retype, erase, and insert lines.

MacArthur and Schneiderman (1986) conducted a study with several LD pupils to determine which features of word processing programs were troublesome, and on the basis of those evaluations, made recommendations to software producers. Their comments included the following:

1. Software designers should write programs that allow for "modeless editing"; that is, where the system is always in insert mode, the arrow keys are used for cursor movement, and the delete key is used to delete the character to the left of the cursor.

2. Designers should make it easy to move text. In the study, students found moving and deleting blocks of text was relatively difficult.

3. One of the more persistent difficulties the students had stemmed from confusion about the correct use of spaces and returns.

4. The menus of word processing programs should be clear. Students need a logical format for knowing how to write, file, and print.

5. Little-used options, such as print formats, should have default values and be accessed only if users request them.

COMMENTS AND DISCUSSION POINTS

Listed here are a number of comments for instructing LD youngsters in handwriting, spelling, and expressive writing.

Handwriting

- Consider beginning writing with italics or the D'Nealian method. Too much time is spent teaching LD youngsters to first print (manuscript) and then write (cursive). Most of them don't become proficient at either form, much less with both. It might be more practical to select one form and concentrate on it. Indeed, some districts throughout the country are teaching only one type of writing; it will be informative to follow their progress.

- Quite early on, LD youngsters should be instructed to legibly write their vital facts: their name, address, telephone number, and other significant information. Furthermore, they should be taught to write this information on a variety of applications and forms.

- When LD students participate in lecture-type classes, they should be taught to take notes and to organize them for later study.

- LD youngsters should be taught to write out certain pieces of critical information on cue cards that they carry with them. For example, they could write out words or phrases that are necessary to their lives, yet are difficult to remember. One LD individual might write his bus schedule on a card; another might write her address and phone number.

- Concentrate on legibility of the most important symbols. Although it would be admirable if LD individuals wrote everything "with a beautiful hand," we may have to be more realistic and strive for "excellence" on only the most vital numbers or words.

Spelling

- Teach LD pupils to spell words they are reading, whether the material is from basal readers, the home and community, or from stories they have written. It doesn't seem efficient to select one commercial spelling program that features certain words and a basal reading series that emphasizes different words.

- A next-best approach would be to teach the high frequency words and the high probability generalizations (those in the program by Hanna et al., 1971, for example).

- LD youngsters should be taught to use spell-check programs such as *Sensible Speller* that are made for microcomputers.

- LD students should be taught early on, to spell correctly the words they use quite often and the ones that are most important.

Expressive Writing

- Early on, teach LD youngsters to write words and simple sentences. As with reading, writing should be taught in context. We probably place too much emphasis on making simple strokes and letters that are not too relevant. The process of writing means more when something has been said.

- Schedule a time each day for pupils to write. As with reading, one of the reasons that most LD youngsters *can't* write is because they *don't* write. We might consider scheduling a daily sustained silent writing period as many schools now have sustained silent reading periods.

- Integrate writing instruction with language, reading, grammar, and spelling instruction. We should also concentrate on good writing during mathematics and other classes as well.

- Teach pupils to use a word processor as soon as possible. There are some simple programs—for example, the *Bank Street Writer* and *Kidwriter*—available for youngsters.

Take advantage of some of the recommendations from Graham and Harris (1988):

— Expose students to a broad range of writing tasks. When possible, writing should be aimed at an authentic audience.
— Create a social climate conducive to writing; teachers should be accepting and encouraging.
— Aid students in developing the processes central to effective writing. Emphasize the importance of planning, sentence generation, and revising.

— Help students develop explicit knowledge about the characteristics of good
writing. Consider direct instruction in the structural elements representative
of a particular genre.
— Assist students in the development of goals for improving their written
products. Have students evaluate their own or others' writing according to
specific criteria.

REFERENCES

Alexander, N. (1983). A primer for developing a writing curriculum. *Topics in Learning
& Learning Disabilities, 3*(3), 55–62.

Beck, R. (1986). *Precision teaching project.* Great Falls, MT.

Blandford, B.J., & Lloyd, J.W. (1987). Effects of a self-instructional procedure on handwriting. *Journal of Learning Disabilities, 20,* 342–346.

Blankenship, C., & Hansen, C. (1972). *Teaching LD youngsters to type: Data.* Experimental Education Unit, University of Washington, Seattle, WA.

Botel, M.; Holsclaw, C.; Cammarota, G.; & Brothers, A. (1971). *Spelling and writing
patterns,* rev ed. Chicago: Follett Educational Corp.

Brigham, T.A.; Graubard, P.S.; & Stans, A. (1972). Analysis of the effects of sequential
reinforcement contingencies on aspects of composition. *Journal of Applied Behavior
Analysis, 5,* 421–429.

Broderbund Software. (1982). *Bank Street writer.* San Rafael, CA.

Bryant, N.D.; Drabin, I.R.; & Gettinger, M. (1981). Effects of varying unit size on spelling
achievement in learning disabled children. *Journal of Learning Disabilities, 14,* 200–
203.

Carpenter, D. (1983). Spelling error profiles of able and disabled readers. *Journal of
Learning Disabilities, 16,* 102–104.

Carpenter, D., & Miller, L.J. (1982). Spelling ability of reading disabled LD students and
able readers. *Learning Disability Quarterly, 5,* 65–70.

Cruickshank, W.M.; Bentzen, F.A.; Ratzeburg, F.H.; Tannhauser, M.T. (1961). *A teaching method for brain-injured and hyperactive children.* Syracuse, NY: Syracuse University Press.

Davis, W.E. (1983). Competencies and skills required to be an effective resource teacher.
Journal of Learning Disabilities, 16, 596–598.

DeMaster, V.K.; Crossland, C.L.; & Hasselbring, T.S. (1986). Consistency of learning
disabled students' spelling performance. *Learning Disability Quarterly, 9,* 89–96.

Deno, S.L.; Marston, D.; & Mirkin, P.K. (1982). Valid measurement procedures for
continuous evaluation of written expression. *Exceptional Children, 48,* 368–371.

Duvall, B. (1981a). What the literature says about handwriting. Research report presented
to Seattle Pacific University, Seattle, WA.

———. (1981b). *Learn to write: Italic style.* Great Falls, MT: Can Do Publications.

Edgington, R. (1967). But he spelled them right this morning! *Academic Therapy Quarterly,
3,* 58–59.

Eisman, E. (1962). Individualizing spelling. *Elementary English, 39,* 478–480.

Elbow, P. (1973). *Writing without teachers.* London: Oxford University Press.

Evans, G.W., & Oswalt, G.L. (1968). Acceleration of academic progress through the
manipulation of peer influence. *Behaviour Research and Therapy, 6,* 189–195.

Finholt, B., & Hansen, C.L. (1975). Tactics to improve writing fluency and legibility. Program Project Quarterly Report, Experimental Education Unit, University of Washington, Seattle.

Fitzgerald, G.; Landis, F.; & Milich, R. (1986). Computer-assisted instruction for students with attentional difficulties. *Journal of Learning Disabilities, 19,* 376–379.

Gardstrom, M., & Lovitt, T. (1979). A creative writing program for second-grade volunteers. In T.C. Lovitt & N.G. Haring (Eds.), *Classroom application of precision teaching.* Seattle, WA: Special Child Publications.

Gerber, M.M. (1986). Generalization of spelling strategies by LD students as a result of contingent imitation/modeling and mastery criteria.

———. (1984). Orthographic problem-solving ability of learning disabled and normally achieving students. *Learning Disability Quarterly, 7,* 157–164.

Gettinger, M.; Bryant, N.D.; & Fayne, R.R. (1982). Designing spelling instruction for learning-disabled children: An emphasis on unit size, distributed practice, and training for transfer. *Journal of Special Education, 16*(4), 439–448.

Giordano, G. (1984). Analyzing and remediating writing disabilities. *Journal of Learning Disabilities, 17,* 78–83.

Glover, J.A. (1979). The effectiveness of reinforcement and practice for enhancing the creative writing of elementary school children. *Journal of Applied Behavior Analysis, 12,* 487.

Goldiamond, I. (1965). Self-control procedures in personal behavior problems. *Psychological Reports, 17,* 851–868.

Graham, S., & Freeman, S. (1986). Strategy training and teacher- vs. student-controlled study conditions: Effects on LD students' spelling performance. *Learning Disability Quarterly, 9,* 15–22.

Graham, S., & Harris, K.R. (1988). Instructional recommendations for teaching writing to exceptional students. *Exceptional Children, 54,* 506–512.

Graham, S., & Miller, L. (1979). Spelling research and practice: A unified approach. *Focus on Exceptional Children, 12*(2), 1–16.

Guerin, G.R., & Maier, A.S. (1983). *Informal assessment in education.* Palo Alto, CA: Mayfield.

Hagin, R.A. (1983). Write right—or left: A practical approach to handwriting. *Journal of Learning Disabilities, 18,* 266–271.

Hall, N. (1964). The letter mark-out corrected test. *The Journal of Educational Research, 58*(4), 148–157.

Hammill, D.D. (1986). Correcting handwriting deficiencies. In D.D. Hammill & N. Bartel (Eds.), *Teaching students with learning and behavior problems,* 4th ed. Boston: Allyn and Bacon.

———. (Ed.) (1987). *Assessing the abilities and instructional needs of students.* Austin, TX: PRO-ED.

Hammill, D.D., & Larsen, S.C. (1983). *Test of written language,* rev. ed. Austin, TX: PRO-ED.

Hammill, D.D., & Leigh, J.E. (1983). *Basic school skills Inventory—diagnostic.* Austin, TX: PRO-ED.

Hanna, P.R.; Hanna, J.S.; Hodges, R.E.; & Peterson, D.J. (1971). *Power to spell,* Boston: Houghton Mifflin.

Hansen, C.L. (1978). Writing skills. In N.G. Haring, T.C. Lovitt, M.D. Eaton, & C.L. Hansen, (Eds.), *The fourth R: Research in the classroom.* Columbus, OH: Merrill.

Hansen, C.L., & Lovitt, T.C. (1973). Effects of feedback on content and mechanics of writing. Paper read at NIE Symposium, Seattle, WA.

Harting, E. (1974). Using feedback and reinforcement to improve handwriting. Unpublished data submitted to T.C. Lovitt, Experimental Education Unit, University of Washington, Seattle.

Hermreck, L. (1979). A comparison of the written language of learning disabled and non-learning disabled elementary children using the Inventory of Written Expression and Spelling. Unpublished master's thesis, University of Kansas, Lawrence.

Hopkins, B.L.; Schutte, R.C.; & Garton, K.L. (1971). The effects of access to a playroom on the rate and quality of printing and writing of first and second grade students. *Journal of Applied Behavior Analysis, 4,* 77–87.

Johnson, C. (1988). *The Written Expression Test.* East Aurora, NY: United Educational Services.

Kamil, M.L.; Langer, J.A.; & Shanahan, T. (1985). *Understanding reading and writing research.* Boston: Allyn and Bacon.

Karracker, R.J. (1971). Token reinforcement systems in regular public school classrooms. In C.E. Pitts (Ed.), *Operant conditioning in the classroom.* New York: Thomas C. Crowell Co.

Kauffman, J.M.; Hallahan, D.P.; Haas, K.; Brame, T.; & Boren, R. (1978). Imitating children's errors to improve their spelling performance. *Journal of Learning Disabilities, 11,* 217–222.

Kosiewicz, M.M.; Hallahan, D.P.; Lloyd, J.; & Graves, A.W. (1982). Effects of self-instruction and self-correction procedures on handwriting performance. *Learning Disability Quarterly, 5,* 71–78.

Kottmeyer, W. (1959). Teacher's guide for remedial reading. New York: McGraw-Hill.

Kottmeyer, W., & Claus, A. (1980). *Basic goals in spelling,* 6th ed. New York: McGraw-Hill.

Lahey, B.B.; Busemeyer, M.K.; O'Hara, C.; & Beggs, V.E. (1977). Treatment of severe perceptual-motor disorders in children diagnosed as learning disabled. *Behavior Modification, 1*(1), 123–141.

Larsen, S.C., & Hammill, D.D. (1976). *Test of written spelling.* Austin, TX: PRO-ED.

Lovitt, T.C. (1984). On writing a book. *Journal of Precision Teaching, 5*(1), 3–9.

Lovitt, T.C., & Fantasia, K. (1983). A precision teaching project with learning disabled children. *Journal of Precision Teaching, 4,* 85–91.

Lovitt, T.C.; Guppy, T.E.; & Blattner, J.E. (1969). The use of a free-time contingency with fourth graders to increase spelling accuracy. *Behaviour Research and Therapy, 1,* 151–156.

MacArthur, C.A., & Shneiderman, B. (1986). Learning disabled students' difficulties in learning to use a word processor: Implications for instruction and software evaluation. *Journal of Learning Disabilities, 19,* 248–253.

Maloney, K.B., & Hopkins, B.L. (1973). The modification of sentence structure and its relationship to subjective judgments of creativity in writing. *Journal of Applied Behavior Analysis, 6,* 425–433.

Maloney, K.B.; Jacobson, C.R.; & Hopkins, B.L. (1975). An analysis of the effects of lectures, requests, teacher praise, and free time on the creative writing behaviors of third-grade children. In E. Ramp & G. Semb (Eds.), *Behavior analysis: Areas of research and application.* Englewood Cliffs, N.J.: Prentice-Hall.

Mann, P.H.; Suiter, P.A.; & McClung, R.M. (1979). *Handbook in diagnostic–prescriptive teaching,* abridged 2nd ed. Boston: Allyn and Bacon.

Mather, N. (1985). Courseware review. *Journal of Learning Disabilities, 18,* 497.

Moran M.R. (1981). Performance of learning disabled and low achieving secondary students on formal features of a paragraph-writing task. *Learning Disability Quarterly, 4,* 271–280.

Morocco, C.C., & Neuman, S.B. (1986). Word processors and the acquisition of writing strategies. *Journal of Learning Disabilities, 19,* 243–247.

Morris, N.T., & Crump, W.D. (1982). Syntactic and vocabulary development in the written language of learning disabled and non-learning disabled students at four age levels. *Learning Disability Quarterly, 5,* 163–172.

Newland, T.E. (1932). An analytical study of the development of illegibilities in handwriting from the lower grades to adulthood. *Journal of Educational Research, 26,* 249–258.

Nodine, B.F.; Barenbaum, E.; & Newcomer, P. (1985). Story composition by learning disabled, reading disabled, and normal children. *Learning Disability Quarterly, 8,* 167–179.

Poplin, M.S.; Gray, R.; Larsen, S.; Banikowski, A.; & Mehring, T. (1980). A comparison of components of written expression abilities in learning disabled and non-learning disabled students at three grade levels. *Learning Disability Quarterly, 3,* 46–53.

Poteet, J.A. (1980). Informal assessment of written expression. *Learning Disability Quarterly, 3,* 88–98.

Roit, M.L., & McKenzie, R.G. (1985). Disorders of written communication: An instructional priority for LD students. *Journal of Learning Disabilities, 18,* 258–260.

Saltzman, J. (1981). Despite all the calligraphy, handwriting is mostly lousy. *The Bulletin,* January, 19–22.

Schulz, B. (1984). Writing needn't be a scrawl, says teacher in Bothell. *The Seattle Times.* February 1, Section G.

Silverman, R.; Zigmond, N.; Zimmerman, J.M.; & Vallecorsa, A. (1981). Improving written expression in learning disabled students. *Topics in Language Disorders 1*(2), 91–99.

Skinner, B.F., & Krakower, S.A. (1968). *Handwriting with write and see.* Chicago: Lyons & Carnahan.

Stevens, K.B., & Schuster, J.W. (1987). Effects of a constant time delay procedure on the written spelling performance of a learning disabled student. *Learning Disability Quarterly, 10,* 9–16.

Thomas, C.C.; Englert, C.S.; & Gregg, S. (1987). An analysis of errors and strategies in the expository writing of learning disabled students. *Remedial and Special Education, 8*(1), 21–30.

Thurber, D.N., & Jordan, D.R. (1978). *D'Nealian handwriting.* Palo Alto, CA: Scott, Foresman.

Torrance, E.P. (1974). *Torrance tests of creative thinking technical manual.* Lexington, MA: Personnel Press.

Towle, M. (1978). Assessment and remediation of handwriting deficits for children with learning disabilities. *Journal of Learning Disabilities, 11,* 370–377.

Trap, J.; Milner-Davis, P.; Joseph, S.; & Cooper, J.O. (1978). The effects of feedback and consequences on transitional cursive letter formation. *Journal of Applied Behavior Analysis, 11,* 381–393.

Travers, R.M.W. (Ed.) (1973). *Second handbook of research on teaching.* Chicago: Rand-McNally.

Vallecorsa, A.; Zigmond, N.; & Henderson, L.M. (1985). Spelling instruction in special education classrooms: A survey of practices. *Exceptional Children, 52,* 19–24.

Vanderwark, M. (1985). Word processing and word processing related software for the learning disabled. *Journal of Learning Disabilities, 18,* 559–561.

Yudkovitz, E. (1979). A visual error-scanning approach to spelling disorders. *Journal of Learning Disabilities, 12*(8), 55–58.

Zaner-Bloser Evaluation Scales. (1979). Columbus, OH: Zaner-Bloser.

Zimmerman, E.H., & Zimmerman, J. (1962). The alteration of behavior in a special classroom situation. *Journal of the Experimental Analysis of Behavior, 5,* 59–60.

Chapter 9

The House of Cards by Jean Baptiste Simeon Chardin (*c.* 1735). National Gallery of Art, Washington, Andrew W. Mellon Collection.

MATHEMATICS

MAIN IDEAS

- Typical plans for instructing mathematics in regular and remedial settings
- Characteristics of learning disabled youngsters in mathematics and comparisons of their performances with nonhandicapped students
- Formal and informal assessments of mathematics and information on objectives
- Approaches for instructing mathematics from practitioners and researchers
- Recommendations for using calculators and computers with LD youngsters and reviews of programs

OVERVIEW

To many individuals, mathematics means to add, subtract, multiply, divide, and perhaps deal with a story problem or two. Certainly, there is more to math than that. Although the applications of numbers is a vital part of mathematics, as is knowledge about time, money, measurement, and story problems, so are such topics as patterns, sets, geometry, probability, statistics, and problem solving. Yet many teachers believe that the curriculum for LD students should include little more than the basic topics. Further, few teachers are required to take courses specifically in mathematics, and for every 20 workshops that are offered on reading or the language arts, only one is scheduled in mathematics. It shouldn't come as a surprise then, that the math performances of LD youngsters are often lower than their communication skills.

   The first section of this chapter summarizes contents from a typical textbook on mathematics instruction. The second section notes some characteristics of LD pupils in math and presents data on the differences between LD and non-LD pupils. The third section deals with formal and informal assessment and presents criterion scores of "successful" and "unsuccessful" adolescents and adults in a wide variety of mathematics skills. Section four reviews techniques and approaches that have been recommended for LD students, and section five reviews intervention programs that were designed for LD students. It includes comments and reviews on the use of calculators and computers in mathematics instruction for LD pupils. At the end of the chapter are comments on mathematics instruction for LD pupils.

MATHEMATICS INSTRUCTION

This section reviews mathematics instruction for non-LD students as well as their LD peers. Regarding the instruction of LD students, Cawley, Fitzmaurice, Shaw, Kahn, and Bates (1979a) reported that when a group of teachers of LD students were surveyed, over 50 percent of them considered themselves inadequately trained in such topics as solid geometry and measurement of time, area, weight, liquids, and temperature. That same proportion admitted their unfamiliarity with methods to conduct error analyses and with most of the current methodological and theoretical approaches for mathematics instruction. Cawley and coauthors also showed data from a state's competency test to indicate that, overall, 47 percent of the LD students passed the communication section, while only 16 percent passed the mathematics section. Their lowest scores had to do with measurement and "life skills."

Regular Education

This section presents an outline and brief discussion of the major topics from a typical mathematics book, *Guiding Children's Learning of Mathematics* (Kennedy, 1984). That text covers eight major areas, which are generally featured in most basal mathematics programs. According to Kennedy, those topics encompass the 10 basic skills highlighted by the National Council of Supervisors of Mathematics: problem solving; applying mathematics in everyday situations; alertness to the reasonableness of results; estimation and approximation; appropriate computation skills; geometry, measurement; reading tables, charts, and graphs; using mathematics to predict; and computer literacy.

Basic Skills
Problem solving, applications, and estimation.   Problem solving is accomplished when an individual uses strategies and skills to determine the answer to an unfamiliar problem. Children need opportunities to learn how to analyze problems, devise and carry out plans for their solutions, and review the reasonableness of the results. Kennedy lists the following strategies for accomplishing this skill:

— Looking for patterns
— Drawing diagrams or pictures
— Making models

— Constructing tables or graphs
— Guessing and checking
— Accounting for all possibilities
— Acting out the problem
— Writing a mathematical sentence
— Restating the problem
— Identifying wanted-given information
— Breaking set
— Changing your point of view

As children learn each of the basic mathematical skills, they need opportunities to try out their new knowledge for solving problems. Kennedy recommends that teachers take advantage of in- and out-of-school situations to show how computing, measuring, graphing, and other skills are used in everyday situations and in solving unfamiliar problems. Kennedy suggests a four-step problem solving process understanding the problem, devising a plan, carrying out the plan, and looking back. Kennedy also suggests that children be encouraged to estimate measures, quantities, and time.

Calculators and computers. More and more math experts believe that calculators enhance mathematical achievement and should be given to children as soon as they come to school. Kindergarten and first-grade children can learn to use them as aids for counting; older children can use them for computing with whole numbers and fractional numbers expressed as decimal fractions. More advanced pupils can use calculators to investigate areas of mathematics they might otherwise avoid because of the amount of paper-and-pencil computation needed to perform them. Kennedy recommends four-function calculators with an eight-digit readout for elementary students, and with memory, square root, and percent keys for high school pupils.

Experts also believe children should learn to use computers for solving problems and dealing with numerical, written, and graphic information and as one way of getting drill and practice in mathematics. Computer-managed instruction systems help teachers assess and evaluate children's knowledge and understanding of mathematics, place children in learning sequences, maintain records, and do other routine tasks. (A discussion of microcomputers and mathematics appears later in this chapter.)

Numbers and operations. In elementary schools, most of the time spent on mathematics is devoted to numbers and operations. Children learn that whole numbers are used to count objects in collections or sets, that fractional numbers are used when considering part of a unit or of a set, and that integers are used to express temperature, time, distance, altitude, and in other situations in which both direction and magnitude must be indicated. After children learn to count, they learn to read and write numbers and to use number lines to relate sequence and counting. They also learn about the ordinal uses of numbers (for example, first, third, middle, last).

The basic number operations are addition and multiplication and their inverses, subtraction and division. In order to perform each operation, children learn an algorithm (set of rules or procedures) for processing numbers. Most of us are familiar with the algorithms we refer to as "borrowing" or "carrying."

As children become more familiar with numbers, they learn about the properties that apply to certain basic operations: Commutative property, when the order of addends is changed (for example, $3 + 4$ yields the same answer as $4 + 3$); associative property, which applies to addition and multiplication (e.g., $[3 + 4] + 6 = 3 + [4 + 6]$); and distributive property, which applies to multiplication and division. For example, in the problem, 36×4, the product of 4 and 6 is recorded first; then the product of 4 and 30 is recorded. The sum of these partial products is then recorded. In division, $36 \div 3$ can be explained as $36 \div 3 = (30 + 6) \div 3 = (30 \div 3) + (6 \div 3) = 10 + 2 = 12$.

Youngsters learn that fractions represent parts of a unit that has been subdivided into equal sizes. Later, they learn how fractional numbers can be expressed with common fractions, decimal fractions, and percent. They also learn to express ratios, to indicate division, and to express abstract fractional numbers.

Measurement.   The two measuring processes are discrete—involving objects that can be counted—and continuous—involving objects that are measured. Continuous measurements are made with two systems—the English (customary) system and the metric. Although the latter has attained more status in the United States since 1975, neither education nor industry has totally made the switch to metrics, which is the system used in most of the world.

Children learn about the following continuous measures:

— Linear measures: meter and kilometer or yard and mile
— Weight: kilogram or ounce. Children also learn that weight is the force exerted on an object because of gravity, and mass is the quantity of matter of which the object is composed.
— Capacity: liters or quarts
— Temperature: Celsius or Fahrenheit

Techniques for measuring areas of squares, rectangles, parallelograms, and triangles and for measuring perimeters of various shapes are included in elementary school programs. Volume measuring techniques for closed three-dimensional figures are introduced in fifth and sixth grade.

Time and money are also important aspects of measurement. Children learn the concept of time (duration and sequence of events) and the mechanics of reading clocks and calendars. Learning about money involves learning the values of coins and bills and how to add, subtract, and convert them.

Geometry.   The study of geometry begins when children are taught to examine two- and three-dimensional figures. During preschool and kindergarten, they learn the spatial relations of proximity, separation, order, and enclosure. Later, models—cubes, prisms, pyramids—are arranged to introduce specific geometric concepts.

Students classify figures according to the shapes of objects or the number of edges and vertices. As they mature, they learn more sophisticated geometric language.

Among the geometric topics generally introduced in elementary schools are common plane figures, segments, angles/rays, symmetry, congruence/similarity, coordinate graphing, and parallel/perpendicular/intersecting lines. Children first learn to recognize common shapes such as square, circle, triangle, and rectangle. Next, they determine each shape's general characteristics, such as number of sides. By the sixth grade, they should be able to classify common figures according to their characteristics and be able to explain why a square is both a rectangle and a parallelogram. The deductive level of geometry is not developed until some time later.

Number theory. Number theory introduces children to odd and even numbers, prime and composite numbers, and concepts such as least common multiple (LCM) and greatest common factor (GCF). Children use LCM to determine the lowest common denominators when adding and subtracting unlike common fractions. Knowledge of GCF is helpful when simplifying common fractions.

Besides being important in and of itself, number theory is included in children's mathematics programs because many pupils enjoy working with it; they may learn that work with prime and composite numbers leads to interesting areas of investigation. Also, they have many opportunities to work with basic facts of the four operations, to practice computational skills, and to develop further a mathematics vocabulary.

Related to number theory, pupils learn that tests of divisibility are used to determine whether a number can be divided by a given number. These tests save time in factoring composite numbers, for the tests enable students to determine quickly whether one number is a factor of another.

Statistics and probability. The National Council of Teachers of Mathematics (Schulte, 1981) gave four reasons for studying statistics and probability in schools. According to them, these concepts provide the following:

—Meaningful applications of mathematics at all levels
—Methods for dealing with uncertainty
—Some understanding of the statistical arguments, good and bad, with which we are continually bombarded
—Interesting, exciting, and motivating topics for most students

As an introduction to statistics, kindergarten children might make surveys to determine their favorite television shows, video games, or the kinds of pets they have. Later in school, children's skills in handling data are nurtured as they collect, organize, display, and interpret information from a variety of sources.

In fifth or sixth grades, students learn such probability terms as *event, impossible event, likely event, certain event,* and *equally likely event.* Correspondingly, they learn that the more likely an event is to occur, the higher the number assigned to it. The numerical measure that refers to that likelihood is that event's probability.

Tables and graphs.   Youngsters learn that tables and graphs are used to organize data so that trends and patterns can be determined, and problems involving the data can be solved. Among the graphs children learn to make and interpret are object, picture, bar, and line graphs. Object and picture graphs are used by kindergarten and first-grade children to organize information about themselves, such as their favorite ice-cream flavors and birth months. Older students use bar and line graphs to organize and display data they gather and to make more sophisticated interpretations of data in tables and graphs.

Scope and Sequence of Programs.   Most mathematics curricula in elementary schools instruct the elements discussed in the preceding paragraphs. Typical programs are accompanied by scope and sequence charts. The scope refers to the topics introduced in the curriculum, and the sequence to the grades at which aspects of those topics are introduced. As an example, see Figure 9.1, a scope and sequence chart from *Direct Instruction Mathematics* (Silbert, Carnine, & Stein, 1981). Note that the scope of the curriculum is indicated by the 11 topics across the top, and the sequences in which they are introduced are indicated across each grade level.

Remedial Education

The following paragraphs outline and discuss *Project Math* (Cawley et al., 1976), a comprehensive program designed specifically for LD students of elementary

John F. Cawley is currently on the faculty of the University of Buffalo. Cawley's major contribution to the field has been his extensive work in mathematics instruction for LD youth. He and colleagues have published *Project Math,* specifically designed for handicapped youth. One of his more popular books is "Cognitive Strategies and Mathematics for the Learning Disabled."

■ **FIGURE 9.1** ■ Skill Hierarchy for Elementary Mathematics Instruction

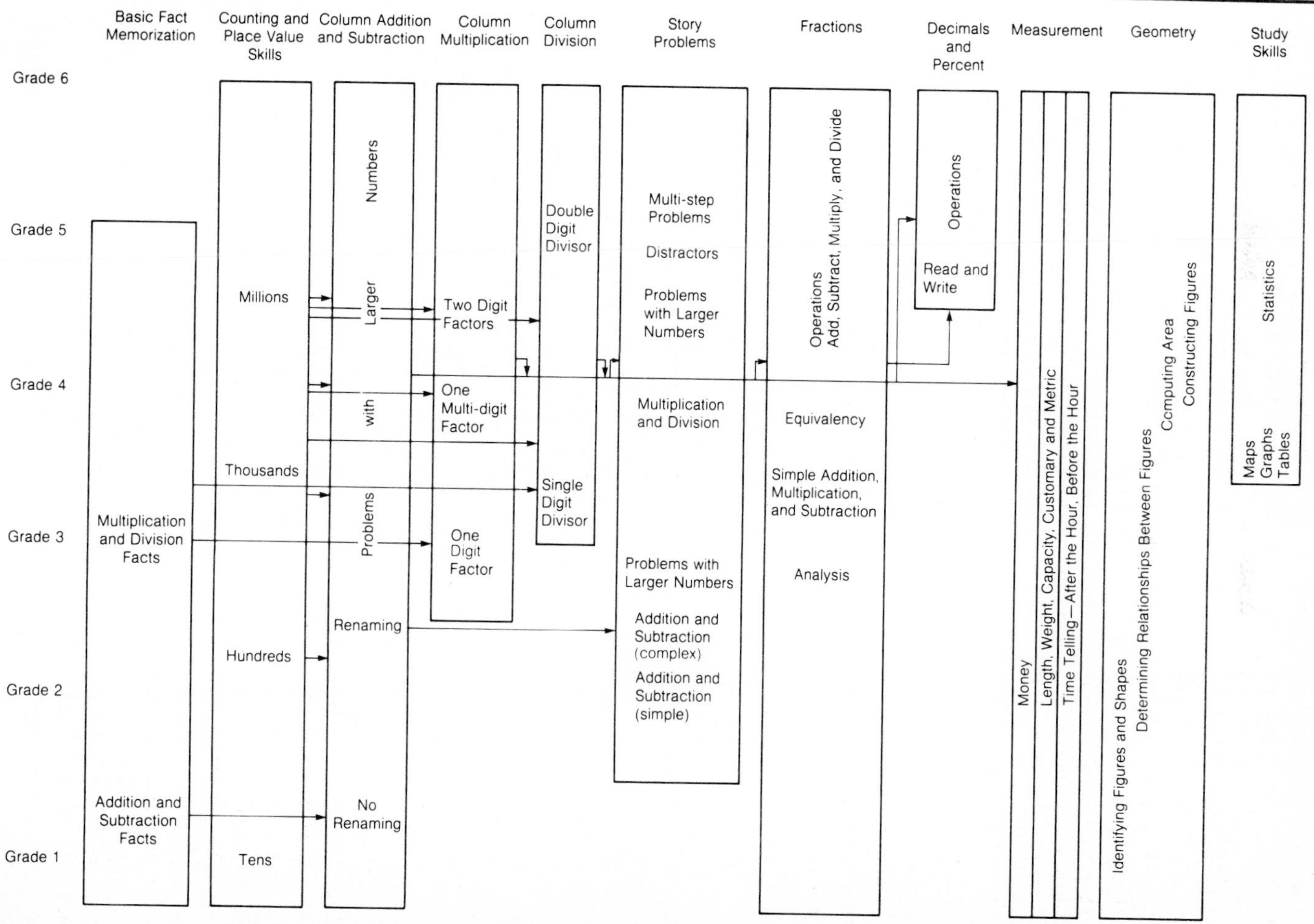

Source: Reprinted by permission from J. Silbert, D. Carnine, and M. Stein, *Direct Instruction Mathematics* (Columbus, OH: Merrill, 1981), p. 45.

age. Although similar in design to programs developed for nonhandicapped youngsters, *Project Math* emphasizes the applicability of the program to the needs of children who have problems learning mathematics. The major difference between *Project Math* and others is less one of content than of the methodology and sequencing of instruction.

According to Cawley and colleagues, most special education programs place excessive emphasis on teaching symbolic operations to children who have inadequate foundations in the concrete, manipulative realm. They feel that too much attention is paid to achievement and not enough to learning. Accordingly, the authors recommend an alternative model that enables learners to break out of their rote, mechanical, "computational set" and to grasp the principles underlying mathematical operations. The model provides multiple options, with reference both to the use of alternative modalities of learning and to methods of problem solving and focuses on enhancing the affective as well as the cognitive growth of the learner.

Goals and Organization.   The authors of *Project Math* have specified the following goals for the program:

— Provide teachers with a number of instructional options to circumvent children's handicaps to learning.
— Enhance learner's chances for success in a total mathematics program.
— Provide learners with a substantial mathematics curriculum designed to facilitate their use of mathematics in daily life.
— Maximize instructors' opportunities for individualizing instruction.
— Provide a framework in which mathematics content can be used as a tool for enhancing the development of children socially, emotionally, and academically.
— Provide a supplement to the regular mathematics program for youngsters who are not actually handicapped but who might profit from the techniques in such a program.

The organization is sequenced in an interrelated fashion across six major areas or "strands" of mathematics: geometry, sets, patterns, measurement, numbers, and fractions. Each strand contains a developmental sequence of mathematics concepts beginning at the concrete, manipulative level and progressing to more abstract, symbolic levels.

The geometry strand introduces basic topological concepts: order, constancy, basic two- and three-dimensional shapes, lines and paths, and similarities. Students are exposed to such basic topological terms as *inside, outside, on,* and *next to.*

Instruction in the sets strand leads children from simple classification tasks (such as sorting objects according to size or color) to operations involving superordinate sets. The patterns strand focuses on the recognition and understanding of systematic patterns of relationships, which help develop readiness for quantitative processings tasks.

The measurement strand emphasizes concepts involving height, temperature, time, speed, and distance, which are dealt with through activities that are commonly experienced. This approach reflects the authors' belief in the importance of developing functional mathematics skills.

The basic concepts in the numbers strand include cardinal property and place value and provide the basis for the operations of addition and subtraction. This strand emphasizes understanding of the concepts involved rather than rote memory.

The fractions strand lays the foundation for understanding of part–whole relationships by extending the learner's concept of numbers to those that represent parts of a group or parts of a whole thing. Learners begin with their own experiences (for example, examining parts of the house) and then note the interrelationships among these parts as well as the relationship of each part to the whole.

Components. *Project Math* has four levels that are differentiated according to the mathematics content covered. A multiple option curriculum has been designed for each level. Each includes instructional guides (and learner activity books), a mathematics concept inventory, and a verbal problem-solving component.

The *instructional guide* component provides directed activities in each of the six strands of mathematics. Each instructional guide is coded according to level, strand, and sequence. A key element in the guides is the "interactive unit," (Cawley et al., 1978), which provides for a combination of teacher "inputs" and learner "outputs." The purpose of these units is to provide instructional options for the teacher—as well as learning options for the student—by using different combinations of modalities of stimuli and learner responses. An interactive unit is graphically presented in Figure 9.2.

There are five basic modalities in an interactive unit:

— The present mode, in which children are shown displays such as pictures or pictorial activity sheets.
— The construct mode, in which pictures of objects are physically manipulated (stacked, arranged, sorted).
— The state mode, in which oral discourse is used.
— The graphic symbolic mode—in which written or drawn symbols are used.
— The identify mode, in which only nonverbal responses such as pointing are required.

With these input and output options, a variety of instructor–learner interactions can be arranged, allowing teachers to select alternative learning combinations for students. These multiple options enable instructors to circumvent difficulties in other areas such as reading, speaking, or writing that may impede mathematics performance. A poor writer, for example, could still attain mathematical understandings by working primarily in the present, identify, and construct modes and avoiding the writing required in the graphic symbolic mode.

■ FIGURE 9.2 ■   *Project Math* Interactive Unit (addition of two single digit numbers)

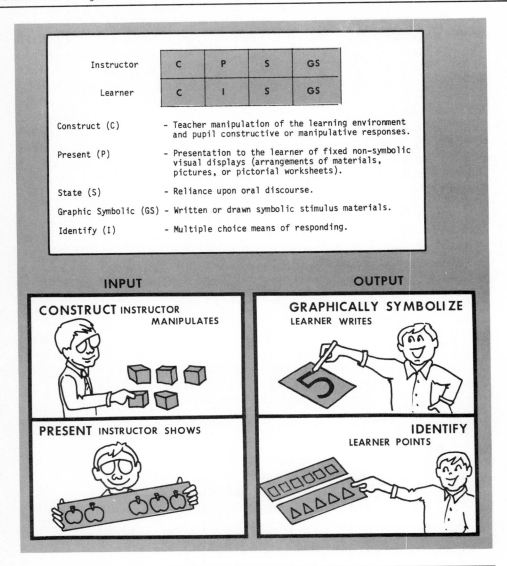

Source: Reprinted by permission from John F. Cawley, Anne M. Fitzmaurice, Robert A. Shaw, Harris Kahn, and Herman Bates, III, "Mathematics and Learning Disabled Youth: The Upper Grade Levels," *Learning Disability Quarterly, 1,* 1978, p. 39.

The *mathematics concept inventory* (MCI) is an assessment instrument of *Project Math*. It enables instructors to evaluate the status of individual students in terms of what they understand and what they can do relative to the major concepts in the program. The MCI serves both as a screening device for placing children in the program and as an assessment device to evaluate student progress after particular sequences have been instructed.

The *verbal problem-solving* (VPS) component of *Project Math* represents an attempt to go beyond computation and focus on the cognitive strategies that underlie problem solving. At Levels I and II, picture manipulatives are used to mediate orally presented verbal problems. For these levels, children do not have to read, and the major goal is to facilitate the process of problem solving rather than to compute correct answers. At Levels III and IV, when students are able to note relevant information and identify appropriate processes, they are introduced to written problem solving.

A major intent of the VPS component is to train children to attend to the information-processing requirements of verbal problems. Errors involving miscounting or other incorrect arithmetic operations are therefore of less concern diagnostically than errors that involve incorrect attention to the relevant information necessary to solve the problem.

Project Math encourages teachers to devise alternatives to the problems provided and to use the story mats for enrichment of language and reading activities. Figure 9.3 presents a set of four mats from Level II of the program. Whereas the general theme is maintained for all the mats, the different figures and roles allow for considerable variation in the types of problems that can be constructed. This flexibility allows teachers to come up with dozens of problems that differ along several dimensions.

Cawley and colleagues (1979b) recommend a number of other formats for instructing problem solving:

— Writing out problems in a rather traditional way ("John delivered 6 apples . . .")
— Embedding information for solving problems within stories
— Using a "cloze" procedure in which learners fill in missing information in problems
— Developing matrices as formats for creating problem-solving activities.

Like the example matrix in Table 9.1, the matrices can be organized according to selected characteristics. From them, teachers can diagnose youngsters' capabilities and design corresponding sets of problems that may differ according to sentence structure, reading level, information processing (for example, direct or indirect addition), and computational complexity.

LD PUPILS AND MATHEMATICS

Characteristics of LD Pupils

In *Teaching Mathematics to the Learning Disabled,* Bley and Thornton (1981) noted 11 major behavioral categories in which LD youngsters may deviate from normal development and, as a result, have difficulties in areas of mathematics.

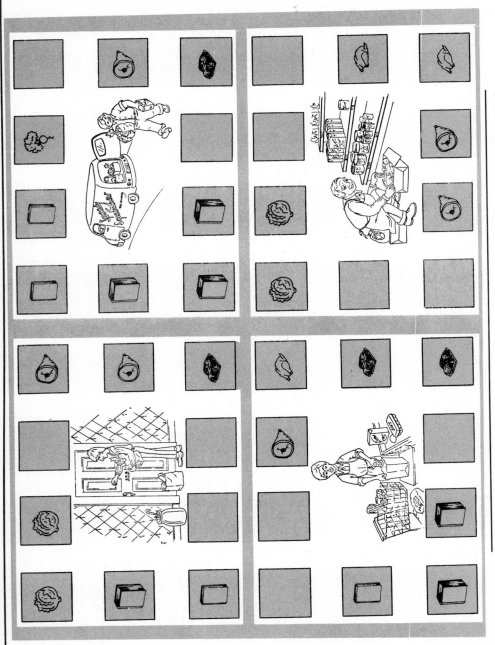

Source: Reprinted by permission from John F. Cawley, Anne M. Fitzmaurice, Robert A. Shaw, Harris Kahn, and Herman Bates, III, "Math Word Problems: Suggestions for LD Students," *Learning Disability Quarterly*, 2, 1979, p. 31.

■ TABLE 9.1 ■   *Problem-Solving Matrix*

	Second		Third		Fourth		
	Direct	Indirect	Direct	Indirect	Direct	Indirect	
Simple sentence	1	2	3	4	5	6	Single digit
Simple sentence with prepositional phrase	7	8	9	10	11	12	
Simple sentence	13	14	15	16	17	18	Two digit × one digit, no regrouping
Simple sentence with prepositional phrase	19	20	21	22	23	24	
Simple sentence	25	26	27	28	29	30	Two digit × two digit, no regrouping
Simple sentence with prepositional phrase	31	32	33	34	35	36	
Simple sentence	37	38	39	40	41	42	Three digit × two digit, no regrouping
Simple sentence with prepositional phrase	43	44	45	46	47	48	

Source: Reprinted by permission from John F. Cawley, Anne M. Fitzmaurice, Robert A. Shaw, Harris Kahn, and Herman Bates, III, "Math Word Problems: Suggestions for LD Students," *Learning Disability Quarterly*, 2, Spring 1979, p. 40.

(See Table 9.2.) Many of the behaviors in the "perceptual" category are among those advanced by theorists who maintain that neurological differences are related to learning disabilities. The behaviors in the memory and integrative categories are ones many language specialists cite as contributing to learning disabilities. Beside each of the 11 categories (for example, Figure-Ground) are examples of how a problem can be noted as either a visual or an auditory deficiency. Note that these characteristics may not apply to all LD youngsters, and conversely, many of them may be apparent for youngsters who are not learning disabled.

McLeod and Armstrong (1982) surveyed a number of teachers to determine the characteristics, with regard to mathematics, of LD youth of secondary age. They learned that LD youngsters of secondary age generally functioned at the level of upper third to upper fourth grade. The types of problems that were the most difficult for these pupils included:

— Upper-level skills of division of whole numbers
— Basic operations involving fractions
— Decimals
— Percents

■ TABLE 9.2 ■   Examples of Learning Disabilities Affecting Performance in Mathematics

	Visual Deficit	Auditory Deficit
Perceptual		
Figure-ground	May not finish all problems on page	Trouble hearing pattern in counting
	Frequently loses place	Difficulty attending in the classroom
	Difficulty seeing subtraction within a division problem	
	Difficulty reading multidigit number (see closure)	
Discrimination	Difficulty differentiating coins	Cannot distinguish between 30 and 13 (see receptive language)
	Difficulty differentiating between or writing numbers (3 for 8; 2 for 5)	Difficulty with decimal numbers
	Cannot discriminate between operation symbols	
	Cannot discriminate between size of hands on clock	
	Difficulty associating operation sign with problem (see abstract reasoning)	
Reversal	Reverses digits in a number (may also be a sequential memory problem)	
	Difficulty with regrouping	
Spatial	Trouble writing on lined paper	Difficulty following directions using ordinal numbers
	Difficulty with concept of before/after, so trouble telling time	
	Trouble noticing size differences in shapes	
	Trouble with fraction concept due to inability to note equal-sized parts	
	Difficulty writing decimals	
	Difficulty aligning numbers	
	Difficulty with ordinal numbers	
	Difficulty writing fractional numbers (may also be reversed)	
Memory		
Short-term	Trouble retaining newly presented material	Difficulty with oral drills
	Difficulty copying problems from the board (may be spatial)	Difficulty with dictated assignments
Long-term	Inability to retain basic facts or processes over a long period	

Table 9.2 Continued

	Visual Deficit	Auditory Deficit
Sequential	Difficulty solving multioperation computation	Cannot retain story problem that is dictated
	Difficulty telling time	
	Difficulty following through a multiplication problem	
	Difficulty following through long division problems	
	Dificulty solving column addition problems	
	Difficulty solving multistep word problems	
Integrative Closure	Difficulty visualizing groups	Difficulty counting on from within a sequence
	Difficulty reading multidigit number (see figure-ground)	
	Difficulty with missing addends and missing factors	
	Inability to draw conclusions, therefore trouble noticing and continuing patterns	
	Difficulty with word problems	
	Trouble continuing counting pattern from within a sequence	
Expressive language	Rapid oral drills very difficult	Difficulty counting on
		Difficulty explaining why a problem is solved as it is
Receptive language	Difficulty relating word to meaning (may be spatial)	Difficulty relating word to meaning
	Difficulty with words that have multiple meanings	Difficulty writing numbers from dictation
Abstract reasoning	Inability to solve word problems	
	Inability to compare size of numbers, using symbols	
	Cannot understand patterning in counting	
	Difficulty with decimal concept	

Source: Reprinted with permission from Nancy S. Bley and Carol A. Thornton, *Teaching Mathematics to the Learning Disabled* (Austin, TX: PRO-ED, Inc., 1981).

— Fraction terminology
— Multiplication of whole numbers

Because these are such significant skill deficits, the authors concluded that many LD youth are not likely to ever function at grade level in mathematics. Consequently, teachers of these pupils must be prepared, at some point, to make the decision to abandon basic-skill instruction and begin instructing life-skill mathematics.

Cawley, Miller, and School (1987) were also concerned about the arithmetic problem-solving abilities of LD students in secondary school. To gather data, they gave pupils problems to solve that differed with respect to two sets of characteristics: direct/indirect or extraneous/nonextraneous. In direct problems, the wording was consistent with the operation to be followed; in indirect problems, the wording and the operation were not in agreement. Also, some problems contained extraneous information and others did not. The data revealed that indirect problems tended to be more difficult for LD students than direct problems and that problems containing extraneous information were more difficult than those without. The authors attributed those difficulties to the teaching methodology and the type of problem-solving experiences that are generally emphasized in school curricula.

Reasons for Failure

In an attempt to account for the reasons why many LD youngsters are "off the mark" in mathematics, Cawley and colleagues (1979a) discussed several facets of failure on the part of LD youngsters when it comes to mathematics. Comments on three forms are offered here.

Correlated Failure.   Certainly mathematics is related to reading. LD pupils who have difficulty reading will probably have problems with math, particularly with story problems. Handwriting problems or difficulty in drawing simple shapes can negatively affect performance in mathematics. Math abilities also suffer if a pupil has difficulty comprehending concepts such as time, space, direction, and amount. Thus, for most LD students, the chances of succeeding—or failing—in mathematics are highly related to their abilities and performance in other subjects.

Instructional Failure.   Currently, great numbers of LD youngsters receive the majority of their instruction in resource rooms. All too often, resource teachers are ill-prepared to instruct any mathematics beyond the fundamental computations.

Cawley and coauthors have identified four types of instructional failure:

1. Instruction is inappropriate, incorrect, or too limited to develop the skill being taught.
2. Students are passed on from one skill to another before reaching competency levels.

3. There is a tendency to overcorrect; teachers sometimes correct other concepts youngsters express when they should instead assist students with the mathematics.

4. The assessment of pupils' performances is faulty or incomplete. According to the authors, performances should be analyzed rather than graded.

Individual Failure.   Cawley et al. state that the field of learning disabilities has put forth its greatest effort within the realm of individual failure. Among the learner characteristics they believe have contributed to failure in aspects of mathematics are attentional deficits and problems of encoding, memory, or organization. Some researchers refer to the general area of disability in mathematics as *dyscalculia.*

In order to provide more information on the deficiencies in mathematics of LD youth, Cawley and associates (1979b) analyzed the data from 850 children who took 57 tests. (Not all the youngsters were given all the tests.) Based upon this analysis, the authors showed that, aside from the relative achievement deficits of the youngsters, the results did not suggest a pattern across the various measures of performance that may be associated with or indicative of learning disability.

Comparisons

It is important to review comparative data if one is to know just how deviant LD pupils generally are from their normal mates. Another reason for using comparison data is to determine whether there are qualitative as well as quantitative differences between the performances of LD and non-LD pupils—to learn if the types of errors made by LD pupils are different from those made by nonhandicapped children. A number of studies have compared LD youngsters and other students. Badian and Ghublikian, for example, compared the social/emotional characteristics of youngsters who had poor mathematical computation skills but were average in reading with students who were below average in reading but average in math, and with pupils who were average in both skills. Data showed that the children who were poor in mathematical computation and average in reading rated significantly lower on a personal-social behavior scale than did youngsters in the other two groups. The picture that emerged from the research

. . . is that the child who is a good reader but poor at mathematical computation is frequently inattentive, is disorganized and inexact in manner of working, avoids responsibility, and probably completes assignments less often than peers. [Badian and Ghublikian, 1983, p. 157]

Englert, Culatta, and Horn (1987) investigated the problem-solving performance of LD students and their peers. Both sets of pupils were given a number of addition word problems with irrelevant linguistic and numerical information embedded within them. Their data indicated that the regular class students revealed greater accuracy and speed in solving the problems than did their LD peers. Analysis also supported the conclusion that LD students experienced greater difficulties than did non-LD students in solving problems containing irrelevant numbers.

Derr (1985) examined the development of conservation with LD and non-LD children between the ages of 9 and 12. Youngsters were administered *The Concept Assessment Test—Conservation*. This test assessed pupils' understanding of conservation in six areas: two-dimensional space, number, substance, continuous quantity, weight, and discontinuous quantity. Derr's data showed that 90 percent of the non-LD students understood the concept of conservation, whereas this was true for only 50 percent of the LD youngsters. Of the tests' features, conservation of number was the easiest for the students to do, while the most difficult area was that of weight.

Swanson and Rhine (1985) compared the strategy transformations in mathematics of LD and non-LD boys whose mean age was about 13. Performances of the youngsters were compared on seven strategies: reduction to answers, reduction to rule, method replacement, unit building, saving partial results, process elimination, and reordering. Data revealed that the two groups did not differ in terms of computation, but did differ in their use of strategies to access information and apply it. Non-LD children handled information at a higher rate than did the LD youngsters. The results also indicated that non-LD children spent more time considering an alternative method and grouping mental operations, and less time recalling computation knowledge than did LD children.

ASSESSMENT AND STANDARDS

Formal Assessment

This section includes descriptions of four popular and representative standardized tests in mathematics.

KeyMath Diagnostic Arithmetic Test (Connelly, Nachtman, & Pritchett, 1976). This comprehensive instrument assesses three basic areas of mathematics—content, operations, and applications. Each of these areas has several subtests: content (numeration, fractions, geometry, symbols), operations (addition, subtraction, division, mental computation, numerical reasoning), and applications (word problems, missing elements, money, measurement, time).

KeyMath is designed to be administered individually and takes from 30 to 40 minutes. Except for a few paper-and-pencil computation problems, items are answered orally or by pointing. Four levels of diagnostic information are provided:

— Total test performance
— Area performance in each of the three clusters
— Subtest performance within each cluster
— Item performance within each subtest

A *KeyMath Metric Supplement* is also available.

Stanford Diagnostic Mathematics Test (Beatty, Madden, Gardner, & Karlsen, 1976). This test has two levels: The first is for children from grades two to four, and the second is for youngsters from fourth to eighth grade. Both levels have been used diagnostically with low-achieving pupils. Level one is divided into three categories: numbers and numerals, computations, and number facts. Level two is made up of five subtests: concepts of numbers and numerals, computation with whole numbers, common fractions, decimals and percents, and number facts. These tests are designed to diagnose students' specific weaknesses in working with numbers. The authors maintain that students' difficulties with most aspects of arithmetic, including problem solving and measuring, stem from their weakness in working with numbers. Minimal reading is required of children throughout the test.

Test of Early Mathematics Ability (TEMA) (Ginsburg & Baroody, 1983). TEMA may be used as a diagnostic instrument to determine strengths and weaknesses. According to its publisher, it provides information that leads directly to instruction. Items are designed to measure two major and six related domains: informal mathematics (concepts of relative magnitude, counting, and calculation) and formal mathematics (knowledge of conventional number facts, calculation, and base ten concepts).

Test of Mathematical Abilities (TOMA) (Brown & McEntire, 1984). According to its publisher, TOMA not only offers standardized information about two major skill areas (story problems and computation), but also provides information related to the following diagnostic questions:

1. What are the student's expressed attitudes toward mathematics?
2. What is the student's level of understanding of vocabulary that is used in a mathematical sense?
3. How well does the student (or group of students) understand the functional use of mathematics facts and concepts as they are applied in our general culture?
4. How do students' attitudes, vocabulary, and understanding of mathematics applications in our culture relate to the general level of basic skills shown in the areas of story problems and computation?

Informal Assessment

The distinctions between formal and informal assessment in mathematics may be useful at this time. Commercially available formal tests have items whose scores have been derived from many youngsters, generally from various parts of the country and of various age or ability levels. Those scores are used as norms, against which are compared the performances of youngsters being administered the test. Informal tests may be developed by teachers or others to reflect pupils' abilities on a variety of matters, many of which are of immediate interest to the developer. This section describes several types of informal assessment.

Considerable valuable material that could be used for informal assessment appears in *Direct Instruction Mathematics* (Silbert et al., 1981). For example, there are placement tests for grade levels K through 7. (See Figure 9.4.) To

■ **FIGURE 9.4** ■   *Direct Instruction Mathematics* Placement Tests

---

LEVEL A
For Beginning Kindergarten and
First Graders

TESTER INSTRUCTIONS

I. Counting Skills

  1. Counting by 1s

    Instructions
    "I WANT YOU TO COUNT FOR ME. START AT 1. COUNT AS HIGH AS YOU CAN." Stop student at 20 or when student leaves out or mixes the order of more than two numbers. If student makes an error in counting, give the student another chance to count. Tell student to start again at 1.

    Recording
    Write the highest number said correctly by student on either attempt.

  2. Counting Lines

    Instructions
    a. Point to the lines in box *a* below.
      "LOOK AT THESE LINES.
      I WANT YOU TO COUNT THEM AND TELL ME HOW
      MANY LINES THERE ARE."
    b. Repeat with box *b*.

    Recording
    If student counted lines correctly, write +.
    If student counted only some of the lines correctly, write
    the number counted correctly.

  3. Drawing Lines

    Instructions
    Give student pencil and paper.
    a. "DRAW THREE LINES.
      HOW MANY LINES ARE YOU GOING TO DRAW? DRAW THEM."
    b. Repeat a with six lines.

    Recording
    Write + if correct or write number of lines drawn and counted correctly.

II. Symbol Skills

  1. Numeral Identification

    Instructions
    Point to each numeral below and ask, "WHAT IS THIS?"

    4 2 6 7 3 8 5 9 10

    When the student misses three in a row, stop testing symbol identification and test symbol writing.

Figure 9.4 Continued

Recording
Write a + in the box next to each numeral identified correctly.
Write NR for no response. If a student says an incorrect number, write the number the student said.

2. Numeral Writing

Instructions
Give student pencil and paper.
a. "WRITE THE NUMERAL 4."
b. Repeat step a with these numerals:

2   6   7   3   8   5   9   10

Recording
Write a + for any numeral drawn correctly.

Write a + even if numeral is drawn backward; i.e.   Ɛ   ;

However, write a *b* (for backward) next to the plus.
Stop testing when students miss three in a row and go to Part III.

III. Math-related Language Concepts

1. More-Less

Instructions
a. Tell me which number is *more*, 5 or 7.
b. Tell me which number is *more*, 8 or 3.

Recording
Write + for each question answered correctly.

RECORD FORM—LEVEL A

Student Name _____

Date of Test _____

Tester _____

I. Counting

1. Counting by 1s—highest number counted to ☐
2. Counting Lines
   4 lines ☐   7 lines ☐
3. Drawing Lines
   3 lines ☐   6 lines ☐

II. Symbol Skills

1. Identification |4| ☐ |2| ☐ |6| ☐ |7| ☐ |3| ☐ |8| ☐ |5| ☐ |9| ☐ |10| ☐

2. Writing |4| ☐ |2| ☐ |6| ☐ |7| ☐ |3| ☐ |8| ☐ |5| ☐ |9| ☐ |10| ☐

III. Math-related Language Concepts

more-less
5 or 7 ☐   8 or 3 ☐

Source: Reprinted by permission from J. Silbert, D. Carnine, and M. Stein, *Direct Instruction Mathematics* (Columbus, OH: Merrill, 1981), p. 25.

administer these tests, the teacher asks each pupil, at the appropriate level, to respond to each item; for example, to count by "1's," to count lines, to draw lines, to identify numerals, to write numerals, and to define various mathematics-related concepts. The teacher then records each pupil's performance and from those data makes instructional decisions.

Also included in *Direct Instruction Mathematics* are instructional sequence and assessment charts for all the skills and concepts in the program. Figure 9.5 shows the sequence and assessment chart for subtraction. Such a chart can be used for diagnosis or program evaluation. For the former, the teacher could administer the items on the chart and then require pupils to respond to other items of the types that had been solved incorrectly. The idea would be to zero in on the exact types of problems with which the pupil had difficulty. For the latter purpose, the teacher could give all or some of the problems (along with others of different types) at the beginning and end of the school year to discover which ones had been learned.

Informal tests have been designed to assess children's cognitive development as described in Piaget's theory of development. Three books written for the Nuffield project in Great Britain are sources of Piagetian-type tests. Three of the project guides—"Checking Up I," "Checking Up II," and "Checking Up III"—contain tests for determining children's levels of development (Nuffield foundation, 1971). (A part of the checkup for one-to-one correspondence is reproduced in Figure 9.6.) To administer such an assessment, the teacher assembles a number of items and perhaps develops a script that describes how information will be requested from pupils. The teacher also needs to develop a summary sheet on which to record data about each pupil's performance, the date of the assessment, and perhaps other anecdotal information about the pupil's effort.

Figure 9.7 is a sample set of questions for assessing children's attitudes toward mathematics (Aiken, 1972). Researchers and teachers are aware of the poor attitudes that some children, particularly LD pupils, have toward mathematics, and some consider it a good idea to assess students' feelings about the process. Data from a scale such as the one shown here could be used in a variety of ways. On learning that a pupil was anxious and insecure over math instruction, the teacher might make some adjustments in an attempt to alter those feelings. The teacher could also administer this scale, or one like it, a few times throughout the year to determine if pupils' attitudes were constant or seemed to be affected by certain instructional situations.

An important dimension of informal assessment is to determine the systematic errors pupils make as they compute arithmetic problems—that is, to detect the problems on which they consistently make errors. Cox (1975) conducted a thorough study of systematic errors in the four algorithms (addition, subtraction, multiplication, and division) by skill levels, grade levels, and by nonhandicapped and handicapped populations.

To obtain data, Cox required pupils to respond to a variety of problems a number of times. In addition, for example, the students responded to five problems of each level. (See Table 9.3.) If a pupil missed three of the five problems of the same type in the same way, that was recorded as a systematic error.

■ FIGURE 9.5 ■   *Direct Instruction Mathematics* Sequence and Assessment Chart

Grade Level	Problem Type	Performance Indicator		
1	Subtracting a one or two digit number from a two digit number; no renaming	57 −20	45 − 3	21 − 4
2a	Subtracting a one or two digit number from a two digit number; renaming required	54 −18	46 − 9	70 −38
2b	Subtracting a one, two, or three digit number from a three digit number; renaming tens to ones	382 − 37	393 −174	242 − 6
3a	Subtracting a two or three digit number from a three digit number; renaming from hundreds to tens	423 −171	418 − 83	228 −137
3b	Subtracting a two or three digit number from a three digit number; renaming from tens to ones and hundreds to tens	352 −187	724 −578	534 − 87
3c	Tens minus 1 facts	70 − 1 = □ 40 − 1 = □ 80 − 1 = □		
3d	Subtracting a two or three digit number from a three digit number, zero in tens column; renaming from tens to ones and hundreds to tens	503 − 87	504 − 21	700 − 86
3e	Subtracting a three or four digit number from a four digit number; renaming from thousands to hundreds	4689 −1832	5284 −4631	3481 −1681
3f	Subtracting a one, two, three, or four digit number from a four digit number; renaming required in several columns	5342 − 68	6143 − 217	5231 −1658
4a	Subtracting a two, three, or four digit number from a four digit number; a zero in either the tens or hundreds column	4023 − 184	5304 −1211	5304 − 418
4b	Hundreds minus 1 facts	700 − 1 = □ 400 − 1 = □ 800 − 1 = □		
4c	Subtracting a one, two, three, or four digit number from a four digit number; a zero in the tens and hundreds column	4000 −1357	2001 −1453	8000 −4264
4d	Same as 4c except 1,000 as top number	1000 − 283	1000 − 82	1000 − 80
4e	Same as 4c except 1,100 as top number	1100 − 241	1100 − 532	1100 − 830
4f	Subtracting involving five and six digit numbers; renaming	342,523 − 18,534	480,235 − 1,827	38,402 −15,381
5a	Thousands minus 1 facts	5000 − 1 = □ 3000 − 1 = □ 1000 − 1 = □		
5b	Subtracting from a number with four zeroes	80000 − 826	50000 − 8260	10000 − 284

Source: Reprinted by permission from J. Silbert, D. Carnine, and M. Stein, *Direct Instruction Mathematics* (Columbus, OH: Merrill, 1981), p. 141.

■ FIGURE 9.6 ■   Sample of a Checkup Test Used to Determine Children's Levels of Cognitive Growth

Summary Checkup OC†	Typical Replies
One-to-one correspondence and transitivity	a [Children with an immature understanding of OC]
Objective	*The child may argue that because the line now looks different there are not as many bricks as counters. He may say:*
Transitivity: if A = B and B = C, then A = C.	*"There are fewer counters because the line is shorter,"*
Material	*or*
A collection of counters, say twelve (A)	*"There are more because the line is longer."*
A collection of small bricks (B)	*Children may also say:*
A collection of small miscellaneous objects (C)	*"There are more counters because they are close together."*
Part 1	b [Children with a developing understanding of OC]
Procedure	*The children will say that there are as many bricks as counters but will not be able to justify their reply.*
The teacher should spread out nine counters on the table and ask the child: "Can you put on the table as many bricks as there are counters?"	c [Children with a mature understanding of OC]
	Children will say that there are as many bricks as counters. They will be able to justify their reply in the following manner:
Note	*i*
Should the child not be able to establish this initial correspondence, then the teacher should let him have further practice.	*"It doesn't matter if they are in a long line because they are exactly the same bricks as before when they were in front of the counters,"*
Once the child has established a one-to-one correspondence between the two collections the teacher should ask the child if he needs the remaining bricks.	*or*
	"You haven't put any more, and you haven't taken any away."
	ii
	"You can put them back as they were before, and you'll see that they are the same."
Note	*iii*
Should the child, with the remaining bricks, fill in a space in the line of bricks already arranged, the teacher should remove the remaining bricks and ask the child:	*"The line is longer but there's more space between the bricks,"*
"Are there as many bricks as counters?"	*or*
"Why?"	*"The line is shorter and there's less space between the counters."*
Once the child's reply has been given, the teacher should then tell the child: "We are now going to spread out the bricks."	*Only those children giving replies b or c should go on to Part 2.*
The teacher should do this in such a way that the line of bricks is longer than the line of counters, and then ask: "Are there as many bricks as counters?" "Why?"	

† OC = one-to-one correspondence

Source: Reprinted by permission from the Nuffield Foundation, *Checking Up I* (London: John Murray Publishers, Ltd., 1970), p. 34.

■ FIGURE 9.7 ■   *Mathematics Attitude Scale*

1. I am always under a terrible strain in a mathematics class.	SD D U A SA
2. I do not like mathematics, and it scares me to have to take it.	SD D U A SA
3. Mathematics is very interesting to me, and I enjoy arithmetic and mathematics courses.	SD D U A SA
4. Mathematics is fascinating and fun.	SD D U A SA
5. Mathematics makes me feel secure, and at the same time it is stimulating.	SD D U A SA
6. My mind goes blank and I am unable to think clearly when working mathematics.	SD D U A SA
7. I feel a sense of insecurity when attempting mathematics.	SD D U A SA
8. Mathematics makes me feel uncomfortable, restless, irritable, and impatient.	SD D U A SA
9. The feeling that I have toward mathematics is a good feeling.	SD D U A SA
10. Mathematics makes me feel as though I'm lost in a jungle of numbers and can't find my way out.	SD D U A SA
11. Mathematics is something that I enjoy a great deal.	SD D U A SA
12. When I hear the word mathematics, I have a feeling of dislike.	SD D U A SA
13. I approach mathematics with a feeling of hesitation, resulting from a fear of not being able to do mathematics.	SD D U A SA
14. I really like mathematics.	SD D U A SA
15. Mathematics is a course in school that I have always enjoyed studying.	SD D U A SA
16. It makes me nervous to even think about having to do a mathematics problem.	SD D U A SA
17. I have never liked mathematics, and it is my most dreaded subject.	SD D U A SA
18. I am happier in a mathematics class than in any other class.	SD D U A SA
19. I feel at ease in mathematics, and I like it very much.	SD D U A SA
20. I feel a definite positive reaction toward mathematics; it's enjoyable.	SD D U A SA

Key: SD = Strongly Disagree; D = Disagree; U = Undecided; A = Agree; SA = Strongly Agree.
Source: From Lewis R. Aiken, Jr., "Research on Attitudes Toward Mathematics," *Arithmetic Teacher,* March 1972, p. 47. Reprinted with permission from the *Arithmetic Teacher,* © copyright 1972 by the National Council of Teachers of Mathematics.

Cox's results, summarized in Table 9.4, showed that the average percentages of systematic errors in multiplication and division was much higher for special education students than for nonhandicapped students. The largest number of systematic errors for both kinds of students occurred in understanding the concepts themselves—that is, in knowing when to multiply and when to divide.

When Cox gathered the same data one year later, it was disturbing to note that 16 percent of the youngsters were making the same systematic error.

■ COMMENTARY ■   *Those data certainly pointed out the need for discrete and frequent monitoring of progress, analyses of the data, and instructional adjustments made accordingly.*

■ TABLE 9.3 ■   Sample Problems for Assessing Levels of Skill in Addition

Skill		Example
Level 1:	Adding a two-digit and one-digit number; no renaming.	23 + 2
Level 2:	Adding a two-digit and one-digit number; with renaming.	18 + 7
Level 3:	Adding a two-digit and two-digit number; no renaming.	43 + 16
Level 4:	Adding a two-digit and two-digit number; with renaming.	19 + 24
Level 5:	Adding a three-digit and two-digit number; no renaming.	172 + 26
Level 6:	Adding a three-digit and two-digit number; renaming in the ones column only.	476 + 17
Level 7:	Adding a three-digit and two-digit number; renaming in the ones and tens columns.	345 + 76
Level 8:	Column addition—three two-digit numbers; with renaming.	46 39 + 17

Note: The levels are not in order of increasing difficulty. They are organized by the number of digits and the inclusion or exclusion of renaming.

Source: From L.S. Cox, "Systematic errors in the four vertical algorithms in normal and handicapped populations," *Journal for Research in Mathematics Education, 6,* 1975, p. 206. Reprinted with permission from the *Journal for Research in Mathematics Education,* © copyright 1975 by the National Council of Teachers of Mathematics.

Speed Standards

Some years ago, Wood, Burke, Kunzelmann, and Koenig (1978) conducted a rather thorough study on performance standards. The individuals in their research were "unsuccessful" high school students, "successful" high school students, and average workers in a community. Data from those students and workers were obtained on 40 different types of math skills that elementary teachers believed had "high instructional value." To acquire the data, the researchers prepared worksheets containing several problems of each type. The individuals were then given one minute on each sheet to respond to the problems. (Data from the timings appear in Table 9.5.) When mean data are compared, it is obvious that in nearly every case, the digit-per-minute scores of the successful students are higher than those of the unsuccessful pupils. It is also apparent that the scores of

■ TABLE 9.4 ■ Comparison of the Percentages of Systematic Errors for All Grades Across All Four Algorithms

Grade	Addition	No. of Papers	Sub-traction	No. of Papers	Multi-plication	No. of Papers	Division	No. of Papers
2	10%	596	13%	382	*	*	*	*
3	6%	800	23%	544	6%	278	*	*
4	1%	816	8%	657	8%	725	7%	411
5	1%	208	6%	199	5%	872	5%	845
6	0%	194	6%	100	1%	847	3%	888
Averages for grades 2–6	4%		11%		5%		5%	
Primary sp. ed.	5%	68	15%	33	*	*	*	*
Intermediate sp. ed.	8%	454	24%	296	27%	206	21%	38
Junior high sp. ed.	2%	444	12%	340	11%	287	13%	194
Averages for special education	5%		17%		19%		17%	
Averages for all grades, both populations	5%	3,580	13%	2,551	6%	3,229	6%	2,403

*Classrooms were not tested because no child could meet the requirements for the study.

Reprinted with permission from L.S. Cox, "Systematic errors in the four vertical algorithms in normal and handicapped populations," *Journal for Research in Mathematics Education, 6,* 1975, p. 207. Reprinted with permission from the *Journal for Research in Mathematics Education,* © copyright 1975 by the National Council of Teachers of Mathematics.

the community workers and the successful students are about the same. These data take on particular relevance when the rates of the unsuccessful students are compared with those of the community workers; for on this test of a wide variety of skills, the slow pupils are once again off the mark. Although there were only a few LD students sprinkled in among the unsuccessful students, it is reasonable to assume that their scores were even lower than those of the average lower students.

TECHNIQUES AND APPROACHES

This section describes a few techniques for instructing aspects of mathematics to learning disabled students. Although these approaches have been recommended by educators, they have not necessarily been researched with LD pupils. The section also reviews mathematics studies that have been researched with learning disabled groups.

■ **TABLE 9.5** ■   Timed Mathematics Test Performance Scores

Skill	Unsuccessful Students				Successful Students				Community			
	N	Median	Mean	S.D.	N	Median	Mean	S.D.	N	Median	Mean	S.D.
Numeration/Place Value												
Write numerals 1 to N	94	147	147	50.85	77	148	152	21.65	48	157	155	41.61
10 through more than 100 by groups of 10	72	80	76	47.56	77	116	111	24.27	48	128	120	37.47
Greater than, less than, equal to (whole num)	95	44	42	25.09	77	60	61	19.65	49	47	42	14.25
Rounding to nearest multiple of 5,10,100	95	72	69	31.95	77	83	82	27.97	49	94	94	21.45
Greater than, less than, equal to (dec num)	95	24	22	13.23	77	34	34	10.58	49	25	25	30.26
Rounding decimal numerals to nearest tenth	95	33	34	20.26	77	56	61	28.69	49	63	59	21.66
Addition												
Adding 1 digit and 1 digit numeral	95	76	82	26.18	77	98	104	26.47	49	117	125	29.70
Adding 3 or more 1 digit numerals	95	53	56	20.65	77	72	72	30.40	49	86	89	24.20
Add 3/more numerals with 1,2,3,4/more digits	95	28	28	9.34	77	33	33	9.10	49	37	40	10.19
Adding decimal numerals	95	40	40	14.58	77	52	51	9.72	49	60	58	12.11
Add 3/more digit numerals and 2/more digit numerals with regrouping	95	38	41	14.58	77	43	46	14.73	49	62	60	16.12
Add 3/more digit numerals and 3/more digit numerals without regrouping	95	73	77	21.79	77	83	85	16.92	49	96	99	20.64
Subtraction												
Subtract 1 digit numeral from 1 or 2 digit numeral (answer 0–9)	95	48	48	13.30	77	58	58	15.24	49	65	68	17.00
Subtract any numeral from numeral with 3 or more digits	95	28	28	13.44	77	42	41	12.93	49	56	56	13.62
Subtracting decimal numerals	95	20	21	9.39	77	23	26	11.50	49	41	40	14.55
Subtracting 2/more digit numerals from 3/more digit numeral (without regrouping)	95	61	64	20.35	77	71	70	16.41	49	70	69	17.41
Multiplication												
Multiply 1 digit numeral by 1 digit numeral	94	82	81	30.09	77	90	87	26.63	49	92	89	32.04
Multiply 2 digit numeral by 1 digit numeral (without regrouping)	95	75	75	28.85	77	83	81	20.75	49	86	84	16.72
Multiply 2 or more digit numeral by 1 digit numeral (with regrouping)	95	34	35	17.96	76	40	42	13.71	49	48	45	14.19
Multiply 2 or more digit numeral by 2 or more digit numeral (with regrouping)	95	9.7	9.7	6.77	77	18	17	7.28	49	21	22	8.90
Multiply any decimal numeral with any decimal numeral	94	36	37	20.76	77	39	37	12.61	49	40	40	16.36
Division												
Divide 1 or 2 digit numeral by 1 digit numeral (answer 0–9; no remainder)	95	32	32	16.43	77	44	44	16.00	49	46	47	16.14
Divide whole numerals and write answers as decimal numerals	93	4.5	4.6	3.99	77	7.1	7.8	3.87	49	8.7	9.7	5.81
Divide decimal numerals/decimal numerals and write answer as decimal numeral	93	2.9	8.7	10.22	77	20	18	10.69	49	12	14	11.59
Divide 2 or more digit numeral by 2 or more digit numeral (with remainder)	93	1.1	1.2	89	77	1.9	2.1	1.34	49	2.9	3.4	2.37
Fractions												
Add 2 common fractions with like denominator	95	76	78	43.81	77	88	93	31.92	49	112	108	30.49
Add involving 1 or more mixed numerals	95	22	22	13.61	77	32	30	19.41	49	36	34	13.62

Table 9.5 Continued

Skill	Unsuccessful Students				Successful Students				Community			
	N	Median	Mean	S.D.	N	Median	Mean	S.D.	N	Median	Mean	S.D.
Difference of 2 common fraction/like denominators	95	64	63	38.54	77	84	81	32.32	49	96	92	26.04
Difference involving 1 or more mixed numerals	95	16	17	13.71	77	30	30	18.60	49	32	30	13.44
Fraction which is less than, more than another fraction	95	14	15	8.71	76	24	26	12.32	49	19	21	13.45
Multiply common fraction by common fraction	95	69	76	42.57	77	92	96	38.58	49	77	80	39.36
Divide common fraction by common fraction	101	28	28	22.27	76	53	56	25.71	49	31	40	35.30
Equivalent common fractions	103	4.8	8.3	31.39	77	7.1	8	6.28	49	4.6	7.6	12.79
Money, Time, Standards												
Value/set of coins using $ and decimal point	104	34	37	13.43	77	39	38	10.19	49	40	38	10.60
Time using colon to separate hours and minutes	104	50	49	12.43	49	59	60	14.51				
Lengths measured using English System	104	3.6	3.8	3.17	77	5.7	5.9	3.41	49	6.7	7.8	4.68
Lengths measured using Metric System	104	3.6	3.8	3.17	77	5.7	5.9	3.41	49	6.7	7.8	4.68
Story Problems												
Identifying amounts and units	106	3.5	2.9	1.96	77	4.0	4.5	1.90	49	5.4	6.1	2.62
Identifying knowns and unknowns	106	3.5	2.9	1.96	77	4.0	4.5	1.90	49	5.4	6.1	2.62
Solving word problems involving fractions	106	3.4	3.9	3.38	77	8.3	9.7	5.46	49	9.9	12	8.98

Source: Reprinted with permission from Stillman Wood, L. Burke, H. Kunzelmann, and C. Koenig, "Functional Criteria in Basic Math Proficiency," *Journal of Special Education Technology*, 2(2), 1978, p. 3.

Recommended Instructional Approaches

Six instructional areas are reviewed here: patterns, sets, geometry, numbers and operations, fractions, and measurement. These categories are from the *Project Math* program, and they are also in close agreement with the categories recommended by the National Council of Supervisors of Mathematics.

Patterns. Instruction in patterns and sets may be to mathematics instruction what certain discrimination and awareness activities are to the teaching of reading.

■ COMMENTARY ■ It may well be that not enough time is spent with these fundamental activities with children, learning disabled and otherwise; as a result, many of them never develop understandings of mathematics concepts and perceptions, even though they can add and subtract.

According to Sedlak and Fitzmaurice (1981) patterns can be an extension of classification activities.

A pattern is defined by a repeating sequence of elements. In the listing, *"table cup cup" "table cup cup" "table cup cup,"* the elements are *table* and *cup*. The repetend, or repeated sequence, is *"table cup cup."* The elements can be of any nature, as the following patterns illustrate:

B B 6 B B 6 B B 6
cup saucer cup saucer cup saucer
$$$ ## $$$ ## $$$

Patterns may be composed of numerals, letters, symbols, words, sentences, or combinations thereof. They may be short or long, simple or sophisticated. They may be visual, as indicated by the examples, or auditory. For that matter they could be olfactory or kinesthetic. When youngsters are exposed to the study of patterns, they are not only acquiring a base for the study of mathematics, but they are learning about the symmetry of their environments and their lives.

■ COMMENTARY ■   From what we know about the perceptual, spatial, and temporal deficits of many LD youngsters, we would probably do well to consider more instruction with patterns and relationships.

Sets.   The word "set" means a group in which all members have a common quality, other than the fact that all belong to the same group. This common quality might be something like "redness" or "squareness" or "wheelness." Sets such as these can be referred to as classes or categories.

There are countless sets of numerals: even and odd numbers; numbers divisible by 2, 3, or 4; 2-, 3-, or 4-digit numerals; and prime and palindromic numerals (for example, 696).

Sedlak and Fitzmaurice (1981) have suggested that activities with sets be used to extend language skills, to refine classification skills, and to foster such capabilities as discrimination and attribute recognition. Instruction in sets becomes a matter of joining classes to make bigger classes, breaking classes into smaller classes, and noting qualities belonging to some members of two different classes.

■ COMMENTARY ■   Based on the information we have about the inability of many learning disabled youngsters to categorize and discriminate, their problems with convergent and divergent thinking, their general ineptness for conceptualizing symbols, and their problems with describing the natures and attributes of objects, items, and relationships, it would be prudent to consider more training in sets for our LD pupils.

Geometry.   This branch of mathematics concerns itself with position or location in space. Some of the most basic geometric concepts children must acquire include: "open," "closed," "inside," "outside," "on," "between," "over," "under," "left," "right," "straight," and "curved."

A knowledge of basic two-dimensional shapes—circle, triangle, square, rectangle—provides youngsters with an awareness of these shapes in the environment and, in many cases, a vocabulary with which to communicate about the environment. The same can be said for a familiarity with basic three-dimensional shapes: sphere, cube, prism, cone, and pyramid.

According to Sedlak and Fitzmaurice (1981), facility in working with shapes and the knowledge of relationships between lines (for example, parallelism and perpendicularity) find application in many vocational tasks. Experiences with other geometrical concepts are valuable also in the development of certain perceptual skills and cognitive skills, attributes that are deficient in many LD students.

Kennedy (1984) has recommended that children with learning problems perform the following activities:

— Copy bead patterns
— Deal with enclosures on a line
— Examine open and closed figures
— Deal with enclosures on a plane

He maintains that these activities help youngsters develop understandings of basic geometric concepts and other concepts that are essential for learning about the order of numbers and the configurations of numerals and letters.

Numbers and Operations.   Kennedy (1984) has offered a number of suggestions for learning disabled youngsters with respect to this category of mathematics; only a few are summarized here. For children who commit counting errors by making incorrect one-to-one matches between objects and the counting numbers, teachers can require them to touch and move objects as they are counted. For youngsters who have difficulty remembering the sequence of numbers and the numbers that come before and after a number, teachers can arrange "count on" activities. This activity can begin at a number other than one, but the child must be aware that the number named at which he or she is to start counting is the cardinal number of the set.

For some pupils who have problems counting across decades—that is, from 19 to 20 and 29 to 30—teachers can have them practice counting from a hundreds chart on which all the numerals from 1 to 100 are written. As the pupils count, at each 10's numeral, they back up and also say the preceding numeral (e.g., 19, 29, 39). Later, ask the pupils to begin counting from two or three numerals before the 10's numeral and continue for a few numerals after.

Kennedy has suggested that "low stress algorithms" be used for LD children who have trouble with some of the more standard computational formats. For addition, he recommends the "half-space notation." This algorithm is particularly useful for adding when there are three or more addends. The example in Figure 9.8 shows that all addition is recorded as the work is completed. Each fact in the set of addends has its sum recorded; no mental accumulation of sums is necessary. For example, add 8 + 4, record 12; add 2 + 6, record 8; add 8 + 9, record 17; add 7 + 8, record 15. Now that all addends have been added, record 5 below the line. Count the number of times a ten was recorded at the left of the column; record 3 below the line. The sum for this addition is 35.

For those pupils who have trouble with alignment in multiplication and division problems, Kennedy has recommended the use of grid-lined paper and color cues of green and red to indicate the sequence of operations. In the example in Figure 9.9, the "6" and the lower circle above the "2" are colored green

■ FIGURE 9.8 ■   Low-Stress Algorithm for Addition

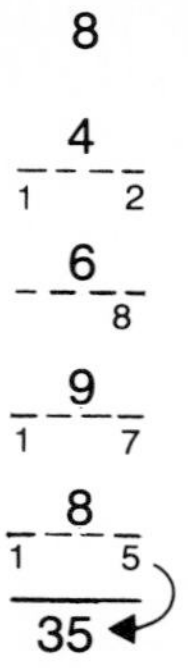

Source: Reprinted with permission from L.M. Kennedy, *Guiding Children's Learning of Mathematics,* 4th edition (Belmont, CA: Wadsworth Publishing Company, 1984), p. 257.

(dashed lines) to indicate that multiplication by 6 is done first. This circle is also where the "carried 5" is written. The "4" in the multiplier and the upper circle are red (dotted lines) to indicate that multiplication by 4 is done next. The answer spaces for each operation are colored to match the colors in the multiplier.

Fractions.   LD students are generally no better at dealing with fractions than they are with other features of mathematics. Early on, they should be introduced to parts of the whole when learning about money (half dollars and quarters), time (half past and quarter past and before the hour), measurement (½, ¼, and ⅛ inches; parts of quarts or liters; partial distances of fields). They should be instructed in part-to-whole relationships in ways that relate to their environments, such as dividing up the class members into teams, working on partial assignments until the total is completed, adding up their contributions with those of their mates in cooperative learning situations.

Kennedy (1984) cautions us that children with visual discrimination or figure-ground weaknesses often have a hard time distinguishing a part from the whole when a geometric region represents a part-of-a-whole situation and when a set of disks represents a part-of-a-set situation. He goes on to remind us that children with memory deficits cannot always retain information acquired during work with concrete models long enough to transfer it to symbolic forms as they learn about numerals for common fractions. For those types of children, he recommends that carefully constructed but simple models can be used and that colors be incorporated to highlight certain features.

In *A Guide to the Diagnostic Teaching of Arithmetic*, Reisman (1978) has explained a number of techniques to arrange for youngsters with learning difficulties. To help pupils compare equivalent regions, for example, she suggested a diagram (see Figure 9.10). With such an aid, the pupil can compare equivalent

■ FIGURE 9.9 ■   Low-Stress Algorithm for Multiplication

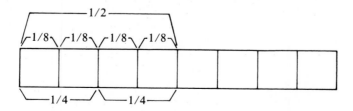

Source: Reprinted with permission from L.M. Kennedy, *Guiding Children's Learning of Mathematics,*
4th edition (Belmont, CA: Wadsworth Publishing Company, 1984), p. 311.

fractions—for example, ½ to ¼ and ¼ to ⅛. If the pupil has trouble adding
fractions, Reisman suggests that he be shown a new algorithm. If, for example,
the problem was ¼ + ¼, the student would compute it as follows:

$$\frac{1 + 1}{4} = \frac{2}{4}$$

Measurement.   Kennedy believes special care is needed to provide a logical
sequence of measurement activities. He recommends, therefore, a three-step

■ FIGURE 9.10 ■   *Instructional Aid for Teaching Equivalent Fractions*

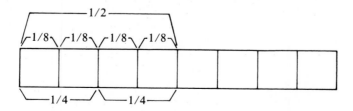

Source: Reprinted with permission from F.K. Reisman, *A Guide to the Diagnostic Teaching of Arithmetic,* 2nd edition (Columbus, OH: Merrill, 1978), p. 160.

progression: exploratory activities, work with nonstandard units, and work with standard units. According to him, the exploratory materials and large nonstandard units provide experiences that help learning disabled children:

— Develop motor skills
— Learn to discriminate on the basis of size, shape, and color
— Sequence materials
— Develop other prerequisite skills for understanding measurement, time, and money

When standard units of measure are introduced, uncluttered measuring instruments should be used.

■ COMMENTARY ■   A number of applied situations should be brought into play when teaching LD youngsters about measurement. They could be instructed about time from plane, bus, or train schedules. They could learn about money by working with budgets, shopping lists, and want ads. They could learn about weights and heights by measuring their own bodies or those of their friends. From these functional opportunities to develop information about measurement, students could also be instructed to form estimations about time and amounts.

Research-Based Interventions

Few research studies have been published on mathematics interventions with learning disabled youngsters. Following are studies that provided instruction of some type, and those that manipulated a reinforcement contingency.

Providing Instruction in Mathematics.   Several studies with the demonstration and permanent modeling (D & PM) technique have been scheduled in addition, subtraction, and multiplication. For this intervention, the teacher shows the pupil, step-by-step, how to solve a problem (demonstration). When the problem is completed, the teacher leaves the answer to the solved problem, along with any preliminary calculations for the pupil to view (permanent model) as she responds to other similar problems.

Blankenship (1978) conducted a study of this type with intermediate age LD youngsters performing problems in subtraction. She was interested in how the D & PM treatment affected the initial acquisition of the pupils and the extent to which they generalized effects and retained them. While the data showed positive initial effects for all pupils, the extent of generalization varied; some pupils generalized to more complex problems, but others did not. However, most of the students did retain their accuracy on instructed and non-instructed problem types one month following the intervention.

Sugai and Smith (1986) used the D & PM technique to instruct subtraction to intermediate age LD students. Whereas the students in Blankenship's research were taught to subtract by the "decomposition method" (borrowing from numerals in the minuend), Sugai and Smith chose the "equal additions method" (adding equal numbers to numerals in the subtrehend). Their data indicated immediate and positive effects on acquisition for all the students. All students were also able to generalize and solve certain problems that were not directly taught. When retention tests were given, about half of the youngsters could still successfully solve the problems.

Rivera and Smith (1987) compiled data from three studies with D & PM. Students in those investigations were LD pupils of intermediate age, and were assigned either addition, subtraction, or multiplication problems. Rivera and Smith were concerned about the effects of the D & PM intervention on initial acquisition and the generalization of the approach to other problems. With respect to the former, the effects of the demonstration and permanent modeling technique were quick and dramatic. Generalization data, however, were mixed; some pupils were affected more than others.

Some years ago, Lovitt, Smith, Kidder, and Evison (1974) investigated the effects of a few manipulatives on subtraction performance among LD pupils of intermediate age. The researchers were interested not only in the extent to which the manipulative—abacus, counting rods, and paper clips—affected types of problems for which it was arranged, but in problems of a different type on which the support was not available. Data showed that all three manipulatives had positive effects on the acquisition of problems, and some generalizations to other problem types were noted.

Lovitt and Curtiss (1968) also arranged three replications in a subtraction study for an eleven-year old LD boy. He was given neither feedback nor reinforcement as he worked the problems during baseline periods. In the phases that followed, however, he was required to verbalize the entire problem and his answer before writing it. That is, for the problem $14 - \underline{\hspace{1cm}} = 6$, he would say "Fourteen minus what equals six?" Then he would complete the statement— "Fourteen minus eight equals six"—and write the answer. Throughout the final phases of these studies he was no longer required to verbalize the problems and solutions. The data indicated that his performances were much more accurate in the second phases than during baselines. In the final phases, his accuracy remained high, and his response frequency greatly increased when he was no longer required to say the problems.

In another type of instruction, Lombardo and Drabman (1985) conducted research with LD students of intermediate age, using a "write" and "write and say" procedure. Throughout the three phases of the research, the youngsters took tests on multiplication problems. In the baseline phase, they did not practice on the words in any particular way. Throughout the second phase, they wrote answers to problems on their practice sheets and if they erred on one, wrote the problem and its answer five times. During the third phase, the pupils were still required to write answers to the problems, but they were also asked to verbalize the problems and answers as they wrote them. The data showed that whereas the performance of only a few youngsters was affected by the write-only condition, nearly all the students were positively changed by the write-and-say procedure.

Fleischner, Nuzum, and Marzola (1987) devised an instructional program to teach problem-solving skills to students with learning disabilities. Their program was developed in response to the recognition that although some LD students have adequate reading and computation skills, they lack the procedural, process, and task-specific knowledge necessary to solve story problems. Students in their research were successful in solving word problems when given a card on which the following five steps were printed:

1. *Read:* What is the question?
2. *Reread:* What is the necessary information?
3. *Think:* Putting together = *add.*
   Taking apart = *subtract.*
   Do I need all the information?
   Is it a two-step problem?
4. *Solve:* Write the calculation.
5. *Check:* Recalculate.
   Label.
   Compare.

Fantasia (1981) developed a similar technique to assist LD boys of intermediate age to solve word problems. Her study included extraneous information, sequential ordering of the problems, and mixed order of the numerical data—all features that were known to influence performance negatively. During a baseline period, no feedback, instruction, or reinforcement of any type was scheduled; the boys were taught a four-step process to rely on as they solved the problems. They were taught to identify:

— What the problem was asking
— The pertinent information needed to solve the problem
— Whether the problem involved parts or the total and one part
— The correct process for solving the problem

Data revealed that there was significant improvement in solving problems during the instructional phases, but there was poor maintenance when the pupils' skills were reassessed 15 weeks after the study.

Manipulating Reinforcement Contingencies.   Some reinforcement contingency has been arranged for a number of studies. In this type of study, there is a cause-and-effect relationship; if the pupil does something, some planned event occurs.

Smith and Lovitt (1976) studied the effects of reinforcement on the performances of LD boys of intermediate age performing various arithmetic processes. In these investigations, following a baseline phase, pupils could earn privileges, contingent on specified levels of performance. Data indicated that the reinforcement contingencies had differential effects. For those pupils who were just acquiring a skill, the contingencies were not effective. The authors recommended that, instead of reinforcement contingencies, some instructional intervention should be scheduled for learners. For pupils who had reached the proficiency stage— they knew how to perform the problems but their rates were not high enough— the contingencies had positive effects.

Lovitt and Esreldt (1970) studied the relative effects on performance of single- versus multiple-ratio schedules. The pupil in their research was a twelve-year old LD boy, and the topic was addition. During the single-ratio conditions, the pupil could earn one point for each twenty correct responses. During multiple-ratio phases, three or four ratios were established, and he could earn proportionally more points the more rapidly he responded. The data, gathered throughout several replications, indicated that the boy consistently responded at higher rates during the multiple-ratio conditions.

In a reverse twist, Lovitt and Smith (1974) withdrew reinforcement in an effort to alter subtraction performance of an LD girl. During a baseline condition, as she worked on subtraction problems of three types, her performances were erratic. At times, all her responses were perfect, but often she made what seemed to be careless mistakes. During the next phase, a withdrawal contingency was instituted for one class of problems. When she committed an error on that type of problem, she lost one minute of free time. Her performance immediately reached perfection for that type, but not the others. When the withdrawal contingency was subsequently instituted for the other types of problems, her performances on those problems also became errorless.

———— USE OF CALCULATORS AND COMPUTERS ————

Recommendations for Calculators

In an attempt to involve schools with current technologies, the National Council of Teachers of Mathematics has made a number of recommendations.

1. Calculators should be routinely available to kindergarten and grade school students during their math studies. Children should be taught, however, that pencil and paper calculations are better methods in some cases, particularly when learning basic mental math skills.

■ COMMENTARY ■   *The author ran a few studies with high-performing sixth graders in an effort to determine the break-even point with respect to using hand-held calculators (Lovitt, 1980). Whereas some of the sixth graders responded to all 78 problem types in a math program using paper and pencil, another group used calculators to solve the problems. The data indicated that it was more efficient to do simple addition and subtraction (commonly scheduled in the first three grades) problems by hand. Long division (usually scheduled in fourth grade) problems are more efficiently done with a calculator.*

2. Because calculators compute negative numbers, decimals, vectors, and similar sophisticated concepts, students casually experimenting with them might come in contact with those features at an early age. Such concepts, therefore, should be taught as they arise.

3. In grades 5 to 8, mathematics instruction should emphasize the ability to approximate and interpret answers, graph theory, and probabilities, and computers should be used as a learning aide.

4. In high school, computers could change traditional math curricula designed strictly to prepare students for calculus. Many students, who have no plans for calculus, could enhance their training in statistics and other fields. Meanwhile, students who are headed for calculus could use computers to learn fundamental concepts of the field without being bogged down by manipulative procedures.

5. Geometry and algebra instruction could be revolutionized by the use of computers. With computer graphics, geometry students can manipulate vectors, three-dimensional space, transformations, and trigonometry with ease. The skill objectives of algebra would have to be redesigned to address the reality of computer programs that can do arithmetic and call up logarithms and trigonometric functions instantly.

6. Students who aren't interested in math or who lack an aptitude for it can use computers in problem-solving classes that heretofore required extensive math mastery.

The Mathematics Council also recommends that students be allowed to use calculators when they take achievement tests. According to Jack Beal of the College of Education at the University of Washington, one reason that calculators are not used more widely in elementary classes is because children are not allowed to work with them when they take achievement tests.

■ COMMENTARY ■   This is certainly a case of backward programming. If test makers, such as ETS, "allowed" youngsters to use calculators during tests, then it is more likely that students would be taught to use them in their classrooms.

S.V. Horton (1984), when a doctoral student at the University of Washington, administered the math section of an achievement test two times to a group of mentally retarded students. The process was a part of his dissertation research on hand-held calculators. On one day students worked with paper and pencil; on the other, they used calculators. The scores for most of the students were much higher the second day.

Reviews of Computer Programs

A number of microcomputer programs have been developed to teach various components of mathematics. Summaries of seven of these programs follow.

Starting Out (published by NTS Software) is a set of two programs developed to introduce preschool and early elementary students to beginning math concepts.

Set I provides an introduction to mathematics that stresses number concepts, counting, sequencing, and beginning addition and subtraction. Set II offers more opportunities to practice with simple addition, subtraction and sequencing. The reviewer (Mather, 1985a) of these programs noted that a major disadvantage was that student records were not maintained. She also pointed out that the tasks were rather indefinite, like endless workbooks; consequently, students may not have felt a sense of accomplishment as they worked on the problems.

Learning About Numbers (published by C&C Software) contains a set of four math games. In the first, exercises range from counting objects to a format in which objects are presented in two boxes and pupils count the objects in each. In the second game, students match analog and digital time with increasing levels of difficulty. The third game has addition and subtraction problems of increasing levels of difficulty, and the fourth has multiplication and division problems. The reviewer (Hummel, 1985a) reported that the program could be useful because the range of exercises was well-matched to the capabilities of many students in typical classes for the learning disabled.

The main objective of *Arithmetic Drill,* another program for microcomputers, is to provide drill on basic addition, subtraction, and multiplication operations. The program has thirty-eight levels, and problems progress from simple addition to multiple-digit multiplication. The difficulty of the program can be altered according to the individual student's performance. Commenting on the program, the reviewer (Mather, 1984a) thought that its graphics were slow, repetitive, and unnecessary, causing the students to spend more time watching than working.

The purpose of *1–2–3–Digit Multiplication* (published by Microcomputer Workshops) is to provide students with drill and practice in multiplication. Either the teacher or the student may choose the size of the multiplier—a one-, two-, or three-digit number. Students work the problems by entering the correct numbers. The reviewer (Mather, 1983) reported that several students had difficulty reading and following the program's directions. Another criticism was that there is no record-keeping system; there were no provisions for maintaining data on the students' response accuracy rate or on number of problems completed.

Long Division (published by Microcomputer Workshops) provides drill and practice in division. Either the student or the teacher may select the difficulty level (in this case, the size of the divisor—one, two, or three digits). The reviewer (Mather, 1984b) had some concerns about unnecessary steps required to participate in the program and was critical of the meager record-keeping system. In her opinion, the program would not be appropriate for students who were having difficulty with concepts that involved regrouping or who were not motivated to respond to the repetitive drills.

Math Blaster (published by Davidson and Associates) is a package of four drill and practice activities with an authoring system for the construction of additional problems. In the first, "Look and Learn," math problems are displayed without answers, and the pupil adjusts the display speed as the program fills them in. In "Build Your Skill," the second activity, the student enters the answers to the problems. In the third activity, "Challenge Yourself," the pupil fills in numbers that are missing from different parts (for example, the addend). The fourth activity of this package, "Math Blaster," is an arcade game, the object of which is to shoot a man out of the cannon at the correct answer. Time adjustments are available with a multiple-choice format, and incorrect answers result in highlighting the correct answer. With a correct response, the answer is blasted away and points are accumulated. According to the reviewer (Hummel, 1985b), a few seventh and eighth grade LD students were aided by this program with respect to the speed and accuracy with which they answered the problems and generalized that learning to other situations.

The program *Money! Money!* (published by Hartley Courseware, Inc.) has four objectives. Pupils are instructed to count money, determine if they have enough to buy an item, determine the most appropriate amount to give for an item, and count change to see if it is correct. The fifteen lessons in the program range from first to fifth grade in difficulty. The reviewer (Mather, 1985b) was concerned about the simple "Y" or "N" responses that were required, the unusual mode in which instructions were presented, and the split screen displays.

—————— COMMENTS AND DISCUSSION POINTS ——————

Based on the programs and research reviewed here, ten points are offered for teachers and researchers to consider regarding mathematics instruction to LD pupils.

- Create, rather early on, a number sense with youngsters. Teach them that numbers sometimes have meanings of their own, and one doesn't necessarily have to add, subtract, multiply, or divide them; for example, the numbers on buses, streets, or uniforms.

- Help youngsters attain reasonable degrees of accuracy on the basic facts in the four math processes as soon as possible. Pupils should be able to perform these calculations in the standard modes—that is, see-to-say and see-to-write—and the usual format—practice sheets. An undue amount of time should not be devoted to ditto sheets, however.

- Instruct LD pupils, early on, in the vocabulary of mathematics so that they can discriminate between the four operations. They should know the meaning of such words and phrases as *more than, less than,* and *altogether* and also know that those terms do not *always* signal the same operation.

- Provide LD youngsters with "medium tech" devices as soon as possible. For example, students should be taught to use digital watches. Far too much time has been devoted to teaching them to tell time with analog watches, "the old-fashioned way." Students should also be taught *about* time—that is, how much of it is spent doing ordinary things. As early as kindergarten, LD youngsters should also be taught to use hand-held calculators. They should not be required to spend long hours adding columns of figures or practicing on lengthy computations.

- Devote a fair amount of time to teaching LD youngsters to estimate. This is particularly important as they rely on calculators. Students should be taught not only to estimate solutions to various computation problems, but to estimate distances, weights, elapsed time, and costs. Although most educators agree with this approach, few strategies or practice exercises for promoting the idea are available in schools.

- Instruct mathematics through situation problems as much as possible. In designing such problems, use words and circumstances pupils know and are familiar with. Students should learn about time, measurement, maps, geometry, and other mathematics features through situation problems, many of which could relate to important aspects of their lives; for example, nutrition, pollution, shopping, budgeting, banking, and time management.

- Identify and teach the types and levels of math problems that people ordinarily use in the normal course of their lives. In a survey of math usage by various occupations, S.T. Horton (1987) discovered that about 90 percent of them used the four arithmetic processes frequently. Some other math activities that were frequently used, in descending order, were decimals, percents, estimations, budgeting, ratio, and various English measures (inches, pounds).

- Integrate mathematics instruction with teaching in reading, writing, spelling, and other subjects as much as possible.

- Teach the metric system. At some point we must bite the bullet and come in line with other countries. According to Horton's survey, few of the respondents used metric measures.

- Train teachers to be more confident when it comes to teaching math. Unquestionably, some of the problems youngsters develop in mathematics are brought on and reinforced by teachers who are themselves incompetent and uncomfortable when it comes to mathematics.

REFERENCES

Aiken, L.R., Jr. (1972). Research on attitudes toward mathematics. *Arithmetic Teacher,* March.

Badian, N.A., & Ghublikian, M. (1983). The personal-social characteristics of children with poor mathematical computation skills. *Journal of Learning Disabilities, 16,* 154–157.

Beatty, L.S.; Madden, R.; Gardner, E.F.; & Karlsen, B. (1976). *Stanford diagnostic arithmetic test.* New York: Harcourt Brace Jovanovich.

Blankenship, C.S. (1978). Remediating systematic inversion errors in subtraction through the use of demonstration and feedback. *Learning Disability Quarterly, 1,* 12–22.

Bley, N.S., & Thornton, C.A. (1981). *Teaching mathematics to the learning disabled.* Austin, TX: PRO-ED.

Brown, V.L., & McEntire, E. (1984). Test of mathematical abilities (TOMA). Austin, TX: PRO-ED.

Carpenter, R.L. (1985). Mathematics instruction in resource rooms: Instruction time and teacher competence. *Learning Disability Quarterly, 8,* 95–100.

Cawley, J.F.; Fitzmaurice, A.M.; Shaw, R.A.; Kahn, H.; & Bates, H., III. (1978). Mathematics and learning disabled youth: The upper grade levels. *Learning Disability Quarterly, 1,* 37–52.

Cawley, J.F.; Fitzmaurice, A.M.; Shaw, R.A.; Kahn, H.; & Bates, H., III. (1979a). LD youth and mathematics: A review of characteristics. *Learning Disability Journal, 2,* 29–44.

Cawley, J.F.; Fitzmaurice, A.M.; Shaw, R.A.; Kahn, H.; & Bates, H., III. (1979b). Math word problems: Suggestions for LD students. *Learning Disability Quarterly, 2,* 25–41.

Cawley, J.; Goodstein, H.; Fitzmaurice, A.; Sedlak, R.; & Althans, V. (1976). *Project Math: A program of the mainstream series.* Wallingford, CT: Educational Services.

Cawley, J.F.; Miller, J.H.; & School, B.A. (1987). A brief inquiry of arithmetic word-problem-solving among learning disabled secondary students. *Learning Disabilities Focus, 2*(2), 87–93.

Connelly, A.J.; Nachtman, W.; & Pritchett, E.M. (1976). *KeyMath diagnostic arithmetic test.* Circle Pines, MN: American Guidance Service.

Cox, L.S. (1975). Systematic errors in the four vertical algorithms in normal and handicapped populations. *Journal for Research in Mathematics Education, 6,* 202–220.

Derr, A.M. (1985). Conservation and mathematics achievement in the learning disabled child. *Journal of Learning Disabilities, 18,* 333–336.

Englert, C.S.; Culatta, B.E.; & Horn, D.G. (1987). Influence of irrelevant information in addition word problems on problem solving. *Learning Disability Quarterly, 10,* 29–36.

Fantasia, K. (1981). An investigation of formal analysis as an intervention to improve word problem computation for learning disabled children. Unpublished doctoral dissertation, University of Washington, Seattle.

Fleischner, J.E.; Nuzum, M.B.; & Marzola, E.S. (1987). Devising an instructional program to teach arithmetic problem-solving skills to students with learning disabilities. *Journal of Learning Disabilities, 20,* 214–217.

Ginsburg, H., & Baroody, A.J. (1983). *Test of early mathematics ability* (TEMA). Austin TX: PRO-Ed.

Horton, S.T. (1987). Community-based mathematics questionnaire. Unpublished manuscript, Lake Washington School District, Kirkland, WA.

Horton, S.V. (1984). A study of the efficacy of teaching educable mentally retarded adolescents to solve subtraction problems with pencil and paper and calculators under several treatment conditions. Unpublished doctoral dissertation. University of Washington, Seattle.

Hummel, J.W. (1985a). Courseware review *(Learning About Numbers: Vol. I). Journal of Learning Disabilities, 18,* 301–302.

Hummel, J.W. (1985b). Courseware review *(Math Blaster). Journal of Learning Disabilities, 18,* 241–242.

Kennedy, L.M. (1984). *Guiding children's learning of mathematics,* 4th ed. Belmont, CA: Wadsworth Publishing Company.

Lombardo, T.W., & Drabman, R.S. (1985). Teaching LD children multiplication tables. *Academic Therapy, 20,* 437–442.

Lovitt, T.C. (1980). Performances of sixth graders on a variety of arithmetic problems. Unpublished manuscript, University of Washington, Seattle.

Lovitt, T.C., & Curtiss, K.A. (1968). Effects of manipulating an antecedent event on mathematics response rate. *Journal of Applied Behavior Analysis, 1,* 329–333.

Lovitt, T.C., & Esveldt, K.A. (1970). The relative effects on math performance of single-versus multiple-ratio schedules: A case study. *Journal of Applied Behavior Analysis, 3,* 261–270.

Lovitt, T.C., & Smith, D.D. (1974). Using withdrawal of positive reinforcement to alter subtraction performance. *Exceptional Children, 40,* 357–358.

Lovitt, T.; Smith, D.; Kidder, J.; & Evison, R. (1974). Using arranged and programmed events to alter subtraction performance of children with learning disabilities. In F.S. Keller & E. Ribes-Inesta (Eds.), *Behavior modification: Applications to education.* New York: Academic Press.

Mather, N. (1983). Courseware review *(1–2–3–Digit Multiplication). Journal of Learning Disabilities, 16,* 622–623.

Mather, N. (1984a). Courseware review *(Arithmetic Drill). Journal of Learning Disabilities, 17,* 190–191.

Mather, N. (1984b). Courseware review *(Long Division). Journal of Learning Disabilities, 17,* 247–248.

Mather, N. (1985a). Courseware review (*Starting Out,* Set I, & *Starting Out,* Set II). *Journal of Learning Disabilities, 18,* 175–176.

Mather, N. (1985b). Courseware review *(Money! Money!). Journal of Learning Disabilities, 18,* 362.

McLeod, T.M., & Armstrong, S.W. (1982). Learning disabilities in mathematics—skill deficits and remedial approaches at the intermediate and secondary level. *Learning Disability Quarterly, 5,* 305–311.

Nuffield Foundation. (1970). *Checking up I.* London: John Murry Publishers, Ltd.

Reisman, F.K. (1978). *A guide to the diagnostic teaching of arithmetic,* 2nd ed. Columbus, OH: Merrill.

Rivera, D.M., & Smith, D.D. (1987). Influence of modeling on acquisition and generalization of computational skills: A summary of research findings from three sites. *Learning Disability Quarterly, 10,* 69–80.

Schulte, A.P. (Ed.) (1981). *Teaching statistics and probability, 1981 Yearbook.* Reston, VA: National Council of Teachers of Mathematics.

Sedlak, R.A., & Fitzmaurice, A.M. (1981). Teaching arithmetic. In J.M. Kauffman & D.P. Hallahan (Eds.), *Handbook of Special Education.* Englewood Cliffs, NJ: Prentice-Hall.

Silbert, J.; Carnine, D.; & Stein, M. (1981). *Direct instruction mathematics.* Columbus, OH: Merrill.

Smith, D.D., & Lovitt, T.C. (1976). The differential effects of reinforcement contingencies on arithmetic performance. *Journal of Learning Disabilities, 9,* 21–29.

Sugai, G., & Smith, P. (1986). The equal additions method of subtraction taught with a modeling technique. *Remedial and Special Education, 7*(1), 40–48.

Swanson, H.L., & Rhine, B. (1985). Strategy transformations in learning disabled children's math performance: Clues to the development of expertise. *Journal of Learning Disabilities, 18,* 596–603.

Wood, S.; Burke, L.; Kunzelmann, H.; & Koenig, C. (1978). Functional criteria in basic math skill proficiency. *Journal of Special Education Technology, 2*(2) 29–36.

Chapter 10

The Artist's Son Jean by Pierre Auguste Renoir (1900). Courtesy of The Art Institute of Chicago, collection of Mr. and Mrs. Martin A Ryerson.

INSTRUCTIONAL APPROACHES FOR LD YOUTH

OUTLINE

Cognitive Training

Self-Management Instruction

Teaching Learning Strategies

Attribution Retraining

Adapting and Modifying Materials

Cooperative Learning Techniques

Tutoring

Comments and Discussion Points

MAIN IDEAS

- Cognitive training that focuses on attending, reading, vocabulary, writing and spelling, and mathematics and a discussion of research on information processing

- Self-management instruction that includes self-recording, self-evaluating, self-selecting, and various combinations

- Teaching learning strategies, including information on general principles, specific areas of intervention, and generalization

- Attribution retraining, including information on general guidelines and specific interventions

- Adapting traditional materials using a variety of approaches, such as study guides, graphic organizers, visual spatials, and microcomputers

- Cooperative learning interventions, including characteristics of such programs and data on several variations

- Tutoring, including information on administrative issues and descriptions of programs

OVERVIEW

A number of instructional approaches for LD youth and others cut across several subjects (for example, science, social studies, reading, writing, and mathematics), and they are applicable for students at both the elementary and secondary levels. The strategies described in this chapter represent the most advanced instructional research in the field of learning disabilities. These approaches, and others yet to emerge, could indicate the wave of the future when it comes to designing instructional practices for learning disabled students.

In the first section of this chapter, studies on cognitive and metacognitive strategies with LD youngsters are reviewed. In the second section, representative self-management studies of three types are summarized: Those that pertain to self-recording, those that deal with self-evaluating, and those that are concerned with self-selecting. The third section is a summary of research on learning strategies with LD students, and the fourth is concerned with attribution retraining. The fifth section in this chapter deals with modifying and adapting materials for LD youngsters. The next two sections deal with the topics of cooperative learning and tutoring. The chapter ends with comments about the instructional approaches and their interactions.

COGNITIVE TRAINING

Palincsar and Brown (1987) stated that metacognition reflects individuals' understanding of their own cognitive system—that is, the way in which they think. It indicates their knowledge of cognitive resources and the use of self-regulatory mechanisms such as planning strategies, monitoring their effectiveness, and evaluating those strategies. As discussed in Chapter 1, in recent years, the cognitive/metacognitive approach has had a tremendous impact on research and practice in learning disabilities. A few of the more representative investigations of that type are reviewed here.

Areas of Intervention

Attending.   Bornstein and Quevillon (1976) taught three hyperactive preschool boys a series of self-instructions designed to keep them on-task with classroom activities. There were four types of self-instructions:

— *Questions about the assigned task:* "What does the teacher want me to do?
— *Answers to the self-directed questions:* "I'm supposed to copy that picture."
— *Verbalizations to guide the child through the task at hand:* "OK, first I draw a line through here. . . ."
— *Self-reinforcement:* "I really did that one well."

Children who followed this plan showed a marked increase in on-task behavior immediately after receiving self-instructional training, and their behavior maintained over a considerable period of time.

Reading.   In Gelzheiser's (1984) experiment, LD students were given rules for enhancing retention of isomorphs: sort to study, study by groups, name the groups, and cluster to recall. Results of that research showed that LD students profited from this instruction, their gains in recall were correlated with the extent they used the strategy.

Pflaum and Pascarella (1980) conducted research on word meanings with middle school LD students. Their intervention had two components: assisting students to determine when they made errors that disrupted the meaning of what was read and teaching them methods for correcting those errors. The data showed that students who could read at third grade level or above gained considerably from the instruction.

Wong and Jones (1982) carried out a reading comprehension study with junior high LD and non-LD students. Their instructional approach involved the following steps:

1. Find and underline main ideas in the passage.
2. Think of questions about this information.
3. Answer the questions.
4. Review the questions and answers to evaluate the sum of the information provided.

According to Wong and Jones, the intervention helped LD students to predict more important idea-units, to answer more comprehension questions correctly, and to recall more information generally than did the control students.

Kurtz and Borkowski (1985), working with sixth graders, were interested in the relationship between metacognition and learning strategies. They arranged two interventions to study those connections. One pertained to the acquisition of a strategy (students received instruction on the use of superordinates, identification of main ideas, and developing topic sentences). The second intervention required youngsters to learn an executive function. In addition to the summarization instruction, students were taught to regard:

— The value of monitoring reading performance
— The importance of deliberate strategy selection
— The flexible use of strategies
— The need to work slowly

Data from these investigations revealed that students who had received the latter training performed better than those in control groups.

Miller (1985) used an error detection task with fourth graders to determine the extent to which training in self-instruction influenced comprehension monitoring during reading. The results showed that students who received training in both general and specific statements regarding error detection were significantly more accurate on both immediate and delayed checks than were students in didactic conditions where errors were simply pointed out. The data suggested further that pupils with learning problems profited most from interventions that emphasized self-control training.

Paris, Cross, Jacobs, Oka, DeBritto, and Saarnio (1984) studied the awareness of third and fourth graders for reading generally, and the use of reading strategies to improve their reading. Students in their study were instructed to understand what a strategy is; to use metaphors to describe strategies; to work in groups as they studied the strategies; to work with guided practice in the application of strategies; and to use the strategies as they read content books. Results of the investigation showed that students who received the training—whether of low, medium, or high ability—increased their awareness of the goals of reading and their knowledge of the roles of reading strategies. Further, their competencies as readers increased more than twice those of students in control groups.

Hansen and Pearson (1983) conducted research on comprehension with fourth grade remedial readers. The purpose of their research was to determine the effects of an elaborating strategy on reading comprehension. To achieve this goal, the teacher posed a series of questions to youngsters before they read. The questions were aimed at activating word knowledge about the topic of the passage and assisting children to relate to their own knowledge the content of the material that would be read. Data from the study showed that inferential questioning increased learning, suggesting that the trained pupils had internalized the activation of prior knowledge, the making of predictions about text, and the construction of inferences.

Vocabulary. Pressley, Johnson, and Symons (1987) claimed that elaborative techniques can dramatically facilitate learning of facts and knowledge of relationships between pieces of information. Examples of this type of research are the investigations of Mastropieri and her colleagues, who have studied mnemonic elaborations involving the keyword method, and O'Sullivan and Pressley, who used a keyword method for understanding and recalling word meanings.

Mastropieri, Scruggs, and Levin (1985) noted superior learning of scientific facts by LD junior high school students when they used a keyword–mediator depiction to learn the material. For example, to learn that the hardness of bauxite is one, the child views a picture containing buns (as in "one-is-a-bun") and a box, since box is a word that acoustically resembles bauxite and can be used as a keyword. Scruggs, Mastropieri, Levin, and Gaffney (1985) extended this research, showing that LD junior high students could acquire three pieces of information about minerals with slightly more complex pictures. The overall conclusion from their work with poor learners using keyword–mediators is that mnemonic elaborations have an enormously positive impact on those individuals.

O'Sullivan and Pressley (1984) investigated the keyword strategy with LD youngsters in an approach requiring students to recode, relate, and retrieve the information to be remembered. For example, to remember the definition "loud" for the word *forte,* the following steps are followed. First, the target word is coded into a word (the keyword) that sounds like the target word and is easily pictured, such as a fort. Next, the keyword is related to the target word's meaning by means of an interactive picture (for example, a fort with guns loudly blazing). In the study, the students who received instruction on this strategy and were informed of its uses and limitations, were more successful than others when recalling word meanings.

Writing and Spelling.   Harris and Graham (1985) taught twelve-year-old LD pupils three aspects of composition using the following sequence of steps:

☐ Review the current use of the word class.

☐ Discuss the significance of each word class.

☐ Describe the contribution of each word class to the makeup of a story.

☐ Practice on the various word classes and receive feedback.

This set of procedures enhanced productivity as well as the quality of writing for the majority of the students.

Raphael, Kirschner, and Englert (1985), working with fifth and sixth graders, were concerned about the extent that knowledge of text structures enhances writing. In their study, some pupils were instructed in groups, and others were instructed individually. Information about text structures (for example, cause–effect, compare–contrast) was given to both groups of youngsters, and they were taught to use that knowledge as they planned, drafted, and revised their papers. Data from that research revealed that students' performances in the treatment groups surpassed those in control groups, and those who received instruction on text structure individually had better scores on the writing measures than did those in the social condition.

Englert, Hiebert, and Stewart (1985) investigated the effects of teaching LD students to spell new words by using spelling patterns from known words—that is, the analogy strategy. Their training sequence had four steps:

1. Identify a known word that rhymes with the unknown word.

2. Identify portions of both words that are spelled the same.

3. Spell the new word using the rhyming element of the known word.

4. Apply the new skill to complete cloze sentences requiring the use of transfer words that rhyme with common words.

Their results indicated that the experimental group, which had received instruction in the strategy, was significantly superior to a control group in spelling high-frequency sightwords and a set of transfer words that were not taught.

Mathematics.   Lovitt and Curtiss (1968) conducted research of this type with an eleven-year-old boy who was classified as behaviorally disordered. In three separate studies, the boy was instructed, following a baseline, to read an arithmetic problem aloud and then answer it. In the third phase of each study, he was not required to verbalize the problems and solutions. Data showed that his performances in the second phases were much better than those during baselines, and his performances held up throughout the third phases.

Research on Information Processing

One emerging theoretical framework for describing LD children's performance on cognitive tasks has been the *information-processing theory*. Within the information-processing framework, individuals learn through various intervening stages of cognition: encoding, organizing, storing, retrieving, comparing, and generating (reconstructing) information. According to Swanson (1987), one of the reasons for the recent interest in information processing is that for three decades, research on LD children has provided neither theoretical nor practical directions toward a science of learning disabilities.

Swanson makes a case for information processing by outlining four ways in which that theory can contribute to our understanding of learning disabilities.

1. *Common denominator.* Information-processing theory may provide a framework for identifying common processing patterns in children identified as learning disabled. A research area that may yield valuable information in identifying common patterns among LD children would focus on how LD children access, execute, and coordinate mental components across various academic tasks. Such research would study the extent to which LD children experience difficulty with self-regulating mechanisms such as checking, planning, monitoring, testing, revising, and evaluating during their attempts to learn or solve problems. That line of inquiry may reveal that learning disabilities are the result of a unique way of regulating or coordinating mental processes rather than specific types of processing deficiencies.

2. *Subgroup selection.* The establishment of subtypes is based on the assumption that learning disabilities can be assigned to categories having some unitary causes and well-defined effects. Although past efforts to cast LD students into subtypes has not yielded such conclusions, this may be a reality when information processing attributes are assessed.

3. *Mental components underlying academic change.* The theory may provide for a clarification and identification of the mental processes required on selected classroom tasks. There may be operations of three kinds: attentional (relate to visual searches), memorial (relate to storage, searching, and retrieval), and executive (relate to judgments about stimulus attributes.)

4. *Hemispheric processing.* "LD students' information processing difficulties may be *indirectly* reflected in such behavioral indices as laterality, EEG, and eye movement data" (Swanson, 1987, p. 163). This theory may provide a means of conceptualizing the neurological deficiencies noted in LD children.

Swanson maintains that improvement in the learning ability of LD children necessitates not only the deployment of strategies, but also an executive mechanism that automatically accesses and combines learning skills—that is, information processing components—when they are needed. He speculates that the dramatic differences observed in the performances of nondisabled and LD students may often be due to differences in underlying knowledge bases (for example, cognitive structure prior to learning), rather than to basic differences in control processes.

Swanson lists the following processes as meaningful links between information processing abilities and classroom performances:

- *Encoding:* Input information is initially analyzed.
- *Elaboration:* Connections with the material to be learned are made to previously stored information.
- *Transformation:* rules are applied to the new information (for example, *i* before *e* except after *c*).
- *Storage:* Input information is added to existing information.
- *Retrieval:* Information that was previously stored is made available.
- *Searching:* Information is accessed by determining the presence or absence of additional properties.
- *Comparing:* Information is recognized to be either old or new, same or different, as previously stored information.
- *Reconstruction:* The recalled information is based on concepts that tie together fragments or pieces of stored information.

SELF-MANAGEMENT INSTRUCTION

This section reviews three components of self-management: self-recording (including counting and charting), self-evaluating (comparing one's performance to a standard, or commenting on the quality of the performance), self-selecting (interventions, schedules, reinforcers, contingencies, and goals). The final part reviews studies dealing with a combination of the self-management components.

Self-Recording

Hallahan and colleagues, working out of the Learning Disabilities Institute at the University of Virginia, have conducted a number of self-recording studies. In one study (Hallahan & Sapona, 1983), an eleven-year-old LD boy was instructed to monitor his on- and off-task behavior by using an audiotape recorder to cue his self-recording. When he heard a tone, which occurred randomly, he recorded "yes" or "no" to indicate whether he was or was not paying attention. Experimenters measured time on task and academic productivity during handwriting and math sessions. Their results gave evidence that the student's on-task behavior increased dramatically with self-monitoring, and his academic productivity increased correspondingly.

In another study by this group (Rooney, Hallahan, & Lloyd, 1983), LD youngsters mainstreamed into regular class were taught to self-monitor their attending during a language arts activity. Similar procedures were arranged in

Daniel P. Hallahan, a student of Cruickshank's at the University of Michigan, is on
the faculty of the University of Virginia and
the director of the Learning Disabilities Institute. Hallahan, with a number of colleagues at Virginia, has published widely in
Learning Disabilities. One of his major interests has been with cognitive behavior
modification and self-management.

this research, and again, self-monitoring led to noticeable improvements in attention. In yet another investigation by the Virginia researchers (Hallahan et al.,
1979), an eight-year-old LD boy was instructed to self-monitor his on- and off-
task behavior during handwriting and math. Like other studies in this series, an
audiotape recorder was used to cue his self-recording. The data indicated that his
on-task behavior increased dramatically for both subjects, and at the same time,
his academic response rates increased. In an attempt to wean the youngster from
relying on the tape recorded signal to self-monitor attending, he was instructed
to self-record without the tape-recorded signals. Still later, self-recording was
discontinued, and he was simply asked to praise himself when he was on task.
The authors reported high levels of on-task behavior and academic output during
both conditions. When data were obtained some time after the experiment, they
revealed a continued high level of being on-task.

Other researchers, McLaughlin and colleagues, for example, have conducted
similar studies with LD youth. McLaughlin and Malaby (1974) reported that self-
recording procedures were effective in controlling assignment completion throughout the school day for three pupils with low completion rates. In another study,
McLaughlin, Krappman, and Welsh (1985) claimed that when four special education students of intermediate age recorded, once a minute, whether or not they
were on task, that activity was generally increased.

Self-Evaluating

Klein and Gory (1976) instructed a class of third grade students in an inner city school to self-evaluate workbook performances. Students were taught to use answer keys and to circle their incorrect answers. The data indicated that when pupils' performances during the self-evaluating phase were compared with those during baseline and recapitulation phases, the poorest students demonstrated marked improvement in the self-evaluation phase. This was not the case with higher achieving pupils.

Turkewitz, O'Leary, and Ironsmith (1975) instructed a number of disruptive children to evaluate their academic and social behaviors in a special setting. Initially, they were given points contingent on accurate self-rating. This requirement was then faded until the children had control over the distribution of points. The data indicated that although appropriate social behaviors were not generalized to the regular classroom, generalization was demonstrated in a control period of the special class, and maintenance was noted when the token system was abandoned.

Self-Selecting

Lovitt and Curtiss (1969) conducted research with a twelve-year old pupil with behavior disorders. The lad and his mates were in a Premack-type classroom, in which points were given for performance in several academic areas, and the points could be redeemed later for free time. Throughout some phases of the study, the teacher determined the points; at other times, the boy made the decisions. In one experiment, he gave himself a few more points than his teacher would have. In the subsequent study, the teacher specified the same number of high points that the pupil had previously given himself and compared his performance rates during that phase with those when he again determined his ratios. Data from these experiments gave evidence that the student's academic rates were higher during phases when *he* specified the points, regardless of what they were.

Lovitt (1973) conducted other research in which mildly handicapped students determined their own schedules; throughout certain phases they chose the time to work on their subjects. In this research, academic data were obtained during conditions when the teacher specified the schedules and when they were set by pupils. Results showed that the pupils' academic rates were higher in those phases when *they* selected the schedules.

Schunk (1985) conducted research with sixth graders in mathematics, all of whom had been identified as LD. Three groups of youngsters were organized for this study: Some set their own goals, some had the goals set for them, while for others, there were no goals. Those who determined their goals had a band within which to specify them (number of pages completed per session). The study showed that participation in goal-setting enhanced the self-efficacy and skill development of the children. (Schunk describes self-efficacy as the personal judgment of one's performance capabilities in specific situations that may contain ambiguous, unpredictable, and stressful features.)

More detailed analysis of the results suggested that participation in goal setting may be more beneficial for children with cognitive deficiencies, who hold low expectancies for success, than for children who are more self-assured as they approach tasks. In any event, according to Schunk, unrealistically high or low goals will not facilitate self-efficacy or skill development.

Combined Components of Self-Management

A number of studies have arranged multiple components of self-management. Tollefson, Tracy, Johnsen, and Chatman (1986) conducted such a study with LD adolescents. Although their training program was carried out in a resource room, their objective was to generalize a goal-setting strategy to the regular classroom. Four interrelated phases were involved in their project to teach self-regulation:

— Setting realistic academic goals
— Developing plans to reach those goals
— Implementing the plans, monitoring progress toward the academic goals, and evaluating progress by personal standards
— Accepting responsibility for success or failure to attain goals

Data were obtained on the number of assignments completed and on the youngsters' attributions for success or failure. According to the authors, the results were not significant with respect to the goal-implementation strategy, since training generalized to the regular classroom for only three of the five students. The attribution data, however, indicated that students relied on effort attributions more frequently than ability, task difficulty, or luck attributions to explain success, presumably as a function of their treatment.

Seabaugh and Schumaker (1981) taught four self-control skills to LD and non-LD junior and senior high students in an alternative school using a counseling format of behavior contracting, self-recording, self-monitoring, and self-reinforcement. The students applied the subskills directly to their work after the first counseling session and met with their teacher weekly to review progress and set new goals. The results showed that the number of lessons completed by the students increased from an average of one-half lesson per day to four per day. In a follow-up study, Seabaugh and Schumaker (1983) found that the weekly sessions could be faded to biweekly meetings as long as the students continued to write their own goals and to review their progress on alternate weeks.

Lovitt (1973) conducted a study that involved a number of self-management components. In that project, nine remedial second graders in a resource room read from the *Sullivan Programmed Reading Series*. This material facilitated elements of self-management: Youngsters moved through the program at their own pace, checked their answers to each frame, and went on to the next if correct or wrote in the correct answer if incorrect. Another feature of self-management was having the children record the times (from a digital clock) when they began and ended a session. Gradually, five other self-management features were incorporated in the study:

1. Count frequency of correct and incorrect answers.
2. Use time finder to determine how long was spent on reading each day.
3. Note that time on the record sheets.
4. Use a rate plotter to chart the correct and incorrect rates.
5. Evaluate the rates from day to day.

These self-management components were taught the youngsters over a 23-week period by their resource room teacher. Following that time, the students were sent back to their regular class with their Sullivan programs. In that situation, as they continued their work on the Sullivan program with the self-management procedures, the youngsters could earn their way back to the resource room once a week *if* their performance rates in reading were satisfactory.

TEACHING LEARNING STRATEGIES

According to Deshler and Schumaker (1986), learning strategies are techniques, principles, or rules that enable students to learn, solve problems, and complete tasks independently. Deshler, Schumaker, Lenz, and Ellis (1984) offered a rationale for instructing study skills when they stated that, for a variety of reasons, many LD students do not spontaneously employ or generate sophisticated task-specific strategies when they are needed.

Donald D. Deshler is on the faculty of the University of Kansas. He was the first editor of the *Learning Disability Quarterly* and is director of the Institute for Research in Learning Disabilities at Kansas. He, along with colleagues Shumaker, Clark, Alley, and others, have had a tremendous impact on the field, particularly at the secondary level with their learning strategies curriculum.

Research from Deshler and colleagues at the Learning Disabilities Institute at the University of Kansas has indicated, however, that once LD students are taught specific strategies, many of them are able to use them effectively. In addition to showing that LD adolescents can learn task-specific strategies, these researchers gave evidence of positive results as the students made use of the strategies. Increases were noted in classroom test scores, course grades, scores on district competency examinations, and teachers' perceptions of students' classroom performances.

Principles for Intervention

Based on their research, Deshler and coworkers have developed materials for teaching learning strategies. Commercially available programs are organized into three strands. Strand One pertains to *acquisition;* it is designed to help students acquire information from written materials through the strategies of word identification, visual imagery, self-questioning, paraphrasing, interpreting visual aids, and reading skills. Strand Two, which focuses on *storage,* is designed to enable students to identify and store important information through the strategies of listening and notetaking, first-letter mnemonic, and paired-associates. Strand Three deals with *competence* and is intended to facilitate written expression and demonstration of competence. Six strategies are used in this strand: sentence writing, paragraph writing, theme writing, error monitoring, assignment completion, and test taking.

The following instructional principles have guided the implementation of learning strategy interventions:

1. Match instruction with curriculum demands. Study pupils' needs and types of instruction being offered; design training from that information.
2. Rely on structured teaching methodologies. Strategies must be learned to an automatic, fluent level.
3. Promote generalization deliberately. After students demonstrate mastery of a learning strategy in a resource room, take them through a set of generalization steps designed to broaden their understanding of the strategy and to increase their facility to carry out regular classroom assignments.
4. Apply "critical teaching behaviors." Provide appropriate positive and corrective feedback, use advance organizers throughout the instructional sessions, ensure high rates of active academic responding, encourage student involvement in discussions, provide regular reviews of key instructional points and checks of comprehension, monitor student performance, require mastery learning, communicate high expectations to students, and explain reasons for instructional activities, and facilitate independence.
5. Develop scope and sequence arrangements for teaching the strategies. Organize the instruction of learning strategies from grades 7 through 12.
6. Maintain a realistic point of view when instructing strategies. Don't attribute the poor performance of certain students solely to learning strategy defi-

ciencies; they may be failing for other reasons. The primary intervention for those students may be something other than training in learning strategies.

Areas of Intervention

Following are summaries of studies conducted by Deshler and colleagues to evaluate certain of their learning strategies.

Information Gathering.   Schumaker, Deshler, Alley, Warner, and Denton (1982) conducted research on *Multipass,* which is an information-gathering approach. The procedures for instructing this strategy (and most others from the Kansas group) include the following steps:

- ☐ Test the student's current level of functioning.
- ☐ Describe the strategy.
- ☐ Model the strategy.
- ☐ Rehearse the strategy steps verbally.
- ☐ Practice on reading ability-level material.
- ☐ Practice on reading grade-level materials.

Multipass requires students to "pass through" their material three times. Those passes are referred to as survey, size-up, and sort-out. In the survey stage, students familiarize themselves with the chapter's organization and main ideas. Size-up means that students are expected to gain specific information and facts from a chapter without reading it from beginning to end. Sort-out is intended to help pupils test themselves on the material in the chapter.

The results of research with a few LD adolescents on *Multipass* showed that students learned the strategy and relied on it when they read ability-level and grade-level textbooks. Furthermore, students' grades on tests covering the textbook material improved after they learned the strategy.

Visual Imagery.   Clark, Deshler, Schumaker, Alley, and Warner (1984) conducted research on another learning strategy—visual imagery—with a group of LD adolescents. This approach is designed to increase reading comprehension, by requiring students to create mental pictures from the text passages they have read. As with most other strategies from the Kansas group, an acronym was developed to help students remember the approach's critical steps. In this case, the acronym is RIDER:

R   Read the first sentence
I   Imagine a picture in your mind
D   Describe the image
E   Evaluate your image for its completeness
R   Repeat the process in the next passage

Positive results where shown when this strategy was arranged for LD students.

Error Monitoring.   Error monitoring, an approach designed to enable students to detect and correct errors in writing, was investigated by Schumaker, Deshler, Nolan, Clark, Alley, and Warner (1981). This strategy was developed in response to data indicating that LD adolescents had great difficulty detecting errors in their performance. The error-monitoring strategy calls for four steps:

1. Read each sentence separately.
2. Ask yourself the COPS questions
   C   capitals, are they correct?
   O   overall appearance, how is it?
   P   punctuation, is it correct?
   S   spelling, how is it?
3. When you find an error, circle it and put the correct form above the error.
4. Ask for help if you are unsure of the correct form.

Self-Questioning.   The self-questioning strategy (Clark et al., 1984) is designed to help students form questions about passages as they read them and to enhance their recall of the content. For this strategy, the acronym is RAM:

   R   Read the passage and ask "wh" questions
   A   Answer your questions
   M   Mark answers with appropriate symbols

Results of a study on this strategy (Nolan, Alley, & Clark, 1980) gave evidence that LD students can learn the strategy and apply it in reading both ability-level and grade-level materials. Their comprehension scores were much higher in posttest conditions than during baselines.

Generalization of Learning Strategies

A major concern of those who instruct learning strategies has to do with generalization, for the primary reason for teaching these approaches is to provide pupils with a structure they can draw on as they go from one situation to another. If students do not generalize a strategy, they have lost in two ways: The transfer technique failed to take, and they failed to acquire another skill (for example, reading) when they were being "taught" the strategy.

Ellis, Lenz, and Sabornie (1987b) referred to four types of activities that can be arranged to help students acquire and then generalize learning strategies:

—*Antecedent:* activities that can be arranged to promote generalization of the new strategy prior to direct instruction

—*Concurrent:* activities that reinforce the acquisition of the skill to the extent that it becomes a generalized procedure
—*Subsequent:* activities that should be addressed after the student has mastered the strategy, but is not habitually using it
—*Independent:* activities facilitated by teachers to promote the pupil's self-regulatory skills

Ellis and coauthors have also suggested that self-management instruction—self-recording, self-monitoring, self-evaluation, self-goal setting, and self-reinforcement—be considered as an approach for assisting youth to acquire and generalize learning strategies.

Schumaker, Deshler, Alley, and Warner (1983) evaluated the effects of a two-year program to instruct learning strategies in which a number of previously described approaches were involved. Analyses of their data revealed that when instruction on strategies made up 75 percent of the instructional time in resource rooms, students showed significantly better performance on tasks that required use of the strategies—that is, they were able to generalize. Performances of students who were taught strategies equaled or exceeded those of non-LD pupils on some tasks. More important, the pupils who had received extensive instruction in strategies gained almost twice as much in certain basic skills as did students in other programs.

Ellis, Lenz, and Sabornie (1987a) reviewed studies that investigated approaches for enhancing the generalization of learning strategies. In one, Schmidt (1984) investigated the degree of direct instruction necessary to achieve mastery levels of generalization and maintenance of writing strategies that were taught to LD adolescents. The results showed that when the effects of various generalization techniques were compared, the most powerful features were the provision of feedback relative to the use of the strategy for regular classroom assignments and the provision of a simple cue by the regular classroom teacher to use the strategy. For those students who required more intensive interventions, self-control and cooperative planning procedures effectively promoted generalization.

In another study, Beals (1984) sought to determine the feasibility and effects of teaching learning strategies in the regular classroom. That research was in response to the fact that most efforts to instruct learning strategies had taken place in special classrooms. Beals' approach for instructing these strategies was to set up cooperative learning situations for LD, slow-learning, and regular-achieving adolescents and to teach four reading and writing strategies. Results indicated that LD students were capable of reaching mastery performance levels when the strategies were taught in large group settings and that they could generalize the use of those skills to other tasks in the same environment.

In a third study, Ellis (1985) examined the effects of teaching LD adolescents an executive strategy for self-generating task-specific strategies. (Students had learned three strategies prior to this training.) To acquire this executive strategy, pupils were taught to assess the demands of the classroom and their ability to meet those demands, generate a plan to meet those requirements, and implement and monitor the plan. Ellis' results demonstrated that LD students' grades in targeted regular classes significantly improved as a function of the training, and content teachers' perceptions of the quality of their work were significantly higher.

ATTRIBUTION RETRAINING

A number of researchers and teachers believe that the attributions of learning disabled youth, as a group, are different from those of non-LD students. Some authorities claim that LD youngsters are more inclined to attribute their failures to ineptness or to plain bad luck. When they do succeed, LD pupils are more apt to attribute success to someone else or to good luck than are their non-LD mates. Noting this attribution as yet another area of deficiency or difference, several educators have recommended that LD youth be retrained so that their attributions are more in line with those of non-LD students.

Guidelines for Intervention

Ellis, Lenz, and Sabornie (1987b) have pointed out the relationship between attribution retraining and the acquisition of learning strategies. They suggest a sequence of instructional steps to follow to capitalize on this association. First, teach students to elicit statements that reflect effort attributions. Second, teach them to attribute their difficulties to ineffective strategies. Finally, arrange for them to experience a fair amount of success with effective strategies.

Licht (1983) has recommended the following factors be considered in attribution retraining:

— Attributing one's failures to ineffective task strategies
— Adapting instructional methods to match the child's attributions
— Teaching a new definition of ability
— Increasing the incentive value of academic achievement

Borkowski, Weyhing, and Turner (1986) made the following recommendations for incorporating attributional statements into strategy training in the classroom:

1. Retraining needs to be intensive, prolonged, and consistent.
2. Retraining should initially center on task-specific beliefs because antecedent beliefs are more resistant to change than more transient program-specific attributional beliefs.
3. It is essential to inform educationally handicapped students about the importance of strategy-based effort for successful performance.
4. Retraining attributions should be emphasized during strategy instruction.

Specific Interventions

Reid and Borkowski (1985) compared the effects of three conditions designed to retrain attributions of hyperactive and LD children. One intervention, the executive condition, emphasized general self-control as well as specific strategy training appropriate for certain tasks. For the executive-plus attribution condition, students were presented all the instruction for the executive condition and given attributional training that included

— Discussion regarding beliefs about the causes of failure
— Opportunity to use of the self-control steps to perform successfully a previously failed task
— Reflection on long-standing beliefs about the causes of success

Children in the control condition received most of the effective strategy instructions but were not given self-control or attributional instructions.

Data from that research, which were in the form of scores on tests of strategy generalization, showed wide differences in performances. Generally, the scores of children in the executive plus attribution conditions were greatly improved.

Using LD students, Weyhing (1986) assessed the impact of retrained attributional beliefs about specific strategies on the subsequent use of newly acquired comprehension strategies. Pupils in the experimental group received instructions on the use of a summarization strategy and attribution training along with it. Results indicated that students who received training in the reading strategies, plus attribution instruction, performed significantly better on paragraph summaries, following training, than pupils who were in control situations.

Shelton, Anastopoulos, and Linden (1985) undertook research to determine whether altering causal attributions for failure would enable "helpless" LD fourth graders to deal more effectively with failure in an experimental reading situation. They assigned 16 "helpless" LD students to an attribution training group or to an assessment control group. Their results revealed that following training, students in the attribution training group demonstrated greater reading persistence, showed significant increases in effort attributions for failure, and revealed more internal attributions for achievement situations when compared to pupils in the control group. Treatment gains lD effort attributions and for reading persistence were maintained in follow up arrangements.

Schunk (1981) studied the modeling and attributional effects on achievement of nine-year-old youngsters who were low performers in arithmetic. For that research, students received either modeling of division operations or didactic instruction. Both treatments were followed by a practice period, during which half of the children in each instructional condition received effort attribution for success and difficulty. The results showed that both instructional treatments enhanced division persistence, accuracy, and perceived efficacy, but cognitive modeling produced greater gains in accuracy. Moreover, children's effort attribution had no significant effect either on perceived efficacy or on arithmetic performance. The treatment that combined modeling with effort attribution produced the highest congruence between efficacy judgment and performance.

Fowler and Peterson (1981) studied the effects of attributional retraining on 28 children between the ages of 9 and 13. The children, who were identified as "learned helpless" and were reading below grade level, were assigned to one of four treatments: partial reinforcement with single failure lengths (relatively easy material), partial reinforcement with multiple failure lengths, partial reinforcement with multiple failure lengths and indirect attribution retraining, and partial reinforcement with multiple failure lengths and direct attribution retraining, which involved covert rehearsal of self-instructional statements. The results showed significant increases in reading persistence for children who had received direct attributional retraining, as compared to pupils in other conditions.

ADAPTING AND MODIFYING MATERIALS

It is often necessary to adapt or modify instructional features for LD youngsters mainstreamed into content classes such as history or science, for many of them have difficulty acquiring information presented in those classes. A number of features—tests, schedules, assignment length, amount or type of assistance offered, grades, and mode of presentation or response—can be altered. This section focuses on adapting textbook passages.

The primary reason for modifying textbook passages for LD youngsters is that so much of the information presented in classes is offered via textbooks, which many LD students have difficulty reading. To illustrate those points, Zigmond, Levin, and Laurie (1985) learned from their surveys that more new information is presented to students by textbooks than by other means, such as lectures, films, trips, or videos. They also learned that 85 percent of secondary age LD students have difficulty reading.

Lovitt, Horton, and Bergerud (1987) set out to determine just how well a student must read in order to gain information from texts. To do so, they required LD and non-LD youth in middle and high school science and social studies classes to read orally from their texts. They then correlated those rates to a number of achievement variables and learned that a minimum oral reading rate of 135 words per minute was required in order to comprehend the material adequately. The majority of LD youths read at rates generally well below that standard.

Tape Recording

One method for adapting texts has been to record passages and play them back so that youngsters listen to the text rather than read it. Mosby (1979) used this approach with social studies passages and related tests over the course of a school year. According to him, the results showed increased year-end scores on an achievement test for students called "high-audio students" over students called "low-audio students." Wiseman, Hartwell, and Hannafin (1980) used audiotaped material as a primary means for teaching subject matter to LD adolescents. They found that recall of textbook information was facilitated when students listened to tapes and when the information was presented in a conversational manner rather than a verbatim reading from the text. Sawyer and Kosoff (1981) used a variation on this approach when they demonstrated that use of time-compressed verbatim recordings of short reading passages was an effective method for delivering content to LD boys.

Schumaker, Deshler, and Denton (1982), however, reported data that were not supportive of recording taping materials and requiring youngsters to listen to the tapes. They reported that when LD adolescents listened to verbatim tapes of content materials, they received poorer grades on chapter tests than they did when they read unmodified materials. These data would seem to indicate that LD youngsters are no better listeners than they are readers.

Advance Organizers

Another approach for adapting materials is to develop and instruct youth to use advance organizers. Lenz, Alley, and Schumaker (1987) conducted a study on this topic with seven secondary content teachers and seven LD adolescents. Training sessions, held in LD resource rooms during the students' regularly scheduled attendance period, focused on 12 components of the approach:

- Teachers informed students of the purpose of advance organizers.
- The task's physical parameters were clarified in terms of actions to be taken by the teacher.
- The task's physical parameters were clarified in terms of actions to be taken by the students.
- Teachers identified the topic of the learning task.
- They identified subtopics related to the task.
- Background information was provided.
- The concepts to be learned were stated.
- The concepts to be learned were clarified.
- Students were motivated through rationales.
- Teachers introduced or repeated new terms or words.
- They provided an organizational framework for the learning task.
- They stated the outcomes desired as a result of engaging in the learning activity.

After the pupils learned to use these advance organizer components, they attained higher scores in their content-area subjects.

Precision Teaching and Study Guides

At the University of Washington, Lovitt and colleagues conducted eleven studies on adapting materials. Lovitt, Rudsit, Jenkins, Pious, and Benedetti (1985) assessed the effects of two methods of adapting materials in seventh grade physical science classes. Six students formed the experimental groups: two high, two medium, and two low (LD) students. They were taken from the regular classroom by a researcher to a nearby room where they studied the materials. Meanwhile, the regular teacher worked with the remaining students in the classroom.

The researchers used the precision teaching (PT) approach in some classes and the study guide (SG) method in others. For the PT approach, vocabulary words from a passage were randomly printed several times on 8½" × 11" sheets. After seeing or hearing the items, the pupils said or wrote the definitions to those words during one-minute timings. They practiced on the sheets until criterion rates were achieved.

For the SG approach, several main ideas from the passage were printed on a sheet, with some of the words being left out. As the instructor lectured from the sheets and discussed the items, the students wrote in the missing words. When the sheets were completed, students spent time reviewing the main ideas.

To determine the effects of the treatments, all the pupils were given pretests and posttests on a chapter in their science book. Data revealed that both treatments—PT and SG—were equally effective. Students in the experimental groups significantly outgained the pupils who did not receive the special training. Furthermore, while gains were noted for all levels of youngsters, the greatest gains came from the low LD students.

Lovitt, Rudsit, Jenkins, Pious, and Benedetti (1986) ran another study with seventh grade physical science classes in which several LD youngsters were mainstreamed. This experiment combined the PT and SG techniques. Unlike the preceding study, where the experimental treatments were conducted by a researcher in a separate room, the regular teachers administered the special programs to *all* youngsters in their classrooms. Six chapters from the textbook were used, with adaptations alternately available. As in the preceding research, students were administered pretests and posttests on the chapters' contents. The data indicated that the scores of LD youngsters and others were significantly better on chapter tests when adapted materials were assigned.

Benedetti (1984) conducted a study on adapting materials in a resource room with 33 LD students in seventh and eighth grades. Three small groups of students were involved; the author carried out instruction for one group, another graduate student worked with the second group, and a special education teacher, the third. Control and experimental groups were arranged in each class. The teacher lectured the control students on the important points from a physical science textbook and asked them to contribute to the discussion. Precision teaching vocabulary sheets and study guides were scheduled for the experimental groups.

Benedetti's data indicated that the posttest scores of the experimental students were significantly higher than those for the control students. Furthermore, analyses of differences between the scores of the two groups, undertaken two weeks after the posttest, indicated continued superiority for the adapted materials group.

In a continuation of those studies, Horton and Lovitt (in press) ran a set of experiments on study guides with three teachers: a science teacher and social studies teacher in middle school and a high school social studies teacher. Three classes for each teacher were involved, and there were LD, remedial, and regular students in each class. Study guides were scheduled in those classes for some passages; for others, pupils took notes on their reading.

Study guides were printed on sheets that contained main ideas from a passage, with a few words left out. During the sessions when the guides were used, the teacher showed her copy on an overhead projector, using it as the framework for discussion. As each main idea was introduced, students discussed it and filled in missing words on their sheets. For the alternate treatment, the pupils reviewed the material they had read, wrote notes on it, and studied those notes.

This experiment involved three studies. In the first, the study guides were prepared by research personnel and directed by classroom teachers. In the second, the guides were developed by the research staff and directed by the students. For both types, pupils looked up missing information on their guides in their texts and wrote it in. In the third study, the teachers wrote out a few key words for each study-guide item, and students expanded on them by including those words as they wrote questions and answers. The pupils then studied the completed items. The outcome measures were multiple-choice tests that followed each condition (study guides versus regular classroom notetaking). Results from these experiments indicated that study guides, whether teacher-directed, student-directed, or student-expanded, produced significantly higher performances than notetaking for LD, remedial, and regular students.

Meadows (1988) conducted research on study guides as an approach for adapting materials, with five classes of seventh grade regular and LD students in social studies. The focus was on the comparative effects of three ways in which to offer study guides: teacher directed, pupil directed, and cooperatively directed. The first two treatments were identical to those explained earlier (Horton & Lovitt, in press). For the third intervention, groups of four were established and given points for group and individual achievement and participation. Data showed that the three treatments had equal effects. This was generally true for high, medium, and low achieving students.

Graphics

Horton, Lovitt, and Bergerud (in press) conducted a series of investigations using graphic organizers as the adaptation method. The design of these studies was nearly identical to the Horton and Lovitt (in press) research, except that four teachers instead of three participated—two teachers from a middle school and two from a high school. A social studies and a science teacher from each location were involved.

This set of experiments was like the preceding: The investigations were run by regular teachers, who had LD, remedial, and regular students in their three classes, and the adaptation interventions were compared to notetaking conditions. Three studies comprised the experiment: teacher-directed researcher-developed materials, a student-directed researcher-prepared materials, and student-expanded material.

To construct the graphic organizers, material from various passages was organized in a series of boxes, circles, and lines to show sequences and relationships. The outcome measure was an incomplete graphic which the students were expected to fill in. Data indicated that regardless of who designed the graphic organizers or directed study from them, youngster's scores—LD, remedial, and regular—were significantly higher in conditions where graphics were scheduled.

Lovitt, Stein, and Rudsit (1985) conducted another study involving graphic adaptation of materials with small groups of LD seventh graders. The intervention was a visual–spatial game similar to those explained in the *World of Facts* program by Engelmann and colleagues (1986), and the subject was again physical science. The main ideas and vocabulary from a passage were graphically printed on a sheet; words and ideas were enclosed by boxes and circles and connected by lines.

The game format was an important feature of this intervention. After the students studied the material on their printed sheets, they were given blank sheets on which there were circles, boxes, and corresponding numbers, but no words. The students were divided into two teams that took turns rolling a pair of dice. If a team member supplied the word that corresponded to the number of the dice roll, the team was awarded a point. Results indicated that the posttest scores of the experimental students were significantly higher than those of a comparison group of LD students who attended lectures on the topic and were asked to become involved in discussions over the material.

Bergerud, Lovitt, and Horton (1988) conducted research in a resource room for high school LD youngsters using two adaptation approaches—study guides and graphic organizers, which were compared with a notetaking condition. Four classes, with a total of 49 youngsters participated in that research; the subject was physical science. The outcome measure was a combination of a multiple-choice test and a graphics test. Results indicated that the graphic organizers assisted secondary students to achieve significantly better scores on posttests than did either the study guides or the notetaking treatments. Although the differences between study guides and notetaking favored the former, the differences were not significant.

Microcomputers

Horton, Lovitt, and Givens (1988) conducted a study in which microcomputers were used to display material for LD and remedial youngsters in a high school social studies class. During some conditions, all the material—text passages, study guides, and tests—was provided by computer. For other phases, students took notes from textbooks, studied them, and took a multiple choice test using paper and pencil. The data showed that the posttest scores were significantly higher when the pupils worked with the microcomputer than when they read from the textbook and took notes.

In another microcomputer study, Horton, Lovitt, and Slocum (in press) investigated the effectiveness of two treatments designed to teach the locations of 28 Asian cities to LD and remedial students enrolled in a ninth grade world geography class. In one treatment, students were shown the locations of 14 cities by completing a computerized map tutorial. In the other intervention, students were asked to learn the locations of 14 cities by referencing an atlas and transcribing the information to a work map. Results showed that the computerized map tutorial produced significantly higher performances than the atlas condition for both LD and remedial students.

In yet another example of using microcomputers to adapt materials, Higgins (1988) conducted a study with regular, remedial, and LD youngsters in ninth grade Washington state history classes. Her study included three treatments. In one, the students used a hypertext program on microcomputers to study textbook passages. For it, they read passages from the screen, accessed specially marked words that provided more information either in narrative or graphic form, and took tests on the computer. In a second treatment, a teacher provided the same information in the traditional format of lecture, notetaking, and discussion. In the third treatment, some instruction was offered via the microcomputer and by the teacher's lecture. Data showed that posttest and retention test scores were highest for all three groups of students—regular, remedial, and learning disabled—who received instruction in the total microcomputer hypertext condition.

COOPERATIVE LEARNING TECHNIQUES

In recent years, cooperative learning situations have been set up in numerous classrooms across the country. This approach has become a particularly popular way in which to instruct classes that include LD youngsters. As a rationale for establishing cooperative learning situations in classrooms, Johnson, Johnson, Holubec, and Roy (1984) elaborated on a crisis in socialization, based on the following points:

—The dramatic increase through the 1960s and 1970s of the frequency with which juveniles were involved in serious crimes against property.
—The rise of more than 250 percent in the suicide rate among teenagers and 150 percent among children 5 to 14 years of age over the past 20 years.
—The presence of a permanent criminal underclass that is totally out of touch with the rest of society and is especially antagonized by the usual symbols of authority, property, and office.
—A general social malaise characterized by a loss of confidence in the future and in our ability to solve society's problems.
—Changes in the family through divorce and other factors that affect twice as many youngsters as was the case 20 years ago, causing children

to spend less time with their parents, more time with their peers, or simply alone in a confusing world. [1984, p. 4]

Characteristics of Cooperative Learning

A number of differences exist between traditional learning and cooperative learning situations. Johnson and coauthors (1984) have identified the following characteristics of cooperative learning groups:

1. To foster positive interdependence among group members, goals are structured so that students need to be concerned about the performance of all group members as well as their own individual performances.

2. To achieve individual accountability, every student's mastery of the assigned material is assessed, each student is given feedback on his or her progress, and the group is given feedback on how each member is progressing so that the other members know whom to help and encourage.

3. The membership is typically heterogeneous in ability and personal characteristics, whereas traditional learning groups, on the other hand, often attempt to assemble homogeneous members.

4. All members share responsibility for acting as group leaders.

5. Members share responsibility for one another's learning, and members are

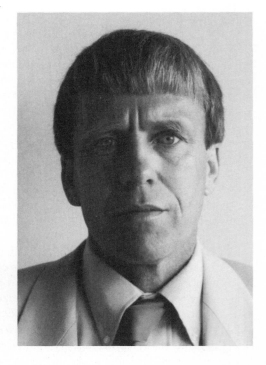

David W. Johnson is on the faculty of the University of Minnesota. Along with his associate, Roger T. Johnson, they have published widely on cooperative learning. They have been particularly concerned about the integration of handicapped youngsters in regular classrooms. One of their publications, *Circles of Learning,* is a comprehensive explanation of their methods.

expected to provide one another with help and encouragement in order to ensure that all participants do their assigned task.

6. The goals focus on bringing each member's learning to the maximum and on maintaining good working relationships among members.

7. The students are taught directly the social skills they need in order to work collaboratively.

8. The teacher observes the group, analyzes the problems the members have in working together, and gives feedback on how to relate with others so as to manage the group tasks.

9. The teacher structures procedures for groups to determine how effectively they are working together. Conversely, in traditional situations, little attention is given to the way in which groups work.

Cooperative Learning Studies

Johnson, Johnson, Warring, and Maruyama (1986) reported on two studies that involved cooperative learning. Study 1 was with sixth graders, among whom were several children with severe learning and behavioral problems. Three conditions were established. In the *cooperative–controversy* approach, groups of four students were divided into two-person teams with one above-average and one below-average reader in each. One pair was given materials that provided a rationale for hunting and killing wolves, and the other pair received materials that offered justifications for protecting wolves. Each member of the pair was assigned a different role. On the hunting side, one student was a "hunter" and the other a "dairy farmer." On the protecting side, one member was a "conservationist," and the other a "researcher." After students learned their respective roles, they interacted with the other pair by presenting their positions and discussing their differences. Then students reversed perspectives and argued the position of the opposing pair.

In the *cooperative debate* approach, similar groups were formed, but each student was given an individualistic goal of learning all the information and writing a group report. Each pupil was also given a competitive goal: to be the one who could best present information to the group. The basic difference between this condition and cooperative–controversy was that the former represented pure cooperation, whereas the second was a combination of cooperation and competition.

In the *individualistic* approach, students were instructed to work on their own without interacting with anyone but the teacher. They were told to learn the material at as high a level of excellence as possible and to write a group report.

Study 2 involved fourth graders, including a number of mildly handicapped children. Two conditions comprised this study. In an *intergroup cooperation* emphasis was placed on how well the entire class achieved. Students were instructed to learn the material and then ensure that all other members of their group knew it as well. For every day that all the class members reached their goal, the class was awarded 10 points. The condition of the other group was *intergroup competition,* in which emphasis was placed on which group achieved the highest score. Students were instructed to learn the material and then ensure that all group members knew the material as well. Feedback indicated which group was ahead in the competition. The difference between the two studies was that in the first, pupils worked for the entire class, whereas in the second, they worked for themselves.

The studies included four dependent variables: class structure (the extent pupils sat by someone), class unstructured (the extent a student played with someone in class), outside of class (the extent students were with someone in school but not in class), and in the home (the extent students interacted with someone at home).

The results of Study 1 showed that the students in the cooperative–controversy condition made more cross-handicap choices for structured and unstructured classroom activities than did students in other conditions. The results of Study 2 showed that pupils in the intergroup competition condition made more cross-handicap choices for structured, unstructured, and out-of-class activities. In both studies, nonhandicapped students in pure cooperation conditions indicated more constructive interaction with handicapped peers than they did in the mixed cooperative and competitive conditions.

Johnson and Johnson (1980) reviewed three other studies that dealt with cooperative learning. In the first, Armstrong, Johnson, and Balow (1981) compared cooperative with individualistic instruction in language arts for fifth and sixth grade youngsters, many of whom were LD. The results indicated that the LD students were far less isolated in the cooperative condition than in the individualistic condition. The regular students in the cooperative condition evaluated their LD peers as more valuable and smarter than did regular students in the individualistic condition. Nonhandicapped students in the cooperative condition also believed that they knew their LD peers better, chose them for friends more often, felt that they had been helped more frequently by them, and were less inclined to want them removed from the classroom.

In the second reviewed study, Cooper, Johnson, Johnson, and Wilderson (1980) examined the relationship between regular classroom students and LD students and students with behavior disorders under cooperative, competitive, and individualistic conditions in science, English, and geography classes. The researchers claimed that more students reported helping and receiving help from their handicapped peers in cooperative conditions than in others. Moreover, nonhandicapped students in the cooperative and competitive conditions chose handicapped peers for friends more frequently than they did in the individualistic condition.

The third study reviewed by the Johnsons was conducted by Nevin, Johnson, and Johnson (1980), who studied the effects of individual and group contingencies on nonhandicapped students' acceptance of handicapped classmates. The research focused on first, seventh, and ninth graders, all of whom were low achieving or special needs students, many in special education. Results from the investigation showed that group contingencies promoted greater social acceptance of handicapped students by their nonhandicapped classmates than did individual arrangements.

Slavin, Madden, and Leavey (1984) set up a study with third, fourth, and fifth grade youngsters who were receiving special education services for learning problems and were in regular classes. There were also a number of nonhandicapped students in the classes. Three conditions were arranged in their research. Under the first condition—team-assisted individualization (TAI)—groups of four or five pupils of all types were assembled, and pupils within groups were assigned to their proper levels in a math program. Following placement, they studied in small groups, corrected one another's papers, and assisted one another. Meanwhile, the teacher spent some time with students who were having problems. At the end of each week the teacher computed a team score (the average number correct on all the tests and the average number of units completed). Under individualized instruction—the second grouping—the same materials were used for pupils, but the students worked individually and checked their own answers. There were no team scores. The third group was a *control*. These pupils used traditional methods for learning math and read from traditional texts. For them, the teacher directed group-paced instruction.

The four measures in the research study pertained to sociometric status, mathematics achievement, attitudes toward school, and teacher ratings. Results revealed that both a combined cooperative-individualized program and an individualized instruction program without cooperative teams had significant effects on social acceptance, socially related behavior ratings of mainstreamed students, and their attitudes about mathematics, but not on their achievement. Achievement was generally better, however, for students in experimental groups than for those in the control group.

Anderson (1985) designed a study with only LD pupils. They were all boys between the ages of 10 and 15. Cooperative learning tasks were administered in a series of 17 sessions (for example, "Each person in your group has been given a clue to a murder mystery. As a group, you are to decide who committed the crime, where it was done, and what the motive was.") Peer acceptance was measured by a sociogram, while cooperation was measured by a forced choice cards task. The results showed significant improvements in peer acceptance and cooperation.

TUTORING

Tutoring[1] is a generic term, ordinarily indicating that one person is assigned to teach another. For our discussion, both parties (pupil-tutee and teacher-tutor)

---

1. For those interested in reading more about tutoring for and with exceptional children, see *Cross Age and Peer Tutoring: Help for Children with Learning Problems,* an excellent monograph written by Jenkins and Jenkins (1981); the equally valuable monograph *Peer Tutoring: Implementing Classwide Programs in the Primary Grades,* by Cooke, Heron, and Heward (1983); the excellent review "Research on Children Tutoring Children: A Critical Review" by Devin-Sheehan, Feldman, and Allen (1976); and the more recent "Special Education Students as Tutors: A Review and Analysis" by Osguthorpe and Scruggs (1986).

are students. If they are the same age, that is peer tutoring; if different ages, that is referred to as cross-aged tutoring.

There are a number of reasons for setting up tutoring programs with LD or other remedial students:

— Increase the time tutees spend on tasks
— Increase the number of opportunities for tutees to respond and, correspondingly, the amount of feedback and reinforcement they can acquire
— Allow tutees to work with pupils who may in some respects be good models
— Facilitate socialization between tutors and tutees
— Aid tutors to acquire information on the subjects they are tutoring
— Aid tutors to learn about teaching, generally
— Raise the esteem of tutors, either nonhandicapped or handicapped

Administrative Issues

Peer or cross-age tutoring situations have been arranged to teach most of the basic skills, some social behaviors, and some rather sophisticated academic skills as well. When establishing tutoring situations, some important administrative concerns must be considered.

1. Take care not to violate the privacy act (Buckley Amendment), which deals with access to information about students. In some tutoring situations, the tutor may have access to information about the tutee that could be in violation of the amendment.

2. Obtain parents' permission before setting up tutoring situations with their children, as either tutors or tutees.

3. Plan scheduling carefully when setting up tutoring programs. Although it is important to get the most benefit from the program, it is also necessary to schedule sessions at times that are not critical for the tutors to be absent from their own classes. Scheduling is also a factor for the classroom teachers, particularly when pupils from two classes are involved.

■ COMMENTARY ■   As mentioned earlier, many teachers are weary of pull-out programs. Even an excellent tutoring program can be just one more annoying scheme unless it fits in well with the "total picture." A former first grade teacher in Great Falls, Montana, solved the pull-out problem by engaging all of the pupils (and the teacher) in the sixth grade class in a special program. After they received training, they were set up as tutors of her first graders in reading programs. This plan also freed the sixth grade teacher for planning or grading papers while the students were tutoring.

4. Match the tutors and tutees properly in order to profit the most from the situation. They must be matched not only on the basis of academic skill and

need, but in terms of social compatibility. If possible, they should be paired on the basis of need and tolerance for reinforcement and feedback, and the willingness and ability to dispense and accept those components.

5. Assemble the appropriate materials and set aside times to teach the tutors. It's not enough to gather together sets of tutors and tutees, assign them to one another, and tell them to begin. Constant monitoring is required to keep tutoring programs on the right track. In this respect, Cooke et al. (1983) stated that student gains were increased when peer tutoring programs were highly structured, when there was an emphasis on repetition, when mastery levels were reached before advancing to next step, when review programs were incorporated, and when tutors were provided training.

6. Keep in touch with the parents of tutors and tutees. Some parents of tutors might be critical of such programs if they believed their children were missing out on instructional time of their own. Parents of tutees might be just as critical if they thought their children were being taught by someone other than a professional.

Some Representative Programs

Cooke, Heron, and Heward (1983) established a three-year federally funded peer tutoring project conducted in primary classrooms of a regular public school. Although the youngsters in their research were not necessarily LD, many of them needed extra help and probably could have qualified as handicapped had the usual tests been administered. The researchers were specifically concerned with teaching sight words and math facts. In their monograph, the authors explained how to select the sight words or facts for the tutees, how to pretest them, how to set criteria, and how to match tutors and tutees, assemble materials, train tutors, chart progress, monitor tutors, and report progress.

Another federally funded tutoring project emphasized a new twist. In this program, directed by Osguthorpe, Eiserman, and Shisler (1985), mildly handicapped youngsters were instructed to tutor younger, nonhandicapped children. The data indicated that after a two-week tutoring phase, the tutors interacted more frequently with nonhandicapped peers during free-play time than did students in a control group.

In 1984 a cross-age tutoring program was established in every school in the Lake Washington School District. In the elementary schools, tutors were high-performing students from the intermediate grades. They came to the resource room to work with LD and other pupils in need of assistance. Generally, they concentrated on the basic skills. In the secondary schools, tutors and tutees of every age worked on most subjects, but mostly U.S. history, English, and math. Ordinarily, two or three periods a day were set up in one room for tutoring. A professional teacher monitored all the activities. In the secondary programs, both the tutors and tutees signed contracts to the effect that they would fulfill their part of the arrangement, and both sets received credit for their participation.

COMMENTS AND DISCUSSION POINTS

- All of the strategies and approaches discussed in this chapter are becoming important in the education of LD youngsters, but these children need substance along with ideas. They must have content and some ability to read, compute, and write.

- It's difficult to determine how much instructional time should be devoted to special strategies at the expense of simply teaching marketable skills. We need to keep in mind the fact that the acquisition of learning strategies is a means toward an end, not an end.

- The identification and involvement of the practices explained here represent the cutting edge of instruction for LD youth today. Hopefully, the interest in these processes will stimulate research and replace less serious concerns, such as *where* to educate LD students.

- The practices outlined in this chapter—self-management, cognitive training, learning strategies, attribution retraining, adapting materials, cooperative learning situations, and tutoring—are interrelated. And some researchers are of the belief that attribution and cooperative learning are related to the acquisition and generalization of learning strategies.

- Training in self-management is perhaps the most generalizable technique when it comes to learning skills that will be useful after graduation. To a great extent, this also holds true for attribution retraining and cooperative learning. Other techniques, however, are more useful while individuals are in school.

- While the long-term gains of instructional strategies may be difficult to ascertain, they should have a positive lifetime effect. For example, if youngsters were taught to be excellent self-managers in school, we might expect them to be more independent as adults and more able to cope with the many difficulties of life.

- There is more to attribution than meets the eye. It may be quite appropriate to retrain youngsters so that they believe that when they succeed it is because they used the proper strategy and had practiced it enough or, conversely, if they fail, to believe that it is because they used a faulty strategy or had not practiced enough. But we shouldn't get too carried away with this approach. Sometimes it is better for youngsters to simply accept the fact that they made a mistake or failed.

- We should be sensible in setting up cooperative learning situations. Some instructional situations *should* be arranged cooperatively (for example, music, sports); others are best suited for *solo* learning (reading, writing, and arithmetic). If we set up cooperative learning arrangements in situations that aren't cooperative by nature, we should at least consider our objectives: Are we trying to teach pupils a subject and give them some content, or are we trying to teach them to behave in harmony? Both objectives are admirable, but in some circumstances they may be incompatible.

- Research on self-recording should go beyond counting the number of instances or minutes that pupils appear to be working. They may not be accomplishing anything even though they seem to be attending. Researchers and practitioners should measure a more important variable, for example, production.

■ Similarly, researchers concerned with learning strategies should be more concerned with the *effects* of acquiring those strategies. As it is, some researchers pay more attention to the students' acquisition of the strategies than to the effects those strategies have on a negotiable product.

REFERENCES

Anderson, M.A. (1985). Cooperative group tasks and their relationship to peer acceptance and cooperation. *Journal of Learning Disabilities, 18,* 83–86.

Armstrong, B.; Johnson, D.W.; & Balow, B. (1981). Effects of cooperative vs. individualistic learning experiences on interpersonal attraction between learning-disabled and normal-progress elementary school pupils. *Contemporary Educational Psychology, 6,* 102–109.

Beals, V.L. (1984). The effects of large group instruction on the acquisition of specific learning strategies by learning disabled adolescents. Unpublished doctoral dissertation, University of Kansas, Lawrence.

Benedetti, D. (1984). The effectiveness of an instructional adaptation on the acquisition of science information by learning disabled students. Unpublished doctoral dissertation, University of Washington, Seattle.

Bergerud, D.; Lovitt, T.; & Horton, S. (1988). The effectiveness of textbook adaptations in life science for high school students with learning disabilities. *Journal of Learning Disabilities, 21,* 70–76.

Borkowski, J.G.; Weyhing, R.S.; & Turner, L.A. (1986). Attributional retraining and the teaching of strategies. *Exceptional Children, 53,* 130–137.

Bornstein, P.H., & Quevillon, R.P. (1976). The effects of a self-instructional package on overactive preschool boys. *Journal of Applied Behavior Analysis, 9,* 179–188.

Bursuck, W.D., & Epstein, M.H. (1987). Current research topics in learning disabilities. *Learning Disability Quarterly, 10*(1), 2–7.

Clark, F.L.; Deshler, D.D.; Schumaker, J.B.; Alley, G.R.; & Warner, M.M. (1984). Visual imagery and self-questioning: Strategies to improve comprehension of written material. *Journal of Learning Disabilities, 17,* 145–149.

Cooke, N.L.; Heron, T.E.; & Heward, W.L. (1983). *Peer tutoring: Implementing classwide programs in the primary grades.* Columbus, OH: Special Press.

Cooper, L.; Johnson, D.W.; Johnson, R.; & Wilderson, F. (1980). The effects of cooperative, competitive, and individualistic experiences on interpersonal attraction among heterogeneous peers. *Journal of Social Psychology, 111,* 243–252.

Deshler, D.D., & Schumaker, J.B. (1986). Learning strategies: An instructional alternative for low-achieving adolescents. *Exceptional Children, 52,* 583–590.

Deshler, D.D.; Schumaker, J.B.; & Lenz, B.K. (1984). Academic and cognitive interventions for LD adolescents: Part 1. *Journal of Learning Disabilities, 17,* 108–117.

Deshler, D.D.; Schumaker, J.B.; Lenz, B.K.; & Ellis, E. (1984). Academic and cognitive interventions for LD adolescents: Part II. *Journal of Learning Disabilities, 17,* 170–179.

Devin-Sheehan, L.; Feldman, R.S.; & Allen, V.L. (1976). Research on children tutoring children: A critical review. *Review of Educational Research, 46,* 355–385.

Duvall, B. (1981). Peer tutoring. Presentation at Precision Teaching Conference in Kalispell, MT.

Eiserman, W.D.; Osguthorpe, R.T.; & Shisler, L. (1985). Increasing social acceptance: Mentally retarded students tutoring regular class peers. *Education and Training of the Mentally Retarded,* December, 235–240.

Ellis, E.E. (1985). The effects of teaching learning disabled adolescents an executive problem solving strategy. Unpublished doctoral dissertation, University of Kansas, Lawrence.

Ellis, E.E.; Lenz, B.K.; & Sabornie, E.J. (1987a). Generalization and adaptation of learning strategies to natural environments: Part 1: Critical agents. *Remedial and Special Education, 8*(1), 6–20.

Ellis, E.E.; Lenz, B.K.; & Sabornie, E.J. (1987b). Generalization and adaptation of learning strategies to natural environments: Part 2: Research into practice. *Remedial and Special Education, 8*(2), 6–23.

Engleman, S.; Davis, K.; & Davis, G. (1986). *Your world of facts I: A memory development program.* Tigard, OR: CC Publications.

Englert, C.S.; Hiebert, E.H.; & Stewart, S.R. (1985). Spelling unfamiliar words by an analogy strategy. *The Journal of Special Education, 19*(3), 291–306.

Fowler, J.W., & Peterson, P.L. (1981). Increasing reading persistence and altering attributional style of learned helpless children. *Journal of Educational Psychology, 73,* 251–260.

Gelzheiser, L.M. (1984). Generalization from categorical memory tasks to prose by learning disabled adolescents. *Journal of Educational Psychology, 76,* 1128–1138.

Hallahan, D.P.; Lloyd, J.; Kosiewicz, M.M.; Kauffman, J.M.; & Graves, A.W. (1979). Self-monitoring of attention as a treatment for a learning disabled boy's off-task behavior. *Learning Disability Quarterly, 2,* 24–32.

Hallahan, D.P., & Sapona, R. (1983). Self-monitoring of attention with learning-disabled children: Past research and current issues. *Journal of Learning Disabilities, 16,* 616–620.

Hansen, J., & Pearson, P.D. (1983). An instructional study: Improving the inferential comprehension of good and poor fourth-grade readers. *Journal of Educational Psychology, 75,* 821–829.

Higgins, K. (1988). Hypertext computer-assisted instruction and the social studies achievement of learning disabled, remedial, and regular education students. Unpublished doctoral dissertation, University of New Mexico, Albuquerque.

Harris, K.R., & Graham, S. (1985). Improving learning disabled students' composition skills: A self-control strategy training approach. *Learning Disability Quarterly, 8,* 27–36.

Horton, S.V., & Lovitt, T.C. (In press). Using study guides with three classifications of secondary students. *Journal of Special Education.*

Horton, S.V.; & Lovitt, T.C.; Bergerud, D. (In press). The effectiveness of graphic organizers for three classifications of secondary students in content-area classes. *Journal of Learning Disabilities.*

Horton, S.V.; Lovitt, T.C.; & Givens, A. (1988). A computer based vocabulary program for three categories of students. *British Journal of Educational Technology, 19*(2), 131–143.

Horton, S.V.; Lovitt, T.C.; & Slocum, T. (In press). Teaching geography to high school students with academic deficits: Effects of a computerized map tutorial. *Learning Disability Quarterly.*

Jenkins, J.R., & Jenkins, L.M. (1981). *Cross age and peer tutoring: Help for children with learning problems.* Reston, VA: CEC publications.

Johnson, D.W., & Johnson, R.T. (1980). Integrating handicapped students into the mainstream. *Exceptional Children, 47,* 90–98.

Johnson, D.W.; Johnson, R.T.; Holubec, E.J.; & Roy, P. (1984). *Circles of learning: Cooperation in the classroom.* Alexandria, VA: Association for Supervision and Curriculum Development.

Johnson, D.W.; Johnson, R.T.; Warring, D.; & Maruyama, G. (1986). Different cooperative learning procedures and cross-handicap relationships. *Exceptional Children, 53,* 247–252.

Klein, R.D.; & Gory, E.L. (1976). The differential effects of noncontingent self-evaluation upon academic performance. In Brigham, Hawkins, Scott, & McLaughlin (Eds.), *Behavior analysis in education: Self-control and reading.* Dubuque, IA: Kendal/Hunt.

Kurtz, B.E., & Borkowski, J.G. (1985). Metacognition and the development of strategic skills in impulsive and reflective children. Paper presented at the meeting of the Society for Research on Child Development, Toronto.

Lenz, B.K.; Alley, G.R.; & Schumaker, J.B. (1987). Activating the inactive learner: Advance organizers in the secondary content classroom. *Learning Disability Quarterly, 10,* 53–67.

Licht, B.G. (1983). Cognitive-motivational factors that contribute to the achievement of learning disabled children. *Journal of Learning Disabilities, 16,* 483–490.

Lloyd, J.; Saltzman, N.J.; & Kauffman, J.M. (1981). Predictable generalization in academic learning as a result of preskills and strategy training. *Learning Disability Quarterly, 4,* 203–216.

Lovitt, T.C. (1973). Self-management projects with children with behavioral disabilities. *Journal of Learning Disabilities, 6*(3), 15–28.

Lovitt, T.C., & Curtiss, K.A. (1969). Academic response rate as a function of teacher- and self-imposed contingencies. *Journal of Applied Behavior Analysis, 2,* 49–53.

Lovitt, T.C., & Curtiss, K.A. (1968). Effects of manipulating an antecedent event on mathematics response rate. *Journal of Applied Behavior Analysis, 1,* 329–333.

Lovitt, T.C.; Horton, S.V.; & Bergerud, D. (1987). Matching students with textbooks: An alternative to readability formulas and standardized tests. *B.C. Journal of Special Education, 2*(1), 49–55.

Lovitt, T.; Rudsit, J.; Jenkins, J.; Pious, C.; & Benedetti, D. (1985). Two methods for adapting science materials for learning disabled and regular seventh graders. *Learning Disability Quarterly, 8,* 275–285.

Lovitt, T.; Rudsit, J.; Jenkins, J.; Pious, C.; & Benedetti, D. (1986). Adapting science materials for regular and learning disabled seventh graders. *Remedial and Special Education, 1,* 31–39.

Lovitt, T.; Stein, M.; & Rudsit, J. (1985). The use of visual spatial displays to teach science facts to learning disabled middle school students. Unpublished manuscript, Experimental Education Unit, University of Washington, Seattle.

Mastropieri, M.A.; Scruggs, T.E.; & Levin, J.R. (1985). Memory strategy instruction with learning disabled adolescents. *Journal of Learning Disabilities, 18,* 94–100.

McLaughlin, T.F.; Krappman, V.F.; & Welsh, J.M. (1985). The effects of self-recording for on-task behavior of behaviorally disordered special education students. *Remedial and Special Education, 6*(4), 42–45.

McLaughlin, T.F., & Malaby, J.E. (1974). Increasing and maintaining assignment completion with teacher and pupil controlled individual contingency programs: Three case studies. *Psychology, 11*(3), 45–51.

Meadows, N. (1988). The effects of individual, teacher-directed and cooperative learning instructional methods on the comprehension of expository text. Unpublished doctoral dissertation, University of Washington, Seattle.

Miller, G.E. (1985). The effects of general and specific self-instruction training on children's comprehension monitoring performances during reading. *Reading Research Quarterly, 20,* 616–628.

Mosby, R.J. (1979). A bypass program of supportive instruction for secondary students with learning disabilities. *Journal of Learning Disabilities, 12,* 187–190.

Nevin, A.; Johnson, D.W.; Johnson, R. (1980). Effects of group and individual contingencies on academic performance and social relations of special needs students. Unpublished manuscript, University of Minnesota, Minneapolis.

Nolan, S.; Alley, G.R.; & Clark, N. (1980). *Self-questioning strategy.* Instructional Materials #1, Institute for Research in Learning Disabilities, University of Kansas, Lawrence.

Osguthorpe, R.T., & Scruggs, T.E. (1986). Special education students as tutors: A review and analysis. *Remedial and Special Education, 7*(4), 15–25.

O'Sullivan, J.T., & Pressley, M. (1984). Completeness of instruction and strategy transfer. *Journal of Experimental Child Psychology, 38,* 275–288.

Palincsar, A.M., & Brown, D.A. (1987). Enhancing instructional time through attention to metacognition. *Journal of Learning Disabilities, 20,* 66–75.

Paris, S.; Cross, D.R.; Jacobs, J.E.; Oka, E.R.; DeBritto, A.M.; & Saarnio, D.A. (1984). Improving children's metacognition and reading comprehension with classroom instruction. Symposium presented at the annual meeting of the American Educational Research Association, New Orleans.

Pflaum, S.W., & Pascarella, E.T. (1980). Interactive effects of prior reading achievement and training in context on the reading of learning-disabled children. *Reading Research Quarterly, 16*(1), 138–158.

Pressley, M.; Johnson, C.J.; & Symons, S. (1987). Elaborating to learn and learning to elaborate. *Journal of Learning Disabilities, 20,* 76–91.

Raphael, T.; Kirschner, B.; & Englert, C. (1985). Teaching expository reading and writing skills: Impact of process writing and text structure; instruction on teachers and students. Paper presented at the National Reading Conference, San Diego, CA.

Reid, M.K., & Borkowski, J.G. (1985). A cognitive-motivational training program for hyperactive children. Paper presented at the society for Research in Child Development, Toronto.

Rooney, K.J.; Hallahan, D.P.; & Lloyd, J.W. (1983). Self-recording of attention by learning disabled students in the regular classroom. *Journal of Learning Disabilities, 17,* 360–364.

Sawyer, D.J., & Kosoff, T.O. (1981). Accommodating the learning needs of reading disabled adolescents: A language processing issue. *Learning Disability Quarterly, 4,* 61–68.

Schmidt, J.L. (1984). The effects of four generalized conditions on learning disabled adolescents' written language performance in the regular classroom. Unpublished doctoral dissertation, University of Kansas, Lawrence.

Schumaker, J.B.; Deshler, D.D.; Alley, G.R.; & Warner, M.M. (1983). Toward the development of an intervention model for learning disabled adolescents. *Exceptional Education Quarterly, 4*(1), 45–74.

Schumaker, J.B.; Deshler, D.D.; Alley, G.R.; Warner, M.M.; & Denton, P.H. (1982). Multipass: A learning strategy for improving reading comprehension. *Learning Disability Quarterly, 5,* 295–304.

Schumaker, J.B.; Deshler, D.D.; & Denton, P.H. (1982). An integrated system for providing content to learning disabled adolescents using an audio-taped format. Research Report No. 66, Institute for Research in Learning Disabilities, University of Kansas, Lawrence.

Schumaker, J.B.; Deshler, D.D.; Nolan, S.; Clark, F.L.; Alley, G.R.; & Warner, M.M. (1981). Error monitoring: A learning strategy for improving academic performance of LD adolescents. Research Report No. 32, Institute for Research in Learning Disabilities, University of Kansas, Lawrence.

Schunk, D.H. (1981). Modeling and attributional effects on children's achievement: A self-efficacy analysis. *Journal of Educational Psychology, 73*, 93–105.

Schunk, D.H. (1985). Participation in goal setting: Effects on self-efficacy and skills of learning-disabled children. *The Journal of Special Education, 19*, 307–317.

Scruggs, T.E.; Mastropieri, M.A.; Levin, J.R.; & Gaffney, J.S. (1985). Facilitating the acquisition of science facts in learning disabled students. *American Educational Research Journal, 22*, 575–586.

Seabaugh, G.O., & Schumaker, J.B. (1981). The effects of self-regulation training on the academic productivity of LD and NLD adolescents. Research Report No. 37, Institute for Research in Learning Disabilities, University of Kansas, Lawrence.

Seabaugh, G.O., & Schumaker, J.B. (1983). The effectiveness of fading teaching input in self-control procedures with LD adolescents. Unpublished manuscript, University of Kansas, Lawrence.

Shelton, T.L.; Anastopoulos, D.A.; & Linden, J.D. (1985). An attribution training program with learning disabled children. *Journal of Learning Disabilities, 18*, 261–265.

Slavin, R.E.; Madden, N.A.; & Leavey, M. (1984). Effects of cooperative learning and individualized instruction on mainstreamed students. *Exceptional Children, 50*, 434–443.

Swanson, H.L. (1987). Information processing theory and learning disabilities: A commentary and future perspective. *Journal of Learning Disabilities, 20*, 155–166.

Tollefson, N.; Tracy, D.B.; Johnsen, E.P.; & Chatman, J. (1986). Teaching learning disabled students goal implementation skills. *Psychology in the Schools, 23*, 194–204.

Turkewitz, H.; O'Leary, K.D.; & Ironsmith, M. (1975). Generalization and maintenance of appropriate behavior through self-control. *Journal of Consulting and Clinical Psychology, 43*, 577–583.

Weyhing, R.S. (1986). Effects of attributional retraining on beliefs about self-efficacy and reading comprehension in learning disabled adolescents. Unpublished master's thesis, University of Notre Dame, Notre Dame, IN.

Wiseman, D.E.; Hartwell, L.K.; & Hannafin, M.J. (1980). Exploring the reading and listening skills of secondary mildly handicapped students. *Learning Disability Quarterly, 3*, 56–61.

Wong, B., & Jones, W. (1982). Increasing metacomprehension in learning disabled and normally achieving students through self-questioning training. *Learning Disability Quarterly, 5*(2), 228–238.

Zigmond, N.; Levin, E.; & Laurie, T.E. (1985). Managing the mainstream: An analysis of teacher attitudes and student performance in mainstream high school programs. *Journal of Learning Disabilities, 18*, 535–541.

Chapter 11

Peasant Girl with a Straw Hat by Camille Pissaro (dated [18]81). Courtesy of the National Gallery of Art, Washington, Ailsa Mellon Bruce Collection 1970.

SOCIAL BEHAVIOR

────────────── MAIN IDEAS ──────────────

- Social characteristics of LD individuals that pertain to social status, perceptions, competencies, interactions, and attributions

- Approaches for assessing social and emotional traits: behavioral observation codes, behavioral checklists, sociometric devices, behavioral rating scales, student records, interviews, and adaptive behavior scales

- Types of interventions for social behaviors—including manipulating antecedent or consequent events, self-control and instructional procedures, commercial programs—and information on selecting and implementing programs

────────────── OVERVIEW ──────────────

There is general agreement that the lack of social competence poses a major obstacle to the successful integration of exceptional individuals into normal settings and roles. In particular, many LD individuals are lacking in the skills required to "get along with others." There is less agreement, however, with respect to how they should be trained in social skills and by whom.

The first section of this chapter provides a discussion of the social and emotional characteristics of LD youth. The next section surveys various ways to assess the social and emotional behaviors of LD youth.

The third section discusses various types of programs, commercial and otherwise, that have been designed to teach social and emotional skills to LD youngsters. The chapter ends with remarks on the studies and programs reviewed in the chapter and comments on what could be done in respect to the assessment and instruction of social skills.

——— SOCIAL CHARACTERISTICS OF LD STUDENTS ———

According to Greenspan (1981), there have been three approaches to defining social competence: outcome oriented, content oriented, and skill oriented. As he explains it, the *outcome-oriented approach* to social competence is characterized by an emphasis on the individual's ability to attain desired social objectives. Indices selected by proponents of this approach would include measures of school performance, dating and marriage, work history, earned income, and the like.

The *content-oriented approach* is characterized by the identification of behavior traits believed to contribute to socially successful outcomes. Some behavioral indicators are appropriate regulation of antisocial behavior and morality and prosocial tendencies, and behaviors along continuums of "niceness–nastiness" and "social activity–inactivity."

The *skill-oriented approach* is recognized by an emphasis on the interpersonal processes used in gaining social objectives and mastering one's social environment. Some measures describe individual's ability to make sense out of interpersonal situations, the ability to engage effectively in complex interpersonal interactions, and the ability to use and understand people.

Greenspan has developed a three component structure to explain social awareness: social sensitivity, social insight, and social communication. Figure 11.1 is an illustration of that model. In it, social sensitivity is divided into two constructs: role-taking and social interference. Social insight is made up of three: social comprehension, psychological insight, and moral judgment. Social communication is made up of two constructs: referential communication and social problem-solving.

▪ FIGURE 11.1 ▪   Model of Social Awareness

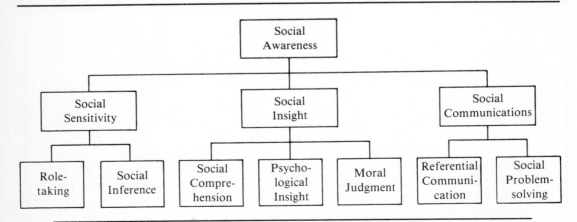

Source: Reprinted by permission from S. Greenspan, "Defining Childhood Social Competence: A Proposed Working Model," in B.K. Keogh (Ed.), *Advances in Special Education*, Vol. 3 (Greenwich, CT: JAI Press), p. 17.

According to Schumaker and Hazel (1984b), when LD youth are compared to their nonhandicapped peers, their social behaviors tend to be less acceptable in a number of situations. For example, they are less able to predict the consequences for their behaviors, they misinterpret social cues more often, they are less able to adapt their behaviors to the characteristics of their listeners, and they perform certain inappropriate social behaviors at significantly higher levels. Numerous studies have compared the social skills of LD and non-LD students with regard to five interrelated social categories: status, perceptions, competencies, interactions, and attributions.

Status

Bryan (1974) combined the peer-nomination approach with the "Guess Who" technique to compare the social status of LD and non-LD students in grades 3 through 5. In the peer-nomination approach, the students were asked to identify classmates who were friends and those who were not. The "Guess Who" technique asked pupils such questions as: "Who finds it hard to sit still in class? Who is handsome or pretty?" The data indicated that LD students received significantly fewer votes for social acceptance and significantly more for rejection. Bryan also concluded that LD girls, particularly white LD girls, were especially rejected by their peers.

Scranton and Ryckman (1979) assessed the sociometric standing of primary-aged LD and non-LD students by asking them three questions that indicated positive choices of their classmates and three that asked for negative choices. They reported significant differences between LD and non-LD youngsters on both positive and negative questions. Their data, like those of Bryan, revealed that LD girls were less likely to be positively chosen and more apt to be rejected than were LD boys.

Sabornie and Kauffman (1986) also relied on sociometric techniques to compare the social status of LD adolescents and non-LD pupils in physical education classes. Their analysis showed that although LD pupils in general scored lower in sociometric status than non-LD students, the two groups did not differ significantly. In fact, there was considerable overlap between the two groups.

Garrett and Crump (1980) likewise used sociometric devices to compare social attributes of LD and non-LD students. Their study was more extensive than the previous ones since they explored the relationship of teacher preference and social status among children, as well as the accuracy of self-appraisal of social status among LD and non-LD students. Their results showed that LD students received significantly lower social status scores than non-LD pupils and that LD students were less preferred by teachers than their non-LD classmates. However, they observed no significant differences in the accuracy of self-appraisal of social status between LD and non-LD students.

The results of studies using peer-acceptance scales or similar procedures tend to support the peer-nomination studies. Bruininks (1978), for example, reported that both LD boys and LD girls received significantly lower peer ratings than did non-LD students.

A few studies of LD high school students have suggested a slightly different pattern with respect to sociometric status. Sabornie (1983), for example, reported nonsignificant differences in sociometric status between LD high school students and a matched non-LD group.

Perceptions

Epstein, Cullinan, and Nieminen (1984) studied teachers' perceptions of LD and non-LD girls of three age groups: 7 to 8 (referred to as younger), 10 and 11 (middle), and 13 and 14 (older). Their data, from a behavior problem checklist, indicated that it was difficult to discriminate between non-LD and LD girls on the basis of emotional and behavior problems at the older or middle-age levels. At the youngest age, however, the personality problem type of disorder (for example, feelings of inferiority, social withdrawal) differentiated between the two. According to the researchers, this finding suggested that girls identified as LD by age seven or eight may be more severely handicapped than those identified later on.

Garrett and Crump (1980) used a modified Q-sort to examine teacher attitudes toward LD and non-LD students in grades 4 through 6. Teachers were asked to sort the names of their students onto a form containing a nine-column pyramid approximating the normal curve that ranged from most to least preferred. The data showed that teachers' preferences for LD students were significantly lower than for non-LD students.

Dudley-Marling and Edmiaston (1985) reported inconsistent results from studies using videotapes to examine LD students' social status. Results often vary depending on what the teachers are told they are watching. For example, it is not unusual that if judges are told that videotapes of normal children are of LD youngsters, they will tend to view the youngsters less favorably than will other judges who are told that the children are non-LD. The researchers concluded that teachers and parents were more likely to assign negative traits to young LD children than to non-LD children.

McConaughy (1986) studied parents' perceptions of their adolescent boys by asking them to fill out their child behavior checklist. Data from that instrument evidenced that, on the average, LD boys showed significantly lower levels of social competence and more behavior problems when compared to non-LD boys. The LD boys were significantly lower than the normative samples in their partic-ipation in activities, their social involvement, and their performance in school. At the same time, the LD boys had high scores compared to non-LD boys on several scales that reflected immaturity, hostility–withdrawal, aggressiveness, and hyperactivity. The total number of behavior problems was within the clinical range of the checklist, which thus suggests severe behavior disturbance.

Gresham and Reschly (1986) studied the perceptions of teachers, parents, and peers for LD and non-LD youngsters, using rating scales. The results indicated that teachers, parents, and peers rated mainstreamed LD children as deficient in task-related, interpersonal, and self-related social skill domains. Data also showed that LD children were more poorly accepted by peers in play and work situations. Teachers and parents maintained that LD children demonstrated the poorest social skills in task-related behaviors that included attending to instruction, completing tasks, staying on task, following directions, and working independently. Their results further suggested that LD children demonstrated significant deficits in such interpersonal and self-related behaviors as accepting authority, helping others, expressing feelings, and having positive self-attitudes.

Competencies

Schumaker, Hazel, Sherman, and Sheldon (1982) investigated social competencies of LD, non-LD, and juvenile delinquent (JD) high school youth by arranging role-playing situations. They gathered data on eight skills:

— Giving positive feedback
— Giving negative feedback
— Accepting negative feedback
— Resisting peer pressure
— Negotiating conflict situations
— Following instructions
— Carrying on conversations
— Solving personal problems

The following is a typical scene arranged to acquire data from pupils: "You feel that your mom has been on your case about nothing and you decide to tell her. She has been yelling at you a lot lately about little things like leaving the cap off the toothpaste. I'll play your mom and we will act out the situation." The results from these activities showed that the non-LD youths performed markedly better than the other two groups on seven of the eight skills. LD youths performed significantly better than JD youths on one skill, resisting peer pressure. Further analyses revealed that females generally scored higher than males and that the LD group was heterogeneous with regard to social skills.

Gerber and Zinkgraf (1982) compared the social-perceptual abilities of elementary age LD and nonhandicapped children by giving them a test of social inference—that is, the children were shown several pictures and asked to explain what was happening. According to the results, the LD children scored consistently lower on social perception than their non-LD peers regardless of age. Furthermore, younger children generally scored lower than older students.

Cartledge, Stupay, and Kaczala (1986) assessed empathy and social skills of elementary-aged LD and non-LD children. To measure empathy they played a tape of four stories for the youngsters. Students listened to each story twice: first, to identify how the stories made *them* feel, and then, to identify the feelings of the story's main character. The stories expressed four emotions—happiness, sadness, anger, and fear. To assess social skills, the researchers asked classroom teachers to rate their students on a social behavior assessment scale covering environmental behaviors, task-related behaviors, interpersonal behaviors, and self-related behaviors. Data revealed that the mean scores for the non-LD students were higher on the empathy assessment than those for LD pupils. Non-LD students were also more proficient in every category of social skills. The correlation coefficients for LD students' empathy scores and social skill ratings were low or near zero; none were statistically significant. Most of the relationships for non-LD students were moderate, and many were statistically significant.

Jones (1985) compared the performances of LD youngsters ages 10 to 13 to those of nonhandicapped students on two tests. He administered the *Piers-Harris Children's Self-Concept Scale* (Piers & Harris, 1969) for a "conscious" measure and a human figure drawing test for the "unconscious" self-concept. Results indicated that the handicapped students had significantly more negative conscious and unconscious self-concepts; higher anxiety levels; more negative perceptions of their intellectual abilities, school status, and popularity; and more feelings of insecurity, inadequacy, guilt, impulsivity, and immaturity. Data also showed that LD students believed that their intellectual, academic, and physical characteristics were significantly inferior to those of their non-LD mates. Jones maintained that those results suggested a negative "school-related self-concept": The high anxiety levels of handicapped students regarding their intellectual abilities and school status negatively influenced their self-concepts, which in turn negatively influenced their academic achievements.

Interactions

Bryan and Pflaum (1978) studied the social interactions of fourth and fifth grade LD and non-LD children by asking them to teach a laboratory game to classmates and kindergarteners. Interactions between the two children playing the game were videotaped, and data were gathered in regard to linguistic complexity, accuracy, completeness of game instructions, and social content. Data showed that LD pupils used shorter sentences, a smaller proportion of complex sentences, and fewer modifiers than non-LD children. Further, females were generally sensitive to age differences, using more complex language when speaking to peers than to younger children. The LD males generally failed to make such distinctions; indeed, they often used more complex language when interacting with younger children. A study by Skrtic (1980) represents many studies of teacher-pupil interactions. He claimed that although the frequency of interactions between LD children and their teachers and peers may not differentiate the LD students from their peers, the quality of those interactions differs. Skrtic concluded that teacher interactions with LD students were more likely to focus on academics, and that positive teacher interactions with non-LD students were more likely than negative. Positive and negative interactions were fairly evenly distributed for the LD pupils.

Weiss (1984) investigated social understanding of unrehearsed interactions that occurred within a school setting between peers of four types: nonaggressive learners (those who were achieving up to par), aggressive learners, nonaggressive LD, and aggressive LD. To compare judgments made from real-life incidents that offered a full range of social cues with judgments made from limited stimuli, the same scenes were described verbally. The results indicated no differences between the opinions of the aggressive and the nonaggressive boys, suggesting that aggressive perceivers do not necessarily project their own characteristics onto others. The author reported, however, that both aggressive and nonaggressive LD boys interpreted all scenes as more unfriendly than did their non-LD mates.

Attributions

Licht (1983) stated that when LD children are confronted with difficulty, they are more likely than their peers to attribute their problems to insufficient ability and less apt to associate them with insufficient effort. Conversely, when LD children *do* experience success, they are less likely than non-LD children to view their achievement as a reflection of their ability. Licht concluded that, in light of the low opinion that LD children hold of their own abilities, it is not surprising that they express lower expectations for future success than their peers and correspondingly show a greater decrement in expectancies that follow failure. (Chapter 10 contains more detail on attributions.)

ASSESSMENT

This section covers various ways to assess the social and emotional behaviors of LD youth. In order to measure social skill functioning adequately, according to Schumaker and Hazel (1984a), an instrument must assess a person's behaviors and the consequences of those behaviors, overt behaviors and cognitive behaviors, the quality of behavioral responses (sequences, timing, contexts, and content), whether the skills are present in the individual's repertoire (revealing a performance deficit versus social skill deficits), the person's physical appearance, and the use of skills in situations of interest.

Assessment Devices

According to Schumaker and Hazel (1984a) four assessment devices have generally been selected to assay social skills of LD youth: behavioral observation codes, behavioral checklists, sociometric devices, and behavioral rating scales.

Behavioral Observation Codes. For this type of assessment, students are typically asked to complete an interactive task, such as interviewing someone or teaching someone a game, and their social behaviors are observed as they carry out the task. Occasionally, students' social attributes are observed in natural situations.

There are a number of advantages to this type of assessment:

1. It can provide data on what a youth does under natural or near-natural circumstances.

2. It can be sensitive to changes in behavior due to social skills instructions.

3. It can be arranged frequently, over a period of time.

This form of measurement, however, also has some potential disadvantages:

1. It can be time consuming.

2. It can be unreliable unless the observers are carefully trained.

3. It can influence the behaviors of the pupils being observed.

Stephens described setting up an environment wherein social skills are likely to occur. He arranged circumstances to observe the sharing of toys and equipment in a play situation:

> During a free-play or recess period, have the target student play with some available toys or equipment alone for a short time. Then send another student over to play with the same toys or equipment. Observe whether the first (target) student willingly allows the second to play with the toys, and if he plays together with the second student. Or, establish a small group activity, such as drawing pictures with one set of magic markers or pens given to target student for all to share. Observe target student for sharing behavior. [Stephens, 1978, p. 293]

A variation on the idea of setting up a "real" social situation is to show the youngsters pictures of social scenes. Edmonson, deJung, Leland, and Leach (1974), for example, developed *The Test of Social Inference,* which calls for interpretations to be made from pictures depicting various social situations. Each picture is accompanied by a standard set of questions that are verbally presented by the examiner and to which the student responds verbally. The assumption behind this test is that students with high social inference ability are able to infer many dimensions in a given social situation, make sense of the situation, and respond appropriately to it.

Yet another variation on this theme is to show videotaped sequences to youngsters. Weiss (1984) describes an assessment situation in which students are shown several taped scenes depicting a variety of social interactions between two or three boys. Students are asked to tell examiners whether the boys in the film are engaged in interactions that are neutral, friendly, cooperative, teasing, horse-play, fighting, or hostile.

Behavioral Checklists.   This approach lists a number of behaviors that could occur under certain circumstances. An observer watches the student throughout an interaction and checks the behaviors that occur. Checklists are generally easy to use, can be used repeatedly, and can provide focus for subsequent instruction. Further, the observer can record incidents that precede and follow the target behavior. Disadvantages of checklists include the following: the frequencies that behaviors occur will probably not be detected; interesting behaviors that are not on the list could occur, but will not be recorded; and the quality of the behavior will probably not be picked up.

One instrument for rating specific behaviors is the *Walker Problem Behavior Identification Checklist* (Walker, 1970). This list of behaviors is designed to identify children with behavior problems severe enough to classify the students as emotionally disturbed. It contains fifty items, which are grouped into five scales of disturbed behavior: acting-out, withdrawal, distractibility, disturbed peer relations, and immaturity. Examples from each of these categories are listed in Table 11.1. A novel (but debated) feature of this scale is that its scoring system discriminates between boys and girls since it allows for more problem behaviors for boys. In terms of social skill instruction, this checklist provides a pupil profile that might enable examiners to identify problem areas.

Sociometric Devices.   Sociometric assessment asks youngsters, in a variety of ways, to identify individuals in the class whom they do and do not like. The most and least socially accepted children are determined by these votes. When Scranton and Ryckman (1979) gathered sociometric data from a group of youngsters, they asked some of the following questions:

□ Who are the children in your class that you like the best?
□ If you were to have your seat changed, who would you like to have sit in the seat next to you?
□ Who are the children in your class that you most like to play with?
□ If you were to have your seat changed, who *wouldn't* you like to sit by?

Hill M. Walker and colleagues at the University of Oregon have made major contributions in the social skills area. They have published a number of assessment devices and instructional programs in this area. Two of their more significant social skills training programs are the ACCEPTS Program for younger children and the ACCESS Program for adolescents.

■ TABLE 11.1 ■   Sample Items from Walker Problem Behavior Identification Checklist

1. Complains about others' unfairness and/or discrimination towards him.
2. Is listless and continually tired.
    ⋮
10. Is overactive, restless, and/or continually shifting body positions.
11. Apologizes repeatedly for himself and/or his behavior.
    ⋮
21. Habitually rejects the school experience through actions or comments.
22. Has enuresis. (Wets bed.)
    ⋮
31. Has rapid mood shifts: depressed one moment, manic the next.
32. Does not obey until threatened with punishment.
    ⋮
41. Does not complete tasks attempted.
42. Doesn't protest when others hurt, tease, or criticize him.

Source: Copyright © 1970, 1976, 1983 by Western Psychological Services. Reprinted from the *Walker Problem Behavior Identification Checklist, Revised 1983* by permission of the publisher, Western Psychological Services, 12031 Wilshire Boulevard, Los Angeles, California 90025. Reprinted by permission.

□ Who are the children in your class that you *do not* like to play with?
□ Who are the children in your class that you *do not* like?

This popular method has some advantages. The data rather accurately reflect the likes and dislikes of the youngsters' peers below the ages of 9 and 10. These data have been highly related to other measures of social acceptance. Moreover, the data are relatively sensitive to changes in a youngster's social abilities. The disadvantages, however, tend to outweigh the advantages. These disadvantages include:

1. The data are not as sensitive to youngster's perceptions over the age of 9 or 10.
2. At the secondary level it is difficult to determine in which class to conduct such assessments since the students are in several classes.
3. The results may vary according to the proportion of handicapped youngsters in the class.
4. The data provide little, if any, diagnostic information.
5. Such assessments cannot be used too frequently because children's opinions on one day influence their choices on subsequent administrations.

Behavioral Rating Scales.   For this form of assessment, a number of behaviors or descriptive items are listed, and respondents are asked to determine the *extent* to which those attributes are noted. They may rate the behavior on a five- or seven-point scale, where the highest number indicates that the behavior occurs quite frequently, and the lowest occurs only rarely or not at all. A variation is to have respondents check either *yes* or *no* to indicate their reaction to the item. Rating scales provide a relatively quick method for assessing skills. They could furnish normative data to be used as standards for socially inept individuals and may provide information on the extent or quality of the behavior. Moreover, the data often lead to subsequent treatment. The relationships between these data and behavioral observations, however, are not always significant. Furthermore, important social behaviors that are not on the list will not be evaluated. A third disadvantage is that the reliability across examiners is often not high.

An example of behavior rating is the "Peer Acceptance Scale" (Goodman, Gottlieb, & Harrison, 1972). For this assessment, three faces—smiling, frowning, and one with a question mark—are placed beside the name of each child in the classroom. As the investigator reads the name of each child, the pupils are instructed to (a) circle the smiling face if they thought the classmate selected them for the free-play period, (b) circle the frowning face if they thought the classmate rejected them for the free-play period, or (c) circle the face with a question mark if they thought the classmate neither selected nor rejected them.

Perhaps the most widely used behavior rating scale is the *Piers-Harris Children's Self-Concept Scale* (Piers & Harris, 1969). This scale, made up of 80 declarative statements, requires respondents to indicate whether the item describes the way they feel about themselves. About half of the items are worded positively and half negatively to decrease the probability that youngsters would believe that one type of response or the other was more acceptable.

Another popular scale of this type is *The Child Behavior Checklist* (Achenbach & Edelbrock, 1983), which is designed to obtain parents' reports of their children's social competence and behavior problems. Parents provide information for 20 social-competence items covering the child's activities, involvement with social organizations and friends, and school performance. Parents also rate children on 118 behavior problem items, using a numbered scale to indicate how true the item is.

Another rating scale is *The Social Behavior Assessment* (Stephens, 1979), an inventory of 136 social skills divided into the areas of environmental behaviors, task-related behaviors, interpersonal behaviors, and self-related behaviors. Each of the major categories is further divided into subcategories and skills. Children are rated on a three-point scale from 1 to 3, with 1 representing an acceptable performance.

Observation Techniques

Two other approaches for assessing social and emotional behaviors of handicapped students that should be mentioned are student records and interviews.

Student Records.   According to Hammill (1987), student records are one of the most important, yet most overlooked sources of information. According to him, a thorough review of records could yield a wealth of information and may expedite the delivery of services to a child by shortcutting the administration of several tests and getting right to the point. Because of legal and regulatory measures, the records of individuals are not as easily accessed as they were in the past; however, legally responsible individuals can still study these files.

■ COMMENTARY ■   *It does make sense that we should study all available information on youngsters before scheduling our favorite scales, checklists, and tests. Too often, teachers or psychologists, those called on to assay the attributes of children, do not seek out sources from the past.*

Interviews.   Hammill has described interviews as broad-based assessment techniques that can be scheduled to gather information from parents, teachers, other professionals, and from the students themselves. Interviews can be scheduled to convey information as well as to gather it and can help to establish an atmosphere that will promote an ongoing exchange of information. Whether highly structured or loosely organized, interviews should be planned and purposeful; the interviewer should have specific goals in mind. Teachers and psychologists can use interviews to assess student abilities, aspirations, reinforcers, and other factors that can contribute to planning programs.

Adaptive Behavior Evaluation

In yet another approach to evaluating social and emotional behaviors of LD youth, Weller and colleagues (Weller, Strawser, & Buchanan, 1985) presented a model for determining the extent to which individuals adapt to their environments. This approach requires teachers or other examiners to evaluate students according to the following adaptation/functional attributes:

— Effect of their problems on abilities in other learning areas
— Interrelatedness of academic problems with socialization skills
— Alteration of future life needs and the ability to cope in adult situations
— Amenability of the problems to remediation or compensation
— Effect of the problems on children's socialization skills with peers and adults
— Demonstration of major strengths and weaknesses in various areas of learning
— Consistent avoidance as opposed to ineffective attempts to behave in the problem areas.

Weller and colleagues suggest that teachers and others should take these circumstances into account when determining placement, programming, and research efforts for LD individuals.

Weller believes that the adaptive behavior model encompasses four functional domains. Brief descriptions of these domains follow.

Social coping incorporates behaviors that individuals use to deal with environmental situations such as social problem solving, change and disorganization, space-and-time orientations, and social cause-and-effect relationships.

Relationships include those behaviors used when relating to peers and authority figures. They refer to the degree of involvement in interpersonal activities, the awareness individuals have of interpersonal interactions, and the expectations they have of themselves and others.

Pragmatic language involves the use of language in social situations. Behaviors of this type are the understandings and uses of gestures and humor, the expressions and interpretations of feelings, and the appropriateness and descriptiveness of social communications in general.

Production refers to how individuals act in various classroom and work settings. Included in this category are behaviors related to how working time is spent, how learning is transferred from one task to another, how tasks are organized, what strategies are used for which types of chores, and what types of tasks yield the most productive results.

INTERVENTIONS

According to Schumaker and Hazel (1984b), social competence involves the generative use of a variety of cognitive and overt social skills that lead to positive consequences for individuals and those who interact with them. They are strong advocates of social skills training. They are of the opinion that social skills include such cognitive functions as empathizing with the feelings of others, discriminating and making inferences about social cues, and predicting and evaluating consequences for social behavior. According to them, children with social problems exhibit a high incidence of the following: dropping out of school, being delinquent, having mental health problems, and being given bad conduct discharges from the armed forces. In other words, Schumaker and Hazel believe that, in general, LD individuals have problems in sizing up social situations, knowing what to do, and being able to do something about those situations.

Vaughn (1985) has also commented on the poor social skills of many LD youth by pointing out the following social deviations: at risk for being social rejects and isolates, frequently uninvolved and ignored, frustrated and lonely because of poor social relationships with peers and adults, having a lowered self-concept. In a plea for social skills training, Vaughn urged that learning to instruct social skills become part of our teacher education programs and that teachers arrange situations to instruct those skills directly to learning disabled students.

Zigmond and Brownlee (1980) offer further reasons for instructing social skills to LD students, particularly adolescents: They may need such training to derive maximum benefit from academic instruction, and this type of training may facilitate efforts to mainstream LD individuals and improve their prospects for employment.

Some have maintained that mainstreaming would, of itself, enhance social development of LD students, thus sidestepping the issue of providing direct social skills instruction. Gresham (1982) has some pessimistic evidence on this score. When he reviewed several studies on mainstreaming to determine its inherent effect on social skills, the data indicated that learning disabled children *did not* become better accepted or less rejected, nor did they interact more positively or derive benefits from modeling. In light of those outcomes, Gresham has called for an increased emphasis on directly fostering the social skills of handicapped youth.

Gresham (1982) has recommended that social skills training be arranged depending on the needs and characteristics of the individuals. He suggests three issues that can contribute to the social skills deviations of youth.

1. Do students possess the necessary social skill in the first place? It would be unreasonable to ask youngsters to display social behaviors they were unable to perform.

2. Do students possess the desired social behavior, but not always display it? Students may be unsure or inconsistent as to when, where, and to what extent to engage in the behavior.

3. Does lack of self-control interrupt their ability to demonstrate desired behaviors? Students may be able to perform the behavior at the appropriate time, but too often, competing behaviors interfere.

Depending upon the dimension in which the student's social skills problem falls, Gresham provides the following advice: for the first situation, model and teach the desired behavior; for the second, manipulate antecedents and consequences to solicit the appropriate rate for the behavior; and for the third, teach students self-instructional techniques.

Schumaker and Hazel (1984a) reviewed a number of research articles to identify the social skills that had most often been taught to LD individuals. They identified three *cognitive* social skills through this process:

— Choosing socially acceptable behaviors (for example, when asked to select which of several behaviors to use, LD individuals were significantly more likely than their non-LD peers to choose less socially acceptable responses)
— Discriminating social cues (for example, LD youngsters are not adept at interpreting cues from facial expressions, "body language," and tone of voice)
— Role-taking skills (for example LD individuals generally perform less well than their non-LD peers on tasks where they need to take into account the thoughts and feelings of others).

■ COMMENTARY ■   By *cognitive,* Schumaker and Hazel are referring to what individuals say they would or would not do in some situation or another. Cognitive skills are not necessarily the same as performance skills. As we all know, there are differences between saying and doing.

Madden and Slavin (1983) reviewed several studies on social skills training to determine how skills have been taught. They grouped the techniques into five categories: *coaching* (teaching specific social skills to students and providing feedback), *modeling* (teaching through some form of guided example), *reinforcement* (managing antecedents and consequences for individuals and for group contingencies), *cognitive behavior modification* (managing behaviors by teaching self-monitoring techniques), and *cooperative interventions* (arranging situations whereby students work together for a common goal rather than for individual rewards).

Schumaker and Hazel (1984b) have offered three categories of social skills interventions. Their schema, much like those of Gresham (1982) and Madden and Slavin (1983), is made up of three components: procedures for manipulating antecedent or consequent events, self-control procedures, and instructional procedures. Brief descriptions and examples of these programs follow.

Procedures Manipulating Antecedent or Consequent Events

According to Schumaker and Hazel (1984b), this procedure focuses on changing environmental events in order to increase the probability of appropriate social behaviors occurring in the future, while decreasing the probability that inappropriate behaviors will occur. Strain, Shores, and Timm (1977), in an example of manipulating an antecedent event, demonstrated that when peers were asked to encourage behaviorally handicapped preschoolers to engage in social interactions, the frequency of those involvements increased. Broden, Hall, Dunlap, and Clark (1970) have provided an example of manipulating a consequent event, demonstrating that when reinforcement was contingent on appropriate social behaviors, those behaviors increased. Similarly, Rosenbaum, O'Leary, and Jacob (1975) have shown that group contingencies influenced the social behaviors of children; when reinforcement was dependent on the acceptable performances of several youngsters, their behaviors generally improved.

Another example of using a consequence to alter a socially inappropriate behavior is found in research by Lovitt, Lovitt, Eaton, and Kirkwood (1973). The subject of the study was an emotionally disturbed boy who occasionally blurted out a sexual or bathroom-type word. The intervention was to remove his friend on each inappropriate outburst. When the boy let loose one of his words, the friend, who was sitting nearby, went up to him and said, "Jon, I don't want to sit by you when you behave like that." Whereupon the friend picked up his materials and moved away. Later, he took his seat near Jon when the latter spoke to him about something appropriate. This technique was effective and long lasting.

Self-Control Procedures

Students themselves are given responsibilities for their instruction in self-control procedures. They may record the extent to which certain social behaviors occur, evaluate aspects of their performance, select features of their own training (for example, schedule or intervention), or administer some other instructional component.

There is a vast literature on self-management, a fair portion of which pertains to the management of social skills. Kaufman and O'Leary (1972), for example, have demonstrated that self-control procedures can curtail disruptive behaviors of non-LD youngsters.

Layne, Rickard, Jones, and Lyman (1976) have shown how a self-management procedure can alter behaviors of behaviorally disturbed youngsters. Following a baseline condition, the boys were instructed to assess several behaviors that had to do with being organized and productive. They were given checklists on which they responded to the following questions:

1. Are all necessary supplies available?
2. Are all assignments complete?
3. Are papers organized in your notebook?
4. Did you arrive on time?
5. Did you obtain missed work if you had been absent?

The data indicated that not only did the students respond accurately to those queries, but they showed significant improvement in their schoolwork. [Chapter 10 also discussed self-management research with LD students.]

Instructional Procedures

Schumaker and Hazel (1984b) identified three types of instructional procedures—descriptive, modeling, and rehearsal–feedback—that have been arranged to influence social skills of LD youth.

Descriptive Procedures.   In the descriptive approach, teachers typically explain to students how certain skills should be appropriately performed. They might initially offer a rationale for learning the skills, then define the steps for displaying the skills, give examples of each, and discuss possible consequences for engaging or not engaging in them.

In one intervention of this type, Porterfield, Herbert-Jackson, and Risley (1976) arranged contingent observation periods for disruptive youngsters. Their intervention went into effect contingent on behaviors of five types—aggression, crying and fussing, tantruming, destructive use of toys, and creating a dangerous situation. Contingent observation has four elements:

□ The caregiver briefly describes the form and inappropriateness of the behavior to the child and tells him how he should have behaved.

□ The caregiver moves the child to the periphery of the activity, sits him on the floor without play materials, and tells him to observe the appropriate social behaviors of the other children.

□ After noticing that the child has been watching quietly for a brief period of time, the caregiver asks the child if he is ready to rejoin the play activities and behave properly.

□ The caregiver gives the child positive attention for behaving appropriately with the group.

Data evidenced that this procedure was quite successful.

Modeling Procedures.   In the modeling approach, social skills are demonstrated for the youth either by the teacher, a videotape, or by another student. Some of the programs require students to verbalize the steps of the method as they watch the model and then attempt to engage in the activities themselves.

Csapo's (1972) research showed how modeling can be effectively arranged for a group of emotionally disturbed youngsters. Peers were selected to act as role models for the disturbed students. They were asked to sit beside the misbehaving pupils, with whom they were matched, and show them how to behave properly. Their disturbing mates were instructed, in turn, to model the behaviors of their peers. When the disturbed students behaved as they should, their peers were told to praise them for their specific deeds. Csapo's results were impressive; behaviors for all disturbed children improved.

Rehearsal and Feedback Procedures.   Rehearsal and feedback is a two-stage approach. Following the verbal rehearsal of skill steps to ensure that individuals know the sequence by memory, the learner is typically provided with feedback on the efforts to comply with the program steps. An example of this technique is the *SIGEP* program (Trupin, Gilchrist, Mauiro, & Fay, 1979). When it is scheduled, children are taught the meaning of the SIGEP letters, and instructed to say them when proper occasions arise:

— Stop and think: Strategies are taught to avoid impulsive or angry responses that get in the way of good thinking.
— Identify: Information is gathered; the facts and feelings of the situation are identified; and the problem is defined.
— Generate: Children are instructed to think more broadly and creatively by brainstorming many ways to solve a problem.
— Evaluate: Each solution is evaluated according to its consequences, and with consideration of fairness and the rights and feelings of others.
— Plan: After a solution has been chosen, a plan is developed for carrying out the necessary action.

Commercial Social Skills Programs

Schumaker and Hazel (1984b) have noted that most research programs on social skills training and the majority of commercial social skills programs rely on combinations of the approaches just discussed. Few of these programs are based on only one of the three general methods just identified. Following are brief descriptions of six commercial social skills programs at the elementary and secondary levels. The components of the Schumaker and Hazel schema presented earlier in this chapter are also noted where they are included.

Elementary Level.   The goals of *Aware* (Elardo & Cooper, 1977) are to assist children to increase their ability to understand the thoughts and feelings of others, become more accepting of individual differences, improve problem-solving skills, and increase respect and concern for others. The specific skills to be taught in the program include:

☐ Describe and discuss feelings.

☐ Discuss fears and anxieties.

☐ Describe positive characteristics about self.

☐ Describe physical differences.

☐ Generate alternative solutions to conflict.

☐ Make and keep friends.

The teacher follows suggestions in the handbook for each topic and guides the class in discussions and role-playing situations. This program has several instructional components, as described earlier by Schumaker and Hazel (1984b)—descriptions, modeling, rehearsal-feedback, and manipulating antecedent events.

The intended goals for *Developing Understanding of Self and Others*—DUSO (Dinkmeyer & Dinkmeyer, Jr., 1982) are for students to increase their ability to express their feelings and learn to discuss relationships between feelings, goals, and behaviors. The eight units focus on the student's understanding of self, feelings, others, independence, goals, resourcefulness, emotional maturity, and choices and consequences. The program includes a wide variety of materials and activities—singing, drawing, responding to stories, role playing, discussing situations, interacting with puppets—and has the following components from the Schumaker and Hazel (1984b) schema: descriptions, rehearsal–feedback, and manipulation of antecedent events.

One of the most popular social skills programs for elementary age pupils is *The ACCEPTS Program* (Walker, McConnell, Holmes, Todis, Walker, & Golden, 1983). The goals of the curriculum are for students to learn about initiating and maintaining positive relationships with others, increasing peer acceptance, increasing success in regular classrooms, and coping with social environments. Among the specific skills are listening to the teacher, doing your best work, using the right voice, taking turns talking, and making friends. The teacher follows five steps in teaching the skills:

1. Define the skill.
2. Model a number of positive and negative examples.
3. Lead role-playing activities.
4. Assess mastery of content through role-playing situations.
5. Establish contracts with students to try the skills in situations outside the class.

Three features from Schumaker and Hazel's reference are emphasized in this program: description, modeling, and rehearsal–feedback.

Secondary Level.   A popular approach for adolescents is *Asset* (Hazel, Schumaker, Sherman, & Sheldon-Wildgen, 1982). The primary goal is for group members to increase specific social interaction skills—giving positive feedback, giving negative feedback, accepting negative feedback, resisting peer pressure, solving problems, negotiating, following instructions, and conversing. Lessons on these skills follow this format:

□ Review notes sent home to inform parents of progress.
□ Review previously learned skills.
□ Discuss positive and negative examples of the target skill shown on videotape.
□ Examine skill sheets that contain steps for carrying out the target skill.
□ Practice the target skill by rehearsing the steps verbally and by role playing.

Features from Schumaker and Hazel that form the structure of this program are descriptions, modeling, manipulating consequent events, rehearsal–feedback, manipulating antecedent events, and self-control.

The goals of *Skillstreaming the Adolescent* (Goldstein, Sprafkin, Gershaw, & Klein, 1980) are for students to improve their prosocial and interpersonal skills and their abilities to manage and plan. Specific skills taught in the program include: starting a conversation, asking a question, asking for help, expressing one's feelings, asking permission, using self-control, answering complaints, dealing with contradictory messages, and deciding on one's abilities. The format for teaching the skills has seven components:

1. Define and discuss the skill.
2. Distribute cards that contain the steps for engaging in the skill.
3. Model appropriate use of the skill.
4. Organize role-playing situations.

5. Give and invite feedback.

6. Provide social reinforcement.

7. Assist students in planning homework assignments.

Four features from the Schumaker and Hazel list are emphasized—descriptions, modeling, rehearsal-feedback, and manipulating consequent events.

The goals of *Social Consequences Series* (Interpretive Education, 1979) are to instruct youth about the social consequences of work, the home, and the school. Specific skills in the program focus on eight characteristics: dependability, interpersonal relations, customer relations, family problems, home conflicts, responsibility, authority, and peer group pressure. The overview serves as an advance organizer, and activities progress from easy to hard. Problem solving is taught by having students identify the problem, generate alternatives, and identify consequences. Features from Schumaker and Hazel in that program are descriptions, modeling, and manipulating consequences.

PROGRAM SELECTION AND IMPLEMENTATION

Schumaker, Pederson, Hazel, and Meyen (1983) identified a set of questions for teachers to ask as they select a social skills curriculum for the mildly handicapped students:

☐ Does the curriculum promote social competence? Do students improve socially in the opinions of others as a result of the program?

☐ Does the curriculum accommodate the learning characteristics of the mildly handicapped? Does the program take into account the learning strengths and weaknesses of the students?

☐ Does the curriculum target the social skill deficits of the mildly handicapped population? Does the program focus on the specific skills of youngsters in the consumer's school?

☐ Does the curriculum provide training in situations as well as skills? Are students given opportunities to practice their acquired skills in real situations?

☐ Does the curriculum incorporate instructional methodologies found to be effective with the mildly handicapped? Have instructional features, deemed as effective, been blended into the program?

Researchers at Utah State University have for some years studied various aspects of social skills. Based on findings from their investigations, Young (1987) has suggested a number of instructional guidelines for setting up quality social skills programs and for increasing the probability that learning acquired from those efforts will generalize to other situations.

1. Organize social skills instruction with groups of students, some of whom are handicapped and others nonhandicapped. Data indicate that these heterogeneous combinations are the most beneficial, particularly when the net effect to all pupils is taken into account. (For additional comments on the arrangement of groups, see the material on cooperative learning in Chapter 10.)

2. Provide students with many opportunities to practice their skills, particularly during the initial period of training. It is essential that students practice their new skills a number of times and in a wide variety of settings.

3. Use peers in both social skills instruction and for encouraging the use of social skills in the natural environment. It has been demonstrated that handicapped and nonhandicapped secondary students can effectively provide social skills instruction. Often, those peers are more motivating, hence influential, than are regular teachers, especially at the secondary level.

4. Extend effective social skills training to the home and community by involving parents and others. Parental involvement is an extremely effective strategy for extending the use of social skills to the home and community, for they can reinforce and give feedback for social skills that have been introduced at school.

5. Train students to self-evaluate and self-monitor their social skills performance. When they are taught to self-evaluate and self-record their social behaviors, the probability is increased that those traits will generalize to situations other than those in which the skills were trained. (See material on self-management in Chapter 10.)

6. Teach specific social skills through direct instructional methods. That is, demonstrate the precise behavior of concern, not one that is closely related. Demonstrating specific skills for students and providing guided and independent practice opportunities designed to develop fluent use of skills increases the probability that behaviors will change.

With respect to which social skills should be taught, and where and when to teach them, Lovitt (1987) advocates that teachers should first survey the social skills of their pupils and note which behaviors are in the most need of instruction. Teachers should then identify the places and times of day that the identified skills are most likely to occur. Table 11.2 demonstrates how this procedure can be followed. The left column of the table lists 14 social skills that the teacher in this example wanted to develop, and the top row shows 9 situations in which the teacher felt these skills were most likely to occur. Within this matrix, the teacher wrote in "Xs" to indicate that the probability is high that the behavior is likely to occur in the listed circumstance.

Once teachers have prepared this type of a plan for a class or an individual, the next step is to decide how to assist pupils to develop the skills (for example, modeling or reinforcement or some other approach discussed in this chapter). Although a matrix such as is shown in Table 11.2 is useful, teachers should seize

■ TABLE 11.2 ■   Matrix for Identifying Social Skills and Likely Situations for Their Occurrence

Skill	Bus	Opening Exercises	Reading	Lunch	Recess	Music	Dance	Drama	Sports
Saying please/thank you				X	X				
Looking/acting interested	X	X	X		X	X	X	X	
Asking questions	X	X	X	X		X	X	X	X
Giving compliments	X	X	X	X	X	X	X	X	X
Being generally positive	X	X	X	X	X	X	X	X	
Asking for help			X	X	X	X	X	X	X
Offering assistance			X	X	X	X	X	X	X
Providing support						X	X	X	X
Taking turns	X	X	X		X	X	X	X	X
Being cooperative			X			X	X	X	X
Accepting criticism			X			X	X	X	X
Apologizing	X				X				X
Accepting apology	X				X				
Overlooking "goofs"		X		X	X	X	X	X	X

Source: Reprinted by permission from Tom Lovitt, "Social Skills Training: Which Ones and Where to Do It?" *Journal of Reading, Writing, and Learning Disabilities, 3,* 1987, p. 216.

each opportunity to work on the designated behaviors, whether they occur during the high probability times or during regular classes.

This type of social skills instruction has been referred to as *incidental teaching,* since it takes place along with instruction on another subject. Teaching in this manner contrasts with the approach some teachers now rely on to instruct social skills. That is, teach one skill at a time as it is introduced in a published program; teach it to all the students whether they need it or not; and instruct it at a set time of day, just as is done with reading, writing, and math. Proponents of incidental teaching believe it is a far more natural and flexible way in which to instruct social skills, for they are important in every activity, not just during a designated period.

COMMENTS AND DISCUSSION POINTS

- We need to be more aware of the many types and categories of what are referred to as "social skills." There are dozens of social circumstances out there—social dealings at home, on the job, in the community. It would help to have a chart or taxonomy to organize social traits with reference to various situations. Certainly Greenspan's work (1981) is a step in that direction.

- Although a number of aims or standards are available for most of the academic subjects, we don't have many for the various social skills. It would help to have data on how skilled individuals should be with respect to certain social behaviors or with certain combinations of behaviors.

- Some interesting research could be conducted with socially or emotionally gifted persons. We could learn about the standards for skills or sets of characteristics shared by those individuals.

- More accurate and inexpensive ways to assess social attributes are needed. For example, there must be better ways to judge individuals' status among their friends than to rely on sociometric techniques, checklists, or rating scales. One alternative would be to simply observe and listen to people to see how they get along. Moreover, if we want to know how individuals go about making friends, we could ask them how they do it and watch them in the process. If we want to know how people *don't* get along, we could also watch that process. We could also observe individuals interacting at the dinner table, on the bus, as they stand in lines, as they call one another on the phone, or as they negotiate. As we observe those situations, we could take notes and ask participants to explain their behaviors and motives. We certainly wouldn't have to administer a test in order to acquire information about social graces. We have been duped into adopting a test mentality, believing that all we need to do is to select the proper test, have a qualified individual administer it, analyze the data, and then act on the findings. Commercial tests often distort reality. They pretend to see, hear, think, and make decisions for us. But they don't. As a result (because of the disuse syndrome), we "unlearn" how to see, hear, think, and make decisions.

- According to Shumaker and Hazel (1984b), results of most research on social skills are based on data that were collected from tests or surveys in contrived situations. The information from those unnatural assessments has often been the basis for choosing the contents of social skills programs. When it comes to making inferences to the real world, the validity of those data, therefore, is questionable.

- Schumaker and Hazel (1984b) have also informed us that changes in social skills have typically been assessed in contrived situations by relying on measures taken immediately before and after training. Rarely have changes been shown in naturally occurring interactions in natural environments during extended periods following training. Surely we can improve on that.

■ Although the group research on social skills shows that in general, LD pupils are worse off in practically every type of social skill than their non-LD peers, many of them are socially normal, even gifted. We should spend some time discovering why some LD youngsters are socially adept.

■ The overlap between the performances of a group of LD children and a group of non-disabled youngsters on about any social skill is quite large. A significant proportion of the non-LD youth are as much in need of social skills training as are their LD mates.

■ Teachers or instructors of social skills should be on the lookout for events and circumstances in the world in which evidence of inappropriate, adequate, and exemplary social skills are noted. Advice columns in newspapers are filled with incidents that could serve as themes for instructing social skills.

■ Schumaker and Hazel (1984b) reported that changes in overt behaviors have rarely been related to improved social relationships, social standing, social confidence, and individuals' satisfaction with their own lives. Researchers would do well to incorporate measures of these attributes in their studies.

■ We need to consider incidental teaching when it comes to instructing social skills. It seems inappropriate to set up specific times of the day to teach social skills, just as we teach reading and math. We should instead work to develop social skills as occasions occur naturally throughout the course of the day.

■ Youngsters should be encouraged to self-manage their social behaviors as much as possible. When individuals are trained to pinpoint crucial social behaviors, to record and graph the frequencies with which those behaviors occur, and to select their own interventions, the chances are greatly increased that the effects on those target behaviors will generalize to several situations.

■ Some individuals can go a long way on very little content, if they have adequate social skills. The classic example is from the movie *Being There*, in which Peter Sellers had learned a number of lines when watching television and repeated them over and over in various situations. Because he didn't say anything beyond those lines, managed to say them at the proper time, and had reasonably well-developed social skills, people thought he was wise. We might take this example into account as we set out to develop social skills—but without carrying it too far.

REFERENCES

Achenback, T.M., & Edelbrock, C. (1983). *Manual for the Child Behavior Checklist and Revised Child Behavior Profile*. Burlington, VT: Queen City Printers.

Broden, M.; Hall, R.V.; Dunlap, A.; & Clark, R. (1970). Effects of teacher attention and a token reinforcement system in a junior high school special education class. *Exceptional Children, 36*, 341–349.

Bruininks, V.L. (1978). Actual and perceived peer status of learning-disabled students in mainstream programs. *The Journal of Special Education, 12,* 51–58.

Bryan, T.H. (1974). Peer popularity of learning disabled children. *Journal of Learning Disabilities, 7,* 621–625.

Bryan, T., & Pflaum, S. (1978). Social interactions of learning disabled children: A linguistic, social and cognitive analysis. *Learning Disability Quarterly, 1,* 70–79.

Cartledge, G.; Stupay, D.; & Kaczala, C. (1986). Social skills and social perception of LD and nonhandicapped elementary-school students. *Learning Disability Quarterly, 9,* 226–234.

Csapo, M. (1972). Peer models reverse the "one bad apple spoils the barrel" theory. *Teaching Exceptional Children,* Fall, 20–24.

Dinkmeyer, D. & Dinkmeyer, D., Jr. (1982). *Developing understanding of self and others— revised* (DUSO). Circle Pines, MN: American Guidance Service.

Dudley-Marling, C.C., & Edmiaston, R. (1985). Social status of learning disabled children and adolescents: A review. *Learning Disability Quarterly, 8,* 189–204.

Edmonson, B.; deJung, J.; Leland, W.; & Leach, E. (1974). *The test of social inference.* New York: Educational Activities, Inc.

Elardo, P., & Cooper, M. (1977). *Aware: Activities for social development.* Menlo Park, CA: Addison-Wesley.

Epstein, M.H.; Cullinan, D.; & Nieminen, G. (1984). Social behavior problems of learning disabled and normal girls. *Journal of Learning Disabilities, 17,* 609–911.

Garrett, M.K., & Crump, W.D. (1980). Peer acceptance, teacher preference, and self-appraisal of social status among learning disabled students. *Learning Disability Quarterly, 3,* 42–48.

Gerber, P.J., & Zinkgraf, S.A. (1982). A comparative study of social-perceptual ability in learning disabled and nonhandicapped students. *Learning Disability Quarterly, 5,* 374–378.

Goldstein, A.P.; Sprafkin, R.P.; Gershaw, N.J.; & Klein, P. (1980). *Skillstreaming the adolescent.* Champaign, IL: Research Press.

Goodman, H.; Gottlieb, J.; & Harrison, R.H. (1972). Social acceptance of EMRs integrated into a nongraded elementary school. *American Journal of Mental Deficiency, 76,* 412–417.

Greenspan, S. (1981). Defining childhood social competence: A proposed working model. In B.K. Keogh (Ed.), *Advances in Special Education,* Vol. 3. Greenwich, CT: JAI Press.

Gresham, J.M. (1982). Misguided mainstreaming: The case for social skills training with handicapped children. *Exceptional Children, 48,* 420–433.

Gresham, J.M., & Reschly, D.J. (1986). Social skill deficits and low peer acceptance of mainstreamed learning disabled children. *Learning Disability Quarterly, 9,* 23–32.

Hammill, D.D. (Ed.) (1987). *Assessing the abilities and instructional needs of students.* Austin, TX: PRO-ED.

Hazel, J.S.; Schumaker, J.B.; Sherman, J.A.; & Sheldon-Wildgen, J. (1982). *Asset: A social skills program for adolescents.* Champaign, IL: Research Press.

Interpretive Education. (1979). *Social consequences series.* Mt. Kisco, NY.

Jones, C.J. (1985). Analysis of the self-concepts of handicapped students. *Remedial and Special Education, 6*(5), 32–36.

Kaufman, K.F., & O'Leary, K.D. (1972). Reward, cost, and self-evaluation procedures for disruptive adolescents in a psychiatric hospital school. *Journal of Applied Behavior Analysis, 5,* 293–309.

Layne, C.C.; Rickard, H.C.; Jones, M.T.; & Lyman, R.D. (1976). Accuracy of self-monitoring on a variable ratio schedule of observer verification. *Behavior Therapy, 7,* 481–488.

Licht, B.C. (1983). Cognitive-motivational factors that contribute to the achievement of learning-disabled children. *Journal of Learning Disabilities, 16,* 483–490.

Lovitt, T.C. (1987). Social skills training: Which ones and where to do it? *Journal of Reading, Writing and Learning Disabilities, 3,* 213–221.

Lovitt, T.C.; Lovitt, A.O.; Eaton, M.D.; & Kirkwood, M. (1973). The deceleration of inappropriate comments by a natural consequence. *Journal of School Psychology, 11,* 148–154.

Madden, N.A., & Slavin, R.E. (1983). Mainstreaming students with mild handicaps: Academic and social outcomes. *Review of Educational Research, 53,* 519–569.

McConaughy, S.H. (1986). Social competence and behavioral problems of learning disabled boys aged 12–16. *Journal of Learning Disabilities, 19,* 101–106.

Piers, E.V., & Harris, D.B. (1969). *Manual for the Piers-Harris Children's Self-Concept Scale.* Nashville, TN: Counselor Recordings and Tests.

Porterfield, J.K.; Herbert-Jackson, E.; & Risley, T.R. (1976). Contingent observation: An effective and acceptable procedure of reducing disruptive behavior of young children in a group setting. *Journal of Applied Behavior Analysis, 9,* 55–64.

Rosenbaum, A.; O'Leary, K.D.; & Jacob, R.G. (1975). Behavioral intervention with hyperactive children: Group consequences as a supplement to individual contingencies. *Behavior Therapy, 6,* 315–323.

Sabornie, E.J. (1983). A comparison of the regular classroom sociometric status of EMR, LD, ED, and nonhandicapped high school students. Unpublished doctoral dissertation, University of Virginia, Charlottesville.

Sabornie, E.J., & Kauffman, J.M. (1986). Social acceptance of learning disabled adolescents. *Learning Disability Quarterly, 9,* 55–60.

Schumaker, J.B., & Hazel, J.S. (1984a). Social skills assessment and training for the learning disabled: Who's on first and what's on second? Part I. *Journal of Learning Disabilities, 17,* 422–431.

Schumaker, J.B., & Hazel, J.S. (1984b). Social skills assessment and training for the learning disabled: Who's on first and what's on second? Part II. *Journal of Learning Disabilities, 17,* 492–499.

Schumaker, J.B.; Hazel, J.S.; Sherman, J.A.; & Sheldon, J. (1982). Social skill performances of learning disabled, non-learning disabled, and delinquent adolescents. *Learning Disability Quarterly, 5,* 388–397.

Schumaker, J.B.; Pederson, C.S.; Hazel, J.S.; & Meyen, E.L. (1983). Social skills curricula for mildly handicapped adolescents: A review. *Focus on exceptional children, 16*(4), 1–16.

Scranton, T.R., & Ryckman, D.B. (1979). Sociometric status of learning disabled children in an integrative program. *Journal of Learning Disabilities, 12,* 402–407.

Skrtic, T.M. (1980). The regular classroom interactions of learning disabled adolescents and their teachers. Research Report No. 8, Institute for Research on Learning Disabilities, University of Kansas, Lawrence.

Stephens, T.M. (1978). *Social skills in the classroom.* Columbus, OH: Cedars Press.

———. (1979). *Social behavior assessment.* Columbus, OH: Cedars Press.

Strain, P.S.; Shores, R.E.; & Timm, M.A. (1977). Effects of peer social initiations on the behavior of withdrawn preschool children. *Journal of Applied Behavior Analysis, 10,* 289–298.

Trupin, E.W.; Gilchrist, L.; Maiuro, R.D.; & Fay, G. (1979). Social skills training for learning-disabled children. In L.A. Hamerlynck (Ed.), *Behavioral systems for the developmentally disabled: II institutional, clinic and community environments.* New York: Brunner/Mazel.

Vaughn, S. (1985). Why teach social skills to learning disabled students? *Journal of Learning Disabilities, 18,* 588–591.

Walker, H.M. (1970). *Problem behavior identification checklist.* Los Angeles: Western Psychological Services.

Walker, H.M.; McConnell, S.; Holmes, D.; Todis, B.; Walker, J.; & Golden, H. (1983). *The Walker social skills curriculum: The ACCEPTS program.* Austin, TX: PRO-ED.

Weiss, E. (1984). Learning disabled children's understanding of social interactions of peers. *Journal of Learning Disabilities, 17,* 612–615.

Weller, C.; Strawser, S.; & Buchanan, M. (1985). Adaptive behavior: Designator of a continuum of severity of learning disabled individuals. *Journal of Learning Disabilities, 18,* 200–204.

Young, K.R. (1987). Future directions in social skills training, or where should we be going and why? *The Special Educator, 7*(7), 1–3.

Zigmond, N., & Brownlee, J. (1980). Social skills training for adolescents with learning disabilities. *Exceptional Education Quarterly, 1*(2), 77–83.

PART IV

EXPANDING DIRECTIONS

Chapter 12

Little Girl in White by James McNeill Whistler (*c.* 1890/1900). Courtesy of the National Gallery of Art, Washington, Chester Dale Collection.

LEARNING DISABILITIES IN EARLY CHILDHOOD

OUTLINE

Rationale for Identifying
    Preschoolers

Screening and Assessment
    Instruments

Screening, Predicting, and Follow-up

Types of Early Intervention
    Programs

Interventions with Preschoolers

Microcomputer Programs

Comments and Discussion Points

MAIN IDEAS

- Theoretical, clinical, and fiscal justifications for early childhood interventions and discussions of successful programs
- Screening and assessment instruments
- Screening for learning disabilities and predicting which youngsters will fail, representative screening programs, ability of teachers to predict success of children, criticisms of this predictive approach, and alternative methods
- General types of early intervention programs
- Examples of interventions with preschoolers that includes information on research studies, measurement issues, and institutes on early childhood research
- Microcomputer programs for preschoolers who have language disorders and are mildly handicapped and recommendations for implementing programs for these youngsters

OVERVIEW

Perhaps the biggest growth area in education over the past three decades has been the instruction of preschool children. This growth has been more pronounced for LD and other handicapped preschoolers. Although most educators, parents, and government officials agree that some sort of education is imperative for handicapped preschoolers, there is considerable debate on a number of issues.

    In this chapter justifications for establishing preschool programs are offered and several of the issues that pertain to this topic are addressed. The first section offers justifications for being concerned with preschoolers who are developmentally delayed or learning disabled, for determining who they are, and to what extent they are disabled or delayed. The second section describes some common instruments for screening and assessing preschoolers. The third reviews representative studies that screened preschoolers in an effort to determine who would or would not succeed in school and then followed up those youngsters' progress. The fourth section is a brief discussion of the types of programs arranged for handicapped preschoolers. Research on selected preschool intervention programs is discussed in the fifth section, and a few microcomputer programs for preschoolers are reviewed in the last section. Comments on programs and research for preschool youngsters with learning disabilities conclude the chapter.

———— RATIONALE FOR IDENTIFYING PRESCHOOLERS ————

According to a number of psychologists and educators, it is important to assess youngsters in their early years because during that time, developmental disorders of different types and degrees are first suspected and can be recognized. Since the preschool years represent a critical period during which reasonable prevention and intervention efforts are most effective, professionals and families must respond to the needs of preschoolers whose development is characterized by certain obvious deviations (*Learning Disability Quarterly,* 1986).

During the preschool years, learning disabilities are frequently noted as specific deficits in language and speech development, in reasoning abilities, and in other behaviors required in early academic achievement. These deficits may occur concomitantly with problems in self-regulation, social interaction, or motor performance. Various signs of learning disabilities may be seen in the same child at different stages and as a result of a variety of circumstances.

Theoretical and Clinical Bases for Early Interventions

Guralnick and Bennett (1987) have offered a detailed argument for early childhood interventions. According to them, findings from diverse areas of inquiry support the notion that the early years are special ones and that environmental events can substantially alter the course of development during that period. Developmental psychologists, working in laboratories in the 1950s and 1960s, discovered that, contrary to prevailing thinking, infants were extraordinarily competent beings who processed information and actively participated in their own development. Neuropsychologists speculated that a significant proportion of an individual's intellectual competence was determined by four years of age. This concept further stimulated interest in the early period. Psychoanalysts also focused attention on early childhood relationships by emphasizing both the primacy of early happenings and the long-term and pervasive consequences adverse early experiences might have on later social and personality development. Indeed, when research reports suggested that the long-term prognosis of children raised in deprived environments could be significantly altered through early intervention,

Michael J. Guralnick is currently the Director of the Child Development and Mental Retardation Center and Professor of Psychology and Pediatrics at the University of Washington. He is a former president of the Council for Exceptional Children's Division for Early Childhood and of the American Association of University Affiliated Programs. Over the years, Dr. Guralnick has conducted research and demonstration projects in early childhood intervention, mainstreaming, social skills development, and peer relations. He has most recently provided a thorough analysis of the effectiveness of early intervention for at-risk and handicapped children in an anthology edited with Dr. Forrest Bennett.

many considered those reports as confirming evidence for both the importance and malleability of early childhood development.

In the face of this evidence, some educators were swept away by the notion that most delayed youngsters could be rehabilitated if environments were properly altered early on. Because of these overly optimistic expectations, many educators were later disillusioned when programs failed to meet their expectations. Consequently, several educators began championing the genetic cause, proclaiming that heredity played a more important role in development than did environment.

Currently, there is a respect for the power of genetic factors in governing complex psychological processes and for recognizing the limits of environmental events. Nonetheless, recent investigations have clarified and extended views about environmental interventions and can now provide a rationale suggesting the importance of the early years.

Researchers have learned, for example, that parental characteristics such as responsivity contingent on child initiations, the quality and quantity of verbal interactions, the provision of numerous toys and materials, the expression of warmth and affection, and maternal sensitivity are all associated with a child's development. More specifically, Guralnick and Bennett (1987) mentioned a few parent–child language strategies that appear to have instructional value: adjustments in pitch, in semantic and syntactic complexity, care in pacing and in reducing disfluencies, sensitive timing of modeling and imitation, and the creation of conversational sequences that expand and add clarity to the form and function of children's language. All of these seem to contribute to the remarkable achievement of learning language during the early years of life. In fact, as added emphasis, the researchers warned that if parents do *not* make these adjustments, there is a chance that their children's language will not develop properly. Two important factors that have profound significance on language development are discussed here.

Developmental Continuity.   One developmental model suggests that continuity originates from early contingent parental responsiveness, which creates a generalized expectancy in infants that they can have an effect on their environment. In other words, infants learn to count on their caregivers. As a consequence, very young children who experience a higher level of responsiveness are more likely to explore and interact with their environments, to probe continually and extract information from their social and physical surroundings, and generally, to create a highly favorable and stimulating environment for themselves. Guralnick and Bennett (1987) speculate that the quality of children's affective, social, and motivational processes emerge from the quality of these early interactions. In turn, these processes serve to influence subsequent interactions of both a cognitive and noncognitive nature, further strengthening behavioral dispositions and establishing positive directions for development. The integrity and coherence of children's interactions with their world during this period suggest that it may be difficult to achieve substantial modifications at a later time.

■ COMMENTARY ■   *Other psychologists and educators would strongly debate this point, maintaining that any time is a good time to learn. Certainly, the data are not all in on this issue.*

Sroufe's position on this matter is certainly in line with that of Guralnick and Bennett. He, too, stressed the importance of early experience:

> We cannot assume that early experiences will somehow be canceled out by later experience. Lasting consequences of early inadequate experience may be subtle and complex, taking the form of increased vulnerability to certain kinds of stress, for example, or becoming manifest only when the individual attempts to establish intimate adult relationships or engage in parenting. But there will be consequences. [Sroufe, 1979, p. 840]

Early Experience of Handicapped Children.   Guralnick and Bennett (1987) argue that the early years may be even more crucial for children with behavioral handicaps; for the disabilities they display and the conditions surrounding their handicaps may serve to intensify the significance of early experiences. The researchers are aware that although there are seriously handicapped children who are highly resilient and capable of overcoming a difficult period in early childhood, the probability is great that their abilities to cope, adapt, and reorient themselves may be limited and fragile.

Guralnick and Bennett point out that certain characteristics of handicapped children make it extremely difficult for parents to create social and physical environments that are likely to encourage development. Following are examples of a few problems that may arise in this regard and their probable consequences.

Disruptions in caregiver–child interactions.   Research and conventional wisdom indicate that establishing secure attachments during neonatal and early infancy periods between handicapped children and their caregivers is difficult to accomplish for at least two reasons. The difficulty arises, for one, because of certain characteristics of handicapped children, especially their inability to signal and display affective responses that engage the caregiver. Many handicapped children are simply not as ingratiating as are their nonhandicapped peers. The second reason pertains to the fact that the parents' awareness of their child's handicap, and the disruptive and stress-producing processes that often accompany this awareness, may interfere with the formation of secure attachments. The presence of a handicapped youngster in a family strongly tests the fabric of that unit.

Related complications and factors.   Most of the problems that handicapped children experience during this early period are neither transient nor circumscribed. Several of them are long lasting and are likely to affect or cause other problems.

Although many secondary complications do not become apparent until children enter different phases of their lives, the roots of these problems can often be detected during the early years. Difficulties in establishing relationships with one's peers, an important predictor of later adjustment problems, is perhaps the most vivid example. In a real sense, these difficulties are partly reflections of other problems that seem to be evident in the early years—for example, communicative disorders, lack of responsiveness of peers, an inability to appropriately initiate social interactions, and even emotional problems. Guralnik and Bennett (1987) underscored Sroufe's (1979) earlier remark when they warned that the failure to intervene early, to ensure that the initial placement is of the least restrictive nature, will surely have lifelong consequences.

Successful Interventions

Another justification for early interventions, according to Guralnik and Bennett, is the success that has been achieved with a number of programs. Although some of those intervention projects are not as elegant as one might like, there is cause for optimism. With that in mind, Guralnik and Bennett offered the following advice when evaluating such studies:

> Whether or not such studies are available [that provide conclusive proof as to the merits of early intervention], it is important to attempt to identify program elements that appear robust across studies, to consider carefully patterns that may appear and internal consistencies that may emerge, and to weigh outcomes in terms of their logical and developmental credibility. Isolated bits of evidence may seem tangential

and circumstantial at first glance, but in their totality may help establish important directions regarding the effectiveness of early interventions. [1987, p. 24]

(Summaries of a few successful interventions are included later in this chapter.)

Fiscal Reasons for Early Childhood Programs

Yet another reason—beyond remediation—for the early identification and treatment of youngsters with developmental disorders has to do with money. The costs of setting up early intervention programs must be carefully weighed against the long-term benefits, for the expenses of special education are considerably higher than those for regular education.

When Kakalik, Furry, Thomas, and Carney (1981) calculated the costs of special education and related services, they learned that the expenses for special education were 2.17 times greater than those for regular education and related services. In the same year, Sweinhart and Weikart (1981) conducted a cost–benefit analysis of early intervention programs and reported that the reduced need for special education services and increases in lifetime earnings were among the significant benefits of those projects. They claimed that the cost per child for a two-year intervention program was $5,984 (in 1979 dollars), and the benefits were as follows:

— A savings of $3,353 per child because children with preschool instruction required fewer years of special education
— Increased lifetime earnings of $10,798 per child, projected from improved educational status
— An estimated $668 per child as the value of the mothers' released time while their children attended preschool

These benefits amounted to a return of 248% on the original investment.

In yet another study that determined costs, Weiss (1981) acquired evidence to show that the INREAL (INclass REActive Language) intervention program made a per pupil difference of $1,283.76 for the three years of that project. Moreover, the data indicated that the intervention made a difference of $3,073.16 for each bilingual pupil for that period.

——— SCREENING AND ASSESSMENT INSTRUMENTS ———

This section describes a few commonly administered screening and assessment instruments. Screening instruments are designed to provide teachers or other caregivers with an initial and rather broad overview of preschoolers' traits or behaviors. Information gained from screening is intended to indicate that either the preschooler is developing on schedule or is in need of further assessment. The idea is to provide a general picture of competence, not to offer specific evidence as to what a child's problems might be. Certainly screening instruments are not intended as devices that suggest what should be done to remediate the problems.

Assessment devices are given after a child has been screened and indications from that initial instrument suggest the need for further testing. One purpose of preschool assessment instruments is to pinpoint rather specifically the nature and extent of the child's problems. Several assessment devices are quite global in that they have subtests in a variety of areas, such as motor, cognitive, language, and social skills. Other assessment instruments are more focused in that they pertain to only one or a few domains. In addition, some preschool assessments suggest treatments that may be scheduled to deal with certain problems.

Johnson and Beauchamp (1987) conducted a survey to determine the following about preschool assessment: what preschool instruments were currently being used, why they were chosen, and what components of those instruments were considered most important. To obtain this information, the authors surveyed teachers in preschool programs who had received technical assistance from the Precise Early Education of Children with Handicaps (PEECH) outreach project. The researchers found that the most commonly used instruments were the *Brigance Diagnostic Inventory of Early Development* (46 percent), the *Learning Accomplishment Profile* (39 percent), and the *Systematic Classroom Observation Assessment Programming* (26 percent). The most common reason given for selecting a particular assessment was that the test was already in place (46 percent). The components of the instruments that influenced the selection included scope of test (25 percent), applicability of test (24 percent), and ease of administering test (22 percent).

Esterly and Griffin (1987) conducted a more intensive nationwide survey to learn which assessment instruments were administered most often. Following is a list of the top ten:

— *Basic School Skills Inventory-Diagnostic* (Hammill & Leigh, 1983)
— *Kaufman Assessment Battery for Children* (Kaufman & Kaufman, 1982)
— *Test of Early Language Development* (Hresko, Reid, & Hammill, 1981)
— *Developmental Indicators for the Assessment of Learning—Revised* (Mardell-Czudnowski & Goldenberg, 1983)
— *Learning Accomplishment Profile* (LeMay, Griffin, & Sanford, 1977)
— *Inventory of Early Development* (Brigance, 1978)
— *Bender Visual Motor Gestalt Test* (Koppitz, 1975)
— *Developmental Test of Visual Motor Integration* (Berry & Buktenica, 1967)
— *Bruininks-Oteretsky Test of Motor Deficiency* (Bruininks, 1978)

Screening Tests

Denver Developmental Screening Test (Frankenburg, Dodds, & Fandal, 1975). The DDST is administered individually and is primarily intended to aid in de-

tecting delayed development in children between the ages of 2 weeks and 6 years
and 4 months. The test consists of 105 items arranged in four sections: personal-
social, fine motor-adaptive, language, and gross motor. Each test item is represented on the test form by a horizontal bar placed along the age continuum to
indicate the ages at which 25 percent, 50 percent, 75 percent, and 90 percent of
the children passed an item in the standardization sample. A delay in development
is considered when a child fails any item that 90 percent of the children can
normally pass at a younger age. From 15 to 20 minutes are required to administer
the DDST.

The Bankson Language Screening Test (Bankson, 1977).   The intent of the BLST
is to provide examiners with measures of children's psycholinguistic and perceptual
skills. Made up of 17 nine-item subtests, the BLST is organized into five general
categories that assess a variety of areas: semantic knowledge, morphological rules,
syntactic rules, visual perception, and auditory perception. The selection of subtests in the BLST was based on a review of those areas that language specialists
frequently test and remediate in younger children. Test results may be reported
in terms of percentile ranks, which are provided for children 4 through 7 years
of age. The BLST should be given to individuals, and requires from 30 to 60
minutes to administer.

The Kindergarten Language Screening Test (Gauthier & Madison, 1983).   The
KLST is designed to identify children who have language deficits which might
impede their academic progress. According to the publisher, the teacher can
pinpoint these children in five minutes. Expressive and receptive language competencies are assessed by testing children's knowledge of their name, age, body
parts, and number concepts, their ability to follow commands and repeat sentences, and their spontaneous speech. The KLST is to be individually administered
and is designed for children between the ages of 48 and 83 months.

Screening Children for Related Early Educational Needs (Hresko, Reid, Hammill,
Ginsburg, & Baroody, 1988).   SCREEN is an academic screening test for children ages 3 through 7. It is constructed to provide both global and specific ability
scores that can be used to identify educationally relevant abilities in the areas of
language, reading, written language, and mathematics. According to the publishers, SCREEN is particularly useful in identifying mildly handicapped students.
The five standard scores obtained with SCREEN can be used to document student
growth and program effectiveness. It should be given to individuals, and it requires
from 30 to 45 minutes to administer.

Assessment Devices

Brigance Diagnostic Inventory of Early Development (Brigance, 1978).   The inventory includes 98 skill sequences for the following areas: psychomotor, self-
help, speech and language, general knowledge and comprehension, and early
academic skills. The inventory is to be individually administered. The time re-

quired to administer it depends on how many skills are assessed. The inventory is based on observable functions, sequenced by task analysis, correlated with child development from birth through six years and with curriculum objectives. According to its publisher, it can be applied directly to individualized instruction.

Battelle Developmental Inventory (Newborg, Stock, Wnek, Guidabaldi, & Suinicki, 1984). The BDI is an individually administered assessment battery of key developmental skills. The full BDI takes 60 minutes or less for children under 3 and over 5 and about 90 minutes for children 3 to 5 years old. The full BDI consists of 341 test items grouped into five domains: personal-social, adaptive, motor, communication, and cognitive. One of the primary functions of the BDI is to identify children who are handicapped or delayed in certain areas of development.

The Preschool Language Scale (Zimmerman, Steiner, & Evatt, 1979). The PLS is an individually administered Binet-type measure of language development suitable for youngsters from up to 7 years old. Verbal items from existing intelligence tests and developmental tests were adopted by the authors and grouped into subtests of auditory comprehension (to measure receptive language) and of verbal ability (to measure expressive language and articulation). Items are placed within each subtest at age levels ranging from two to seven years.

The examiner instructs the child in each task, and results are recorded on a point scale. Age scores are determined by combining credit for items below the level at which all items are passed with those items passed before the age level at which all items were failed. Ratio quotients for either subtest or for the total scale are computed by dividing the age score by the chronological age of the child and multiplying that by 100. Total administration and scoring time is approximately ten minutes.

The Test of Language Development—Primary (Newcomer & Hammill, 1987). TOLD has seven subtests that measure different components of spoken language. A picture vocabulary and an oral vocabulary subtest are intended to assess the understanding and meaningful use of spoken words. Subtests on grammatic understanding, sentence imitation, and grammatic completion assess differing aspects of grammar. Word articulation and word discrimination are supplemental tests that measure the abilities to say words correctly and to distinguish between words that sound similar. The TOLD, designed for children between the ages of 4.0 and 8.11, is intended to identify children who have language disorders and to isolate their particular disorder. It is to be individually administered and requires from 30 to 60 minutes to give.

The Test of Early Language Development (Hresko, Reid, & Hammill, 1981). The TELD, which is to be administered individually, measures the spoken language abilities of children between the ages of 3.0 and 7.11. It is intended to provide information that is directly related to the semantic (content) and syntactic (form) aspects of language. The 38 items on the test assess different aspects of receptive and expressive language requiring a variety of semantic and syntactic tasks. The test takes about 15 minutes to give.

Test of Early Socioemotional Development (Hresko, & Brown, 1984).   The TOESD is a battery of four components designed to evaluate the behavior of children ages 3.0 to 7.11 years. According to its publishers, the TOESD can be administered for four purposes: to identify young children suspected of having behavior problems, to document the degree of behavioral difficulty observed in these children, to identify specific settings in which problem behaviors most often occur, and to evaluate the impressions a child makes on different observers. Three scales make up the test: a 30-item student scale completed by the child, a 34-item parent rating scale completed by the parents, and a 36-item teacher rating scale to be completed by the teacher. In addition to those data, an accompanying sociogram provides information about peer perceptions of the child being evaluated. The test can be administered individually and requires about 50 minutes to deliver.

Kaufman Assessment Battery for Children (Kaufman, & Kaufman, 1983).   The K-ABC is a clinical instrument for the evaluation of children between the ages of 2½ and 12½. It was developed from research and theory in neuropsychology and cognitive psychology. Made up of 16 subtests, the K-ABC, yields scores in five global areas: sequential processing, simultaneous processing, mental processing composite (sequential plus simultaneous), achievement, and nonverbal (those mental processing subtests that require no verbal response). Its publisher claims that the K-ABC is especially sensitive to the diverse needs of minority and exceptional children. The test is to be individually administered and requires from 30 to 90 minutes to give, depending on how many subtests are scheduled.

The Miller Assessment for Preschoolers (Miller, 1982).   The MAP is an assessment battery designed for children between the ages of 2 years 9 months and 5 years 8 months. The intent of the test is to identify children who exhibit mild to moderate developmental problems which may later affect their academic success. According to the publisher, MAP may be given to children who demonstrate more severe developmental deficiencies to obtain a developmental overview, as well as a thorough profile of their strengths and weaknesses. Five developmental domains are assessed by the MAP: neural foundations (standard neurological items), coordination (fine, gross, and oral motor), verbal (expressive and receptive language), nonverbal (sequencing, memory, and visual-spatial perception), and complex tasks (involving two or more domains). The test is to be administered individually and requires from 20 to 30 minutes to give.

Miller and Sprong (1986) compared four norm-referenced tests based on their widespread use in screening programs: *Comprehensive Identification Process* (CIP), *Denver Developmental Screening Test—Revised* (DDST-R), *Developmental Indicators for the Assessment of Learning—Revised* (DIAL-R), and *Miller Assessment for Preschoolers* (MAP). The theoretical model underlying the CIP, DDST-R, and DIAL-R is primarily cognition/language with a small portion of items assessing motor performance. MAP is based on a neurological/developmental model with a smaller portion of items assessing cognition and language. The tests were compared on ten criteria: description of normative sample, adequacy of sample size, item analysis, reporting of measures of central tendency and variability, concurrent validity, predictive validity, test-retest reliability, interexaminer reliability, and adequate description of test procedures and tester qualifications. Miller and Sprong concluded that, to varying degrees, the DIAL-R and MAP met most of the ten psychometric criteria. The DIAL-R met six criteria in full, and two partially. The MAP met seven criteria in full.

SCREENING, PREDICTING, AND FOLLOW-UP

For some time, researchers have testified to the benefits of early screening and identification of learning difficulties (for example, Book, 1974; Book, 1980; de Hirsch, Jansky, & Langford, 1966; and Maitland, Nadeau, & Nadeau, 1974). Arguments for screening procedures are also noted in the more recent literature (for example, Badian, 1986; Edmiaston & Mowder, 1985; and Gallerani, O'Regan, & Reinherz, 1982). These researchers have argued that screening techniques are particularly important in predicting learning problems and developing specialized early intervention programs (de Hirsch et al., 1986; Gallerani et al., 1982; & Lichtenstein, 1982). In 1976 Makins reported that 47 percent of the local education associations were using screening procedures and an additional 27 percent were planning to implement them. That proportion has continued to this date.

Summary of Screening Projects

In one study that involved only a single instrument for screening, Wood, Powell, and Knight (1984) examined the predictive validity of the *Gesell School Readiness Screening Test*. The results from that test, obtained by certified examiners of 84 kindergarten children, were compared with subsequent school successes. The results gave evidence that the Gesell procedures were effective in predicting child success or failure in kindergarten 78.6 percent of the time.

In a similar study, Steinbauer and Heller (1978) conducted a screening and follow-up project with a number of youngsters. The students were given the *Boehm Test of Basic Concepts* in kindergarten, and as second or third graders, they were administered the *Stanford Achievement Test* (SAT). The grade scores obtained from the SAT were then correlated with the Boehm scores. The resulting coefficients indicated a strong association between deficiencies in early concept mastery as measured in kindergarten and academic achievement in the second and third grade. The results prompted the authors to recommend the Boehm as an early predictor of school attainment.

A number of other screening studies administered multiple tests and followed up youngsters for longer periods of time. The pioneering work of de Hirsch, Jansky, and Langford (1966) is the most widely known predictive index based on a combination of variables. When this battery of 37 tests was administered to over 400 kindergarteners, a predictive index correctly identified over 75 percent of the children who failed in reading at the end of second grade. The researchers reported that there were five excellent predictors for success: letter naming, word matching, picture naming, copying designs, and sentence repetition. Satz and Friel (1974) developed a similar battery and reported successful classification of over 90% for both high- and low-risk students at the end of second grade.

Book (1974) administered three tests—*Metropolitan Readiness Test* (MRT), *Bender-Gestalt* (B-G), and *Slosson Intelligence Test* (SIT)—to a group of 725 children in kindergarten and followed them through second grade. This screening program, designed to obtain the greatest predictive value for the least investment of time and money, relied on the following sequence of activities: Kindergarten children were screened with the MRT. Those whose scores indicated potential difficulties were then tested on either the SIT or B-G to determine more specific difficulties in intelligence and perceptual-motor development. Next, children were assigned one of six diagnostic categories in order to define a need for further evaluation, program placement, and program planning. Book proudly announced that at the end of second grade, only one child had failed to make as much progress as was predicted, and 27 children did better than expected.

In a later study, Book (1980) investigated the group test performances of 472 children identified during kindergarten as educationally high, moderate, and low risk, and followed their progress from grades one through four. Predictive measures at the end of kindergarten were the *Kindergarten Evaluation of Learning Potential, Bender-Gestalt,* and *Slosson Intelligence Test,* whereas follow-up measures were group achievement tests administered in April of each school year. Book reported significant differences in achievement between the high- and low-risk groups; furthermore, significant correlations were noted between risk group designation and achievement performance in the first four grades. Findings supported the predictive validity of the screening procedures for group test performance through grade four, in the sense that students appeared to perform consistently at the same level year to year in a regular class instructional program.

Other studies not only relied on tests to screen youngsters, but also took into account other information. Jansky and de Hirsch (1972) found that sex, color, socioeconomic status, teacher competence, and chronological age were factors that affected the accuracy of prediction. According to Satz, Taylor, Friel, and Fletcher (1978), socioeconomic status was an important predictor of reading, ranking highest in some follow-up studies.

The presence of several minor physical anomalies in a child is also a predictor of poor academic school performance. An accumulation of deficits, which may be compensated for singly but are overwhelming in combination, were related to later school achievement (Galante, Flye, Stephens, & Stephens, 1972). Such deficits included an unusual birth history, eye muscle imbalance, abnormal EEG, and an adverse home environment. According to Badian (1984), male sex and later birth position were associated with poor school achievement. She also suggested that month of birth was a significant factor, with birth in the hottest months associated with reading disability.

The purpose of Badian's 1986 research was to investigate the relationship of screening test scores and biographical factors with later reading achievement. That study, the *Holbrook Screening Battery,* was administered to over 200 kindergarten boys. When the scores were related to pupils' reading scores in grade 3, it was discovered that the screening test identified 91 percent of the 178 good readers (valid negatives), and 43 percent of the 30 poor readers (valid positives), with an overall hit rate of 84.1 percent. The screening test failed, however, to predict 57 percent of the poor readers (false negatives), and 55 percent of the youngsters who had appeared at risk but later became good readers (false positives).

Guidabaldi and Perry (1984) investigated the concurrent and predictive validity of the *Battelle Developmental Inventory* (BDI), a test designed to assess the growth of children from birth to age 8. This inventory assesses five domains—cognition, communication skills, psychomotor ability, personal-social skills, and adaptive behavior. Several input formats, including structured tasks, direct observation, teacher report, and parent report are embodied in the BDI.

For their study, Guidabaldi and Perry randomly sampled 124 children comprising an entire grade level in a school district; samples were taken during both the kindergarten and first grade school years by using a comprehensive battery of assessments. Results of these assessments indicated a consistent pattern of relationships between separate BDI domains and assessments that purported to measure similar constructs. An especially revealing finding, according to the authors, was that the BDI evidenced higher predictive values of achievement in first grade than did other assessments. The data were interpreted to support the BDI as a valid multifactored assessment for use in educational, clinical, and research endeavors with young children.

Hall and Keogh (1978) conducted a four-year longitudinal study in an effort to provide more support for early identification of youngsters with deficits. The research involved 30 at-risk and 30 non-risk kindergarteners of similar chronological age and ethnic background. Most of the risk youngsters were boys; none of them had physical or sensory impairments. The children were selected on the basis of behavior observations and teachers' ratings.

At the end of the first and second grades, achievement data and teachers' ratings were collected. Those scores, following both grades, significantly favored the non-risk youngsters. At the end of grade three, the staff developed a profile of behavioral/temperamental characteristics of the children by asking their teachers to comment about them.

From those data, three patterns emerged: one for girls, and two for boys. The girls were found to be generally at risk educationally, "looked like" average peers in behavioral and motivational areas, and were particularly low in academic aptitude. One behavior profile of at-risk boys was characterized by intense reaction, uncertainty in quality of mood, generally disruptive classroom behavior, and good academic aptitude. The second group of risk boys were generally seen as more behaviorally adaptive and less academically able than the first group of boys. In relation to risk girls, they were perceived as more variable on behavioral and motivational indices and as having specific rather than general learning problems.

Hall and Keogh stressed the point that their screening approach to early identification, like others, was valuable only if it led to appropriate, effective, and positive educational responses. "Early identification as a goal in itself is indefensible, as it may work to the disadvantage rather than to the advantage of many children. When developing early identification programs, the real question is not just 'how?', but more importantly 'why?' " (Hall and Keogh, 1978, p. 68).

Teachers' Predictive Ability

The following investigations pertained to the ability of teachers to predict youngsters' success or failure in school. Colarusso, Gill, Plankenhorn, and Brooks (1980) maintained that there was considerable evidence to indicate that teachers are able to identify children with potential learning problems, but they tended to err in the direction of false positives. Such an error results in some children being unnecessarily placed in intervention programs. Overall, the researchers found that teachers agreed on the following descriptors: hyperactive, disruptive, aggressive, short attention span, and lack of self-discipline.

Keogh, Tchir, and Windeguth-Behn (1974) reported that there were some differences in teachers' descriptions according to the socioeconomic status of the school district; teachers from lower status schools were in less agreement for high-risk characteristics than were teachers in middle status school districts.

■ COMMENTARY ■ *The evidence from those two studies might suggest that early identification based on teachers' observations of behavior, even if rather accurate, provides little information that could be directed toward designing intervention strategies for children at risk for school failure. It might well be, however, that these teachers were asked the wrong questions. Possibly, if they were queried on how they would intervene with children who were either failing now or might in the future, they would have valuable suggestions.*

Criticisms of Screening and Predictive Studies

A number of criticisms of the screening and predictive process appear in the literature. Badian (1986), for one, commented that a common problem of these studies is the matter of predictive validity, as measured by correlation coefficients. Although she acknowledges that correlation coefficients are useful statistics, they do not provide predictive information for individual children. Even a relatively high correlation of .6, which is commonly found between a predictor and the reading criterion, means that only one-third of the variance in reading performance can be attributed to the predictive measure.

A number of researchers (for example, Coleman, 1978) have noted that another concern over preschool screening for possible developmental delays is related to false labeling—that is, the over-identification of children as handicapped. A child expected to fail may succeed (false negatives), and inappropriate labeling or placement may result. On the other hand, there is the failure to identify children who may, in fact, require further evaluation or services. Children expected to succeed may fail (false positives), and in this case, interventions that should have been provided are not, and undetected problems may escalate.

A third criticism of many screening tests is that their focus is too narrow. Whereas most screening assessments have emphasized intellectual, language, perceptual-motor, and developmental skills, there has been less information regarding social and emotional behaviors. Studies have shown that early problems in those areas are related not only to later social or emotional adjustment, but to academic functioning as well (for example, Reinherz, Kelfer, Griffin, & Holloway, 1977). Perry, Guidabaldi, and Kehle (1979) found that ratings of affective social characteristics and specific academic measures for children entering kindergarten had equal or higher predictive values than did global measures of intelligence.

Yet another criticism of predictive screening is directed at reliance on a medical approach. Lindsay and Wedell (1982), for example, have reminded us of the limitations of medical screening. They pointed out that the evidence on medical screening for certain disorders detectable at birth was impressive. For example, the identification in the neonatal stage of children with persistently high levels of phenylalanine (PKU) is reliable and enables medical personnel to take direct action. Lindsay and Wedell commented, however, that although medical screening data can be highly efficient for certain profound handicaps, they may be of dubious value as a predictor of mild psychoeducational difficulties. They noted further that levels of prediction are likely to be poor with many children from lower socioeconomic homes.

Alternative Approaches for Screening

A number of alternative approaches have been recommended for screening preschoolers. For one, Schaer and Crump (1976) have suggested that screening tests be followed by checklists that would provide detailed information on at-risk children (positives). Those scoring above the cutoff (negatives) would then be grouped according to the presence or absence of characteristics likely to be associated with later reading failure (or success). When Schaer and Crump retrospectively considered such an approach, the identification of poor readers increased from 45 percent to 93 percent, and of good readers from 91 percent to 98 percent.

Lindsay and Wedell (1982) proposed an alternative assessment strategy based on sequences of educational objectives rather than standardized instruments. They argued that the use of task-centered assessment and intervention techniques should be the main focus of attempts to deal with the needs of children with learning difficulties.

With respect to the ordinary one-shot approaches to screening, Lichtenstein (1982) reported that in view of available ". . . evidence, it appears that extensive assessment of young children at a single point in time is a poor investment of system resources" (p. 72). Alternatively, he recommended that children, particularly those who require special services, should be assessed often.

■ COMMENTARY ■   The views of Lindsay and Wedell and of Lichtenstein both fall in line with proponents of curriculum-based assessment, who argue that educators should measure what they teach and should do it rather often.

————— TYPES OF EARLY INTERVENTION PROGRAMS —————

This section discusses the four major types of programs for infants and preschoolers insofar as locations are concerned. It then identifies and briefly describes six curricular models for structuring preschool programs.

Locations of Programs

There are four locations in which infant and preschool programs are developed. This section cites representative projects that fall into each category (Bryand & Ramey, 1987).

Center-Based, Child- and Parent-Focused.   The *Milwaukee Project* served youngsters from 3 to 6 months old, who came from economically depressed areas. They were provided cognitive-language orientation in a structured environment where prescriptive teaching techniques were used. Their mothers were offered vocational and social education programs. The interventions took place in the home and at the center.

In *Project CARE,* the children were about 3 months old and from families of lower income. The focus of the intervention, which took place in the center and at home, was on language and cognitive development and adaptive social behavior. Parents were given assistance on responsive parenting and behavior management.

Children in the *Carolina Abecedarian Project* were 3 months of age and from lower income families. Their intervention was offered at the center and focused on language, cognitive development, and adaptive social behavior.

The *Field's Center-Home Visit* program involved infants from birth, most of whom had teenage mothers. The intervention for the children relied on activities designed from Denver and Bayley test items, and parents received training in child development and in job skills. The interventions were scheduled both at the center and in the homes.

Center-Based, Parent-Focused.   In the *Birmingham Parent-Child Development Center* (PCDC), the infants were from 3 to 5 months old and from lower income families. Mothers received training in parenting and child development at the center.

For the *Houston PCDC,* youngsters were about one year old and from low-income families. Mothers were given training in several topics: child development, parenting, home as learning environment, parent-child activities. This training was initially provided in the homes, then later at the center.

In the *New Orleans PCDC,* infants were about 2 months old and from lower income homes. Mothers were trained at the center on matters of child development.

Home-Visit, Parent-Focused.   Infants of 3, 7, or 11 months were in the *Ypsilanti-Carnegie Infant Education Project.* Most of them were living with families in which no one was employed. The focus of this intervention was on the mothers as teachers of their children. Emphasis of the Piagetian-based interventions were on fine and gross motor skills.

Youngsters in the *Family-Oriented Home Visiting Program* were from 17 to 24 months of age and were from lower income families. The home interventions emphasized teaching style, competence, language, and behavior management.

From birth, infants were involved in the *Field's Home Visit Study.* Many of the mothers were unwed teenagers and from the lowest socioeconomic strata. The curriculum activities, which were modeled for the mothers, were adapted from Denver and Bayley test items.

School-Based, Child-Focused.   Whereas the three preceding types of programs were for infants, the following programs were designed for preschoolers.

The youngsters in the *Perry Preschool Project* were 3 and 4 years of age at the beginning of the program. Most of them were living in homes in which no one was employed. Their curriculum was Piagetian-based and emphasized concrete activities and language experiences. (There is more information on this program later in the chapter.)

Youngsters in the *Early Training Project* were 3 and 4 year olds who were living in lower socioeconomic status homes. Their curriculum focused on perceptual and language development and the acquisition of basic concepts. Instructors at this project emphasized improving motivation for achievement and for extending the delay for gratification.

Children in the *Academic Preschool Project* were 4 years old, and most of them were living with parents on welfare. The intervention of this project was based on direct instruction techniques and focused on the rapid attainment of basic academic concepts.

Curricular Models

The following paragraphs sketch six common curricular models of preschool programs. These models were identified in a nationwide survey conducted by Esterly and Griffin (1987).

The *child development* model stresses self-initiated exploration of materials, dramatic play, field trips, learning centers, and unit planning. There is particular emphasis on social-emotional behaviors and the attainment of developmental milestones. The teacher's role in this model is to provide instruction appropriate for children's levels of development.

The *psychoeducational* model emphasizes the development of personality, motivation, and self-concept. Advocates of this approach maintain that learning is the result of an interaction between the environment and maturation. For this method, the teacher serves as a model and facilitator.

The *behavioral* model is based on concepts from reinforcement theory. The adherents of this view maintain that the child's environment is most important and can be arranged to bring about desired behaviors. Major considerations of this model are reinforcement, repetition, measurable goals, observable behaviors, and data-based programming decisions. The teacher's role in this approach is to arrange situations so that desired behaviors will occur.

The *cognitive-developmental* approach concentrates on the sequential hierarchy of developmental stages of children's intellectual structures. An emphasis of this program is on the child's interaction with concrete activities during the early years. The teacher's role is to stimulate children so that they are active, rather than passive, learners.

The *diagnostic-prescriptive* model emphasizes heredity and maturation equally and recognizes the complementary role of these components. Advocates of this approach maintain that in order for learning to take place, there must be a match between the skills being taught and the developmental stage of the child. The teacher's role in this model is to monitor closely children's attainment of developmental milestones. Proponents of this plan frequently administer tests and use the results to help them design proper programs.

The *perceptual-motor* programs place emphasis on spontaneous learning in structured environments. For this approach, materials are sequenced to promote error-free learning, and sensory, motor, and language development is emphasized. The role of the teacher is to ensure that children have properly mastered fundamental perceptual skills before being advanced to academic activities.

INTERVENTIONS WITH PRESCHOOLERS

Research Studies

This section describes representative intervention studies with preschoolers and comments generally on research with mildly handicapped preschoolers. Highlights from papers that deal with research issues involving preschoolers are also presented, along with summaries of current research on preschoolers being conducted at three major universities.

Weiss: INREAL Intervention.   In a widely referenced intervention study, Weiss (1981) reported on a three-year study to measure the effectiveness of a treatment with language-handicapped and bilingual (Spanish-speaking) children ages 3 to 5.

The method was referred to as a "naturalistic and nonstigmatizing method." She employed a randomized block design, with both experimental and control groups receiving pre- and post-treatment measurement. Students in the experimental classes were provided the INREAL program, techniques of which were based on Piagetian developmental psychology. The program's two major objectives were to increase children's language development and to prevent later language-related problems.

Language specialists provided instruction by going into the classrooms and entering into the children's learning situations by reacting to their natural communications and interactions. They did not manipulate the situations to elicit predetermined utterances from the children. The specialists interacted with children by using five psycholinguistic techniques: self-talk, parallel talk, verbal monitoring and reflecting, expansion, and modeling.

The overall preschool and kindergarten data from that research revealed that the INREAL treatment markedly influenced language performance gains for both age groups. The data also indicated that the treatment positively influenced the language performance gains of the bilingual children.

Follow-up data indicated that INREAL was effective in reducing later learning problems that were language-related. Furthermore, Weiss claimed that the program was responsible for reducing retention-in-grade of the participating students and the need of resource room services.

Schweinhart and Weikart: Perry Program.   In 1981, Schweinhart and Weikart reported on their fifteen-year study of 123 children who were followed from age 3 to 19. The youngsters in their research were from families of low educational attainment and low occupational status, and their parents were of low cognitive ability—all predictors of later academic difficulties.

The experiment lasted from 1958 to 1962, and the children were assigned to either an experimental or a control situation so as to equate the groups on initial cognitive ability, sex ratio, and socioeconomic status.

Children in the experimental group (the Perry Project, referred to earlier) attended a group preschool program for 12½ hours a week for one school year. Staff personnel also visited those youngsters and their mothers at home for 1½ hours per week.

The 1981 data, reported on children between the ages of 3 and 15, were in respect to 48 different measures covered by IQ tests, school achievement tests, child rating scales, parent and youth interviews, and school records. Following is a summary of those data:

1. The average child who attended preschool went to kindergarten with an IQ of 95; the average child who did not attend preschool went to kindergarten with an IQ of 84.

2. Children who attended preschool had a stronger affinity for school (as shown by increased motivation during elementary school, and at age 15, a higher value placed on schooling), had greater aspirations for college, a greater willing-

ness to talk to parents about school, devoted more time to homework, and had a higher self-rating of their school ability.

3. The achievements in school of the experimental youngsters at age 14 were significantly higher than those of the control children.

4. The children who received preschool education required and received fewer years of special education services during the course of their schooling: Of the control group 39 percent had received special education services for one year or more, compared with 19% of the experimental group.

5. The parents of youngsters who attended preschool were more pleased with the school performances of their youngsters, at age 15, than were parents of non-preschoolers.

6. It appeared that preschool education led to improved classroom conduct and personal behavior, as rated by elementary school teachers, and to a decrease in teenagers' delinquent behavior.

This program is still thriving and has become the accepted plan for the pre-primary special education program of the Ypsilante, Michigan, public schools. According to an article in the *Phi Delta Kappan* (Harper, 1987), the program is growing both in size and reputation as an effective early-intervention program for high-risk preschool children.

The preprimary special education program in Ypsilante helps students who develop more slowly than their peers because of medical or physical problems stemming from accidents or illness before birth, at birth, or in early infancy. The program is based on the premise that children develop and mature at varying rates and that an approach for dealing with slow-developing children should be grounded in established principles of child development and language acquisition.

Students are grouped into classes according to their developmental levels. Those at a level between that of the average 2½ to 4 year old, are placed in the morning sessions; those functioning at levels typical of 4½ to 5½ year olds attend the afternoon session. The students' days are structured, with the instruction being geared toward encouraging oral communication and developing functional, expressive, and receptive vocabularies, but much time is left for informal play and conversation.

The success rate of the preschool is good: More than 50 percent of the participating children advance to regular kindergarten programs; another 35 percent require only speech and language services when they leave the preprimary program; and only 15 percent require a special program, but they have the advantage of having been served earlier than many other preschool children.

Dale and Cole: Experimental Education Unit.   Dale and Cole (1988) also reported on their intervention study at the Experimental Education Unit at the University of Washington. More than 60 preschoolers and 20 kindergarteners, all of whom were developmentally delayed, participated in the research. Pupils were randomly assigned to two types of classes: direct instruction (DI) and mediated learning (ML).

DI is based on task analysis and features the systematic and explicit instruction of academic skills such as language, reading, and mathematics, with a goal of maximizing academic learning time. The instructional procedures of DI, like the content, are direct; it is teacher managed and fast paced, utilizing a highly structured presentation of material with frequent opportunities for student response and reinforcement or correction.

ML emphasizes the development and generalization of cognitive processes of input, elaboration, and output rather than specific academic content. Units are organized around such cognitive processes as comparison, classification, perspective changing, and sequencing. These processes are assumed to underly academic learning.

A systematic classroom observation system, developed by the project staff, evidenced gains for pupils in both programs, but there were differential effects for specific measures: DI led to greater gains on the *Test of Early Language Development* and the *Basic Language Concepts Test,* whereas ML led to greater gains on the *McCarthy Verbal and Memory Scales* and the mean length of utterance measure.

Guralnick and Groom: Social Interactions. Guralnick and Groom (1988) arranged a study to compare the peer-related social interactions of mildly developmentally delayed children in a mainstreamed program to their interactions occurring in settings in which there were only other delayed children. The handicapped youngsters were, on the average, 4½ years old. Two groups of nonhandicapped children were involved: One was younger than the delayed children (matched on maturation) and the other was the same age (matched on chronological age).

The delayed youngsters were first observed in mainstreamed situations with nonhandicapped peers and later in settings in which there were only handicapped children. The major finding from this research was that the delayed children engaged in peer-related social interactions at a much higher rate when they participated in mainstreamed playgroups in comparison to specialized programs. Data also revealed that the peer-related social play of the nonhandicapped children was much more frequent and qualitatively of a more sophisticated type than that of the delayed children. With respect to social interactions between handicapped and nonhandicapped, the mildly delayed children were not selected by the nondelayed children as play partners as frequently as were the nonhandicapped children. However, the delayed children chose to interact more often with nonhandicapped children, of the same chronological age, than with other groups.

Casto and Mastropieri: Meta-Analysis. Casto and Mastropieri (1986) conducted a meta-analysis of 74 research studies with handicapped preschool children. Those studies took place between 1937 and 1984 (most since 1970). The majority of the children in the reviewed research were categorized as mentally retarded or as having a combination of handicaps. The most frequently measured outcome was IQ.

The authors' overall conclusion from the analysis was that early intervention programs resulted in moderately large immediate benefits for handicapped populations. The data supported the immediate benefits of early intervention programs applied to a wide variety of children, conditions, and types of program. Casto and Mastropieri cautioned that the effect sizes of reviewed studies, when only high quality investigations were considered, was noticeably lower than that for other studies.

The meta-analysis yielded the following rather specific conclusions:

☐ Parents can be effective interveners, but they are probably not essential to intervention success.

☐ There are few data to support the notion that "earlier is better."

☐ There is a trend to favor the more structured programs, but the data are inconclusive.

☐ Longer, more intense programs are associated with intervention effectiveness for handicapped populations.

☐ For handicapped populations, the immediate benefits of early interventions are apparent as long as two years later.

Casto and Mastropieri advanced one note of caution: "In the past, reviewers have used data from disadvantaged and at-risk populations to make statements about intervention efficacy with handicapped children. The results of this meta-analysis suggest that for most variables this may be appropriate; however, this practice has also led to many erroneous conclusions about efficacy" (1986, p. 422).

Measurement and Evaluation Issues

Fewell and Vadasy (1987) described the early training project designed by Susan Gray to serve poor rural children. The authors noted that early researchers concluded that they could increase the intelligence of children through their intervention efforts. Fewell and Vadasy reminded us of the disappointment these researchers later experienced when the children's early IQ gains were not maintained. Much later, however, Gray and others discovered that the individuals who were in the experimental preschool classes were less likely to be sent to special education and stayed in school longer than did the control pupils. Based on this information from Gray, Fewell and Vadasy argued that, in evaluating preschool intervention programs, researchers should select measures of programs that are likely to reflect gains over time.

Fewell and Vadasy emphasized the point that although we can teach children to acquire certain behaviors under specified conditions, we cannot assume that those skills will be internalized or generalized, or that they will be transformed into more complex skills. According to them, spontaneous internally motivated learning has not been a goal of the preschool interventions, and it should not surprise us that it was not a by-product of our instructional approach.

Fewell and Vadasy concluded that if we establish the unrealistic goal of eliminating developmental disabilities by raising IQ scores, then we are set up for failure. If we look only at child outcomes such as IQ scores for evidence of program impact, they continued,

> . . . we will fail to capture the effects our programmatic supports have upon the family's broader ecological system and interactions—information that can be extremely valuable in planning tomorrow's programs for handicapped children and their families. Our present and future concern must be to clearly understand the transactional nature of development as we set our goals for early intervention, then to make sure that our measures of effectiveness are sensitive and comprehensive enough to document the outcomes in all their complexity. [Fewell and Vadasy, 1987, p. 94]

In a second paper, Wolery (1987) stated that preschool programs should engage in evaluation activities that included impact assessments. He argued that the focus of impact studies should be on the effects of intervention strategies rather than programs, should compare two or more accepted strategies, and should analyze program components. Wolery noted that such impact studies would allow answers to the question, "What interventions are most appropriate for which infants/children under given conditions?" rather than "Is early intervention effective?"

Wolery described a seven-step process for conducting such studies:

1. Specify purpose of the evaluation study.
2. Specify objectives of the program to be evaluated and develop goal-attainment scales.
3. Generate questions and identify measurement sources related to the program's progress on each objective and suspected area of need.
4. Develop multiple measurement strategies to answer questions.
5. Collect data from each measurement source.
6. Analyze and summarize data by objective and question.
7. Report data from the evaluation study to the program decision makers.

In a third paper, Dunst, Lesko, Holbert, Wilson, Sharpe, and Liles (1987) described a systemic model that is designed as a framework for conducting intervention studies. They maintained that this model would facilitate the increased balance of power, using conventionalized interactive competencies. Their intervention model emphasized the following:

— The types and forms of competencies that permit the child to exercise control over the environment in a socially adaptive manner
— The role that caregivers play in encouraging competence
— The contexts in which the interventions take place in order to ensure the functional display of newly acquired competencies

The systemic model is intended to provide one way to integrate and operationalize both theoretical and empirical evidence, thus suggesting the most efficient way to accelerate child development.

The assessment process associated with the intervention model of Dunst and coauthors is designed to map a child's topography of the types and forms of social and nonsocial interactive competencies. A feature of their assessment is that individual responses of children are important only to the extent that they serve as exemplars of a certain type and form of interactive competency. The purpose of their ". . . assessment strategy is to discern the manner in which a particular child manifests interactive competencies at each level of performance in order to identify appropriate intervention targets. The focus is not on whether the child can produce certain preselected overt indicators of interactive behavior but rather how the child demonstrates his or her interactive competencies" (Dunst et al., 1987, p. 28).

Dunst and colleagues maintained that one of the most useful teaching techniques for fostering interactive competencies is incidental teaching, which, according to them, ". . . refers to interactions a child has with the social and nonsocial environment which arise either naturally or through afforded opportunities, where child initiation with the environment provides a basis for both sustaining and elaborating on the child's topography of behavior" (p. 31). According to the researchers, incidental teaching episodes provide the structure for instructing targets every time opportunities arise, and those opportunities come up every time the child is in the presence of another person and emits a behavior that can be used to sustain and elaborate on the child's topography of behavior. (See remarks on incidental teaching in Chapter 11.)

Institutes on Early Childhood Research

Over the past ten years three institutes on early childhood research have been established. Their general purposes have been to identify service needs of young handicapped children and their families and to evaluate current intervention models and develop or validate new or alternative approaches (Reevers, 1987). The research activities of these institutes have encompassed a number of critical issues, including the physical, mental, and emotional development of infants with disabilities; the needs of their families; the development of new instructional programs and intervention models; and the evaluation of the benefits and cost-effectiveness of early intervention services.

The Early Childhood Research Institute at the University of Pittsburgh has concentrated on developing and evaluating instructional programs for teaching social skills to handicapped preschoolers. Specific topics of the institute's research include peer social skills, communication skills, independent performance, disruptive behavior, and parent training.

The Early Intervention Research Institute at Utah State University has concentrated on studying the benefits and cost-effectiveness of early intervention services for handicapped preschool children. The results of this project are intended to help researchers and policymakers to judge programs more effectively and to compare the costs, benefits, and overall effectiveness of newly developed programs with those of programs previously studied.

The major focus of the Institute for Research on Early Education for the Handicapped at the University of North Carolina has been to detail the characteristics and needs of children, from birth to age 5, who have moderate to severe handicaps. The institute has completed research projects on the following: young children with handicaps from two-parent families versus single-parent families resulting from divorce and separation, parent-child interaction styles, and development of a model of family-based intervention.

MICROCOMPUTER PROGRAMS

A number of microcomputer programs have been designed for preschoolers with language disorders. This section reviews these programs and a variety of programs suitable for mildly handicapped preschoolers.

Programs for Preschoolers with Language Disorders

According to Meyers (1987), many children with language delay or disorders lack these prerequisite skills: speaking and understanding the sounds, words, and sentences of language; recognizing letter shapes and words; and evidencing eye-hand coordination and fine motor control. She maintains that the longer children's disabilities keep them out of the meaningful dialogue of language, the less motivated they will be to learn the complex rules of spoken and written language. Meyers contends that computers, particularly when equipped with synthesized speech output, can change all this. She pictures the computer as a language scaffold, supporting children's use of language to communicate meaning. By using computers, children can bypass the skills that were once prerequisites and immediately experience the use of spoken and written language to convey their own messages. Computers allow language-disabled toddlers to participate immediately in the normal process of learning language. Synthesized speech output can function as a voice for toddlers, thus allowing them to name objects and events and talk about ongoing play. Children repeat the words they want to know on the computer and gradually learn to say them on their own.

Meyers recommends the PEAL Software *Exploratory Play Disk,* which promotes language learning by allowing children to use language to talk about typical play routines. To operate this program, children touch the color pictures on an overlay covering a membrane keyboard. The computer "says" the vocabulary for the picture touched in synthesized speech output, and an identical graphic appears on the computer monitor screen.

Meyers endorsed another PEAL software disk, *KEYTALK,* which is designed as a language scaffold for children just beginning to read and write. Using *KEYTALK,* children immediately begin to write and read meaningful text. When they begin the program, they see a blank writing page along with the six commands that are needed to control the software displayed at the bottom of the page. As they type, the computer "says" the letters in speech output. When children hit the space bar after each word, the computer "says" the word, and when they type in punctuation, the computer "says" the whole sentence. Children can read the text on the monitor screen as many times as they want, using the speech output. Furthermore, children can print their writing, save it, and find it again. Children using this program learn the keyboard, letter names and shapes, sight vocabulary, and visual scanning as they write meaningful text about topics of their choice.

Myers believes the most important characteristic in using the computer as a language scaffold is that all of the language made available by the software and hardware can be used meaningfully by the children. She maintains that this is what motivates children to construct internalized grammars for spoken and written language; they learn language in order to get something done—to communicate or understand interpersonal messages.

Programs for Mildly Handicapped Preschoolers

The following programs, which are suitable for mildly handicapped youngsters, are reviewed by Meyers (1987) in her guide to the selection of microcomputer technology for special education and rehabilitation.

Animal Hotel is a multi-leveled memory game similar to the game "Concentration." Users choose the level of challenge by selecting from different time requirements and difficulty levels to find animals who are staying in hotels. Individual scoring is provided after each practice session. *BearJam* can be scheduled to enable exceptional children to develop basic skills and perhaps have fun in the process. By interacting with an animated bear, children learn to recognize basic shapes, colors, and the concepts of same, different, and similar.

CAPTAIN: Cognitive Training System was designed to train basic cognitive function. More specifically, the program focuses on developing attention, concentration, memory, visual, motor, and reasoning skills. "CARIS" introduces reading skills to low readiness children, very young children, or learning disabled students. The program addresses the problems of the beginning reader through noun and verb selection, followed by an animated cartoon illustrating the meaning of the sentence the child has formed.

Color Find, a drill-and-practice program designed for handicapped preschoolers, provides practice in recognizing and matching both primary and secondary colors. *Early Childhood Series* consists of five parts: "Letters and Words" provides practice in word/picture matching, letter and word recognition, and alphabetical sequencing; "Body Awareness" provides names of body parts and seasonal clothing; "Shapes and Patterns" gives practice in visual discrimination, forms, and patterns; "Fun With Directions" focuses on directionality and sequencing; and "Knowing Numbers" provides practice in number recognition, the concepts of greater and less than, and subtraction. *Memory Building Blocks* is a program designed to help students discover the power of memory strategies that work best for meeting the challenges of five "Concentration" type games— "Pictures," "Words," "Colors," "Shapes," and "Tunes"—included in the program.

Sarah and Her Friend, an animated graphic adventure for prereaders, is designed to teach cause and effect and basic learning patterns. Its more specific objectives for children include the following:

— Define their world and their place in it
— Explore many choices and possible sequences
— Discover the outcomes of their choices
— Reinforce basic learning patterns (first, middle, last; top, middle, bottom; before and after; matching)
— Expand their imaginations
— Create their own plots
— Develop basic computer literacy

SimpleCom I: Yes/No Communication is designed as a step toward more sophisticated communication for nonverbal individuals; whereas "Time Tutor" patiently quizzes children on telling time in two directions: looking at an analog clock and typing the time and then moving the clock's hands to match a digital display.

The *Visuospatial Skills* package consists of ten computer programs designed to remediate impairment of visuoperception and visuomotor integration skills. The programs present tasks that require unilateral and bilateral control, and those programs can also be used to train attention.

Recommendations

Warren and Horn (1987) have advanced four recommendations with respect to microcomputers and the education of handicapped preschoolers:

1. Microcomputer technology cannot substitute for good teaching; designers of software should incorporate the features of excellent instruction.
2. Systems and instructional management applications should be vigorously pursued. Designers need to find ways for integrating microcomputers into ongoing practices.
3. There is a substantial need for knowledge on how to use a range of hardware and software simultaneously within the classroom environment to accomplish individual learner and classroom-wide goals.
4. Efforts should be directed toward narrowing the information and literacy gap with reference to microcomputers, teacher training, and continuing education efforts.

COMMENTS AND DISCUSSION POINTS

- Identification programs for preschool children should be based on skills and be-haviors that are important and common. Test items should reflect either those behaviors that are currently important for youngsters, or ones that will be later. Too often, preschoolers are assessed on trivial or irrelevant behaviors.

- Not only should assessments be directly related to the lives of youngsters, they should be frequently administered, particularly in the case of high-risk youngsters. These assessment data indicate development and inform caregivers about the effects of their interventions.

- Once language, social, motor, or other developmental deficits are identified, instruc-tion should be designed immediately to deal with them. Efforts should be underway to either remedy the problems, to the extent possible, or provide assistance in coping with them prosthetically or otherwise. It is quite inappropriate for educators to test children as preschoolers, then predict which ones will fail, and wait a year or so for the report to come in.

- For many preschoolers, assessments and subsequent interventions should be inter-disciplinary. Although it isn't necessary for professionals of all types to deal with every preschooler, high risk or not, certain specialists should be called on as they are needed. Depending on the type of concerns, personnel from neurology, pedi-atrics, pharmacology, nutrition, psychology, and other disciplines should be consulted.*

- Throughout the entire process of assessment and treatment, families of preschoolers should be encouraged to participate. Initially, they should be consulted when it comes to assessment, for they know more about their youngsters than anyone else. Later, when information from other assessments is gathered, it should be tied in with the families' knowledge and presented to them in ways that are understand-able. Still later, when intervention programs are designed, their knowledge and experience should be considered.*†

- Parents should be provided training and information by professionals on determining where their handicapped child is in reference to critical states of development. Further, parents should be instructed on how to work with their child so that developmental milestones are achieved.†

- Since language is at the heart of learning, every program for handicapped infants or preschoolers must reflect that emphasis. Teachers and parents, through obser-vations, workshops, or other means, should become aware of the critical importance of language in the child's total intellectual, social-emotional, academic, and motor development.

- When setting up an intervention program for preschoolers, there should be a high adult–child ratio, to the extent possible. One way to achieve this is to engage qualified paraprofessionals.†

---

*Suggested by Karnes & Lee (1978).

†Suggested in *Learning Disabilities Quarterly* (1986).

- It is extremely important to take transfer of training into account when intervention programs are arranged, for teachers cannot assume that transfer will occur. To increase the probability that preschoolers will make use of trained behaviors in other situations, teachers must involve strategies designed for that purpose: teaching in multiple settings, encouraging youngsters to self-manage, relying on several managers in multiple settings.

- When intervention programs are established, researchers must evaluate them. They must obtain multiple measures of these programs. As researchers have pointed out, IQ scores, when used as the single measure of programs, are inadequate indexes of interventions. Others have suggested that more appropriate measures would be those that indicated the types of social interactions the pupils were capable of, the extent to which they were independent, and how well they manipulated their environments. Whatever measures are chosen to evaluate programs, they should be tied to later development. Some researchers, in attempts to explain the benefits of preschool programs, have indicated the extent their youngsters were later placed in regular education classes, reacted positively to school, or considered going to college.*

- When evaluating new interventions, researchers should compare them with other widely used or highly acclaimed programs. (Of the few intervention studies, too many of them have been a comparison of BMWs with Fords.) Furthermore, when these interventions are evaluated, researchers should attempt to identify their vital features, those that are most related to development.

- Considerably more effort should be devoted to developing exemplary programs for preschoolers. More time is now spent devising and validating instruments that predict failure or success of preschoolers than on designing approaches for assisting them.

REFERENCES

Badian, N.A. (1984). Reading disability in an epidemiological context: Incidence and environmental correlates. *Journal of Learning Disabilities, 17,* 129–136.

Badian, N.A. (1986). Improving the prediction of reading for the individual child: A four-year follow-up. *Journal of Learning Disabilities, 19,* 262–269.

Bankson, N.W. (1977). *Bankson language screening test.* Austin, TX: PRO-ED.

Book, R.M. (1974). Predicting reading failure: A screening battery for kindergarten children. *Journal of Learning Disabilities, 7,* 52–55.

Book, R.M. (1980). Identification of educationally at-risk children during the kindergarten year: A four-year follow-up study of group test performance. *Psychology in the Schools, 17,* 153–158.

Brigance, A.H. (1978). *Brigance diagnostic inventory of early development.* North Billerica, MA: Curriculum Associates.

Bryant, D.M., & Ramey, C.T. (1987). An analysis of the effectiveness of early intervention programs for environmentally at-risk children. In M.J. Guralnick & F.C. Bennett (Eds.), *The effectiveness of early intervention for at-risk and handicapped children.* New York: Academic Press.

Casto, G., & Mastropieri, M.A. (1986). The efficacy of early intervention programs: A meta-analysis. *Exceptional Children, 52,* 417–424.

Colarusso, R.; Gill, S.; Plankenhorn, A.; & Brooks, R. (1980). Predicting first-grade achievement through formal testing of 5-year-old high-risk children. *The Journal of Special Education, 14,* 355–363.

Coleman, L. (1978). Problem kids and preventive medicine: The making of an odd couple. *American Journal of Orthopsychiatry, 48*(1), 56–70.

Dale, P.S., & Cole, K.N. (1988). Comparison of academic and cognitive programs for young handicapped children. *Exceptional Children, 54,* 439–447.

de Hirsch, K.; Jansky, J.J.; & Langford, W.S. (1966). *Predicting reading failure: A preliminary study.* New York: Harper and Row.

Dunst, C.J.; Lesko, J.J.; Holbert, K.A.; Wilson, L.L.; Sharpe, K.L.; & Liles, R.F. (1987). A systematic approach to infant intervention. *Topics in Early Childhood Special Education, 7*(2), 19–37.

Edmiaston, R.K., & Mowder, B.A. (1985). Early intervention for handicapped children: Efficacy issues and data for school psychologists. *Psychology in the Schools, 22,* 171–177.

Esterly, D.L., & Griffin, H.C. (1987). Preschool programs for children with learning disabilities. *Journal of Learning Disabilities, 20,* 571–573.

Fewell, R.R., & Vadasy, P.F. (1987). Measurement issues in studies of efficacy. *Topics in Early Childhood Special Education, 7*(2), 85–96.

Frankenburg, W.K.; Dodds, J.B.; & Fandal, A.W. (1975). *Denver developmental screening test.* Denver: Ladoca Project and Publishing Foundation.

Galante, M.B.; Flye, M.E.; Stephens, R.N.; & Stephens, L.S. (1972). Cumulative minor deficits: A longitudinal study of the relation of physical factors to school achievement. *Journal of Learning Disabilities, 5,* 75–80.

Gallerani, D.; O'Regan, M.; & Reinherz, H. (1982). Prekindergarten screening: How well does it predict readiness for first grade? *Psychology in the Schools, 19,* 175–182.

Gauthier, S.V., & Madison, C.L. (1983). *Kindergarten language screening test.* Austin, TX: PRO-ED.

Guidubaldi, J., & Perry, J.D. (1984). Concurrent and predictive validity of the Battelle Developmental Inventory at the first grade level. *Educational and Psychological Measurement, 44,* 977–985.

Guralnick, M.J., & Bennett, F.C. (1987). A framework for early intervention. In M.J. Guralnick & F.C. Bennett (Eds.), *The effectiveness of early intervention for at-risk and handicapped children.* New York: Academic Press.

Guralnick, M.J., & Groom, J.M. (1988). Peer interactions in mainstreamed and specialized classrooms: A comparative analysis. *Exceptional Children, 54,* 415–425.

Hall, R.J., & Keogh, B.K. (1978). Qualitative characteristics of educationally high-risk children. *Learning Disability Quarterly, 1,* 62–68.

Harper, J.A. (1987). Preventive preschool programming that works. *Phi Delta Kappan, 69*(1), 81–82.

Hresko, W.P., & Brown, L. (1984). *Test of early socioemotional development.* Austin, TX: PRO-ED.

Hresko, W.P.; Reid, D.K.; Hammill, D.D.; Ginsburg, H.P.; & Baroody, A.J. (1988). *Screening children for related early educational needs.* Austin, TX: PRO-ED.

Jansky, J., & de Hirsch, K. (1972). *Preventing reading failure.* New York: Harper and Row.

Johnson, L.J., & Beauchamp, K.D.F. (1987). Preschool assessment measures: What are teachers using? *Journal of the Division for Early Childhood, 12*(1), 70–76.

Kakalik, J.S.; Furry, W.S.; Thomas, M.A.; & Carney, M.F. (1981). The cost of special education: Summary of study findings. Prepared for the U.S. Department of Education, The Rand Corporation, Santa Monica, CA.

Karnes, M.B., & Lee, R.I. (1978). *Early childhood: What research and experience say to the teacher of exceptional children.* Reston, Virginia: The Council for Exceptional Children.

Kaufman, A.S., & Kaufman, N.L. (1983). *Kaufman assessment battery for children.* Circle Pines, MN: American Guidance Service.

Keogh, B.; Tchir, C.; & Windeguth-Behn, A. (1974). Teachers' perceptions of educationally handicapped children. *Journal of Learning Disabilities, 7,* 367–374.

Learning Disabilities Quarterly. (1986). Learning disabilities and the preschool child: A position paper of the National Joint Committee on Learning Disabilities. *9,* 158–163.

Lichtenstein, R. (1982). New instrument, old problem for early identification. *Exceptional Children, 49,* 70–72.

Lindsay, G.A., & Wedell, K. (1982). The early identification of educationally "at-risk" children revisited. *Journal of Learning Disabilities, 15,* 212–217.

Maitland, S.; Nadeau, J.B.E.; & Nadeau, G. (1974). Early screening practices. *Journal of Learning Disabilities, 7,* 645–649.

Makins, V. (1976). Bullock plus one. *Times Educational Supplement.* Feb. 6, pp. 21–23.

Meyers, L.F. (1987). Bypassing the prerequisites: The computer as a language scaffold. *Closing the gap, 5*(6), 1 and 20.

Miller, L.J. (1982). *Miller assessment for preschoolers.* Circle Pines, MN: American Guidance Service.

Miller, L.J., & Sprong, T.A. (1986). Psychometric and qualitative comparison of four preschool screening instruments. *Journal of Learning Disabilities, 19,* 480–484.

Newborg, J.; Stock, J.; Wnek, L.; Guidubaldi, J.; & Suinicki, J. (1984). *Battelle developmental inventory.* Allen, TX: DLM Teaching Resources.

Newcomer, P.L., & Hammill, D.D. (1987). *Test of language development—primary.* Austin, TX: PRO-ED.

Perry, J.D.; Guidubaldi, J.; & Kehle, T.J. (1979). Kindergarten competencies as predictors of third-grade classroom behavior and achievement. *Journal of Educational Psychology, 71,* 443–450.

Reevers, C. (1987). Institutes on early childhood research. *Counterpoint,* September/October, 15.

Reinherz, H.; Kelfer, D.; Griffin, C.L.; & Holloway, S. (1977). Developing a tool for assessing social-emotional functioning of preschool children. Paper presented at the annual meeting of the American Association of Psychiatric Services for Children, Washington, D.C.

Satz, P., & Friel, J. (1974). Some predictive antecedents of specific reading disability: A preliminary two-year follow-up. *Journal of Learning Disabilities, 7,* 437–444.

Satz, P.; Taylor, H.G.; Friel, J.; & Fletcher, J.M. (1978). Some developmental and predictive precursors of reading disabilities: A six year follow-up. In A.L. Benton & D. Pearl (Eds.), *Dyslexia.* New York: Oxford University Press.

Schaer, H.F., & Crump, W.D. (1976). Teacher involvement and early identification of children with learning disabilities. *Journal of Learning Disabilities, 9,* 91–95.

Schweinhart, L.J., & Weikart, D.P. (1981). Effects of the Perry preschool program on youths through age 15. *Journal of the Division for Early Childhood, 4,* 29–39.

Sroufe, L.A. (1979). The coherence of individual development: Early care, attachment, and subsequent developmental issues. *American Psychologist, 34,* 834–841.

Steinbauer, E., & Heller, M.S. (1978). The Boehm test of basic concepts as a predictor of academic achievement in grades 2 and 3. *Psychology in the schools, 15,* 357–360.

Walker, H.M. (1970). *Walker problem identification checklist.* Los Angeles, CA: Western Psychological Services.

Warren, S.F., & Horn, E.M. (1987). Microcomputer applications in early childhood special education: Problems and possibilities. *Topics in Early Childhood Special Education, 7*(2), 72–84.

Weiss, R.S. (1981). INREAL intervention for language handicapped and bilingual children. *Journal of the Division for Early Childhood, 4,* 40–51.

Wolery, M. (1987). Program evaluation at the local level: Recommendations for improving services. *Topics in Early Childhood Special Education, 7*(2), 111–123.

Wood, C.; Powell, S.; & Knight. R.C. (1984). Predicting school readiness: The validity of developmental age. *Journal of Learning Disabilities, 17,* 8–11.

Zimmerman, I.; Steiner, V.; & Evatt, R. (1979). *Preschool language scale.* San Antonio, TX: Psychological Testing Corporation.

Chapter 13

The Artist's Daughter with a Parakeet by Berthe Morisot (1890). Courtesy of The National Gallery of Art, Washington, Chester Dale Collection 1962.

SECONDARY EDUCATION AND LIFE TRANSITION

MAIN IDEAS

- Characteristics of LD adolescents and adults with respect to academic, social, and vocational abilities

- Academic, social, and vocational assessment of LD adolescents and adults

- Places and circumstances where LD adolescents are instructed: special teachers who manage instruction, special teachers who support regular teachers, regular teachers who have groups of LD youngsters, consulting teachers and remedial teachers who collaborate with regular teachers, consulting teachers who collaborate with regular teachers, special and regular teachers who team teach, and regular teachers who are provided in-service support

- Curriculum for LD adolescents: general considerations, program options, and program descriptions

- Transition programs for LD youth and adults: rationale for these programs, setting up transition programs, career education programs, and postsecondary options for learning disabled youth

- Follow-up studies during and after school years

OVERVIEW

There is as much debate centered on LD secondary students as there is with their elementary age counterparts when it comes to *where* their education should take place, but there is much more debate over secondary students with regard to *what* they should be taught. Such placement and curricular issues and many others are dealt with in this chapter.

The first section of this chapter reviews studies that relate to the characteristics of LD adolescents, and the second section covers a few popular and representative tests for secondary age individuals. The third section pertains to delivery systems (such as resource rooms) selected for providing instruction to LD youth, while the fourth provides an outline of the curricular options that are recommended for LD adolescents. The final sections relate to the transition phase for adolescent LD youth, postsecondary programs, college programs, and follow-up studies. The chapter ends with comments that relate to secondary and transition matters.

CHARACTERISTICS OF LD ADOLESCENTS

This section discusses the deficiencies that are characteristic of LD adolescents. Three sets of characteristics are presented. The first is the academic deficiencies of secondary age LD individuals. The second set relates to social skills deficiencies, and the third, to vocational skills deficiencies.

Academic Deficiencies

The major academic difficulties experienced by LD adults, according to Blaylock's (1981) report on the self-descriptions of those individuals, are outlined in Table 13–1. Difficulties are noted in five areas: oral language, reading, writing, mathematics, and nonverbal activities.

■ COMMENTARY ■   It is discouraging to note that the same problems (at least for groups of individuals) were apparent for younger LD students. The problems didn't just happen and didn't manifest themselves differently for these LD adults; they were noted for LD youngsters of elementary age. As the earlier chapters on academic and social skills make clear, Blaylock's LD adults as a group have generally been subaverage performers in every area for quite some time.

Gregory, Shanahan, and Walberg (1985) compared the data of LD and non-LD tenth graders from a national study, "High School and Beyond." Of the total population sampled (30,000), 800 or 2.7 percent were LD. They learned that whereas white students were underrepresented in the LD group, black and Hispanic individuals were overrepresented. There were no significant differences in the proportion of Asian American pupils in either group.

With regard to performance, data from the survey revealed that non-LD pupils significantly outperformed LD students in all academic measures: math, science, civics, vocabulary, reading, and writing. Furthermore, the LD group indicated more school-related problems, attempted and completed less homework, prepared less for class, enrolled in fewer advanced courses, received lower grades, and had lower educational aspirations. Data also revealed that LD pupils were less motivated toward work generally and toward school in particular. Finally, LD pupils exhibited more problems with self-image, locus of control, independence, and the law.

To add to the string of negative characteristics, it is widely known that LD adolescents, as a group, don't attend school as often as their non-LD mates.

■ TABLE 13.1 ■   Areas of Functional Difficulties of LD Individuals

Problem Area	Specific Difficulties
Oral Language	
1. Receptive problems	Listening, auditory perception, auditory comprehension, auditory memory, and auditory discrimination
2. Comprehensive problems	Difficulty understanding conversation, judging grammar, and idiom; problems with abstract language
3. Memory problems	Difficulty remembering steps in a task, directions, and information, such as telephone numbers
4. Expressive problems	Word retrieval, sequencing, pronunciation, and formation (not related to motor speech function or intelligibility); poor knowledge of sounds, words, and syntax
Reading	
1. Decoding problems	Lack of automatic decoding skill, leading to poor pace
2. Comprehension problems	Rate and remembering as well as understanding; difficulty with main ideas, titles, reasons, inferences, and context
Writing	
1. Handwriting problems	
2. Spelling problems	
3. Problems with syntax and morphology	
4. Problems with written connected formulation	Poor organizational skills; problems with planning and developing priorities
Mathematics	
1. Calculation	Problems with calculation, despite good conceptual grasp
2. Conceptual problems	Problems with nonverbal abilities and concepts
3. Language-related problems	Problems in math related to poor reading
Nonverbal Activities	
1. Orientation	Poor sense of direction, lack of map-reading skills, and problems imitating movements (could be two-dimensional or three-dimensional problems); some time-orientation problems
2. Visual–motor problems	Difficulty with daily living skills
3. Social perception	Few friends; inappropriate comments, inappropriate use of personal space, and inadequate social behavior

Source: Reprinted by permission from J. Blaylock, "Persistent Problems and Concerns of Young Adults with Learning Disabilities," in W. Cruickshank and A. Silver (Eds.), *Bridges to Tomorrow: The Best of ACLD* (New York: Syracuse University Press, 1981).

Zigmond, Levin, and Laurie (1985) reported that secondary LD students "fail" their regular education courses more often because of poor attendance than for any other reason. Zigmond and coauthors recommended, therefore, that considerable attention should be given to motivating LD youngsters to attend school regularly. They argued that this issue was far more important than providing teachers with new or different techniques for managing LD youngsters in content classes.

Owings and Stocking (1985) were also concerned about the academic standings of mildly handicapped youth and their prospects for staying in school. They reported data from a national longitudinal study of 30,000 sophomores and 28,000 seniors that included students with self-identified handicaps. Of those sophomores with mild handicaps, whether enrolled in special education or regular education, 45 percent were in the lowest quartile on combined vocabulary, reading, math, and science tests, compared to only 19 percent of the nonhandicapped students. Moreover, the dropout rates for the mildly handicapped were relatively high: 22 percent of the handicapped, as compared to 12 percent of the nonhandicapped, had dropped out of school between their sophomore and senior years.

Algozzine, O'Shea, Stoddard, and Crews (1988) compared the reading and writing scores of LD tenth graders with those of nonhandicapped youngsters on

■ TABLE 13.2 ■   Mastery of Reading and Writing Skills by Tenth Grade Students

	Special Class		Regular Class	
Skill Area	Number	Percent Mastery	Number	Percent Mastery
Reading				
Who, what, when	735	67%	888	95%
Pictures, maps, signs	724	66%	809	87%
Identify informed sources	677	62%	856	92%
Written directions	617	56%	836	90%
Indexes/dictionary	614	53%	814	87%
Cause and effect	581	49%	842	90%
Diagrams and tables	540	48%	724	78%
Main idea (implied)	529	46%	821	88%
Paragraph conclusion	500	46%	769	82%
Main idea (stated)	439	40%	768	82%
Facts and opinions	430	39%	768	82%
Writing				
Money orders and checks	865	79%	892	96%
Request information/messages	742	68%	870	93%
Complete forms	700	64%	833	89%
Letters	493	45%	724	78%

Source: Reprinted by permission from B. Algozzine, D.J. O'Shea, K. Stoddard, and W.B. Crews, "Reading and Writing Competencies of Adolescents with Learning Disabilities," *Journal of Learning Disabilities, 21* (1988), p. 157.

the *Florida State Student Assessment Test—II*. There were about 1,000 LD students in the sample (78 percent boys) and an equal number of non-LD pupils. As expected, the nonhandicapped students demonstrated higher degrees of competence in communication (91 percent mastery) than did the LD students (49 percent mastery). Table 13.2 gives a summary of the scores in several reading and writing skills. All the scores of the non-LD students were higher. The best scores in reading for the special students were in skills that involved the literal recall of facts (for example, "who, what, when"), and their lowest scores were those that required interpretations or judgments ("main ideas"). The highest writing scores for the LD pupils were for "money orders and checks," and the lowest, for writing "letters."

In addition to comparing the communication scores of the two groups, the researchers were also interested in how potential employers judged the measured skills. Surveys from 240 individuals provided data showing that, in general, reading was considered slightly more important than writing. Some skills that were rated as very important were "following written directions," "obtaining information from graphs or tables," "obtaining information from pictures or maps," "writing accurate messages," and "writing requests." (See Table 13.3 for a summary). It was interesting that the reading and writing skills on which the LD pupils performed the best were the same ones the employers cited as the most important.

■ TABLE 13.3 ■   Relative Importance of Reading and Writing Skills in the World of Work

Communication Skill	NVI	VI	Ranking
Reading			
Follow written directions	6%	85%	1
Obtain information from graphs or tables	18%	66%	2
Obtain information from pictures or maps	17%	62%	3
Determine main idea	24%	51%	4
Identify cause and effect	25%	50%	5
Obtain information from references	32%	45%	6
Distinguish facts and opinions	34%	39%	7
Obtain information from directories	44%	30%	8
Writing			
Write accurate messages	5%	80%	1
Write requests	10%	67%	2
Note an assignment	15%	63%	3
Complete forms	22%	55%	4
Write formal letters	37%	41%	5
Complete check and stub	52%	30%	6
Complete money order	75%	12%	7

Source: Reprinted by permission from B. Algozzine, D.J. O'Shea, K. Stoddard, and W.B. Crews, "Reading and Writing Competencies of Adolescents with Learning Disabilities," *Journal of Learning Disabilities, 21* (1988), p. 158.

Based on their data, the researchers recommended that educators consider gearing curricula in reading and writing to those ". . . skills that handicapped adolescents will find useful in adult life (e.g., reading directions in recipes or reading labels on food, reading magazines or the newspaper, writing bowling scores or addressing personal letters)" (Algozzine, O'Shea, Stoddard, & Crews, 1988, p. 159).

Social Skills Deficiencies

Bryan (1976), in summarizing the results of several studies, stated that LD adolescents were less attuned to the affective states of others, more egocentric, and less competent at perceiving others' affective moods than their non-LD peers. She also noted that LD pupils were often unaware of the impact of their behavior on others. Bryan speculated that since LD individuals are often neither stimulating nor concerned with the nuances of others' emotional states, they are not highly sought after as friends.

According to Kronick (1978), other socially inappropriate behaviors of many LD persons include sharing intimate family secrets with casual acquaintances and responding with lengthy dialogues to comments from passersby. She also reported that LD adolescents experienced significantly greater difficulty in labeling non-verbally expressed emotions than did academically achieving youth. Kronick later concluded (1981) that when one takes a lifetime into consideration, social disabilities tend to be far more handicapping than academic deficits.

Keilitz and Dunivant (1986) reported that adolescents with learning disabilities had significantly higher rates of delinquent behavior and engaged in more violence, substance abuse, and school disruption than non-LD adolescents. According to these researchers, the likelihood of arrest and adjudication was also substantially higher for LD adolescents. On a more positive note, Keilitz and Dunivant claimed that an academic treatment program with which they were associated was effective in improving the academic skills and decreasing the delinquency of LD youth who had been officially adjudicated. They remarked that although the youngsters' academic achievement improved, presumably as a result of the remediation program, those changes neither altered the adolescents' attitudes toward school nor were primarily related to their reduced delinquency. It was suggested instead that the participants developed attachments to their LD specialists during the course of remediation and that this bonding led to a reduction in delinquency and better attitudes toward school.

Vocational Skills Deficiencies

Mathews, Whang, and Fawcett (1982) assessed several occupational skills of LD and non-LD high school students. To obtain data on their skills, examiners assessed the youth in a simulated office. There, role-playing tests were administered to measure the participant's performances in 13 different skills. An experimenter played the role of the employer, and the students were asked to act out the job-related tasks as if they were in an actual employment situation. Each session was audiotaped and later scored.

The findings of the study showed low levels of employment-related skills for both groups. The non-LD students, however, performed significantly better on seven of the 13 job-related skills: participating in a job interview, accepting criticism from an employer, providing constructive criticism to a coworker, explaining a problem to a supervisor, writing a letter to request an interview in response to a help-wanted advertisement, writing a letter to follow up a job interview, and completing a federal income tax form. (Note that three of the seven skills involved writing.)

The scores of the non-LD youth were higher, but not significantly so, in three areas: getting a job lead from a friend, telephoning a potential employer to arrange a job interview (when there is not a job opening), and telephoning a potential employer to arrange a job interview (when there is a job opening). Data showed that the two groups were the same when it came to accepting suggestions from an employer, and the LD students were higher than the non-LD pupils in two features: complementing a coworker on a job done well, and accepting a compliment from a coworker.

Krishnaswami (1984) is of the opinion that the many learning and social difficulties of LD youth have considerable impact on their social and interpersonal functioning, self-concept, and leisure activities. She maintains that from a vocational rehabilitation perspective, it is apparent that many of their social and educational problems have a direct bearing on employability and job-readiness. More specifically, when commenting on the vocational attributes, Krishnaswami stated that many LD youth tended to be immature vocationally and also lacked the occupational information needed to make career decisions. She was of the opinion that the ability to choose goals is not one of the strengths of LD individuals and is further complicated by the fact that decision-making is extremely difficult for many of them.

ASSESSMENT FOR LD ADOLESCENTS

Many of the approaches for testing explained in other chapters (Chapter 3 and Chapter 11—that is, rating scales, checklists, and curriculum-based assessment— are also used to assess secondary age individuals. Furthermore, many of the standardized tests explained in other chapters (Chapter 7 and Chapter 9)—for example, *Reading for Mastery* and *KeyMath*—are arranged for learning disabled adolescents and adults. Only a few representative tests developed for adolescents or young adults are outlined in this section.

Academic and Social Assessment

Test of Adolescent Language—2 (Hammill, Brown, Larsen, & Wiederholt, 1987).   The TOAL—2 is designed for youth between the ages of 12.0 and 18.5.

Phyllis Newcomer is on the faculty of Beaver College. She is also the editor of *Learning Disabilities Quarterly*. Newcomer has assisted in the development of a number of tests of LD youth. She has also published in several areas, including writing and the development of competencies for professionals in learning disabilities.

Most of the subtests can be administered to a group, but two are to be administered individually. On the average, it takes about 100 minutes to give the test. TOAL—2 is made up of eight subtests: listening/vocabulary, listening/grammar, speaking/vocabulary, speaking/grammar, reading/vocabulary, reading/grammar, writing/vocabulary, and writing/grammar. TOAL—2 is designed to accomplish four purposes:

1. Identify students who are significantly below their peers in language proficiency and who may profit from supplemental help.
2. Determine the particular kinds of language strengths and weaknesses that individual students might possess.
3. Document students' progress in language as a consequence of special intervention programs.
4. Serve as a measurement device in investigations where researchers are studying the language behavior of adolescents.

Fullerton Language Test for Adolescents (Thorum, 1980).   The FLTA, an individually administered test that requires about 45 minutes, was designed for youth between 11 and 18 years of age. The FLTA assesses receptive and expressive language skills and provides a comprehensive profile of the student's language competency. A major purpose of the FLTA is to distinguish normal from language-impaired adolescents and adults in such language-related skills as auditory synthesis, morphology competency, oral commands, convergent production, divergent production, syllabication, grammatic competency, and idiom.

Weller-Strawser Scales of Adaptive Behavior: For the Learning Disabled (Weller & Strawser, 1981). The WSSAB, developed for students of elementary and secondary age, assesses adaptive behaviors in the areas of social coping, relationships, pragmatic language, and production. Information from the subtests allows the examiner to determine the severity of the student's disability and to identify specific areas of adaptive behavior that require remedial attention. The WSSAB should be administered individually, and requires about 20 minutes to give.

Social and Prevocational Information Battery (Halpern, Raffeld, Irvin, & Link, 1975). The SPIB, developed for mildly handicapped individuals from grades 6 through 12, consists of a series of nine tests designed to assess knowledge of life skills and competencies regarded as important for community adjustment. The tests cover job search skills, job-related behavior, banking, budgeting, purchasing, home management, physical health care, hygiene and grooming, and functional signs. According to the publisher, the skills tested are directly related to five long-range goals of work-study or work-experience programs in secondary school: employability, economic self-sufficiency, family living, personal habits, and communication. The tests are orally administered to groups and require from 15 to 25 minutes per test to administer.

Vocational Assessment

According to Irvin (1988), vocational assessment ". . . is a comprehensive, multidisciplinary process that educators and rehabilitation professionals can use for a variety of purposes. It can be used, for example, to identify vocationally relevant characteristics of students. It can also be used to document relevant educational, training, and placement needs of individual students. Finally, it is appropriate as a strategy for identifying the necessary and available resources to address those needs" (p. 111).

Irvin maintains that vocational assessment should provide, at the minimum, relevant information on the following:

— Individual competence in so-called prevocational areas such as work habits and attitudes
— Training needs of individuals in specific vocational areas; that is, skills for specific job roles rather than training on generic "tool use" or equipment operation
— Characteristics of training strategies that are effective for individuals in schools and other settings
— Placement options during and following training

There are four types of vocational assessment in schools. They are briefly described in the following paragraphs.

Vocational Evaluation Center Model. For this approach, vocational assessment centers are established. Students referred to those settings are administered a battery of assessments—aptitude tests (verbal, spatial, motor), work sample tests (sorting, folding, tool use), and interest inventories. For this approach to be successful, there are three requirements: emphasis on the use of evaluation results to direct skill training, involvement of classroom tryouts and work samples based directly on the contents of vocational training programs, and use of vocational evaluation as part of a comprehensive service for students receiving special education.

Curriculum-Based Model. For this model, vocational assessment takes place primarily in the classroom, school, and community settings where career or vocational education occurs. All professionals who provide training participate in the ongoing evaluations, conduct the assessments, and make the educational decisions. The major emphasis of the curriculum-based model is on an instructional approach in which competencies, interests, and values are addressed within a comprehensive curriculum throughout the school years. With this model, assessment and training are exactly in accord with written IEP objectives. Irvin argues that when the content and formats of assessment are derived directly from the curriculum, the results of assessment have immediate implications for educational judgments, such as what to teach, how to teach, and where to teach.

Comprehensive Model. This approach is a combination of the center- and curriculum-based models. It relies on features of the curriculum-based approach as the primary strategy for educational decision making. When that approach fails to provide enough information for placement or training, or for some other educational or administrative component, a referral to an evaluation center is suggested. In the comprehensive approach, assessment data collected in centers must be communicated immediately to instructional personnel in schools or communities to facilitate their use in program planning. Interdisciplinary team meetings of the vocational assessment staff are essential if results from center-based assessments are to be of value.

Conceptual Model. The three-stage approach proposed by Stodden and Ianacone (1981) is an example of this model. Their first stage, "readiness," involves preassessment activities addressing student awareness, exploration, and decision making. Students from grades K through 9 explore, become aware of, and learn about the values of roles and the nature of work in our society. As a result of these activities, students learn about employability issues, personal-social behaviors, and general academic preparation.

The second stage of the model, "assessment," involves an in-depth evaluation of students' performance on work roles and specific work-related and work skills. Students are provided a number of opportunities to experience the information, skill, value, and role demands of real work in classroom, school, and community settings throughout the secondary school years. Assessment is continuous, direct, and derived from multiple sources in multiple settings.

The third component, "application," involves formatting and interpreting assessment information for use in the secondary school program. Assessment information is organized and presented to meet the needs of several audiences (for example, parents, support services staff, and administrative personnel).

DELIVERY SYSTEMS

This section describes seven types of programs that are arranged to offer services to LD adolescents. To a certain extent they are listed from most to least restrictive with respect to involvement with regular youngsters; special teacher management of content instruction is the most restrictive, while in-service help by regular teachers is the least. Included in the descriptions are comments on the possible advantages and disadvantages of each program.

When schools arrange programs for LD adolescents, they ordinarily offer a blend of approaches. It would be very unusual for a district to operate its program with only one of these options, as will become clear when two actual programs for LD adolescents are examined later in this chapter.

Special Teacher Manages Content Instruction

When this approach is chosen, special education teachers operate much the same as elementary school teachers, in the sense that they manage most of the instruction. Although there are fewer situations of this type than there once were, it is not unusual to find special education teachers who offer instruction in secondary content areas such as physical science, U.S. history, algebra, and language.

Possible advantages include the following:

- The classes are generally small.
- There can be more flexibility in terms of time, since several subjects may be taught in one large time block.
- The materials can be individually selected.
- Pupils' modes of receiving information and responding to it can be taken into account.
- Teachers can make adjustments in the ways pupils are tested and graded.
- Special teachers may have considerable experience dealing with pupils who display wide ranges of ability and motivational levels.
- Special teachers may have a great deal of experience managing unruly and unmotivated youngsters.
- Special teachers may be more attuned generally to the social and emotional problems of handicapped youth. Special teachers may have experience in setting up cooperative learning groups, instructing study skills, and arranging peer tutoring situations.

There are also some possible disadvantages:

☐ Special education teachers may not have enough information or sufficient formal training to teach certain subjects.

☐ Special teachers might be required to plan for five or six different subjects.

☐ Youngsters in those special classes are not likely to be associated with more able students who may serve as models.

☐ Teachers might be too easy on the students and not expect enough from them.

☐ Teachers might grade their special students too easily, thus giving them a distorted idea of how grades are earned.

☐ Students might not earn the required credits when enrolled in these special classes.

Special Teacher Supports Regular Teachers

For this model, resource teachers support the instruction offered in the content classes. In effect, they run study halls. LD youngsters bring their assignments from history, math, language, and other classes to the resource room, and there, special teachers help them. Quite a few districts schedule this approach.

Some possible advantages include the following:

1. Resource teachers can help students keep up in their classes, and as a result, students may make better grades, which, in turn, may encourage them to come to school more often and stay in school longer.

2. Youngsters are able to spend some time with regular students.

3. Special education teachers might modify some of the materials and the means whereby students respond to them and perhaps suggest the modification techniques to content-area teachers.

4. The special class might serve as a sanctuary for certain handicapped youth, since their teachers can assist them on matters beyond U.S. history and math.

Following are some possible disadvantages:

1. There might be too many youngsters to help with too many assignments, and special teachers may become frantic trying to assist them all.[1]

---

1. We have data from resource teachers in a middle school in which teachers work with 25 students. On most days, they see only 10 of the students, and often, 3 or 4 pupils take up 75 percent of the time.

2. Some students fail to bring in their assignments and thus waste the teacher's time.

3. Resource teachers must collect and have available the materials required in all the various subjects.

4. Regular teachers might place too much responsibility for helping low-achieving students on special teachers.

5. Because LD youngsters know they can work on assignments in the resource room, they might loaf during the regular class period.

6. Resource teachers might be so busy patching up students with respect to their academic assignments that they might not be aware of their other problems in classes (for example, asking questions, contributing to discussions, and acting interested).

Regular Teacher Manages Modified Classes

In these instances, regular science, history, math, or language teachers are assigned classes made up of low achieving students. They might use the same texts and materials as those found in the regular classes, or they might select texts or other materials that are different but have about the same coverage as those used in the regular classes. There are several such situations around the country.

Following are some possible advantages:

□ Teachers of these modified classes were presumably trained in the subjects they teach.

□ The class sizes may be lower than the usual.

□ Teachers should be able to work with others in the same department and gather ideas and materials from them on how best to serve LD students.

□ Students should be able to earn credit for required courses.

□ The teachers may be able to modify materials, tests, methods of grading, and other instructional features.

Among the possible disadvantages are the following:

□ Teachers might not want to be assigned to these "lower track" classes.

□ The size of modified classes might not be smaller than the "regular track" classes, yet the youngsters might be more difficult to manage.

□ It is unlikely that there will be many superior students in these classes who could serve as models.

□ There might be a stigma attached to these classes, causing other students and teachers in the school to look down on them.

Consulting Teacher and Remedial Teacher Collaborate with Regular Teachers

This system is advocated by Laurie, Buchwach, Silverman, and Zigmond (1978), but has not been widely adopted. In this collaborative approach, consulting teachers provide services to content-area teachers who have LD youth mainstreamed into their classes, and remedial teachers assist LD youngsters with the basic skills—reading, mathematics, and writing—in a special room. Proponents of this model call for regular and consulting teachers to move through an eight-step sequence in order to modify regular situations to accommodate special students:

1. Determine the requirements for "making it" in the regular classes, with respect to how the classrooms are organized, how they are managed, and other general features.
2. Specify the course requirements and expectations that the LD students are not achieving.
3. Speculate as to the possible reasons for those failures.
4. Brainstorm possible classroom modifications that might alleviate the problems; in so doing, propose procedures that teachers can easily adopt into their practices.
5. Reject the alternative of removing youngsters from regular classrooms and dealing with them elsewhere.
6. Detail management and instructional plans for LD or other low-achieving students.
7. Put those plans into operation.
8. Obtain data on relevant behaviors of the youngsters and evaluate effects of the modifications.

Some possible advantages of this approach include:

□ It is better able to serve a wide range of pupils' needs.
□ It allows two special teachers to assist each other.
□ It provides continuity of programming, because of "bench strength."

Following are some possible disadvantages:

□ Since so few systems rely on this approach, it would be difficult to find a suitable model.
□ Hiring two special teachers is rather expensive.
□ Sorting out the responsibilities of the two teachers and determining who would do what is time consuming and could cause conflicts.

☐ Regular teachers might rely too heavily on the specialists and thus never become competent in dealing with the academic and motivational variability common to most classes.

Consulting Teacher Collaborates with Regular Teachers

For this type of program, LD youngsters are enrolled in regular content classes, and their teachers receive assistance from a consultant. The consultant comes into the class and provides assistance or consultation or, more commonly, meets with teachers before or after school or during preparation periods to offer advice on management and instructional matters. According to Powell (1981), consultants might assist regular teachers to provide study and social skills instruction and possibly help them adapt materials and tests for slow learners. This option is becoming popular throughout the country.

Following are some possible advantages:

☐ Students remain in regular classes with their peers, some of whom might serve as proper models.

☐ Pupils are instructed by teachers who were presumably trained in their specialty.

☐ The consultant might be able to assist regular teachers to adapt instructional features for all types of students, not just those with learning disabilities.

☐ Consultants can observe all the happenings of regular classes when they visit them and thus be more understanding of teachers and students.

☐ Consultants might learn a few tactics for teaching from the regular instructors.

The possible disadvantages include the following:

☐ LD youngsters might rely too much on the consultants and, as a result, fail to learn about modifying or adapting aspects of instruction.

☐ Some consultants are not able to work well with people and thus are not welcome in classrooms.

☐ Consultants might not have much information regarding instruction to offer teachers.

☐ Consulting teacher programs can be expensive because consultants do not have youngsters on their caseloads.

☐ Some regular teachers might resent the fact that consultants have more flexible working arrangements.

☐ Some teachers don't want others in their classes and are not interested in consultation assistance.

Special and Regular Teachers Team Teach

In the team teaching approach, described by Proctor (1986), regular and special teachers combine their classes and team teach the content subjects. There are not many of these arrangements, but the numbers are growing.

Some possible advantages are the following:

☐ Pupils benefit from the content experience of the regular teacher and the management and instructional modification experience of the special teacher.

☐ There is an opportunity to group youngsters by ability level.

☐ Special and regular students can be instructed in the same room.

☐ Special and regular teachers may learn from one another.

☐ There is the probability of continuity if one teacher is absent.

☐ There is a strong chance that the teacher is often on his or her "best behavior" when the peer teacher is near.

Some possible disadvantages include the following:

☐ It is sometimes difficult for administrators to work out the "numbers game" when two teachers are involved.

☐ A fairly large room is required.

☐ Some teachers don't work well with others.

☐ It takes time and patience to set up the structure so that both teachers know their roles.

Regular Teachers Are Provided In-Service Help

In this approach, the least restrictive of the delivery systems for LD students, youngsters of all types are enrolled in regular content-area classes. The teachers of these classes receive in-service assistance designed to help them manage youngsters of diverse needs. This practice is common.

Some possible advantages are the following:

☐ If the in-service programs are carefully planned and based on teachers' needs, there is some chance that teachers will acquire skills to manage their current group of handicapped youngsters.

☐ If teachers develop a repertory of teaching tactics from the in-service training, they may be able to assist handicapped students, slow learners, and others in years to come.

☐ When it is up to teachers to develop skills for managing the many and varied needs of youngsters, there is a chance that they will attend carefully to the in-service instruction.

□ Handicapped youngsters are instructed alongside nonhandicapped students in these situations.

Following are some possible disadvantages:

□ If the in-service programs are poorly planned, do not pertain to teachers' needs, are poorly presented and organized, are too few, held at inconvenient times, or have no follow-ups, the teachers will not acquire the necessary information, and they will resent the waste of their time.

□ Some in-service programs are very expensive.

Mainstreaming LD Students

Zigmond, Levin, and Laurie (1985) reported on four studies that have considerable bearing on the instruction of LD adolescents, particularly those served in regular classes. In Study 1, they surveyed the attitudes of regular high school teachers who had LD youngsters in their classes. The data indicated that 65 percent of the teachers reported that LD students differed from the others in their classes; 78 percent of the teachers believed that the primary problem of LD students was their lack of proficiency with the basic skills; 41 percent maintained

Naomi Zigmond studied at Northwestern University with Myklebust and is on the faculty of the University of Pittsburgh. Her research has centered on learning disabled adolescents. On that topic she has surveyed existing services for LD youth and recommended alternative programs. Zigmond has been particularly interested in mainstreaming situations. Recently, she and Kerr have developed a school survival curriculum for LD youth.

that LD students should be placed in regular classes; but 25 percent thought that they did not place extra demands on the teacher.

In Study 2, Zigmond and coauthors were concerned with the extent that mainstream teachers accommodated LD adolescents in their classes. The data revealed that 85 percent of the teachers believed that the ability to read was the main problem of LD students, 55 percent said that the students did not place extra demands on them. With reference to practices and policies, 96 percent reported that they made no adjustments at all to ensure that LD students received necessary information from texts, other materials, or lectures; 71 percent made no adjustments in the assignments for the LD pupils; 71 percent made no adjustments in testing those students; and 60% didn't make adjustments in grades for them. Other data from Study 2 revealed that 51% of the teachers claimed that textbooks were the materials that students used the most during class time, and 83% reported that their tests were written.

In Study 3, Zigmond and colleagues studied the grades of LD students in mainstreamed classes. These results showed that more than 80 percent of the students passed at least half of their subjects; at least one third of them passed all their classes; and 65 percent of the students were failing at least one course.

■ COMMENTARY ■   Keep in mind that according to Study 2, about 40 percent of the teachers made adjustments in grades for the LD youth. This was about the only instructional feature they adjusted.

Attendance patterns of LD students in mainstream classes was the theme of Study 4. It was reported that more than half of the failed grades of LD students could be attributed to attendance problems.

■ COMMENTARY ■   Most educators and researchers are in agreement that not only is there a relationship between attendance and grades, but there is a definite linkage between attendance and dropping out of school.

Following is a summary of the major conclusion Zigmond and coauthors made from the four studies: Recognizing the need to make the mainstream experience successful for learning disabled students, some might interpret the data from the first three studies to suggest that in-service programs should be established to provide high school teachers with techniques for accommodating LD students in the mainstream. Sessions could include techniques for reducing the heavy demands on reading and writing in assignments and tests, for arranging for small group or individualized instruction and for introducing peer tutoring into high school classes. Although such techniques might be useful to teachers and LD students, it would be unwise to focus on only new techniques and to neglect the data on grades and attendance patterns. Data suggest that the main problem is not to accommodate LD students in high school classes, but to get them to show up in the first place.

   In line with that conclusion, the researchers recommended that schools reconsider the merits of a common grading policy that punishes students for nonattendance and contributes substantially to making high school a defeating experience. Zigmond and coauthors are of the opinion that a less punitive system would be to base grades on achievement and merit. That approach would refocus both teachers and students away from a custodial emphasis (keeping students in school) to an instructional emphasis (making the activity of classrooms meaningful and worthwhile). The researchers argued that in the end, a new grading system would provide teachers, administrators, and students with a much clearer picture of the extent to which the secondary school curriculum was comprehended by all students, not just the mainstreamed learning disabled.

CURRICULUM FOR LD STUDENTS

Studies on Skills Needed

As indicated earlier, there are debates not only on *where* LD adolescents should be instructed, but on *what* they should be taught. This section describes some curricular themes that are available for educating LD youth. As is true with the types of delivery systems, it is rare for a school to opt for only one of these curricular approaches; the majority of secondary schools rely on several.

   In an effort to determine what constituted effective programs for LD students, Touzel (1978) surveyed the literature and asked the opinions of a number of experts in the field. From those data, it was apparent that the experts agreed on the following points:

1. There should be a philosophy and set of goals in which the main components include survival skills, individualization of the goals and needs of each student, career and vocational development, and the development of a healthy self-concept.
2. The philosophy and goals should include input from a variety of sources and be influenced by assessment and projections of present and future needs.
3. The curriculum should be derived from a variety of sources.
4. The evaluation of programs should include the follow up of graduates and drop-outs, using a variety of sources that included ecological observations.

   Touzel pointed out that the relevant literature was very light on functional coping and survival skills and on approaches for developing self-concepts. She concluded that the current state of the curriculum for secondary LD youngsters was inconsistent and that virtually nothing had been written on philosophies, goals, curricula, or evaluation procedures.

   Salend and Salend (1986) surveyed the literature on instructional and social skills and developed a questionnaire that was sent to regular and special education teachers at the junior and senior high levels. They wanted to know which behaviors the teachers believed secondary youngsters should exhibit in order to achieve satisfactorily in schools. Table 13.4 shows the teachers' rankings of behaviors for three functions.

In the survey, the special education teachers were generally more stringent than the regular teachers, and junior high teachers more so than those at the senior high level.

■ COMMENTARY ■   It is difficult to account for the latter, but it isn't surprising that special education teachers were more concerned about these socially and academically related behaviors than

■ TABLE 13.4 ■   Teachers' Ranking of Behaviors for Secondary School Success

---

Function 1.0: Exhibit appropriate work habits

1.1   Attend class regularly
1.2   Follow directions
1.3   Bring necessary materials to class
1.4   Attempt to complete tasks before giving up
1.5   Ask for help when it is appropriate
1.6   Complete homework
1.7   Demonstrate adequate attention span
1.8   Communicate their needs
1.9   Remember more than one direction at a time
1.10 Begin an assignment after the teacher explains it to the class
1.11 Complete work on time
1.12 Work without being easily distracted

Function 2.0: Respect others and their property:

2.1   Refrain from stealing others' property
2.2   Respect others' property
2.3   Respect adults
2.4   Tell the truth
2.5   Respect others' feelings
2.6   Refrain from speaking when others are talking
2.7   Display proper health and hygiene habits
2.8   Be aware of the effects of their behavior on others
2.9   Work well with others

Function 3.0: Follow school rules:

3.1   Obey class rules
3.2   Refrain from cutting classes
3.3   Avoid getting in fights
3.4   Refrain from cheating on tests
3.5   Refrain from cursing
3.6   Demonstrate appropriate behavior in large group settings
3.7   Refrain from boastful comments concerning inappropriate behaviors
3.8   Seek teacher permission before speaking

Source: Reprinted by permission from S.J. Salend and S.M. Salend, "Competencies for Mainstreaming Secondary Level Learning Disabled Students," *Journal of Learning Disabilities, 19* (1986), pp. 92–93.

were the regular teachers, for they might have been more aware of the adverse consequences than would be likely for individuals who were not adept in those areas.

Zigmond, Sansone, Miller, Donahoe, and Kohnke (1986) have stated that in addition to motivating secondary LD students by considering their interests, teachers must make the acquisition of new skills as important and immediately useful as possible. Adolescents, like the rest of us, respond positively when given reasons for learning skills. Following are some reasons that could be communicated to LD adolescents for needing certain skills taught at school:

—To find a job
—To perform on a job
—To survive as an adult
—To assist in learning a more desirable skill
—To be mainstreamed into a regular class
—To enter college or some type of postsecondary training
—To complete the courses and earn the credits required for high school graduation
—To enjoy or participate in a desired leisure activity
—To function like their normal peers
—To participate in extracurricular school activities
—To help cope in times of stress
—To be better able to live with others, particularly with one's own family

McBride and Forgnone (1985) surveyed the instructional programs for LD and other handicapped youth by studying the short-term objectives written for them on their IEPs. Their study included fifteen youngsters from grades 6, 7, and 8 in each of the three groups—learning disabled, emotionally handicapped, and educable mentally retarded—in categorical and cross-categorical resource room programs. Their findings revealed that over 90 percent of the objectives for LD youngsters in both types of programs were academic. Only 10 percent of the objectives were sociobehavioral. The distribution of academic and sociobehavioral objectives for EH youngsters was about equal in either type of program. As for the EMR youth, about 75 percent of their objectives had to do with academics and 25 percent to self-help/basic living in both situations.

■ COMMENTARY ■   It is more than a little interesting to note that labels *do* influence programs. This, in spite of the fact that it is highly probable that treatment needs overlapped among the groups. Certainly, a number of educators and researchers would recommend large doses of social skills training for many LD adolescents.

Program Options

Following is a brief review of a number of program options available for LD students. Some are very common, others are not. A few of the latter should probably be arranged more often than they are.

Basic Skills.   For this option, which is fairly popular, teachers concentrate on the fundamental academic skills: reading, arithmetic, writing, and spelling. Programs of this type are much like those offered in elementary schools. In fact, teachers committed to the basic skills approach use many of the materials for teaching reading, mathematics, and other academic subjects that are discussed in this book. When these programs are scheduled for LD students, the idea is that many of the young people will not be able to achieve in content courses unless they can read and calculate at certain levels of proficiency. However, Schumaker, Deshler, Alley, and Warner (1983), who reported data on this topic, warned that when teachers emphasized basic skills instruction, LD adolescents gained only .2 of a year in reading and math during a year of teaching.

Functional Academics.   The focus of this approach, which is more popular with the MR than the LD, is on teaching information believed to be needed in society beyond high school. The assumption is that students cannot succeed in content-area programs and therefore need an altered curriculum that prepares them for the world beyond high school. (This is in line with a previously noted recommendation of Algozzine et al., 1988.) Components of functional reading include reading directions and attempting to follow them, scanning material for specific pieces of information, reading recipes, reading popular magazines and newspapers, and reading application forms and bus schedules. Functional math skills include writing checks and maintaining a checkbook; estimating times, distances, and amounts; using hand-held calculators and digital watches; making change; and following recipes. Among the functional writing skills are filling out forms, writing personal notes and memos, and writing simple paragraphs.

Learning Strategies.   According to Alley and Deshler (1979), learning strategies (study skills) are the techniques, principles, or rules that facilitate the acquisition, integration, and retrieval of information across situations and settings. (See Chapter 10.) The researchers base their support for this approach on four assumptions:

1. Knowledge and situations are transitory; therefore, students should be taught strategies that can be applied to a variety of situations.
2. Current educational practices have not been successful.
3. Learning strategies have been effective with non-LD students.
4. Instruction in learning strategies is compatible with notions of the least restrictive environment.

Although proponents of study skills do not completely agree on the components of that process, such programs generally feature reading comprehension strategies, skimming, scanning, notetaking, test taking, paragraph writing, and time management. Supporters of study skills instruction maintain that if youngsters are taught to rely on sets of strategies, they can draw on them in many of the content subjects in secondary schools.

In some schools study skills are taught in resource rooms. Special teachers instruct various strategies and expect LD youngsters to rely on those strategies when they go to regular classrooms for history and science. In some cases, the resource teachers instruct the study skills *and* contact regular teachers periodically to check on the students' use of the techniques. In other schools, study skills are taught by regular teachers within the context of their subjects. Although there are few, if any, data to compare those approaches, it is likely that the latter design would be most effective, since LD youngsters (or others for that matter) are not keen on generalizing learnings from one situation to another. (See comments on generalization in the Epilogue.)

Social Skills.   Few would debate the importance of being able to get along with others, and few would argue that being adept socially was one of the strong suits of LD adolescents. (See Chapter 11.) As indicated elsewhere in this section, it is necessary to have reasonably developed social skills when living with family members and when engaged in the work place. Getting along socially is probably more important than having technical, physical, or organizational skills.

Social skills are complex arrangements of components; they include listening to others, expressing needs and opinions in noninflammatory ways, working with others for a common goal, complimenting others, accepting criticism without blowing up, controlling emotions, negotiating, taking turns, maintaining conversations, providing assistance at the proper time, knowing when to be candid, and "reading" social situations accurately.

Prevocational.   Prevocational offerings are traditionally scheduled more often for mentally retarded youngsters than for the learning disabled. A few schools, however—particularly since the current emphasis on the transition of handicapped youth from school to adult life—have arranged prevocational experiences for LD adolescents. Among the areas generally included in prevocational curricula are purchasing, budgeting, looking for a job, interviewing for a job, managing a home, writing checks and banking, grooming and general health care, and reading functional signs.

Work-Study Programs.   When this option is offered, LD students are placed on job assignments either in the school or in the neighborhood during part of their school day. Although programs of this type are more popular with mentally retarded youngsters, some districts involve LD students. One of the prime reasons for offering work study programs, according to some authorities, is that the best single predictor of finding a job after graduation is the number of jobs that people had obtained competitively while in school or shortly thereafter.

■ COMMENTARY ■   In one classroom survey, we found students averaged six "funky" jobs between the ages of 16 and 21, most of which were of the service type and were low paying.

Home Living.   For this program option, students are taught the basics of living by themselves or with others in a house or apartment. Programs of this type are more popular with mentally retarded than with LD youth. In these programs students are taught to operate such machines as dishwashers, clothes washers and dryers, microwaves, and stereos. They are also instructed to maintain and clean their living quarters, to care for lawn and garden areas, and to arrange routines so that they know when to carry out their chores.

An emphasis of these programs is to assist individuals to work independently, to work with others, and to work alongside others. (This component is highly related to the social skills theme). Individuals in such programs learn to share time and space in the home, to give in, to express their desires, and to negotiate.

■ COMMENTARY ■   It is of great importance to assist LD pupils with home living skills, for according to a number of researchers (for example, Edgar, 1988), many of them are likely to be unemployed for extended periods of time and, consequently, will live at home. An informative survey would be to ask adults who have young adults living with them a few questions: How do they get along as a family? What would the sons or daughters need to do differently in order to make communal living more tolerable? That information would be of value in planning social skills and home living type programs.

Knowing Your Neighborhood.   This social studies component of some programs for mentally retarded students is not a common one for LD youth, even though they too need to know about their immediate and not-so-immediate environment. Since many of the learning disabled are likely to be living at home for long periods of time, it is important for them to know ways to spend their leisure hours profitably. They need to know the locations of museums, galleries, parks, recreation centers, and shopping malls, and how to get to them. If they can move about in their communities and sensibly occupy their leisure hours, they will learn from the experiences, have more to talk about when interacting with others and will possibly make a few friends.

■ COMMENTARY ■   Certainly another argument to support the involvement of certain LD students in community endeavors is that when they are away from their homes, they are allowing their parents to have a few hours of privacy. This might contribute to more positive subsequent interactions between family members.

Networking.   This program option related to social skills training is rarely, if ever, chosen for LD students, despite the fact that they need to be able to build social networks for a number of reasons. For one, a number of experts in the business of "follow-ups" (for example, Edgar, 1988) claim that most people, whether they are learning disabled or not, locate jobs through networks. They find more jobs through their families and friends than through formal job finding agencies or advertisements in help wanted columns.

■ COMMENTARY ■   This was certainly corroborated by the classroom survey referred to earlier; 80 percent of the students' jobs were obtained through family or friends. Given instruction in learning to network, LD students would benefit vocationally and in other ways, too. For example, students could be required to locate something or find out about something and be told to identify the people they asked in order to come up with the desired information. As they learn more about the topic, they can be guided to ask more sophisticated questions and begin to focus in on the answer or alternatives that will enable them to make a decision.

In the meantime, they might gain socially and linguistically from the process.

Employment Adaptability.   Mithaug, Martin, and Agran (1987) described an instructional option designed to teach students generic employment adaptability skills. The model, designed to teach students to adapt, is made up of decision making, independent performance, self-evaluation, and adjustment. According to the authors, failure to adapt to dynamic work environments results in unsatisfactory work experiences and job terminations. Failure to adapt to dynamic home and community environments results in unsatisfactory relationships and disorganized living activities.

The researchers are critical of current instructional practices for many of the mildly handicapped, claiming that the dominant instructional approach assumes a level of student dependency that reinforces behaviors incompatible with independence and student initiative.

■ COMMENTARY ■   Under current practices, many of the mildly handicapped learn to be *special* and to demand lots of attention. Many of them learn that unless the instruction is one-on-one, it isn't important.

Opportunities for students to express preferences, make choices, and behave spontaneously and autonomously are not ordinarily provided. Mithaug and associates maintain that programs are needed that enhance self-direction and that teach problem-solving skills in classrooms, community sites, and work settings. They suggest that these approaches should focus on generic adaptability skills, rather than on specific work skills that apply only to the environment targeted in the student's transition program.

It is the intent of the adaptability model to prepare students to respond appropriately to five major features associated with employment generally: working on tasks employees may or may not enjoy, earning money, working on tasks that match employees' skills and abilities, completing tasks quickly and accurately, and completing tasks that must be done.

Description of Actual Programs

The following paragraphs review secondary programs for LD adolescents in two Seattle area high schools, both of which rely on a number of delivery systems and offer several of the curricular options just outlined.

Liberty High School.   Four special education teachers serve 81 LD students in grades 9 through 12 at this suburban school. They divide their duties as follows: One teacher is responsible for ninth and tenth grade resource room English and two periods of prevocational classes. The second teacher instructs twelfth grade resource room English, U.S. history, contemporary issues, and two prevocational classes. A third teacher has two periods of eleventh grade resource room English, one period of ninth grade social studies, and two periods of vocational work. The fourth teacher offers ninth grade general science, resource room math, and study skills.

Prevocational classes are team taught by two teachers. Included in these classes are six weeks of job shadowing and an exploration of career choices. In addition, a vocational class offers a half-day of unpaid job experience.

One of the special teachers and a regular science teacher team teach a ninth grade general science class and a contemporary issues class, in which no particular ratios of LD to non-LD students are established. In these situations, the regular teacher is responsible for organizing the content and presenting the materials, and the special teacher assists individual students and offers suggestions for alternate instructional methods. The team teachers are also responsible for offering study skills instruction in the content classes.

The regular classes into which LD youngsters are mainstreamed are those required for graduation, some of which are modified to better suit the needs of slower youngsters. The math department offers such classes in general math, business math, and pre-algebra, whereas the social studies department schedules modified U. S. history and Northwest studies classes. The science department offers a survival science class. The English department does not offer a modified English class; consequently, four periods of English are taught in the resource room by a special teacher. LD youngsters are also enrolled in classes that are not required for graduation and are not modified: vocal music, physical education, home living, and industrial arts.

Hazen High School.   At Hazen, one part-time and two full-time teachers serve 70 LD students from grades 10 to 12. One full-time teacher works primarily with the students in a study skills program. There, they work on time management, reading study skills, test taking, positive presentation of self, notetaking, paraphrasing, effective speaking, and effective listening. Those students are mainstreamed for all their subjects. In order to incorporate the study skills into content classes, this teacher is allotted time for consultation with regular teachers and is also given extra time to consult with the parents of LD students.

The other full-time teacher supervises the vocational track students (lower LD youngsters and the MR students) who are not mainstreamed into regular classes. They are enrolled in classes at the Renton Vocational and Technical Institute, where they take a diversified occupations class, and a prevocational class.

At Hazen High School, several classes are taught by special teachers in resource rooms: U.S. history, language arts, math, and Pacific Northwest history. These classes are for moderately functioning LD youngsters and a few MR students.

Some modified classes are also offered at Hazen—that is, classes for lower functioning students, taught by regular teachers. The math department offers basic math, consumer math, and math maintenance; the science department schedules modified life science and general science classes; and the social studies department offers a modified U. S. history class. The English department offers three levels of composition and four levels of language arts classes. Rather than offering modified classes, they schedule accelerated classes. The thinking is that the slower youngsters will be able to fit into their regular classes.

This program places a strong emphasis on the transition from high school to a career or further education. Toward that end, the vocational track teacher works closely with outside agencies to provide career counseling prior to and following graduation.

Some concluding remarks seem to be in order from the sketches of the two high school programs.

1. There was little emphasis on basic skills instruction in either of the programs.

2. Both programs relied on a number of delivery systems to instruct their LD youngsters: resource rooms, modified classes, team teaching situations, and consultation with regular teachers.

3. The schools went to considerable effort to offer LD youngsters the courses required for graduation.

4. These high schools scheduled prevocational or vocational experiences for the LD youth.

5. Several content classes were taught by the special education teachers.

6. Language arts departments seemed the most reluctant to offer modified classes.

TRANSITION

Transition is now a widely used term that generally indicates the movement of individuals from youth to adulthood. It refers to many behaviors—social, educational, vocational, and others—that undergo change from the school years to being an adult. Whereas most educators look upon the transition period as that which follows the age of 18 or when youngsters exit school, there are several who recommend that training efforts for this era begin much earlier than that time.

Rationale for Arranging Transition Programs

The practical reasons for being concerned about the transition years for the LD population come from studies and casual observations of those youngsters who have exited schools, either by graduating or dropping out. In too many instances, the quality of lives being led by those individuals is not high.

Postsecondary Problems.   Many LD graduates or drop outs are not living independently, but are housed with their relatives or others. Many of them are
unemployed, while many of those who are employed are earning substandard
wages. Numbers of them who have had job experiences have also had extended
periods of unemployment. Few are able to profit from the recreational and
educational opportunities in their neighborhoods. For many LD citizens, the
picture is grim.

Kiernan and Ciborowski (1986) reported data from the Department of
Health and Human Services, Administration on Developmental Disabilities. They
estimated that there were 3.9 million persons with developmental disabilities, and
of that number, more than 2 million were over the age of 18. Estimates of students
with special needs exiting special and vocational education programs each year
range from 95,000 to 200,000, but from 46 percent to 88 percent of these students
(depending on which study is consulted), do not enter competitive employment
situations after leaving school. These data are in agreement with those of Sitlington
(1981), who reported that in 1976, only 40 percent of the handicapped were
working as compared to 74 percent of the general population, and that 85 percent
of the employed handicapped earned less than $7,000 per year.

Kiernan and Ciborowski (1986) also reported data from a survey of 1,629
facilities and organizations throughout the country for persons with developmental
disabilities. The data showed that the average earning for those engaged in
competitive employment was $3.74 per hour for full-time and $3.46 per hour for
part-time employment (72 percent went into entry-level positions in food services,
assembly, and maintenance). When those data are used to calculate annual wages,
the figure comes to $7,333 for full-time employment, and $3,392 for half-time.
Meanwhile, the national median incomes for full- and part-time work in 1986
were $16,068 and $4,524.

In addition to those practical reasons for becoming more involved in the
transition years, transition programs have been stimulated by the legal mandate
from P.L. 99–457, amendments to the Education of the Handicapped Act (EHA).
In extending the discretionary programs authorized under the EHA, Congress
specified that particular attention be accorded special groups of handicapped
children and youth (minorities, preschool handicapped, and secondary school and
older handicapped youth). The law amends the authority for secondary education
and transitional services to clarify that programs should serve not only handicapped youth currently in school but also handicapped youth who recently left
school.

The bill also clarifies the concept of "transition" to denote services that are
provided throughout a handicapped student's years in school. Moreover, it expects
educators to be concerned about the improvement of vocational and life skills of
handicapped youth and about arranging studies of handicapped youth dropouts.

Prompted by the concern for LD adults, the National Joint Committee on
Learning Disabilities drafted a position paper. According to them, the following
concerns must be addressed when considering the problems of adults with learning
disabilities:

□ Learning disabilities are both persistent and pervasive throughout an individual's life. Manifestations of a learning disability can be expected to change throughout an individual's life span.

□ At present there is a paucity of appropriate diagnostic procedures for assessing and determining the status and needs of adults with learning disabilities.

□ Older adolescents and adults with learning disabilities frequently are denied access to appropriate academic instruction, prevocational preparation, and career counseling necessary for the development of adult abilities and skills.

□ Few professionals have been prepared adequately to work with adults who demonstrate learning disabilities.

□ Employers frequently are not sensitive to the needs of adults with learning disabilities.

■ COMMENTARY ■ *Telling an employer that one is LD is different from stating that one is physically handicapped. The employer can see that. A problem with telling employees, or for that matter college people, that a youth has learning disabilities is that many informers and those being informed have different ideas as to the condition known as learning disabilities.*

□ Current advocacy efforts on behalf of adults with learning disabilities are inadequate.

□ Federal, state, and private funding agencies concerned with learning disabilities have not supported program development initiatives for adults with learning disabilities. [*Learning Disability Quarterly*, 1986, p. 164]*

Recommendations for LD Adults. The National Joint Committee on Learning Disabilities has made a number of recommendations for assisting LD adults:

□ Programs must be initiated to increase public and professional awareness and understanding of the manifestations and needs of adults with learning disabilities.

□ Selection of appropriate education and vocational training programs and employment for adults with learning disabilities should be predicated on a clear understanding of how their condition influences their learning and performance.

□ Throughout the school years, individuals with learning disabilities must have access to a range of program and service options that will prepare them to make the transition from secondary to postsecondary or vocational training settings.

□ Alternative programs and services must be provided for adults with learning disabilities who have failed to obtain a high school diploma.

□ Adults with learning disabilities must assume an active role in determining the course of their postsecondary or vocational efforts.

---

*Reprinted by permission from "Adults with Learning Disabilities: A Call to Action," position paper of the National Joint Committee on Learning Disabilities, *Learning Disability Quarterly*, 9 (1986).

▫ Appropriate federal, state, and local agencies as well as postsecondary and vocational training programs should continue to develop and implement effective programs that will allow adults with learning disabilities an opportunity to attain career goals. Also, consistent with Section 504, postsecondary programs, colleges, vocational schools, employers, and governmental agencies should be aware of the nondiscriminatory testing requirements for the handicapped. If adults with learning disabilities are to gain access to and profit from postsecondary or vocational training programs, innovative planning and collaborations will be necessary among agencies and personnel working with and concerned for their needs. Such planning consortia should include adults with learning disabilities and perhaps their families.

▫ Development of systematic research programs that will address the status and needs of adults with learning disabilities is essential for the provision of appropriate services.

▫ Curricula relating to the problems and needs of adults with learning disabilities must be developed and incorporated in preparation programs for professionals in such disciplines as education, vocational and rehabilitative counseling, social work, psychology, medicine, and law.

▫ Mental health professionals must be aware of the unique personal, social, and emotional difficulties that individuals with learning disabilities may experience throughout their lives. [*Learning Disability Quarterly,* 1986, pp. 166–167]*

Establishing Transition Programs

Brody-Hasazi, Salembier, and Finck (1983) laid out the following objectives for planning and evaluating transitional activities:

1. Develop and implement assessment procedures that identify functional skills and interests related to current and future employment and training opportunities in the community.
2. Provide necessary support services to ensure access to mainstream vocational classes.
3. Provide at least four work experiences, six to eight weeks each, in identified areas of interest and skill for students between the ages of 15 and 18.
4. Assist students to locate and secure employment prior to graduation.
5. Provide supervision and follow-up services to students in full-time or part-time employment until graduation (or the student's twenty-second birthday).
6. Develop individual transition plans with appropriate adult service agencies—that is, vocational rehabilitation, community college, state employment service, or mental health—for students who need continued service following graduation.

---

*Reprinted by permission from "Adults with Learning Disabilities: A Call to Action," position paper of the National Joint Committee on Learning Disabilities, *Learning Disability Quarterly, 9,* Spring 1986.

The information from certain studies should be considered when designing transition programs for youth. For example, Minskoff, Sautter, Hoffmann, and Hawks (1987) investigated employer attitudes toward hiring the learning disabled. The evidence indicated that, generally, employers were less pleased with LD individuals than with other handicapped persons; only one-half of the employers stated that they would hire workers with learning disabilities.

When employers were asked if they would make allowances for handicapped workers, 72 percent responded affirmatively. Of those willing to make adjustments, most chose to provide more support and encouragement, extra time for training, more detailed directions, and more effort to identify jobs suited to the individuals' abilities. The choices employers least frequently selected to accommodate LD individuals were reduced work demands and more involvement in their personal lives. Employers in the service/government job class were the most willing to hire LD workers, while employers in the professional/technical/managerial class were the most resistant.

When employers were asked what they knew about learning disabilities, they most frequently selected the inability to read. The second most frequently selected item was the likelihood of emotional problems. Minskoff et al. noted that only 16 percent of the employers believed that LD persons could not do jobs well; yet only 51 percent expressed a willingness to hire them.

Salzberg, Agran, and Lignugaris-Kraft (1986) obtained opinions from employers of different types of jobs about behaviors that are generally important for entry-level work and about behaviors that may differ in their importance across jobs. In the survey, employment supervisors from five types of jobs, commonly obtained by workers with developmental disabilities, rated the importance of 23 work-related behaviors. Those behaviors were analyzed within three clusters: nonsocial production-related behaviors, task-related social behaviors, and personal social behaviors. Table 13.5 shows the mean ratings of the importance of those behaviors for the five types of jobs.

According to Salzberg and coauthors, their study affirmed data from others who also found that worker productivity was a prime concern of employers and that employees who produced faster were likely to be more highly valued than slower producing employees. The researchers believed that their findings suggested that certain social behaviors were also critical for employment success. "In fact, the importance ratings of the four top task-related social behaviors were essentially equivalent to the ratings of the four nonsocial production-related behaviors" (Salzberg, Agran, & Lignugaris-Kraft, 1986, p. 312). The researchers entertained the possibility that these social skills (for example, following directions) were highly rated because they related directly to worker productivity. Following instructions, helping coworkers, providing necessary information to coworkers, and asking for assistance are all related to carrying out job tasks.

Salzberg and colleagues concluded by saying that the debate about the relative importance of task skills and social skills for successful employment may be inappropriate, in that worker productivity may be the outcome of their interaction. They contended that their results pointed to a core of critical skills that is common across different entry-level jobs and that core of skills could provide

■ TABLE 13.5 ■   Mean Ratings of Importance of Work-Related Behaviors

| Behavior | Mean Importance Rating by Job Type | | | | | Mean Rating across Job Type |
	Janitor	Dishwasher	Maid	Food Service	Kitchen Helper	
Task-Related Social Behaviors						
Asking supervisor for assistance	4.26	4.32	4.42	4.09	4.52	4.32
Clarifying instructions	4.34	4.28	4.23	4.29	4.30	4.30
Response to criticism	4.34	4.10	4.10	4.21	4.36	4.23
Getting information before job	4.30	4.10	4.03	4.35	4.30	4.22
Carrying out immediate instructions	4.08	4.10	4.10	4.27	4.46	4.20
Carrying out delayed instructions	4.23	4.06	3.87	3.97	4.18	4.08
Offering to help co-workers	3.92	4.03	3.94	4.15	4.39	4.08
Using weak or phony excuses	3.86	3.61	4.07	4.25	4.10	3.98
Referring inquiries to qualified personnel	3.87	3.94	3.90	3.98	4.12	3.96
Providing information	3.87	3.60	3.82	4.15	4.21	3.94
Having friends around during work hours	3.55	3.22	3.93	3.97	3.75	3.70
Talking—not working	3.43	3.13	3.73	4.00	3.34	3.52
Mean	4.04	3.90	4.01	4.14	4.17	4.05
Personal Social Behaviors						
Using social amenities	3.73	3.75	4.03	4.18	4.33	4.00
Listening without interrupting	3.81	4.03	4.13	3.85	3.91	3.94
Expressing appreciation to co-workers	3.91	3.74	3.65	4.13	4.24	3.94
Acknowledging	3.78	3.84	3.73	3.97	4.34	3.93
Using objectionable language	3.90	3.30	4.20	4.33	3.75	3.90
Arguing	3.60	3.57	3.57	3.88	3.87	3.70
Talking about personal problems	2.83	3.31	3.60	3.61	3.19	3.29
Mean	3.14	3.68	3.83	3.99	3.97	3.82
Nonsocial Production-Related Behaviors						
Getting to work on time	4.44	4.50	4.55	4.73	4.61	4.56
Responding to job emergencies	4.54	3.90	4.20	4.68	4.30	4.34
Working at expected rates	4.29	4.16	4.42	4.21	4.39	4.29
Working continuously	4.13	4.13	4.04	4.00	3.90	4.04
Mean	4.35	4.17	4.32	4.41	4.31	4.31

Source: Reprinted by permission from C.L. Salzberg, M. Agran, and B. Lignugaris–Kraft, "Behaviors That Contribute to Entry-Level Employment: A Profile of Five Jobs," *Applied Research in Mental Retardation, 7* (1986), pp. 206–307. Copyright 1986 Pergamon Journals Ltd.

a base for a generally applicable employment preparation curriculum for handicapped individuals.

Career Education

Although it may seem early to begin training youth to make the transition from school to work during the elementary school years, this viewpoint is held by many educators, and is in accord with recent legislation regarding transition training.

Professionals who advance the cause of "career education" are certainly supportive of this view.

One of the more prominent special educators who has proposed career education for the handicapped, including the learning disabled, has been Brolin at the University of Missouri. According to Kokaska and Brolin, "Career education is the process of systematically coordinating all school, family, and community components together to facilitate each individual's potential for economic, social, and personal fulfillment and participation in productive work activities that benefit the individual or others" (1985, p. 43).

Brolin and colleagues have developed an approach for fostering career education referred to as "life-centered career education" (LCCE). This competency-based method for providing handicapped individuals with educational services was developed as a result of work with special and career education experts, professional workers from various agencies and organizations, parents, and many others.

The LCCE Curriculum for grades K through 12 is designed to help students acquire 22 major competencies that can be broken down into three curricular areas: daily living, personal–social, and occupational, as shown in Table 13.6. The table also includes instructional opportunities for the various competencies at the junior high and senior high level.

The LCCE model of career education includes four stages of career development: awareness, exploration, preparation, and placement. *Career awareness,* as the program is outlined, should be emphasized in the elementary years. When

Donn E. Brolin, who is at the University of Missouri, has written in the areas of career education and vocational education for the mildly handicapped. His major contribution to this field has been the development of the life-centered career education approach. A close collaborator of Brolin's has been Charles Kokaska.

■ TABLE 13.6 ■ Competency-Based Instructional Opportunities

Competency	Junior High	Senior High
Daily Living Skills		
Managing family finances	Business, math	Home economics, math
Selecting, managing, and maintaining a home	Home economics, vocational education	Home economics
Caring for personal needs	Home economics, health	Home economics
Raising children—family living	Home economics	Home economics
Buying and preparing food	Home economics	Home economics
Buying/caring for clothing	Home economics	Home economics
Engaging in civic activities	Social studies, music	Social studies, music
Utilizing recreation and leisure	Physical education, art, music, counselors	Physical education, art, music
Getting around the community (mobility)	Home economics	Driver's education
Personal–Social Skills		
Achieving self-awareness	Music, physical education, counselors	Art, music, counselors
Aquiring self-confidence	Art, music, physical education, home economics, counselors	Physical education, counselors, social studies, art, vocational education, music
Achieving socially responsible behavior	Physical education, counselors, music	Social studies, music
Maintaining good interpersonal skills	Counselors	Music, counselors
Achieving independence	Counselors	Counselors
Achieving problem-solving skills	Math, counselors	Science, counselors
Communicating adequately with others	Language arts, music, speech, physical education	Language arts, speech, music, art
Occupational Skills		
Knowing and exploring occupational possibilities	Vocational education, home economics	Counselors
Selecting and planning occupational choices	Business, vocational education, counselors	Counselors
Exhibiting appropriate work habits and behaviors	Vocational education, math, home economics, art	Home economics, vocational education, music
Exhibiting sufficient physical-manual skills	Vocational education, physical education	Vocational education, physical education, art
Obtaining a specific occupational skill	Vocational education, home economics	Vocational education, home economics
Seeking, securing, and maintaining employment	Counselors	Counselors

Source: Reprinted by permission from C.J. Kokaska and D.E. Brolin, *Career Education for Handicapped Individuals*, 2nd ed. (Columbus, OH: Merrill, 1985), p. 51.

learning daily living skills, for example, students must become aware of how to manage and use money appropriately, how to manage and maintain a home, how to take care of personal needs, how to purchase and prepare foods, and how to do dozens of other tasks.

Brolin and colleagues contend that *career exploration* begins at the elementary level, but should receive greater emphasis during the junior high years. During this phase students begin a more careful self-examination of their unique abilities and needs in relation to their vocational interests, leisure, and recreational pursuits.

The *career preparation* period, according to Brolin and coauthors, begins in the early grades and continues throughout life, but for most individuals, the high school years are critical for reaching necessary levels of competence in the three major curricular areas. Continuing to follow through with daily living skills as an example, educators should monitor and promote a curriculum that helps students master skills in that area by enrolling them in classes such as home economics, business, health, driver's education, and physical education.

Career placement can occur during the secondary or postsecondary years. Work-study programs, for example, provide students with opportunities to be placed in actual jobs as if they were employed as regular workers. All the previous stages are pulled together during the career placement phase, and educators identify whether students need to refine any of the competency skills. This stage of the career education program, may extend intermittently over several years for many students; therefore, the involvement of community resources is crucial to the students' life career development and success.

Postsecondary Options for LD Youth

Since the writing of Section 504 of the Rehabilitation Act of 1973, PL 94–142 in 1976, and its amendments, PL 99–457, in 1986, more postsecondary options have been available for LD youth. In part, this has come about because of the changes in attitudes and aspirations that many parents and educators have for LD youth. But without question, the possibilities for LD youth, and other handicapped individuals, have increased because of the aforementioned laws.

Specific provisions of Section 504 related to postsecondary education, for example, the regulation that prohibits discrimination against handicapped persons in recruitment, admission and treatment after admission. According to that regulation, colleges and universities are required to make "reasonable adjustments" to permit handicapped students to fulfill academic requirements and to assure that disabled students are not excluded from programs because of the absence of auxiliary aids (Scheiber & Talpers, 1985). In this section, a few of the options available to LD youth who exit the common school are reviewed, with particular emphasis on two- and four-year college programs.

Vocational Education.   Postsecondary vocational education can hold the key to an independent and productive life; it can provide professional training that leads to a marketable skill and a vocational future. According to Scheiber and Talpers, a number of LD students have been guided into unskilled occupations, with little effort undertaken to determine their vocational capabilities. Recently, however, legislation, vocational educators, and advocacy groups have expanded vocational education opportunities for disabled youth, including those with learning disabilities. A significant move in this direction was the passage in 1984 of the Perkins Vocational Education Act, which called for sufficient appropriate support services to foster successful participation of disabled students in regular vocational programs.

Vocational training is available in a number of occupational areas—for example, agriculture/agribusiness, marketing and distribution, health, business and office, trade and industry, and occupational home economics. Courses and experiences in these and dozens of other areas are offered in a variety of settings— community and junior colleges, two-year technical institutes, area vocational or vocational-technical centers, and private schools.

A number of agencies have been established to provide assistance with respect to the many vocational training options. One is the National Association of Vocational Education Special Needs Personnel in Arlington, Virginia; another is the National Network for Curriculum Coordination in Vocational Technical Education in Columbus, Ohio. In addition to those national networks, a few special centers offer regional assistance. One is the Materials Development Center of the Stout Vocational Rehabilitation Institute in Menomonia, Wisconsin, and another is the "Missouri LINC" in Columbia, Missouri.

Military Service.   Another option available to LD youth is a tour of duty, if not a career, in the military services. Before considering joining a branch of the service, however, the youth should prepare to take the "Armed Services Vocational Aptitude Battery." It is a series of tests that measures individuals' reading, spelling, math, general, and mechanical knowledge, and it is intended to screen out individuals who cannot perform adequately in the basic skill areas.

■ COMMENTARY ■   It is interesting to note that personnel in branches of the military are not covered by Section 504.

For youth who do not have a vocational plan, need some organization to their lives, or simply want time to think over the business of being an adult before settling down, the service is an option to consider.

The service is definitely worth considering if the youth plans to attend college at some time, but is short on funds. What with the signing of a new G.I. bill, every youth who enters the services for a two-year hitch or longer can contribute $100 a month for one year to his or her educational fund. In return, the veteran is eligible for up to $25,000 in tuition and other higher education costs.

Colleges.   A number of college choices are available for some LD youth. They can enroll in public or private junior colleges or community colleges or in some four-year colleges and universities. Opportunities for LD students in graduate and professional schools are opening up, and support services are being developed.

One such service is the HEATH Resource Center, the National Clearing-house for Handicapped Individuals, in Washington, D.C. This center can provide a list of state agencies responsible for postsecondary education and information about financial aid as well as grant and loan programs for state residents.

Among the preparatory programs established to prepare LD youth for colleges and universities are the Hilltop Preparatory School in Rosemont, Pennsylvania, and The Landmark School in Prides Crossing, Massachusetts. Another preparatory program is Project ASSIST (Adult Services Supporting Instructional Survival Tactics), described by Dalke and Schmitt (1987). This transition program was developed at the University of Wisconsin at Whitewater to help LD high school students adjust to the university. The project has a five-week, noncredit, post–high school, precollege summer program that emphasizes affective support, diagnostic evaluation, academic reinforcement and instruction, strategy training, awareness of support services available on campus, and a general campus awareness. Following are the goals of the program:

1. Provide an opportunity to explore and address the emotional factors involved in losing a familiar support system of family, teachers, and friends.
2. Provide an educational experience similar to what is expected in college.
3. Familiarize students with the layout of the campus and community.
4. Familiarize students with the procedures and functions of the college system.
5. Identify and describe organizational agencies and related services available to students.
6. Enhance academic performance while providing prerequisite skill instruction to college level courses.
7. Provide direct instruction in study skills, time management, notetaking, and library usage.

Students rated the affective support component of the program highest and most helpful and the math sessions of the academic instruction least helpful. Results showed that those who attended the summer program did better in school than those who did not.

To point out the necessity for support programs such as this throughout the county, White, Alley, Deshler, Schumaker, Warner, and Clark (1982) claimed that 67 percent of the individuals diagnosed as learning disabled while in elementary or secondary school planned to enroll in postsecondary education. Lischio (1984) reported that over 500 two- and four-year institutions have listed supplemental post secondary services for LD youth.

FOLLOW-UP STUDIES

Perhaps the best way to learn about the effectiveness of programs for the mildly handicapped, and others, is to follow up those individuals who have left school, either as graduates or as dropouts. If a significant number of LD youth from a particular program are getting along well, perhaps doing as well as non-LD individuals, then it would appear that that type of program was a good one. If, however, large numbers of LD youngsters were not doing too well when followed up, then it would seem that their program was not such a good one.

■ **COMMENTARY** ■   *One of the problems of following up LD youth, with respect to their programs in school, by asking either them or their caregivers to identify the programs they were in, is that many of them can neither identify their program by name (for example, prevocational or meta-cognitive) nor describe what they did, except in the most general of terms.*

Although most educators, researchers, and parents would agree that it is important to follow up youngsters, there are few such studies. (See, for example, Touzel's conclusions with regard to follow-up studies.) There are several reasons that may account for this fact, but the main one is that most school districts operate on a here-today-gone-tomorrow basis. When school officials are asked why they don't routinely follow up their graduates and dropouts, they explain that they have troubles enough managing the handicapped youngsters who are *in* school, without taking on the burden of following up those who are *out*. There are probably other reasons to account for the rarity of follow-up studies:

☐ They aren't as glamorous as other types of research; therefore, they are not funded as readily or sought after by publishers.

☐ They are difficult to carry out. Good follow-up researchers are much like detectives and must be prepared to go wherever their clues lead them.

☐ The data from follow-up studies are often not clear-cut—that is, immediate actions to be taken from them are not always apparent.

■ **COMMENTARY** ■   *This is unfortunate, because follow-up data are the best sources for making revisions in programs. Without those data, programs for secondary LD students are changed or not changed rather whimsically.*

Follow-Up During the School Years

This section reviews data from two follow-up studies that pertained to LD youngsters in their final years of school. The students had been identified as LD about five years before the follow up.

In one of the studies, Levin, Zigmond, and Birch (1985) documented the progress of 52 LD adolescents four years after they entered a special education program in the ninth grade. The students should have been in twelfth grade at the time of follow up. The data indicated that 16 were still in a special education program, 7 were in regular classes full time, 24 had dropped out of school, and 5 could not be located. (The dropout rate of 51 percent for the LD students is high when compared to 36 percent for the general population in Pittsburgh.)

Thirty-four of the 52 students were retested on the "Peabody Individual Achievement Test" (the 23 who were in school and 11 dropouts). The data revealed impressive gains for all students, although about half the achievement had taken place in the first year of the LD program. The reading scores of those in regular class were the highest; next were the scores of those in special classes. The lowest scores were those of the dropouts. The math scores of the LD youngsters in regular classes were higher than those in other groups, but interestingly, the math scores of the dropouts were higher than those for the special education pupils.

When the dropouts were interviewed and asked their reasons for leaving school, the majority reported that they had been encouraged to leave before graduation because of persistent academic, behavior, or attendance problems. Three quarters of the dropouts were unemployed, two were in vocational training programs, six were working toward their equivalency diplomas, and one was considering a return to school.

In a similar follow-up study, Leone, Lovitt, and Hansen (1981) surveyed ten LD boys when they were old enough to be twelfth graders. One difference between this study and the one preceding was that these students were labeled as LD in the intermediate grades, whereas the students in Zigmond's research were not identified as LD until junior high school.

During follow-up interviews by Leone and coauthors, the boys were asked to read orally from a newspaper and from books they had read while in the special education class. As part of the follow-up proceedings, data from the students' school files were examined. Comparable information was also gathered from a non-LD group, students much like the LD pupils except they had never been in special education.

Data indicated that the oral reading rates of the LD youngsters were quite adequate, and much higher than their rates while in special classes. The rates were significantly lower than those of the non-LD students, however. Other data from the follow up revealed that the mean grade point average of the former special education students was over 2.5 (on a four-point scale); only three of the students were absent from school more than 20 days in two years (their grade point averages were among the lowest), and the absence rate for the normal cohorts was higher.

Follow-Up After School Years

Some studies have been undertaken to follow up LD and other handicapped pupils after graduation. In one of these studies, Schalock, Wolzen, Ross, Elliott, Werbel, and Peterson (1986) followed up handicapped individuals of several types in Nebraska. Regarding LD youth, summary data from their survey showed: 72 percent were employed, 71 percent were their own primary source of income, 28 percent relied on parents or relatives for primary financial assistance, and 54 percent were living in a supervised situation. The authors claimed that the number of semester hours in vocational programs appeared significantly related to the major outcome variables, as was the level of family involvement. They recommended that special education programs should increase their emphasis on fostering independence as well as productivity.

In another follow-up study of this type, Edgar and Levine (1986) surveyed former special education students of all types, including learning disabled, who had either dropped out or graduated from public school between 1976 and 1984. In order to acquire data on the current status of those individuals, the parents of identified students were interviewed over the phone. Summary data on the 827 LD/BD individuals in this survey showed 32 percent of the dropouts were employed, whereas 61 percent of graduates were employed; and 65 percent of all the LD youth were living at home or with a relative, and only 16 percent were living alone or with a spouse.

To gain a broader perspective on the drop-out situation, consider the data in Table 13.7 These data, from the Ninth Annual Report to Congress, show the percentage of LD students who graduated with a diploma, graduated through certification, reached maximum age, and dropped out of school. According to Blackorby, Kortering, Edgar, and Emerson (1987), youth do not one day decide

■ TABLE 13.7 ■   Proportion of LD Students, 18 Years and Older, Leaving School

State	Graduation with Diploma	Graduation through Certification	Reached Maximum Age	Dropped Out	Other
Alabama	59.86	9.00	0.13	23.59	7.42
Alaska	39.70	1.19	0.00	12.69	46.42
Arizona	53.44	2.57	0.90	24.46	18.62
Arkansas	60.45	13.74	0.79	18.46	6.56
California	17.44	23.79	0.46	23.58	34.73
Colorado	57.13	1.48	0.09	21.48	19.81
Connecticut	92.76	3.51	0.70	0.41	2.62
Delaware	49.17	10.21	0.00	38.96	1.67
District of Columbia	70.71	25.25	0.00	0.00	4.04
Florida	42.09	12.35	0.38	32.83	12.35
Georgia	52.88	6.19	0.18	35.60	5.15
Hawaii	43.48	33.48	2.17	13.48	7.39
Idaho	52.31	3.89	0.00	35.77	8.03
Illinois	68.46	0.33	0.33	30.87	0.00
Indiana	55.26	2.29	0.08	23.97	18.39
Iowa	64.49	2.72	0.00	19.99	12.80
Kansas	72.34	1.23	0.10	20.49	5.84
Kentucky	66.78	1.26	0.49	21.91	9.56
Louisiana	29.59	18.37	0.70	36.19	15.15
Maine	74.21	11.19	7.30	7.30	0.00
Maryland	22.49	0.00	0.00	28.59	48.92
Massachusetts	0.00	64.19	3.34	26.65	5.82

TABLE 13.7 Continued

State	Graduation with Diploma	Graduation through Certification	Reached Maximum Age	Dropped Out	Other
Michigan	65.03	9.91	0.00	24.79	0.27
Minnesota	46.61	22.76	0.07	20.07	10.49
Mississippi	29.57	41.93	0.76	23.83	3.91
Missouri	46.25	10.99	0.07	35.33	7.37
Montana	66.67	7.14	0.00	20.78	5.41
Nebraska	83.84	11.71	0.00	2.79	1.67
Nevada	53.47	34.14	0.00	11.78	0.60
New Hampshire	43.79	7.45	0.93	41.77	6.06
New Jersey	74.12	0.00	0.21	23.10	2.57
New Mexico	61.61	3.01	0.00	27.46	7.92
New York	43.94	7.27	2.44	46.34	0.00
North Carolina	61.46	6.51	0.13	26.66	5.24
North Dakota	72.02	1.79	1.19	19.05	5.95
Ohio	68.49	0.00	0.09	15.44	15.98
Oklahoma	72.75	1.49	0.59	17.01	8.16
Oregon	43.56	3.87	0.00	20.27	32.30
Pennsylvania	53.27	2.67	0.13	19.86	24.07
Puerto Rico	3.11	7.77	1.04	68.91	19.17
Rhode Island	50.74	0.00	0.46	42.09	6.71
South Carolina	48.90	11.13	2.88	22.56	14.53
South Dakota	0.00	70.66	0.63	22.71	5.99
Tennessee	13.89	8.97	0.29	57.60	19.25
Texas	33.91	37.97	0.00	28.12	0.00
Utah	77.83	2.56	0.43	15.14	4.05
Vermont	59.04	0.60	0.00	36.14	4.22
Virginia	57.06	8.21	0.00	24.49	10.24
Washington	50.12	4.93	1.02	29.40	14.54
West Virginia	75.98	0.19	0.00	11.87	11.96
Wisconsin	89.43	0.00	0.00	5.22	5.35
Wyoming	68.01	2.36	0.00	16.84	12.79
American Samoa	—	—	—	—	—
Guam	65.08	0.00	0.00	33.33	1.59
Northern Marianas	—	—	—	—	—
Trust Territories	—	—	—	—	—
Virgin Islands	—	—	—	—	—
Bur. of Indian Affairs	—	—	—	—	—
U.S. & insular areas	49.66	12.65	0.57	25.63	11.50
50 States, D.C. & P.R.	49.65	12.66	0.57	25.62	11.50

Some states reported only total students exiting the educational system and did not report data by reason for exit. As a result, the proportions for the U.S. and insular areas and the 50 states, D.C. and Puerto Rico will not sum to 100 percent. Data as of October 1, 1987.

Source: *Ninth Annual Report to Congress on the Implementation of the Education of the Handicapped Act.* Washington, DC: OSERS, U.S. Dept. of Education, 1988.

to drop out of school: "Rather, mildly handicapped students who fail to graduate from high school usually start falling behind in credits earned, have attendance problems, and are released for short or long terms due to behavior problems early in their high school experience. They are released for a designated period of time and eventually go through standardized reentry procedures into their high school programs, alternative programs, or in another regular high school. For many of these students, this pattern continues until the student does not return to school or their age mates graduate and they choose not to return to school" (1987, p. 22).

The authors made the following recommendations for reducing the numbers of dropouts in Seattle:

1. A significant proportion of the funds allocated for secondary level special education programs should be earmarked for dropout prevention and intervention programs.

2. Additional counseling and teaching staff should be hired to work with these students. In particular, vocational counselors should be engaged.

3. Special emphasis should be given to 9th grade students since this was the year that most students dropped out.

4. The high school curriculum, for many of these mildly handicapped students, should be revised. Many of them should be in vocational rather than college preparatory programs.

—————— COMMENTS AND DISCUSSION POINTS ——————

- It is important to remember that secondary LD youngsters are no more all alike than are all elementary LD students. They differ in respect to academic abilities, social competencies, motivational levels, styles of attribution, abilities to generalize, and in every other conceivable way.

- Attendance is a big part of the problem with LD adolescents. In fact, as pointed out by some, the number-one concern with these individuals is simply persuading them to show up for school. Most teachers and researchers would agree that the finest learning strategies and other top-of-the-line techniques are of no value unless individuals show up.

- Grading is also a big concern for LD adolescents. Although there are a number of alternatives—pass/fail; grading on basis of effort, attendance, or achievement; and all sorts of combinations—no one has set out to determine the purposes for grading in the first place and then obtained data on the extent those purposes were met by one method or another. Related to grading is the debate about the type of diploma LD youngsters should receive, particularly if they were graded in some way different from the non-LD students.

- Related to these two concerns is another critical matter when it comes to educating LD youngsters—that is, the determination of exit criteria. What are they to achieve academically? How are they to behave socially by the time they graduate (with whatever grades or diploma they are given)? Should some of them be kept in school to the maximum age limit, or should they be graduated at the same time as non-LD youngsters of their age?

■ How to keep these youngsters in regular classes is a concern. What are the "best practices" when it comes to mainstreaming LD citizens into social studies and science classes? How should regular teachers be assisted to put those ideas into operation?

■ Peer tutoring is a popular way in which to teach LD youngsters more about their content courses. Schools should exercise caution in setting up these programs, however, so that they take into account the "big picture." Not only should LD youngsters profit from the program, but so should non-LD participants. There must be something in the program for everybody. To determine these net effects, data of several types must be gathered and analyzed. The same cautions could be made for every program that is brought into schools; all should be evaluated.

■ The service options in this chapter (for example, team teaching) should be considered and related to the needs and abilities of the districts' goals and resources. Too often schools set up programs of one type or another without considering the many options.

■ More LD students should be involved in vocational programs than is currently the case. Too many school districts run all their LD students through remedial/college-bound–type programs. Although this approach is proper for some, it is not for others. A fair number of these LD youth should receive more training in job-related activities.

■ Districts need to coordinate job placement sites. In some locales, school people stumble all over themselves when identifying training or actual job sites. There are representatives in the community from the vocational department, from business education, special education, and others. Not only is this an inefficient use of school time, but it isn't a good way to establish community support for job-related programs.

■ Large numbers of LD youth should be involved in programs that provide instruction in home living and learning about the community. These activities are commonplace for most MR youth, but they are often denied LD students, simply because they have been labeled as LD. As indicated by data in this chapter, many of our LD citizens will spend large chunks of their lives living with their relatives.

■ Many LD youth should be exposed to other new curricular ideas that were touched on in this chapter. According to some researchers, they should be involved in programs that teach adaptability; and according to others, they should be taught to network.

■ Districts should devote more time and effort to gathering and analyzing follow-up information. These data should be routinely acquired and studied before new or different programs are arranged. Follow-up data should be the key to all program and curricular decisions. The merit of any secondary program should be determined by the success of its graduates.

■ With respect to motivating LD youth to stay in school, perhaps we need to enlarge or extend our notions of mainstreaming. Now it includes reentry into content classes.

It should also include the involvement of extracurricular activities: music and drama groups, athletic organizations, clubs of various types, and school elections. For most adolescents, those "extras" are the main reasons for staying in school.

■ *We might do well to consider a track or two for our LD people, so as to prepare them as best we can for the world after school. If we do, we should guard against the fault of most tracking systems—that is, once on a track, few get off. Provisions would have to be set up so that individuals were not in the same track for everything, and they could—based on performance, motivation, and other factors—shift from one track to another.*

REFERENCES

Algozzine, B.; O'Shea, D.J.; Stoddard, K.; & Crews, W.B. (1988). Reading and writing competencies of adolescents with learning disabilities. *Journal of Learning Disabilities, 21,* 154–160.

Alley, G., & Deshler, D. (1979). *Teaching the learning disabled adolescent: Strategies and methods.* Denver: Love Publishing.

Blackorby, J.; Kortering, L.; Edgar, E.; & Emerson, J. (1987). Special education dropouts. Unpublished manuscript, University of Washington, Seattle.

Blaylock, J. (1981). Persistent problems and concerns of young adults with learning disabilities. In W. Cruickshank & A. Silver (Eds.), *Bridges to tomorrow: The best of ACLD.* Syracuse, NY: Syracuse University Press.

Brody-Hasazi, S.; Salembier, G.; & Finck, K. (1983). Directions for the 80's: Vocational preparation for secondary mildly handicapped students. *Teaching Exceptional Children,* 206–209.

Bryan, T. (1976). Peer popularity in learning disabled children. *Journal of Learning Disabilities, 5,* 307–311.

Cobb, R.B., & Phelps, L.A. (1983). Analyzing individualized education programs for vocational components: An exemplary study. *Exceptional Children, 50,* 62–63.

Dalke, C., & Schmitt, S. (1987). Meeting the transition needs of college-bound students with learning disabilities. *Journal of Learning Disabilities, 20*(3), 176–180.

Drake, G.A., & Witten, B.J. (1985). Facilitating learning disabled adolescents' successful transition from school to work. *Journal of Applied Rehabilitation Counseling, 15,* 34–37.

Edgar, E.E. (1988). Personal communication. Experimental Education Unit, University of Washington, Seattle.

Edgar, E.E., & Levine, P. (1986). Washington state follow-up studies of postsecondary special education students in transition. Unpublished manuscript, Experimental Education Unit, University of Washington, Seattle.

Gregory, J.F.; Shanahan, T.; & Walberg, H. (1985). Learning disabled 10th graders in mainstreamed settings: A descriptive analysis. *Remedial and Special Education, 6*(4), 25–33.

Halpern, A.; Raffeld, P.; Irvin, L.K.; & Link, R. (1975). *Social and prevocational information battery.* Monterey, CA: CTB/McGraw-Hill.

Hammill, D.D.; Brown, V.L.; Larsen, S.C.; & Wiederholt, J.L. (1987). *Test of adolescent language—2.* Austin, TX: PRO-ED.

Humes, C.W., & Hohenshil, T.A. (1985). Career development and career education for handicapped students: A reexamination. *The Vocational Guidance Quarterly*, 31–40.

Irvin, L.K. (1988). Vocational assessment in school and rehabilitation programs. In R. Gaylord-Ross (Ed.), *Vocational education for persons with handicaps*. Mountain View, CA: Mayfield Publishing Company.

Keilitz, I., & Dunivant, N. (1986). The relationship between learning disability and juvenile delinquency: Current state of knowledge. *Remedial and Special Education, 7*(3), 18–26.

Kiernan, W.E., & Ciborowski, J. (1986). Survey of employment for adults with developmental disabilities. *Remedial and Special Education, 7*(6), 25–30.

Kokaska, C.J., & Brolin, D.E. (1985). *Career education for handicapped individuals* (2nd edition). Columbus, OH: Merrill.

Krishnaswami, U. (1984). Learning to achieve: Rehabilitation counseling and the learning disabled adult. *Journal of Applied Rehabilitation Counseling, 15*(4), 18–22.

Kronick, D. (1978). An examination of psychosocial aspects of learning disabled adolescents. *Learning Disability Quarterly, 1*, 86–93.

Kronick, D. (1981). *Social development of learning disabled persons*. San Francisco: Jossey-Bass.

Laurie, T.E.; Buchwach, L.; Silverman, R.; & Zigmond, N. (1978). Teaching secondary learning disabled students in the mainstream. *Learning Disability Quarterly, 1*, 62–72.

Learning Disability Quarterly. (1986). Adults with learning disabilities: A call to action, a position paper of the National Joint Committee on Learning Disabilities. *9*, 164–168.

Leone, P.; Lovitt, T.; & Hansen, C. (1981). A descriptive followup study of learning disabled boys. *Learning Disability Quarterly, 4*, 152–162.

Levin, E.K.; Zigmond, N.; & Birch, J.W. (1985). A follow-up study of 52 learning disabled adolescents. *Journal of Learning Disabilities, 18*(1), 2–7.

Lischio, M.A., (Ed.). (1984). *A guide to colleges for learning disabled students*. New York: Academic Press.

Mathews, R.M.; Whang, P.L.; & Fawcett, S.B. (1982). Behavioral assessment of occupational skills of learning disabled adolescents. *Journal of Learning Disabilities, 15*(1), 38–41.

McBride, J.W., & Forgnone, C. (1985). Emphasis of instruction provided LD, EH, and EMR students in categorical and cross-categorical resource programs. *Journal of Research and Development in Education, 18*(4), 50–54.

Minskoff, E.H.; Sautter, S.W.; Hoffmann, F.J.; & Hawks, R. (1987). Employer attitudes toward hiring the learning disabled. *Journal of Learning Disabilities, 20*(1), 53–57.

Mithaug, D.E.; Martin, J.E.; & Agran, M. (1987). Adaptability instruction: The goal of transitional programming, *Exceptional Children, 53*, 500–505.

Owings, J., & Stocking, C. (1985). High school and beyond: Characteristics of high school students who identify themselves as handicapped. Washington, D.C.: National Center for Education Statistics, U.S. Department of Education.

Powell, T.H. (1981). Mainstreaming: A case for the consulting teacher. *Journal for Special Educators, 17*, 183–188.

Proctor, J. (1986). Sharing learning: An alternative to resource rooms. *Language Arts, 63*, 67–73.

Salend, S.J., & Salend, S.M. (1986). Competencies for mainstreaming secondary level learning disabled students. *Journal of Learning Disabilities, 19*(2), 91–94.

Salzberg, C.L.; Agran, M.; & Lignugaris-Kraft, B. (1986). Behaviors that contribute to entry-level employment: A profile of five jobs. *Applied Research in Mental Retardation, 7,* 299–314.

Schalock, R.L.; Wolzen, B.; Ross, I.; Elliott, B.; Werbel, G.; & Peterson, K. (1986). Postsecondary community placement of handicapped students: A five-year follow-up. *Learning Disability Quarterly, 9,* 295–303.

Scheiber, B., & Talpers, J. (1985). *Campus access for learning disabled students: A comprehensive guide.* Washington, D.C.: Closer Look, The Parents' Campaign for Handicapped Children and Youth.

Schumaker, J.B.; Deshler, D.D.; Alley, G.R.; & Warner, M.M. (1983). Toward the development of an intervention model for learning disabled adolescents. *Exceptional Educational Quarterly, 4*(1), 45–74.

Sitlington, P.L. (1981). Vocational and special education in career programming for the mildly handicapped adolescent. *Exceptional Children, 47,* 592–598.

Stodden, R., & Ianacone, R. (1981). Career/vocational assessment of the special needs individual: A conceptual model. *Exceptional Children, 47,* 600–608.

Thorum, A.R. (1980). Fullerton language test for adolescents. East Aurora, NY: Slosson Educational Publications.

Touzel, S.W. (1978). Secondary LD curricula—a proposed framework. *Learning Disability Quarterly, 1,* 53–61.

Weller, C., & Strawser, S. (1981). *Weller-Strawser scales of adaptive behavior for the learning disabled.* Novato, CA: Academic Therapy.

White, W.J.; Alley, G.R.; Deshler, D.D.; Schumaker, J.B.; Warner, M.M.; & Clark, F.L. (1982). Are there learning disabilities after high school? *Exceptional Children, 49,* 273–274.

Zigmond, N.; Levin, E.; & Laurie, T.E. (1985). Managing the mainstream: An analysis of teacher attitudes and student performance in mainstream high school programs. *Journal of Learning Disabilities, 18*(9), 535–541.

Zigmond, N.; Sansone, J.; Miller, S.E.; Donahoe, K.A.; & Kohnke, R. (1986). *Teaching learning disabled students at the secondary school level: What research and experience say to the teacher of exceptional children,* CEC monograph. Reston, VA: The Council for Exceptional Children.

PART V

EPILOG

RECOMMENDATIONS

In this final section of the book, a number of recommendations pertaining to the field of learning disabilities are reviewed. The first part of this section covers recommendations from a number of texts and journals in the field of learning disabilities. The second part contains 18 personal recommendations.

SURVEY OF TEXTS AND JOURNALS

In order to identify the concerns of experts in the field of learning disabilities, Addis and Lovitt (1987) surveyed journals and textbooks published from 1980 through 1987. They scanned articles from three journals—*Academic Therapy, Learning Disability Quarterly,* and the *Journal of Learning Disabilities*—and leading textbooks in learning disabilities. A total of 154 journal issues and 13 textbooks were examined with respect to their recommendations for the field.

For this study, they searched for articles or passages that pertained to future directions, anticipated needs, or administrative trends. They did not review statements in discussion sections that often refer to future needs, but restricted their survey to articles, chapters, or portions thereof that dealt specifically with recommendations and current needs.

On occasion, the identification of these recommendations was explicit; the author simply stated, "I believe that the field must include research in the area of . . ." or "Following are . . . recommendations for LD researchers to consider." Examples of less explicit references to recommendations included one of the following: "In the area of subtyping, we have discovered that . . . ; however, it is critical that we determine . . ." or "The definition of learning disabilities is still highly controversial; it is a problem that requires resolution." In addition to locating articles or passages that made recommendations, they identified the recommendations by type.

For the journals, their surveys showed that there were articles that focused on recommendations in 59 of the total 154. References about recommendations appeared in all 13 textbooks. Table 1 shows the number of articles and textbooks that referred to recommendations during the eight years from 1980 to 1987. The data do not indicate a trend insofar as recommendations are concerned. There were bursts of interest in this topic for journals in 1981, 1983, and 1986. One of those periods was in 1985 and 1986 when the *Journal of Learning Disabilities* ran a ten-article series entitled, "The Future of the LD Field."

Needs and Recommendations in Survey Literature

Analysis of the passages and articles suggested nine categories. Following is a brief description of each.

■ TABLE 1 ■ Total Number of Journal Articles and Textbooks Per Year

Year	AT	LDQ	JLD	Total Journal	Books	Totals
1980	1	3	3	7	0	7
1981	2	6	2	10	2	12
1982	0	1	2	3	1	4
1983	1	5	5	11	3	14
1984	1	4	4	9	1	10
1985	1	3	2	6	3	9
1986	1	0	11	12	0	12
1987	1	0	0	1	3	4
Totals	8	22	29	59	13	72

Need for a Better Definition of Learning Disabilities.   The need for an unambiguous definition of learning disabilities was the most prevalent concern noted throughout the LD literature. Furthermore, the literature indicated that the definition must reflect the many subtypes and severity of learning disabilities. In addition, the definition must be such that all those who are *not* learning disabled are excluded.

According to the literature, the definition of learning disabilities is important because:

1. It helps determine the prevalence of learning disabilities, which is necessary for federal funding and efficient management of LD programs.
2. It is necessary for more precise differential diagnosis and treatment of LD subtypes.
3. It allows for more precise experimental research designs, which in turn allows for more accurate generalization of findings and more accurate indications of the effects of LD programs.
4. It helps eliminate false positives being included as learning disabled (for example, emotionally disturbed, mentally retarded, and underachievers).
5. It facilitates consistent diagnosis and treatment of LD individuals throughout the various regions of the country.

Need to Measure the Efficacy and Validity of Many Theoretical Approaches. Several approaches (for example, skills-oriented, task-oriented, holistic-oriented, and additive-oriented) are available to determine the cause, to assess, and to treat LD students. In addition, cause, assessment, and treatment can be approached as intrinsic (intra-individual) or extrinsic (environment, family, and society). Other major approaches include cognitive, metacognitive, behavioral, attitudinal, and motivational. The literature indicated a need to measure the efficacy and validity of these approaches so that practitioners could better select treatments for certain types of individuals.

Need for Higher Quality Research.   The literature suggested several areas of future improvement in research. It called for less subjective and systematic bias. In line with the need for a better definition of learning disabilities the literature suggested more precise definitions of operational terms and constructs. Furthermore, it recommended better research designs and methodologies, including better instances of experimental control and explanations of treatment variables, better sampling techniques and explanations of subjects, more attention to reliability, and more concern for concepts of validity.

Need for Higher Standards for Recruitment and Training.   Two methods of improving the LD field were expressed: the need for higher standards of recruitment and training and the need for more rigorous instruction (particularly at the graduate level) in measurement, statistics, and research design. Several authors cited the overall lack of quality of many research studies and attributed this to poor recruitment and training.

Need for More Accurate Diagnosis.   The literature indicated that the development of better diagnosis of learning disabilities is dependent upon an unambiguous and exclusive definition of learning disabilities. A more accurate diagnosis may require the development of better tests or perhaps the involvement of curriculum-based assessment rather than standardized tests. As a corollary, the literature suggested a need to solve the problem of bias (logical fallacies/subjective thinking) and the invalid use of test data in diagnosis.

Need for More Adult LD Education.   In this category, five general recommendations were offered:

— More and higher quality research in the area of adult learning disabilities
— More adult education centers to locate and train LD adults
— Modified vocational interest tests to accommodate LD adults
— Better training of educators in adult LD education
— Better vocational training of school-aged LD children

Lack of an Objective Classification.   A few articles or books indicated the lack of an objective way to classify individuals as learning disabled, in contrast to others (noted earlier) who believed that an unambiguous definition of learning disabilities must be written. The former group is of the opinion that a clear definition of learning disabled *does not exist* and the field should stop wasting time in the pursuit of one.

Proponents of this viewpoint have suggested that attempts at classification have led to many false positives—that is, a misclassification of LD individuals among those who are emotionally disturbed (ED), mentally retarded (MR), or underachievers (UA). These proponents also maintained that the LD classification is often associated with stigmatization.

Two methods for resolving the problem of "objective" classifications have been suggested: a cross-categorical methodology that allows for more common assessment and treatment methods among LD, ED, MR, and UA individuals and an elimination of the LD category by encouraging more integration of those individuals into regular classes.

Need for More Research in Specific Areas. Listed in order of prevalence, the following questions represent areas recommended for future research:

- What does longitudinal research indicate regarding the long-term effects of various types of LD instruction?
- What are the results of prevention and early intervention programs?
- Are resource rooms effective?
- What are the operational differences between LD and non-LD students?
- Are computers useful for LD students?
- Should minimum competency tests for teachers be required?
- Should teacher training be generic or categorical?
- Are pull-out programs effective?
- Is mainstreaming effective?
- Should there be minimum competency testing for students?
- What is the prevalence of learning disabilities among bilingual students?
- Can learning disabilities be predicted?

Other Concerns. Following are other concerns that were expressed in the literature (in order of prevalence):

1. There is a need for more interaction with disciplines such as psychology, neurology, sociology, and counseling.
2. More and better programs are needed to enhance public awareness, including better advocacy and lobbying.
3. The LD field needs to be less deficit-driven and more aware of the abilities and talents of LD individuals.
4. There should be less politicization within the LD field.
5. There is a need for more and better legislation pertaining to LD youth.

Table 2 shows the number of articles and textbooks that pertained to these nine categories for each year of the survey.

LD Issues in the Literature

Bursuck and Epstein (1987) carried out a survey similar to that of Addis and Lovitt to determine the critical research priorities in learning disabilities. To

■ TABLE 2 ■   Future Needs Recommended per Year

Future Need	1980	1981	1982	1983	1984	1985	1986	1987	Total	% of Total
Better definition of LD	3	3	1	6	2	6	5	1	27	14.9
Examine theoretical approaches	2	1	0	3	1	7	7	0	21	11.6
Better quality research	2	3	0	3	3	3	5	0	19	10.5
Higher training standards	2	0	2	3	2	2	3	2	16	8.9
More accurate diagnosis	1	0	0	5	2	1	4	0	13	7.2
More adult LD education	1	0	0	2	2	6	1	0	12	6.6
No objective classifications	0	0	0	2	2	2	2	0	8	4.4
More specific research (12 items*)	0	5	1	9	1	12	6	1	35	19.3
Other concerns (5 items*)	1	0	2	5	3	7	12	0	30	16.6
Totals	12	12	6	38	18	46	45	4	181	100.0

*See text for itemized listing of items.

acquire this information, the authors reviewed all the issues from the 1984 *Learning Disability Quarterly* and the *Journal of Learning Disabilities* and a number of textbooks on learning disabilities. They noted the major research issues in those articles and passages, and came up with a list of 25 major topics.

That list of topics was then sent to 78 professionals who were either authors of textbooks on learning disabilities or were on the editorial staffs of the journals represented in the survey.

Following is a rank order of the top ten issues, according to the survey:

— Long-term effects of treatment programs for pupils with learning disabilities
— Assessment and remediation of academic problems of the learning disabled
— Generalization of intervention effects across settings
— Screening and identification of learning disabled students
— Assessment and remediation of perceptual disorders of the learning disabled
— Definition of learning disabled
— Preparing teachers of students with learning disabilities
— Mainstreaming pupils with learning disabilities
— Preventing learning disabilities
— Assessment and training of social skills

—————————— PERSONAL PERSPECTIVES ——————————

Following are brief discussions on 18 topics I believe are most critical in the LD field. Some are the same as those noted in the previous section. Moreover, I have written on some of these topics in "Comments and Discussion Points" at the end of various chapters in this book. Although there is considerable overlap among the 18 points, I have cast them into three categories: assessment, program, and research. When it seemed appropriate—that is, when the information on one topic seemed to lead to another—I arranged the topics within those categories in a sequence.

- **Definition:** When it comes to finding *the* definition of learning disabilities, we should forget about it, at least for now. Although this is a very high priority, as indicated by our survey and that of Bursuck and Epstein, it shouldn't be. Far too much time, money, and space in textbooks and journals has been taken up by this futile mission. Those concerned with this goal have sought the answer by administering one test after another, giving multiple tests, and like alchemists of old, carefully selecting and combining subtests and items from many tests. The thinking is, apparently, that if *the* proper battery of tests, subtests, or items can be blended and then administered and if the proper multivariate analysis is employed, then we will be able to tell who is *really* learning disabled and who isn't (the pretenders!). And further, if our tests and measurements are highly sophisticated, we will know about the many subtypes of learning disabilities. Wrong!

- **Assessment:** Although I'm recommending a moratorium when it comes to drafting *the* definition of learning disabilities (at least one that comes from standardized tests), I'm all for assessment. I'm calling for assessment that is *worthwhile, direct, sensible,* and *frequent.* The worthwhile part actually precedes the assessment. This means that we, the teachers, should elect to teach youngsters traits, skills, and facts that are important rather than trivial. *Direct* means just that. We should test what we teach; not what we don't teach. (Some would call this curriculum-based assessment.) The sensible part refers to the manner in which we assess. The type of assessment should match what has been taught and what the learner is supposed to do with that information or behavior. An example of an assessment that doesn't make sense would be to teach someone to make a stew and measure their ability to do so with an essay test. Requiring the cook to list the ingredients and steps for preparation or to actually make the stew would be a more sensible assessment. The frequent part of our formula simply means to do it often. With each assessment, pupils and teachers are able to judge the effects of a treatment, how much they have improved, and other matters.

- **Placement:** We worry a great deal about where to put the learning disabled: in a self-contained room, resource room, or regular classroom. This has been going on for years. Those who advocated "mainstreaming I" in the 1960s, "mainstreaming II" in the 1970s, and now the regular education initiative in the 1980s argue that most, if not all, LD youngsters should be educated in regular classrooms by regular teachers. By now you know their arguments: Handicapped children will be with nonhandicapped peers who will serve as models; handicapped youngsters will interact with the nonhandicapped; and handicapped students will not be stigmatized or isolated. Other reasons are advanced from time to time.

    Since the data are not all in on this matter, we must take a few important issues into account as we consider the question of placement. One, placement is, to a great extent, teacher relevant. There are good and poor regular teachers, just as there are good and poor special teachers. Likewise, there are good and poor plumbers, pilots, and preachers. So to argue that LD youth should be sent to regular classes, regardless of the quality of instruction, doesn't make sense. Two, it doesn't make any difference where we learn certain things; placement is rather irrelevant. Take reading, for example. Students could learn to read (with a good teacher) in a regular or special classroom. Furthermore, they could learn to read at home, at church, at a library, or on a bus. Three, the placement options become fewer as we specify more instructional objectives, and this is where the problems over placement arise. When we list several objectives for our instruction, some of which are educational and others social, we must be realistic and be prepared to compromise, for the acquisition of certain behaviors in certain places may go counter to the learning of other behaviors in that same setting. Phrased another way, we need to evaluate the net effect.

- **Motivation:** How quickly we forget. I read an article recently about the "LeBoeuf System" (Ridenhour, 1988). According to him, "What gets rewarded is what gets done." Wouldn't Fred Skinner be amazed at that! What a revelation. But don't laugh; Mickey LeBoeuf gets from $5,000 to $7,000 a night for talking to business people about that. Skinner and other operant folk have been saying for years that we do what we were reinforced for doing. But we teachers have forgotten those lessons. Many of us believe that if we can just make the materials, the lectures, and the general environment more appealing, then youngsters will be turned on to education. Or we are of the opinion that if we offer instruction in just the "right way," our instruction will take. And of course the arguments rage as to what the right way happens to be. To some, it is cooperative learning, and for others, peer tutoring. Still others tout reciprocal teaching, direct instruction, a multisensory approach, or something else.

    But all too often we forget about reinforcers and their power. We forget that there is a great chance that if we can find pupils' reinforcers, arrange them contingent on desired behaviors (or bits thereof), the desired responses will occur. So, we should do the following:

    — Spend some time identifying potential reinforcers for youngsters
    — Take time to identify the responses that are possible for pupils to run off
    — Take time to learn about the proper arrangement and nurturing of contingencies (in other words, if this occurs, then this will happen)

We definitely need motivation analysts for LD youngsters at the secondary level, for we haven't begun to tap into what their "payoffs" are. Some of the more apparent reinforcers seem to be talking, loafing, bragging with chums, listening to rock music (particularly the type that their parents find repulsive), thinking about and looking at their bodies and those of others, talking about and driving cars. Perhaps school psychologists could be retrained as motivation analysts and stop giving tests.

- **Self-Management Instruction:** This is the key to it all! If youngsters can be taught to manage aspects of their lives, they will profit in several ways. If they are taught (then allowed) to pinpoint behaviors of concern, to count and chart the frequencies of those behaviors, to set aims and evaluate progress, and to select certain instructional features, then benefits of all types are possible.

For openers, students will become more independent, hence less dependent on teachers. Moreover, they will become better organized, more socially acceptable, more positive about themselves, and generally, better citizens. To continue, youngsters will have developed *the* transition skill. If they learn to identify crucial problems and to deal with them, they will be better prepared to move from the world of school to the world thereafter. But before leaving the fold, self-management experiences will help them to become organized, to deal with their classes, to earn better grades, to stay in school, and to graduate. Those same self-management skills will serve them well as they enter the world of work, as they negotiate about their communities, and as they live with their relatives.

Teachers should, incidentally, attempt to develop self-management skills as they teach other subjects: science, social studies, English, industrial arts, home living. Youngsters should be taught to self-manage in the contexts of school; instruction in that important topic should not be undertaken apart from those activities.

We should keep in mind that as we train or assist youngsters to be good self-managers, our ultimate goal is not to develop compulsive citizens who are so dedicated to their routines that they are inflexible. (Inflexibility, by the way, seems to be a characteristic of many LD adults. They get into a groove and can't get out of it.) By assisting LD youth to generate options—a vital component of good self-management training—we are helping them to become efficient and flexible citizens.

- **Home Living:** I touched on this point in Chapter 13, but it merits a few more words. As indicated there, many, if not most of our LD people need to be trained for home living, particularly on how to live with their relatives. This opinion is based on the fact that many of them will live extended periods of their lives with their parents or other relatives, because they cannot afford to move out. From interviews, we know too that those youth (and most others who are not learning disabled) do not get along with their relatives. Therefore, the learning disabled need to be trained to interact properly with those they live with.

On a related theme, they need to be trained:

— To work outside the home as much as possible to help defray living costs
— To help at home with chores
— To discuss and negotiate critical family matters
— To know about the resources in their communities (particularly those that are inexpensive and reasonably wholesome and productive) so that they can learn from them

In addition to their learning about social, leisure time, and occupational matters, LD youth should be taught some straightforward skills about running a home: to clean it; to shop for groceries and other essentials; to wash, dry, and fold clothes; to care for the yard; to care for elders and youngsters; to care for pets; to do some minor repairs of fences, screens, small electric motors, bikes, and toys; and to cook. A considerable amount of time in schools should be spent on teaching these functional skills. A great proportion of their math and reading assignments could be directed toward those and other practical activities.

- **Vocational Training:** We have to face the facts, that despite the increased opportunities for LD youth to attend colleges, great numbers of them will not. For many, it will be quite a task just to stay in high school. According to Edgar's interviews, a number of LD dropouts said that they would "drop back" in if they could receive vocational training. (One wonders about that, however. Would they, in fact? Do they know what vocational training is?) But earning money is a big reinforcer for high school students, who want to be able to buy a car, snacks, tickets to rock concerts, and stylish clothes. Furthermore, they want to buy those items on their own; they don't want to rely on mom or dad.

  When it comes to vocational training, some maintain that we should first teach prevocational skills—such as showing up for work, being organized, being able to ask questions, and other behaviors that are supposedly important across a number of jobs. Other vocational experts maintain that the way to train folks for work is to identify jobs they could possibly obtain, analyze them, and train youth to do those jobs. Both strategies have merit. Yet another approach that vocational people could take would be to emphasize frequency. They could make an effort to place individuals into a number of different jobs during their training period; first in this job, then another, and another. As indicated in Chapter 13, when I interviewed young adults about their vocational histories, they had had, on the average, six low-paying jobs before they secured their current position.

  Of course, there could be some training on specific skills besides these vocational experiences, at the school, but that training could be designed from incidents on the job. If it were determined that the individual was not able to do something on a couple of sites, then perhaps services could be set up back in school to help that student perform those chores. (See forthcoming comments on "Generalization.")

- **Transition Strategies:** Any number of strategies are available for youth while they are in school. Dozens of approaches are available in reading, writing, notetaking, memory, test taking, and time management. Several sessions are scheduled on these topics at every conference, and that is fine. We need to find ways to help our LD citizens stay in school. But what about later? It seems to me that if LD youth are in such need of these metacognitive prosthetics to stay in school, they are in need of them to function out of school. To a great extent, this is where self-management training comes into play. As you recall, I referred to it as *the* transition strategy.

  But we need other approaches, ones that are more specifically focused. Think, if you will, of the daily circumstances we face and about which it would be helpful to offer our LD friends a strategy or two: dealing with advertising, handling criticism, handling stress, managing time, stating beliefs and opinions, knowing when to hold and when to fold, being a wise shopper, identifying our reinforcers and those of others, and hundreds of others.

- **Positive Focus:** Although we don't know how to *really* define LD youngsters (and heaven knows we have tried), we do know that they don't do as well as their non-

LD mates in oral and silent reading, reading comprehension, spelling, mathematics, history, science, geography, industrial arts, music, or family living. We know that, generally, their social and study skills aren't as keen as those of non-LD children, that their cognitive abilities (plain and meta) aren't up to standard either. Because of these many deviations and deficits (at least when groups of LD are compared to groups of non-LD youth), we teachers, in all good faith, set out to remediate as many of the "shortfalls" as possible so that learning disabled youth will be as normal and wonderful as we are. Poplin (1984) and I believe that we should reconsider this total remedial approach to learning disabilities. One reason for considering an alternative might be obvious if we thought of a day in the life of an LD youth. First, the teacher sets out to remediate his reading, then his math, and then his language, social skills, and soccer playing. Toward the end of the day, she attempts to remediate his metacognitive deficits. That lad is in a remediation mode throughout the day. Is it any wonder that the self-concepts, self-images, self-esteems, and attributions of these youngsters are out of whack?

Poplin and I, and I imagine many others also, are of the opinion that we should spend some time concentrating on these youngsters' positive qualities. If, for example, a girl is inclined toward mechanics or a boy, to being a chef, we teachers should nurture those skills. And if an LD child doesn't have a negotiable behavior, we should locate one and promote it. I can't help but think that if every youngster, LD or otherwise, had at least one art, trade, skill, or technique about which he or she was fairly competent, that would do more for that youngster's adjustment than would many of remediation hours to which the child is subjected. Perhaps that accent on the positive would go a long way toward actually helping the remediation process. If children knew that they could excel in something, that might help them become competent in other areas as well.

- **Blending New Practices with Old:** Teachers are besieged by numerous hucksters (some noble, others not) who are selling educational wares. Some are marketing social skills, a number are hawking reading programs, while others are pushing study skills. Hundreds of other product lines are brought to the attention of teachers through catalogs, in-service training, workshops, summer courses, and conferences. Many of these drummers contend, or at least intimate, that if teachers would buy and then use their product, good things will happen: Time will be saved, children will learn more and at a faster pace, their students will be more tractable, and all in all, it will be a better life. Not a few teachers solve this matter quite easily. They don't pay any attention to the salespersons and certainly do not fuss around trying to involve their students in any of the new or different ideas.

Yet some teachers actually want to try out a few of these practices. But which ones should be selected and to what extent? Although not an easy matter to settle, I'll lay out a few steps to follow, using a rather specific example that might help. First, the teacher should take a look at his class or situation and write down, if he hasn't already, what he wants his youngsters to learn. For one thing, he might want to enhance pupils' ability to acquire information from textbooks.

Second, he should acquire data on the extent his pupils gain from textbooks from his current practice. If he had instructed his youngsters to use a reading skills study approach as they read from texts, he should gather data for several days from pupils as they read and followed the procedures. The teacher would, of course, chart the performance scores for each youngster.

Third, the teacher would schedule the new technique. In this case, he might have attended a workshop on the use of study guides. For a few days he would rely on this technique instead of the usual approach.

Fourth, he would decide whether or not to incorporate the new technique into his routine by analyzing the data. If the teacher learned, from scanning each students' chart, that his lower students performed much better when the guides were in effect, but there were no differences for the others, he might opt to use the guides with only his lower pupils.

- **Medicine**: We need to keep up with medical advances. Most teachers have rather distorted ideas about the medical profession. We either think too little of it or too much. Regardless, we need to follow medical progress with respect to our field. For example, we should know about the current happenings in neurological assessment. The medical assessments of a generation ago were crude and often unrevealing; neurologists administered Bender Gestalts, analyzed WISC subtests, gave Reitan's, and other batteries. From those data they sought to determine whether there was a brain injury and, if so, to pinpoint the location and extent of the damage. Those data were often unreliable, hence not too helpful.

  Today, what with the computerized tomographic methods for accurately and unobtrusively observing brains, not only are the data more reliable, but there is a great chance that neurologists and others will learn considerable amounts about which areas of the brain are responsible for certain activities and to what extent those brains are either damaged or different. In time, those data might actually suggest specific treatments.

  For another example from the medical community, we need to keep up with pharmacologists. Those scientists are constantly seeking drugs that will act on discrete areas of the brain and that are no more powerful than necessary so as not to effect functioning in areas that are not targeted. Toward those ends, they have not only come up with better drugs, but have developed more efficient ways in which to dispense them (for example, wafer transplants).

  On yet another line, members of the medical community are learning more about the causes of mental retardation and learning disabilities. To date, a number of dietary, metabolic, and toxic causes have been identified. These discoveries have immediate impact, for teachers now know which conditions to avoid, and in a few instances, they know how to monitor the strength or intensity of those variables.

  On a more futuristic note, I recently read about fetal cell transplants—the possibility of taking cells from aborted fetuses and transplanting them into individuals. So far, medical researchers have considered their use for Parkinson's disease, diabetes, and Alzheimer's disease. If that process proves successful with those conditions, it could be that fetal cell transplants would be effective for certain types of brain damage (or differences) that result in learning disabilities.

- **Follow-Up Studies**: I commented on the need for follow-up studies in Chapter 13, but more emphasis on that subject might be in order. To summarize the situation, there are too few of them, and many of those that have been conducted prompted little action. The main reason to carry out follow-up studies is simple. With respect to the education of LD youth, we need to know what they are doing once they leave school, either as graduates or dropouts. It's important to know about their quality of life: Whether they work, where they work, what they do with their leisure time, how they get along with others, and how pleased they are with life. Once we know how they are getting along, we should take that information back to the schools. If the follow-up data indicate that life is generally dismal for the LD leavers, then something should be done: Modify the current program, put in another one, or blend the two. And once changes were made, school personnel should continue to follow-up groups of students to determine whether those modifications had positive effects.

Not only should schools carry out follow-up studies to learn about the lives of LD learners, but they should schedule *follow-along* studies. They should keep track of their LD citizens (and others) as they move from one grade to another, from one educational level to another, and from one school to another. The purpose of those assessments is much the same as that of the follow-ups—that is, to make instructional adjustments so that LD youth will continually receive the best instruction and assistance possible.

In Chapter 13, I gave a reason or two that might account for the infrequent follow-up studies, but the main reason is that schools rely on the "out-of-sight-out-of-mind" philosophy; once students are gone, schools forget about them and focus their efforts on the new crop. This is short sighted. Schools need to develop the follow-up components to their marketing plans. Most businesses have discovered (some too late) that it is very important to follow-up their customers to determine, basically, whether or not they are pleased with the company's product or service. Even my car dealer contacts me once in a while to see if I am pleased with the company's service.

■ **School and University Collaborations:** Quite a number of researchers and a few educators have for some time lamented the fact that the lag between the discovery of an approach and its implementation is so great. Not only is there quite a gap between the time that a discovery is noted and that information is blended into school practice, but often, when that translation does take place, there has been a considerable loss; the original process has been drastically diluted. Several reasons have been advanced for this state of affairs, but in the main, it seems that the two sectors—schools and universities—have rarely set out to collaborate.

Following is a common route taken by educational researchers:

— Identify an interesting research topic from a published investigation.
— Draft a proposal to conduct the research.
— Check out the procedures, statistical analyses, and general design with an expert to see if everything is in order.
— Contact administrators in a school district, and present the proposal to them.
— Explain the procedures to building principals and possibly a few teachers.
— Run the study in selected classes, if all went well in the preceding step.

—Wrap up the study, and send thank-you notes to the participating administrators and teachers.
—Present data from the research at a meeting of university researchers.
—Write up the study, and submit it to a prestigious journal.

(That sequence of events is far more considerate than the path taken by numerous researchers.)

I will now list another set of steps that could be followed by university researchers and school personnel:

—Personnel from the university study the needs of selected schools and identify four themes through this process: study skills, social skills training, self-management, and adapting materials.
—University personnel review literature on the topics and develop designs or protocols that approximate situations in common schools.
—University personnel design studies on the topics, but in so doing, alter the circumstances from the original research so that they are more like those of schools, yet preserve the integrity of the original designs.
—School personnel provide in-service training on the topics and send teachers off to conduct further experiments.
—University personnel follow-up efforts of the teachers as they carry out the studies.
—School personnel gather data from the school sites and send them to the University for analysis.
—From those data, university personnel suggest modifications to schools regarding future in-services and researches on those topics.
—Teachers who conducted the research, staff from the schools, and individuals from the university collaborate to write up the studies for school and university-type journals; they also collaborate to present data at conferences.
—The university seeks information from schools on other topics about which they can collaborate.

Indeed, more could be written on this topic. Certainly the second process I described is not the only way to go about setting up collaborations between schools and universities, but this process should be studied and developed, for the rewards for youngsters and education could be significant.

■ **Comparison Studies:** We don't need any more comparison studies in the field of learning disabilities. As the careful reader of this text and others like it will agree, there are no surprises from studies of that type. Let me summarize, with an example, how comparison researchers ply their trade. In fact, I'll give them more credit than they deserve when it comes to selecting subjects and conducting their "research." First, 1,000 youngsters of about the same age were available from which to draw subjects. Second, the researcher identified 25 LD students among them. Third, the researcher went back into that pool of youngsters (975 were left) and randomly identified 25 non-LD students who served as the contrast group for the LD students. Fourth, data were obtained from those two groups of youngsters (LD and non-LD) on some trait, skill, or behavior. Fifth, the data from the groups were analyzed. When a *t*-test or other statistic was used to determine differences between groups, there were significant differences. When the data from the two groups were plotted on a frequency distribution, they looked like the data in Figure 1. Weener (1981) reviewed 47 research studies that compared regular classroom children with LD children. In most of those studies, more than 20 percent of the LD children scored above the mean of the non-LD group, as noted in Figure 1. Weener concluded his analysis by saying that "... as long as categorical thinking and mean difference tests dominate research methodology, researchers will probably continue to make misleading categorical statements based on group averages" (1981, p. 23).

To go back to our example, the comparison researcher must have known that this would happen before beginning the study. Data such as those illustrated in the figure are common when comparisons in language, reading, social/emotional, mathematics, and most other traits are determined. Across the board, if performances of a group of the learning disabled are compared with those of a group of non-handicapped, the mean differences will favor the non-learning disabled and may even be significant, but there will be a fair amount of overlap between the two groups.

Not only are data from these comparison studies not interesting, they could be misleading. If, for example, a teacher reviewed studies of this type that had to do with a component of language and was informed that the LD students were off the mark, she might schedule some language treatment for her group of LD students.

■ FIGURE 1 ■   Typical Frequency Distribution of Data on LD and Non-LD Students

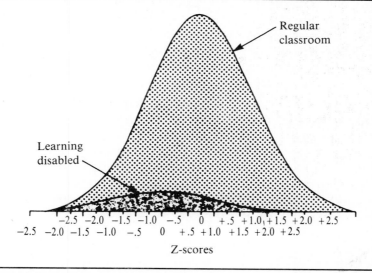

Source: Reprinted by permission from P. Weener, "On Comparing Learning Disabled and Regular Classroom Children," *Journal of Learning Disabilities, 14* (1981), p. 230.

If she took that approach, there would be three probable consequences: Some LD youngsters would develop a skill they should have developed, other youngsters were "taught" a skill they had already developed, and some non-LD youngsters were not taught a skill when they should have been.

■ **Single Subject Research:** After a comparison study has been run (or better yet, instead of scheduling one in the first place), the wise teacher or researcher should conduct a series of studies on individuals. For this, they can rely on techniques of applied behavior analysts who have recommended that we concentrate on individuals rather than groups. Following are a few steps to be taken after a study has found significant differences between LD and non-LD pupils on some language attribute:

— Identify some (if not all) of the students in both groups—LD and non-LD— who were significantly off the mark for that behavior.
— Arrange a situation whereby data are obtained from those youngsters for a few days, during which time the circumstances remain about the same.
— Plot those data individually.
— Analyze the data and other aspects of the youngsters' performances.
— Design treatments for the youngsters based on analyses of the data.
— Arrange those treatments with the pupils.
— Continue to plot the data individually.
— Inspect the data after each session to determine if there are effects.
— Change the treatment for individuals if it is not effective.
— Continue scheduling treatments until the aims are reached.

These are the kinds of simple, yet elegant experiments that are needed. Teachers must know *what* to arrange for their pupils so that they will improve. They don't need to be told that their LD students aren't up to standard; they know that. I suppose that the main reason there are so few intervention studies and so many comparison studies has to do with time and imagination. One doesn't have to be too quick or diligent to run off a comparison study, but it takes considerable wit and effort to identify and schedule treatments.

■ **Interventions:** We need more interventions. We should have many more ideas (ones backed by data) that can be put into operation to help youngsters learn and develop. Most of us have very few strings on our fiddles when it comes to intervention ideas. We are, to continue the musical metaphor, "one-note Johnnies." When asked how to assist youngsters in oral reading or to encourage others to stay in their seats more often, many of us would come up with one, possibly two potential solutions, and that is it. To some teachers, the matter of instructional interventions comes down to flash cards and time out. When they want to teach some skill, they use flash cards. When they want to get rid of some behavior, they count on time out. Although those are successful tactics on certain occasions, they won't always work.

It is becoming more and more important for teachers to amass a considerable supply of potential techniques for developing skills and managing behaviors, for the range of ability of the students with whom they work is increasing. Whereas the variability in regular classrooms has always been large, it is increasing because of the mildly handicapped, bilingual, and other "difficult-to-teach" youngsters who are entering those classes. Teachers must have several recipe boxes (or computers) full of potential tactics. Once teachers have hundreds of tactics at their disposal, it would be a good idea if they knew *when* to use them. Not an easy task, but the teachers/researchers will be helped considerably, over a period of time, if they keep data on the performances of their charges. They will learn that treatment *X* seems to work best with one type of student, and intervention *Y* is best for others.

- **Alternative Treatments:** These comments are for researchers who are attempting to come up with techniques that can be recommended to teachers. They should take a bit more care in the description and selection of alternate treatments, (realizing there are not many of them). Most researchers are very proud of the treatment they are investigating. They are eager to come up with effects and will be pleased if others latch onto their tactic. In their efforts to disseminate their product, these researchers explain their procedure in some detail. They note the origin of the approach, tell us how to prepare materials to administer it, and offer step-by-step activities for carrying it out. Sometimes they even include pictures or diagrams to show us what they have in mind.

  But when it comes to describing the alternate treatments, the one in competition with their favorite, researchers are often terse and vague. They tend to use one of the following clichés to describe these competing treatments: "The teacher relied on traditional procedures"; "The procedures were those commonly found in public schools"; or "Procedures common to most basal reading programs were in effect." Now, really!

  Such was the case in many of the early cooperative learning studies: A rather elaborate cooperative intervention would be explained and administered, only to be pitted against a briefly explained and weak alternative. Not unexpectedly, when the data were analyzed, they indicated that the former procedure was vastly superior. Later, when even better cooperative learning strategies were run against respectable opponents, the differences in the data were virtually nil.

- **Generalization:** Teachers and researchers alike have been frustrated when they taught LD youngsters (or those of other types) to do something properly in one setting, only to find the students failed to exhibit the behavior when they went some place else. A student who, for example, was taught to get around in one grocery store, may be unable to negotiate in another store.

  The arguments rage among those concerned about teaching generalization. (Unfortunately, there are as few of them as there are intervention developers.) Some contend that individuals should be taught all the required skills in simulated environments (for example, schools) to a high level of competency, then be sent out into the world. In the case of grocery stores, teachers would identify, with task analysis procedures, all the behaviors required for successful grocery shopping, teach them at school, and then send the student to actual stores. The other camp of generalization trainers would teach pupils in those settings where the behaviors would be ultimately displayed. They would teach at one grocery store, then another, and another. They would contend that if training had taken place in enough real settings, generalization to others would occur.

The data are inconclusive when it comes to training generalization, but we could speculate that a third approach to this matter might be worth trying. That would be to train certain behaviors in simulated environments until aims were reached, and then teach other skills *in situ*—that is, in "grocery stores." The obvious problem of this strategy is one of determining which behaviors to teach in which settings. But difficulties notwithstanding, we must attend more to the matter of generalization training with LD citizens, for generally, they are not noted for their strengths in this area.

So there you have it. The study of learning disabilities is indeed an adventure. It is certainly not a simple, straightforward story. It has had its ups and downs, its agreements and controversies, and its heroes and villains. It is a frustrating field in that we are today debating some of the issues that were raised two or three decades ago. This is particularly true with respect to definitions and placement.

But on the bright side, there are many more options today than there were 20 to 30 years ago. There are certainly more choices when it comes to assessment and curriculum. There is more sophistication today than there once was with respect to medical aspects in particular and etiology in general. There is more concern now than there once was with a wider age range of youngsters. There are certainly more journals and books available on learning disabilities today than there were in the 1950s. All of these expansions are causes for optimism in our field.

But our future will be enlightened even more by the young women and men who have chosen learning disabilities as their career. Whereas there were only a handful of men and even fewer women several years ago who set standards, policies, and other matters in learning disabilities, there are today dozens of superb minds who will in the years to come contribute significantly to the field. A few are noted here: C. Blankenship, C. Bos, D. Carnine, C. Darch, S. Deno, E. Ellis, C. Englert, D. Fuchs, L. Fuchs, K. Lenz, J. Lloyd, G. Lyon, M. Mastropieri, C. Mercer, J. Patton, E. Polloway, M. Poplin, S. Robinson, J. Schumaker, D. Smith, H. Swanson, J. Torgesen, C. Weller, B. Wong. Therein lies our future, for they are among the best and brightest in education.

REFERENCES

Addis, G., & Lovitt, T.C. (1987). Recommendations in the field of learning disabilities. Unpublished manuscript, University of Washington, Seattle.
Bursuck, W.D., & Epstein, M.H. (1987). Current research topics in learning disabilities. *Learning Disability Quarterly, 10,* 2–7.
Poplin, M. (1984). Summary rationalizations, apologies, and farewell: What we don't know about the learning disabled. *Learning Disability Quarterly, 7,* 130–134.
Ridenhour, R. (1988). The LeBoeuf system. *Northwest, 19*(3), 19–20, 46.
Weener, P. (1981). On comparing learning disabled and regular classroom children. *Journal of Learning Disabilities, 14,* 227–232.

Index